WATER MIRROR ECHO

Also by Jeff Chang

We Gon' Be Alright: Notes on Race and Resegregation

Who We Be: A Cultural History of Race in Post–Civil Rights America

Total Chaos: The Art and Aesthetics of Hip-Hop

Can't Stop Won't Stop: A History of the Hip-Hop Generation

Photo courtesy of the Bruce Lee Family Archive.

WATER MIRROR ECHO

BRUCE LEE AND THE MAKING OF ASIAN AMERICA

JEFF CHANG

MARINER BOOKS
New York Boston

For all materials courtesy of the Bruce Lee Family Estate:
Bruce Lee: copyright © 2025 Bruce Lee Enterprises, LLC. All rights reserved.
Shannon Lee: copyright © 2025 Shannon Lee. All rights reserved.
Linda Lee Cadwell: copyright © 2025 Linda Lee Cadwell. All rights reserved.
Brandon Lee: copyright © 2025 Brandon Lee. All rights reserved.

"Song of the King" from *The King and I*. Lyrics by Oscar Hammerstein II. Music by Richard Rodgers. Copyright © 1951 by Richard Rodgers and Oscar Hammerstein II. Copyright Renewed. WILLIAMSON MUSIC owner of publication and allied rights throughout the world. International Copyright Secured. All Rights Reserved. Reprinted by Permission of Hal Leonard LLC.

Without limiting the exclusive rights of any author, contributor or the publisher of this publication, any unauthorized use of this publication to train generative artificial intelligence (AI) technologies is expressly prohibited. HarperCollins also exercise their rights under Article 4(3) of the Digital Single Market Directive 2019/790 and expressly reserve this publication from the text and data mining exception.

The material on linked sites referenced in this book is the author's own. HarperCollins disclaims all liability that may result from the use of the material contained at those sites. All such material is supplemental and not part of the book. The author reserves the right to close the website in their sole discretion following September 2025.

WATER MIRROR ECHO. Copyright © 2025 by Jeff Chang. All rights reserved. No part of this book may be used or reproduced in any manner whatsoever without written permission except in the case of brief quotations embodied in critical articles and reviews. For information, address HarperCollins Publishers, 195 Broadway, New York, NY 10007. In Europe, HarperCollins Publishers, Macken House, 39/40 Mayor Street Upper, Dublin 1, D01 C9W8, Ireland.

HarperCollins books may be purchased for educational, business, or sales promotional use. For information, please email the Special Markets Department at SPsales@harpercollins.com.

The Mariner flag design is a registered trademark of HarperCollins Publishers LLC.

hc.com

FIRST EDITION

Interior designed by Jen Overstreet

Library of Congress Cataloging-in-Publication Data has been applied for.

ISBN 978-0-358-72647-0

Printed in the United States of America

25 26 27 28 29 LBC 5 4 3 2 1

To the memory of Eugene Y.T. Chang, Viviane Oh, Nasty Nes Rodriguez, and Dawn Bohulano Mabalon

I'm writing you all this from another world, a world of appearances. In a way the two worlds communicate with each other. Memory is to one what history is to the other, an impossibility. Legends are born from the need to decipher the indecipherable.

—CHRIS MARKER

CONTENTS

BOOK I: WATER

Introduction: The Lives of Bruce Lee — 1

Part I: War Child, 1940–1950
Chapter 1: Anchor Baby — 12
Chapter 2: The Dead and the Diseased — 24
Chapter 3: The One Who Can't Be Stopped — 30

Part II: The Orphan, 1950–1959
Chapter 4: The Kung Fu Guy — 40
Chapter 5: Talk with Your Hands — 49
Chapter 6: Days of Being Wild — 55
Chapter 7: Dualities — 65

Part III: Learning America, 1959–1961
Chapter 8: A Return Passage — 74
Chapter 9: The Power Broker — 84
Chapter 10: The Student — 91
Chapter 11: A Central District Story — 99

Part IV: The Man Who Thinks He Can, 1961–1962
Chapter 12: Blood on the Floor — 110
Chapter 13: Dance Away — 117
Chapter 14: The Ghosts and the Moon — 125
Chapter 15: American Fictions — 131

Part V: Simplicity Directness Freedom, 1962–1964
Chapter 16: Mavericks — 142
Chapter 17: Homecoming — 149
Chapter 18: Things Disclose Themselves — 155
Chapter 19: This Is It! — 164

Part VI: A Bigger Stage, 1964–1965
Chapter 20: Openings — 176
Chapter 21: Training Floor — 184
Chapter 22: The Boxer from Toisan — 191
Chapter 23: The Fight — 199

BOOK II: MIRROR

Part VII: Broken Mirrors, 1966–1967

Chapter 24: The Screen Test — 212
Chapter 25: Number One — 227
Chapter 26: The Sum of All Projections — 236
Chapter 27: Mirrors and Smoke — 245

Part VIII: Warrior State of Mind, 1967–1969

Chapter 28: The Names, Part 1 — 256
Chapter 29: The Names, Part 2 — 263
Chapter 30: Stand! — 271

Part IX: Above and Below Sunset, 1968–1970

Chapter 31: Plateaus — 284
Chapter 32: The Seeker — 293
Chapter 33: What Is Freedom? — 302

Part X: Action Action, 1970–1972

Chapter 34: Water Above, Mountain Below — 310
Chapter 35: A Journey from the West — 317
Chapter 36: The Teacher and the Warrior — 324
Chapter 37: The Fighter's Instant — 332

BOOK III: ECHO

Part XI: The New Hero, 1971–1972

Chapter 38: Us Against the World — 342
Chapter 39: The Mid-Pacific Man — 352
Chapter 40: Yellow-Faced Chinese — 360
Chapter 41: Fists and Mayhem — 368

Part XII: Watch Me Now, 1972–1973

Chapter 42: The World Stage — 376
Chapter 43: The Cost — 386
Chapter 44: Representations — 393
Chapter 45: The Proud Dragon — 398
Chapter 46: The Weight — 403
Chapter 47: The Names, Part 3 — 414
Chapter 48: The Light of Stars — 423

Part XIII: Afterlives, 1973–Now

Chapter 49: The World Is a Ghetto — 432
Chapter 50: Melancholia and Memory — 436
Chapter 51: How We Use Our Hands — 443

Acknowledgments — 454
Author's Note — 458
Notes — 461
Index — 523

BOOK I
WATER

Photo courtesy of the Bruce Lee Family Archive.

A monk asked Chao Chou, "Does a newborn baby also have sixth consciousness?"

Chao Chou said, "Like tossing a ball on swift-flowing water."

The monk also asked T'ou Tzu, "What is the meaning of 'Tossing a ball on swift-flowing water'?"

T'ou Tzu said, "Moment to moment, nonstop flow."

—PI YEN LU

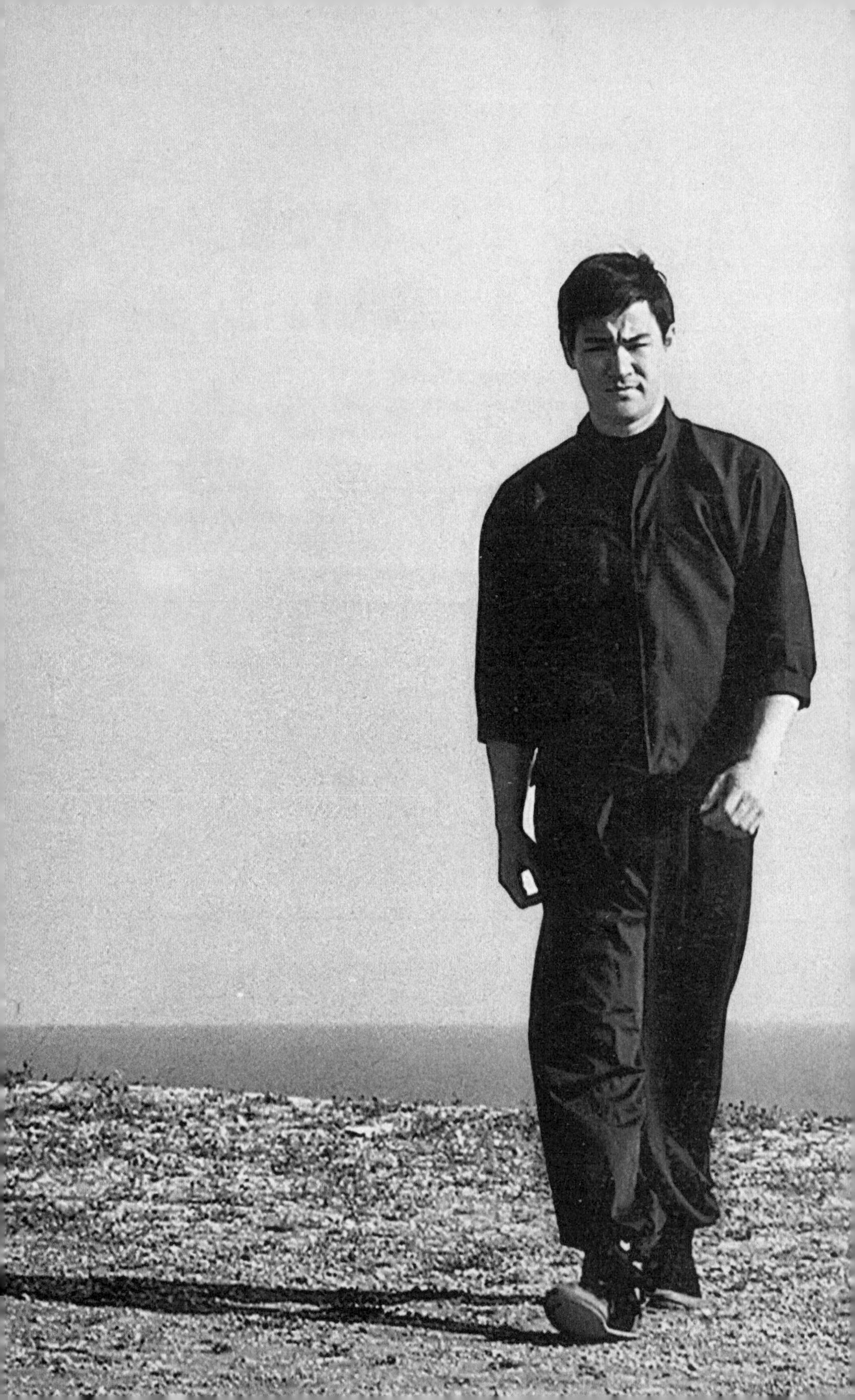

The Lives of Bruce Lee

> The first thing the colonial subject learns is to remain in his place and not overstep its limits. Hence the dreams of the colonial subject are muscular dreams, dreams of action, dreams of aggressive vitality.
>
> —FRANTZ FANON

Photo courtesy of the Bruce Lee Family Archive.

Picture him, rising from stillness to movement.

Wearing a jade pendant around his neck, a sign of a promise he has made to his mother that he will not engage in violence. Watching as his fellow workers are pummeled by thugs paid for by his boss. Taking a stray punch and turning his cheek, flush with rage.

His chain is severed. Jade pendant shattering on the concrete. Released from his pacifist vow, his face contorts, he lets out a wildcat scream and explodes into motion.

With a back crescent kick he drops a man. Flattens another with a roundhouse kick and an elbow. Stomps his foot into the chest of a third. Whips around to finish him with a hook kick.

Nine men line up against him.

He waves a finger. "You bastards can't push us around."

Steps over the bodies of the men he's KOed. Grabs the hem of his pants. Crouches into a ready position.

Picture him again, eyes cocked, lip upturned in a sneer. *Bring it on.*

One pulls a knife and charges. He kicks away the knife, then the knife man. Raises his eyes. Sets his teeth. "Well, I'm waiting."

Three men up—four kicks, two punches—three men down. Three more surround him. In three kicks he levels them all. He crouches again—sharp and taut.

Picture him, the Bruce Lee we know.

This was the moment of his rise: the 1971 film, *The Big Boss*. Blocked by Hollywood's low ceiling of expectations, Bruce had returned to Southeast Asia, specifically Hong Kong—to fight and to be seen, which he had come to see as the same struggle. His very presence on-screen was a protest.

In just two years, Bruce would become the biggest global Asian star born in America since Anna May Wong, the pioneering siren who had died all but broken by Hollywood. In his lifetime, Bruce Lee popularized Asian martial arts and philosophy to millions through the most unlikely of forms—the American action film. He helped decenter American whiteness, opening up the free-flowing global popular culture we all now enjoy.

Then, at the age of thirty-two, in the prime of his life and at the threshold of success, he suddenly died of cerebral edema. It was a cruel interruption, an irresoluteness that would freeze his image in amber. He became an idea for each of us to imbibe, molded to the shape of all our lives like spirits to a cask, felt at the scale of history.

More than a half century later, Bruce is still with us. His movies have generated hundreds of millions of dollars, the basis for an economy of filmmakers, merchandisers, publishers, and toymakers that is thriving. His stature has far exceeded that of all his film contemporaries.

In global impact Bruce Lee is closer to Muhammad Ali or Bob Marley. He is a symbol of unity flexible enough to signify postwar ethnic and religious peace in the Balkans. Young activists erected a bronze statue of him in the city of Mostar, Bosnia and Herzegovina, because he was, an organizer said, "the one thing we all have in common." He stood for "our idea of universal justice—that the good guys can win."

The image of Bruce Lee endures above time and place. But what do we know of the man? Ali's and Marley's lives seem to us inseparable from their accomplishments. Not so for Bruce.

Picture him, born in a segregated American hospital. A swaddled baby wailing on a movie set. Flickering child star, the celebrated orphan of Hong Kong. Teenage dance floor king. Street-fighting thug. Fresh-Off-the-Boat immigrant. Lonely bookworm. Forgotten waiter. Cadet. Lover. Fatherless child. Suburban dad. Chinese Tonto. Kaftaned hippie. Hollywood guru. Depressed recluse. All this before he becomes our hero.

Bruce Lee is perhaps the most famous person in the world about whom so little is known.

He burst into the popular imagination at a hinge moment in history, during which a massive shift in relations between America and the Third World was underway.

Bruce was born in San Francisco, on the eve of a world war that would draw the United States decisively into Asia and the Pacific. He grew up during an era of decolonization. He became a fighter amid a generation of fighters, close to the realities of war, instability, and migration. He returned to the States as Americans were "looking to the East." He became an actor at the dawn of an awakening among racialized minorities, a revolution of perception through which they would demand to be seen on their own terms.

At the same time, Asians in America were inspired by young Blacks who had rejected the term "Negro." They renounced the diminutive "Oriental" as an archaic slur and began to call themselves "Asian American." The "Orient" was the distant, exotic "East"—but compared to what? Looking from Asia and the Pacific, Europe and the Americas were the Far East.

Those who called themselves "Asian American" had been raised to believe that to be American was to be white—that Americanness was inseparable from whiteness, the ideal to which they were required to assimilate, and from which they were excluded. No more. They saw themselves as warriors against the wars in Southeast Asia who were also fighting for recognition and civil rights at home in America.

They were an imagined community of peoples originating from the Asiatic

Barred Zone, a portion of the globe that Americans had once drawn a red line around to exclude immigration. They were now confined to living in segregated districts in the continental United States. They were seen as alien, as "all alike." They decided to claim difference *and* solidarity.

"Asian American" was a conscious provocation, an Ali-styled dare: *What's my name?*

"Asian American" said, *You bastards can't push us around.*

That attitude proved necessary time and again.

Eighty years after Bruce Lee's birth, President Donald Trump unleashed violence upon Asian Americans when he began to fling around words like "China virus" and "Kung Flu." As the pandemic spread, hatred did too. Thousands of incidents of violence were reported across the country. Neighborhood patrols and self-defense groups formed, and the image of Bruce Lee appeared everywhere in Asian America again. He represented safety, survival, and pride.

The idea of the Asian American sometimes feels confoundingly, impossibly diverse. Today there are twenty-five million people of Asian, Native Hawaiian, and/or Pacific Islander descent living in the States. That includes a bewildering array of ethnicities, cultures, languages, and religions. But not everyone sees the distinctions. That blindness feels so pervasive as to be normal. And it is an ignorance that can be denigrating or deadly. When violence targets them, it makes them Asian Americans.

But the idea of Asian America has also allowed disparate communities to name a We, shaped not just by mass mistaken identity, but by stories of war and migration, violence and displacement, segregation and exclusion. It has provided a clean page on which to compose a history of common experience. Asian America is not just about self-defense, melancholia, and loss. It is a process of becoming, a joyful act of creation, a leap into the making of history.

I am part of the first generation after the advent of the Asian American, which was also the first generation After Bruce. Growing up, for me and many others, the idea of Asian America and the idea of Bruce Lee were inseparable. He made us real. Because of his image, we became flesh-and-blood.

We made zines about him. We rapped about him in a thousand songs. We turned *They Call Me Bruce* and *Finishing the Game* into cult films. We photoshopped him rocking headphones behind a pair of turntables and slapped that image onto T-shirts. We bought and traded collectible toys of him. We wore yellow jumpsuits with black stripes to Halloween parties. We overpaid for Nike Kobe 5 Protros.

We taught our kids his *nunchaku* routines and put the videos of them on social media. We forwarded our friends deep fake videos of him playing Ping-Pong with those same *nunchakus*. When we got our own film and TV deals, we put him back on the screen. Remaking Bruce was part of the process of making Asian America.

Yet to so many others, we—this rousing, sublime We of Asian America—remain a mystery. Alien, without past or presence.

In 2021, as violence against Asian Americans was exploding, and after the half-Desi American Kamala Devi Harris had taken the oath of office for the vice presidency, a study found that 42 percent of Americans could not name a single prominent Asian American, not even Harris. Bruce Lee and his screen successor, Jackie Chan, a Hong Kong native who has never claimed Americanness, were the top two. Just when we were being seen as victims of American violence, even the most famous of us remained unseen.

It is hardly a leap to suggest that so little is known about Bruce Lee because so little is known about Asian America.

Much of the Bruce Lee story is neither extraordinary nor unique. He lived through war and hunger in Asia and racial segregation and exclusion in the United States. He was a survivor, a migrant, and a minority.

In the mid-sixties, Bruce was trying to assimilate into white America while Black Americans were challenging white supremacy. He was far from a radical. As far as we know, he never used the term "white supremacy" or "Asian American" in his lifetime. The Black Panther Party for Self-Defense offices opened less than two miles from where his Jun Fan Gung Fu Institute stood. But they never crossed paths. When Huey P. Newton and Bobby Seale were at Merritt College selling Mao's Little Red Book to fund the party, Bruce was already in Los Angeles, costarring as the Oriental sidekick in an all-American TV show, *The Green Hornet*.

But he shared with the Panthers and the newly named Asian Americans an impulse to fight for freedom and justice. He proudly identified as a warrior. In martial arts, he discovered a dialectic of violence and creativity—the engine that would propel his unrelenting drive. The term *gung fu*, which the Cantonese used as a blanket term for all the Chinese fighting arts, in fact, translates into "skill acquired through hard work." *Gung fu* evokes time and focus devoted to craft with only a distant promise of achievement. This ethic was how he approached fighting and acting, and here is where the unique part of the Bruce Lee story begins.

During his lifetime he had a marginal Hollywood career and, as a teacher of martial arts, an even more marginal occupation. In Hollywood and the emerging West Coast counterculture, Bruce navigated fascination and revulsion with "the Oriental," a corpus of distorted images that limited Asian American opportunity and mobility.

He stood just five feet eight in leather wingtip shoes. His feats of physical mastery seemed so extraordinary because he appeared so ordinary. When he demonstrated them on-screen they were doubly astonishing because he also appeared so foreign, so alien. In the States, no one who looked like him had ever been *seen*.

But Bruce was not satisfied to out-punch, out-kick, and outlast everyone. He also wanted to be regarded as a poet and philosopher, to build upon an inheritance of expression, focus, and risk cultivated by his parents and grandparents. He wanted to be seen not just as a body, but as a mind and a soul. He wanted to reveal the beauty and sagacity of Asian ideas, and to have those worldviews taken seriously.

In America Bruce slowly came to the realization that that might never happen. It did not matter if he married a white American woman and had mixed-race kids, or if he became a teacher to Hollywood's most powerful men. He was still incapable of becoming one of them.

Unwilling to accept his fate, he returned—perhaps retreated—to Hong Kong and Southeast Asia, where he attained stardom, then superstardom. He came back across the Pacific to star in *Enter the Dragon*, a bridge he was building to a destination he would never reach, a future of visibility that Asian Americans had just begun to build. Only in death would he achieve all he had set out to do.

But his image would also begin to make legible the lives of those who were invisible like him—especially Asian lives, and specifically Asian *American* lives. He became a muse and a mirror. His words would echo. In this way Bruce Lee's story is still continuing, more than fifty years after his death. He is still making Asian America.

Some treatments of Bruce foreground the time of his dying, as if that was what made his life worth telling. But through the fights he fought, the paths he broke, and the many lives he lived, Bruce Lee changed everything. And to take a true measure of him we must place his story alongside the equally epic story of Asian America.

Some have told the story of Bruce as an Asian, others the story of him as an American, like the flicks from Hong Kong and America made after his death in the genre called Bruceploitation. But many of the tellings terminate in mythmaking. They make the man into a legend above time and place, as if his success had always been preordained. They make him transcendent but also unknowable.

They miss an important piece: Bruce was an Asian in America at the dawn of Asian America. He was not only living in between two worlds, but in a third place, one with its own history, meaning, and direction. The lives that he lived there expose the true size of the obstacles he faced, describe the complicated character of the man he became, and delineate his unprecedented achievement. Restoring Bruce to history in this way returns him to a human scale.

The final mystery of Bruce Lee is not in the question of how an ordinary man came to live an extraordinary set of lives. That answer can be found in biography. Nor does it lie in how he died so suddenly. That question may never be resolved satisfactorily. The lingering question is why Bruce Lee continues to matter. That mystery is entwined with the mystery of Asian America's emergence, swift expansion, and continuing significance.

The rise of Bruce Lee and the rise of Asian America would mirror each other. When Bruce returned to the States in 1959 for the first time since his birth, he learned quickly how debased Asians were there. But their struggles and dreams became his, and they molded who and what he became to the world. As the first global icon produced by Asian America, he would provide the measure of the distance they had traversed as well as how far they had yet to go.

By seeing Bruce Lee we can better understand Asian America. By seeing Asian America we can best understand Bruce Lee.

Bruce's best-known aphorism—which he said so often that a screenwriter friend wrote it into a television role for him—is: "Be water, my friend."

From an early age, water loomed large in Bruce's imagination. His father exposed him to the slow-moving shadowboxing art of *tai chi chuan* and the canon of classical Chinese books, including Laozi's *Tao Te Ching*. To his father, the old Taoist master Laozi[*] was a model for living. To Laozi, *water* was a model for living:

> Under heaven nothing is more soft and yielding than water.
> Yet for attacking the solid and strong, nothing is better.
> It has no equal.
> The weak can overcome the strong.
> The supple can overcome the stiff.
> Under heaven everyone knows this.

One of the *gung fu* arts most influenced by the *Tao Te Ching* was *tai chi chuan*. Its name comes from the core idea of Chinese cosmology: *tai chi* 太極, or "the Great Ultimate." It is the mother of *yin* and *yang*, the opposing forces of the universe. They form dualities such as water and fire, moon and sun, black and white.

The symbol for *tai chi* divides *yin* and *yang* and whirls them together into an endlessly revolving circle. A white dot resides within the head of the black swirl, a black dot within the head of the white. In each one is the other. The one also depends upon the other. They create each other. Pushed far enough, the one becomes the other. Together *yin* and *yang* constitute the Tao 道—"the oneness," "the Way"—which flows everywhere and sustains life.

Water is the agent of *yin* energy—tranquil, adapting, and dark. Young Bruce seemed to his father a burning ball of pure *yang* energy—excited, advancing, and bright. The father felt the son needed the element of water in order to grow, to mature. The son would soon learn this himself.

---

[*] It could also not have been lost on father or son that Laozi had been born with the surname Li and that Confucius had called him "Dragon."

One day when the Li* children were at Lai Yuen amusement park splashing around in a shallow water pool, young Bruce was annoying his older sister, Phoebe, with his incessant teasing. She grabbed him by the hair, giggling, and plunged his head underwater. When he came up gasping for air, he was so distressed that, for the rest of his life, the boy who would grow up to be so fearless never learned to swim. From then on, the thought of water's power—its ability to flow, transform, and destroy—possessed Bruce.

His fear was primal, and in Chinese cosmology, it meant something. Water, from antiquity, was a sign of trouble and peril. In the oracle called the *I Ching: The Book of Changes*, the twenty-ninth hexagram is 坎, *ham*: water over water. The Taoist professor Alfred Huang writes that this hexagram—by doubling the element of water—suggests the act of plunging into a deep pit, "falling but not drowned; in danger but not lost." He names it "Darkness."

Water and its darkness would be Bruce's profound teacher. It reminded him of the universe beyond him, its vastness without him. When he told his students, "Be water," he was also pushing himself to confront and reconcile with his own darkness. It forced him to see what he was not—or, to be precise, what he was not yet.

But that line about water was just part of a longer passage of Taoist writing Bruce Lee encountered as a young man, a riddle to which he would constantly return for guidance, and which helps us make sense of his lives and his afterlives:

Moving, be like water.
Still, be like a mirror.
Respond like an echo.

---

* For this text, I am standardizing Li Hoi Chuen and Grace Li's names in the old British style. The family will be identified as Li to refer to their time in Hong Kong and Lee in the United States. Their children will later be identified by the Americanized "Lee."

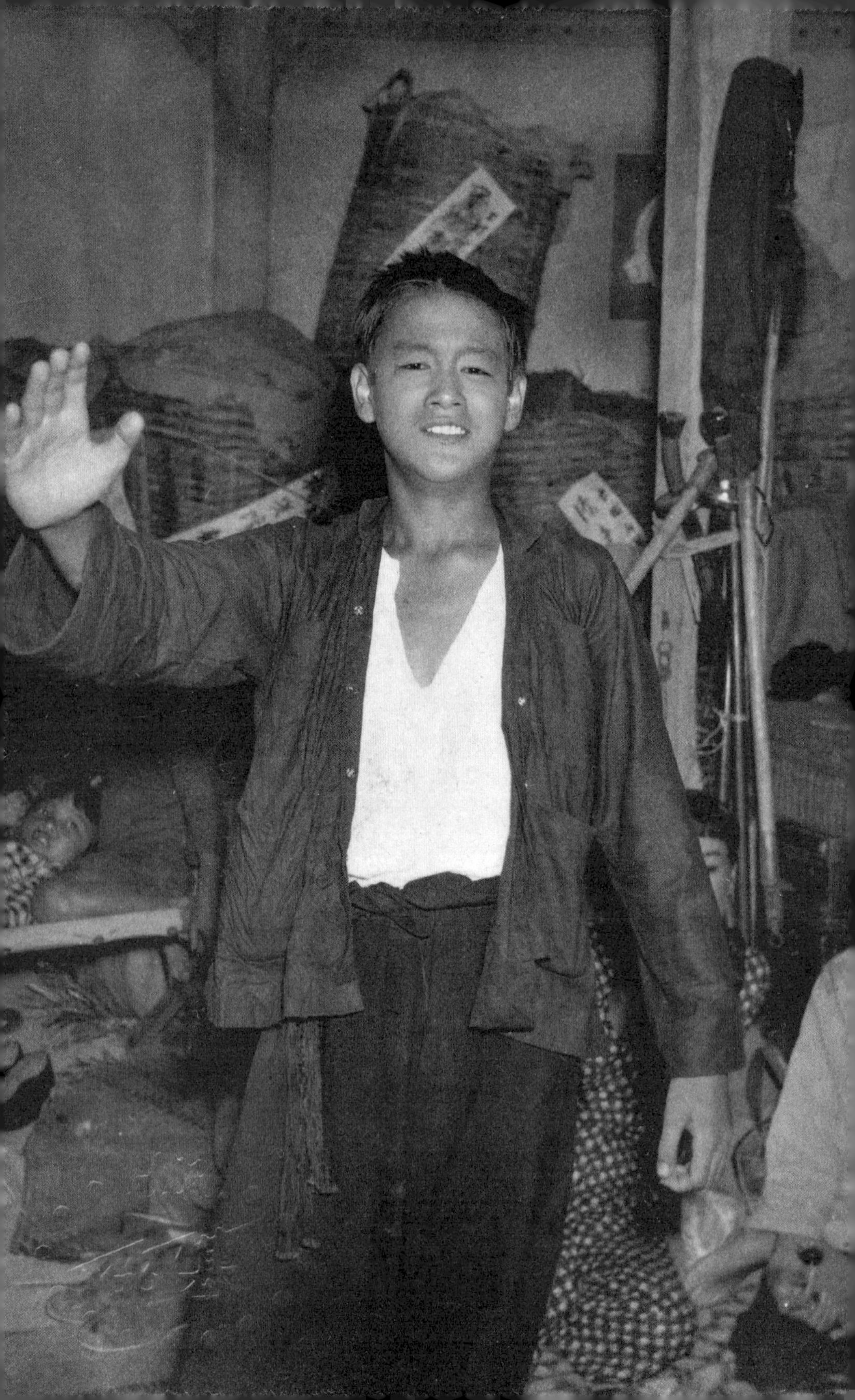

PART I
War Child

1940–1950

"You reckless monster!" cried Monkey. "You think I am small, not knowing that it's hardly difficult for me to become taller; you think I'm without weapon, but my two hands can drag the moon down from the edge of Heaven. Don't be afraid; just have a taste of old Monkey's fist!"

—WU CHENG'EN

The child actor, possibly from *Infancy (The Birth of Mankind)*, 1951.
Photo courtesy of the Bruce Lee Family Archive.

CHAPTER 1
Anchor Baby

"That I should be an American-born Chinese was accidental," Bruce Lee once mused, "or it might have been by my father's arrangement."

He had been born in San Francisco's Chinatown on November 27, 1940, at the Chinese Hospital, at 7:12 a.m.—an auspicious time, many have noted, in the Chinese astrological hour of the Dragon in the year of the Dragon. He was birthed in a hospital built just a generation before by Chinese Americans to remedy their exclusion from the city's basic health services. Had he been born today, Bruce Lee might have been called—in the divisive language used to describe immigration—an "anchor baby,"* a child whose foreign-born parents had chosen to bear in the United States to secure citizenship for themselves. This dubious idea requires a belief in migrant families as the devious architects of decades-long, multigenerational conspiracies. But migration and immigration were always so much simpler and so much more complex.

The year before, on November 18, 1939, Bruce's parents, Li Hoi Chuen and Grace Li Oi-Yu, had boarded an eastbound steamship called the SS *President Coolidge*, crossing the dark waters of the Pacific from a region besieged by war for the promise of work in the United States of America. Two summers earlier, Japan had invaded China. Bombs were falling a hundred miles away from Hong Kong in Guangzhou, and thousands were fleeing toward the setting sun, where the British flag waved over the anxious colony. Hoi Chuen's livelihood, the Cantonese opera, had collapsed. When the skies turn crimson with threat, what else is a performer to do? The couple was leaving behind three toddlers in the care of Hoi Chuen's mother.

Li Hoi Chuen had been born Li Moon Chuan, the sixth child of eight, most likely on March 27, 1902, in the hour of the Tiger in the year of the Tiger, in the village of Jun'an, in the Shunde district of Fatshan, in China's Pearl River Delta. Fatshan was known for producing silk, iron, ceramics, insurrectionists, and opera singers. Performers learned the Four Arts: singing, speech, choreography, and martial arts. In times of peace, the opera singers floated down the river in red junks, stopping at villages along the way to perform. In times of war, the opera singers took up

---

* The phrase was invented in the late 1980s to describe the US-born Vietnamese American children of refugees. By the 2000s, demagogues were using "anchor baby" to describe the children of migrants from Mexico and Latin America, whipping up anti-immigrant hysteria the same way the term "Chinese exclusion" had a century before. "A Profile of a Lost Generation," *Los Angeles Times*, Dec. 13, 1987; Gabe Ignatow and Alexander T. Williams, "New Media and the 'Anchor Baby' Boom, *Journal of Computer-Mediated Communication* 17 (2011), pp. 60–76.

arms alongside the insurrectionists. Hoi Chuen was born into an era of combat and chaos that came to be known as "the golden age of Guangdong's martial arts."

His father, Li Jun Biu, was a poor fisherman who, because of a childhood illness, spoke in a low whispery rasp so rarely that most thought him mute. He worked sometimes as a security guard, escorting valuable transports. Family lore described him as the source of Bruce's fighting prowess. Hoi Chuen's mother, Lok Gong Mui, had been a *mui jai*, a servant girl to a wealthy family. She kept the family together with a discerning eye.

Almost every day, the boy joined his father on the water to catch fish. Because of his father's condition, Hoi Chuen also became the fishmonger selling the daily catch. As the waters downriver from the city became increasingly polluted, Hoi Chuen's grandfather arranged for him and his fifth brother to work at Fatshan's Siu Chen Wan Teahouse, a solid hedge against starvation. From the age of ten, Hoi Chuen cheerfully took diners' orders and chanted them in a musical voice across to the kitchen. If the father had been nearly voiceless, the son's voice would end his family's misfortune.

One day a famous opera singer named Siu Sang Yik sat down to eat in the restaurant. Amused by the boy's stagey mien, the performer invited him to join his theater troupe. The family agreed, and to mark his new destiny, Moon Chuan was renamed Hoi Chuen. The boy grew up in Siu's company, washing their laundry and studying the craft, learning the stories, the songs, the acrobatics and martial arts necessary for the stage.

The training was unrelenting, marked by episodes of corporal discipline. But by his twenties, Hoi Chuen had achieved fame with the celebrated Hing Chung Wah Opera Troupe. He was soon a major draw—dubbed one of the four great *chou sang* ("clown masters")—calming rowdy riff-raff in crowded theaters and rousing genteel guests at posh parties with his acclaimed village-accented "rusty voice."

Grace Ho Oi-Yu, born Ho Pak Yung in Shanghai on December 12, 1907, was a beautiful and downwardly mobile flapper. She had grown up in the ostentatious wealth of Shanghai, China's glamorous, cosmopolitan face to the world. But the specifics of Grace's ancestry remain shrouded in mystery.

Her grandmother was Lady Sze Tai, a woman who had married Charles Henri Maurice Bosman, a Dutch-Jewish merchant who sold Chinese laborers to harvest sugar in Guyana and build railroads in the United States. He went bankrupt and deserted the family. Lady Sze remarried a Chinese businessman and gave birth to Grace's father, Ho Kom Tong. He and Grace's uncle, Sir Robert Hotung, built lucrative businesses in shipping, insurance, real estate, and opium, working all sides of the wars in southern China to become two of the richest Chinese of their time.

Grace would later tell US immigration officials she was the daughter of Ho Kom Tong and an unnamed English mistress, one of twenty-nine children he had by fourteen women. Stories still circulate that Kom Tong's mistress was German, or that Grace had been adopted into the family. But it is more important to note that, when she was young, her mother and father both disappeared from her life. She might have become another impoverished wartime orphan but for being adopted by Kom Tong's thirteenth mistress, Cheung King-sin.

Instead Grace grew up among Shanghai's elite in the French Concession, was educated in colonial schools, and spoke Cantonese, Mandarin, English, and French. When she moved to Hong Kong Island in her teens, it was to a grand estate on Victoria Peak, the colony's most exclusive address, to live with her aunt Clara Hotung, Sir Robert Hotung's wife. By all accounts, she was beloved by the family. She dressed plainly but enjoyed the good life. She had an impeccable reputation but a streak of unpredictability.

"She liked drinking beer very much, sometimes with meals," recalled Robert Lee Jun Fai,* Grace's youngest son. "She also liked to knit sweaters."

One night, Hoi Chuen came with his troupe to perform at their mountaintop mansion, delighting the high-society crowd with song, comedy, and daring *wushu*. In his presence, Grace was enchanted. She pursued the man several years her senior, and in so doing, scandalized her family. The two eloped. Grace was cut off from her inheritance and exiled from the Peak. She and Hoi Chuen crossed the harbor to live in Kowloon, home of the Nine Dragons. Years later she would sometimes pull out a picture to show her children and their spouses of her younger self wearing a glamorous Western gown, sitting in a horse-drawn carriage.

Not long after the war erupted, Hoi Chuen and Grace began a family, having three children in less than two years. They lost their first, a son named Li Jung Teung, when he was three months old. Phoebe Li Chow Yuen came next in late 1937, born out of wedlock to a woman with whom Hoi Chuen had an affair, but whom Grace agreed to adopt. Agnes Li Chow Fung was born to Grace forty days later. On the day they boarded the steamship, their youngest, Peter Li Chung Sum, was barely more than two weeks old.

Hoi Chuen had signed a guarantee of work with the Mandarin Theatre in San Francisco. He and his company would tour the States, receive room and board and a small fortune by Chinese standards, and be welcomed as stars. The performances would raise funds for wounded soldiers and refugees in China. If all went well, the Lis could return in a year with enough to care for their young family for a while. Hoi Chuen's mother had also warned Grace that her son could be tempted by other fruits while he was gone. She assured Grace she could care for the three young children and saw the couple off.

But as they said goodbye to their family and boarded the ship in the winter of 1939, who could say what awaited them in America and to what they might return?

---

* I am rendering their names in the modern style with the English name first, followed by surname and Cantonese name.

So much was up to fate. Migrants—by circumstance and self-selection—must be gamblers. Hoi Chuen and Grace's journey would be the reason that Bruce Lee was born American.

Migration is simply the freedom to move. Only man-made laws can make a natural thing illegal. From its founding by settler migrants, immigration to the United States was largely open. After the 1845 potato blight, a wave of Irish arrived, unleashing a national anti-immigrant backlash. But it was the Chinese who fixed the young nation's will to shut its doors after the discovery of gold at Sutter's Mill in California in 1848.

The first Chinese arriving at what they called Gold Mountain—some 250 years after the first Filipinos had landed at California's Morro Bay—were not even thought of as immigrants. An "immigrant" was a migrant who went to another country intending to stay. A "sojourner" was what the rich men wanted—faceless, movable, exploitable labor to build levees that created farmland, grow crops and harvest them, establish commercial fisheries, lay railroad tracks through deadly terrain, wash laundry, and pour tea, only to be repatriated when they were no longer needed.

In 1862, the newly elected California Governor Leland Stanford declared, "Asia, with her numberless millions, sends to our shores the dregs of her population." He called for more whites to settle in the state and for government to ban the "inferior race." Three years later the same Leland Stanford, as president of the Central Pacific Railroad, became the nation's biggest recruiter of Chinese workers. The eastern portion of the transcontinental railroad had made barons rich off the labor of European immigrants in the North and Black slaves in the South. The western segment would be completed by more than twelve thousand Chinese workers, 80 percent of Stanford's workforce. More than a thousand would die in the process.

After the Civil War, a long depression left many white workers jobless. Across the West the cry went up, "The Chinese must go!" It was the slogan of the Workingmen's Party, led by Irish American organizer Denis Kearney, and it was heard at increasingly violent demonstrations. In July 1877, a rally descended into three days of mob rioting across the San Francisco Bay Area, leaving four dead and many Asian businesses destroyed. Targeting Blacks and Chinese was how the Irish, and other European immigrants, became white and American.

Tabloids ran cartoons of the Chinese "coolie"—"unsophisticated," "imitative," "ape-like," but wearing "a cunning smile of triumph at his discomfited rivals," as he grabbed coal mine veins, staked gold panning spots, and stole farmland from white men. At their peak of immigration, the Chinese were less than 1 percent of the US population. But the "Yellow Peril" occupied an outsized portion of the American imagination.

16 WATER MIRROR ECHO

The Yellow Peril: *Nach einem Entwurf Sr. Majestät des Kaisers Wilhelm gezeichnet von Hermann Knackfuss.* "After a design by His Majesty Kaiser Wilhelm drawn by Hermann Knackfuss," 1895. The angel tells the nations of Europe, "Join in the defence of your faith and your homes!" Courtesy New York Public Library. Public Domain.

A flurry of laws were passed to restrict the civil rights of Asians—limiting access to schools, outlawing cultural practices, preventing them from owning land or homes, and banning their testimony against whites in cases before the court. In 1861, Nevada banned marriage between whites and "any Black person, mulatto, Indian, or Chinese." In 1875, Congress passed the Page Act, which banned sex workers from "China, Japan or any Oriental country." President Ulysses S. Grant made explicit the bill's intent to stop the immigration of all Asian women, "few of whom," he said, "are brought to our shores to pursue honorable or useful occupations." In 1879, the state constitution of California was amended to include Article XIX, entitled "Chinese," which barred their employment in any business or government agency, and forbade their "introduction into this State." In 1882, Congress passed the Chinese Exclusion Act, the first time the country excluded an entire group of people because of their race.

Anti-Asian terror only escalated after the Exclusion Act. In Rock Springs, Wyoming, in 1885, white coal miners burned and looted workers' quarters, wounded fif-

---

* It was not repealed until 1952, by a vote on Proposition 14 on the California ballot.

teen, and killed twenty-eight. In 1887, in Oregon, thirty-four men were ambushed at Hells Canyon, stripped of their gold, and murdered, some of them scalped, their bodies dumped into the Snake River, washing up miles downstream to tell of their slaughter. Across the West, from Pasadena, California, to Seattle, Washington, white rioters burned down Asian settlements, rounded up their Chinese, Filipino, South Asian, or Japanese residents, and told them: *leave or be lynched*. Between 1850 and 1906, there were over 340 purges. Bruce would return to this time of terror as the setting for a television series project about a Chinese migrant wandering the old West that he called *Ah Sahm*, later *The Warrior*.

Exclusion produced new language—words needed to be invented for novel functions like "deportation"—and a new regime of papers. All Chinese Americans were required to carry "certificates of residence" and "certificates of identity" that verified their status as legal immigrants. They would be issued only after the applicant was vouched for by at least one white witness. Anyone without these papers became, in the historian Erika Lee's words, "America's first undocumented immigrants." When migrants began crossing the Canadian and Mexican borders, Congress formed the precursor of today's Border Patrol, gangs of white deputies who called themselves "Chinese catchers."

The Immigration Act of 1917 created the "Asiatic Barred Zone"—covering one-third of the earth's surface from Afghanistan to Oceania—to stop nearly all immigration from almost every Asian and Pacific Island nation.* President Calvin Coolidge declared, "America must be kept American," and signed the Immigration Act of 1924, which, the scholar Mae Ngai wrote, sealed into the law "a racial hierarchy of desirability," and "perfected Asiatic exclusion."

On December 8, 1939—as the SS *President Coolidge* transported Hoi Chuen and Grace beneath the newly opened Golden Gate Bridge—the Asiatic Barred Zone, certificates of identity and residence, and the anti-Chinese section of the California constitution were all still the law of the land.

At the San Francisco docks the Lis were segregated from citizen passengers, then ferried to the Angel Island immigration station in San Francisco Bay, where, for three decades, most Chinese migrants had been detained. At Ellis Island in New York Harbor, where European immigrants arrived, only 2 percent of immigrants would be turned away. But at Angel Island, Chinese were not treated as hopeful new Americans. They were seen, Mae Ngai wrote, as "proxies for foreign troops"—in the same way Japanese Americans would be treated during World War II, and South Asian, Arab, Sikh, and Muslim Americans after 9/11.

---

* Japan and the Philippines were excluded because of their peculiar diplomatic relationships with the United States. The Philippines was a US territory, and the United States had a separate agreement with Japan. But exclusion was accomplished by other means.

On Angel Island, the Lis dropped their luggage and proceeded to an administrative building, where they were separated from white migrants, then from each other. In a stuffy room, Hoi Chuen and a dozen other Asian men were stripped and inspected by medics for hookworm. They were led to a crowded men's quarters, full of bunks already mostly occupied by hundreds of other Chinese migrants. Many had been waiting for a month or more to hear about their cases.

Carved into the barracks' walls were hundreds of poems, a graffiti feed of throttled hope. One captive named Chan had cut these words into the wood:

America has power but not justice.
In prison, we were victimized as if we were guilty.
Given no opportunity to explain, it was really brutal.
I bow my head in reflection, there is nothing I can do.

For these reasons, the Lis had already carefully prepared papers for their arrival. Hoi Chuen's non-immigrant visa listed his purpose for visiting as "theatrical work only." Grace's papers described her as an "actress (wardrobe woman)."

The Mandarin Theatre staff had received approval from the Department of Labor to admit them. But the Immigration and Naturalization Service required that they secure a bond of one thousand dollars each[*] that ensured they were "over 16 years of age," remained "in possession of proper visas" and "free [of] contagious disease," and would not become "public charges"—bureaucratese for "recipients of government funds or services."

After being cleared, the Lis were ferried back to San Francisco, shadowed by an immigration official. They were met at the pier by a theater representative, who produced more papers for yet another official. Once cleared, they headed directly to Chinatown to take their residence in the Mandarin's quarters in a blind alley at 18 Trenton Street, a block from the Chinese Hospital.

That day, Hoi Chuen later told his children, he had come to understand how unfree the Chinese were in America.

Of all the Chinatowns around the world—from London's East End to Dunedin, New Zealand, to Havana, Cuba—San Francisco's was perhaps the largest and the most storied. It was a place of quarantine and isolation, but also refuge—"Heartland Asian America," in the words of one community leader. Restaurants, groceries, and pharmacies lined Grant and Jackson Streets. The Lis lived steps away from the Chinese Hospital. Like most Chinese in America, they would experience the country mainly through its Chinatowns.

---

[*] This is more than twenty-two thousand dollars in 2024 dollars.

Hoi Chuen's job exceeded mere entertainment. Bruce later explained, "At that time, the Chinese inhabitants in the States, [who had] mostly migrated from Guangdong, were very much homesick. Nostalgia was held towards everything that was associated with their homeland."

The Cantonese opera had first come to San Francisco in 1852, when the Hong Fook Tong played to a house full of appreciative white spectators. But as anti-Chinese sentiment spread, city officials across the West stopped the performances. In the year of the Exclusion Act, when police in Portland, Oregon, arrested opera musicians for violating a noise ordinance, the Chinese audience rioted. "The opera," Frank Chin wrote, "is made of the soul of the Cantonese. It speaks from and to the heart of their deepest matter."

In the heart of Chinatown at 1021 Grant Avenue, Mandarin Theatre was doing daily battle with the Liberty Theatre and the Great China for audiences. Each afternoon, hawkers passed out handbills touting the night's shows and stars. Crowds filled the seats—the Mandarin and the Great China each boasted more than seven hundred—until final bows near midnight. Landing Hoi Chuen and his company was a coup for the Mandarin.

The performances they gave are lost to time. Perhaps some of Hoi Chuen's best known were included—*Chivalry in Red*, *Flying Across the Yumen Pass*, or *Legends of the Heroes of the Ming Palace*. But they were talked about for years. When Bruce returned to San Francisco at the age of eighteen, many Chinatown residents still fondly recalled his parents and received him warmly.

As a national hub, the Mandarin sent companies they had booked to other Chinatowns. Hoi Chuen was soon bound for Seattle and New York City. But the cross-country trip was tense and taxing. "They weren't allowed to get off the train whatsoever," said Robert Lee. "The only time they could get off was when they arrived at the station in New York." In each city, immigration officials tailed them until they got back on the train.

Sometime in the spring of 1940, Grace learned that she was with child. Throughout her pregnancy, her Chinatown friends looked after her. "When your mother was ready," one of them told Bruce, "we just walked her across the street." In New York City, Hoi Chuen celebrated the news of his third son backstage with his company.

With the help of a friend, Lau Yee Nam, they picked the English name of "Bruce." A white midwife named Mary Glover filled out the birth certificate for Grace, Americanizing her surname as "Lee," rather than "Li," the more common anglicization in Hong Kong. In the United States, the Lis became the Lees.

The boy's Chinese name, "Jun Fan," would amass meaning like layers of strata. The second part of Bruce's name, "Fan," signified "foreign" or "border." It was also a contraction of the colloquial Cantonese name for San Francisco, "Sam Fan," 三藩, forever associating Bruce with his birthplace. He was also the third son, 三. For the rest of his life Bruce would favor the nickname "Ah Sahm," "the third," for himself and characters he played.

Following friends' advice, Grace and Hoi Chuen matched the first part of Bruce's name, "Jun," to the first part of Hoi Chuen's father's name, Jun Piu. In this rendering, "Jun Fan" (震藩) suggested "power shocking the foreigners," perhaps representing their patriotic hopes for their son. But it could also have meant "an earthquake jolting San Francisco," linking the boy's destiny to the 1906 catastrophe.

This name was a particular favorite of the Lees' Chinatown friends. The quake had unleashed fires that incinerated official immigration records, allowing countless Chinese a way to elude the Exclusion Act. Those with citizenship could now give or sell their names to "paper sons" and "paper daughters" who were not blood kin. To the migrants and their descendants, earthquakes represented freedom of movement.

But in Cantonese custom it would have been disrespectful for a child to share the same first name as his grandfather.* So, later, on Bruce's immigration papers Hoi Chuen wrote in a different "Jun," 鎮—meaning "to guard," perhaps a more appropriate way to honor his father, the watchman. Bruce later abandoned this name, too, choosing a third "Jun," 振, which was closer in meaning to the first—to "shake, inspire, or rise with force."

Jun Fan, 振藩—ascending powerfully in the borderland.

Speaking in 1867, just after the Civil War, as the United States was struggling to shape its future, the Black abolitionist Frederick Douglass said of the Chinese, "They will cross the mountains, cross the plains, descend our rivers, penetrate to the heart of the country, and fix their homes with us forever."

Douglass and the Black freedom movement had pushed the country to grant citizenship to all born on its soil, an idea called "birthright citizenship." If the United States was to make good on the Declaration of Independence's promise of what Douglass termed "absolute equality," it needed to become a multiracial democracy. Douglass said, "I want a home here not only for the negro, the mulatto, and the Latin races, but I want the Asiatic to find a home here in the United States, and feel at home here, both for his sake and for ours. Right wrongs no man." Douglass's expansive vision for America did not prevail then. Between 1890 and 1919, as sixteen million people immigrated from Europe, only 315,000 were accepted from South Asia and East Asia.

---

* Traditionally, each generation is given a similar first name to mark that generation. To have Bruce share a name with his grandfather would be giving the baby a genealogical stature equivalent to his grandfather and his grandfather's generation.

To exclusionists who wished to preserve a white settler nation, Asians born in the States—the "American-born Chinese," the first "second generation"* of Asian Americans—represented a new problem.

Wong Kim Ark, a humble San Francisco–born Chinatown cook who had been among the first American-born Chinese, was perhaps the original "anchor baby." In 1894, he journeyed to China, filling out extensive reentry papers that included the attestations of three white witnesses of his US birth. But upon his return, immigration officials detained him on the steamer on which he had arrived, ruling that the Chinese Exclusion Act denied him birthright citizenship.

For five months Wong Kim Ark was imprisoned in the harbor. A US attorney questioned whether his loyalties lay with the "country of his birth" or "the country of his father," and asked, "Is it possible that any Court in the United States will deliberately force upon us as natural born citizens, persons who must necessarily be a constant menace to the welfare of our Country?" Wong chose to fight his case up to the Supreme Court. In March of 1898, a 6–2 majority affirmed his citizenship and upheld the idea of birthright citizenship for all.

Chinatowns and other Asian settlements had already demonstrated the cultural possibility of an Asian America; birthright citizenship opened the legal possibility. Both pointed toward Douglass's freedom dream. But for generations of Asians born in America, the same racist hysteria that fueled their exclusion and segregation planted within them a consciousness of marginality stronger than the law.

In 1936, a second-generation Chinese American from San Francisco's Chinatown was asked by a white historian a question that would bedevil many generations hence—did he consider himself American or Chinese? "I have no choice," the exasperated young man answered. "I have a right to vote, but it is an empty gesture." The historian came away pessimistic for the future of Chinese in America: "Here no matter how much they adopt our traditions, they can never hope to enter fully into a birthright."

After Wong Kim Ark won his day in the Supreme Court, he moved to Texas for a new start. But he was jailed there for four months by immigration officials who refused to believe he was a citizen. He continued to visit China, but on every return was required to fill out a form entitled "Application of Alleged U.S. Citizen for Reentry into the United States," and subjected to what historian Erika Lee called "a barrage of humiliating interrogations." When his sons applied for entry to the country, they were detained at Angel Island. Two of them were rejected because

---

* I use "second generation" here to describe those born in the United States, in keeping with the US Census Bureau's definition: "The first generation is composed of individuals who are foreign-born. The second generation refers to those with at least one foreign-born parent." Such a definition has also become standard in Asian American and other immigrant communities. When used to describe the American-born, the term "first-generation American" alienates—that is, makes *alien* or *Other*—immigrant parents.

officials refused to believe his children were his own. One won his appeal. The other submitted himself to deportation.

Still holding his certificate of identity, Wong Kim Ark booked a final ship passage to Toisan. Like his son, he gave up on America. In today's dehumanizing language, he "self-deported." Citizenship had afforded him no reassurance, no peace. The Asian—no matter their birthplace—might always be seen as alien, as Other, might never be American.

In 1941, with Hoi Chuen's work complete, the Lees prepared to return to Hong Kong and filed papers to verify Bruce's US citizenship status.[*]

Hoi Chuen and Grace had worked with the Mandarin Theatre staff to hire an immigration law firm—somehow named White & White—to help them fill out Form 430, the application for a Citizen's Return Certificate, on behalf of their son, whom they listed as "Lee Jun Fon (Bruce Lee)." A Chinese American friend named Esther Eng secured his birth certificate.

The application, dated March 31, 1941, included pictures of infant and mother. Baby Bruce is dressed in a knit sweater. His eyebrows are raised, cheeks puffed, lips pursed as if drawing an expectant breath, alert and ready for anything. Grace is in a dark dotted blouse, posing as she would for all her official photos—her head tilted slightly, smiling sweetly for the camera, patient and proud.

When an immigration official asked Hoi Chuen why they had filed these papers, he answered through a translator in Cantonese, "I thought it would be a good thing since he was born here so that he could come back here to study English." During their interrogations, the "alleged father" and "alleged mother" were asked to corroborate their ages, places of birth, address in San Francisco, marriage date, the names of their sons, alive and dead, and their daughters.

Hoi Chuen was asked, "Has Lee Jun Fon any other name?"

He joked, "The doctor gave him an American name, but I can't pronounce it."

Grace was asked, "Do you intend to have Lee Jun Fon remain with you until he grows to manhood?"

She said, "When he is able to go to school, I intend to have him come back here and attend school."

Both were advised, "If Lee Jun Fon remains abroad for more than six months he may be obliged to submit definite proof that he has not expatriated himself, if he should wish to reenter the United States."

Did they understand? Each of them answered through their translator—yes. In

---

[*] While the biographer Matthew Polly has speculated that the Lees may have overstayed their visa, US Immigration documents show that on January 3, 1940, their "Public Charge and Departure" bond was secured by the Mandarin Theatre and their stay was officially extended through June 24, 1941. They were not in the country "illegally" at the time of their departure.

the section of Form 430 asking the reason for Bruce's departure, the lawyers typed: *a temporary visit abroad.*

The Lee family was free to return to Hong Kong. But Bruce was an infirm infant, unready to travel. A Chinatown friend, the movie director Esther Eng, approached Hoi Chuen with an offer for a part, not for him but for his newborn son.

The Cantonese performing arts were entering a new era. Cinema was displacing the opera. Before Hoi Chuen had left for the States, his first film, *Robbing the Dead*, had opened. He and other stars would leave the stage for the film set. In Chinatown, the Mandarin's dominance would be toppled by the film-oriented Grandview Theatre, owned by Esther's business partner Joseph Sunn Jue.

Born Ng Kam-ha in 1914, the year that DeMille's, Chaplin's, and Sessue Hayakawa's Hollywood careers began, Esther Eng was a character in a Chinatown full of them—a liberated third-generation Chinese American who spoke and read Cantonese fluently and was a lesbian proto-feminist. She wore her hair in a crew cut and dressed in men's clothing. Her closest friends called her "Brother Ha." Like her contemporary Anna May Wong, she was an original.

At the age of twenty-one, Esther had used her father's investment to rent a Sunset Boulevard film studio and produce a movie called *Heartaches*. Billed as "The First Cantonese Singing-Talking Picture Made in Hollywood," it became a sensation in Hong Kong, Guangzhou, and Singapore, and rallied support for the Chinese national defense.

In this first golden age of Hong Kong cinema, she made five feature films. As the war in China grew, she returned to the United States permanently to make resistance-oriented movies with Joseph Sunn Jue at their Grandview studio in Chinatown. By the time Eng reached out to Hoi Chuen, she had been hailed on both sides of the Pacific as a pioneering Chinese woman director.

Set in San Francisco, Eng's movie *Golden Gate Girl* was a multigenerational family story whose outlines felt familiar to Hoi Chuen and Grace. A stern Chinese American patriarch deplores his daughter's romance with an opera singer and has him deported. But his daughter dies tragically after giving birth. His granddaughter grows up to join the theater, and the two maintain a strained relationship. In the end, the patriarch reconciles with her and her opera-actor father, who has returned to America to perform and raise funds for China's defense.

In his very first on-screen appearance, Bruce is the theater-loving granddaughter as an infant. He appears wrapped up tightly in a bassinet, cross-dressed with a girl's crown on his head, wailing irritably into a soft blanket. Born into a world swirling with art, war, and migration, the hope of free movement and the realities of utter subjection, this baby is restless, loudly straining at comforts and constraints.

CHAPTER 2
The Dead and the Diseased

When it came to Bruce, Grace admitted, "I think I spoiled him because he was so sick."

Death had haunted her and Hoi Chuen. Their first son, Li Jung Teung, had come into the world disease-stricken and doomed. "After he was born," said Bruce's younger brother, Robert Lee Jun Fai, "my mom said he would constantly look into the light. And he didn't blink much. Then, maybe a week later, he passed."

When Peter was born, he too was chronically ill. It would be the same with Bruce and with Robert, born after the war as the couple's last surviving child.*

"When we were young, we would get sick," Robert recalled. "All of a sudden, we would get a fever and then the temperature would just go up sky high." All the Lee boys seemed afflicted. "Bruce almost didn't make it," Linda Lee Cadwell, Bruce's widow, later wrote in her biography *Bruce Lee: The Man Only I Knew*. "As a child, he never ate much and for a long time remained thin and, apparently, delicate."

Hoi Chuen blamed otherworldly forces. "He believed," Robert said, "that the gods had something against our family." He and Grace visited temples to make offerings to appease the deities. To divert the demons from the boys, their parents called them by feminine nicknames. Peter was called "Curly," after his unusual hair. Bruce became Sai Fung, "Tiny Phoenix," because the phoenix was the *yin* counterpart to the masculine dragon. Hoi Chuen and Grace pierced Bruce's left ear, and sometimes dressed him, as in Esther Eng's movie, in girl's clothing.

In her biography, Linda attributed Bruce's weakness to the change in the weather, moving from the temperate climate of San Francisco to the tropical climate of Hong Kong. But as Robert recalled, "Hong Kong was on the verge of falling to enemy attack at that time. Life was very hard and there was cholera." Disease and infant mortality stalked China, close on the heels of war.

One of the most famous images of the twentieth century is "Bloody Saturday," taken on August 28, 1937, by a photojournalist named H. S. Wong moments after Japanese warplanes had bombed a crowded railway station in Shanghai. Wong was known to his colleagues by the nickname "Newsreel" because he always traveled with a Leica and an Eyemo 35mm film camera and always seemed to be exactly where news was being made.

That afternoon two thousand civilian refugees had gathered at Shanghai South

---

* Later, after Bruce, Grace would lose two more children, a girl named Fengping, born after Bruce, and another child, born after Robert.

"Bloody Saturday." H. S. "Newsreel" Wong, Shanghai, August 28, 1937. Public Domain.

station, hoping for train passage westward to safety. But in the photo, there is just one lonely living thing, a scared baby screaming in distress, horribly burned, and bathed in blood. The baby sits at the edge of the train platform, framed by debris and ruin, buckled structures, steel strewn like rolls of toilet paper. Just outside of the frame, black smoke filled the sky and the child's mother lay dead.

Wong said, "It was a horrible sight. People were still trying to get up. Dead and injured lay strewn across the tracks and platform. Limbs lay all over the place."

"I noticed," he said, "that my shoes were soaked in blood."

Wong descended onto the steaming tracks, took photos and reels, and saw a man place the crying baby on the station platform. After he snapped the photo, he heard more warplanes returning. A man he presumed to be the child's father gathered up the baby, and they fled for shelter.

This was the world to which Hoi Chuen, Grace, and Bruce were returning. Bruce would spend his first four years of life in a fallen city as a war child.

When they departed San Francisco on the *President Pierce* steamer on April 4, 1941, a century had passed since Hong Kong had been ceded to the British after the First

Opium War and four years since the start of the Second Sino-Japanese War. A surge of refugees had doubled Hong Kong's population to over 1.6 million. It would not take long for war to crash directly into their lives.

On December 8, hours after the Japanese attacked Pearl Harbor, they stormed into Singapore, Thailand, Malaya, the Philippines, Guam, and Hong Kong. The British had left the colony's defense to an outnumbered patchwork army of ten thousand British, Canadian, and Punjabi soldiers, supplemented by Chinese volunteers. On Christmas Day, Japanese soldiers entered a makeshift hospital at St. Stephen's College, bayoneted doctors and wounded soldiers, and raped and slaughtered nurses. Later that afternoon, Governor Sir Mark Young surrendered.

In the streets the soldiers and the military police made a sport of their savagery—beating, judo-throwing, and shooting countless Chinese. They tore through private homes, looting families' belongings and ravaging women. The head of one hospital estimated that he and his staff had treated thousands of rape victims. The regime publicized the torture methods they used on uncooperative Chinese and staged public executions. Tens of thousands perished in the occupation.

The Japanese conscripted Hong Kong's farmers to build tunnels and bunkers and expand the airport for warplanes. Food production collapsed. Rice itself became a spoil of war. The regime seized Hong Kong's rice reserve and shipped it to Japan, then introduced severe food rationing. Hong Kongers lamented the lack of "firewood, rice, oil, and salt," and came to name this era of famine, fear, and death the "Three Years and Eight Months." Their bitterness lasted a generation.

Bruce's sister Phoebe recalled one night vividly. After dark fell, the curfew sirens sounded, signaling to Hong Kongers it was time to lower their curtains, put out their candles, and go to sleep. But on this night, the Lis continued a lively mahjong game. Japanese soldiers broke down the door and commanded the family to stop. When Bruce's aunt protested, the soldiers beat her and her husband. Grace objected too, and was slapped black and blue. The soldiers forced the humiliated adults to grovel as the Li children watched.

During the war, the family's small apartment—down a small Yau Ma Tei alley called Mau Lam Street—was full, packed with as many as a dozen people. Hoi Chuen had lost two of his older siblings in those dark years, a sister and a brother. He took in his deceased brother's wife and her five children, and provided for his two surviving sisters, their spouses, and their children. With his own four children, including frail Bruce, and Hoi Chuen's mother to care for, he and Grace needed to keep them all from starving.

The Japanese cultural ministry was renaming streets, places, and buildings, and replacing English instruction with Japanese. But it was also invested in fostering the appearance of pan-Asian solidarity, naming their imperial project the "Greater East Asia Co-Prosperity Sphere." The Japanese knew the Chinese had resented British rule, which coupled contemptuous messages of white superiority with destructive neglect. They converted news outlets into a propaganda arm. One newspaper editorialized, "Thanks to Japan, we are now a free people, and the shapers of our own destiny. The question of color is dead."

The cultural ministry forced all entertainers to register, and sent agents to enlist performers, Robert recalled, to "create an atmosphere of prosperity with singing and dancing and to whitewash an illusion of peace." Kosuke Kawada, a radio host who represented the Japanese cultural ministry, offered Hoi Chuen and other Cantonese opera artists the opportunity to continue performing in exchange for food rations. Caught between Japanese patronage and Chinese pride, between supporting the resistance and feeding his family, Hoi Chuen chose to keep acting.

"My father never received a salary. They only paid him in rice bags," Phoebe recalled, mimicking him tossing one over his shoulder.

The Japanese tried to pressure Hoi Chuen and other prominent Chinese performers to appear in a feature-length propaganda film, *The Battle of Hong Kong: The Day England Fell*, which would present the occupation as liberation from British rule. It would be the only film made in Hong Kong during the war. But this time, Hoi Chuen "courageously refused," the biographer Matthew Polly wrote. "The wise decision saved his career—those who appeared in the movie were blacklisted after the war as collaborators."

Hong Kong emptied again, losing a million people as deportees and refugees crossed the straits back to Macao and the mainland and the death toll mounted. But the Lee family hunkered down. They survived on thin *pok chang* pancakes they made from tapioca starch. When Hoi Chuen brought home his rice ration, they added water to make *jook*, a pot of soup that would feed everyone for a day.

Newsreel Wong's bloodied baby was seen by hundreds of millions and would be credited with aligning the Allies against Japan. But for the West this image was twinned with another, much older image. The West pitied the abject War Child, but abhorred the Sick Man of Asia.

The Sick Man was a powerful racist trope linking Chinese to contagion, impurity, and revulsion. It dated back to the 1700s, when the Qing empire was at its height, New York was a minor British colony, and frustrated Europeans were trying to force open trade with an indifferent China to gain access to her riches.

Its origins were steeped in a terrible irony. To combat outbreaks of smallpox across his dominion, the Qianlong emperor had commissioned a national study. The resulting report represented the best thinking in epidemiology in the world, including advanced ideas like contact tracing and inoculation.

It also featured detailed woodblock reproductions meant to aid doctors in the diagnosis and treatment of the disease. But when these images found their way back to Europe, they were separated from the study and recast in the context of racist pseudo-sciences like phrenology and eugenics. European mass audiences—

absurdly—received them as confirmation that the Chinese were a dirty, disease-ridden people.

A century later, in the mid-1800s, the balance of power between China and Europe had shifted. The British were harvesting opium in India to trade for silk, tea, porcelain, and silver from China. Chinese of all classes had become hooked on the narcotic. Qing leaders saw opium addiction as an epidemic, an economic drain, and a national crisis, and banned it.

But the British refused to stop the illegal trade—opium pried China open to even more exploitation. In 1839, Manchu leaders blockaded Western drug boats in the Pearl River, seizing and destroying their opium caches. Britain and her European allies met them with diplomatic pressure, troops, and gunships, and years of war began.

Two Opium Wars across two decades pushed China into steep decline. Britain, France, Russia, and the United States forced China to legalize opium and the coolie labor trades, and pay cash reparations for their war costs and lost drug shipments. Hong Kong passed into the ownership of the Crown. "The Sick Man of Asia" became an enduring epithet.

War set migrants in motion. At the end of the nineteenth century, after outbreaks of smallpox and bubonic plague spread through southern China, "The Sick Man of Asia" trope followed the Chinese across the Pacific. The Chinese body itself—once exotic and desirable, now pathetic and detestable, laid low by ravenous, repugnant, infectious appetites—was seen as so outside the realm of normal, it was not so much inhuman as anti-human. In San Francisco, the top health officer and physician proclaimed that the Chinese would "breed and engender disease wherever they reside," and called them "moral lepers."

As smallpox struck San Francisco in 1875, officials reduced funding for sanitation and hospitals. One city health official pointed the blame away from budget cuts to "the presence in our midst of 30,000 of unscrupulous, lying, and treacherous Chinamen, who have disregarded our sanitary laws, concealed or are concealing their cases of smallpox." Leaders passed a resolution to declare Chinatown a "public nuisance." Business leaders plotted to empty Chinatown of the Chinese.

On March 6, 1900, reports surfaced of a Chinese American who had died of the bubonic plague. The next day, city officials quarantined Chinatown, an area home to one in five of the city's residents. At sunrise, angry crowds of Chinese cooks, servants, and laundrymen hoping to get to their jobs outside of Chinatown gathered at the cordon. Police truncheoned Chinese who tried to leave, while escorting out whites. Health officials voted to encircle Chinatown with barbed wire, and seriously discussed burning it down to the ground. Instead, they began building a high wall around the radius of Chinatown.

As Chinese American leaders lodged formal protests, Mayor James Duval Phelan, a loud Asian exclusionist, argued the quarantine was essential to protect white San Franciscans. His opponents—no more ethical or enlightened—included business interests, who argued that Phelan's quarantine would crush the economy, and the surgeon general of the navy, who believed that the plague was "a disease peculiar to the Orient" to which whites were likely immune. As for the Chinese inside the police lines and on the wrong side of the rising wall, the journalist David Randall wrote, their imprisonment left them "isolated, unable to escape either the disease or the white men they did not trust or understand."

The Sick Man of Asia trope would persist as an evolving meme of white superiority and Chinese humiliation.

As we watch the swagger and blur of Bruce Lee on-screen now, it is hard to imagine him ever having been sickly. There he is in the 1972 movie *Fist of Fury*, as Chen Zhen, avenger of China, standing on the *dojo* mat, bare-chested, sinewy, and ripped, the Chinese body revivified, one man standing against the aggressors.

We look down—as if we sit alongside all the Hong Kongers who survived the occupation, all the Asians whose forebears faced pogroms on American soil, all the ghosts before and after carrying that racial shame—and witness the unfolding drama.

At the center, Chen crouches and flexes, and the motion seems to ripple through all of his opponents, as if he is conducting an anxious orchestra. When two of them abruptly attack, he springs into action, dispatching man by hapless man with throws, punches, elbows, spinning kicks, and the thunder crack of the *nunchaku*, that crop-threshing instrument of Okinawans and Filipinos that they transformed into a weapon of resistance against Japanese imperialism.

After Chen Zhen has left the school's *sensei* writhing on the mat, he wags his finger at the rest of the *dojo*: "We Chinese aren't the sick men." He smashes the frame of a brush painting bearing the insult "Sick Man of Asia," tears it to pieces, and force-feeds their words back to them.

"You'll eat the paper this time," Chen says. "Next time I'll make you eat the glass."

Legend has it that when this scene first played in the theaters of Southeast Asia, riots broke out, chairs were ripped out and tossed, and audiences roared a century of hunger.

CHAPTER 3
The One Who Can't Be Stopped

In the summer of 1945, the surrender of the Japanese brought the occupation to an end. The sickly boy suddenly blossomed into an energetic one, a perpetual sound-and-motion machine. Each day from when the birds began singing and the dogs started barking until they all went to sleep, Bruce's mind and body needed constant stimulation. As he rushed to and fro, his family exclaimed, *"Mou si ting, cho m'ding!* 無時停、坐唔定—he can't be stopped, he won't sit still!"

The family's fortunes turned dramatically. During the worst of the war, as people cleared out of Hong Kong, the frugal Hoi Chuen had saved enough to quietly purchase a couple of dozen housing units. Now shelter for returnees and refugees was inadequate, and rents soared. Grace managed the units, as well as the family's other investments, with skill and acumen, bringing them steady income for years to come.

The Li family settled into a second-floor, four-thousand-square-foot apartment on Nathan Road in the heart of Kowloon. Its entryway opened to a high-ceilinged foyer filled with carved teakwood furniture. There were two rooms, the first with double bunk beds and dressers that opened to a bathroom and a balcony.

The other room, a friend recalled, "tripled as a dining room, living room, and sleeping area," with bunks and a large round dining table. It too connected to the balcony, where more bunks were stationed. On the balcony, a corner was curtained off for a bathing area. In the back was a tiny kitchen with a two-burner stove and small living quarters for the help, Ngan Ma and her son, Wu Ngan, who was Bruce's age and constant companion, and went by Ngan Jai.

The flat was near Whitfield Barracks, where the Gurkha soldiers were housed and the British military force stored its arms. During the war, shrapnel from a shelling had permanently scarred their veranda. But now, living here at the border of the Yau Ma Tei and Tsim Sha Tsui districts felt safe. The house was alive—the adults chitchatting over domestic tasks, the children ducking and darting here and there, a constant stream of visitors at the door.

The number in residence swelled to as many as twenty at a time, including a second live-in maid, a driver on retainer, and a loud menagerie of house pets—cats, birds, dogs, chickens, goldfish, and rabbits. "My family was, as you say, 'well to do,'" Bruce recalled in a later interview. "We had servants, always someone to do everything for you—wait on you hand and foot. I suppose I was spoiled."

L-R: Grace Li, Phoebe Lee, Bruce Lee, Agnes Lee, Li Hoi Chuen, Peter Lee. Photo courtesy of the Bruce Lee Family Archive.

He tortured his siblings with tricks, luring them into traps that ended with him drenching them in water or giving them electric shocks. He jumped on his parents' bed so much he broke the springs, twice. He rained ice cubes and fruit down on the weekend crowds of passersby on Nathan Road. He stole mangos from the neighbor's garden. He offered his cousin and uncle his dog's poop to eat, telling them it was chestnuts. He swallowed the rubber nipple from his baby brother Robert's bottle and thought he would die.

One evening when his nanny left for errands, he rearranged the furniture and turned out the lights. When she returned, she stumbled through the dark room, banging into everything and cursing him to heaven. Grace scolded him and issued her punishment, but when alone, she chuckled at his demented mischief.

Bruce was a chatterbox, pestering his parents, siblings, and nannies with impertinent questions. Why did he have to apologize to his nanny? Why did he have to go to school? Why do girls get spanked with rolled-up newspapers and boys with bamboo sticks? Unceasingly entertaining and exasperating, pure *yang* energy, Bruce earned a permanent nickname from the family: *Mou Si Ting*, the One Who Can't Be Stopped.

Even at rest, his sister Agnes said, "Bruce was a sleepwalker. We slept in bunkers, and many times I would see him climb down from the top bunk in the middle of the night, and while in a sound sleep, go strolling off."

Once in his sleep in the deep of night, he descended the bunk, walked out onto the balcony, and climbed onto the railing. His mother and siblings gathered to watch, breathlessly. Grace desperately whispered to them, warning them not to call out to him lest he awake and plunge to the street below. Finally Bruce climbed down, went back into the room, and climbed into his bunk. The next day, Phoebe asked him why he had dared to do something so dangerous, but Bruce had no memory of it. He had been out cold.

Young Bruce treated the classroom with indifference. He was behind his peers because he had been held back a grade. But Hoi Chuen knew there was a wild fantasy world going on in the boy's head. Comic books, martial arts serials, and pulp tales of the Monkey King and other Chinese heroes calmed the boy's racing mind. When Bruce was at a table or on the floor copying images of swordsmen and dragons with a steady drawing hand, the household received a moment of relief.

Hoi Chuen told Bruce fantastic stories of ancient *tai chi* heroes. He took Bruce along with him to his sessions with his *tai chi sifu*, master Liang Tzu-peng, and the child tried to imitate the men. When Hoi Chuen hung out with his performing friends, he called out to Bruce, "Show some moves to your uncles!"

Phoebe and young Bruce were awestruck by their father's artistry. She studied opera with her father, but Bruce seemed especially transported. Hoi Chuen sometimes invited his children to accompany him to his performances in Hong Kong and across southern China, where he sat them in the VIP seats near the musicians alongside the stage.

At one show, Phoebe watched as Bruce slipped trance-like into the rhythms and melodies, imitating the dancers' gestures and movements. In the next moment, to the laughter of the crowd, the boy was being escorted off the stage by company members. Near the end of the war, Hoi Chuen secured bit parts for Phoebe, Agnes, and Bruce in one of his plays. It was the boy's first conscious, permitted taste of the limelight, and he wanted more.

Hong Kong became the new center of the Chinese film industry, taking in Shanghai's displaced capital, skill, and talent. As a *chou sang*, one of Hong Kong's most celebrated comic actors, Hoi Chuen was well positioned for the new opportunities. Because film studios could efficiently convert the stage performances into movies, Cantonese opera provided ready content, staging, and production to meet a bottomless demand for postwar escapism. Hoi Chuen starred in over one hundred films, playing, in the words of the film critic Stephen Teo, "generals, magistrates, and fools." The pay was better than the opera, the audiences bigger, and he could also bring the kids to his movie shoots.

Bruce gladly took on the task of delivering food or snacks from the house to the set. The studio was an ideal playground for his nonstop imagination. He roamed across the back lot and climbed on ladders to tinker with the lights. He charmed nearly everyone he met. The director Yu Leung asked Hoi Chuen if he could cast six-year-old Bruce in a movie. Hoi Chuen agreed, and the father and son played a father and son under the lights. The movie, *Wealth Is Like a Dream*, premiered in the colony in 1948, three days before Bruce's eighth birthday.

Grace recalled, "At two o'clock in the morning, I'd call out, 'Bruce, the car is here,' and he'd leap up and put on his shoes and go off very cheerfully. There was no trouble getting him up when it came to making a film. When I had to get him up for school in the mornings, however, it was quite a different story."

"During summer vacations, we let him make more movies," she said on another occasion. "Bruce liked it so much that he said, 'You know, Mom, I don't want to go to school. I want to make some money!'"

Phoebe recalled that when Bruce was young her mother went to a fortune teller. He told Grace that she would have three living sons, a prophecy that would be fulfilled when Robert was born. But he went on: "One of your sons will be a Black Dragon, the dragon of floods and deep waters. The Black Dragon is like a general, he influences a lot of people and he is above everyone. When he reaches his thirties, they will take him back to the heavens. If you don't believe me, just see."

Young Bruce would soon be embodying some of Hong Kong's deepest postwar fears and hopes.

After the Japanese surrendered to the Allied nations, Hong Kongers did not enjoy the independence that came to India, Pakistan, Vietnam, Indonesia, and Burma. Intent upon maintaining a presence in China while the Communists and Nationalists jockeyed for power, Western powers restored control of the territory to the British. "They were the minority," Bruce would later say, "but they ran the city."

As the civil war in China drew to its conclusion in 1949, an even larger wave of migrants poured across the border. Some days, a hundred thousand might gather at the Lo Wu bridge in Shenzhen to await crossing. Between 1945 and 1950, Hong Kong's population swelled from 600,000 to 2,237,000. The colony would be reshaped by this new generation—a brimming, restless, questing demographic not unlike the West's Baby Boomers.

After the war Hong Kongers were all too aware of their political precarity, caught between the imperial designs of China and Great Britain, abandoned by one and neglected by the other. While Beijing long-gamers looked toward the day when the colony would return to Communist China, the British elite, who made up less than 1 percent of Hong Kong's population, returned to rule with Cold War calibration and domestic neglect. Free marketeers from Europe and the United States saw the colony as the perfect place to build a rat lab for unfettered capitalism.

"There is literally nothing here," the famous economist Milton Friedman once said. "Hong Kong has in that sense no past. Hong Kong also has no future."

But through many successive waves of in-migration, Hong Kongers kept alive their own creation story. The first people of Hong Kong, according to myth, were a people from Guangdong called the Lo Ting, who had risen up in AD 411 behind a brave Cantonese leader named Lu Xun to fight the oppressive Western Jin dynasty. Their army got as far as the Yangtze River, but was finally routed and forced to flee all the way through the southeastern borderlands beyond the empire's edges to the caves of Lantau island.

There, the stories say, the outcast and isolated Lo Ting ate so much fish they began to grow fish heads and scales. These merpeople lived between land and water, moving deftly between the two to stay ahead of angry gods and outside marauders. One story had them tattooing themselves to look like dragons to evade the Water God. Hard-coded into the Lo Ting mythology were ideas, the journalist Louisa Lim wrote, that the Hong Kong people were "children of a rebel, born of insurrection," and Hong Kong was, in the words of one of her interview subjects, "the safe haven, the refuge for those escaping from injustice and tyranny."

Hong Kong's burgeoning postwar film industry was making movies for a rapidly growing audience that was young, poor, and undersheltered. Through the cinema's flickering images, a new generation bolstered by war refugees could begin to process mass trauma, channel their vast yearnings, and bind themselves together in a new identity.

Before the war, the movies of Hong Kong's first golden age had often been serious, nationalist, and patriotic, committed to the fate of the mainland. After the war, sentimental and moralistic family melodramas became popular. But the children of the post-1949 generation, those of Bruce's age, were a different breed altogether—wild, independent, even anarchic.

Young Bruce sometimes came to the film set with Ngan Jai. There, they befriended the son of a stuntman, a boy named Unicorn Chan who would also become a child star. The three roamed the streets, looking for adventure.

"They either went off shooting marbles together," Robert Lee recalled, "or were walking down Nathan Road and kicking the rat collection bins that were hanging off the lampposts along the side of the road."

Film directors saw in these children the volatility of the rising young city. In his little body, Bruce somehow perfectly distilled their typhoon energy and war-hardened attitude. In *Wealth Is Like a Dream*, Yu Leung cast Bruce as one of a pair of uneducated, unsheltered orphans roaming the streets and living by their wits in the naked city. In at least half of the twenty movies he made in Hong Kong, Bruce would play the orphan, the impoverished urchin, or the abandoned child—sometimes all three in the same role.

Here was an emerging Hong Kong postwar cinematic archetype: the derelict child, hungry, tough and tender-hearted, but also hurt, angry, and explosive, desperately searching for a parental figure. Like Hong Kongers themselves, the postwar child stood between abandonment and neglect. But this child would not be a mirror of the colonizer's image, an automaton without past or future made to produce wealth for someone else. The child was a Galeano mirror, the face of the unseen and forgotten.

Bruce's breakout movie came when he was just nine years old, in the 1950 drama *My Son Ah Cheung*, best known as *The Kid*.

Yuen Po-Wan's "Kiddy Cheung" was one of the most popular daily *manhua* comic strips of the time, featuring a primitively drawn orphan whose personality exploded off the page. Ah Cheung is street-smart and naïve, navigating an adult world of greed and hypocrisy, swinging between good and evil, impatient but irrepressible.

Director Fung Fung cast Bruce in the starring role of Kid Cheung, opposite his father. Hoi Chuen played Hung Park-Ho, a stingy, dull-witted sweatshop owner. Hung is a capitalist so self-absorbed that he doesn't even know his son Charles and foreman Four-Eyed Joe are harassing the seamstresses and embezzling his goods under his nose.

Kid Cheung lives with his uncle Ho and two young cousins. Uncle Ho represents the hard luck of Hong Kong's multitude. He is educated and upright, but destitute, hawking books on the street. He lands a job with Hung as a secretary and a tutor to his children, and Hung arranges for Ah Cheung to enter an elite school. But when the Kid shows up, he is bullied by his wealthy schoolmates. Encircled, he fights them all, is beaten soundly, and expelled.

The Kid goes to work at Hung's factory but discovers Charles's and Four-Eyed Joe's thievery. In retaliation, they fire the boy and his uncle. An embittered Kid Cheung runs away and falls under the sway of Flying Blade Lee, played by the director as a Sino-Japanese War veteran, gangster, and smuggler. Under Flying Blade, the Kid becomes a prosperous street thief.

Now sporting a fedora like Flying Blade, flush with cash and seeking approval, the Kid returns to see his desolate uncle. The old man curses him out for following the wrong crowd, calling him a "bad guy."

The Kid's mood sours. "Uncle, you look like a rich man," he says.

"What? How?" Uncle asks.

"A rich man sneers upon a poor man," the Kid says, mimicking Uncle Ho's sanctimony. "'Bad guy, bad guy, BAD GUY!'"

The Kid is immediately guilt-stricken and offers to buy Uncle Ho tea to talk it out. But Uncle isn't done lecturing him.

"Ah Cheung, look at you—dressed like a hoodlum," he says. "You're young. Someday..."

"'Someday, someday, someday,'" the Kid explodes, "I don't care about 'SOMEDAY'!"

Uncle disowns him. Kid Cheung vows to visit his young cousins, but Uncle threatens to beat him if he does. The Kid turns to leave but, in a last gesture of contrition, tries to give Uncle a large roll of money. Uncle knocks it away. Shaking with emotion, the Kid pulls a knife on him.

"Stab me then!" Uncle Ho shouts.

Mortified, the Kid flees.

He reappears soon after to deliver a large bag of food to his cousins. When the children ask him where he's been, the Kid names a faraway heaven without hunger and strain: "America."

Then he's gone.

Bruce had brought to his performance as the Kid the poise and firecracker precocity of one for whom the stage is an inheritance. Perhaps the presence of his father inspired him toward an unforgettable performance.

Despite being beaten down in his first filmed fight scene, Bruce is memorable in the next. He dispatches a rival boy in the factory with a block, a punch, and a broom. Then he brushes his thumb across his nose and smirks—a move he has picked up from Fung Fung's Flying Blade Lee—and we shudder with recognition, knowing how he will use this same gesture in the future.

The camera loves his round, elastic face. He arches his back, puffs out his chest like a peacock, and struts around chin up with a little ditty-bop. To entertain his cousins, the Kid jumps onto a chair, slaps on sunglasses, and delivers a bulge-eyed, jut-jawed, ape-faced impression of his fatuous classroom teacher. His delighted cousins erupt in disobedient laughter, mutinous child's play undoing the adult world.

Hong Kong family melodramas of the 1950s tried to advance values of collectivism and mutuality. But Bruce's nose-swiping Kid is not infatuated with a far-off cause. He is a tiny rebel trapped in an eternal present controlled by overwhelming powers that threaten to erase him.

"Disappearance," wrote the journalist Louisa Lim, "is the ultimate fear of Hong Kongers."

But the Kid stares down existential threat with a pride, instinct, and swagger that belie his age and size. The audience is prepared to accept a tragedy. The Kid is just like them—meaning there is no way he can win.

Yet *The Kid* attempts a filmic resolution. Flying Blade Lee's gang attacks Charles and Four-Eyed Joe, and the seamstresses, outraged at their corruption and sexual abuse, go on strike at Hung's factory. Treated kindly by Mei, one of the women unionists, Kid Cheung joins their picket and helps to unite the gang and the workers. The women win the strike, the criminals are banished, and Flying Blade Lee gives the Kid the money he has stolen from Hung so that Ah Cheung, Uncle Ho, and his cousins can return to their ancestral village. Mei and the seamstresses see them off as they stride toward an Edenic Chinese pastoral beyond time and strife.

It was a pat ending—but for Hong Kongers in 1950, a happy one. As the Kid, Bruce had transfigured their self-image from pitiable war child into redeeming orphan.

The Kid drew large audiences and inspired critics to call young Bruce a "prodigy" and "child genius actor." His star appeal was sealed, and his rise would parallel the rapid expansion of the Hong Kong film industry. In the new decade, Hong Kong would nurture a film culture and a fighting culture. The big dreamer who played the little scrapper on-screen wanted to be in the middle of both.

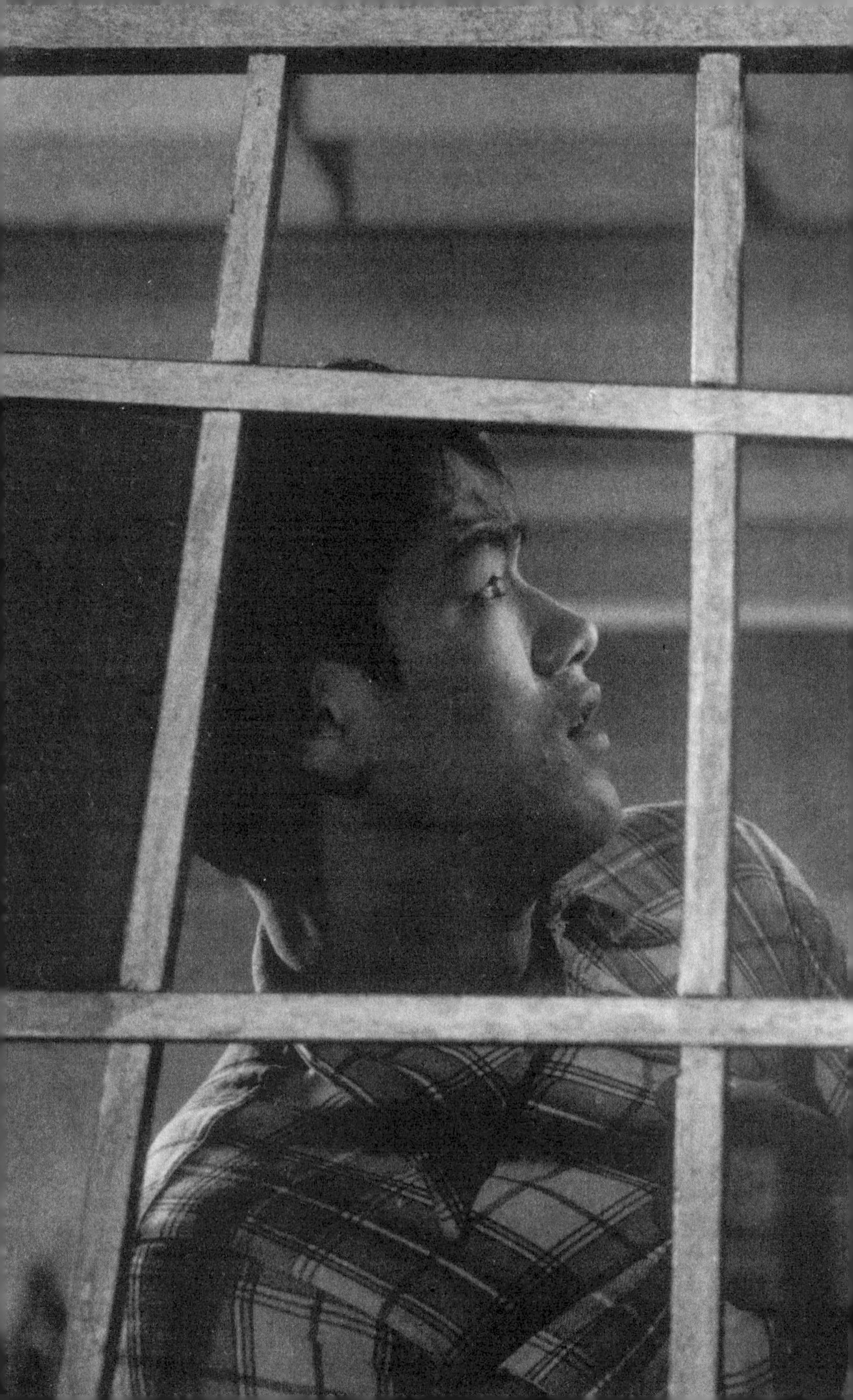

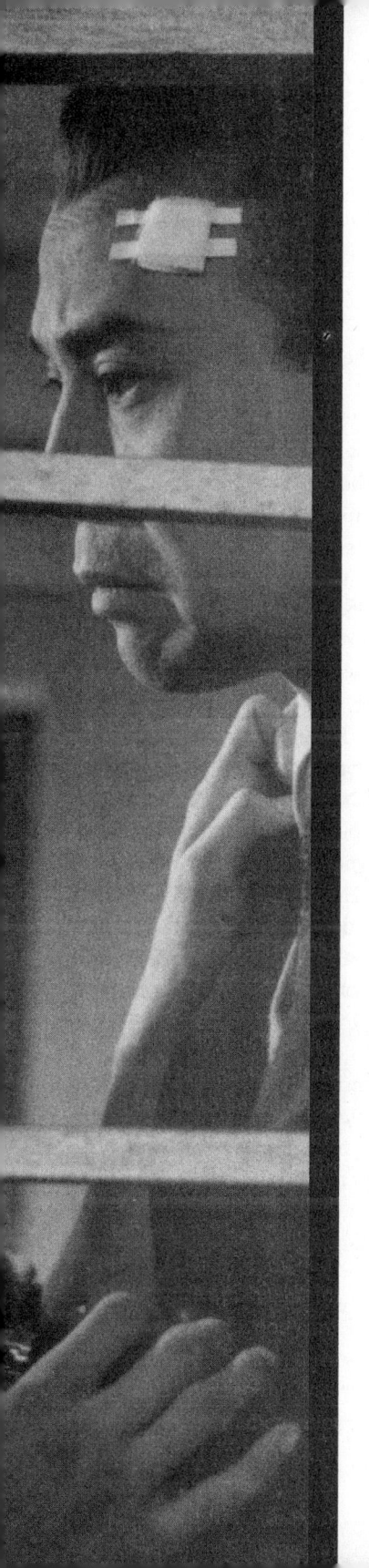

PART II
The Orphan
1950–1959

> The smaller man usually makes up for the balance of power by his greater agility, flexibility, speed of foot, and nervous action.
>
> —GEORGE F. JOWETT

The Orphan, 1960. Bruce Lee with Ng Cho-Fan.
Courtesy of the Bruce Lee Family Archive.

CHAPTER 4
The Kung Fu Guy

There was a time when even Bruce Lee yearned to be the Kung Fu Guy, admired and respected.*

It is 1949, the year of China's revolution—or the year of its fall, depending on your perspective—and Bruce is turning nine years old, ten by the Chinese count. This birthday is significant. Ten finally places Bruce beyond the reach of malicious spirits. His doting mother still calls him by his feminized nickname—Sai Fung, Tiny Phoenix—and will continue to even when he is an adult, even after he has passed. Bruce won't complain because he loves his mother. But he doesn't need that name anymore to be protected, much less all that *yin* energy. He is restless for a new name. In the movies, he is called "Little Li Hoi Chuen," "Li Yum" (triple gold), and "Genius Child Star." Soon he will have a more suitable one bestowed by the lesser gods of movie marketing. Soon, but not yet.

Bruce's left earring may ward off otherworldly forces, but at Tak Sun, his all-boys private primary school, it has attracted playground teasing and hallway bullying. Boys are simple. They don't know—or don't care—about the difference between self-defense and aggression. They'll circle you, cheer when you raise your fists against another, and respect you only for what you can show.

Picture Bruce alone in bed staring at the ceiling. He is small, restive, languishing at the bottom of the class. He is nearsighted and self-conscious. The insults might never lose their bite. In the next room his brother Peter spreads his books across the dining table, engaged in the daily work of defining what it means to be a Li boy—diligent, studious, handsome, pleasing to peers and teachers, uncles, aunts, and elders alike. Peter doesn't fight in the halls, he wins fencing trophies.

At this birthday party in 1949, Bruce is in the center of the frame, talking and laughing even louder and faster than he normally does, receiving red envelopes from his father's friends and the children they have brought with them, many of whom he doesn't know. Some, like Unicorn Chan and Wu Ngan, have been with him forever. Others have never met real movie stars before. William Cheung Cheuk-hing, born seven weeks before Bruce, observes how the boy's presence fills the room, how everyone fusses over him.

William is the second son of his father's second wife and thus twice cursed.

---

* Shout-out to Charles Yu's *Interior Chinatown*. I'm using "Kung Fu Guy" in tribute to his book and the archetype, while *"gung fu* guy" refers to actual martial arts practitioners.

When his older half brother, the first son of the first wife, is in a rage, which is often, he kicks William and his other siblings around. William calls him King Kong, and King Kong's aggression makes William also want to be a Kung Fu Guy. Perhaps Bruce, the boy who stands up to bullies on the big screen, can help him.

Bruce is called to the center of the room. William notices that the smiling boy has long arms and walks on the tips of his toes with a little bounce. William is built like a square red brick, Bruce like a green bamboo shoot. Both of them have high foreheads—to the Taoists, a sure sign of intelligence. William's nose pinches up like a bulldog's. Bruce has cat lashes, shiba eyes, and Valentino lips. As mother and child stand in front of the ancestral altar, Grace explains to the crowd that Bruce is now free of the curse, and they no longer need to dress him or refer to him as if he were a girl. William feels his hopes sinking. When he sees the birthday cake dedicated to "Tiny Phoenix," all he can feel is sorry for Bruce.

The following year, Bruce makes his star turn in *The Kid*, and for the first time the marquees bill him as "Siu Loong," the Little Dragon, the masculine name Bruce has wanted. The movie's runaway success makes it stick. He is cast as the lead for Chin Chien's 1951 Grandview Pictures film, *Infancy*, also known as *The Birth of Mankind*.

He plays another young tough, more interested in comic books than schoolwork, whose mother is more interested in mahjong than her children. He wins fights with the other boys, but not with his mother, who beats him mercilessly. After running away from home, he follows fraudulent mystics and underground thieves. One day he attempts to rob a woman but is shocked to discover his target is his own mother. Fleeing again in shame, he is hit by a car and killed. The movie is transparently, didactically, tediously Confucian, and it flops at the box office.

To her son, who at the age of ten has already experienced the magnificent highs and bottomless lows of minor stardom, Grace offers some wisdom: "The life of a famous film star is not so comfortable as you imagine. Their lives are abnormal."

In the fall of 1951, Grace and Hoi Chuen enroll him at La Salle College, one of the top schools in the colony. The instruction is in English, the students are Chinese and British, and Peter is already the school's golden child.

At La Salle, all the other boys soon know about Bruce's movies, the famous folks he knows, and the pet monkey he bought with his own money, because he can't stop talking about these things. To classmate Robert Wang—who will become one of Hong Kong's most important barristers, but in that moment is a refugee boy looking for a protector—Bruce is "a loner," "nerdy, temperamental, and aloof," who is "about fighting and being even better than the best." Bruce lets Robert tag along when he's out making himself known.

Sometimes when Bruce can't get kids to pay him any attention, he picks a fight with them. But respect is different from submission, and submission is different from admiration. To Michael Lai, a fellow child actor who will become a famous composer but in that moment is an admirer, young Bruce is "everyone's leader." When he wins, he rubs his thumb across his nose and gives a show. When he loses, he's *ngaa chaat*—boasty but still entertaining. To James Wong Jim, who will also become a Cantopop legend but in that moment is just the target of a boy who once wore an earring, Bruce is a "total ruffian, a Teddy Boy from head to toe."

One day, for some reason, Bruce beats down his brother and the offended Wong Jim jumps in to save his family's dignity. But Bruce whips him too and finishes him off by making him eat dirt. Wong Jim gathers his cousin and three other boys Bruce has terrorized and together they hatch a plan of vengeance. In the bathroom they surround Bruce as he's coming out of a stall and pants him. Seeing Bruce's birth defect and private shame, their jaws drop, and they gleefully pour back into the halls with a new name for him, "Lee One Ball."

For weeks, Bruce chases them after school. They turn to throw stones at him before scattering again like koels. The path of pursuit is recursive—hunter becoming hunted and back around again until all are prey.

Everyone knows the pecking order, and at the top is a hulking Britisher who swaggers through the school demanding lunch money from the Chinese kids. Bruce starts carrying a pocketknife. Sometimes he uses it to slash the tires of the bicycles of the boys he is beefing with. But on the day the white boy comes for him, Bruce is ready: OK, *follow me.*

Leading him into the bathroom, Bruce thrusts his knife up against his bully's pale stomach. He glares up at the boy's face and demands the British boy strip to his underwear. Bruce takes his clothes, pushes him into a stall, and warns him, *You better not come out!* Bruce tiptoes out of the bathroom, then runs out of the school, tossing the boy's uniform behind a bush.

When the British boy does not show up at his pickup spot, his desperate parents alert the school administrators, then the police, who hop right to it. They search the school up and down, until at last they find him snoring in the bathroom stall. The next day all the Chinese kids are buzzing about the white bully who got what was coming to him, and about Bruce, who finally delivered it. Grace and Hoi Chuen, of course, are also alerted to Bruce's misbehavior.

By now, William Cheung is learning an art called Wing Chun from real *gung fu* guys—an actual grandmaster from Fatshan named Yip Man and his contentious disciples. When William hears about Bruce's exploits, he is impressed. But the same incident has earned Bruce an epic parental whipping, an order to report to Peter every day after school, and a ban from acting. Just when his name is on the lips of movie audiences across Hong Kong and all the other kids in Kowloon, Bruce's screen life is over.

Picture him in his bed, still dreaming of being the Kung Fu Guy, beyond shame and reproach.

• • •

In the decade after the war, Chinese refugees and returnees quadrupled the colony's population from 600,000 to 2.4 million. Half of Hong Kong's population was under the age of twenty-one, nine years lower than the United States in the middle of its Baby Boom. While white America's youth were enjoying—and rebelling against—the fruits of the affluent society, Hong Kong's youth faced much different conditions.

In the last six months of 1949, the number of squatters swelled from 45,000 to 300,000. Housing stock was dangerously insufficient. Old slums filled with new arrivals. When those were full, open fields, tracts, and hillsides became dense shantytowns of wood and metal. Governor Alexander Grantham defended the colonial administration's neglect, saying there was "no reason for turning Hong Kong into a glorified soup kitchen for refugees from all over China."

As if called down by angry gods, a season of massive fires followed. At the start of 1950, a blaze swept through Kowloon's infamous Walled City at Junction Road, destroying over 2,500 shanties, a Buddhist temple, and countless more businesses, legal and illegal—kitchen-table tailor shops, unlicensed dental services, day care centers, brothels, opium dens, gambling parlors, even film studios—leaving 3,500 families and 17,000 persons without shelter. Another fire in Tung Tau left 25,000 homeless. Then, on Christmas Day in 1953, a kerosene stove fire in a lean-to overtook the encampment on the slope of Shek Kip Mei, killing two and leaving an astonishing 53,000 people homeless. During the 1950s, over 190,000 Hong Kong squatters would be displaced by the fires.

Colonial administrative disdain had marked Hong Kongers' lives. In 1841, when Hong Kong had been taken by the British as part of the plunder from the First Opium War, it was merely an afterthought scribbled into the margins of a treaty. One writer thought his country had been fleeced by China and famously called Hong Kong "a barren rock with hardly a house upon it . . . it will never be a mart of trade." Generations of imperials ignored Hong Kong. As the Empire retreated from Burma, Ceylon, Singapore, and India after World War II, it all but abandoned the colony to become a dog-eat-dog free-for-all.

European and American free marketeers came to see neglect as a virtuous form of laissez-faire. "Hong Kong has no other public, moral, intellectual, artistic, cultural or ethical purpose as a society of individuals," said one US economist. "It is just one big bazaar."

The war's end brought moneyed elites from cities like Shanghai and Beijing. But it also brought the Triads, the organized criminal syndicates of southeastern China, who took up in the broad cracks where governance failed, like the Walled City.

"By 1951 and '52, they started recruiting young people—some as young as 10," William Cheung recalled. By the time he and Bruce were 14, he says, the Triads had rooted across the colony.

"They recruited young people to do their dirty jobs," William said. "They would use the 'good guy, bad guy' tactic. They would get the bad guy to bully you and the good guy would come along and say, 'Look, I can take care of you. Join the gang and you'll be OK.'" They demanded protection dues, established elaborate initiation rituals, and maintained military-like control, but also provided an anchoring certainty against the chaos.

This city on fire seemed to foreshadow the story of another, half a world away and two decades later: the burning Bronx, where gangs filled the spaces that government abandoned until an impoverished, underhoused young precariat came together to rise from the rubble. In the Bronx of the 1970s, the violence would recede before the youths' salving creativity, producing the hip-hop movement. In the Hong Kong of the 1950s, a culture of fight took hold among the colony's restless youth.

In the media, a revival of martial arts tales took over. Writers like Louis Cha, writing under the pen name Jin Yong, seemed to transmute Hong Kongers' dramas of exile and return into rip-roaring *wuxia* serials set in a mythical Chinese past. They fueled an explosion of newsprint tabloids. In 1948, the return of the 1920s film franchise showcasing the fictional Shaolin hero Fong Sai Yuk would lead to over a dozen movies in the next decade. The following year, *The True Story of Wong Fei-Hung*—based loosely on the life of a Cantonese doctor and Hung Gar *gung fu* master, directed by Wu Pang and starring Kwan Tak-Hing in exhilarating kung fu combat with swords, staffs, and empty hands—tapped into a mass desire to escape the ashes of the present for a world of good and evil where injustice could be overcome through heroic action. A landmark in Hong Kong's postwar culture, it launched a hundred more films.

In Macao, a real-life showdown—staged weeks after the Shek Kip Mei firestorm as a charity for its victims—pitted a *tai chi* master against a White Crane *gung fu* fighter and became the media event of the year. In sweaty rooms and on breezy apartment rooftops, in temples, shantytowns, and union halls, young men and women trained intensely in the myriad martial arts schools that had migrated to the colony from all over China. To British authorities and the respectable classes, the *gung fu* craze was a sign of decadence. Street fighting was quickly made illegal.

But by 1954, it seemed nearly everyone else in Hong Kong dreamed of being a Kung Fu Guy.

At La Salle, Bruce was required to wear a tie and a jacket. In family photos, he is in his uniform—a clean, pressed white shirt, khakis, and penny loafers, his hair slicked back, flashing his perfect smile. Another shows him carrying a fencing sword. But he quickly resumed being the un-Peter—disruptive and underachieving.

Sometimes he paid other students to do his homework for him. Sometimes he browbeat them into doing it. The martial arts he was picking up in snatches on movie sets did not just bolster his status in the school halls, they serviced a thin fiction that Bruce was becoming a proper scholar.

One of his teachers, Brother Henry Pang, thought he saw in young Bruce a nonconformist who needed guidance. "I had ways of controlling Bruce and his hyperactive problems," he recalled. "When he would come to school in the morning I would say, 'Bruce, please open all the windows. Please, Bruce would you clean all the blackboards.' He loved to do things and he needed a way to drain some of his phenomenal energy."

But once, while the La Salle Brothers were in an after-school faculty meeting, Bruce exploded into the room, running around their table twice before darting into a phone booth, where he made himself as small as he could. When Brother Henry came over to ask him the meaning of such behavior, Bruce said that a group of boys were coming to beat him up. Later, the truth came out—he had started a fight with some junior Triad types, then fled into the teachers' conference room when the odds turned against him. Bruce finally wore down the patience of even Brother Henry, who sent a pleading note to another Brother: "I cannot stand it anymore. Please watch over him!"

Peter noticed that Bruce seemed never to be alone: "He was always talking and liked to make jokes so he always had lots of friends."

The fighting and the friendships went together. Steve Lee Ka Tai, who later became a stuntman on Bruce's movies, said, "In that era, who wouldn't fight? We would be fighting for a marble, a toy car afterwards, we just made it up. It was natural naughtiness. It was never serious, just spitting mouth water, and no one holds grudges."

Even James Wong Jim recalled, "In the end, we were all exhausted and decided to make good at the tuck shop, treating [Bruce] with a bottle of Coke and a dish of beef noodles, forgetting about the past."

Grace hired her son a tutor. But then the tutor called the house, asking, "Where's Bruce?" She already knew. "Bruce was generally off with friends, fighting in the street," she recalled. "I'd ask him where he'd been, and he'd tell me he just finished studying."

The attention-craving child, Linda Lee Cadwell later wrote, "needed a mentor who would assist him in finding a direction to channel this unique and incredible energy." But the boy's needs had exceeded what his father could give.

By 1950 Li Hoi Chuen was one of the most in-demand film actors in Hong Kong, appearing in as many as ten movies a year. When he wasn't at the studio, he was distant. Robert Lee recalled, "We did not know much about Dad's life and work because despite his comical image onstage he was taciturn at home."

Hoi Chuen was often up early for *tai chi* in King's Park with the men, returning to read scripts alone, and then locking himself away with a musician to prepare for an upcoming performance, only emerging for dinner with the family. At the table, each child was to recognize their elders one by one—father, mother, uncle, aunt, sister, brother—before they were allowed to eat. Bruce's was the longest list to recite, an increasingly irritating obligation.

In the evenings, Hoi Chuen's showbiz friends visited, and they withdrew to the bedroom to fill their pipes with opium tar. "He would sort of toke at night and then burn a lot of incense just to cut the smell," Robert said. Bruce's siblings had learned to live with their father's habit. For Phoebe, who sometimes helped Hoi Chuen pack his pipe, it was a sign of their status. "Only rich people could smoke opium at the time," she said.

But to Bruce, that sickly sweet after-dinner smell was a reminder of his father's neglect. Opium absorbed all of his father's attention, made him slow and stupid, and shut him down. Bruce knew he would never be Peter, but at least on the set he had experienced joy and accomplishment before his father. Hoi Chuen's addiction was a betrayal. Bruce responded by withdrawing in his own way.

One day Grace received a call from the school. "They asked me, 'Why hasn't he come to school lately?'" she said. "I was disappointed with him again and again."

At home she was beleaguered. "His father was sick," she recalled. "As a result, I had to deal with all the troubles [Bruce] caused.

"I told Bruce that it did not matter much if he did not like to study at school, but he had to tell me wherever he went to play so that I could contact him if necessary," she said. "I told him that it would be very embarrassing for me when the school authority or the police came to find him and I, as his mother, did not know where he was. After that, Bruce still played truant, but he told me where I could find him."

On Perth Street outside La Salle, Bruce and his crew ran things. He would lead them to the gates of King George V School, where they taunted the white preps, trying to start fights.

"We had what we call '*man chok yee sik*,'" said Michael Lai, "which is to say we had much national or ethnic pride. Nationalism, as they say. We like to beat up English boys." Bruce would never lose the feeling of growing up a colonial. "The white kids have all the best jobs and the rest of us had to work for them," he said years later. "That's why most of the kids become punks."

The boys soon set their sights on nearby Junction Road in Kowloon City, straddling the notorious Walled City. Along the road, with its bustling shops, and on the rooftops, which connected several buildings at a time, young men gathered to dance to music, flirt with girls, and spar with each other. The tabloids called them teddy boys after London's rock-and-roll delinquents, or worse, *fei zai*, teen hoodlums.

Bruce fell in with a gang of sorts that called themselves the Junction Road Eight Tigers, a clique of Chinese, Portuguese, and mixed-race teens that included the son of a famous opera singer and the brother-in-law of a prominent politician. He was one of the younger boys, and far from the leader. William Cheung remembered the Tigers as not hardened criminals but adolescent thrill-seekers. They talked trash with other gangs but avoided the Triads.

In the meantime, William had developed a rep. People said he had won so many street fights, even the Triads avoided him. In fact his father was a police detective, who, through shared ancestral village ties, was close to leaders of the Sun Yee On Triad. William was protected. But like Hoi Chuen, his father was distant.

One bloody night, after protecting his mother and brother from his half brother King Kong in a domestic fight, William ran away from home. He walked the streets of Sham Shui Po before knocking on the door of the fourth-floor apartment where Yip Man and his lover, Song Lian, lived. For a time William slept in the same hallway where Yip Man held his classes.

When Bruce and William met again one warm day on Junction Road, it was what each of them needed. William knew a lot about fighting and didn't have lots of friends. Bruce had lots of friends and didn't know a lot about fighting. William was living a life Bruce only played on-screen. Bruce enjoyed the ease and attention William desired. After school, before heading to Yip Man's classes, he began meeting Bruce and the Tigers.

William got Bruce into situations. They entered a stationery store and William grabbed a bunch of pencils and put them into Bruce's shirt pocket. Then he snatched some more, and waved them at the shopkeeper. Blocks later, in the corner of an alley, William was laughing while Bruce hunched over, panting and sweaty.

Bruce and his father, Li Hoi Chuen, clash in *Wealth Is Like a Dream*, 1948. Photo courtesy of the Bruce Lee Family Archive.

Cooks chased them with cleavers after they fled roadside food stalls without paying. Casino security guards chased them with truncheons after they tossed money boxes in the air. William picked fights on Junction Road, and Bruce developed a taste for blood.

When Bruce got home, he told Robert about their adventures, bragging that he was averaging two fights a day. "He would just walk down the street and people would look at him funny," Robert said. "If somebody is around the same age, someone he can fight with, he'll look right back and say, 'What the eff you looking at?'"

He filled pen cavities with blades, removed toilet chains, and tied them around his waist to whip out in brawls. "Those days, kids improvised all kinds of weapons—even shoes with razors attached," he said. "I kept wondering what would happen to me if my gang was not around when I met a rival gang."

The more they hung out, the more Bruce wanted to know what William knew. Bruce had heard a story about a man who had come to challenge Yip Man in his studio. When the *sifu* declined, the man refused to leave and became so belligerent that Yip Man killed him with a single punch. It didn't matter if the story was true—Bruce believed it could be.

One day he returned to the house as the family was preparing for dinner. He was covering one of his eyes with his hand. Instead of coming to the table, he went straight to the bedroom to avoid his father. He had been beaten in a Junction Road rooftop fight with a junior *gung fu* student. Grace devised a cover story for him.

Bruce told his mother he needed to learn martial arts so he could defend himself against school bullies. *Wing Chun*, he told her, *is what I need to learn*. Perhaps it was a good idea, she thought. *Gung fu* might protect him and teach him some discipline. She found him the fifteen dollars for the class, and assured him, *I will talk to your father*.

During a warm autumn day in 1954, William took Bruce to meet Yip Man at his apartment in Sham Shui Po.

CHAPTER 5
Talk with Your Hands

In Hong Kong's postwar youth culture, 1954 marked a turning point.

Gung fu schools—especially Southern Shaolin styles (in Cantonese, *sil lum**), like Choy Li Fut, White Crane, Hung Gar, and Wing Chun—filled with a generation of what martial arts historians Ben Judkins and Jon Nielson called "angry, often near delinquent, young men." They developed a fight culture they called *beimo*, "comparison fights." They called their blood sport "Talking Hands," from a street saying, *"Mou gong hau, gong sau"*: "Don't talk with your mouth, talk with your hands." When the British authorities outlawed the fights and deployed police to break them up, the culture went underground and evolved quickly.

Challenges were issued by students of one school to another or by fighters to other fighters. Sometimes brokers made matches. Venues were chosen, such as rooftops or back alleys hidden from the street. Referees were selected, rings drawn, and rules set. Sometimes there was to be no kicking, sometimes no punching, sometimes there were no rules at all. Audiences flocked in, some to cheer on their friends, some to gamble, some to do both. Referees stopped fights quickly, because it was the merciful thing to do and the best way to control a crowd, but most of all, it was dull and embarrassing to watch someone unable or unwilling to fight back.

William Cheung had been inducted into this world of Kung Fu Guys through a friend's older brother, a stocky eighteen-year-old Western-style middleweight boxer named Wong Shun Leung. Soon Wong would be known simply as Gong Sau, "the King of Talking Hands." But before he had attained that name and status, he had to go through his own ritual of humbling. He had heard about an old man who taught an old style originated by a woman. He set up a challenge with the old man and invited his brother and William to come to the Restaurant Workers Union Association hall to watch him pound the guy.

When the three walked in, the little old man stood to greet them. He was balding, perhaps five foot four and 120 pounds. Wong Shun Leung looked down on him with scorn. The little old man said to Wong, "Look, you're much younger than me. You can start throwing punches first."

Wong danced and threw a few fast jabs. The old man dodged them easily. Then he intercepted and trapped one of Wong's jabs, pulled Wong off-balance, and tossed the young man to the ground. Wong got back up and threw another punch. And

---
* In this text, I will use Shaolin and *sil lum* interchangeably.

was tossed again. He got back up and threw another punch. And was tossed again. Looking up at the old man after being tossed this third time, Wong saw that he had Popeye-sized forearms, legs like agarwood trunks, and power and speed that defied age. He, his brother, and William fled the union hall as fast as they could. Later he returned to beg forgiveness—William followed—and Yip Man agreed to let them become his students.

Yip Man had been born in Fatshan in 1893, the same city as Bruce's father, during the high period of Cantonese fighting arts, but unlike Hoi Chuen he had grown up in relative comfort. His parents were property owners whose clan hall stood on the town's main street. Decades after the Qing had massacred the town's poor, the colorful town of singers and fighters had returned to its rebellious fighting ways. Yip Man's generation of martial artists was a more bourgeois group. As one popular saying went, "The poor study literature, but the rich play at martial arts."

When Yip Man was eleven or twelve, Chan Wah Shun, an elderly master of the still insular *gung fu* art of Wing Chun, rented space at the family hall to live and teach the lessons he had first learned from his *sifu*, the legendary Dr. Leung Jan. The young boy was excited to learn from Chan, who had been Leung's most senior student. But Chan rebuffed him, telling him rich kids never made good pupils.

When the boy pressed, Chan told him he could pay for his classes and named a price so high he thought it might scare him away. But Yip Man showed up one day with a bag of silver taels enough for a dowry or multiple plots of land. The stunned *sifu* suspected the money was stolen and took the boy to his father, who said that his wife had given Yip Man the money so that the skinny, sickly boy could learn Wing Chun. Chan was now obligated to take him. But Yip Man rewarded his *sifu* with unwavering commitment and became the last of just sixteen students Chan would accept during his lifetime.

At fifteen, Yip Man was sent to study at a Catholic school in Hong Kong, the prestigious St. Stephen's College. There he developed a rage against the British colonists and their South Asian conscripts. One legend had Yip Man defending the honor of a Chinese woman by taking out an entire detachment of Indian cops. His reputation grew, and Yip came to the attention of Leung Jan's son, Leung Bik, who taught him more advanced aspects of Wing Chun.

Yip Man returned to Fatshan as warlords and Nationalists contended for China, with a desire to do nothing but enjoy himself and practice Wing Chun. He sold his family's properties and was living the good life. It was only when he was nearly forty years old—after southern China had descended into chaos under the Japanese, and his money began running low—that he began teaching Wing Chun to support himself.

Soon after, a *sifu* named Wan Dai Hu from a nearby Choy Li Fut school challenged Yip Man to a public fight. Choy Li Fut was the most popular style in Guangdong province, and fighters from any other style who sought prestige would inevitably need to contend with its followers. Wan used long swings to attack Yip, who angled in closely to avoid them. Then when an opening came, Yip stepped in and attacked Wan's head and center line with rapid-fire punches. Wan could not continue and the judge called the fight. Yip Man had won a victory for himself, his school, and his style.

But his classes could not pay all his bills. He took a job as a police captain with the Nationalists, a choice that landed him on the Communist kill list. Just before Guangdong fell to Mao's army, he fled with his eldest daughter to Macao and then Hong Kong. When the borders closed, he was separated from his wife and his four other children.

Friends at the Restaurant Workers Union Association in Sham Shui Po gave him a home, and he amused himself by watching the men teach each other martial arts in the union hall. As one of the many stories goes, Yip Man was sitting in the corner making fun of one of the teachers, Leung Sheung, who was renowned for his skill in White Eyebrow, Southern Dragon, and Choy Li Fut styles. A challenge followed. By the end of the night, the man in the corner had revealed himself to be a grandmaster and Leung Sheung had become Yip Man's first Hong Kong student. In 1950, at the age of fifty-seven, Yip Man was teaching Wing Chun at the union hall with Leung Sheung by his side.

When his students asked, Yip Man told them a story. During the time of the Qing emperor Kangxi, he said, the Shaolin temple—the mythical home of *gung fu*—was at its greatest strength. Threatened by the power of the warrior-monks, the Qing army attacked the temple repeatedly. Each time it was repelled. Only through the treachery of a turncoat abbot were the Qing forces able to rout the Shaolin, burning the temple to the ground and scattering the monks across the countryside.

Among them was an abbess named Ng Mui, one of the Five Elders, who wandered the land until she finally settled at the White Crane Temple on a mountain called Tai Leung. There she saw a fight between a crane and a snake and, inspired by their movements, integrated them with her own boxing style to develop a new form of fighting.

At the foot of Tai Leung lived a Cantonese family named Yim, who had also fled far from their native region after the patriarch, Yim Yee, was framed for a crime he had not committed. He and his daughter made and sold tofu soup, and that was how Ng Mui came to meet Yim Yee and his beautiful daughter, Yim Wing Chun.

This young woman told Ng Mui a sad story: she was in love and betrothed to marry a Fujianese salt merchant from the coast named Leung Bok Chau. But a gangster wanted her for his own and swore to her father he would take her by force if necessary. After Wing Chun told her story, Ng Mui promised to teach the young woman everything she knew.

Wing Chun went up the mountain every day to study and train with Ng Mui. When she was away, the gangster brought his crew to visit Yim Yee and demanded his daughter give herself to him. Yim Yee told them she was a fierce martial artist and had vowed that if any man could beat her, she would marry him. This made the tough guys laugh, and the gangster agreed to return for a challenge.

When the day arrived the gangster and the young woman faced off. Every time he attacked, she stopped him, controlled him, and repulsed him. When he tried to overpower her, she tossed him and beat him bloody. His gang members tried to defeat her as well, but she thrashed them all. They scampered away, never to return.

Ng Mui prepared to leave Tai Leung, but before she left, she went to see Wing Chun. She told the young woman, *Use this style and develop it, but only to overthrow the Qing and restore the Ming Dynasty.*

The young woman asked her, *What name shall I give it?*

Ng Mui answered, *Give it your name.*

With this underdog lineage, Wing Chun was for everyone. Small or big, woman or man, priest or skeptic, rich or poor, it was the great equalizer. Yip Man told his students that he had been hit by Chan Wah Shun, who had been hit by Leung Teong, who had been hit by Wong Wah Bo, a Red Junk actor who had felt the slap of the Long Pole from his peer Leung Yee Tai, both of whom had been hit by Leung Bok Chau, who had been taught all the fist ways by his brave wife Yim Wing Chun, and she by Ng Mui—seven generations of salters, butchers, herbalists, singers, street vendors, moneychangers, and other flesh-and-blood fighters, an unbroken line that now included them as well.

The martial arts had begun as intimate knowledge, passed from elder to adult to child, through clans and villages. In time, styles, techniques, and systems in fighting and weaponry became associated with religious sects, secret societies, criminal enterprises, and political dissidents. By design, they were closed; why surrender any advantage to another?

But then, in the Boxer Uprising, which lasted from 1899 to 1901, underground armies of martial artists—some of whom claimed their training had given them supernatural powers—were slaughtered by gun-wielding Europeans. Successive waves of foreigners made incursions into China. Pride became shame. At the end of the nineteenth century, China's "century of humiliation," self-defense had become a national matter. The next generation bitterly critiqued the mystical, secretive aspects of the fighting arts. They called for them to be brought into the light, modernized, and taught widely, strategically, and scientifically, and the study of martial arts spread in schools across the country.

By 1954, migration had made Hong Kong the undisputed center of Chinese martial arts, where dozens of different styles and schools flourished. Waves of migrants would disperse these fighting arts around the world. Later, the colony's burgeoning film industry—and one fighting star in particular—would do the rest.

Within the year, Yip Man's friends at the union had been voted out of leadership and he was forced to find new places to teach. He moved classes to his apartment building, where the students sometimes trained on the roof in the rain. His first Hong Kong students, mostly transient restaurant workers, gave way to young upstarts from across the colony.

Wing Chun suited their impatience. Yip Man counseled that motion, energy, and time were not to be wasted. Other styles required their students to learn many forms—choreographed sets of signature movements—before a fight philosophy and a repertoire of useful tools could be unlocked. But Yip Man had streamlined his system. Ben Der, a schoolmate of Bruce who later became a Wing Chun *sifu* in the San Francisco Bay Area, said, "In a short time, you'd be able to defend yourself."

Bruce asked William Cheung what made Wing Chun different from the other styles. "Wing Chun was one of the only *gung fu* made by a woman," William answered. "How can a woman fight a man? Because Wing Chun is very scientific. Everything is very precise."

Some of the other styles looked dramatic with arcing punches and eye-pleasing poses. But even the little Monkey King, fighting bare-fisted with the gigantic Demon of Havoc, knew that a long reach might not always land so hard and true as a short one. Wing Chun was direct, built for sensitivity, and suited for close combat in tight spaces. Coordination, balance, and reflexes were as important as speed and power.

It was aggressively minimalist. Yip Man taught students proper body structure and positioning through just three basic forms. To strengthen their fundamentals, he had students work on a close hand-to-hand practice called *chi sao*, "sticking hands." Advanced students added one-on-one drills and solo practice on the *mook yan jong*, a wooden dummy.

The youths appreciated Yip Man's focus on efficiency and effectiveness. Hawkins Cheung, who began training with Yip Man around the same time Bruce did, said, "Yip Man trained us to fight, not be technicians." When Yip's eager young students questioned him, Hawkins said, the teacher had an ironic smile and a ready answer: "Don't believe me as I may be tricking you. Go out and have a fight. Test it out." They took him up on it.

"We learned," Hawkins said, "by getting hit."

But they also hit back with the ferocity of contenders, and their exploits became the best marketing plan for the old man who let the angry young men fight.

Yip Man was amused by young Bruce. William had told Yip that Bruce was a movie star and the son of a movie star. He assigned his third Hong Kong student, Chu Shong-Tin, a senior instructor, to teach Bruce, and then named William his *ah hing* (older brother) and assigned him to work further with Bruce to refine his basics. Chu showed him the first form, *siu lim tao*, or "A Little Idea."

Designed in part to filter out serious students from casual ones, the form requires a student to sink deeply into a horse stance and hold in stillness while slowly advancing and withdrawing one's hands, elbows, and arms. But although the form forced the always moving Bruce to quiet his mind and relax his body, he was hardly deterred. "His devotion to *gung fu*," Linda later wrote, "was total."

William had joked with Bruce that being a fighter was not a good idea because he needed to take care of his face. "I never thought he was serious because he was a famous movie star," he said. But Bruce was always practicing, even when they were hanging out on Junction Road.

"Every time we go out Bruce would have two dumbbells, doing numeric punching," said Cheung. "And it was really embarrassing because in the street, everybody would look at him and would laugh, but he didn't care. I said, 'Bruce, why do you do that?' He would say, 'I lost so many years, I have to catch up.'

"So he would be sitting there, we would be drinking Coca Cola, and he would hold the cup with one hand, and the other hand be doing his *lap sao* and punch, and then he would train the other hand. He was very annoying."

Wing Chun focused Bruce's eddying energies. He picked a fight with a boy who had once clobbered him. This time Bruce finished off his opponent and boasted, "*I've* been learning Wing Chun."

After a while, Bruce was allowed to try *chi sao* with some of the senior students. But when sticking hands with them, he fast learned how much he still did not know. When they got in on him, they left Bruce's chest and arms full of red, black, and blue bruises. Frustrated, Bruce violated the unwritten rules of practice, pinching or even punching back. He couldn't control himself.

"When he started doing *chi sao* and sparring with the seniors, he was trying too hard," Cheung said. "He was always hurting his sparring partner."

Years later, Bruce still bristled thinking about those early days. "Those bastards enjoyed overpowering us, and as we weakened they used to slap us on our chest and face. I got so mad one day that I decided to dish out the same medicine to them," he said. "In a few months, I got my revenge, and did I dish it out to them! I really picked on them after that."

Yip Man was impressed by Bruce's enthusiasm and skill. But complaints mounted about the disrespectful kid with the famous name. As the chorus of angry seniors grew, Yip Man decided he had to step in. He warned Bruce to calm down or he would have to leave the school.

Yip Man and Bruce Lee. Photo courtesy of the Bruce Lee Family Archive.

CHAPTER 6
Days of Being Wild

At home, things were getting worse. Li Hoi Chuen's opium addiction had left him more withdrawn. Many in the community were talking. Opium smoking was against the law, but, they said, he would never be arrested because he was famous. Police began coming by the house to blackmail Hoi Chuen.

Bruce hated his father's habit. He would remember this period as one in which his father had abandoned him. He withdrew further from the family, spending more time in the streets.

Grace was frustrated. "On a few occasions," Robert recalled, "Mom told me after drinking a lot of beer that she had thought about running away from home." But abandoning the children in the way Hoi Chuen had was simply unfathomable to her.

She was also bothered by what she saw as Bruce's growing indifference to the family's needs. Over dinner one night, she admonished him, "You are such a useless child, you do not have much affection for us."

Bruce shot back, "If we were in the forest and there was a tiger, I would immediately fight the tiger and free all of you."

"He wanted Mom to understand that was the way he had been silently guarding the family," Robert said. "In this regard, he was just like Dad. He held everything in his heart without saying anything."

In 1953, after two years, Bruce's parents lifted his film ban. The Hong Kong movie industry he returned to was growing by leaps and bounds. Each year, Hong Kong was generating over two hundred films for sixty screens. Ticket sales doubled during the 1950s. In Asia, only Japan's movie business was larger.

Bruce appeared in five movies in 1953 and six more in 1955. No longer a child star, he was now a character actor in large ensembles, usually playing hard-luck kids. In *The Guiding Light* (1953), his character is so poor he is sold into slavery. In *An Orphan's Tragedy* (1955), his father is framed and imprisoned and he is raised by a blacksmith. In *Love, Part 2* (1955), he is the hungry son of a vagabond street performer.

The biggest critical and box-office success of this period, *In the Face of Demolition*, was released on his thirteenth birthday. It is set in a crumbling, overcrowded apartment building after a typhoon, where residents come together to rebuild their condemned home. Ng Cho-Fan, who would play a major role in Bruce's early acting career, starred in the movie, exhorting the residents to come together with the cry "All for one and one for all!"

Hoi Chuen's idea of parenting had been to place Bruce with a film company he hoped might moderate his son's ways. Ng's left-leaning collective, Union Film Enterprises, specialized in family melodramas meant to inspire national pride. Perhaps Hoi Chuen hoped his spoiled son might learn to appreciate his good fortune. Perhaps he—whose acclaimed performance in the 1948 movie *Two Opium Addicts Sweep a Long Dike* had been informed by his own habit—understood how unsteadily his son lived at the margin between fantasy and reality. Perhaps he wanted the sheltered boy who thought he belonged to the streets to realize he had a role to play in his own family melodrama.

One night when Hoi Chuen was on set, the police came to the family's door, Robert recalled, "like stormtroopers." They searched the house, turned up Hoi Chuen's drug paraphernalia, and threatened to arrest him. To make them go away, Grace gave them five hundred dollars, which, Robert said, was "enough to feed our family of more than a dozen for a few months." The next day Grace issued an ultimatum to Hoi Chuen—*stop the opium smoking or leave*. Ashamed, he began the painful process of withdrawal, weaning himself off the drug by drinking rice wine infused with smaller and smaller doses of cooked opium, fitfully working his way down the long path back to health.

But Hoi Chuen's epiphany had come too late for Bruce. At La Salle, the Brothers had let Bruce repeat Form 4,* Robert said, "as a courtesy to our parents." But the teen was increasingly acting out.

During a PE class, the teacher had the boys run laps around the field, then followed after the slowest to whip them with a grass reed. He caught Bruce fooling around and lagging and snapped at Bruce's calves. Bruce recoiled in pain. Then, enraged, he stopped, turned, pulled a switchblade from his pocket, and chased the teacher in the opposite direction all the way to the principal's office, where he was finally disarmed and disciplined.

One day at morning assembly, as the students lined up on the lawn for their principal's review, a boy named David taunted Bruce. Soon the class lines had dissolved and a circle had formed around the two as they faced off.

David threw punches at Bruce's head, but missed. Bruce danced around, his friend Robert Wang recalled, then "landed a series of Wing Chun punches onto David's face, knocking out a couple of his teeth before grabbing the half-dazed opponent by the collar and ramming his knee into his chest."

David writhed on the ground, humiliated before his classmates. But the fight, Wang said, "did not make [Bruce] any more popular. Everyone was intimidated by him. No one wanted anything to have to do with him. He was trouble."

---

* This would be the equivalent of tenth grade in the U.S.

His constant fighting and his tendency to skip afternoon classes had made him unmanageable. By the end of the 1955–56 school year, the La Salle Brothers had finally decided to expel Bruce.

Grace quickly and quietly found another school for him in the autumn—St. Francis Xavier, a Catholic institution that had just relocated to Hong Kong from Shanghai.

Bruce befriended Hawkins Cheung, a classmate who lived just blocks away, had also grown up with a driver and house servants, and was also studying Wing Chun. Out from under Peter's shadow, Bruce quickly established himself, in Robert's words, as "king gorilla, boss of the whole school." Hawkins made jokes about Bruce's long, thick, knuckle-dragging arms, but no one else would.

What mattered most to both was that the school was a short distance from Yip Man's school. "Everyone wanted to be top dog," said Hawkins. "Everyone had to find his own source, and not let the others know what we learned. We would purposely hide a trick that we would get from Yip Man, the Seniors, or friends from other styles."

After formal classes, Bruce, Hawkins, and William Cheung sometimes went up to the rooftops at night to continue. "When we weren't fighting others, we fought each other," said Hawkins.

Yip Man's classes were now so popular that his senior students arranged for him to move to a larger studio on Lee Tat Street, in Yau Ma Tei, even closer to where Hawkins and Bruce lived. But they were also upset about the new cohort of younger students. To them, Bruce especially epitomized the school's unwanted changes. He had brought dozens of St. Francis Xavier students to Yip Man's door, well-off kids vying to be respected like Bruce and Hawkins. When word got around that Bruce was not pure-blooded Chinese, the *sifu* had a full-blown revolt on his hands.

The seniors directly appealed to the old man's nationalism. "They told Yip Man, 'Look, Bruce is not full Chinese. He shouldn't be training here,'" said William. "But the whole reason is that they didn't want to be tapped by Bruce."

Yip Man came from a time when the arts were taught in secrecy. He also knew that teaching one mixed-race kid would hardly shatter Chinese civilization. But it would certainly affect his lifestyle. His senior students paid his rent and living expenses. He told William to take Bruce to train separately with Wong Shun Leung.

Wong, some whispered, was paying the price for his own excesses. In *beimo* matches with the Chow Gar Praying Mantis and Pak Hok Pai White Crane *gung fu* clans, he had allegedly been so brutal that a high-level summit of school leaders needed to be convened in Mongkok. A chastened Wong had retreated from challenge fights and was working to make amends with the other schools. But these same fights—not to mention grand tales of him fighting with British authorities—had made Gong Sau's name legendary. For Bruce, being expelled from Yip Man's immediate circle of seniors wasn't so bad. Yip Man had not cut him off. He would simply be learning directly from a different *sihing*, someone more potent than all of them—the King of Talking Hands.

On his first day on Wong's practice floor, Bruce showed up with William, hair slicked back, sporting a floral shirt. Gong Sau's first impression of the "Elvis-like youngster" was withering: "He leaned his body to one side with his hand on the wall. The other hand was in the back pocket of his trousers. His body was supported by one of his legs only. He swayed his body continuously. His manner was very frivolous as though he thought that he was smart. I really did not like his appearance. After he went away, I told Cheung that I did not welcome this young man." The next time Bruce showed up, he was respectful and deferential, and his training began in earnest.

Bruce met with Wong Shun Leung and William Cheung almost every day. He valued his training time with *sihing* Ah Leung so much that, when William was not with him, he sometimes stood at the bottom of the staircase to tell other students their teacher was not in, then bounded back up the stairs for uninterrupted time.

Bruce proved a diligent student. He observed Wong's short-distance punch and decided to build his forearm strength with steel bars and sand-filled weights. "Sometimes I waited for him outside his school to take him to my house. On our way, I would put his bag on my back, and he would punch at it. He did it all the way from Sham Shui Po to Tsim Sha Tsui like an idiot, but he did not care about other people's comments," Wong said. "That was Bruce Lee, competitive and aggressive . . .

"In nine months' time, he seemed to surpass me," Wong said. "Therefore, I enjoyed practicing with him very much."

As Bruce grew from a slim, mischievous kid into a handsome teen, he began to receive a lot of attention. In the floating world of the colony's film industry, he worked alongside beautiful actors like Margaret Leung, whose father was also a famous opera star and whose stage name was Man Lan, and Amy Chan, whose face would soon grace the celebrity tabloids under the name Pak Yan. Bruce became self-conscious in a different way. Peter noticed the amount of time Bruce was spending in front of the mirror, combing his hair and fixing his tie.

"He always had a lot of girls going for him," Peter said. But when they flirted with him, Bruce, the boys' boy, didn't know how to act. Shy and awkward, he couldn't make conversation. Instead he invited them to feel his muscles.

Ben Der, a classmate, threw parties at his house and invited Bruce to attract girls to come. "This is the guy they want to know, so then they want to know us," Ben chuckled. They put on Nat King Cole, then Elvis records, but it was only when they played cha-cha that the girls wanted to dance and the party got started.

Havana's cha-cha craze had belatedly crossed the Pacific, rooted itself in Manila, and spread across Southeast Asia. By the spring of 1956 it was the sound of the tea shops where teens like Bruce, Man Lan, and their hip actor friends flocked on weekends. A wave of Latin-tinged musical rom-coms followed—notably the ecstatic *Mambo Girl*, starring Grace Chang—and made cha-cha a sign of the postwar generation's ascent to modernity.

Bruce and Hawkins learned the dance from Filipino friends. True to form, Bruce was soon keeping a list of 108 different steps on a small card in his wallet. "He went to my Filipino friend's dance instructor to learn more steps," Hawkins recalled. "I later went to the same dance instructor and tried to persuade him not to teach Bruce."

On the cool rooftops at night, above the noise and neon, Bruce practiced cha-cha with Hawkins and William. Bruce told them that he would add Wing Chun hand movements and enter all of the contests: "I'll do a *chi sao* cha-cha, *bil sao* cha-cha, *pak sao* cha-cha, *heun sao* cha-cha!"

Grace was not altogether happy about this development. Robert recalled, "One time brother Bruce secretly went to a dance and came back in the early hours of the morning. He snuck in near where the servants slept, so they got up and told Mom. She took a thick and heavy door latch and waited for brother Bruce. When she saw him coming back, she got furious and beat him hard with the latch." She forced him to kowtow before the altar tablets and "admit his fault sincerely to the ancestors."

Bruce finally received her approval to attend weekend afternoon dance parties with friends, especially Pearl Tso—the daughter of Walter Tso Tat-Wah, who had produced and costarred in the Wong Fei-Hung movies, and Eva Tso, his godmother and his mother's best friend, who had shepherded young Bruce into the movie life, spoiled him as much as Grace had, and called herself his "second mother." Pearl was an accomplished ballet dancer and Bruce's first real crush.

When the music came on, he took her hand and stepped into the space where he was the most comfortable—at the center of the party, all eyes on him. The guys tried to analyze how he did it—*he has such high arches he never leaves his toes, he's getting the steps from some secret Filipino masters, he just has rhythm.* To the swooning girls, Bruce was simply poetry in motion.

Before long, Robert said, "he had several girlfriends. I think about four or five. He would date one and then the other, back to this one."

Bruce gave them autographed Hollywood-style glamour portraits of himself—like the ones from his idols Elvis Presley and James Dean he once had written away to America for. In all those hours he hadn't spent studying math, he had practiced drawing chivalrous warriors, brave swordswomen, and powerful dragons in magnificent detail. He had also perfected a distinctive form of handwriting. His characters were tall and balanced, their end strokes tailing into long flourishes, bespeaking refined aspirations, as if what he really wanted was the life of an artist,

Bruce and Margaret "Man Lan" Leung, *Darling Girl*, 1957. Photo courtesy of the Bruce Lee Family Archive.

scholar, or poet. In black marker, he inscribed lines from Chinese love poems and signed his name.

Among the most striking images of Bruce Lee's youth are a series of promotional photos he took with Man Lan for her 1957 star vehicle, *Darling Girl*.* Released on the heels of *Mambo Girl*, it was a comedy about a spoiled rich girl in which Bruce made a brief appearance in a ballroom scene. He first appears seated at a back table—bespectacled, dressed in a soft wool vest and clean white shirt, looking like a schoolboy Jerry Lewis. When the band strikes up a tune, Man Lan's character runs over to grab his hand, an impetuous move meant to drive the boy she likes into fits of jealousy. Bruce stumbles out awkwardly, but when the couple hits the dance floor and the band peaks, they lock in and exuberantly chase each other back and forth across the floor. The promo pictures show Man Lan and Bruce in perfect finger-snapping, short-stepping, low-kicking symbiosis. Against a white background, above the scrum of daily life, they are suspended in the timeless romance of youth.

Bruce decided to enter the All Hong Kong Cha-Cha Championships. But he had a problem: too many girls wanted to be his partner. Rather than choose one and risk losing them all, Bruce tapped Robert, the little brother whom he still

---

* He had also done cha-cha in the 1956 movie *Too Late for Divorce*.

called "Gau Jai," Little Dog, then just ten years old. They practiced every day for three months, then showed up at the nightclub in dark formal suits to the chuckles of the other contestants. But their performances were irresistible, and the judges crowned them the colony's finest.

On another night Bruce entered a cha-cha contest at a Nathan Road club. William and Hawkins cheered as he advanced to the solo finals, then edged out a Filipino dancer to win. But Bruce had somehow offended the dancer's crew, and soon they were circling Hawkins, William, and him near the club's exit doors, loudly yelling and challenging him to a fight.

"I just used Wing Chun cha-cha to beat you in your cha-cha game," Bruce snarled, "you think I can't use Wing Chun to beat you?" And the three bopped on out of the club.

Emboldened and hungry for cred, Bruce was often hanging out with his crew in Shek Kip Mei looking to start shit. "You didn't have to ask Bruce twice to fight," Robert said. Every time he won, Bruce reminded his opponent just how poor his *gung fu* was. He was amassing enemies all across town.

On Junction Road, Bruce had become William's backup in his beefs with rival Triads. When the two stumbled upon the son of a high-ranking member of the Sun Yee On being attacked by members of the 14K, they jumped in to defend him. "He never backed out of any fight," William said. "Some of the other boys with us would run away. He would be so angry with them afterwards that he would not speak with them."

Bruce saw himself as Ah Sahm, the third brother to his big brothers, Ah Hing William and Ah Leung, his version of "all for one, one for all." But privately he brooded that they had become bored of practicing with him. When they did *chi sao* and got inside Bruce's hands, they left his nose bloody, his lips swollen, and his chest black and blue. This ritual thumping only increased his obsession with the pecking order. Bruce constantly asked Ah Leung to compare his skills to others.

One day, however, Wong said, "He asked too much." Bruce had asked, *Could I beat William or even you?* "I felt that he had fallen into the state of bewitchment," Wong recalled. "I feared that he would lose the aim in learning *gung fu*."

Many years later, a journalist asked William Cheung if Bruce had a big ego. "Not really. Looking from another angle, I think Bruce more or less had an inferiority complex," William said. "That's why he tried so hard."*

In 1958, St. Francis Xavier's Brother Edward recruited him to be one of the school's three representatives in a boxing tournament against English teens from

---

* Dan Inosanto was being interviewed at the same time. He replied to Cheung's comment, "I agree. I was going to say the same thing. He had to come on stronger to overcome it."

St. George and King George V. After learning the Queensberry Rules from Brother Edward, Bruce prepared under Wong Shun Leung's tutelage. Photos show him and his opponent, a British teen named Gary Elms who was the reigning titleholder in his weight class, wearing cartoonishly large gloves.

When the fight bell rang on the afternoon of March 29, Elms bounced around like the young Wong Shun Leung once had with Yip Man. But Bruce held his Wing Chun ready position, even as catcalls poured down from the audience. The little boxing tourney had unexpectedly become a contest of Western versus Chinese boxing, the strong men of Europe versus the sick men of Asia.

Elms lost his patience and attacked. But Bruce used *pak sau* and *heun sau* techniques to fend him off. Then, with an eruption of chain punches, he knocked the English boy down in the first round. Elms recovered and took the fight the distance. "After two rounds it seemed like their abilities were about matched," recalled Robert, who attended the fight. But Bruce won a unanimous decision and his supporters erupted with joy. Still, he left unsatisfied that his punches had not been more decisive, blaming the overstuffed gloves, his blood hunger unsated.

Two months later, at the urging of his Wing Chun classmates, Bruce issued a challenge to the Lung Chi Chuen Choy Li Fut school and enlisted Ah Leung to train him. But this time, he did not tell his mentor what kind of fight it was. When the day arrived, Wong found a large crowd heading up to a Junction Road rooftop with them, and suddenly realized what a spectacle Bruce had created. He had even arranged an undercard match and placed himself in the main bout facing a man named Chung, Lung Chi Chuen's assistant teacher.

Both sides pressed Wong to serve as referee. He reluctantly agreed, set the terms, and drew an eighteen-by-eighteen-foot ring. The first bout was forgettable. Then Bruce and Chung stepped up.

Bruce took his stance, asking-hand forward. Chung showed his left in a sword finger, balling his right into a fist at his waist. Chung drew first blood, connecting with a right to Bruce's left eye. Bruce struck Chung's chest but took another punch to the eye.

Angered, Bruce swung wildly. By the end of the first round, Chung appeared weathered, but he had succeeded in wrecking Bruce's face. Bruce's left eye was black and swollen, his lips were puffing, and his nose was bleeding. As the two fighters retreated to the corners and the audience jeered, Bruce's shoulders drooped.

In Bruce's corner, Wong the referee became Ah Leung the trainer, and saw that his fighter had turned desperate. "If I am hurt too badly, my father will notice," Bruce moaned. "I think we better take it as a draw and end the match."

Now Ah Leung went full Gong Sau on Bruce. "Bruce, if you do not continue it means that you surrender," he said. "Your opponent is wheezing now. If you withdraw, how will you face your classmates?"

It had become a test not just of the boxer but of the trainer. Ah Leung met his slumping fighter's eyes. "If you fight on, you will win," he said. "You are now in a *fight*, not a *performance*."

Bruce nodded, with a fresh look of determination, and the second round began.

He planted himself on his back leg and raised his hands to the ready position. Once, twice, three times he feinted, unsettling Chung. When Chung tried another right, Bruce shot a left at Chung's mouth, then stepped in with a swift right, knocking out Chung's front tooth. Chung stumbled, and Bruce unleashed a barrage of straight punches. Chung went down, falling against the water tank, and his students rushed in to stop the fight. Bruce threw his fists in the air and his classmates cheered.

For years afterward, Wong pondered what he had done. Would Bruce have been better off losing? Would winning make even more trouble for him in the future? "I was a judge, I should have not let emotion control me," Wong wrote later. "I also should not have forced Bruce to go on."

Yet he had not wanted to see his student discouraged. At least, Wong thought, Bruce had learned something: "It taught him that one could not naturally become a successful man. One had to fight."

For Bruce, there would still be the reckoning at home. In the next room his father raged—as if suddenly wakened from a long sleep—over the boy's disgraceful conduct. But Bruce was feeling something he had never felt before. He lay on his bed, holding a cold egg to his eye with one hand and writing in his diary with the other: "Against Chinese boxer student of Lung Chi Chuen (4 years training). Results: Won (that guy got fainted, one tooth got out, but I got a black eye)."

Finally, he had become the Kung Fu Guy.

After his 1958 rooftop fight, Bruce wanted bigger challenges.

"If you want to learn to swim you can't do it on dry land," he told Robert. "The only way to learn real fighting is to do it in the street."

William Cheung's brawling had entangled him in serious Triad and police politics, and his mother sent him to live with his retired father on a farm in the New Territories. Bruce and Peter drove out to meet him, and they talked about old times. But not long after, William's father concluded he was going to get himself killed and sent him to Melbourne. It was time for Bruce to become the top dog.

One day, he watched an old *tai chi* instructor give a demonstration, asking people from the audience to punch his stomach. Bruce recalled, "I didn't like the way this old man smiled when the young volunteer couldn't hurt him." He volunteered to go next. When the instructor showed his stomach and grinned, Bruce let loose a right to the man's ribs. The old man collapsed, moaning. "You know I was such a smart-assed punk," Bruce said, "I just looked down at the old man and laughed, 'Sorry I missed. Next time don't show off.'"

One of his classmates described to him a beef he had with a man named Li, a former associate of William's who was now teaching at a different school. Bruce volunteered to exact revenge. All Wong Shun Leung could tell him was to stand down if Li did not agree to a contest. That weekend, Bruce showed up at Li's school with eight of his classmates. Wong, who had followed them at a remove, watched as Bruce taunted the teacher and his students. Li refused Bruce's challenge.

"You cowards! Go home, why even practice kung fu?" Bruce said, breaking into a wild cha-cha to mock them. "I'll let you beat me. I won't fight back. OK?"

Li turned to Wong.

"Bruce, cool down," an embarrassed Wong said. "Your behavior is not very good. If Master Yip knows it, he will not be happy." But when Wong turned back to reassure Li, Bruce and another classmate were behind him miming in slow motion Li being knocked out. To Wong's relief, the teacher and his students left.

Soon Wong Shun Leung and even Hoi Chuen found themselves placating even more angry *sifus* whose students Bruce had challenged. Then, late in 1958, the influential parents of one of Bruce's badly bruised victims went to the police. Summoned to St. Francis Xavier, Grace Li found a police detective seated with the headmaster. The policeman told her that if Bruce fought again, he would be arrested and charged. The headmaster added that, at the rate Bruce was going, he would not graduate.

At home, Hoi Chuen yelled at Bruce again. *You have wasted your life and all your opportunities. I regret having a son like you. You have brought us only shame. What will you do with yourself?*

Bruce was cornered. *I'm no good at studying,* he cried. *I'm only good at fighting. I will fight to make a name.* His parents gaped in disbelief. They dismissed him and conferred privately. *Bruce cannot continue like this. Peter says he has enemies who could kill him. How could he stay?*

Grace recalled that US Immigration had warned them their son needed to return to exercise his American citizenship. When he turned eighteen, his Selective Service requirement would be active. Hoi Chuen had a large network of friends to call upon across the Pacific, in Honolulu, Seattle, and San Francisco.

They resolved: *His future is in America.*

CHAPTER 7
Dualities

Through cha-cha, Bruce had won the admiration of the girls. Through street fighting, he achieved status among the guys. He was leading a double life. Who was he—button-down boyfriend material or *fei zai* street punk? What did he want from people—adoration, respect, fear? Perhaps the screen would be the best place for him to wrestle with such contradictions, if his exasperated parents would agree to let their son act again.

Across British-occupied Asia, unrest was spreading. In Hong Kong, political clashes between Nationalist- and Communist-affiliated youth led the British colonial administration to intercede with what they euphemistically termed "forms of social defence," an agenda to contain the wild energies of a rebellious, belligerent generation. On the eve of the sixties, the island colony hoped to leave behind its difficult postwar decade for a more optimistic one.

Bruce's personal troubles seemed to mirror Hong Kong's uncertain fate. Hoi Chuen's friends, the actor Ng Cho-Fan and the director Lee Sun-Fung, had become two of the biggest names in the industry. They were producing a movie to meet the moment—*The Orphan*, a reimagining of the cinematic archetype of the decade they were leaving behind. Based on Auyeung Tin's popular novel *A Solitary Swan in a Sea of Humanity*, they hoped to make for postwar Hong Kong what *Rebel Without a Cause* had been to the United States, an authentic cry of youth and a defining social statement. They wanted to offer Bruce the starring role of Ah Sahm, a distressed teen standing on society's blade edge between good and evil, troubled past and hopeful future.

Hoi Chuen had entrusted Ng and Lee to mentor Bruce through the seven movies he had made during his La Salle years. But this time Bruce's father, intent upon seeing Bruce graduate, was displeased that the role was for a *fei zai* delinquent. Ng explained that his China-backed investors were ready to provide three hundred thousand dollars, one of the biggest budgets the industry had seen. Then he showed Hoi Chuen his script, saying that, like his other Union movies, *The Orphan* would be a message movie for the masses. There would be hardened gangsters, an earnest reformer, a miserly tycoon and his insufferable family, and a tragic war orphan whose coming-of-age would allegorize Hong Kong's own fate. Hoi Chuen's resistance crumbled. In the latter part of 1958, Bruce began preparing for his biggest role since *The Kid*.

The Orphan opens with images of the teeming city—stately buildings, shiny new cars, and uniformed youths planting a garden of vegetables in their hillside orphanage—a colony striving to become a world-class metropolis. Ng Cho-fan plays Ho See-Kei, the principal of the Kwan Yau Orphan School. He is a man haunted by the war. Japanese bombs have killed his wife and daughter as well as, he believes, his son To-Tsai and the infant's nanny, Ah Ng. His Confucian sense of responsibility has shifted into leading the orphanage with missionary zeal.

Bruce is the orphan. He answers to the name Ah Sahm, "the third," the third brother in a gang of thieves led by Big Brother in the unforgiving streets of Hong Kong, the third place between Britain and China. Ah Sahm's fate is buffeted by circumstance, saved through coincidence, and always triangulated by relationships that ricochet him between right and wrong. The role seemed to have been tailor made for the third son of Hoi Chuen and Grace who fancied himself third sibling to Wong Shun Leung and William Cheung, caught between ruination and respectability.

We meet Ah Sahm as he is fleeing police, carrying a coat he has stolen. He stumbles into See-Kei, who confronts the boy but trades him pocket change for the coat, and allows him to escape. The coat belongs to a tycoon named Cheung Kit-Chiong. See-Kei finds Cheung and returns it.

Soon afterward Ah Sahm steals the purse of a music teacher named Yiu So-fung, played by famed actress Pak Yin, and See-Kei is chasing the boy again. When the principal catches up to Ah Sahm, the flannelled teen is at an afternoon club, absorbed in a frenetic cha-cha. See-Kei takes him to a restaurant to talk him into returning the purse.

The scenes between them showcase Bruce's comic patrimony, fizzy energy, and Chaplinesque physicality, and are some of the best of his screen career. See-Kei tries to control him, but the skittery Ah Sahm's eyebrows flash in disbelief, his lips curdle into contempt. Ah Sahm accedes to See-Kei's instruction but makes a grand exit, singing himself to the door and rocking an even campier cha-cha, stumbling over a final stairstep with an "Aiya!"

Later, while See-Kei lectures him about proper conduct, the bored teen drums out a fast beat on the table with his hands. He can't sit still. See-Kei invites him to enroll at his school. "What will I study?" Ah Sahm asks. "Dancing?" He jumps up to do a cha-cha and his "Ah Fei" delinquent dance, shaking like Elvis and screaming like Little Richard.

Then Ah Sahm's fortunes sink. He is beaten by Big Brother for losing the stolen goods. He is caught and jailed by the police. See-Kei bails him out and enrolls the orphan in his school.

Ms. Yiu has become the music teacher there, and one night, after she spots the homesick boy running away to visit his guardian, she snitches him out to See-Kei. In the movie's most riveting scene, the outraged Ah Sahm confronts Ms. Yiu in her classroom. He pulls a switchblade, and with feral laughter, threatens his classmates and slashes her dress across her chest. It takes the entire school to subdue him, and See-Kei locks him in a toolshed, an improvised jail.

Big Brother frees Ah Sahm and commands the teen to kidnap the tycoon Cheung's son, precipitating a massive police search. Cheung blames See-Kei for the kidnapping, because he has harbored Ah Sahm. At Cheung's home, See-Kei promises to help. But he sees Ah Ng there—his son's lost nanny is now Cheung's servant—and learns that Ah Sahm is actually To-Tsai, his missing son.

Ah Sahm pays for his sins when Big Brother savagely slashes off his ear, and he flees the gang to run back to the school. Ah Sahm is finally reconciled with See-Kei, his father, and Ms. Yiu, and apologizes publicly to his classmates. Together with the police they raid the gangster hideout, kill Big Brother, and save Cheung's son.

The movie closes with the students performing Ms. Yiu's maudlin song: "We are orphans in a sea of humanity. We have lost the warmth of a family."

"Dry your tears, pick up your courage," they sing. "Look! In the world to come, who will be the masters?"

In the final scene, Ah Sahm is a student watering the garden, bandaged like Van Gogh, tamed, rehabilitated, and finally productive, just as Bruce's father and mother and so many other adults once hoped he might be.

Ng had cannily tapped Bruce for *The Orphan* because of his explosive dualities: the cha-cha dancing and street fighting, the charm and aggression, the petulance and the need to be loved. Some scenes, like Ah Sahm's knife attack, seem lifted directly from Bruce's La Salle years. Bruce's recklessness, his desire for a father figure, and his yearning for redemption are all on display in his performance. The Orphan's sins are absolved, and his typhoon energies harnessed into the labor necessary for the colony's ascent from chaos into modernity.

When *The Orphan* was released in Hong Kong, on March 3, 1960, his performance drew rave reviews.[*] One reviewer rhapsodized over Bruce's breakout performance and his "charisma and rebellious temperament," comparing him to James Dean. That reviewer was Chang Cheh, who, six years later, would direct the martial arts epic *The One-Armed Swordsman*, launching the golden era of *wuxia* film which would make Bruce's return to Hong Kong possible.

At that moment, Chang was a director and screenwriter for MP&GI, better known as the Cathay Organization, and determined to make a movie with Bruce. But after dispatching a production manager to find Bruce, he was told the teen had disappeared to America.

Bruce shared none of the glory of what might have been his second breakthrough film. While *The Orphan* was taking in four hundred thousand Hong Kong

---

[*] In time, *The Orphan* would be ranked by the Hong Kong Film Awards as one of the top one hundred Chinese movies of all time.

dollars in its first week and drawing enthusiastic audiences, he would be living half a world away from the stardom that might have been his.

Years later, Bruce wrote, "A Chinese boy growing up in Hong Kong knows that if he disgraces himself he brings disgrace upon all his kin, upon a great circle of people." After his eighteenth birthday, with his exile looming, Bruce suddenly pivoted. The cold war with his father finally began to thaw.

Prodded by Grace, Hoi Chuen had retired from acting and finally kicked his opium habit. He cared for a menagerie of pets—dogs, fish, birds, and turtles—and tended a collection of plants and flowers. One day Bruce told his father about the Wing Chun he had been learning and, for the first time, demonstrated for him some of his forms.

After a long time in thought, Hoi Chuen said, "I can see how this form compares to *tai chi*. I am proud of the skill you've developed. As long as practice doesn't get in the way of your studies, you should continue." His father had freed him from Peter's shadow to discover his own path.

As Bruce's departure neared, he signed up for additional English classes at the nearby YMCA. His mother's admonition about the vicissitudes of a career in the movies had acquired new meaning. Linda later found these English entries in his diary from just after his eighteenth birthday:

November 30, 1958—now I try to find out my career—wether [sic] as a doctor or another? If as a doctor I must study hard.

December 1, 1958—learn more mathematics.
learn more English (conversation).

Robert recalled, "In my memory I had never seen him so quiet while he was at home."

In a small notebook, on whose first pages he had listed eighty-two cha-cha steps—"Waltz step," "Charleston step," "samba step"—Bruce transcribed passages from a pamphlet titled *The Modern Commando Science of Guerilla Self-Defense for the Home Front*, published in 1943 by Britain's most famous tough guy, George F. Jowett: "Pay absolutely no attention to his size, his arrogance, fierce facial contortions, nor his vicious language... THE BIGGER THEY ARE, THE HARDER THEY FALL."

Such transcriptions helped him practice the English he had ignored for so long. The notebooks and journals also marked a new interiority and the start of a wide-ranging intellectual life. To his collection of *wuxia* novels, he added fighting and self-defense pamphlets, but also classical Chinese novels, histories, and poetry. *Gung fu* was reintroducing him to the best ideas of his heritage.

In small, neat Chinese characters, he copied "A Theory of Fighting" from an Eagle Claw *gung fu* manual. He redrew illustrations he had found in another book of bodily flows of *qi*, pressure points, and vital attack points. He copied another classical poem. "Blades may cross yet I am not dazzled by them," it read. "Surrounded and beset on all sides, yet I do not fear."

He transcribed some of the historian Sima Qian's most famous lines, replacing "businessman" with "*gung fu* man": "A good *gung fu* man always hides his assets so that he may appear as without valuables; a good man who values morals always looks as if he is someone without knowledge and seeks advice."

It was a humbled Bruce who returned to Wong Shun Leung to ask to train again. Wong—and soon after, Yip Man—welcomed him back. Almost every afternoon, Bruce practiced with Wong for two hours. On weekends the two went to the Shatin Hotel, where Bruce danced cha-cha all night. He asked Wong if it would be OK for him to learn some Shaolin forms in case he was asked to perform them in the States. "You should learn it as if you are learning a dance," Wong said, "then it'll not disappoint you."

Bruce invited a close friend of his father's to *yumcha* brunch, an older actor named Siu Hon-Sang who had acted and done fight choreography for the Wong Fei-Hung films and taught Northern Shaolin styles at the Jing Wu Athletic Association. In the bustling restaurant, the teen peppered his amused elder with questions about acting and martial arts. Then he proposed a deal: "Uncle Siu, I'll be your cha-cha *sifu*, you be my kung fu *sifu*."

"First, you must have martial arts virtue," Uncle Siu told him. "This virtue finds expression in politeness, cultivation in temper, and respect for teachers. No matter what achievement you will get, in China you must not forget your masters who have helped a great deal in molding you."

After Bruce indicated he understood, Uncle Siu agreed to Bruce's terms. He taught Bruce two Northern Shaolin boxing forms, *gung-lik kune* (power fist) and *jeet kune* (sectional fist), and two weapons forms, *bagua dao* (eight diagram broadsword) and *wu hu qiang* (five tiger spear). He gifted Bruce with the *Jing Wu Anniversary Book*, a sought-after history of the famed republican martial arts school cofounded by Huo Yuanjia, the legendary fighter whose life and death would inspire *Fist of Fury*.

In turn, Bruce tried to teach Uncle Siu some dance steps. "It would take a few weeks or a month for ordinary people to learn those moves, but Bruce learned *gung-lik* in three nights," Siu recalled. "But I still cannot even dance to a beat of cha-cha!"

On the training floor Bruce was unhappy with his progress. His *sihing* William Cheung was in Australia, but Bruce still nagged Wong Shun Leung about whether he could best him. "Actually these questions are meaningless," Wong told him. "Our greatest enemy is our own self."

Bruce would remember this period as one in which he was forced to confront his demons. "From boyhood to adolescence, I presented myself as a troublemaker and was greatly disapproved of by my elders. I was extremely mischievous, aggressive, hot-tempered and fierce," he wrote. "I never knew what it was that made me so pugnacious. The first thought that came into my mind whenever I met somebody I disliked was 'Challenge him!'"

But his fear of failure always threatened to send him into an emotional tailspin. "The moment I engaged in combat with an opponent, my mind was completely perturbed and unstable," he wrote in a 1962 paper for an English class that he entitled "A Moment of Understanding." "My one thought left was somehow or another I must beat him and win.'"*

"Loong, relax and calm your mind. Forget about yourself and follow the opponent's movement," Yip Man counseled him. "Above all, learn the art of detachment."

Bruce was reconsidering *qigong, tai chi,* and internal *gung fu,* the so-called "soft" styles which he had once rejected as weak, boring, and useless. He was trying to understand his *yin* qualities—stillness, receptivity, yielding, what he would come to call "the principle of gentleness." But he also wondered if these went against his true self.

"Loong," Yip Man said, "preserve yourself by following the natural bends of things and don't interfere. Remember never to assert yourself against nature. Never be in frontal opposition to any problem but control it by swinging with it. Don't practice this week. Go home and think about it."

He meditated, practiced alone, then quit in frustration and headed down to the harbor, where he secured a junk and steered himself into the water. He thought over his years of training, became upset with himself again, and punched the surface of the water.

"Right then at that moment, a thought suddenly struck me," he wrote. "Wasn't this water, the very basic stuff, the essence of *gung fu*?

"I struck it just now, but it did not suffer hurt. Again, I stabbed it with all my might, yet it was not wounded. I then tried to grasp a handful of it, but it was impossible. This water, the softest substance in the world, could fit into any container. Although it seemed weak, it could penetrate the hardest substance in the world.

"That was it! I wanted to be like the nature of water.

"Suddenly a bird flew past and cast its reflection on the water," he wrote. "Shouldn't it be the same then that the thoughts and emotions I had in front of an opponent passed like the reflection of the bird over water? This was exactly what Professor Yip Man meant by being detached—not being without emotion or feeling but being one in whom feeling was not sticky or blocked.

---

* Bruce Lee wrote this paper in spring semester 1962 for English 103 class, taught by Professor Margaret Walters—and likely also for another class—at the University of Washington. This original paper was edited just slightly—mainly grammatical fixes—when Linda republished it in *Bruce Lee: The Man Only I Knew,* p. 38, and *The Bruce Lee Story,* pp. 37, 39. From here, this shall be referred to as the "Tao of Gung Fu" paper.

"Therefore, in order to control myself I must first accept myself by going with, and not against, my nature. I lay on the boat and felt that I had united with Tao. I had become one with nature."

Ben Der told Bruce he was having one final blowout party at his house. He, too, was moving to the United States. He had emptied his house and even had his parents knock out some walls so that he could throw the biggest farewell party Kowloon had ever seen.

St. Francis Xavier showed up, including many of the fresh new Wing Chun students. Bruce arrived with Wong Shun Leung and Hawkins Cheung. Wong posted up in the corner, looking mean and impressive. But when the music came on, Hawkins and Bruce charged into the center of the dance floor. Ben laughed at the memory. "Those girls went crazy!"

Some of the St. Francis Xavier boys—and not a few of the girls—agreed, yes, Bruce could be self-centered and aggravating. But they would also remember exactly what he had said to them with all the bravado he could muster: "I am going to become famous in America." And on this night, as he lifted a girl over his head and twirled her around while the others laughed and screamed at him to put her down and Ben's mother came running out of her room to scold him, they all knew that they did not want to be anywhere else but right there, right then.

"I mean, this is the showmanship, you know?" Ben Der remembered with a wistful smile more than sixty years later. "Put it this way, that was the happiest moment in my life."

On the evening of April 29, 1959, Bruce went down to the dock to board the SS *President Wilson*, bound for San Francisco. The night before, he had woken his little brother. "Doggie, I have to leave here to study in America," he confessed to Robert. "I don't know what it'll be like over there."

Bruce seemed so downcast that after he left the room Robert lay awake in bed thinking about how to cheer his brother up. He dug out a picture of himself wearing cowboy-like trousers and suspenders, scratching his nose. On the back, he wrote, "To dearest Bruce, please don't be sad in the ship. From your loving brother, Robert."

Some of his friends had come to join his family to see him off, including Hawkins, Wu Ngan, Unicorn, and Pearl. Hoi Chuen stayed home, saying that the tradition in his village was for fathers never to see their sons off. Privately, out of Bruce's earshot, he expressed worry. "I hope he makes it," he confessed. Grace would be the parent to accompany Bruce to the dock, hug him, slip a hundred dollars into his pocket, and give him their final message—*do not return unless you have made something of yourself.*

I'm going to make it, Mother, he answered. *I really am.*

At 10:00 p.m., the horn sounded, the steamship pulled away from the dock, and the streamers fluttered down into the bay. Grace's shoulders shook with sobs. From the rail, Bruce waved goodbye to his family and friends and he, too, wept.

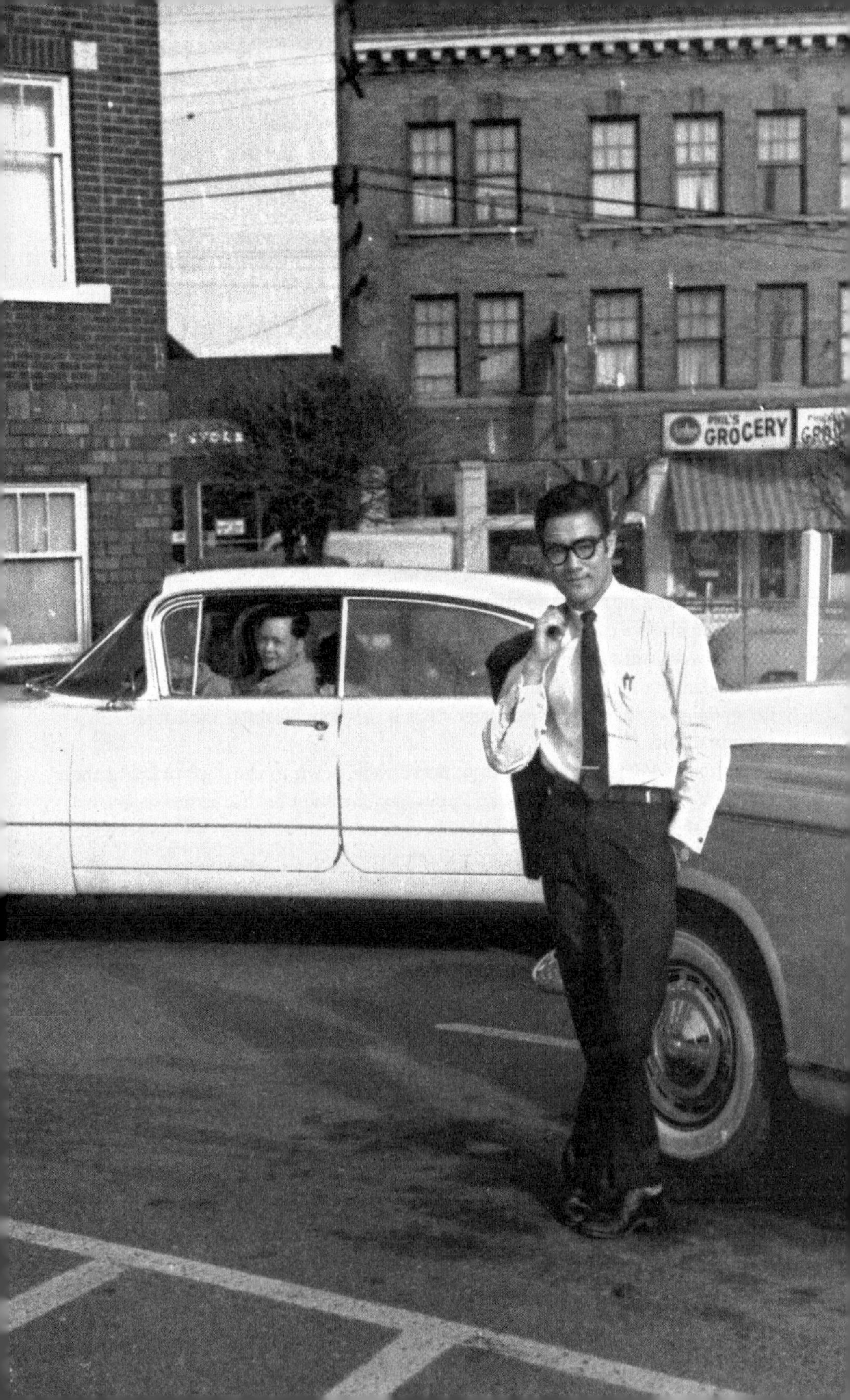
GROCERY

PART III
Learning America

1959–1961

> But the Chinese do not come in the name of liberty as oppressed, nor are they willing to renounce their old allegiance.... It is also plain that, by their mental organization, they have no capacity for or appreciation of the blessings of liberty.
>
> —JAMES DUVAL PHELAN

Bruce and Ping Chow, Seattle, 1959.
Photo courtesy of the Bruce Lee Family Archive.

CHAPTER 8
A Return Passage

Bruce had been a colony star, a name in the streets, or so he had thought. Now the roads and rooftops, the friends and adversaries—all that had contoured his everyday was gone.

"The first friend I made after boarding the ship," he wrote, "actually turned out to be an Indian man." In Bruce's telling, he soon had the man begging for cha-cha lessons. But then the man "ran into his friend and in the end, I was alone again."

He made his way down the levels to steerage, where he met the travelers with whom he'd share the eighteen-night journey. Mr. Deng gave him advice on how to avoid seasickness. Mr. Chang turned out to be a student of Choy Li Fut and the older brother of a school classmate. He made a note to himself to spend more time with Chang.

He decided to take a shower. But having bathed much of his life with just a bucket of water on the veranda, he couldn't make sense of the faucets. He turned on the hot water until he scalded himself, then the cold water until he froze. He tramped up to the bar for a drink but fled when he found out how much a Coke would cost.

At the end of the night, he pulled out a notepad and scribbled his thoughts in Chinese. "After I got into bed, I felt like the entire bed was swinging back and forth and it was rather uncomfortable," he wrote. "Hopefully this won't lead to seasickness!"

He wrote as if the next morning he might be reading back these tales of his follies to everyone around the breakfast table. But here he was in a bargain bunk alone, and that life was disappearing in the darkness beyond the horizon. He wrote a poem to himself:

> Once a friendship of several years is split up
> Some feelings of melancholy arise from being separated from the pack
> It's uncertain when the return date will be
> To whom can I relay my sorrow and worries?

The ship pulled into Tokyo Bay, the first stop on its journey. Bruce was greeted at the Yokohama dock by his brother Peter, who was on break from classes in Australia. The two caught the commuter train into a bustling Japan that was no longer an imperial scourge but a place of promethean creativity, the home of Kurosawa, Mizoguchi, and Godzilla. Bruce was mesmerized.

"On the roads there were cars driving in both directions continuously. The streets were packed with lively crowds and bursting with activity. In the markets there were a myriad of colorful neon lights that were changing every moment," he wrote in his diary. "Compared to this, Hong Kong is really nowhere even close."

He shared a meal of chicken *donburi* with Peter and his worldly friends, who already seemed at home in the new postwar Asia. They shopped for stylish shoes and terry cloth shirts and ended the night at a jazz club. Bruce left to catch the train back to the ship, his solitary reflection in the window, the lamplights slipping one by one into the distance. Then it was back into the darkness of the Pacific.

When the ship docked next in Honolulu, Bruce was disappointed to learn that no one from his family had written him. But Hoi Chuen had ignored the small things and taken care of the big things. Someone was always there for Bruce: to greet him, take him around, buy him meals, even chat him up. In turn Bruce never passed up an opportunity to show off his martial arts skills, sometimes blindfolding himself to exchange hands. "He was young and I was young," one of his father's friends remembered, "but I could not even touch him."

Back on the ship, Bruce discovered a place to be each evening—beside the bandstand in the upper-deck dance hall under the lights. Every night he dressed in a white button-down dress shirt and dark pleated slacks. He stared at himself in the mirror, slicked his hair back, adjusted his collar, and went up to take his spot at the edge of the dance floor, awaiting the time when the formal-wear crowds streamed in from the banquet room.

When the band kicked in, the eighteen-year-old from the lower levels could show first-class passengers what could be done with light feet, loose hips, and a 1-2 cha-cha-cha. Before long, the band members invited him to do what he would have done anyway—formally teach cha-cha to the guests. From then on he was King of the Night—leading lines of passengers through the steps, taking the odd lucky matron for a whirl, smiling for photos like a Disneyland cast member.

Sometimes during the band breaks, Bruce stepped onto the emptied floor to perform *gung fu*. But as he punched and kicked through his forms, the guests just sipped their drinks and stared. They had no idea what he was doing.

One night the ship hit rough waters. "There was a dance party at night but people could not dance, and many liquor bottles and such were falling all over as well," he wrote. "After I taught cha-cha for 15 minutes there was another emergency rescue exercise. I had to go below deck again and put on a life jacket. It was quite annoying!"

Before sleep each night, he retrieved his notepad to write letters he might never send and doodle things he missed—a hanging punching bag, a small punching bag, a wall-mounted punching bag, a jump rope, dumbbells, grips and rings, a wooden dummy. To journey to faraway lands the Monkey King had conjured clouds to spring across. To prepare himself for his new life across the ocean, Bruce composed lists—seven ways to warm up for training, six methods for directing *qi*, six *chengyu* four-character idioms to memorize:

開門見山. ["Open the door, see the mountain"—always come straight to the point.]

口是心非. ["The mouth says 'Yes,' the heart says 'No'"—beware duplicity.]

見異思遷. ["Seeing a foreign object, the thinking shifts"—don't be swayed by the shiny, new, and novel.]

弄巧成拙. ["Trying to be clever, making a fool of oneself"—avoid self-defeating acts.]

杌隉不安. ["The condition of the state is dangerous and restless"—remain aware and prepared.]

嚴於律己. ["Forgive others but not yourself"—be generous with others but critical, exacting, and disciplined with oneself.]

There was another, one that spoke to all the teachers he had ever obeyed or ignored: 飲水思源—"when drinking water, consider the source."

On May 17, 1959, as the ship passed under the Golden Gate Bridge, Bruce snapped a picture from the deck and posed with friends he had made on the cha-cha floor.

Some things had changed since his parents' arrival. In 1940, after a suspicious fire, the Angel Island immigration station had closed. In 1943 Congress had voted to repeal the Chinese Exclusion Act, a nod to the role China played as an American ally against Japan. The repeal was cosmetic. Congress replaced complete exclusion with an annual quota of just 105 visas for immigrants from Asian countries. Anti-Asian sentiment still ran deep. In 1952 Congress ended restrictions on naturalization for other Asian ethnicities. But total immigration from the entire Asiatic Barred Zone was capped at two thousand a year, ensuring that nearly all immigrants who could become citizens were still from Europe.

There is a photo of young Bruce taken not long after his arrival, on a day of sightseeing with friends. He stands near Fisherman's Wharf, where the city meets the water. Behind him rise Telegraph Hill and Coit Tower, and all around are American automobiles with their high narrow tails, polished tops, and sensuous curves. Bruce sports an orange shirt topped with a green bomber jacket, and the dark dance slacks and pomaded hair of a cruise night.

His posture is curiously tight. He grips his hands at his waist, fixes his mouth, and knits his brows. He is very nearly in a ready position. With a half-step forward he can reach out to shake someone's hand. A half-step back and he is coiled for explosion. In between the before and after, he seems to be waiting.

Bruce at Fisherman's Wharf, San Francisco, summer 1959. Photo courtesy of the Bruce Lee Family Archive.

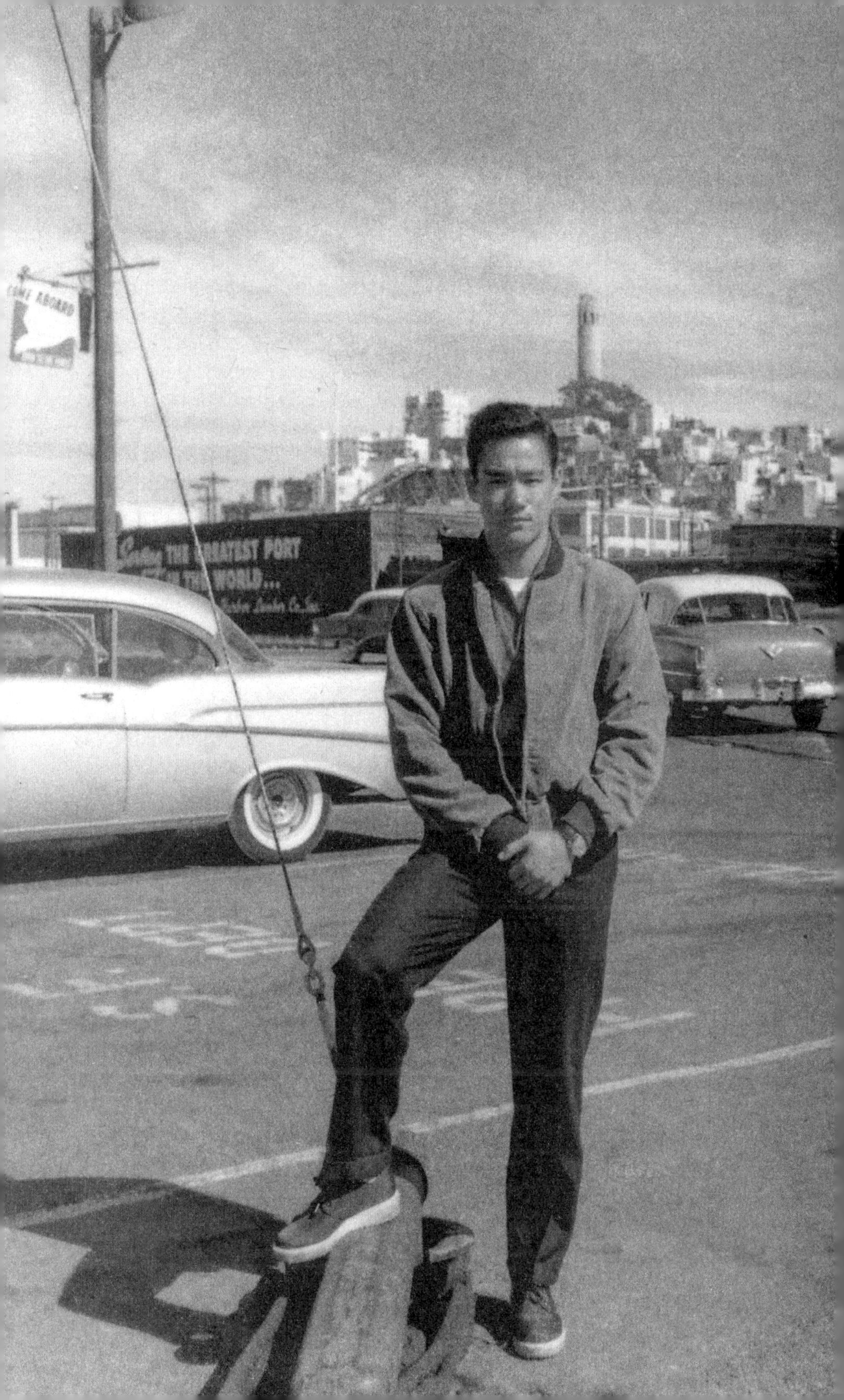
PORT

Perhaps San Francisco would not be so different from Hong Kong—a refuge on a shimmering harbor, enclosed by waters of protection, streets climbing hills of hope, alive to strangers and their struggles. Or perhaps it would be a country of no traditions, a land without ghosts, a place of lonely crowds propelled by an unnamed hunger and melancholy toward the frontier at the setting sun.

On the other side of Telegraph Hill lay Chinatown, where Bruce would reside with his godfather, a gentleman bachelor named Quan Ging Ho. In 1960, thirty-five thousand Chinese lived in San Francisco, most of them within this half-mile-by-quarter-mile space, a sheer human density familiar to a Hong Konger. Chinatown was a city within a city, with its own separate schools, churches, hospital, and telephone exchange. If Bruce followed any street two blocks out of Chinatown, he was crossing unseen borders.

Down the hill in the Financial District businessmen transacted the wealth of the Pacific. Up the hill, ramshackle Chinatown tenements gave way to the mansions of the leisure class. After the 1906 earthquake, the city's leaders wished Chinatown unseen because it separated the homes of the capitalists from their places of work. They proposed removing the Chinese quarter down to Bayview-Hunter's Point, a low, marshy area of slaughterhouses, shipbuilding, and shrimpers at the southern edge of the city.

Instead Chinese merchants mobilized quickly to rebuild, hiring white architects and giving them permission to reimagine Chinatown. They turned the nineteenth-century urban ghetto of brick and wood and iron into an Orientalist movie set—all red and gold paint, curving roofs and skyward-pointing eaves, and decorative faux pagodas. It was an exchange of the aesthetic for the material: *let us live and you can picture us any way you wish.*

In the 1930s federal bureaucrats drew up redlining maps to lock in racial and economic segregation. They worried over "threats of infiltration" by "Negroes and Japs," and were anxious that other "racial concentrations" would spill out of their appointed ghettos into gilded white neighborhoods. But they had no such worry about the Chinese in Chinatown, confident that those Orientals had already learned not to test the existing "topography."

In that sense, little about San Francisco had changed in the century from the first settling of Chinatown to Bruce's arrival.

Hoi Chuen and Grace must have especially been pleased to have Quan Ging Ho as their proxy parent. An accomplished poet and playwright and the principal of Nam Kue Chinese school, he had looked after Grace's well-being when Hoi Chuen was touring. He lived in a two-story white brick building at 654 Jackson Street, in the densest part of Chinatown, around the corner from the Mandarin Theatre, next door to the Great China Theatre, just down the block from the hospital where he had taken Grace to give birth to Bruce. Mr. Quan was well loved in Chinatown.

Now in his mid-fifties, he was welcomed in the classrooms, cafés, and restaurants by day, and the theaters, speakeasies, and nightclubs by night.

Bruce enrolled in English classes at John Adams High School and registered with the Selective Service through Local Draft Board Number 36 on New Montgomery Street. Each day Bruce ascended a staircase to a landing, off which lay a bathroom and kitchen shared with the other residents, and their apartments. He slept on a single bed in a corner of Quan's book-stuffed room.

Mr. Quan got him a job busing tables at Kum Hon restaurant across the street. But Bruce hated the work. It was hectic, messy, and beneath him. Within a week he had gotten himself fired. As Mr. Quan plotted how to rescue this part of Hoi Chuen and Grace's plan, Bruce reconnected with Ben Der. On Friday nights, they went to dances at Galileo High. During the day they practiced Wing Chun in the apartment, pushing each other loudly around the room during their *chi sao* sessions, and disturbing the neighbors.

If Bruce would not succeed at honest labor, Mr. Quan realized, maybe the other of his preoccupations would do. He found Bruce a job teaching cha-cha classes at the Kuomintang building, at the rate of a dollar a head. Soon an organization called the Chinese Association of Dancers offered Bruce more opportunities to teach and perform. This gig left Bruce free most days to wander the largest Chinatown in America—which was still tinier than the least of Kowloon's neighborhoods. California was very big, but the world Bruce had come to was very small.

The couples he taught were mostly a generation older than him. Some were regular folks—workers, nurses, teachers. Some had a little bit of money—traders, doctors, lawyers. Many spoke Toisanese, which meant that they or their people had come from the countryside. Some were second- or even third-generation *jook sing* who answered him only in English.

Bruce spoke proper Cantonese and British-accented English. Around his students, he felt urbane and sophisticated. They could hardly be blamed for the misfortune of being American. They seemed so excited to learn dances that were two years old. This gig would be so easy.

But Bruce was restless. He longed to feel the blood-and-adrenaline rush of a real fight again, to test hands with other *gung fu* men. After Ben Der moved to Florida, Bruce quickly found himself in more trouble.

In 1914, Tomi Mori performed a bit of *jujitsu* in one of the very first Asian American–produced movies, Frank Shaw's *The Oath of the Sword*, the first film depiction of Asian martial arts in the United States. During World War II, white American servicemen encountered Japanese *judo* and Okinawan *karate* on their tours of the Pacific. After the war, urban *dojos* in Honolulu, Phoenix, Seattle, and California spurred the rapid development of Japanese martial arts in the West. By the mid-1950s, regional associations and intercollegiate competitions had sprung up across the country. Critically acclaimed Hollywood movies like John Sturges's *Bad Day at Black Rock* and Samuel Fuller's *The Crimson Kimono* featured *karate* and *kendo*, and sparked more interest in Japanese fighting arts.

Yet in the United States, only a very small number of non-Chinese had been inducted into *gung fu*. In Hong Kong, wartime migration had transformed the fight underground, relocating countless schools and pitting them in fierce competition against each other. But in the States, immigrant exclusion had pinched off the arrival of new styles and challengers and made many Chinatown practitioners resistant to change. Those who read of Wong Shun Leong's *beimo* exploits in the transpacific Chinese-language newspapers were predisposed to dislike the migrant upstarts and their styles.

"All those Chinatown martial arts guys," Ben Der recalled, shaking his head, "they think Wing Chun people are all troublemakers."

Across the bay in Oakland's younger, smaller Chinatown, there was more receptivity. Bruce received an invitation from two middle-aged Oaklanders, Bob Lee and his wife, Harriet, to teach "Hong Kong cha-cha" to their dance association at the Chinese American Citizens Alliance lodge, at Eighth and Harrison. By day the three-story wood-shingled building was where Mrs. Fong kept her famous barbershop, community organizers planned campaigns, and lawyers prepared civil rights lawsuits. During the evenings, entertainment took over.

Bruce guided the fifteen couples through the dance steps. "Everyone who learned from Bruce liked him a lot, and he showed us some very different cha-cha moves than we were used to," Harriet recalled. "He was a pure entertainer."

At intermission, he told them he wanted to show them something else—the art of *gung fu*—and performed a Praying Mantis form at top speed. He explained that *gung fu* was the root of all the Oriental martial arts and the most powerful. He punctuated his short talk with flurries of Wing Chun punches. After the event, Bruce received warm compliments on his cha-cha and his *gung fu*. Unlike on the cruise ship, this audience knew exactly what they had seen.

Bob, Harriet, and their friend George Lee circled Bruce. Bob Lee's younger brother was a highly reputable *gung fu* fighter named James Yimm Lee, who held daily workouts with a group in his Oakland garage. George Lee, a World War II vet and a machinist who had been studying *gung fu* for over a decade, asked, "What kind of *gung fu* was that you did?"

Bruce smiled. "It's called Wing Chun."

The Oaklanders were taken not only by the young man's knowledge, but also his self-confidence. They boasted to Bruce about James, and the next afternoon they raved to James about Bruce. The two needed to meet.

From the moment Chinese had begun arriving in the States, they had practiced *gung fu*. To outsiders, sociologist Ying-Jen Chang wrote, "It was hidden and unrecognized in the forms of the lion dance, the dragon dance, and the *chi lin* dance, as well as the Cantonese opera and the herb store." But it was deeply integrated into the life of Chinatown.

In the earliest days, access to the fighting arts was controlled by clan, village, or family association leaders as well as those who ran Chinatown's underground economies. *Gung fu* men served as bodyguards and security guards. The *kwoons* could function like craft guilds: teaching outsiders what you knew undermined your ability not just to defend yourself, but to make a livelihood.

Later, new *gung fu* schools opened the arts to a Chinese American community in broader need of protection in a fitfully integrating society. In turn, as Chinese America desegregated, so did its institutions. By the middle of the fifties, the *gung fu* schools were making, historian Charles Russo wrote, "a quiet transition of martial arts from the tongs to the public."

Bruce learned the names of the top *kwoons*. Both had opened in San Francisco's Chinatown in the late 1930s and were led by grizzled old enforcers for the Hop Sing Tong. The Wah Keung (Strong Chinese) Kung Fu Club of Choy Li Fut, considered the first *gung fu* school in the United States, was led by a man named Lau Bun. Nearby was the Kin Mon (Sturdy Citizen's Club) school run by T. Y. Wong.

In 1955, T. Y. Wong and his students appeared on Hugh Downs's and Arlene Francis's national NBC daytime show, *Home*, demonstrating *gung fu* for the housewives of America. It was likely the first North American media appearance of Chinese martial arts.

Before long, Native Hawaiian judo black belt and famed waterman Clifford Kamaka would be one of Lau Bun's top students, and two white men—Noel O'Brien and Al Novak—among T. Y. Wong's. A wave of new migration from Hawai'i and Asia would soon push *gung fu* in the United States into a new era, with Bruce joining his migrant peers as heralds of change. But in 1959, Bruce was still just a kid fresh off the boat, itching to test his skills and the patience of his elders.

Lau Bun, the old tong man and *gung fu* master, was an esteemed herbalist and bonesetter nearing the age of seventy. Born in Toisan, his father had been one of the first immigrants to California, sending remittances to China that allowed Lau Bun to live in comfort learning different forms of martial arts. Lau studied Choy Li Fut with Yuen Fai, the master of the Hung Sing school. But the school's affiliation with the Communists brought it into disfavor during the republican era, and in the early 1930s, Lau decided to migrate to the States.

Lau crossed the border from Mexico at Tijuana, made his way to Los Angeles, and took the paper son name of Wong On. But the Border Patrol caught up to his ruse and sent four officers to raid Lau's apartment. Whatever happened next—it was a story that grew with the telling, involving fists, kicks, perhaps even some dead feds—what is agreed upon is that Lau fought off the agents, jumped out of a second-story window, and escaped to San Francisco.

With a Guan Yu–level scowl, he still struck fear into the bravest of hearts. And he still ran his school from a basement off Portsmouth Square with the intensity of a field general. Some said he sent his students out to test their skills by picking fights with Mexicans in the Mission, but he would never tolerate such disorder in Chinatown, because the last thing he wanted in his own community was anything resembling Hong Kong's anarchy.

It was Lau's school, the Hung Sing studio, that Bruce Lee walked toward in the twilight of a late summer day, with a challenge on his mind and chaos in his heart. "When Bruce Lee came to Hung Sing, he didn't know anything about San Francisco," Lau's senior student Sam Louie told Charles Russo. "He came to show off some hands and tried to say to us that Wing Chun was the best."

Lau Bun entered his studio into a scene ready-made for a movie. Seven or eight of his students were yelling at some FOB kid.

Bruce Lee was yelling back.

As Lau stepped in, the noise abruptly ceased. He motioned to his students to stand down, then stared Bruce down with his scowl.

"Did your teacher allow you to talk like that at his school in Hong Kong?" he asked.

Bruce had no answer.

"There is no street talk in here. Take your mouth back up to the street!"

Bruce was frozen.

"Now!"

And back into the darkness he fled.

At the beginning of September 1959, Bruce bade farewell to his godfather Mr. Quan and, luggage in hand, walked down to a car double-parked on Jackson. It had been driven eight hundred miles to San Francisco by another old opera friend of his father, a cook named Fook Yeung, who was picking Bruce up as a favor to Hoi Chuen. Bruce was about to repeat the same mistakes he had made in Hong Kong, so Hoi Chuen and Grace had arranged for their son to move to Seattle—a smaller city with fewer Chinese, fewer martial artists, and therefore fewer distractions.

Bruce would live with a former opera star named Ping Chow and his dynamic wife, Ruby, who ran a restaurant that bore her name. He would work for them to earn his lodging and keep. The Chows promised Bruce's parents that he would earn his high school diploma and university degree. He was to arrive days before classes started.

Fook Yeung was a cook in the Chows' kitchen, a turnabout from his previous life. In his youth, he had been known for the physically demanding, star-making role of the Monkey King. While on an American tour, he jumped ship and found his way up the coast to Seattle, where Ping and Ruby were taking in stage vets stranded by the wars and giving them work.

Yeung was an adept of many *gung fu* styles, including the Red Junk Opera branch of Wing Chun. He taught Southern Mantis styles and helped Ping teach the lion dances to students in the Chinese Youth Club. Bruce knew all of this about the man he called Fook Baak, "Uncle Fook." So upon greeting him, Bruce challenged his uncle to sticking hands. But the wiry Yeung, no bigger than Yip Man, easily and quickly overpowered the youth. Disappointed, Bruce got into the passenger seat and settled in for the long ride.

In the spring and summer of 1959, on the ocean liner and in San Francisco and Oakland, Bruce had learned a little about how much he still didn't know. Now he was bound for Seattle, where he would learn America.

CHAPTER 9
The Power Broker

When Bruce arrived in Seattle, on September 3, 1959, he found a city even more beautiful than San Francisco—bays and lakes of sparkling indigo that met a palette-knife stroke of verdant greens in hemlock, fir, and cedar. But he would learn that crystal days like this were fleeting. Most of the time Seattle would be shrouded in a gray mist, pelted by cold steady rain, a place of intimate distances.

Seattle was the kind of town where, as the community activist Wing Luke once put it, the first English words every Chinese learned were "yes," "no," and "he hit me first." In 1962, Luke became the first person of color ever elected to the Seattle City Council. Many credited his victory to an unusual get-out-the-vote campaign led by Bruce's new boss and landlord, his "aunty" Ruby Chow. She had organized all the Chinese restaurateurs to fill their fortune cookies with messages that started Charlie Chan style with the phrase "Wing Luke says . . ." and concluded with a little bit of humor and a little bit of threat: *It's wise to vote for Wing Luke*. His electoral breakthrough only highlighted how racially segregated the city remained. A century after the first Chinese had arrived, Seattle was still 95 percent white.

The Chows had opened their restaurant, Ruby Chow's Chinese Dinner Club, in 1948, the same year that the Supreme Court struck down racist housing covenants. They had purchased a building at Broadway and Jefferson atop Seattle's storied First Hill, a neighborhood initially settled by the city's white elite during the Chinese Purges. Of the more than sixty Chinese restaurants in town, theirs was the first to open outside Chinatown, let alone in a wealthy white neighborhood.

"People in Chinatown said that we would go up there and be back down in Chinatown in sixty days, bankrupt," Ruby recalled many years later, with not a little ginger in her voice. Instead, after Wing Luke's untimely death in a plane crash, she would become as influential as her late friend.

Born Mar Seung Gum on the fish docks in 1920, the year of the Monkey, Ruby Chow was the first daughter in a family of ten. Her father, Mar Jim Sing, had survived the barbarous 1886 anti-Chinese purge and founded the Seattle chapter of the Hop Sing Tong. As a labor contractor, he held one of the most influential jobs in Chinatown. His wife, Wong Shee, was thirty-three years his junior. She worked as a cook on the dock and sold lottery numbers on King Street, bore ten children in seventeen years, and suffered Jim Sing's regular outbursts of domestic violence.

Ruby was determined to be different. One day, when she was a child, she was standing in the street with her aunties alongside a wealthy young Chinese man and his attendant. An older white man stopped to curse at them. Ruby alone stood up to him, punching the *gweilo* until he ran away. Then she turned to the rich Chinese man and asked, "Why didn't you help?"

"He was calling *you* 'chink,'" the rich man said, "not me."

During the Depression, the family fell on hard times, and men came to make offers to buy the feisty young Ruby. But even when her father pressed, her mother refused. The tong wars intensified. After surviving an assassination attempt, Jim Sing boarded a boat back to China and abandoned his family. At fourteen, Ruby dropped out of Franklin High School, took whatever job she could get, and helped her mother raise her nine siblings.

By the age of seventeen, Ruby was working at a teahouse when she met the man who became her first husband, a dashing man in Western clothes. They left for the bright lights of New York City, where he revealed himself to be a gambler and a wife-beater. Ruby now had two baby boys to feed and found late-night work at the Howdy Club, a drag-and-burlesque revue in Greenwich Village serving a mostly lesbian audience. As her husband fell deeper into debt, she kicked him out and took up a side hustle reading tarot cards, a skill she had learned at the Howdy. Finally she landed a job managing the fabled Nom Wah Tea Parlor.

The war had begun. Chinatown's restaurants were subject to immigration raids. Federal agents gave the undocumented men a choice: submit to the draft and fight for the United States or be jailed and deported. The workers and customers developed an ingenious system of signals. When feds walked in the door, someone dropped a teapot. The kitchen staff fled out the back while everyone in the dining room sat down at a table, the waitstaff tossed their aprons under the table, and together they played the old game, "Which of These Migrants Is Not Like the Other." The baffled *gweilo* always lost, and had to retreat empty-handed.

One afternoon, Ping Chow, an opera actor in New York on a tour date, came by to check out the fine new waitress all the men on the Eastern Seaboard were buzzing about. Suddenly teapots loudly crashed to the floor, everyone took seats, and Ping found himself staring across the table right at the woman herself, Ruby. As the *gweilo* paced angrily around the restaurant, he regaled her with stories of the opera life. The newly divorced Ruby was smitten.

Ping had come of age on the red junks sailing down the Pearl River delta. He dove through rings of knives, flashed long spears and wide blades, danced with high-flying flags, and spun bowls full of flames. He and his troupe had come to perform in Hawai'i, California, and the East Coast. But war closed the borders and they were stuck. If the United States deported them, where would they even be sent? They were stateless.

Ruby advised him to enlist in the army rather than live with the fear of being caught and jailed. They needed bodies so badly now, she said, that if he served in the US military he could apply for citizenship. Ping was falling in love, so he had two good reasons to stay in America.

One morning at the Oswego boot camp where Ping had become a cook, he woke up, couldn't see anything, and feared he was going blind. Of all the women he had dated Ruby was the only one who took the long train ride upstate to care for him. Ping's condition eventually improved, he was honorably discharged, and the couple moved to Seattle to be married.

First they worked for Ruby's brother, Ping flipping hamburgers and stir-frying *chop suey* as Ruby greeted customers. Then they joined with an investor to open a new restaurant in Chinatown. Ping filled the kitchen with opera refugees, and Ruby filled the restaurant and bar with increasingly non-Chinese clientele. She made things happen. "She speaks English as if it were Cantonese," the Asian American writer Frank Chin wrote admiringly of his godmother, "an all-present tense language."

When relations with the investor soured, they gambled everything on the rambling property on First Hill. It had once been a hotel and an Italian restaurant. It seated three hundred patrons, and in the two stories above, she could house her family and dozens more workers and boarders.

From her place in the front of the house, Ruby never forgot a name and wasn't shy about putting people in their place—the well dressed and the ready-to-spend in the high-visibility seats, the rest in one of the back rooms or near the kitchen. She was letting Chinese and other minorities know that they belonged on that historic hill, but they would have to level themselves up to get there.

Success, she told her employees, depended on food, atmosphere, and service. The Ruby Chow's Dinner Club menu featured winter melon soup and Hong Kong-style abalone in oyster sauce alongside New York steak and pineapple spareribs. But instead of *chop suey*, Ruby urged Ping and the cooks to make their favorite home-style dishes, like *haam yu yook baeng*—steamed pork and saltfish cake. The cooks were surprised to find the *lo fan* excited to try Ruby's suggestions, and even more excited after eating them.

She filled the space with gold-leaf statues of Guan Yin, a dragon, and a phoenix. She put in carpeting and covered the ceiling with red-painted egg cartons to quiet the ambience. She gave guests steamed jasmine-tea-scented towels. She took away soy sauce bottles to save them from ruining their meals. She designed red and gold menus that opened from the left to educate them. But the only Chinese character on the menu was Ping's family name on the cover. Inside, *wonton* dumplings were introduced as "ravioli with a delightful Chinese twist." She trained her staff in her way of folding linens, setting a table, and stacking dishes. On a good weekend, a waiter made more than a hundred dollars in tips. The restaurant quickly swelled to more than thirty employees.

It was the era of the Chinese crossover restaurant entrepreneur. Mandarin women of wealth and refinement like Cecilia Chiang in San Francisco, Joyce Chen in Boston, and Madame Wu in Los Angeles brought Northern Chinese food to white diners, running successful restaurants, writing cookbooks, and becoming media personalities. Southern Chinese bootstrapping strivers Ruby and Ping took a similar path. When Bea Donovan launched her popular cooking show on Seattle's KING-TV, a decade before Julia Child, she invited the Chows on as regulars, and Seattle fell in love with the convivial beehive-haired hostess and her laconic husband chef. Soon they had their own TV show. They sealed their fortune by launching the first Chinese frozen food business in the United States.

But Ruby was only beginning to surpass her contemporaries.

One day outside her restaurant, Ruby's children were playing on the sidewalk with her half-white niece when a white woman stopped to lecture the light-skinned girl, "You shouldn't be playing with those Japs." The frightened kids ran to Ruby and recounted what had happened. She settled on a new mission.

"She thought, The *lo fan* are not necessarily prejudiced, they're just ignorant of the ways of other people," her son Mark Chow said. "She was into demystifying us."

Chinatowns across the country were changing. "The tongs are not what they used to be," wrote Frank Chin. "They have gone from warring on the streets for turf, to warring in the courts for corporate control and equal rights." By the late 1950s, the daughter of a Hop Sing Tong founder had swept aside the old leadership of the all-powerful Chong Wah Association to become its first woman head, ushering in a new wave of US-born, bilingual leaders.

Ruby sponsored a girls' drill team and a lion dance troupe, forced the city's matriarchs to open the Miss Seattle beauty pageant to communities of color, and made Chinatown a key site for the citywide Seafair summer festival. At lavish parties, she welcomed Seattle's police, corporate, and city leaders, as well as global celebrities and dignitaries, who considered the Chows' Christmas gala a must-attend event. She knew everyone's secrets and kept them. She was Chinatown's fixer, discreetly managing business deals, immigration cases, housing issues, health care problems, high-profile arrests, and every other kind of trouble an Asian might find with white authority. She was the champion of Chinese American respectability, someone white people could call "a bridge," "an ambassador."

No one had ever leveraged the humble ethnic restaurant to thrust an entire community into the mainstream the way she had. By the time Bruce had arrived with Fook Yeung at his new home on First Hill, Ruby was one of the most powerful Americans of Asian descent anywhere.

Ruby and Ping had agreed to take Bruce in as a favor to their old friends Hoi Chuen and Grace, whom they had often visited in Hong Kong. Among the many things the couples shared was an understanding of how to rear children. The Chows' promise to them was that Bruce would receive his General Education Diploma and go on to earn a college degree.

Ruby was aware that Bruce had been a famous actor and dancer in the colony, but when she took a first look at him, she was unimpressed. He wore thick black eyeglasses to correct his 20/400 vision.* Months of hamburgers, chocolate, and Cokes had left the eighteen-year-old's face ridden with acne. She decided he was unfit to appear on the restaurant floor. She said, "You need to eat better."

She laid down her rules. During the day, go to school and study hard. Be dressed for work and ready by 4:30 p.m. to eat with the staff. Fridays and Saturdays are the biggest days, so forget weekend plans. No women. No weapons. Nothing that would bring shame to this house. "I'm not your mom or dad, I'm your aunty," Ruby said to Bruce. "You're in my household."

She walked him upstairs, above the restaurant and the second floor, where she, Ping, and their younger children slept, to the third-floor attic where he would live with the other workers. Ruby had given Bruce one of the few single rooms not reserved for her own family. But to Bruce, it was hardly better than the ship quarters—lit by a single bulb and a small window, decorated in fading flowered wallpaper, barely big enough to fit a wooden crate for a desk, with a twin bed under the roof that he had to duck beneath each night to go to sleep.

Six days after Bruce arrived in Seattle, Ruby had him in a whole new routine: walking the half-mile north to Edison Technical School for classes each morning and returning in the afternoon to clean the bathrooms, dining room, and kitchen before the restaurant opened. Then he was doing all the things he had hated doing in the San Francisco restaurant—washing dishes, unboxing vegetables, dicing onions, peeling shrimp.

In the kitchen, Uncle Ping was as kind as Aunty Ruby was demanding. Sometimes during lulls, Uncle Fook would set aside his cigar and show Bruce *gung fu* forms. But Bruce had expected to be welcomed by the Chows as an honored guest, and for at least twenty hours a week, he was nothing but Ruby's employee.

The only people in the building who felt he *was* receiving special treatment were the envious bachelor workers who slept in shared rooms, packed into tight bunks. One night in the kitchen Bruce got into an argument with one of the old cooks, who grabbed a cleaver and waved it at him, yelling that he would use it. Bruce stood his ground and seethed, "I dare you." The futility of it all was soon clear, and they all returned to work.

In time Ruby decided Bruce's face had cleared up enough that he could be seen

---

* In 1966, Dr. James Durkins found, "Bruce had 20/400 vision in both eyes that had stemmed from myopia and astigmatism. Essentially, Bruce was very nearsighted and could see clearly only at a distance of two feet or less without the correction of glasses." Dr. James Durkins quoted in Sid Campbell and Greglon Lee, *Remembering the Master: Bruce Lee, James Yimm Lee, and the Creation of Jeet Kune Do* (Blue Snake Books, 2006), p. 119.

At Ruby Chow's. L-R: Bruce, Peter Lee, Ruby Chow, Ping Chow, and other employees. Fook Yeung is sitting on the trash can. Photo courtesy of the Bruce Lee Family Archive.

on the dining room floor and assigned him to set up and bus tables. From the waiters and busboys he learned her singular method of presenting the linens and clearing the tables, and as they had, suffered her wrath when he deviated even slightly.

But as he poured tea and cleaned up after Seattle's white elite—people who made a mess knowing they wouldn't have to clean it up, who called him "boy" or looked through him, who *unsaw* him—he considered why Ruby expected him to be ready to hop to their every request, no matter how rude or disrespectful they were. He began to understand why some of the old men seemed enraged all the time.

Sometimes after work, he was so angry he didn't know what to do. Sometimes he was so tired all he could do was shower and sleep. Sometimes he immersed himself in his studies. Sometimes he opened letters from friends in Hong Kong and sighed over everything he was missing.

He wrote letters to them in English, filling every space of the small blue fold-up aerogrammes. "Now I find out all those stuffs like wing chun and Cha Cha are just for killing time and have a little fun out of it, and that study always comes first," he wrote to Hawkins Cheung. "Yes, that's right your own future depends on how well you have studied . . .

"Now I am really on my own," he added. "I am working as a waiter for a part time job after school. I am telling you it's tough, boy! I always have a heck of a time!"

He turned the paper over and, on the remaining flap, added a last note. "P.S. Give my regards to your folks!" he wrote in big letters. "Also, to all my friends in Hong Kong, there is one last thing to tell you, that is: I didn't forget you!!"

He seemed to be pleading, *Please don't forget* me.

Sometimes he drew heroes from Jin Yong's, Liang Yusheng's, and Ti Feng's *wuxia* pulp novels of bravery, loyalty, and chivalry long into the morning hours.* "Sometimes," he later told his brother Peter's girlfriend Eunice Lam, "I wake up in the middle of the night and sit on the bed and cry my heart out."

---

* Many of these novels are now kept at the Wing Luke Museum in Seattle.

CHAPTER 10
The Student

In the early sixties, Seattle was the kind of town where a young Chinese American girl named Sue Ann Kay, a student at Garfield High School in Central Seattle, could win an essay contest that offered the opportunity to attend Ballard High School in North Seattle for a short time.

For six weeks she and the other prizewinners—a Japanese American girl, a Jewish boy, a Black boy, and a Caucasian girl—could enjoy Ballard's new science classrooms, their new gym for the boys, a remodeled gym for the girls, and a state-of-the-art auditorium. Ballard was the kind of school that boasted all the perquisites of one that merited an "All-American" rating from the educational experts at the University of Minnesota. At the time, only three Black students and one Japanese American were enrolled there as full-time students.

Seattle school administrators sent five white students from Ballard to Garfield High and called it an "exchange program." Garfield was the kind of school where thousands of community members crowded into student assemblies to hear Martin Luther King Jr. test lines for what would become his "I Have a Dream" speech, and, later in 1967, see Stokely Carmichael, after winning a free speech battle against the school board, herald a new era of Black Power consciousness. The school was roughly equal parts white, Black, Asian, and other.

Sometimes Garfield students marked the boundaries between each other with racial epithets. Sometimes they mixed in ways that pointed to the future. During the fifties and sixties, Garfield produced cultural visionaries like Quincy Jones, Ernestine Anderson, Minoru Yamasaki, Robert "Bumps" Blackwell, and Jimi Hendrix. By the seventies, Black and Asian children would no longer need to compose exceptional essays to be bused across town to a wealthy all-white public school.

Seattle was the kind of town where, four months before Congress had passed the landmark Civil Rights Act of 1964, voters defeated by a two-to-one margin a referendum that would have outlawed housing discrimination. Nearly all the people of color in Seattle—about half of whom were Black, the rest mostly Chinese, Japanese, and Filipino—were confined to the inner city, an area called the Central District, from Chinatown in the west to Lake Washington in the east and Madison Valley in the north to Rainer Valley at the southern edge of the city, cross-shaped strokes of color in the middle of a milk-white map.

From Pioneer Square to Yesler Terrace, the Manilatown, Chinatown, and Nihonmachi neighborhoods crossed through working-class Black and Jewish communities. East beyond Thirty-Fourth Street were the white neighborhoods with Lake Washington views, what Seattleites called "the sunrise side of the mountain." Non-whites who could afford it might find homes on "the sunset side of the mountain."

Madison Street marked a northern border between whites and non-whites, Broadway a western one. Edison Tech, like Ruby Chow's, was just on the *lo fan* side of Broadway. But its halls teemed with the Central District's multiracial working class—nurses, mechanics, veterans, those labeled "nontraditional" students. "They were young folks who got kicked out of other schools or got pregnant or this and that," said Leroy Garcia, whose wife, Sherri, was attending. "It was like a delinquent high school sort of a deal."

In the segregated city, Garfield and Edison were cauldrons of amalgamation in the borderland between the white and non-white, and the wealthy and working-class neighborhoods.

Bruce carried around an orange book of English colloquialisms he had bought secondhand. He underlined the ones he had learned:

Above:

above all—chiefly, before everything else.

above-board—not open to question, honest, straightforward, beyond reproach.

above-par—of superior quality . . .

A bad beginning makes a good ending.

A bad excuse is better than none at all.

A bad husband cannot be a good man . . .

After four months of remedial language classes at Edison and Franklin Adult School, he wrote in his diary, now in neat English script:

"I know what is wrong with my speech—stammering. All the time I was so worried on how or what how to make my speech sounds acceptable that I began to talk in an artificial manner and not just saying what I wanted but just to make it sound good. I afraid that people will laugh at me and thus become self-conscious. I should say what I wanted to and won't give a darn as to whether I pronounce right or gramatically. I should say like other people do and also I'm not sure in the lang language."

Sometimes his anxieties over communicating poorly caused him to skip classes.

But Bruce's curiosity was bottomless. Books stacked up around his bed. He studied Chinese books of illustrated forms from Tai Chi Fist, Hung Gar Iron Thread Fist, and Drunken Luohan Fist; Emei and Yuefei *gung fu*; Xingyiquan, Gongzi Fuhuquan, and Wudang Baguazhang. He studied books on deep breathing exercises, Yijin Jing, Baduajin and Five Animals *qigong*; acupuncture, *dit da* bonesetting, and *dim mak* techniques. He collected biographies of Jack Dempsey and Jack Johnson. He notated and marked up fencing and boxing manuals.

But he wasn't going to just read all day every day. He wanted to practice his cha-cha, but his room was too small. He enlisted Ruby's youngest kids, Cheryl, Brien, and Mark, in mischief. Bruce told Mark to smear ketchup all over himself and lie on Cheryl's bed, while he hid in the closet wearing a gorilla mask. When Cheryl and another cousin came in, Mark jumped up, Bruce leaped out, and the girls ran away screaming. Bruce bought a Lone Ranger–style domino mask from a dollar store and hung it in his room. When Mark and Brien asked him what it was for, he showed them his two fingers and then began jabbing them furiously through the mask's empty eyes.

One afternoon, Ruby, Ping, and Bruce were walking in Chinatown. Bruce had fallen behind the Chows. When they turned around to see where he had gone, they saw him dropping into a fighting stance in front of each person who passed and talking himself through what he might do to them. The elder Chows frowned, turned, and continued down the street until they stopped again. They had heard Bruce kicking over garbage cans. What the boy really needed, Ruby thought to herself, was a physical outlet.

Ruby allowed Fook and Bruce to order and install a *mook jong* dummy in the alley behind the kitchen, and the two practiced on it when they weren't working. He attended Uncle Fook's Chinese Youth Club, where he practiced Wing Chun and learned some Southern Shaolin forms. The club also afforded him the opportunity to check out the young girls practicing for Ruby's drill team.

In the heart of the Nihonmachi neighborhood, near Yesler Terrace, Bruce dropped in to watch sessions at the Seattle Dojo, the oldest *dojo* in North America. It was there one weekend that he met the father of Sue Ann Kay, a man named Moses Kay, a second-generation Chinese American who worked for the police department and was searching for a martial arts school for his youngest, his eleven-year-old son, Roger. Bruce so impressed the elder Kay that he invited Bruce to dinner at the house.

Bruce became a frequent visitor. He drew comic book heroes and monsters with Roger, talked about school with Moses's eldest daughter, Jacquie, enjoyed his wife Sue's comfort food, and took Roger, Moses, and Sue Ann out into their backyard to show them some *gung fu*.

Yes, they were far from the source. The Kays were *jook sing*, the Cantonese idiom for American-born Chinese, a metaphor derived from bamboo, which are hollow and segmented inside and don't allow water to flow through, and yet grow together fast, pliant, and massed. In their warm household, Bruce—who had until then simply thought of himself as a Chinese born in America—was beginning to see what it really meant to be an American-born Chinese.

Jesse Glover was a Black man in his mid-twenties, another student at Edison Tech trying to get it together. He had grown up fatherless in Yesler Terrace. Because he was a sickly child and his mother was so protective of him, he had been "robbed," he said, "of the simple pleasure of getting into childhood fights."

At a young age, he became fascinated by *judo* and *jujitsu*, read all the books on them he could find, and tried with a Chinese American friend to re-create the moves shown in the pictures. They practiced not far from the then emptied-out building of the Seattle Dojo. Jesse was six years old when the government forcibly removed his Japanese American neighbors and placed them in wartime concentration camps.[*] He was twelve when he experienced the incident that would shape the rest of his life.

He and two other friends, Ron and Sylvester, were returning from a youth dance at the Georgetown projects, walking home through the downtown area, when they turned a corner and came upon a drunken white policeman, who saw them and began cursing and waving his nightstick at them. They turned and ran into an alley. But then they heard a patrol car screech at the other end and begin reversing toward them. Ron and Sylvester jumped into the window wells of a building, but Jesse was trapped in an open doorway between the cop car and the savage N-word-spewing cop.

He screamed, "Come out, you little Black bastards, or I'll kill you!"

When his friends appeared from their hiding places, the cop wheeled around and brutally beat them. One of the patrolmen placed himself in the way of Jesse, telling him, "Mind your own business." Then the drunken cop whirled around and whipped his nightstick across Jesse's lower jaw.

The three cops flung Ron and Sylvester into the back seat of the car and argued over what to do with them. "Let's take them out and dump them," one said. Jesse feared the cops were about to toss him and his friends into Puget Sound—he couldn't swim—so he put up a ferocious fight until the cops finally subdued him and threw him in the car also. They asked Ron where he lived, drove up the hill, stopped blocks away from the house, and pushed them out of the car. The three boys staggered back to Ron's house.

"When Ron's mother came to the door she found Ron bent over holding his groin, Sylvester holding the corner of his mouth together, and me trying to stop

---

[*] Some use the term "internment camps," which are associated with the imprisonment of "enemy aliens." I have chosen to follow Asian Americans, especially Japanese Americans, who use the term "concentration camps," to capture both the harsh conditions and the fact that most of those incarcerated were in fact American citizens.

my mouth from bleeding," Jesse said. He tried to speak, but was physically unable to tell her what had happened.

"I couldn't figure out what was wrong until I went into the bathroom and looked at the mirror," he recalled. "One of my teeth was sticking through a hole below my lower lip, and three others were deeply embedded in my tongue. My mouth was full of blood and it was very difficult to breathe."

When his mom arrived, Jesse heard her curse—repeatedly—for the very first time in his life. He had to have his mouth wired shut for weeks. "When I left the hospital, I had one burning thought," he recalled, "and that was to somehow kill the man who had beat me up."

After the war, Japanese Americans returned from the concentration camps and reopened the Seattle Dojo, one of a countless number of small acts intended to piece back together their broken community. Jesse asked his Nikkei peers if he could learn *judo* there. But he was told that the *dojo* was only for Japanese.

For the next decade he pursued teachers and schools with a singular focus and little success. When he enlisted in the air force to support his family, he received his first formal opportunity to study the art. Upon his discharge he returned to Seattle, went back to the *dojo*, and this time was accepted and trained by black belts Shuzo Kato and Fred Sato. He competed for the *dojo*, won tournaments, and attained a brown belt.

At the age of twenty-two, Jesse walked into a downtown restaurant and found the policeman who had beaten him so horrifically sitting there.

"I had played it over thousands of times in my mind how I was going to take him apart slowly with my hands," Jesse recalled. "I sat and stared at him for a full ten minutes. With each passing minute a year of stored-up hatred drained out of me, and when I finally got up and left, the only anger I felt was toward myself for the ten years I had spent living on the flimsy foundation of hate."

He concluded, "I knew that to waste him would be to waste myself."

By the time Bruce came to town, Jesse was bored with school and growing discontented with *judo*. Despite his accomplishments, some of the *sensei* seemed reluctant to offer him a chance to test for a black belt. Blocked in this way, he wondered if the skills he had acquired were actually effective. Before long, Jesse recalled, "It had become apparent to me that only the most skillful *judo* men would have a chance in the street."

A *judoka* friend, Leroy Porter, told Glover about Okinawan *kenpo karate* and lent him a book from a *sensei* in Hawai'i. Porter also told him about his studies in a Chinese martial art called *gung fu* which some insisted was the progenitor of *judo* and *karate*. He lent Jesse another book, *Modern Karate Kung Fu*, written by a man named James Yimm Lee, a Bay Area maverick who had loudly broken away from a leading San Francisco *gung fu* school, T. Y. Wong's Kin Mon school, declaring that

Wong's teachings couldn't stand the test of real street fights. Jesse decided he had to visit the Bay Area to meet Lee.

In Oakland, James Yimm Lee welcomed Jesse to his garage studio by asking him to throw a punch, to which Lee responded with a painful counter. Jesse gasped, thinking maybe James had broken his ribs. Then, with a colossal blow, James sent the heavy bag flying. He smiled and invited Jesse to try. When Jesse struck the bag he realized it was full of ball bearings, and he felt like he had broken his hand. On the way back to Seattle, Jesse was convinced that whatever this *gung fu* thing was, he needed to learn it. Another *judoka* friend, Charlie Woo, told him there was going to be a *gung fu* demonstration in Chinatown.

On an autumn weekend Jesse and his roommate, Ed Hart, a white professional heavyweight boxer and a Seattle Dojo black belt, awaited the demo before a stage in front of the Chong Wah Association building. This was a stage Ruby Chow had built. She had overseen nearly every aspect of the cultural life of Chinatown for a decade. At Seafair, the Moon Festival, or Chinese New Year, she had the *jook sing* generation performing a kind of public Chineseness for Seattle.

Jesse's ears pricked up when the emcee announced that the *gung fu* demonstration was next. But first, there would be a dance performance. And suddenly there was Bruce, doing a cha-cha with a young woman from the Chinese Youth Club, pleasing the mothers and grandmothers in the crowd of weekend families. Buoyed by the applause, they did a few more. "I felt like screaming at them to hurry up," Jesse remembered.

When their dancing was complete, the club came out to perform Southern Shaolin forms and demonstrate attacks. A club member narrated in English, sating some of Jesse's curiosity. Bruce returned to the stage for the climax—a Praying Mantis form he had learned from Uncle Fook. Suddenly he was crouching and exploding, pushing and stomping, parrying and popping his knuckles for effect. Jesse and Ed joined the crowd in applause, deeply impressed.

There is no evidence that Bruce was billed as an attraction for this event, even though he was a minor Hong Kong celebrity with a buzzy movie about to be released. Ruby Chow and Fook Yeung were likely the only reasons Bruce was even onstage. Even after *The Orphan* had opened at San Francisco's Sun Sing and Seattle's Kokusai Theatres, neither Chinatown had claimed him. If he was known at all, it was just as the new kid who worked for Ruby Chow.

But for most of his life Jesse Glover had begged, bartered with, even stalked people to secure whatever instruction in the martial arts he could get. He wanted nothing more than to forge a meaningful relationship with a *sifu* or *sensei*. And so Jesse decided to pursue Bruce Lee, an eighteen-year-old, five years his junior, as his guide.

First he needed a plan. He discovered that Bruce was also enrolled at Edison

Tech and lived just a few blocks away from him at Ruby Chow's. He decided to stake out Bruce on his morning walk to school, and to communicate his intentions in what he thought would be a fighterly type of way. Each day as he saw Bruce, Jesse crossed the street ahead of him, stopping to loudly punch or kick each telephone pole he passed. He'll get it, Jesse thought, I do martial arts too. But either Bruce didn't notice Jesse or wouldn't show it.

"After a week or so of assaulting poles I decided that it was time to approach Bruce and ask him about instruction," Jesse recalled. "I couldn't devise a cool approach."

Their encounter one wintry afternoon after school, which Bruce noted in his diary entry for January 8, 1960, would change both their lives, and many more.

"Is your name Bruce Lee?"

"Yes, that is my name. What do you want?"

Picture Bruce now waiting for the stranger, in between the before and after, leaning back on his left foot, his right foot forward, his arms low and ready.

The stranger asks him if he practices *gung fu*. He answers that he does. The stranger asks if he will teach it to him. Bruce is silent.

When he had been preparing to leave Hong Kong, Bruce boasted to Hawkins Cheung that he would make money in the United States by teaching people Wing Chun. Hawkins snorted. "I replied that he didn't have much to teach at the time," Hawkins said. "We had both only learned up to the second Wing Chun form, *chum kiu*, and forty movements on the dummy."

But now here is the stranger, spilling his whole story: he had been seeking a teacher for years, had even gone to meet a man in Oakland, which was too far away, and then he had seen Bruce, and had tracked him down, and just wondered, maybe? Possibly?

This stranger is pleading.

This is probably not how Bruce had imagined it would happen.

But the stranger waits an eternity for Bruce to answer.

Bruce missed his Wing Chun brothers. In San Francisco, he had only pissed off other martial artists. Now he was just reading books and practicing with Fook Baak at the Youth Club. He had been deflated—a necessary humbling, from his parents' point of view—and his confidence was at a low ebb. Jesse was offering Bruce a new direction, a chance to be a real *sihing*. And whether or not he had intended it, Jesse was also pushing Bruce toward a larger kind of redemption, a path of much more profound import.

Martial arts physicalize the natural forces of creativity and destruction. They were invented for people to protect themselves, but also to subdue, punish, control, dominate, and wage war. By themselves they are a means to an end. They are a set of tools, techniques, and technologies that serve a broader aim—for conquest, for god, gold, and glory, or for self-defense against all of that. Perhaps in an enlightened time and place, these ends may become sport, exercise, self-actualization, community building, even spiritual practice.

But at what point does self-defense become aggression? When laws or ethics break down and opposing sides come to irreconcilable conclusions on the answer to this question, these arts are part of the means by which groups, clans, peoples, or nations terminate disputes over claims, rights, and justice. Martial arts always introduce the problem of violence and its ends. What if the first person who had asked young Bruce to teach him *gung fu* had been the drunken racist cop who had brutally disfigured Jesse and his young friends?

Instead, in the decades to come, Bruce Lee—Chinese child star, fortunate son, privileged but lost teenager—would be remembered as the global hero of the downtrodden. That transformation began on the January morning he finally said yes to Jesse Glover.

CHAPTER 11
A Central District Story

The student was ready, the teacher had appeared.

Bruce's first diary entries on "the negro" are full of uncertainty and anticipation: "January 8, 1960—To day after school, a negro came and ask me to teach him Kung Fu. He is a brown belt holder of judo and weighs 180 lb. However, I think he is kind of clumsy. If he practice under my instruction, I'm sure he can achieve distinction."

He told Ruby about his meeting with Jesse and that he was going to teach him some *gung fu*. Ruby chastised him. "You're teaching Black guys this and that, they're going to beat up on Chinese."

Bruce responded, "Well, they can beat up on Chinese anyway. So if I teach them, maybe they're going to have some respect for Chinese."

Their first meetings were awkward, like two circling the ring. Jesse, ready and eager. Bruce, too aware of Ruby's words. But walking home together after classes, they warmed to each other's curiosity, Jesse with question after question, Bruce stopping to show Jesse a block or an attack in halting English, then laying down conditions for further practice—just the two of them somewhere no one else could watch, and only after his work shift ended.

Sunday evening arrived, and by the time Bruce knocked on the door, Jesse had cleared his roommates from his small apartment near Eighth and James. During their four-hour session, Jesse pulled out James Yimm Lee's book, which Bruce studied.

Jesse recalled, "Bruce asked if I knew anything about other martial arts, and I told him that I had done a little boxing in the Air Force and that I was currently practicing judo."

Bruce confessed he knew little about either and asked Jesse to show him something. Jesse tossed him with an *osotogari* throw, then held his breath when Bruce's head barely missed the metal bed corner. Bruce bounced up and said, "OK, hit me any way you can."

"I threw jabs, hooks, and haymakers as fast as I could, but none of them made contact. Each punch was blocked and I always ended up staring at the wrong end of Bruce's fist," Jesse recalled. Bruce showed Jesse part of the Yang *tai chi* 108 movement form and the first Wing Chun form, *siu lum tao*. They made plans to meet again.

When Bruce returned home, he wrote in his diary, "January 10, 1960 —To day I went to the negro's house and teach him a few tricks on Kung Fu and ask him not to use it on Chinese! To night I couldn't go to sleep."

Neither could Jesse.

The two became fast companions, meeting for morning walks and lunch hangouts. In the afternoon they might stop a block north of Ruby Chow's, and Bruce would show Jesse some drills. One day, Jesse followed Bruce to the post office and saw his joy at receiving a letter, a picture, and five dollars from his family.

He recalled, "We spent so much time together in 1960 and '61 that he would often lapse into Chinese and ramble on for several minutes before it dawned on him that he wasn't getting a response. Whenever this happened he would say that it seemed as though I should be able to speak Chinese."

Bruce told Jesse of his admiration for "the slyness of the monkey style, the strong punching and footwork of the Hung [Gar], the tearing grips of the Eagle Claw, the nervous energy of the Southern Mantis, the smooth kicks of the Northern Mantis and Jeet Kune, and the effective swings of the Choy Li Fut."

He said he was studying Chinese philosophy and Chinese martial arts to better understand how the two related to each other. He declared to Jesse that the *I Ching* contained all the secrets of humanity. His enthusiasms poured out of him, sometimes so fast that his thoughts outran his English, his tongue shut down, and his entire body trembled with the swelling ideas.

"The whole time that I knew him I don't think that I ever heard him say my name without stuttering," Jesse said. "He always had to repeat the 'J' in my name several times before he could spit it out."

Bruce told him about his fight brothers, Wong Shun Leung and William Cheung. He said he'd had a "small scrap" on the streets of Seattle, and that he needed to learn to be more patient and to practice his self-defense more. To Jesse's utter disbelief, Bruce admitted that he thought he was "little more than an advanced beginner."

Soon a motley bunch, most of them Jesse's friends from Edison Tech and the Seattle Dojo and all of them older than Bruce, had gathered around him: Ed Hart, Jesse's brawny six-foot-three roommate, "a leg breaker" who, some said, "made money by collecting money"; Howard Hall, Jesse's other roommate, the bookish, bespectacled salesman who had joined Jesse for his first road trip to meet James Yimm Lee; Charlie Woo, a small, kindhearted Chinese American so bullied as a child he was driven to become a second-*dan judoka*; Michael Lee, Jesse's brother and a bodybuilder and athlete of considerable renown; John Jackson, a Black intellectual type immersed in the study of Asian history and philosophy; Pat Hooks, a navy code expert, friends said, with "more fights than hairs on his head and the scars to prove it"; Takamitsu "Tak" Miyabe, who had been born of *samurai* lineage in Auburn–Kent Valley, been raised on a rice farm in Japan during the war, and returned to Seattle to serve in the US Army; Skip Ellsworth, who had learned to knuckle up daily growing up white on an Indian reservation; Leroy Garcia, a red-haired self-described "car freak and motorcycle freak and get-drunk freak and fight freak" of Spanish, Mexican, and Apache descent; and Takauki "Taky" Kimura, a Japanese American sixteen years Bruce's senior, whose family's incarceration during World War II had left him disillusioned and bereft.

Each of them would describe their first encounter with Bruce in the form of a conversion story. James DeMile had walked into an Edison Tech assembly celebrating Asian cultures to kill time between classes.

It had been a rough road to get there. James had fought his way up through childhood in a Catholic orphanage. He had just come off a stint in the air force, where he had been the heavyweight boxing champion. He was half-Filipino and half-white—perhaps the reason he was fighting all the time—and had three inches of height, a hundred pounds of muscle, and five years of life on Bruce.

There were a bunch of guys onstage, whose names he would later learn: Ed Hart was the MC, Pat Hooks and Skip Ellsworth were demonstrating *judo*, and Jesse was the guy serving as the *uke* for a short, skinny young Asian man dressed,

The gang. L-R: Jesse Glover, Bruce, Howard Hall, Pat Hooks. Note the martial arts photos on the wall. Photo courtesy of the Bruce Lee Family Archive.

James remembered, "like a Mormon missionary" in a dark suit, a tie, and thick eyeglasses.

This guy was saying, "You are about to witness the world's oldest self-defense system, Chinese *gung fu*, the ancestor of Japanese *karate* and *jujitsu*. Actually, *gung fu* is more than just a fighting system. Simply to use it to kill or maim an opponent is not its chief purpose. *Gung fu* is a way of life. Its philosophy is based on the integral parts of Taoism and Zen, the ideal of giving in with adversity..."

James tuned out.

Then this guy started doing a form, thrusting and jumping and yelping his way through weird animal poses. When he finished, he described *gung fu* as if it were some fearsome ancient Chinese fighting secret. From the back of the auditorium, James chuckled. This is bullshit, he thought. This kid has a lot to learn about what fighting is really like.

After the demonstration, this guy was holding court with a small group, including some attractive women. James remembered this guy "pawing and poking at the air while bobbing and weaving like a drunken monkey." He left his seat and came down to the front and interrupted whatever it was this guy was talking about.

"Kid, you're going to learn very quickly that fighting over here in America is not a game," James said. "All those fancy moves won't work against a fast street fighter."

Bruce stopped, took a look at James, and responded, "Why don't you take a punch at me?"

"OK," James remembered saying, before falling into a boxer's stance. Then he threw a light fast jab, just to show what he could do. "In a blink, the kid exploded into action, not only blocking my punch but yanking my body towards the floor, engaging my right arm and interlocking it with my left, so I felt like a pretzel," James recalled. "I could not move."

For one last humiliation, Bruce tapped him on the forehead with a smile and a look that said, "Really now?" Bruce Lee had done to James DeMile what he had done to them all, with the same result—adding another follower.

Bruce's new friends were what the sociologists called "social deviants." They had names for themselves: "street punks," "greasers," "devil children." They never expected to rule the world. They were all as coarse as they thought themselves to be, except for an older Japanese American man who hung at the corners of the group, hands in his pockets, a spectral presence.

Takauki Kimura was born in 1924, sixteen years and eight months before Bruce, the youngest son of eight children. His father, Suejiro, was a stoic *issei* man, practical and decent. His mother, Haruyo, had been born into a *samurai* family that had fallen on hard times. They had named him Takeyuki (竹雪, "snow on bamboo")—a homonym for "martial arts" (武行)—but as it had been with Bruce, some things had been lost in the transliteration of names.

By the time Takauki's parents had arrived in the Pacific Northwest in the late 1800s, the whites had vanquished the Indians. Asian migrant workers were doing the kind of labor there that Black and Mexican workers were doing in the rest of the country. The Kimuras had come to the United States hoping to make enough money to retire back to Japan. "Like most other Japanese immigrants of the day, it did not work out that way," their son remembered, in his typically understated fashion.

Migrant work took the family from the forests of southwestern Washington to the high plains of eastern Montana. Suejiro learned English. He found the white men demanding and the Native people welcoming. He became so close to them, the family received invitations to join *potlatch* gatherings.

The Kimuras finally settled back on the coast, in Clallam Bay, at the edge of the Olympic Peninsula. Suejiro found work maintaining railroad tracks after the Chinese were purged. The rail men renamed him "Sam," gave him an old train car to house his family, and made him the head of the work crews.

Through his childhood Taky, as he was called by his white friends, pledged allegiance to the same flag in the same one-room country school. He felt accepted. But he also knew that at the beginning of every school year he would be the one the new boy challenged to fight. Beating up the Jap was the easiest way for a boy to assert his whiteness and establish his place in the pecking order. Defending himself for his classmates' pleasure was Taky's annual fee for membership.

During the summer, Taky and his friends went to pick berries, returning home with baskets of fresh fruit. His father instructed him to give them away to their white neighbors. When Taky asked why, his father admonished him, "We have to be good to them so they will be good to us." Suejiro believed Asians would always be second class. "Don't think you're anything else," he told his *nisei* son.

That infuriated Taky. "We've learned in school that in America everyone is equal," he retorted. "It's *right there* in the Constitution and the Declaration of Independence."

As he neared his eighteenth birthday, Taky was ready to receive a scholarship to Washington State University, where he would study to become a brain surgeon. Then the Imperial Japanese Army attacked Pearl Harbor, Franklin Delano Roosevelt signed Executive Order 9066, and Lieutenant General John DeWitt implemented Civilian Exclusion Orders to imprison those of Japanese ancestry on the West Coast.

Some of the Kimuras' neighbors discussed going to the feds to vouch for "Sam and his family," to say they would volunteer to "watch them." But on the eve of what would have been Taky's graduation, as part of a "relocation" of 120,000 Japanese Americans informed by a century of "removal" of American Indians, the

Kimuras walked past armed infantrymen into a rail station and boarded a train bound for a concentration camp at Tule Lake. They had been given days to pack their lives into suitcases, and sell or secure all that they owned.* They crowded into train cars whose windows were painted black. They traveled in fear and silence.

"I thought I was white," Taky recalled, "until they sent me to the camps."

Taky's brother Eiji volunteered for the 442nd Regimental Combat Team, an all-*nisei* infantry modeled on the segregated Black fighting units, destined to become one of the most decorated and devastated in US history. Taky had volunteered too, but was refused because of his poor eyesight. He joined others in backbreaking work at an onion farm for prisoner's wages.

Tule Lake was the largest of ten concentration camps, all sited on desolate lands. It caged almost twenty thousand Japanese Americans behind barbed wire on a Northern California lake bed. They were housed in a thousand hastily assembled housing blocks surrounded by twenty-eight guard towers. They had been imprisoned on the same desperate terrain where, seven decades before, the US Army had routed the Modoc people in one of the bloodiest of the so-called Indian Wars.

After a year the government remade Tule Lake into what it called a segregation center, a maximum-security prison for Japanese Americans the government labeled "disloyal." The Kimuras, deemed "loyal," were removed again, to the Minidoka camp in Idaho's high desert.

In thin-walled barracks, they suffered through harsh winters when temperatures fell to 20 below, and scorching summers when the mercury climbed above 110. When it was dry, dust storms threatened. After winter storms the camp was, one inmate wrote, "a muddy swamp," turning a basic trip from living quarters to the mess hall, washroom, or toilet into an ordeal. Meals were often made with rotting food delivered by the government. When Taky needed to have his tonsils removed, the dentist had him hold his own spit cup and took them out without anesthesia.

Because the camps were treated with either heavy discipline or official neglect, Japanese Americans ran their own schools, mess halls, and hospital. They maintained their own roads and safety. They organized athletic leagues, Catholic, Protestant, and Buddhist services, libraries, and big-band orchestras.

They screened *samurai* films. Taky took up *judo* with inmates who had studied at the Kōdōkan. If General DeWitt were paying attention, he might have disapproved of prisoners of war teaching, learning, and enjoying the arts of self-defense. For Taky, the *dojo* became a place of pride. He rapidly ascended to a brown belt until he broke his collarbone in a match.

On September 4, 1945, the Civil Exclusion Orders were rescinded. Now the

---

* A 1983 congressional investigation estimated the total property loss suffered by Japanese Americans at $1.3 billion and their net income loss at $2.7 billion, in 1983 dollars.

family had to reintegrate into American life, Taky said, "with no place to go, no home, no food, and no possessions." Of this period, he later wrote, "I don't feel bad about it, it's just something that happened and if you are angry about it now you are only hurting yourself. It was something that was not right, but what are you going to do."

The Kimuras moved to Seattle and prevailed upon a German man to rent them a one-bedroom house. Late at night Taky drifted into the street-racing scene, hanging with the speed demons, gear monkeys, and thrill-seekers at the Mount Baker Tunnel. But during the day, although the economy was booming, he could not find steady work. He tried to join the military and was again rejected. He sat in restaurants where waitresses refused to serve him. He walked into barbershops, waited for hours, and left without his hair cut. He asked his white girlfriend not to put her arm around him in public.

"I had no self-esteem. I ceased to be a human being," Taky remembered. "When a Caucasian came up behind me, I had to step aside and let him pass, since I was not worthy." Even after his family had purchased a grocery store and he was successfully building the business, Taky said, "I was walking around half-ashamed even to be alive.

"They took away my identity," he said, "because if I wasn't white and I wasn't free and I wasn't American, then who was I?"

He went back to the Seattle Dojo and began training again, earning a second *dan*. Getting physical on the mats staved off depression or worse. Jesse and Ed frequented Taky's store and sometimes worked out in the back. They invited Taky to meet Bruce at a practice on a Seattle University baseball field.

"And there he is, bubbling over with pride," Taky remembered, "knocking these big white guys all over the place as easy as you please. And I got excited about something for the first time in fifteen years. So I started training and bit by bit I began to get back the things I thought I'd lost forever."

Taky Kimura was drawn to Bruce like he had been to the drag races at the tunnel. Bruce was exciting, profane, and full of all the fire smothered out of him on the train to Tule Lake.

Taky wanted to be at every practice he could. But he was also painfully self-aware he was twice as old as everyone else. He felt like he was working twice as hard just to keep up. When he arrived from work Bruce ribbed him in front of the guys, "Jesus, Taky, look at how you're dressed! You look like you're sixty."

Still he toiled on. "After a quite a long time, I thought, 'Boy, I must be getting better now' and I was feeling very confident," he recalled. But then Bruce worked with him on a technique, saw Taky struggling, and said, "Ah you'll never get it." Taky thought he overheard Bruce telling the others, "That guy will never make it."

At the next practice he told Bruce he was quitting. Bruce looked at Taky, as if for the first time—seeing his resignation, his reflex to withdraw rather than suffer further despair. He took Taky aside.

"Listen, Taky," Bruce said. "I remember the Japanese zeros when they were flying overhead in Hong Kong. But do you think because I'm Chinese I'm a better man than you? You're no better or worse than anyone else.

"You have the talent," Bruce told Taky, "You just refuse to recognize it."

He devoted more time to Taky during and after practice. He copied Walter Wintle's inspirational poem, "The Man Who Thinks He Can," and gave it to Taky:

If you think you are beaten, you are
If you think you dare not, you don't
If you'd like to win but you think you can't
It is almost certain you won't.*

Taky felt a profound gratitude. That may be why, when Bruce asked Taky if he would drive him and his dates around—one of the privileges Bruce had lost upon exile from Hong Kong—Taky inexplicably agreed. Nearly forty years old, he found himself leaving behind his sleeping wife to be Bruce's driver, fixing his gaze on the stoplights and away from the rearview mirror while Bruce was making backseat moves on the girl of the week.

But it was also Taky who checked Bruce's reckless impulses. One night after a *samurai* movie at the Kokusai, when the two of them were strutting out of the theater in full swordsman swagger, they attracted the hostile stares of some white men.

"Hey, Taky," Bruce said, "those white guys are looking at us funny. Let's go kick their asses."

Taky stopped. "Uh, no, Bruce," he said, "we can't go around just beating up white people."

Another time they had just pulled out of Taky's grocery lot, Bruce driving a bit too slowly, when a motorcycle cop waved them over. As the cop approached the car, he and Taky were talking and laughing. "You think it's a big joke?" the cop yelled. "You're just eating apples and having a good fucking time here, huh?"

Bruce glowered at the cop, balling his right hand into a fist. "Don't do it," Taky said, grabbing Bruce's wrist. Bruce glared at Taky. Then he finally released his grip, exhaled, and turned to the policeman to accept the ticket. After the cop had left he turned to Taky and screamed, "Why do you put up with this shit?"

Taky looked back at Bruce and said nothing. Bruce had received him, Jesse, and the others with something like equanimity, guilelessness, a beginner's mind. But

---

* Later he hung a typed and framed copy of this poem in his Golden Harvest office.

how much of Bruce's uncommon audacity came from ignorance, inexperience, from never having been a minority?

Around that time, Bruce was working out with some of the guys near a school playground where a rainbow group of children were out for recess. He launched into a jokey trolling rant, telling the guys that Chinese were the best race in the world.

"I'm prejudiced for Chinese people!" he declared.

They told him to stop talking shit, which was exactly the reaction Bruce had wanted.

"All Chinese are like this," he said. "Let me show you."

He called out to a boy to come over to the fence. "Hey kid, are you prejudiced for Chinese people?" he asked.

The boy stared first at Bruce and then at his crew—a couple of white guys and a Black man. Then he shouted at Bruce, "No! I'm an American!" And he ran back to the playground.

In America now, who was the student and who the teachers?

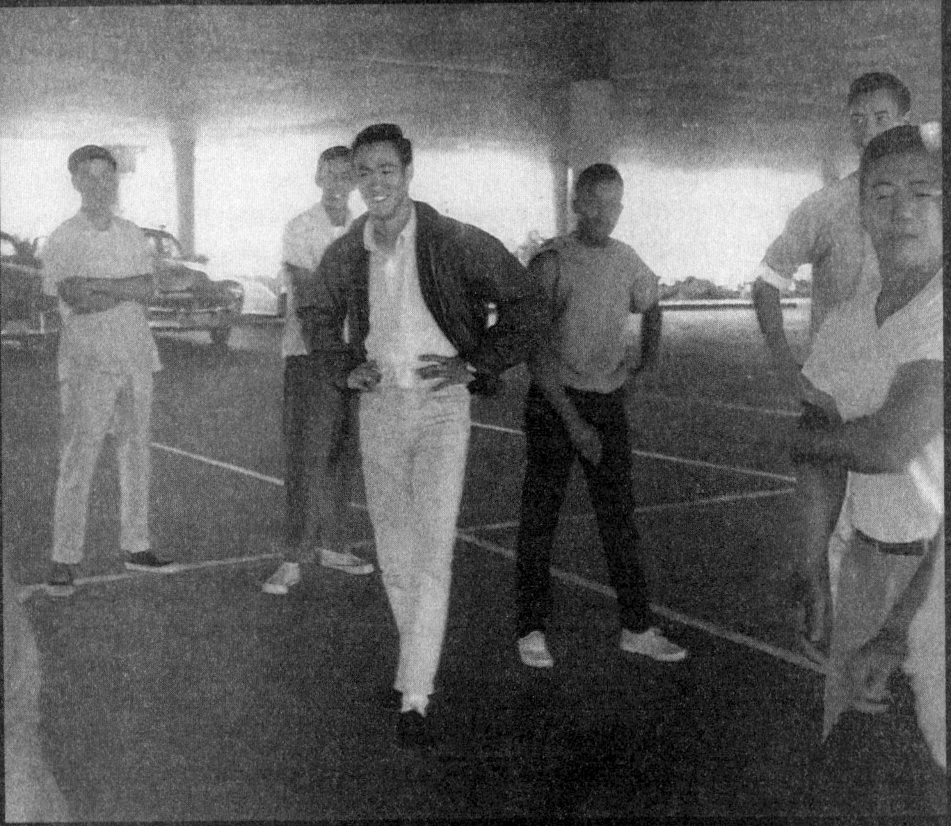

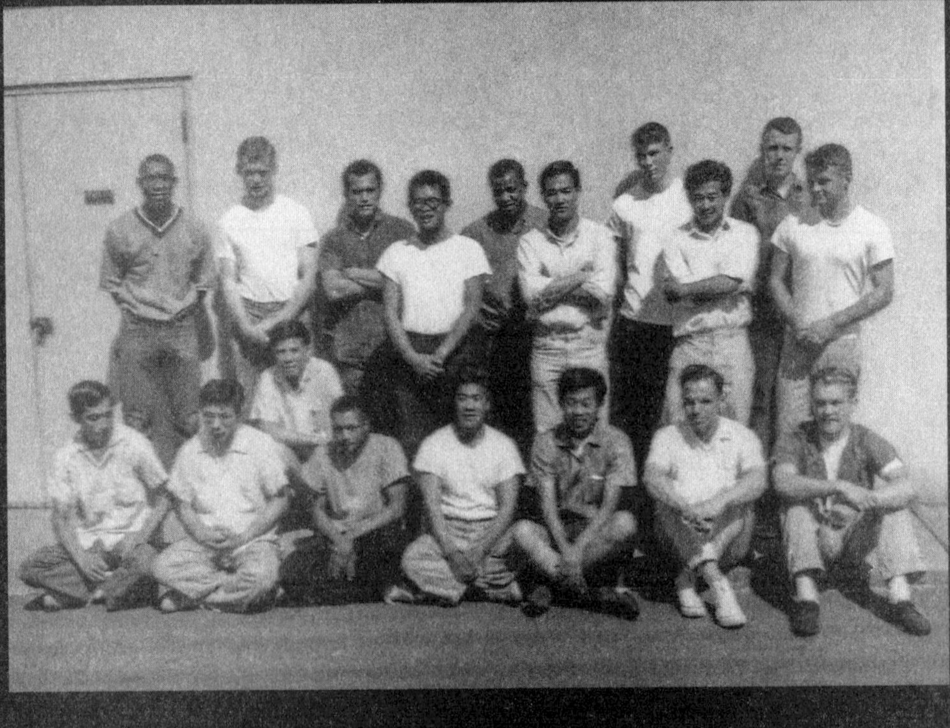

PART IV
The Man Who Thinks He Can

1961–1962

> The boxers will bring to the fight everything that is themselves, and everything will be exposed—including secrets about themselves they cannot fully realize.
>
> —JOYCE CAROL OATES

Working out at the underground garage. Mike Lee (right of Bruce). Photo courtesy of the Bruce Lee Family Archive.

Bruce (top row, fifth from right) and his class. Top: James DeMile (third from left), Jesse Glover (left of Bruce), Doug Palmer (right of Bruce). Bottom: Taky Kimura (second from left), Mike Lee (third from left), Charlie Woo (fourth from left). Photo courtesy of the Bruce Lee Family Archive.

CHAPTER 12
Blood on the Floor

Bruce was the Monkey King in a new land. All the swagger he had lost during his loneliest year was back. He had a gang again. The small Chinese kid with the awkward stutter and the unstoppable hands was—at nineteen years old—the alpha of the alpha Americans.

The gang met to practice wherever they could—first at Jesse, Howard, and Ed's small two-bedroom apartment, then at outdoor parks, the Yesler Community Center gym, and the downtown YMCA. They all wanted to learn from Bruce, because he couldn't be stopped. "I didn't spar with Bruce," Jesse Glover said. "He was too fast."

"I tried to crush Bruce," James DeMile said. "One of my disappointments in those days was that I could never hit Bruce."

To up the ante, Bruce asked several of them to attack him all at once. "He had what they called a 'five-man defense,'" said Leroy Garcia. "Any five of us would circle him and then somebody would go at him with an offensive move. Then when the first guy went off everybody went off. Bruce would defend and attack every one of us all at the same time. He would just turn into a dervish."

In one of these exercises, Leroy landed a successful left-right double kick on Bruce, pulling it at just the last instant so as not to hurt him. "It blew his mind," Leroy laughed, recalling the moment, "and it blew my mind, too!"

Twenty minutes later, Bruce called out, "Roy! Come here!"

He noticed Bruce was still pronouncing his "r" like "w" in that funny Chinglish way, but the thought was quickly replaced by a panic that Bruce was going to teach him a lesson. The two faced off.

With stunning speed Bruce moved in on Leroy, pinching him the way his Wing Chun seniors used to do to him. "You wouldn't hit him going in or out, but you'd have a little red dot on you," Leroy recalled. "When I took a shower that night, I had about 15 red dots on me—my arms, my chest, my cheek."

These sessions were the opposite of the strict, structured instruction of most *gung fu* schools. The guys seemed united in a mission to root out techniques that were showy but useless. They would keep only those that were truly dangerous and effective. Nothing was sacred. Much was permitted.

"We tried not to really hurt each other, but drawing blood was no big deal as long as the person could still work out," James said. "I remember a number of instances where Jesse drew blood from splitting my skull with one of his dynamic back-fists. I remember Ed Hart knocking Jesse over some bags of cement." The scars they took home reminded them that they had never felt more alive than in each other's company.

After workouts, the gang hung out at Taky's grocery or at cheap restaurants in Chinatown, particularly a hole-in-the-wall on King Street called Tai Tung, where Bruce held court over pots of tea and plates of oyster sauce beef and *chow fun*. He told raunchy jokes and corny jokes, stories and more stories.

"Bruce's main interests," Jesse said, "were *gung fu*, cha cha, girls, philosophy, and Chinese history."

One night, the guys noticed him constantly tapping the table and asked him what he was doing. "I'm watching that guy over there eat," Bruce said, "and every time he moves for his fork, I tap, because I'm thinking that's when I'd hit him." Another time, Taky caught Bruce staring at people's feet as they walked by. Bruce explained, "I'm watching that moment just before their foot hits the ground when I would sweep their foot."

Bruce cooked for the guys and cut their hair. Ed helped Bruce write his English and history homework. James lent Bruce his home phone so he could call his mom in Hong Kong. Leroy taught Bruce to drive in his tiny Fiat Bianchina, which Bruce steered with antic recklessness. Leroy hated dancing, so he told Bruce to take his blond wife out for nights on the town. He introduced Bruce to girls: "White girls, all white girls . . ."

"There were several times that Jesse and myself and Bruce went out," Leroy recalled. "My wife would go with Jesse, and I would go with his cousin, a Black lady, and we'd walk through Seattle with a Chinese man, a Black man, and a white man all with the wrong color woman just to see if anyone would say anything."

Bruce showed up with the gang at a movie theatre wearing white contact lenses so that he could appear blind, just as Seattle-born Chinese American actor Keye Luke later would as Master Po in the *Kung Fu* TV series. Movie nights were always Bruce's choice, which meant Zatoichi the blind swordsman or Jerry Lewis. The guys could see why Zatoichi was Bruce's kind of hero. He was modest and gentle, always underestimated, always a reluctant fighter, but swift, efficient, and clean when it came to the kill. His love for Jerry Lewis was just inexplicable to them.

When *The Orphan* came to the Kokusai Theatre for a weekend run in September 1961, he took the gang. Afterward, he told them that the film's climax—when Ah Sahm returns to the orphanage with his ear cut off—"caused old ladies to cry," then cheer. It was a line he had rehearsed.

In his one-man marketing campaign for *The Orphan*, Bruce had somehow scored an interview with Frank Lynch, a columnist for the *Seattle Post-Intelligencer*. He amused the veteran reporter with his enthusiastic descriptions of his earlier Hong Kong films. Lynch would write of Bruce's appearance in *Infancy*: "Everybody in the audience cried then hurried out to tell everybody else what a hell of a picture it was." Of *An Orphan's Tragedy*, he wrote: "The people who saw this bawled and cheered." Under a promo picture of Ah Sahm stabbing his knife at Ms. Yiu, the caption nailed the punch line: "Bruce Lee in 'The Orphan': *People Wept And Cheered*."

Bruce no longer had any ties back to the Hong Kong industry and knew nothing yet of Hollywood. But Jesse recalled Bruce talking as if he were just taking a break from acting: "He said that he could make about thirty thousand U.S. dollars a year if he returned to the Hong Kong film industry, but that he was staying in the U.S. because he thought that the opportunities here were greater."

Bruce had begun sounding like Napoleon Hill, W. Clement Stone, and Elmer Leterman, American confidence men whose popular get-rich-quick, self-help books he had discovered. Perhaps, following Hill, the young optimist was speaking his radiant future into reality. Perhaps the callow worker from Ruby Chow's attic was just talking shit.

Jesse, who had decided that all he wanted was a simple life of freedom and happiness, began to understand that his immigrant friend was quite different from him: "Bruce wanted to be famous, rich, and the best Gung Fu man in the world."

He wrote, "Bruce was then a strange mixture of dreams and reality."

Ruby was certain Bruce was going to get himself into trouble if he were not kept occupied. If he wanted to practice martial arts, she thought, it would be best for him to do so by training the Chinatown kids. Teaching—and the responsibility that came with it—might calm him down. She presented him with a proposal. She would let him clear part of the dining room on Saturday mornings and he could practice right in the restaurant, as long as they put everything back into place afterward.

"That sounds good," Bruce said. "But who will be my students?"

"Just leave that to me."

Ruby rounded up her sons and her daughter, her nieces and nephews, and two more children of a close family friend, eleven in all, ranging in age from seven to fourteen. She bought Bruce and the kids *karate gis* and a tumbling mat.

Bruce asked Fred Sato and another Japanese American *judo* black belt to help him teach the classes. He knew Ruby would be comfortable with them, and he knew better than to ask her if he could invite his gang.

Bruce won the kids over with his ease, confidence, and his thumb-and-finger push-ups. He had taught himself how to do these—a technique called "Supporting the Sky with a Finger"—from a pamphlet by Shaolin Diamond Fist *gung fu* master Yuen Cho Choi. To the wide-eyed *jook sing* children, Bruce was a superhero.

By then, Bruce had expected to move on from Ruby Chow's. He told Leroy that she had brought him to work for her because it was good for her image: his father was a revered Cantonese opera star, and she still prided herself on being Chinatown's chief patron of the arts. Bruce thought that more old opera men would soon replace him and he would move on. "I'm not going to work here for long as all those guys has come back from Hong Kong," he wrote in his diary at the start of 1960. "Thanks to Ruby for looking a job for me."

But the job Ruby promised never materialized. It slowly dawned on Bruce that she wasn't going to help him. He took part-time work from Leroy, stuffing leaflets into *Seattle Post-Intelligencer* newspapers that Leroy and Jesse then delivered. He began saving money to move out—a quest that gave him a perspective of the America outside of the Central District.

Skip Ellsworth needed help with a delivery job, so Bruce went with him to Montana to pick up a load. "We stopped at a cowboy-honky-tonk-tavern restaurant for dinner," Skip recalled. "Bruce generally walked in a very 'cocky' way that would always attract attention." They got into it with "some cowboys that were hanging out under a mercury-light in the parking lot," whom Bruce dispatched quickly.

Working harder than he ever had in his life, Bruce felt he now understood something about laborers and American Chinatowns. Ruby and Ping were building a home for themselves in a white neighborhood, a majestic house on a hill in the Seward Park neighborhood with a lake view. But it was he and the other migrant workers who were making it possible.

He told Jesse that Chinatown ran off exploited labor. Chinese bosses like Ruby imported them, housed them, and paid them cut-rate wages. "Bruce said that this practice was a direct outgrowth of the exploitive practices of the earlier tongs, which had imported illiterate people and kept them on opium until they needed someone killed," Jesse said. Bruce had come to identify with the migrant *lumpen*.

One night, Bruce led the gang in an elaborate performance at a posh all-white restaurant downtown. Wearing his magnificent black gabardine greatcoat with red fox lapels and lining, Bruce arrived pretending not to be able to speak English. Howard, Jesse, and Ed told the waitstaff that he was the son of a Chinese ambassador and they were his entourage of translators.

"It was funny to watch the quick change in people when they found out that Bruce was someone important," said Jesse, who saw the joy Bruce took in carefully plotting and executing the farce. He hadn't just pranked the *gweilo* elite. For a single evening Ruby Chow's busboy could be her equal, usurping all the privileges she worked so hard every day to maintain in white Seattle.

The gang had wearied of moving around, so they discussed where they could keep a regular practice. Leroy Garcia offered his farm in Bellevue, on the other side of Lake Washington, where he had built a log cabin. He was an avid hunter, fisherman, and outdoorsman, a self-described "mountain man." He had a bow to hunt big game and a large collection of firearms. He kept an eleven-inch Ruger on his dashboard to shoot at pheasants each morning on his newspaper delivery route.

When Bruce had first arrived in San Francisco, he had joked with Ben Der, "Over here, they don't fight like we do. They use guns!" Now, as Bruce stood before Leroy's stash of rifles, pistols, and revolvers, he became quiet.

"It's power, Bruce," Leroy said.

Bruce was deep in thought. Finally, he said, "Well, Roy, Samuel Colt made everybody equal."

Leroy laughed and promised to show Bruce how to use them.

When the day arrived, Jesse waited in the yard for the two to emerge. Bruce came out waving a thirty-aught-six, Leroy's Ruger strapped to his side, a ten-gallon hat on his head. Leroy followed, a madman's grin on his face. Here they were: a Black man from the segregated city shaking his head and chuckling at the picture he saw of a redheaded white Mexican Apache mountain man and a Chinese American immigrant dressed like a Wild West gunslinger. Leroy pointed out the hay he had stacked seventy-five yards away, where he had affixed some target sheets, and the three whiled away the afternoon firing bullets into the bales.

One day Bruce told Leroy to take his single-action revolver, remove the bullets, cock it, point it at him, and prepare to pull the trigger. Bruce stood in his *ding bou* ready position, then suddenly leaped forward, grabbed the gun, and threw a half-punch at an astonished Leroy. Now that Leroy understood the drill, they tried it again, Bruce taking a step back each time.

"At seven feet, that was the maximum he could close and turn the gun. He was faster than my reflex," Leroy said. For a long time afterward, Leroy joked, "You notice I keep eight feet between us, Bruce."

For Bruce's birthday, Leroy gave him a .25 automatic, "a purse gun," he called it. Bruce snuck the revolver into Ruby's house, another rule on her list he could check off as broken. Up in his bedroom, he closed the door and went to the window. His eye landed on some birds picking seeds out of the rain gutter. He pulled out his gun and squeezed the trigger, scattering the crying flock. Then he aimed the gun down at Ping's backyard pigeon coop and fired on the caged birds.

He laughed long and hard.

Bruce was indulging his insatiable appetite for new weapons and methods. He devoured everything Fook Yeung could teach him. He practiced internal *gung fu* forms to strengthen his *qi*, and learned flamboyant Eagle Claw, Mantis, Peacock Eye, and back-fist forms that looked great onstage. He picked up Choy Li Fut from a migrant from Hong Kong named Richard Leung who had once defeated many of Yip Man's students. He studied *judo* and advanced concepts of attack from Taky and Jesse's Seattle Dojo *sensei*, Fred Sato.

But the nineteen-year-old was not nearly as rigorous a teacher. Teaching made him new friends, gave him workout partners, and brought him new tutors. But, Ed Hart said, "I don't think he liked teaching very much." In sessions, he showed the guys attacks or closing moves, had them do *chi sao* with each other, then sent them to drill or spar with each other using the techniques. The gang presented him with different bodies, strengths, and skills on which to test all his new ideas.

"Once he discovered an effective technique he would train in it 'til he was confident in its application," said James DeMile, "and regardless of our skill level he would never teach it again . . .

"The main focus to Bruce's training was what interested him at the moment," James DeMile said. "You had to pay close attention to what he said or did since he was really talking to himself."

Bruce's mind was still on Hong Kong. He wanted to show his parents he had made something of himself. He wanted to prove to Master Yip and Ah Leung that he could stand alongside them above the other senior students.

James DeMile began to wonder about what Bruce was not sharing—certainly fighting tactics and concepts, but perhaps also important things about himself. They all agreed he was the best fighter among friends. But if he was withholding things, then what kind of a friend was he?

James fixed on something Bruce had said in passing during a workout. "Why," Bruce had asked him rhetorically, "should I teach someone how to beat me?"

The same demonstration at Edison where James DeMile had met Bruce had left another man enraged and agitating for a fight.

Yoichi Nakachi was almost a decade older than Bruce, held black belts in *judo* and *karate*, and was known for having thrashed a group of knife-wielding thugs in a street fight. While sitting in the audience that day, he had taken personal offense to Bruce's claim that soft styles of Chinese *gung fu* could prevail over hard styles like Japanese *karate*. Yoichi stalked Bruce through the halls of the school, staring him down, and issuing challenges through various messengers. Each time Bruce demurred.

"He doesn't agree with me about these styles," he told Yoichi's friends. "But it's pointless for us to fight."

On the evening of October 28, 1960, Bruce and his crew finished a well-received exhibition at Yesler Gym when Yoichi sent another friend over to reiterate his challenge. Bruce walked away without a word. Down in the locker room, he asked the guys if he should fight.

"We told him that he didn't have to prove anything to us and that it was beneath his dignity to accept the challenge," Jesse said.

But Yoichi continued to pursue Bruce, and even escalated his challenge. He claimed Bruce had not just insulted him, but all Japanese with his disrespectful comments on *gung fu* and *karate*. "Other *gung fu* men started telling Bruce if he didn't fight the *karate* man, they would," Jesse said. "Bruce told them he wasn't going to allow them or anyone else to prod him into a fight."

But four days later, when Bruce was talking up a young woman in the hallway, Yoichi stepped between them. "He challenged Bruce in front of the girl," Leroy recalled. "Well. Bruce lost his philosophical bit."

Jesse hastily brokered arrangements for Yoichi and Bruce to fight at the downtown YMCA. The crews walked to the bus stop, Bruce with Jesse, Ed, and Howard, and Yoichi with his followers, including a black belt named Masafusa Kimura who had once trained with Bruce. On the bus Yoichi sat on the long seat facing Bruce and started dictating fight rules.

"Forget the rules!" Bruce exploded. "I'm going all out on you."

Jesse told Yoichi to back off, then turned to whisper to Bruce, "Don't hit with any deadly hands. Just punch him, kick him."

At the Y, Bruce and the gang, joined by Leroy, who had left work after he got the call, headed straight for the handball court. There, Bruce took off his shoes, stripped down to his undershirt and trousers, and stretched. Yoichi strode in. He had changed into a *gi*. They lined up before each other.

Bruce asked him, "You're the one who wanted this fight, yes?"

Yoichi sneered, "Yes!"

Jesse announced that they would have three two-minute rounds, that he would be the referee, and that Ed would be the timekeeper. Then Ed opened the fight.

Bruce leaned back on his left foot, his right poised lightly, and aimed his right hand toward Yoichi's nose. Yoichi took a forward stance, his right fist at his waist, his left pointing at Bruce. Then he quickly dropped back into a cat stance and attacked with a front kick. Bruce parried it with his right and struck Yoichi's face with a left. He followed with straight punches—one-two-three-four-five times, snapping Yoichi's head back. Bruce's attack carried them all the way across the court and bounced Yoichi off the back wall. He tried to grab Bruce's arms, but Bruce shook him off, and with both fists, one to the face, the other to the sternum, lifted Yoichi into the air. As the *karateka* fell forward, Bruce swung his foot into Yoichi's nose.

"When the kick landed I saw blood squirt from the guy's nose like the hot breath from an angry bull," Jesse said. "I screamed for them to stop."

Yoichi lay stiff, face down on the floor. For an instant Jesse was sure that Bruce had murdered him. As Bruce stood over his opponent, the rest of the guys rushed in to turn the beaten *karateka* over. They propped him up against the wall so that he wouldn't gag on his own blood. His face was purple with bruises. His bottom lip was split from top to bottom. His teeth were red with blood. His eye socket was cracked.

After an interminable wait, Yoichi's eyes flickered. Groggy and disoriented, he asked how long it had taken for Bruce to beat him. Ed glanced at his stopwatch: eleven seconds, it read.

"Twenty-two seconds," Ed said.

Yoichi's friends lifted and carried him off the handball court, bound for Harborview emergency. The crew watched them leave in silence. Even Leroy Garcia had been shaken by the efficiency of Bruce's violence.

"I've seen a lot of fights, been in a lot of fights. I never saw anybody trash another man that badly. It was . . ." Leroy's voice trailed off. "It was an ego adjustment for me."

CHAPTER 13
Dance Away

At Edison Tech, Bruce was an average student, maintaining a 2.6 grade point average. But he had bought into the plan his parents and the Chows had for him. In one of their less adversarial moments, Ruby Chow recalled, "He told me that he wanted to prove to his father that he could go to the university without him."

By the end of 1960, Bruce was on his way to securing his GED. He soon learned he had been accepted into the University of Washington for the spring quarter in 1961. When he sent news to the family in Hong Kong, Hoi Chuen exclaimed, "This is better than winning the lottery!"

He signed up for five classes at U-Dub, including one in theater speech and two physical education classes, one in gymnastics and the other in *judo* with Seattle Dojo *sensei* Shuzo Kato. After classes started, in March 1961, he met with a counselor who asked him what he planned to major in.

"Drama," Bruce answered.

Each morning white students streamed onto campus from the dorms, fraternities and sororities, and the apartments in the University District. But students of color were still largely excluded from the Greek houses and unwelcome as residents in the U District. Many of them commuted from their neighborhoods in the Central District. Those who could afford to drive parked in the southwest lots, and those who could not transferred through multiple bus routes. Everyone came to the Hub, the Husky Union Building, a modern center with Gothic flourishes where a lively scene was always happening.

The Hub's spaces were also segregated by status. At the top were the fraternities and sororities, who filled the Husky Den restaurant. Below them were the dormies, who met in the study lounges. At the bottom were the commuters and students of color, a Venn diagram of outsiders who gathered in the ground-floor cafeteria and around the pool tables and bowling alley in the basement.

When Bruce first arrived on campus, he sat in the cafeteria with Jacquie Kay and others from Chinatown, figuring it all out. Over here were the Black football players playing whist with their white teammates, over there were the Japanese Americans playing bridge or pinochle. Before long, Bruce decided to circulate among the tables, trying to strike up conversations.

Larry Matsuda, a Japanese American who had been born in the Minidoka concentration camp and graduated from Garfield, drove in thirty minutes from his home in Beacon Hill. He found his place in the cafeteria booths with the Asians from the neighborhood. In the Hub, he said, "The lowest among us were the FOBs, Fresh-Off-the-Boats. You just didn't want to be mixed up with them because people might think you're one of them."

Bruce was a FOB, but Larry and his friends found it impossible to avoid him. He was fidgety. His mind always seemed to be racing. Larry invited Bruce to play pinochle with them once, but he was quickly bored.

"He would come up to me and say, 'Hey man!' He used to call me 'Hey man.' I don't think he knew my name," Larry said. "He didn't communicate well in words because he had this thick accent and all these peculiar motions."

There was a rumor that he was a bouncer at Ruby Chow's, but none of them could substantiate it because no one actually ate there. They all dismissed it because he was so thin and unimposing—until he started doing his little demonstrations. One day, Bruce said to Larry, "Hey man! Grab my wrist."

"What?"

"Grab my wrist."

"I grabbed his wrist," Larry recalled, "and he did this and that and his fist was in my face. I said, 'OK! OK! Cool, cool.'

"When he did this, he was trying to communicate with me physically. And my appropriate response to him would have been, 'Hey, Bruce, that's really cool. Show me more,'" said Larry. "But I didn't. Instead it was like, 'Jesus! What are you doing? This is not what we do!'"

Roger Shimomura, a commercial design major who was about to graduate and head to Korea as an army lieutenant, said, "All of us people used to play Hearts in the Union. And everyone would groan, because here comes Bruce, and showing off."

Bruce's martial arts thing, Roger said, "was all very entertaining initially," but it wore off fast. "He was just like a real pain to be around 'cause he was also always doing these tricks and knocking people over and everything else."

But before long all the Central District Asian kids were watching in amazement as Bruce hammed it up at the football players' table, challenging amused Black linemen and white lumberjacks to arm-wrestling matches—and winning. Skip Ellsworth showed up on campus one day and pledged a Greek fraternity. Soon the Central District kids were watching an even more astonishing spectacle: Bruce commanding the attention of the white preppies—"Grab my wrist!"—and entertaining them with the secrets of *gung fu*.

When Bruce and Skip were by themselves, away from the frat boys, they marveled at their new circumstances. Skip had been the white boy on the rez. Bruce was still washing dishes at Ruby Chow's. They laughed together, feeling like they were somehow getting over.

● ● ●

One day in the Hub, Bruce spotted a gorgeous Japanese American woman the Asian guys knew as Roger Shimomura's girlfriend. Her name was Emiko Sanbo, a *sansei* born on May 16, 1940, in Sacramento, California. She had been just two years old when her family was incarcerated in the Tule Lake Segregation Center. After the war, they moved to Washington and she Americanized her name to Amy.

She was book smart and streetwise, focused and driven. As a child, she had received music and dance scholarships. At Garfield High, she was song queen and homecoming queen, and she graduated in 1958 near the top of her class. She performed ballet, jazz, and *shigin* dance, and sang in the choir at the First African Methodist Episcopal Church. She also performed in the Central District nightclubs as part of a vocal swing trio with a Black woman and a mixed-race Black *pinay*.

Her father had passed away when she was just eight, and her single mother had scraped together a living as a house cleaner to pay the rent on a Yesler Terrace apartment next to a brothel. To cover her tuition, Amy worked at the bookstore, the Bank of Tokyo, and the Chinese embassy. After hours, she served cocktails in Chinatown's premier late-night haunt, Bush Gardens, and learned how to hustle the old gangsters at the card tables in the smoky gambling dens. She planned to double-major in Far Eastern studies and English literature, then go to work for the Mitsui Corporation.

"I wanted to do it all," she said. "I was an A-type."

Amy pretended not to notice that Bruce was eyeing her in the Hub. It was comical, though, the way he was trying to discreetly move himself and his books across the room closer and closer to her table. She said goodbye to her friends and started for class, but as she passed Bruce, he shot his hand out and grabbed her arm. He pressed her forearm with his thumb so hard that she dropped her books. She shrieked, but he held on.

"That's enough!" she growled. "Stop it before I get really pissed!"

Suddenly Bruce was on the ground helping her pick up her belongings, and Amy was demanding to know why he had done that. He mumbled something about wanting to show his friend some martial arts thing. What bullshit, she thought as she gathered her books and stormed off. The bruise he left remained for a whole week.

"That's how he introduced himself," Amy said, "with force."

Yet afterward, it seemed she could not escape him. He popped up everywhere, asking her if she was OK, how she was feeling, bringing up random things to keep a conversation going, never saying the two words Amy wanted to hear. "As far as I was concerned," she recalled, "Bruce never apologized. He never apologized to anyone for anything."

She already had multiple *sansei* suitors—Roger, whom she had been dating for three years, and, when he wasn't around, David Fukui, a handsome hipster who drove a BMW and was studying to be an architect. Behind her back the Asian guys joked that she was the kind of girl who "made men out of boys," but when she walked up they turned timid and nervous.

Amy thought Bruce seemed "awkward and kind of dumb." Yet despite herself, she was becoming curious. She asked her friends about him. Their opinions were split. The only consensus was that he was definitely a character.

"He was single-minded," Larry said. "All the guy talks about is *gung fu*!"

In her ballet class, Amy did a *jeté* and landed on a nail, leaving her unable to walk. When she and her poet friend Lonny Kaneko arrived at the campus parking lot one morning they were surprised to find Bruce waiting for them. He offered to carry her across the lot and up the hundreds of stairsteps between where they stood and her class on the other side of campus.

She agreed—for practical reasons, she reasoned.

Lonny took her crutches and book bag, and Bruce swooped her up like John Wayne had Maureen O'Hara in *The Quiet Man*. Each morning that week he met them and did the same. By Friday he was in Lonny's back seat riding home with them so he could carry her up the three flights to her apartment.

Amy watched as Bruce charmed her mother. He chatted up Mrs. Sanbo about the Japanese-language newspaper on the table and turned the discussion toward translating Chinese and Japanese. They wrote in *kanji* for each other. He asked about their family name and learned it was 三寶, "Three Treasures," a powerful idea that linked Asian worldviews. The Buddhist took refuge in the three treasures: the Buddha, the Dharma, and the Sangha. The Taoist strived toward the three treasures of compassion, moderation, and humility. The last of these was explained in an epigraph: 不敢為天下先. *Do not dare to be first under heaven.*

Over tea and *manju*, the three of them talked and laughed together. Well, aren't you a smart boy? Amy thought to herself.

Before the war, Amy's parents had maintained strong ties to Japan, which made them suspicious in the eyes of US government officials.

In July 1943, after most Japanese Americans had been incarcerated, the War Relocation Authority required all of them to fill out a form called "Statement of United States Citizenship of Japanese Ancestry" or "Application for Leave Clearance," but best known as the "Loyalty Questionnaire." Among the forty-odd questions were two that created an impossible jeopardy:

No. 27. Are you willing to serve in the armed forces of the United States on combat duty, wherever ordered?

No. 28. Will you swear unqualified allegiance to the United States of America and faithfully defend the United States from any and all attack by foreign and domestic forces, and forswear any form of allegiance or obedience to the Japanese emperor, to any other foreign potentate, power, or organization?

Those who answered "yes" to both questions, they were told, might qualify for early release. But thousands of Japanese Americans answered "no" to one or both of the questions or simply refused to answer them at all.

The actor George Takei recalled that his parents had answered "no" for a simple reason. "My parents had three very young children," he said. "The only honest answer that they could give as parents was 'No.' They weren't willing to bear arms and fight to defend the country that's holding their children as hostages."

Question 28 was a "sentence with two conflicting ideas," Takei said. "The word 'forswear' assumes that we have a preexisting inborn racial loyalty to the emperor." Its insidious effect was to render all US-born *nisei* enemy aliens and all immigrant *issei* stateless, since American law had already prohibited them from owning land and becoming naturalized US citizens. Joining the Takeis among the five thousand Japanese Americans who responded "no" to both questions were the Sanbos.

As Taky Kimura's family was being removed from Tule Lake to Minidoka as a "loyal" family, the Sanbos were among the new surge of incoming "No-No" prisoners into the maximum-security segregation center. In the fall of 1943, Tule Lake prisoners staged a peaceful protest against the terrible conditions that had caused the deaths of a worker and an infant. They were met with state-of-the-art American tanks and gun-mounted jeeps, clouds of tear gas, brutal troop rampages, and finally, an order of martial law. Amy was just a three-year-old toddler when she strayed too close to a barbed-wire fence and found a screaming soldier warning her to back off, his rifle sights trained on her forehead.

After the war, her parents told her the stories of the family. Her mother came from a family who had been merchants and farmers in the California Central Valley. Her father's brothers were scholars at Stanford University, and the Sanbos descended from a famous line of Zen Buddhists. Amy took pride in her family's history and their decision. She thought of herself and her mother as built differently from the other Asians. Many of them, she thought, were trying to be "blonder than blond." The others, she said, "would huddle together. They would clutch together. They moved this way because they were still frightened."

Bruce seemed different, too. "Bruce had a certain way of walking," she said. "I thought, There's something about this man. He's unusual.

"Bruce was so cocky that it was refreshing," she said. "He was just so free and he liked being Asian. He didn't apologize for it and I liked that.

"At the time I was a cocky female. I didn't think anybody was going to really outdo me. So we were two alike temperaments, I think. Very competitive."

Bruce realized that if he wanted to see Amy outside of the Hub, he needed to visit her in the Suzzallo Library carrels. He just wanted to hang out with her. "I don't think he liked to study," Amy said. "I'd tell him to go away."

When *The Orphan* returned to the Kokusai, Bruce invited Amy and her mom. Afterward, they said nice things about the movie, but he realized that they did not seem as impressed as the guys had been. Amy let him know that she was still seeing Roger Shimomura. Bruce realized he would have to work harder.

"Put out your hand," he told her. Then he placed a nickel in it. "OK, don't let me grab it."

He swung his hand at hers. She laughed. "Ha! It's still there!"

"Look at your hand," he said. She opened her hand and there was a penny there. He flashed the nickel at her and grinned.

Some mornings he cooked up ginger beef in Ruby's kitchen and personally delivered it to her. At school he passed her love poems. He gifted her with a mandarin statuette carved from elephant ivory. When Amy sang at the Hub with her jazz band, he was there in front. After good days, he asked her how much she liked him in comparison to her other suitors. When she grinned slyly, he would say, "I think it's sixty percent Roger and maybe forty percent me."

They made bets over test grades, which Bruce knew he was bound to lose. But Amy was a willing and patient tutor, and his English improved dramatically, along with his confidence. One day, he pulled her into an empty classroom on the first floor of Parrington Hall. But as they laughed and flirted, a middle-aged, six-foot-three, two-hundred-pound man appeared at the door. "You're in my room!" he thundered.

Amy froze and cowered. She realized exactly whose room they had taken. They were in one of the only rooms on campus reserved for a single professor, and this one belonged to one of the university's most accomplished men of letters, the Pulitzer Prize–winning poet Theodore Roethke.

Bruce stood up and said, "I am Sifu Bruce Lee, *gung fu* master." After they shook hands, Bruce lectured for his audience of two on the history and philosophy of *gung fu*, moving to the blackboard to draw the *tai chi* symbol to explain *yin* and *yang*, and showing them different moves to illustrate his points. The poet took a front-row seat and listened, entranced.

"Bruce was one of these people that would get the attention back to himself," Amy recalled. "Theodore Roethke was kind of impressed with him, and I thought to myself, 'Oh. Wow.'"

On days like this Bruce grinned at Lonny. "I think Amy likes me 80 percent today."

Bruce came down to Amy and Lonny's table in the Hub and took out a stack of pages of classical Chinese poems. He read them in Chinese and then gave each a translation and thoughtful exegesis. Amy looked at Lonny, who aspired to be a writer, and saw he was floored. Maybe this weird *gung fu*–obsessed guy had a whole other side to him. Then Bruce read another poem, this one in English:

A girl must be like a blossom
With honey for just one man
A man must live like honeybee
And gather all he can.

To fly from blossom to blossom
A honeybee must be free,
But blossom must not ever fly
From bee to bee to bee.

These were the lyrics from "Song of the King," from the Rodgers and Hammerstein musical *The King and I*. Amy wheeled up and hit him.

"OK," he said, "I've got this silver dollar in my hand. I'm going to hold it and drop it, but I won't tell you when. You try to catch it before it hits the ground."

He dropped it. Amy swept her hand across and caught it.

"No one's ever done that before with me!" he said. "How did you do it?"

"I wasn't looking at your hand. I was looking at your eyes," she said, smirking. "What would you do if I pulled a .45 on you right now?"

He said, "I would run!"

Bruce often stopped by Amy's apartment just to get a few more minutes with her. When he was with her alone, he was different. "He was shy," Amy said. Sometimes he stuttered and then affected a British accent to cover it. This amused her.

After the weather turned warm, Seattle's waters sparkled in the long light, and Roger had graduated and left to serve his country in Korea, she agreed to let Bruce take her to the *bon odori* celebration at the Seattle Buddhist Church. They joined the crowd circling the *yagura* in time to the music, and she noted how quickly he picked up the dance. Later in the evening they drifted into the auditorium where the young couples were. The band played a jazzy cha-cha, and she decided to test his skills.

"I showed him one sequence," she said. "He just got it like that! I thought, He knows. He's no slouch."

He was moving like Fred Astaire—not bad, but still too white. Amy added more hip, tilt, and funk, and Bruce followed her perfectly. She tried something more difficult. Again he followed, adding his own flourishes.

"There was a kinetic genius about him," Amy said. "The nuance, the gesture, the attitude he immediately had—like, I know what he is. And he knew what I was. There was no explanation necessary because we knew each other by movement."

For the rest of that cool evening, song after song, rhythm and gesture, back and forth they went, calling and responding and calling again, young, delighted, and free. Alone later, they fell into each other's arms. Remembering their first night together, Amy said, "I was a dancer. I had no problem showing my body."

But Bruce, the boy who was so confident in public, was suddenly terror-stricken about his private shame. He explained he had a problem and showed her. Amy silenced him, and their night continued. Years later, even after multiple sclerosis had taken its toll on her body, Amy could remember these moments like falling blossoms in a gentle breeze.

"I think he was very guarded. Always," she sighed. "I guess he must have been trained that way that they corrected him constantly, you know? The *gung fu* and all that. He always wanted to make sure that he didn't make an error."

She said, "The only time that we could just cut loose, when I could meet him face-to-face, is when we danced."

CHAPTER 14
The Ghosts and the Moon

At Ruby Chow's, her children, nieces, and nephews greeted each Saturday afternoon with excitement. Before prepping the restaurant for the week's biggest crowd, they had a ceremony.

"In the restaurant entrance, there was a beautiful hand-painted lantern with a tassel," said Trisha Mar, Ruby's half-white niece. Each of the kids took their turn jumping to touch the bottom of the tassel. Then Bruce would crouch and leap into a high kick, letting out a scream and sending the tassel flying with his foot, making the kids cheer. Afterward, they retreated to the kitchen to fold *wontons* for the evening crowd.

But after-hours brought a sense of dread. For years the workers had whispered to each other that the building was haunted—why else would the *gweilo* have sold it to Chinese people? They talked about the migrant worker who saw a pink lady floating in the basement and quit on the spot, fleeing into the night presumably paperless and now jobless. One day Ruby hung an ominous black-and-white print in the second-floor hallway for all to see—an optical-illusion drawing by George Wotherspoon called "Gossip: And Satan Came Also," in which four Victorian women talking with each other are arranged to resemble the face of a laughing devil.

Ruby herself was being visited by ghosts. "My mom was sleeping," Mark Chow recalled, "and a black shadow got on top of her and pinned her down. She couldn't move." Sometimes as Bruce slept, he too felt a powerful force on his chest holding him down. When Peter Lee visited his brother in the summer of 1960, he remembered Bruce seemed possessed at night, just as he had sometimes been in Hong Kong.

"We slept together in an old double bed," Peter said. "Every once in a while, Bruce would be taken with a dream and start punching out and yelling, and once, he literally tore his pajamas apart as he punched and kicked out in a violent demonstration. Then he'd start kicking and throwing the covers off before settling back for the rest of the night. He was tight and tense even in his sleep."

When Ruby and Bruce shared their nocturnal troubles with each other, they realized that they were both afflicted by evil spirits. There were known remedies. Those who practiced *feng shui* geomancy placed mirrors in carefully chosen places to repel ghosts. Like Jean-Michel Basquiat, who had, in his paintings, written invocations and conjured guardian demons for protection, Bruce picked up a pencil and drew a werewolf so scary it frightened Ruby's boys. When he went to sleep, he hung the drawing on his doorjamb, like a talismanic lion at the gate.

Ruby dismissed all of it. She figured she could manage anything in this world or another through sheer willpower. Except Bruce. "He had problems with everybody," Mark Chow recalled. "And my mother was very strong-willed."

It was not just that the boy seemed intent on taking all the girls in Chinatown out for a cha-cha. She had put him in school, given him a job and opened her home, got him *gung fu* students and put him onstage where he wanted to be. But he was spoiled and ungrateful. Even worse, he was embarrassing her. He openly flouted her orders and got into public yelling matches with her. Sometimes he antagonized restaurant guests. Ruby told Ping and her children that Bruce was *saa chen* (沙塵)—flashy, arrogant, full of himself. She warned her drill team girls, "Don't talk to him. He's a bad boy." She stopped introducing Bruce to elders in the community.

One Saturday night, after their tassel ritual, Ruby's children, nieces, and nephews were folding *wonton* dumplings. Trisha and Bruce got into a playful argument and one of them threw a *wonton* at the other. As Billy Potts described the scene, "Someone returned fire and all of a sudden *wontons* were flying through the air. The friends went whooping through the restaurant, pelting each other under the serene gaze of the Eight Immortals statues that looked over the room."

Then, as they realized what they had done, the kids gathered up the *wontons* as fast as they could. But by opening time there were still wet *wonton* dumplings scattered throughout the room. Bruce knew he would be blamed and that another screaming match with Ruby was coming.

Bruce decided that Leroy's house was too far, so they began practicing in a Blue Cross hospital parking lot across from the restaurant, a spot he knew because the Chow boys biked and skateboarded there. The lot descended three floors below street level. While Ruby was catering to the white elite in her dining room, Bruce positioned himself on the other side of the street, forming a *gung fu* underground with the tough guys amid the oil, grease, and exhaust fumes.

As the weather grew colder, he began to think that the only way for him to escape Ruby Chow's would be to transform his *gung fu* classes into a private school. Taky and Jesse asked everyone to pledge ten dollars per month each to Bruce toward renting a space. Taky collected the money and they found a spot in Chinatown at 609 South Weller Street. It was a modest room in a run-down building that would soon be torn down, but Taky said, "I can remember the excitement on Bruce's face as he walked through the doors of his first school, it was like he was a self-made man on his way to greatness."

Bruce wanted the gang to learn traditional *gung fu* forms, in part because he believed the forms would help them build strength, speed, and precision. He also had an image in mind, a radical one at the very fringe of white Seattle—he wanted his motley rainbow crew to publicly demonstrate the diversity of the art of *gung fu*. Leroy did a *bagua* form, Jesse a Hung Gar form, and even twelve-year-old Roger Kay performed a *judo kata*.

The performances also allowed Bruce to market the school. He applied lessons he had learned from watching Ruby, booking the gang for public performances and also angling for a TV show, in hopes of drawing more paying students. In the spring of 1961, they landed a gig with Fook Yeung and Fred Sato to do five half-hour episodes for a show called *The Oriental Art of Self-Defense*, to air live Monday nights on the University of Washington's public television station, KCTS Channel 9. The TV appearances were historic, but did not exactly set the world on fire. In the third episode, Bruce accidentally jabbed Jesse in the eye.

"Oh shit!" Jesse cried, grabbing his face.

The crew fell out laughing; the producers stopped shooting and never invited them back.

In the spring of 1962, Bruce enrolled in the introductory class for Far Eastern Studies, a four-hundred-person survey class taught by George Taylor called "The Far East in the Modern World." Taking the class, he hoped, might impress Amy.

Bruce had already discovered the writings of Alan Watts, the former Episcopalian priest who had left England for the redwood forests at the edges of the military-industrial sprawl of Northern California. He and poets like Jack Kerouac, Allen Ginsberg, and Gary Snyder—who had written into existence the Beat generation in the cafés and clubs of San Francisco's North Beach neighborhood, adjacent to Chinatown—had created an American chic for Taoism and Zen.

"Zen is grounded precisely in this faith or trust that ordinary life is Tao, and is to be accepted or loved as such," Watts wrote. Among its revolutionary attributes, he wrote, were its disdain for dogma—"words and letters" that only encouraged confusion and obeisance—and its insistence on "direct-pointing to the soul of man."

"Thus the Zen masters say that ideas are fingers pointing at the moon of Reality, but that most people mistake the finger for the moon," Watts wrote. "Zen, therefore, does not consist in acquiring new ideas about Reality and our relation to it; it consists in getting rid of ideas and feelings *about* life in order that we may get to life itself."

Bruce had already worn out his copies of *Zen Buddhism* and *The Way of Zen*, underlining dozens of passages in red and blue ink. He read Watts discussing "direct pointing" by citing lines from chapter 56 of the *Tao Te Ching*:

> Those who know do not speak,
> Those who speak do not know.

To Bruce these were all much more refined ways of saying, "Don't talk with your mouth, talk with your hands." In such diamond prose he was finding, as he recorded in permanent ink above this section, "SIMPLICITY DIRECTNESS FREEDOM."

He felt he was awakening to what the masters had written about for millennia—the link between the dust of the universe and the sweat of human effort, the bond between the cosmological and the physical. In a paper he had written for his English class with Professor Margaret Walters and reappropriated for this one, "The Tao of Gung Fu: A Study in the Way of the Chinese Martial Art," he rehearsed ideas he would return to the rest of his life: "The principle of *gung fu* is not a thing that can be learned, like a science, by fact-finding or instruction in facts. It has to grow spontaneously like a flower, in a mind free from desires and emotions. The core of this principle is Tao—the spontaneity of the universe."

Soon his Asian friends noticed that when Bruce was in the Hub he was not just showing off martial arts moves, he was excitedly talking about the form and flow of *yang* and *yin*. Amy found this new development hilarious.

"What can you say to the Far Eastern majors?" she recalled. "It was just gongs going off and all this mystical BS. That is *not* what we were talking about at lunch."

She would interrupt him with a sweetly condescending "Okaaaay, Brucey Woosie." To which Bruce would moan, "You guuuuys." Then he would storm off to find a more receptive audience, like Skip's frat brothers.

Bruce had finally saved enough to buy his first car, a used 1956 gray Ford Fairlane, and was proud to be able to drive her home himself. Unimpressed, Amy called it "a clunker." He sometimes sent one of his *gung fu* students with his car to accompany Amy to the market or other errands. But Bruce's escorts knew what she knew—the whole exercise was pointless. Amy knew these streets and how to handle herself out there better than any of them did.

It seemed to her that Bruce had two different sets of friends, the university folks and the *gung fu* crew, and he did not want to mix them. That was fine with her. "I think he felt comfortable with the *gung fu* people and a little defensive with university guys," Amy said. "With his *gung fu* people he had control."

On the same late summer night in 1961 that Amy and Bruce had attended the *bon odori* celebration, a white Garfield High rising senior named Doug Palmer met Bruce for the first time. Doug had grown up in the Central District, the son of a prominent civil rights attorney, and had boxed since childhood. He had seen Bruce, Taky, and Jesse do a demonstration of *chi sao* and Praying Mantis forms in a Chinatown street fair the week before, asked Jacquie to introduce him, then promptly forgot about it. As he moved through the crowds milling on the street that night, he felt a tap on his shoulder. The six-foot-two teen spun around.

"I heard you're looking for me," Bruce said. He was leaning back on his right foot, one hand casually stroking his chin. Doug remembered, "It was the body language that said he was ready for anything." Bruce thought Doug had wanted a challenge. Instead Doug would soon be riding with Moses and Roger Kay to his first class with Bruce and the crew at Leroy's house.

Bruce was now formalizing his teaching, standardizing a curriculum for beginners. They performed a classic salutation to him, which he returned like a *sifu*. Then, Doug recalled, they limbered up with stretches, and lined up to practice the basic Wing Chun blocks and punches, *pak sau* and *laap sau* and *chaap choi*.

He sat them down to lecture on Chinese philosophy, as he had in Roethke's lecture room. He discussed Zen and Taoist ideas—Doug's notebook was full of scribblings like "Let things be what they are"—but Confucian ones, too. "Follow advice of teacher. Treat him with great respect," Doug wrote. "Conduct yourself [in accordance with the] principle of *gung fu*, by showing forbearance and gentleness in dealing with people." Palmer recalled that Bruce "was addressed as *sifu*, even though he was younger than all of the students except Roger." Only after his lecture would Bruce set them up to fight. He instructed them to stand strong side forward like a fencer, in the opposite of a traditional boxer's stance, then paired them off to spar.

"When Bruce got to the university," Leroy said, "he had a whole new audience."

But what was working for the new students was no longer working for the old gang. James DeMile was unhappy that Bruce had stopped teaching key principles that he used in his own fighting—the *bai jong* stance, the centerline, the use of spring energy. That told him that Bruce did not think of them as equals. For Jesse, the unease was more personal.

"I found it a little difficult to start calling someone who I had been running around with for two years '*sifu*.' To me Bruce had always been Bruce," he said, "just as I had always been Jesse to him."

In the summer of 1962, the gang was invited to be part of a command performance for a distinguished centenarian from the Chinese Canadian community. It was billed as "East-and-West dancing meets Wushu performance night." Set at the eighteen-hundred-seat Majestic Theatre in Vancouver, British Columbia, the show was to be headlined by the Jin Wah Sing Dramatic and Musical Association's star opera actress Tam Sau-Chen. She would sing popular selections and Ping Chow would spin water dishes. Bruce and Eunice Lam would dance the cha-cha, and his multiracial crew would demonstrate the "Shaolin Wing Chun National Art."

As the lights came up, Taky, Doug, Skip, James, and Leroy strode out onstage in blue Chinese outfits and lined up behind Bruce and Jesse. Bruce demonstrated straight punches and back fists, his *kiai*s echoing to the back row, barely pulling his punches on Jesse. The guys then paired off and staged three rounds of full-speed choreographed fights. When they left the stage to thunderous applause, Jesse had "a sore temple, swollen lips, and a bloody nose." But as the crowd roared their approval and he saw Bruce's glow, he realized that he had helped his young immigrant friend achieve something he had deeply desired—to be received as a *gung fu* master by the Chinese in America.

The banquet that followed was sumptuous and hazy. As bottles of Scotch were replaced on the lazy susan one after another, Skip challenged Jesse to a drinking contest. When the crew arrived at the border after midnight and were stopped by customs officials, Skip couldn't remember his name or where he was born, and they were all very nearly detained in a Canadian immigration jail.

They would remember this night as their last grand time together.

CHAPTER 15
American Fictions

Three years after leaving Hong Kong, Bruce was still trying to figure out how he appeared to others. He had been trying on different personas—Chinese boxer, *sifu*, thinker, street fighter, laborer, lover, preppie, performer. Every day was an improvisation.

To the young Chinese, Japanese, and Filipino Americans in the Central District, Bruce and Amy were a power couple, receiving invites to all the best house parties. Bruce looked great on her arm, and she on his, and when the music came on they could show everyone how free two young Asians could be in space and time. But then she would leave him for a minute, turn to find a crowd gathered around him, Bruce on the floor doing two-finger push-ups, and feel the flush of embarrassment rising in her cheeks. She would take a deep breath and, when she had finally had enough, say in her schoolmarmish tone, "Bruuuuuuuuuuuce."

Only then would he stop, get up, and chuckle at her.

At one of the parties the guys wanted to introduce Bruce to a tall Japanese American army man who was visiting friends while on break from Fort Lewis. John Yamamoto was legendary for beating down some rednecks in a backwoods bar who had called him racist slurs. They figured Bruce and John, both fearless and tough, would instantly hit it off. But after Bruce saw Amy checking out the GI, he stepped up to John with some choice words and soon the two were chest to chest, jostling each other.

"Geez, guys, cut it out," Amy shouted, as the guys separated them. But she also came away intrigued by the man who would become her husband.

Bruce felt a sense of urgency. When they were alone he told Amy she was different from the rest, so much more intelligent, more talented, and more mature than all the other girls. He said he felt she understood him. He said he was in love with her. He wanted to marry her and raise a family with her. He wanted to put his grandmother's ring on her finger. Amy changed the subject.

Over the next few months, he proposed to her over and again. She told him he was fun to be around, why couldn't they just leave it at that? She had no intention of settling down. She said she could wait to have children. Maybe she wasn't even interested in having children at all.

But the more Amy brushed it off, the harder Bruce pushed. He brought up Hong Kong. He wanted to take her there to meet his father and his family. He knew they would love her. Amy talked about documentaries she had seen about the impoverishment of the boat people.

"We'll live on the Peak, Amy," Bruce said. "You remember *The World of Suzie Wong*, and that scene when they're on a hill and you look down on the city? That's how we will live. We'll have servants and drivers."

"I can't live like that!" Amy said. "I can't ignore those people on the boats."

"But it'll be wonderful," he said. "Hong Kong is so beautiful."

She was, he told her, the one who could help him make his dreams come true.

Amy was offended. *Where*, she asked, *is the room to pursue my dreams?* She wanted to sing, to write, to dance. *Can you provide for me and my mother?* Bruce said he had big plans, he was going to build *gung fu* schools across America. She told him to stop right there.

"I would always expect some honesty from him rather than pretense and a display," Amy recalled. "Like, this is *me* you're talking to."

Amy was in her last quarter at the university. She was working at the Seattle World's Fair and had so impressed her bosses that they offered her the opportunity to move to New York City upon graduation to join the advance team for the 1964 World's Fair. Bruce was three years behind her in college credits and close to flunking out. He asked her what it would take to convince her to marry him. She told him, "Match me. Match my grades. Match what I do."

In Chinatown, over meals after martial arts practice, Bruce was gloomy. He told the gang that Amy was breaking his heart.

Bruce was asking her to be patient with him, saying that he would get it together, the money, the grades, everything. But she had already begun corresponding with the tall handsome army man from Fort Lewis and was planning her move cross country. Amy wanted no part of Bruce's vague old-world fantasy. She told him she didn't want to see him anymore.

"Bruce was still such a child yet," Amy said. "I think he was too anxious about himself. He was not sure of his masculinity. I understood that about him. But did I want to deal with it? No. It was like babysitting." After graduation, she quietly left town, instructing all her friends not to tell him where she had gone.

"He spent the next few weeks depressed," Jesse recalled. "He didn't do anything during this period except draw pictures of the girl and talk to his close friends about the emotions he felt."

The last time he saw her was in the spring of 1962. When Leroy asked about Amy one day at dinner, a dejected Bruce told him it was over. He had tried to find her but she was gone. A silence fell over the table. Then Bruce felt compelled to add one more thing: Amy's parents had rejected him because he was Chinese.

She would not be there to scoff at these last fictions.

When Bruce had been promoting *The Oriental Art of Self-Defense* the year before, a *Seattle Daily Times* columnist invited him to the office for an interview.

The newspaperman asked Bruce what *gung fu* was useful for. Bruce answered,

"*Gung fu* was used by Taoist priests and Chinese monks as a philosophy, or way of thinking, in which the ideals of giving with adversity, to bend slightly and then spring up stronger than before, are practiced."

The newspaperman protested that it was all just *hai-yah* and *ka-pow!*

"Gung fu is not preoccupied with breaking bricks and smashing boards, such as Karate," Bruce explained. "We're more concerned with having it affect our whole way of thinking and behaving."

Bruce felt he had hooked the newspaperman. He was ready to drop some deeper truths.

"The American is like an oak tree. He stands firm against the wind. If the wind is strong, he cracks," Bruce continued. "The Oriental stands like bamboo, bending with the wind and springing back when the wind ceases—stronger than ever before."

Picture the newspaperman grinning now, and Bruce leaving the office feeling good, maybe even feeling heard, striding a little taller. Maybe he's even a little nicer to the guests in the dining room that evening.

Picture him a few mornings later—stopping at a *Seattle Daily Times* news rack on a First Hill corner, dropping a dime in the slot and grabbing a stack of copies, running back to his room to open up a copy, impatiently flipping page after page to find the story. Picture his excitement at seeing a halftone picture of himself in his *jing mo* and his quotes in bold print, citing his ambition to make the University of Washington the "first university in the western world" to offer *gung fu* instruction.

Now picture the look on Bruce's face as he reads the very strange last sentence, "That would make Lee, Gung Fu, and Chow Mein manufacturers velly happy."

Picture Bruce rereading the lede: "At first Gung Fu sounds like a variety of Chow Mein."

Picture his face as he sees the caption under his picture—it calls him *Mike Lee*—and begins to comprehend the headline, its text and subtext: "Mike Lee Hope for Rotsa Ruck!—U Introduced to Gung Fu."

First Ed Hart had returned to the East Coast, and then Howard Hall. Other students had come and gone. Bruce could no longer make the rent on their space.

He, Taky, and Charlie Woo organized a major push of performances and publicity on campus, attracting enough new members to rent a new space at 420 ½ Eighth Avenue South, at King Street, at a steep discount. Its affordability was the result of urban renewal. The dingy building was the last one standing beside the cleared right-of-way for the soon-to-open I-5 freeway—whose construction had destroyed hundreds of Chinatown, Filipinotown, and Japantown homes and institutions, cleaved the communities from each other, and catalyzed a decline there the same way that the Cross-Bronx Expressway had spurred the tragedy of the South Bronx.

To access their training space Bruce and his students entered a street-level door and descended into the building's dank, poorly lit, unfinished basement. James stopped showing up, and Jesse and Leroy soon followed him.

"I had to make a decision as to what was more important—Bruce as a friend or Bruce as a formal teacher," Jesse recalled. "I chose his friendship and stayed away from the practice sessions."

The three of them opened a new school four blocks away.

"Bruce was a magnetic sort of fellow. But he told us what he wanted to tell us," Leroy recalled, with not a little sadness. "We thought we were as important to Bruce as Bruce was to us, and it wasn't true at all. We were just Act One of the Bruce Lee movie."

One afternoon, James came down to Bruce's space and chatted up some of the students. They asked him why he, Leroy, and Jesse had stopped training with them. "I told them we didn't like what they were doing," James said.

Overhearing this, Bruce came over, outraged. "You have no right to tell my students that!" he shouted.

James backed up and apologized. Bruce glared at him. James met his gaze, but slowly moved his right hand into his pocket, gripping the gun he always packed. He thought to himself, *If this kid even flinches at me, I'm going to shoot him.*

Then Bruce turned away, his students quietly dispersed, and James fled up the stairs into the unsettled night air.

Bruce stopped taking care of his grooming. Ruby Chow was telling friends who asked about her problematic charge, "Oh, he's trying to grow a beard and mustache, trying to make everybody call him *sifu*." But Bruce couldn't be sure that, beyond Taky and Charlie Woo, his other students weren't preparing to leave him too.

Bruce returned to Ruby. She listened to him, then again reminded him that those who needed his martial arts knowledge and skills the most were the Chinatown kids. He began leading children's classes on Tuesday afternoons at the Chinese Baptist Church. He taught Moses Kay's Boy Scout troops.

He ordered the kids to do countless warm-up rounds of push-ups, chicken-walks, and frog jumps. He demonstrated a new *fa jin* technique he called the "one-inch punch" on a teenage boy whom he had given only a thin pillow to cover himself. When Bruce connected with the boy's chest, the teen's hands shot up involuntarily and he punched himself in the face. They laid the boy out with a bloody nose and a bruised sternum.

Years later, Ruby Chow was still seething over Bruce. "If I can't say anything good about anyone, I'd rather not talk about it," she told the biographer Bruce Thomas. But then she had more to say.

"I took care of him for four years. I raised five children and I treated him like a second son. He was just not the sort of person you want your children to grow up like. He was wild and undisciplined. He had no respect. Lots of martial arts people are insecure. Martial arts are supposed to be to defend people, but he used them to be aggressive!"

Bruce was having a hard time concentrating on school, and that increased the danger of him being sent to fight for the United States in a war in Asia.

Just before Bruce had been born, on the eve of World War II, President Franklin Delano Roosevelt had reinstated the military draft. After Bruce turned eighteen, his mandatory Selective Service registration was a reason his parents had cited for sending him back to the States. At that time the war in Korea had ended and the war in Vietnam had not yet escalated. Now the requirement that every able male at the University of Washington participate in the Reserve Officers' Training Corps program was a blunt reminder of his duty.

By the end of 1962, nine thousand US "military advisers" had been deployed to South Vietnam. Pressures were growing to send ground troops. Some in the White House were telling President John F. Kennedy that within five years, the United States might have three hundred thousand men fighting there. The college draft exemption had become serious. School was the one thing that would keep Bruce from being called up.

At the start of the 1960s, American college enrollments of people of color were still paltry, the continuing impact of decades of racial segregation. Less than one in thirty non-whites had completed college, a third of the rate of whites. The booming University of Washington was one of the few places in the country offering something like equal opportunity. But access came with a trap, an aggressive process of "washing out."

Freshmen students were regularly warned that their GPAs would drop by a full point in college. "If your GPA dropped below a 2.0, you'd be on [academic] probation. You'd have to bring it up, or then you'd be gone. You'd be 'washed out,'" recalled Larry Matsuda.

"Freshman English was where they did it to you. They'd tell you, 'In three quarters, half the people in this class are going to be gone,'" he said. "I think Bruce must have felt the pressure from freshman English, because that was the killer."

Matsuda volunteered for the army reserve on a gamble that his part-time service would keep him out of Vietnam. At basic training in Louisiana, a white soldier pointed out a poster featuring an image of a slant-eyed Asian in a rice-paddy hat holding a rifle. "There," he told Lawrence. "There's your picture, dude."

Underneath the image were the words "This Is the Enemy."

By the end of his first year at the University of Washington, Bruce's GPA had dropped to 1.84. Academic probation and the mandatory two years of ROTC service loomed for him, and beyond that, the threat of conscription.

On a snowy day outside the restaurant, Bruce posed stiffly in his oversize ROTC uniform as Taky snapped a picture of him to send to his family. But after dark he posed again for Taky inside the restaurant—his coat unbuttoned, tie loosened, cap askew, rifle on his knee, bandolier slung over his shoulder, looking bored, mocking the absurdity of it all.

"How could a kid from Hong Kong be appointed the ROTC savior of the world?" he cracked.

Taky had once begged to serve his country. Bruce hated the idea. He skipped so many ROTC classes that he was finally required to show up on Fridays for 4:00 a.m. exercises. He went through the motions while chewing a wad of gum, until the drill officer spotted him and told him, "Swallow that, soldier!"

Bruce spit out the gum. "It's bad for my health," he said.

When the drill was done, the officer got up in Bruce's face and yelled, "Next time I say, 'Swallow,' soldier, you'd better swallow!"

"If you speak to me like that again," Bruce growled, "I'll put you on your back!"

The officer glowered at him, then walked away, shaking his head.

In her history of the war in Vietnam, Frances FitzGerald wrote that the United States "seemed to be less of a vessel than a movement."

Unlike Vietnam or other Asian countries, it was not a nation into which its people poured themselves like water into a vessel. The United States was an arrow pointing outward. Americans had little regard for a past or even a present. They never thought of themselves as settled because they were so intent on reaching their limit, then pushing past it. When the nation reached its frontier, it kept on running west into the Pacific. Movement was freedom and optimism.

"Americans ignore history," FitzGerald wrote, "for to them everything has always seemed new under the sun. The national myth is that of creativity and progress, of a steady climb upward into power and prosperity, both for the individual and the country as a whole. Americans see history as a straight line and themselves standing at the cutting edge of it as representatives for all mankind. They believe in the future as if it were a religion; they believe that there is nothing they cannot accomplish, that solutions wait somewhere for all problems, like brides."

At the end of May 1962, the week before Amy was to walk in her commencement exercises, his old teen crush Pearl Tso came to visit him in Seattle. She had blossomed into a graceful young lady, creating a stir everywhere she went in her A-line dress and Jackie Kennedy bouffant. The meeting made Pearl's aunty Grace, Bruce's mother, and Bruce's aunty Eva, Pearl's mother, very happy.

"I think that they all thought that those two would get together," Linda Lee recalled.

Bruce had dashed those hopes the year before when he forgot to pick Pearl up from the Seattle-Tacoma airport after she had flown across the ocean to see him, and she had angrily rebooked herself on a flight to San Francisco the same afternoon. But the two had patched things up. Bruce was clean-shaven again, and this time he remembered to meet her. He took Pearl to visit the Seattle World's Fair and they spent a day traversing the grounds under the world's flags before he took her back to the airport. If Bruce had hoped they might, they never ran into Amy.

Her rejection had shaken him. She had blown up his gauzy nostalgia for Hong Kong and his wispy designs for the future. But Amy had begun her childhood at gunpoint, and had always looked at America in a hard bright light. She had learned to train her gaze on the distance.

Bruce needed to concentrate his powers as she had. He needed a real plan. It was what she had wanted, and what he could not give her. Pearl became the distant muse he needed now that Amy was gone. At the end of September Bruce wrote her in fevered, scratchy drafts on binder paper:

> This letter is hard to understand. It contains my dreams and my way of thinking and way of life. It will be rather confusing as it is difficult to write down exactly how I feel.... I'll do my best to write it clearly, and I hope that you, too, will keep an open mind in this letter, and don't arrive at any conclusion until you are finished.

He then poured out ideas, stream-of-consciousness style. He talked about *yin* and *yang*, the *I Ching*, and Alan Watts. He explained how the inventor Charles Steinmetz came to see spirituality as the highest form of progress. He retold a Hindu parable of the gods hiding the key to enlightenment within man.

He was, as he would later put it, *in his process*. He was finding his higher purpose. He wrote:

> It is a fact that labor and thrift produce a competence, but fortune, in the sense of wealth, is the reward of the man who can think of something that hasn't been thought of before. In every industry, every profession, IDEAS are what America is looking for. Ideas have made America what she is, and one good idea will make a man what he wants to be.

Alan Watts had warned him that ideas were the fingers pointing, and not the moon. But Bruce had also been devouring books like Donald and Eleanor Laird's *The Technique of Handling People*, W. Clement Stone's *The Success System That Never Fails*, and Napoleon Hill's *Think and Grow Rich*, a curriculum he had designed for himself on how to make it in America.

He explained to Pearl what he had never been able to articulate to Amy:

> One part of my life is *gung fu*. This art influences [me] greatly in the formation of my character and ideas. I practice *gung fu* as a physical culture, a form of mental training, a method of self-defense, and a way of life. *Gung Fu* is the best of all martial art; yet

the Chinese derivatives of Judo & Karate, which are only basics of *Gung Fu*, are flourishing all over the U.S. This so happens because no one has heard of this superior art; also, there are no competent instructors....

My aim, therefore, is to establish a first *Gung Fu* Institute that will later spread out all over the U.S. (I have set a time limit of 10 to 15 years to complete the whole project.) My reason in doing this is not the sole objective of making money. The motives are many and among them are: I like to let the world know about the greatness of this Chinese art; I enjoy teaching and helping people; I like to have a well-to-do home for my family; I like to originate something; and the last, but yet one of the most important is because *Gung Fu* is part of myself.

From the way-out to the right-now, from follow-the-flow Zen surrender to sunset-chasing American ambition, from "craving is the root of all suffering" to "if I just believe in myself I can have everything"—perhaps he was testing ideas as he had fight techniques, to see which might stick.

In the pop language of discovery, positive thinking, and self-actualization, he told Pearl:

I feel I have this great creative and spiritual force within me that is greater than faith, greater than ambition, greater than confidence, greater than determination, greater than vision. It all these combined and more! My brain becomes magnetized with this dominating force which I hold in my mind....

When you drop a pebble into a pool of water, the pebble starts a series of ripples that expand until they encompass the whole pool. This is exactly what will happen when I give my ideas a definite plan of action. Right now I can project my thoughts into the future. I can see ahead of me. I dream. (Remember that practical dreamers never quit.) I may now own nothing but a little place down in a basement, but once my imagination has got up a full head of steam, I can see painted on a canvas of my mind a picture of a fine, big five six-story *Gung Fu* institute with branch off all over the states and with thousands and tens of thousands of students taking *Gung Fu* lessons under my self-taught assistant instructors. I am not easily discouraged, readily visualize myself as overcoming obstacles, winning out over setbacks, achieving "impossible" objectives.

Finally he declared, in excited, imperfect grammar:

Probably people will say I'm too conscious of success. Well, I am not. You see, my will to do spring from the knowledge that I CAN do. I'm only being natural, for there is no fear or doubt inside my mind. Pearl, success come to those who become success conscious. If you don't aim at an object, how the heck on earth you think you can get it?

Nineteen sixty-two had been his year of separations.

"A boxer, like a writer, must stand alone," A. J. Liebling, the great ringside scribe, once wrote. "If he loses he cannot call an executive conference and throw off on a vice president or the assistant sales manager."

Eunice Lam—Peter's girlfriend, soon-to-be wife, and later, the crown princess of Hong Kong's literati—had enrolled in classes at the University of Washington, and Peter asked Bruce to look after her. "Gradually, I found Bruce to be a lonely person," Eunice recalled. "He didn't seem to have many Chinese friends. No, I should say he had no friends. I feel the one who treated him best was his Japanese American friend who was very reliable and trustworthy."

At Seward Park, Bruce and Taky spent hours on the dock at the edge of the glistening Lake Washington. They meditated, took pictures of each other, and talked aimlessly. Bruce rented a boat and went floating on the lake. He later composed a poem he titled "Boating on Lake Washington":

> I live in memory of a dream
> Which has come and gone;
> In solitude I sit on my boat
> As it glides freely down the tranquil lake.
> ...
> The sun goes down in flame on the far horizon; and
> Soon the sunset is rushing to its height through
> Every possible phase of violence and splendor.
> The setting of the sun is supposedly a word of peace.
> But the evening like the soft and invisible
> Bonds of affection adds distress to my heart.
> ...
> Lying back on the boat, I try to conjure up the land of dream where
> I may seek for you.
> But, alas, no dreams come, only
> A moving point of fire in the dark,
> The distant light of a passing boat.

When it was time to go, Bruce stepped to the door of his Ford Fairlane, which he had asked his Central District friends to soup up after Amy had left him, and he smiled across the roof at Taky.

"I'll race you," he said.

They steered their automobiles onto the dark empty road back to the Central District and stepped on their accelerators, two American men speeding toward their uncertain futures.

To 李八腳
This trick takes 10 years of 苦練功夫
1st requirement in JKD- is that you must be 1. flexible, 2. agile, & 3. Mobile

PART V
Simplicity Directness Freedom

1962–1964

> To me, great musicians are like great fighters who know self-defense. They have a higher sense of theory going on in their heads. Great fighters are testy, just like great artists; they test everybody.
>
> —MILES DAVIS

Bruce, James Yimm Lee, and Ted Wong. The inscription reads, "To Eight-Feet Lee, this trick takes 10 years of training hard at *gung fu*. Signed, Iron Armor Yimm." Translated by Sze K. Chan. Photo courtesy of the Bruce Lee Family Archive.

Taky Kimura, Bruce, and Linda on Capitol Hill. The arrows are Bruce's notations. Photo courtesy of the Bruce Lee Family Archive.

CHAPTER 16
Mavericks

That the martial arts are now "mixed" has much to do with the mid-century mavericks who came of age on desegregated fight floors in Hawai'i and California, testing and combining different styles and schools like combat scientists. Bruce's encounters with them would change the course of fight history.

In Northern California, a new generation was establishing itself beyond San Francisco's Chinatown and transforming the Bay Area into an American center for Asian fighting arts. Wally Jay was one of them, part of an influential group of fighters from Honolulu who had migrated to the Bay Area after the war.

Born Jay Wah Leong, of Chinese descent, in 1917 in the rough-and-tumble Kalihi neighborhood, Wally Jay had learned boxing from a Black man named Jimmy Mitchell, *jujitsu* from a Latino man named Juan Gomez and a Hawaiian man named Paul Kaelemakule, and *judo* from a Japanese man named Ken Kawachi. Most important was the time he and his Native Hawaiian and Chinese wife, Bernice, spent with the influential *jujitsu* master Seishiro Henry Okazaki, who certified them as black belts and taught them massage therapy, bone-setting, and the healing arts. In 1950, Wally, Bernice, and their family desegregated a neighborhood in Alameda, California, and opened the Island Judo Jujitsu Club studio at their house.

By the summer of 1962, he was driving students from his championship-winning *dojo* to compete in Oregon, Idaho, and British Columbia, with a side trip to the Seattle World's Fair as a bonus. One of the chaperones, Dr. Jane Li, insisted Wally stop to meet her former cha-cha teacher. Wally was incredulous. But like Bob, Harriet, and George Lee, she too had never forgotten Bruce's *gung fu*. "He's really good," she told Wally. "You've got to meet him."

In working-class Honolulu after World War II, the Okinawan and Japanese martial arts were taught not just to Okinawans and Japanese, but to Chinese, Native Hawaiian, Filipino, Korean, Portuguese, and mixed-race kids, as well as white GIs. At the Palama Settlement, the YMCAs, and other floors across the city, Okazaki, Kawachi, and masters like James Mitose and William Chow compared and cross-pollinated *judo*, *jujitsu*, and *kenpo karate* with boxing, *gung fu*, Filipino martial arts, and the Hawaiian combat art of *lua*. The diverse generation of fighters they taught, including Ed Parker, Ralph Castro, Adriano Emperado, and Wally Jay, never knew "pure" forms of the fighting arts.

But what was natural for them, others deemed decadent. When Wally first entered his students in a Northern California *judo* competition, they stood out ethnically—they were half-Japanese/half-Portuguese, Native Hawaiian, Chinese, Filipino, Mexican, white—and were soundly whipped. Big-name Japanese instructors loudly mocked "Wally Jay's *judo*." But by the summer of 1962, Wally's students were taking national titles, he was winning coaching awards, and the old guys were not laughing anymore.

So here he was steering a station wagon full of teens up to the Seattle Chinese Baptist Church. In the middle of the fellowship hall, with his students encircling them, Dr. Li introduced Wally, but Bruce was neither warm or welcoming. He had on his game face.

Wally tensed when Bruce asked his biggest student, a part-Hawaiian teenager named Darrell Sniffen, to hit him. They touched forearms, and Sniffen suddenly made his move. But each time Bruce trapped his hands and tapped the teen on the head to end it. After a couple of rounds, Sniffen stopped, said, "OK, wait a minute," and turned to take off his jacket. At that Bruce's hard facade cracked and he grinned. The teen was fearless, the sign of a great teacher.

"No, no, that's good enough," Bruce chuckled. "You're just frustrated right now."

Wally exhaled and his students fell out laughing. They listened intently as Bruce lectured, and were transfixed when he blindfolded himself and did *chi sao* with their *sensei*. Wally had his students demonstrate grappling and throwing techniques, leaving Bruce impressed.

"What's your nationality?" Bruce suddenly asked.

"I'm Chinese," said Wally.

"I knew it!"

The next day Wally was on the phone to James Yimm Lee, his good friend back in the Bay Area, to tell him about Bruce Lee. James, the Iron Hand practitioner and *gung fu* maverick who had so impressed Jesse Glover, was still hearing about Bruce from his cha-cha dancing brother, Bob, Bob's wife, Harriet, and their friend George Lee. Finally determined to meet the young *gung fu* fighter from Seattle, James learned that his old friend Allen Joe was taking his family up to see the World's Fair. "Check out this cat," he told Allen. "Tell me if he's the real deal."

James and Allen were old friends from Oakland's Chinatown. They had gone to Chinese school together. As Japanese Americans were being sent to concentration camps, they joined other young Chinese Americans enlisting to fight in the Pacific. Allen was the second generation in his family to go to war for the United States.

After they returned, the two became gym rats, hung out at Neptune Beach, Alameda's version of Muscle Beach, and became devotees of the godfather of the California fitness craze, Jack LaLanne. In 1945, the first year the Mr. Northern California bodybuilding championship was desegregated, Allen was the first Asian American and the first man of color to win. Both trained in *gung fu*—James in Southern *sil lum*, Allen in *sam seen kune* (three-line fist). James called Allen "Tiger." Allen called James "Killer."

One warm summer night, Allen showed up at Ruby Chow's at closing time. Allen had been expecting a rough-hewn type of guy, but when Bruce stepped into the bar in a gray flannel suit, he thought, "He looks more like a model than a *gung fu* man." Bruce saw a well-built Chinese man polishing off a second glass of Scotch and assumed Allen had come to challenge him.

Instead, after Allen mentioned Bob and Harriet Lee, cha-cha, and *gung fu*, the two settled into a congenial mood, then went out for burgers and root beer. In Cantonese and English they bantered about fitness, philosophy, and fighting. As they walked back to Ruby Chow's Bruce suddenly stopped and said, "Show me some *gung fu*."

Allen flexed and, exhaling, showed Bruce a *sam seen kune* form. "Pretty good. You look pretty strong," Bruce said. "Now try it again." Moments later he had trapped the bodybuilding champ's hands and was dragging him around the sidewalk like a rag doll.

Inside Ruby Chow's, Bruce showed Allen a gold-covered spiral notebook on which he had inscribed "The Tao of Gung Fu." He had already filled more than seventy pages of it with prose and drawings for a book he wanted to publish.[*] By then Allen already knew what he was going to tell James—*Hey, Killer, this guy is for real.*

James Yimm Lee was five foot six and 160 pounds of pure steel. At Oakland Technical High School he had competed in wrestling, boxing, swimming, and weightlifting, where he had broken state records. Among his many nicknames was "Lee the V," for his build. In elementary school his classmates had elected him student body president. By his twenties, he was no longer known for his diplomacy.

One night James was drinking with some Chinese American buddies in an Oakland dive at 310 Broadway, just south of Chinatown, when a six-foot, two-hundred-pound white guy walked in. He spotted James at the bar and shouted, "Hey, chink! Buy me a drink."

James met the man's eyes and coolly responded, "What's your pleasure, sir?" He nodded to the bartender, who fixed the drink and slid it over. James slapped a dollar bill down beside the glass, picked it up, and tossed the drink in the white man's face. The man screamed in anger, and James floored him with a one-two. His friends leaped up to kick, punch, and stomp on the man until he pulled himself up and stumbled out of the bar.

"Yeah," one of his friends shouted at James, "we showed that *lo fan*!"

He smiled and said, "You guys sure did!" Then he raised his own glass and drained it.

He had been born on January 31, 1920, the same year as Ruby Chow and Taky

---

[*] The notebook included a much longer version of the paper he had written for his Far Eastern Studies and English classes.

Kimura. His father, Yimm Look On, had come to San Francisco after the Exclusion Act and worked as a tailor in Chinatown making special lingerie for the women of the night. After the earthquake, he obtained false identity papers, and as a "paper son" changed his surname from Yimm to Lee.

Later Bruce would tease James, "Hey, James, you're not a real Lee. I'm a real Lee." To which James would retort, "Correct. But I *am* related to your original *sifu*, Yim Wing Chun!"

His mother, Alice Ching, had migrated to Oakland's Chinatown. She had bound feet, and ran a shrimp business that fronted for a thriving Chinese lottery. At her holiday parties, she gifted the white policemen's wives with mink coats. By his teens, James and his seven siblings were no longer living in Oakland's Chinatown, but at 321 Perkins Street, in the comfortable Grand Lake neighborhood.

Just before the war, James—who had by then reclaimed his true family name, an act that could have been taken as a middle finger to anti-Chinese immigration laws—apprenticed as a welder and worked in shipyards from Richmond, California, to Pearl Harbor, where he arrived days before the Japanese attacked. In 1944, he enlisted in the army and saw combat in the Philippines. A bout with malaria brought him near death, and when he recovered, he vowed never again to feel so weak.

In Hawai'i, he had trained with Henry Okazaki, as the Jays had. After he returned to California, he joined T. Y. Wong's Kin Mon School and became one of Wong's best-known students, attracting new students with his Iron Hand demonstrations. He would set up a stack of bricks, name exactly which one in the stack he would break, and then, after bringing his bare hand down on the stack with a cry, extract and offer a stunned onlooker the broken brick.

In 1957, James started a publishing business called Oriental Book Sales to meet a growing demand for information about Asian martial arts. Three years before, Ed Parker, a part-Hawaiian fighter from Kalihi—who had been born under the name Edmund Kealoha Parker Waipa and trained under the famously tough founder of *kenpo karate*, William Chow—opened one of the earliest *karate* schools on the continent.* In 1960 Elvis Presley returned from the army and enrolled in *karate* lessons with Parker. The following year a publication named *Black Belt*, launched by another migrant from Hawai'i named Mitoshi Uyehara, began shipping magazines nationally.

By the end of 1961, James Yimm Lee, Ed Parker, and Mitoshi Uyehara were part of a new vanguard in the Asian martial arts in North America. If Chinatown's older generation had been shadowy, the emerging generation would be showy. If the elders had stewarded the martial arts to defend their communities from a hostile

---

* The first *karate* school in the United States is credited to Robert Trias, a World War II veteran who opened a school in Phoenix in 1946.

America in an era of danger, the younger generation wanted to modernize and popularize them in a nation that was slowly, unevenly desegregating.

The cover of James's first book, *Modern Kung-Fu Karate: Iron, Poison Hand Training*, promised readers they could "break brick in 100 days" and featured a picture of James doing just that. He bought small ads in science magazines like *Popular Mechanics* and boxing's journal of record, *The Ring*, and sold up to a thousand copies of each of his books. By 1961, he had already published four.

In his zeal to promote the arts, James approached T. Y. Wong about doing a book together. His *sifu* agreed, and their book, *Chinese Karate Kung-Fu: Original Sil Lum System*, was published in 1958.* James made some influential marketing decisions. He called *gung fu* "Chinese *karate*," a uniquely Asian American conflation, believing his reading audience would be more familiar with the Japanese art. He popularized the Americanization of the name *gung fu* as "kung fu," choosing the "k" over the native "g" because he liked its alliteration with *karate*.

His book with T. Y. Wong captures the Asian martial arts in America on the verge of a generational rift. It contains growing tensions between the old and new, the secretive and performative, the classical and the spectacular. There are pictures of T. Y. Wong demonstrating basic forms and techniques, and James Lee showing his Iron Hand brick breaking. There is a brief account of Wong's Southern Shaolin lineage but also special profiles of James's heterodox contemporaries from Hawai'i, like Ed and Wally. The book itself exacerbated tensions between the older gatekeepers and the young upstarts.

In this case, these tensions broke over a misunderstanding. The book sold very few copies, likely less than James's investment. But T. Y. Wong, who had expected to see big royalties, accused his student of stealing money from him. James stormed out of Kin Mon, never to return, in a bitter dispute over what some estimated to be no more than ten dollars.

But the disagreement was more than monetary. James wrote, "I wasted three and a half years performing *kata*. Not once during those years did I see the students spar. We were told that this type of training would eventually lead to 'deadly internal strength.' I realized later that the whole repertoire was just a time-killing tactic to collect the monthly fee." For his part, T. Y. Wong would publish a book without James and include a picture of his eight-year-old son breaking bricks, with the caption, "See I can break 'em too!"

James had quit, he said, "in disgust." He indulged the freedom to explore different schools, styles, and masters. With his charm and skill, he found many willing to teach him. "When he wanted to learn something new he would go where it

---

* James used his Chinese name, Kein Heir Lee.

was possible to learn, with no reservations toward the style or method taught by others," said his friend Ralph Castro, another *karate* master from Hawai'i who had moved to the Bay Area. "He could do this without making a pest of himself and was well-liked by everyone who knew him."

James and another former Kin Mon student, a white, three-hundred-pound World War II combat vet named Al Novak, organized the East Wind Modern Kung Fu Club, and set up across the bay in Hayward. Novak had learned *jujitsu* in Honolulu's backyards, and made use of it on Saturdays at the notorious Pearl City Tavern, where navy men like him regularly rumbled with marines. When their storefront business fizzled, they moved back to James's house at 3039 Monticello Avenue, in Oakland's middle-class Maxwell Park neighborhood. James had already outfitted his downstairs garage with weight sets, the heavy bags Jesse Glover had nearly broken his hand on, and spring-loaded strength training devices he had personally designed and built.

The club's students were decidedly outsiders. Many were employed in jobs requiring the knowledge of *fist ways*—they were police, bouncers, security guards. A fair number were not Asian. The Chinatown men left them alone, James's son Greglon Lee recalled, because "they were big brutes. When they saw my dad's students and him, they'd be afraid of them."

James and Bruce finally met in the fall of 1962. The details of their first meeting are lost to time—perhaps it was through a phone call arranged by Allen Joe or Wally Jay, or James attending one of Bruce's dance classes, or Bruce just showing up one day at the Lees' doorstep. Their friendship seemed fated. Katherine, James's wife, had once visited a tarot card reader who told her, "You will meet a mysterious gentleman, and he will become world famous."

When Bruce came down to Oakland to teach the occasional dance class, he stayed with James, Katherine, and their tween children, Karena and Greglon. The two men worked out in the garage and talked all night in the living room about the merits of different schools, martial arts manuals they'd read, and their views on training and fighting. James told Bruce that he wanted his students to be adaptable. His motto was, "You must learn to adapt to the circumstances, and adapt your training methods to the circumstances."

"Circumstances?" Bruce laughed. "Hell, I make circumstances!"

One night James invited Ed Parker, who was in town to see Ralph Castro, to come meet Bruce. The four bonded instantly. Bruce asked Ralph to block a back knuckle strike, and Castro responded by blocking with another back knuckle strike that neutralized him. "You son-of-a-gun," Bruce said, "that's the first time that has ever happened." Once again, he had found his people.

Before Bruce returned to Seattle, James encouraged him to share the writings he had shown Allen—maybe he could publish and sell them as a book. Bruce agreed and vowed to return to Oakland as often as he could. Allen Joe wrote that James "had been searching for the ultimate in martial arts for all those years, studying *sil lum gung fu*, and he discovered it from a man half his age." As for Bruce, Greglon Lee said, "He was smart. He surrounded himself with people twice his age so he could learn from them and they could mentor him."

There was so much to learn.

CHAPTER 17
Homecoming

In Seattle, Bruce was lonely for company. He found a new running buddy in Lanston Chinn, Moses Kay's tough, laconic nephew.

Lanston was also a student at the University of Washington, but he maintained a strong rep in the Central District. In a late-night brawl at a hamburger stand, people said, Lanston had fought off three attackers—one of whom had been wielding a knife. His uncle Moses encouraged him to try a class with Bruce, but Lanston considered himself above the hype. He had come up on the corners with his "Black brothers" in Rainier Valley. But after just one class with Bruce, Lanston was bringing his friends to train with him.

Soon Bruce was driving Lanston to school every morning and hanging out with him all weekend. They both had short tempers, older brothers who were overachievers, and bad study habits. When Bruce promoted his *gung fu* classes around the University District, Lanston was the *uke*, the fall guy. When they went to Asian American parties in the Central District, he was Bruce's wingman.

"Bruce was kind of possessive," Lanston said. "He was always saying, 'Come on!' He had a lot of energy just to just run around and go here, go there. He was always interested in finding out more about every aspect of what was happening in that town."

But at night when Bruce was alone in the attic, he wrote poetry to himself in Chinese:

> It's so difficult when I raise my eyes
> Endless tears fall on my shirt
> Three years of depending on others for food and shelter
> Exhausted my heart wishes to return
> But alas, I stay and endure the rain and wind and punishing frost.

Bruce longed for Hong Kong. He heard the voices of his family only a handful of times a year. Calls cost ten US dollars per minute and were huge productions on both sides of the Pacific. They needed to make an appointment at a calling establishment, and rehearse what to say to each other in a short amount of time. On these calls Bruce tried, above all, to project a narrative of success. But in actuality he was feeling trapped at Ruby Chow's, his GPA was cratering, and military service was threatening.

When Bruce had first entered the University of Washington, he said he wanted to study drama. In his letter to Pearl, Bruce had written that he intended to major in psychology and minor in commercial art. But after two years and six quarters of classes, he had enrolled in only one drama class, one drawing class, and two psych classes—the most important of which, General Psychology, he had flunked. Before he broke up with Amy he was taking five or six courses each quarter. Afterward, his course load dropped to two a quarter, one of which was basic Mandarin Chinese. He was no closer to declaring a major than when he had started.

He wanted to withdraw in the spring quarter of 1963 and go back to Hong Kong. But first, he needed to inform the school of his plans and check on his tenuous status with the ROTC. The draft board informed him that it would not permit him to leave the country.

Bruce had one faculty member in whom he could confide, an English professor named Margaret Curtis Walters with whom he had taken multiple classes. She had grown to like him, despite her suspicions that he might have been plagiarizing some of his writing assignments.

"I'm pretty sure that some of the things he gave me as themes must have been translations of Chinese poetry that he had studied or read or memorized in the past. And in fact I accused him once of doing that and he sort of laughed. He didn't admit it, but he didn't deny it either," she said. "And I think that's how he got through Freshman English 101."

The paper that had impressed and troubled her was an early version of what would become his "Tao of Gung Fu" manifesto, for which he had lifted some lines uncited from various Asian philosophy books. But one day during office hours, when Bruce confided in her his dream of building *gung fu* schools, Professor Walters saw something else in him: "It is not at all commonplace for a boy—because he was just a boy—to have strong ambitions as he had."

When the draft board threatened to deny his return home to Hong Kong, Bruce pleaded with her to intervene on his behalf. She wrote a letter to the board and asked Walter L. Riley, the assistant dean of the College of Arts and Sciences, to call the draft board "to assure them that Bruce Lee was a reputable and honorable gentleman and was not going to skip the country." In early 1963, the draft board cleared Bruce to return to Hong Kong.

Bruce prepared for his homecoming as if for a performance. All the protocols and minor rituals would be freighted with significance—the proffer of gifts, the repaying of a debt, the lavish banquet. He readied himself for all of it, even down to clothing changes. He needed to present an irreproachable image to win over his father and mother.

He went to the bookstore to buy purple University of Washington gear for himself, and to the department store to purchase an expensive car coat for his father. He went to the bank to get cash to prepare red *lai see* envelopes of "lucky money" for his siblings. He would hand a hundred-dollar bill to his mother, the amount she had given him on his departure. After classes broke for spring break on March 25, 1963, he donned his best-tailored suit, paired it with a dark skinny tie, Brylcreemed and styled his hair, then boarded the plane for passage across the Pacific to Honolulu, Tokyo, and finally Hong Kong.

As soon as he walked into the Kai Tak airport receiving area, he was blinded by flashing camera bulbs. Among the many who had come to greet him were his aunty Eva Tso and the famed character actor Mary Wong Man-Lei, the costar of a 1957 movie he was in called *Thunderstorm*, both dressed as if for a gala. Fourteen-year-old Robert had arranged for a reporter and photographer from *Wah Kiu Yat Po* to show up.

Bruce distributed the *lai see* to his siblings. Robert recalled, "We thought Bruce had struck it rich." He hugged his teary mother and gave her a gift, then greeted his father by pointing to the coat, draped over his arm and still in its plastic wrap. "Dad, this is for you," Bruce exclaimed. "I've made my own living. I've come back at my own expense. Aren't you proud of me?"

His entourage took pictures and vied for his attention. Then they all went back to Nathan Road for a banquet, where Bruce changed into his University of Washington fleece for more pictures and regaled them with stories of his American life. No longer did he need to conceal his love for martial arts from his father. He gave a *gung fu* demonstration, and everyone erupted in applause.

Robert noticed how much his older brother had changed. "He was more confident and secure with himself," he wrote. "The new Bruce was more in tuned to everything and everyone around him.

"The glow on our father's face said it all. [He] was smiling like we had never seen before."

Bruce had invited Lanston Chinn and Doug Palmer to visit him in Hong Kong. But Lanston had developed health issues and his mom didn't like Bruce. Doug would be on summer break from his first year at Yale, where he was majoring in East Asian Studies, and sent word he would come.

He arrived in late June for a two-month stay and stepped off the plane into the humidity and grime. Hong Kong and Southeast China were parched by a drought and in severe water crisis. But everywhere was thrumming with life—beggars, refugees, and pushcart vendors, people pouring into the streets to escape the heat of their tiny apartments. Doug remembered that "swarms of people filled the sidewalks, sitting in front of shops, standing at sidewalk food stalls, coolies in undershirts and old ladies in black pajama-like pantsuits rubbing shoulders with businessmen in Western suits." Even after midnight the crowds of Kowloon did not abate, surging forward under the warm glare of neon.

"It was an assault on my olfactory sense, my visual sense," Doug recalled. "It was a magical summer."

Doug stayed with Bruce and Robert in their corner of the main room. He had been studying Japanese and Mandarin, which were of no use. But he won over Bruce's mother and aunts one night as they played a game with dice that had different animals on each face. He was yelling, "*Haai!*," thinking he was saying "crab," but in the seven-toned language he was actually crying, "Vagina!" Because he walked around shirtless at night in the oppressive heat, they called him *jiu lin dak*, "Pig Tit Doug," the first of many nicknames he would acquire.

On the landing to the Lis' apartment entrance, a refugee from China had set up a sleeping pallet. "Every night, if we came home late, Bruce and I had to step over this guy," Doug said. Another beggar with her infant had noticed he was staying there; the good-natured six-foot-two *gweilo* was hard to miss. "She was there every time I came back down," he said. "I'd give her a Hong Kong dime, which is like a penny and a half."

Bruce had warned Doug before coming that, in Hong Kong, "they respect your clothing first before they respect you! Remember to dress sharp." Sure enough, Aunty Eva Tso invited Bruce and Doug to join her on visits to the Peak, the Tai Pak floating restaurant in Aberdeen, and parties with Hong Kong starlets.

While they were both in the States, Bruce had bragged to Eunice Lam that when he returned to Hong Kong he would be shooting films again. But he had no work lined up. An old flame, the actress Pak Yan—whose star was rising after a hit period romance called *So Siu Siu*—called him and said she had been cast as a bad woman for her next movie. "Can you show me how bad women move?" she asked.

They met at the Carlton Hotel. He delighted her with impressions of Ng Cho-Fan, his father in *The Orphan*. He told her of his plans to build a *gung fu* studio in Seattle. "He already had this plan," she recalled him telling her. "He would teach Chinese people first, and not foreigners, [then] Chinese people would not be bullied by foreigners."

As with the other girls, Bruce had told her what he thought she wanted to hear. On the dance floor and in other private places he showed her how to move. But by the light of morning, if he had hoped she might open a door back into the industry for him, he must have realized he would be disappointed.

One night Bruce was returning from a party in Hong Kong Central on the Star Ferry, dressed in a new bespoke tailored suit he had just had made, when two punks sitting behind him began taunting him. "Oh ho," they said, laughing, "look at this pretty boy."

Bruce ignored them. But as he disembarked to walk home, they followed, continuing to taunt him, "Oh, look, pretty boy has to hurry home to mama!" He stepped up his pace, but they closed on him. Suddenly Bruce wheeled around and kicked one of them in the shin, leaving him writhing on the ground. The other backed up, holding up his hands in submission.

Back at the flat he recounted the story for Doug and his family, chuckling as he told it. His cousin Frank replied, "If that had happened a few years ago, Bruce would have beaten both of them to a pulp as soon as he got off the ferry!"

To complete his trip, Bruce needed to see Yip Man. Having become an American *sifu*, he felt he finally understood what Yip Man had been trying to teach him. When he had left Hong Kong, Bruce had been obsessed with *chi sao*, not just because of his nearsightedness—training in sensitivity helped him compensate for this weakness—but also because it was a primary method of comparison. Now he understood it as "a constant energy flow" between two people, like water finding its path—*yin* and *yang*, indeed the Tao itself in action.

"The practitioner should keep the flow constant and fill every possible gap in each rolling and turning," Bruce wrote. "As training goes on, the more this energy becomes like water, and the narrower the crack through which its flow can pass." The lesson was that martial arts expressed the heights of Chinese art and philosophy.

But that was not all he had learned. Bruce went to test hands with his Wing Chun teachers, so that he might show them that he had returned as their equal or better. He wanted to return to Seattle having reached a new level of recognition and accomplishment.

Bruce was welcomed back by his old master, Yip Man's *sibak* Leung Sheung, and Wong Shun Leung. Master Yip even allowed Bruce to take pictures of them together, some on the rooftop, some in a photography studio. In one of them, his master stands in loose Chinese clothes, Bruce stripped to a white tank. They face each other, their arms resting on each other's, captured in the moment of turning just before the contending—Bruce's eyes sharp with intention, Yip Man's sparkling with amusement.

Doug accompanied Bruce to Yip Man's apartment but, as Bruce had asked him, took a seat. Bruce did not want his *sifu* to know that he was teaching non-Chinese. When Bruce and his *sifu* rolled and turned, Doug remembered, "To me, they seemed equal in terms of their ability. In fact, Bruce still could not move his elderly master in sticking hands. He was also unable to best Wong Shun Leung or Leung Sheung. Doug asked if Bruce thought he could beat Yip Man. Bruce dodged the question. "*Sifu* is getting older," he said.

Doug recalled, "I took it to mean that Bruce considered his own physical abilities to be greater at that point but was too polite to say so directly."

But in fact Bruce was despairing, wondering if all he had done in America was for naught. He later told Jesse Glover, James DeMile, and Howard Williams that he had been so frustrated, he thought of quitting martial arts altogether. His dissatisfaction would unexpectedly push him onto a new path.

"I didn't realize it at the time," Doug said, "but he was starting to depart from pure Wing Chun."

• • •

One sunny day Hoi Chuen invited Bruce to King's Park to join him and five friends, older opera and film actors with whom he had long practiced *tai chi*. At the bottom of a sandy hill, they stretched and then broke into pairs and played hand-to-hand. Someone had brought a camera and they all lined up and posed like Father, Son, and the five *gung fu* avengers. With Bruce in the center, asking hand forward, the photo looked like a superhero comic book cover.

The public welcome at Kai Tak had reminded Bruce of the glamour he had left behind. His time with Pak Yan underscored how far his former peers had left him behind. But he was surprised to find his father had lost all ambivalence about the celluloid dreams he once had. Hoi Chuen even seemed to be encouraging him. He told Bruce, "When you become an actor, you can earn big money quickly. But when things are down, you may not see any money for months. So save everything you can to stretch your money when you need it." It was exactly the kind of advice and recognition Bruce had desired from his father as a teen. If he wanted to return to film now, his father had freed him to do so. But his homecoming only seemed to point him back to America.

He visited a fortune teller to divine his future, which seemed as cloudy as ever. The oracle had shocking news: this trip would be the last time he saw his father alive. He flew back across the Pacific, disquieted but resolved.

Bruce with Hoi Chuen and his *tai chi*/opera/*gung fu* film friends at King's Park, Hong Kong. Photo courtesy of the Bruce Lee Family Archive.

CHAPTER 18
Things Disclose Themselves

Back in Seattle for the fall quarter in 1963, Bruce gave Ruby Chow notice that he was quitting the restaurant and moving out. Immediately she hastened his departure. Out of the blue, Doug Palmer's father, Doug Sr., received a call.

"It was Bruce saying his landlord had just kicked him out," he remembered. "He asked if he could stay with us for a few days and [Palmer's wife] Ida said, 'Yes.' Five minutes later he showed up on our doorstep with a suitcase."

Bruce spent a month at their rambling three-story lake-view Craftsman on the sunrise side of the hill in the Madrona neighborhood of Seattle. At the dinner table, where the worldly activist family discussed the issues of the day, he was polite and respectful. But away from it, he was in his element with the four Palmer boys—telling dirty jokes, chopping bricks with his hand, doing two-finger push-ups with Doug's 195-pound brother on his back.

But soon Bruce was startled to learn that, because of his quarter away, his student draft deferment had been revoked. He received notice from the draft board to immediately report for a medical examination for military induction.

In Vietnam, the war had turned. After escalating their guerrilla attacks the previous fall, Viet Cong insurgents had won a major battle southwest of Saigon, shattering the official optimism conveyed in US and South Vietnamese reports. In September, shortly after President Diêm declared martial law and President Kennedy reaffirmed that the US troops would continue to fight, Bruce appeared at the military office with about a dozen other students. He told friends that only two of them—himself and a football player—seemed physically fit enough to serve.

After the physical, he awaited his fate and poured his energies into advancing his dream of a *gung fu* school. Bruce had secured a workspace in the University District at 4750 University Way NE, a modern apartment building on the main commercial strip with a ground-floor storefront that the landlord wanted to convert into a "health studio." Bruce decided the site was perfect and talked the landlord into accepting him and his school.

When Doug stepped into classes in the new location, he realized how focused Bruce had become. The storefront was a massive step up, well lit and spacious—three thousand square feet—with big windows, a solid floor, and a locker-room-style shower and bathroom. After the landlord finished the renovations, Bruce would move into a windowless room in the back, which he would furnish with teakwood furniture he had shipped back from Kowloon. Everything felt right. There was even a Chinese restaurant across the street with a cook named Ah Sahm, who made a mean oyster sauce beef.

Bruce installed punching bags and speed bags. He hung brush scrolls with inspirational quotes. He filled a massive scrapbook with pages of pictures, drawings, and descriptions of different systems of *gung fu*, their founders, and their fighters. He proudly inserted pictures of himself doing *chi sao* with Yip Man. He would use the scrapbook to provide students a context for what he was now calling the Jun Fan Gung Fu Institute, the clearest sign that he was moving on from Wing Chun.

He branded the school with a logo rendered in Ruby Chow's palette of red, gold, and black—the *tai chi* symbol of *yin* and *yang*, around which he drew arrows to indicate their perpetual motion. He hired Ruby's sister to embroider the logo onto student vests and badges. He typed up rules of conduct. He created membership cards and worksheets to track each student's progress. He printed flyers and posted them across campus, instructing interested parties to clip a coupon, fill out their info, and leave them with a friend in the dorms. He drew up a contract to hire Taky as an instructor, offering him a 10 percent share of the profits.

In mid-October, Taky received a notice for Bruce in the mail from the Selective Service in San Francisco. Draft Board 36 had deemed Bruce "unacceptable for induction under current standards," and declared him "IV-F," unfit for military service. He told Professor Walters he had been rejected because of his high arches. But it was his undescended testicle, his middle-school shame, that had disqualified him—an unexpected but satisfactory end to his tangles with ROTC and the draft board. Unlike Larry Matsuda and many other college peers, he would be spared from confronting the meaning of being an Asian fighting an American war against Asians. Freed from the prospect of having to participate in real combat, he could build his own fighting art.

Like Doug, Lanston had noticed changes in Bruce too. The weekend hedonist was now sounding like an old metaphysician.

Bruce had begun teaching centerline theory again, the idea that defense and attack should always begin from one's center, a place of strength and balance. But now he was also saying: "Learn the center. Keep the center. Dissolve the center." He meant: *Learn the rules, master the rules, break the rules.* A design for art and life.

Years later, Bruce told a journalist, "When my tutor assisted me in choosing my courses, he advised me to take up philosophy because of my inquisitiveness. He said, 'Philosophy will tell you what man lives for.'

"When I told my friends and relatives that I had picked up philosophy they were all amazed. Everybody thought I had better go into physical education since the only extra-curricular activity that I was interested in, from my childhood until I graduated from my secondary school, was Chinese martial arts."

The journalist asked, "Are you implying that the two disciplines are not related?"

"As a matter of fact, martial arts and philosophy seem to be antithetical to each other," Bruce said. "But I think that the theoretical part of Chinese martial arts seems to be getting indistinct. Every action should have its why and wherefore; and there ought to be a complete and proficient theory to back up the whole concept of Chinese martial arts."

Bruce's first steps toward his unified theory of martial arts had come in Hong Kong's Victoria Harbour. In Seattle, he was conducting rigorous physical study. He had transcribed the wisdom of the masters and refined his ideas in class papers and personal journals. His disappointing reunion with Yip Man and Wong Shun Leung had also reinforced his faith in his own process.

In the fall of 1963, Bruce enrolled in Philosophy 428, his first philosophy class and the school's only course on Chinese philosophy, taught in the Far Eastern Studies department by a renowned professor of Chinese literature, Dr. Vincent Shih. He and his old friend Jacquie Kay were two of only three Asians in a large survey class of over a hundred students.

As Bruce rediscovered Taoism and Buddhism in the American context, he could also see how these "Eastern" ideas were radicalizing "the West." Alan Watts's books *The Way of Zen* and *This Is It!* brought Bruce into a world of West Coast spiritualists, Beat poets, and a white counterculture looking to the East for ways of liberation and alternatives to stifling bourgeois conformity. These seekers made up most of the students who filled Professor Shih's class. But for Asians in America like Jacquie and Bruce, the cultural turn offered some validation. Perhaps their worldviews and ways of living were not baggage that needed to be shed in a rush to assimilation, but gifts of birthright.

In the Hub, Bruce and Jacquie passionately debated the big ideas they were learning. When Bruce turned their discussions to how Asians could protect themselves, they found common ground: self-defense was key. "We saw this was not a nice world out there," she said. "We're Asians, we're small, and we have a harder way to go in this big *gweilo* world."

For their term paper assignment, the two decided to go head-to-head. Jacquie—who had been the valedictorian at Garfield, and who took notes in Spanish in the Mandarin class they shared so that Bruce couldn't copy them—told Bruce that she was going to write about the idea of *prajñā*, the notion shared by Buddhists and Hindus of a "supreme understanding." Bruce laughed and replied that he was just going to take a quote from Alan Watts and apply it to martial arts. She protested, "You're just taking the easy way out!"

But his paper—another version of the "Tao of Gung Fu" paper that he had turned in to Professors Margaret Walters and George Taylor—dazzled Professor Shih and earned him an A plus. Jacquie only received a B.

"I told you you shouldn't do that for your paper," Bruce cackled. "Just give them what they want!"

And then he glided off to another table as Jacquie steamed.

James Yimm Lee's book publishing offer had given Bruce the promise of a broader public platform. By the fall of 1963 Bruce was working on it in earnest, writing drafts and making drawings. He enlisted James, Taky, and Charlie Woo for photo sessions, and—in a peace offering—invited Jesse Glover and James DeMile to join them too, all of them dressed in their old uniforms. He asked Ed Parker Jr. and Wally Jay to pen testimonials, and they praised the twenty-two-year-old's knowledge and "his incredible speed and snap."

The book they published is a transitional one. Reading it from beginning to end, one can track Bruce's thinking as it changes. At the start he repeats received teachings, illustrating classical *qigong* stretches and *sil lum* stances. By the end Bruce is challenging orthodoxies, even joining James Yimm Lee's beef with T. Y. Wong. In a series of photos, James acts out Wong's *sil lum* forms and Bruce applies easy counters.

He and James agreed: these old *sifus* just complicated things to preserve their own status. "The technique of a superior system of Gung Fu is based on simplicity," Bruce wrote. "It is only the half-cultivated systems that are full of unnecessary wasted motions."

Bruce called the book *Chinese Gung Fu: The Philosophical Art of Self-Defense*. Naming it a "philosophical art" rather than a "fighting art" was deliberate. In Seattle, Bruce had found himself standing between the Central District pugilists, who were obsessed with discovering more effective and efficient ways to crush their opponents, and the University District counterculturalists, who were turning to the "ancient" wisdom of Asia for words of peace and enlightenment. He decided he did not want his book to be just another technical manual for enthusiasts.

Gung fu, Bruce wrote, had evolved from a "no-holds-barred type of fighting" into "a highly scientific and philosophical type of self-defense":

> Its philosophy is based on the integral parts of the philosophies of Taoism (道教), Ch'an (Zen 禪), and I' Ching (Book of Changes 易經)—the ideal of giving with adversity, to bend slightly and spring back stronger than before, and to adapt oneself harmoniously to the opponent's movements without striving or resisting. The techniques of Gung Fu emphasize not power but conservation of energy and moderation without going to either extreme (Yin and Yang 陰陽).

In the middle of the book, as if separating the old from the new, he inserted a three-page essay on *yin* and *yang*—the negative and the positive, the female and the male, the soft and the hard, the dark and the light.

Bruce reads *A Source Book in Chinese Philosophy*. Photo courtesy of the Bruce Lee Family Archive.

In Western philosophy, opposing forces can create contradictions. In this light, the English term "martial art" appears to be a paradox. It describes the cardinal skills of war and the craft of death-making. It also reveals, as Bruce would later put it, the beauty of human expression.

But in the Taoist worldview, dualities are mutual, dynamic, and transformative. Combined within the *tai chi* symbol, *yin* and *yang* form a unity. Bruce wrote, "The sun is not the opposite of the moon, as they complement and are interdependent on each other." Together the forces form the great constant dialectic driving and illuminating the always-changing universe.

By linking fight with philosophy and seeking the integration of body and mind—as his father, Uncle Siu, and Master Yip had encouraged him—the twenty-two-year-old Bruce had begun to articulate his own perspective on the martial arts. In this, he had become like his hero Miyamoto Musashi, the seventeenth-century Japanese swordsman known for his *Book of the Five Rings*, who had, by the age of twenty-two, also opened his own school and composed his first scroll on sword technique.

Reading Daisetz T. Suzuki's essays on Zen and swordsmanship, Bruce found further confirmation that the deepest ideas of Asian philosophy had long intersected with the martial life. For a warrior did not only need to have the right techniques, but the right mindset. Suzuki referred to the teachings of the swordsman Odagiri Ichiun:

> The great mistake in swordsmanship is to anticipate the outcome of the engagement; you ought not to be thinking of whether it ends in victory or defeat. Just let the Nature take its course, and your sword will strike at the right moment.

Electrified by this passage, Bruce pursued the interiority of the warrior in his "Tao of Gung Fu" papers, introducing the Taoist ideas of *wu hsin* and *wu wei* into his philosophy of fight. *Wu hsin* is about attaining a state of "no mind." Quoting Alan Watts, Bruce wrote that it was "a place of 'wholeness in which the mind functions freely and easily, without the sensation of a second mind or ego standing over it with a club.'"

To underscore this point Bruce copied lines—he was a close, omnivorous, and innovative reader but, as Professor Walters had suspected, often indifferent to the protocols of citation—from Eugen Herrigel's *Zen in the Art of Archery*: "The flow of thought is like water filling a pond, which is always ready to flow off again. It can work its inexhaustible power because it is free, and it can be open to everything because it is empty."

Wu hsin, Bruce wrote, following Suzuki, is like a *gung fu* man dealing with ten opponents, one after another: "As soon as he stops to think, his flow of movement will be disturbed and he is immediately struck by his opponent." The fighter needs to act by nature. *Wu hsin* allows *wu wei*—"action without strain." *Wu wei*, Bruce wrote, is spontaneity, the right move in the right moment, "the art of artlessness, the principle of no-principle."

He quoted Evan Morgan's 1933 translation of the Taoist classic *Huai Nan Tzu*: "Placidly free from anxiety, one acts with the opportune time; one moves and revolves in the line of creation." The best analogy, Bruce said, was water. He quoted Morgan:

> Water is so fine that it is impossible to grasp a handful of it; strike it, yet it does not suffer hurt; stab it, and it is not wounded; sever it, yet it is not divided.

Bruce knew Sun Tzu's saying that an effective army was like water, withdrawing from the peaks, rushing to the plains, and shaping its flow to the terrain. In a burst of inspiration he wrote:

It has no shape of its own but molds itself to the receptacle that contains it. When heated to the state of steam it is invisible but has enough power to split the earth itself. When frozen it crystallizes into a mighty rock. First it is turbulent like Niagara Falls, and then calm like a still pond, fearful like a torrent, and refreshing like a spring on a hot summer's day. So is the principle of *wu wei*.

Bruce instructed his students: "If you feel emptiness, strike in a straight line." He was translating philosophy into physicality, trying to teach fluid modes of response—avoid the opponent's strengths, attack his weaknesses, adapt to rapidly changing situations.

Inspired by the spareness of the classics, Bruce was offering a poetics of fight, an evocative way to describe what it felt like to be in the middle of a good scrap—consumed with blood scent, body overtaking mind, intellect and fear converted into adrenaline and presence. On the tightrope between triumph and destruction, time slowed. Things became possible: delight in the motion and counter-motion of bodies; clarity through a radically narrowed aperture of consciousness; ecstasy nearing complete freedom.

But, apart from the *feeling* of fight, wasn't the *function* of fight wholly incompatible with *ahimsa*, the pan-Asian principle of pacifism, compassion, and nonviolence?

Zhuangzi had written that Laozi and Guan Yin "based their system upon nothingness, with One as their criterion. Their outward expression was gentleness and humility. Their inward belief was unreality and avoidance of injury to all things." At the edge of violence, Laozi had noted, the warrior often parts from the wise one. "Good weapons are instruments of fear; all creatures hate them," he said. The enlightened use them only as a last resort.

Bruce attempted to reconcile this problem by writing, "A *gung fu* man aims at harmony with himself and his opponent." *Gung fu* was "like a graceful ballet with movements that maim or kill," whose end was to "'borrow' his [opponent's] force to 'help' him defeat himself. Instead of opposition there is co-operation.'" A fight, in other words, was just a different kind of a dance.

But the *gung fu* he claimed was not cha-cha; it was not a game. As the philosopher and martial artist Barry Allen wrote, "Martial arts are sportslike only in training and dancelike only in demonstration."

Sun Tzu had famously said that the highest art was to defeat the enemy without fighting. But he did not valorize bloodlessness, much less harmony or cooperation. War, he said, was deception. The ends of the art of war were to force the Other into complete and utter submission—even to ruin, disfigurement, or death. Had Bruce

---

* This is from a flyer he made for the Jun Fan Gung Fu Institute entitled "The Chinese Method of Self Defense."

confused triumph over the Other with the pathway to enlightenment and oneness? What were the ethics of the art of war?

Bruce was partial to the warrior's morality. Overcoming one's own "greed, anger, and folly" and fulfilling one's yearnings for "peace, justice, and humanity" were the highest human intentions. But a warrior revealed these intentions in the purity of one's execution of violence, in the terrible act of the death blow.

"Zen discipline is simple, direct, self-reliant, self-denying," D. T. Suzuki had written in a passage that would deeply influence Bruce. "The fighter is to be always single-minded with one object in view: to fight, looking neither backward or sidewise. To go straight forward in order to crush the enemy is all that is necessary for him."

These lines had appeared in *Zen Buddhism and Its Influence on Japanese Culture*, a book published in Japan in 1938, just weeks after the Imperial Army had ravaged and massacred thousands in the Rape of Nanking.

"That is why a victory," Laozi had counseled, "must be observed like a funeral."

One passage from an assigned textbook, Fung Yu-Lan's *A History of Chinese Philosophy*, especially captured Bruce's imagination. Bruce had read these words perhaps as early as March 1960, when he was first probing the relationship of philosophy to fight. In the spring of 1962, they found new resonance as Amy, Jesse, Leroy, and James were leaving him. When everything was falling apart, these words lit the way forward.

They came from the Taoist classic, *The Liezi*. In it, a humble archer named Liezi learns the Tao from masters like Guan Yin. He tells Guan Yin that he knows that an enlightened man—not unlike the Israelite in the Book of Isaiah or Mr. Wiggles in Parliament's *Motor Booty Affair*—can walk underwater and not drown, go through fire and not burn, and tread the entire world without fear.

But, Liezi asks, how?

In fragments Guan Yin answers the question, usually in the form of riddles. This one was so striking, even Zhuangzi would reappropriate it. After Bruce read the words in *A History of Chinese Philosophy*, he tracked them back to *The Liezi* and carefully transcribed them:

If nothing within you stays rigid,
Outward things will disclose themselves.
Moving, be like water.
Still, be like a mirror.
Respond like an echo.

Was this the secret to power? If so, it was power that came through meekness and humility.

When he wrote about these lines in his "Tao of Gung Fu" paper, Bruce linked them to the famous lines from the *Tao Te Ching* that had been taken up by generations of revolutionaries: "The strong and mighty topple from their place; the soft and yielding rise above them all." Pride, status, and domination were folly, he wrote, a "gratuitous waste of energy," a problem of "Western hygiene."

But at the same time, Bruce was also finding in Asian philosophy exactly what the Beat poets thought that they had found—a language of the self consonant with American notions of self-reliance and radical individualism. When introducing Zen to white audiences, D. T. Suzuki had written, "Zen aims at preserving your vitality, your native freedom, and above all the completeness of your being. In other words Zen wants to live from within. Not to be bound by rules, but to be creating one's own rules—this is the kind of life which Zen is trying to have us live."

Suzuki and Watts offered seekers like Bruce's white classmates in Far Eastern Studies an alternative to technocratic Christian rationalism. They didn't have to enlist in America's Cold War. Zen Buddhism and Taoism gave them countercultural instruments for self-actualization. In this way, Bruce was closer to his white classmates in rebellion against their parents' America than his Asian American ones, who practiced Buddhism and Taoism to sustain their traditions, families, and communities in America against erasure.

Bruce was entering into his own personal revolution, where he would oppose everything and everyone he saw as "rigid," "closed," and "despairing."

CHAPTER 19
This Is It!

It was on a winter's morning at the end of 1962, Bruce's year of separations, that she had first seen him.

Bruce was walking up the steps into Garfield High, dressed to the nines in a tan raincoat, a black silk suit, a purple shirt, and a slim-brimmed black hat. He had an entourage with him—Doug Palmer, back from Harvard on Christmas break, and a new girlfriend, another pretty Japanese American. He was looking like he had just stepped out of *West Side Story*, senior co-ed Linda Emery thought as she stared down the hall at him—"a Chinese George Chakiris."

She turned to her best friend, Sue Ann Kay, and said, "Who is *that* guy?"

"Oh, Bruce?" Sue Ann said. "He's a family friend. He's our *gung fu* instructor."

She would not see Bruce again until the following summer, but she would not soon forget him.

Linda Emery was eighteen, strawberry blond, athletic, and also a little nerdy. Born on March 21, 1945, she had graduated in the top ten of her 1963 Garfield High senior class. She and Sue Ann had both been yell leaders, too, part of the in crowd. She was exactly the kind of girl that guys wanted to marry. What many of them didn't see was that she was also defiantly independent. She had learned early to keep her own counsel.

When she was a five-year-old girl living in Everett, a sleepy town north of Seattle, her father suddenly went into cardiac arrest. She found him in the bathroom slumped against the door in the throes of death. The Emerys—her mother, Vivian, her older sister, Joan, and herself—lost the spacious house he had built for them at the edge of an orchard, and moved to the city, renting a place in the Montlake neighborhood, across the bay from the University of Washington.

Her mother met a manager named Dave McCulloch at the Sears department store downtown, who got her a job there as a debt collector and courted her. Soon she had remarried, and they moved into a two-story red-brick Tudor home on Capitol Hill, at 2332 Eleventh Avenue East.

"My mother was a toughie. She was hard on us kids," Linda recalled. But her new stepfather was an alcoholic and much worse, peeping at his stepdaughters in the bathroom through the heat register in the wall. It was an unhappy household.

"When I was a kid at the dinner table, if somebody said, 'Pass the salt,' my mother would be, 'What's wrong, there's not enough salt on it? Well, then, you cook it!' There was just constant bickering," she recalled. "Therefore, I'm kind of a person who does not speak up about things and doesn't answer unless asked, just because I don't want to stir up trouble."

Linda spent as much of her time away from the house as she could—the arboretum, the woods, the Lake View Cemetery, the streets of the Central District. "I remember having that distinct feeling when I was about ten years old that I'm on my own, I can handle myself. I don't need anything from those guys," she said.

Linda's mother paid close attention to Joan, whom friends had dubbed "the cute one," and sent her to Roosevelt High because she worried that Joan was too interested in Black men. Linda, "the smart one," could do what she liked. She took a part-time job at Sears so that she could have her own money to spend. After work she drove her multiracial crew of white, Black, and Asian girls around town in her round-top Plymouth. The summer before senior year she secretly dated a guy who was half-Japanese, but when her mother found out, she was told, *This is not what is expected in our family.*

"I didn't get my broad viewpoint of humanity from her," Linda said.

Sue Ann had become serious about these Sunday morning *gung fu* classes she was taking in Chinatown with Bruce Lee. Linda teased her about them. The petite Sue had turned fearsome. Her legs had hardened into solid tree trunks, and everyone knew she could kick the hell out of someone. What was she learning? What the heck was a *gung fu* anyway?

"Why don't you come out with me sometime," Sue dared Linda, "and find out?" The truth was that Linda had never forgotten her first glimpse of Bruce in the Garfield hallway.

"I'll go," she answered coyly, "for the physicality of it."

In August 1963, the two headed to Chinatown. At first Linda was unimpressed by the musty basement space. *What did I get myself into now?* she thought. But then Sue Ann bowed in and introduced her. Bruce welcomed her and began taking the dozen students through their exercises. Linda found herself drawn into the intensity of the training.

There is a picture of Linda from her cheerleader days—she is aloft in a jeté, her right leg tucked under her, her left extended straight back, her body tilted left, forming a perfect triangle. She reaches toward her left foot, ribbon in her hair, arms spread, flashing a radiant smile, and she looks like she is effortlessly soaring. It would not be long before she was kicking the shit out of her classmates. Bruce was quite taken by the new girl.

After sessions, Bruce led the group down the hill for *dim sum*. One day Linda sat next to Bruce, and when he poured out some tea for her she emptied a packet of sugar in it.

"Oh my god!" Bruce exclaimed. "What are you doing? That's disgusting!"

Linda stared at him in embarrassment. Bruce quickly changed the subject. When she laughed, she was neither demure or showy. She had no artifice, no airs,

Linda Emery, Garfield High School, 1962. Photo courtesy of the Bruce Lee Family Archive.

and she possessed a natural grace. Her smile was like his mother's—it calmed him down. He would daydream about her eyes.

"They were a little blue, a little green, with here and there a fleck of brown," he recalled. "What you call, I think, 'hazel.'"

A few weeks later Bruce moved into the University Way storefront. He had perfected his pitch. In an informational packet featuring pictures of him and Taky in action, he proclaimed:

THIS IS IT!

It was Jujitsu and Judo, then Karate and Aikido. Now comes the highest art of Chinese gung fu, the center of all Oriental arts of self-defense. Its history covers 4000 years and the true art of Gung Fu was not known to the public until 1960, when Mr. Lee Jun Fan was giving demonstrations along the West Coast... Gung Fu has since gained popularity. It is just a matter of time until Gung Fu will be practiced nation-wide.

Gung fu, he continued, "serves to CULTIVATE THE MIND, to PROMOTE HEALTH, and to provide a most efficient MEANS OF SELF-PROTECTION against any attacks."

He offered classes on Tuesday and Thursday evenings and Sunday mornings at twenty-two dollars a month, seventeen dollars for students, and twelve dollars for women and teens. He set up exhibitions at the gym, the frats, the Hub, featuring Sue Ann roundhouse-kicking guys in the groin and tossing them over her shoulder *judo*-style.

"Between classes, I would go to the Hub," Linda said, "and if he was there, which was usually, he was always surrounded by a group of us who were taking classes from him—Sue Ann, Lanston. Bruce would be commanding court at the Hub. He was so fun to be around, could tell jokes like crazy, and give demonstrations at the table and all this stuff."

Linda was on a premed track. But other than her swim class—which, Bruce noted, she took just before lunch so that she always arrived at the Hub with her hair wet and pulled out in pigtails—she found her classes more difficult than she had expected. Her first-quarter English assignment was to write an essay on Orwell's *Animal Farm*. He volunteered to write it for her.

"I got an A," she said. "He thought in Chinese, but he wrote well in English. He could be real sloppy in his speaking English, but he knew how to write perfectly."

Linda and Sue Ann were wide-eyed freshmen, intoxicated with the freedoms of campus life, and he made them feel like they were part of a scene. One day after classes he said to the group, "Let's go see this movie." They went down to the Kokusai, and Bruce made sure that Linda sat next to him.

"Oh, that's you!" she exclaimed, as Bruce appeared on the twenty-foot-high screen in *The Orphan*. She thought to herself, *There's a lot to this guy I don't know*.

When they got bored with the Hub, Bruce led his acolytes out to the university's Sylvan Grove, where four Ionic columns stood, named Loyalty, Industry, Faith, and Efficiency. There he put them through their workouts. There was "plenty of space and soft grass to land on," Linda wrote, the perfect collegiate mise-en-scène. She recalled, "One afternoon, Bruce and I were racing from one end to the other and when we got away from the group he tackled me to the ground. I thought he was going to show me a new maneuver, but instead, he held me down and when I stopped laughing, he asked me if I wanted to go to dinner at the Space Needle. I hesitated a moment, thinking that was a pretty expensive place for all of us to go, and I said, 'You mean all of us?' And he replied, 'No, only you and me.'"

If she had any doubt about his intentions, he handed her a letter after a Sunday class:

Linda,

To live content with small means; to seek elegance rather than luxury, and refinement rather than fashion, to be worthy, not respectable, and wealthy, not rich; to study hard, think quietly, talk gently, act frankly; to bear all cheerfully, do all bravely, await occasions, hurry never.

In other word, to let the spiritual, unbidden and unconscious, grow up through the common.

Bruce

It was a poem he had found by the nineteenth-century Unitarian minister William Henry Channing called "My Symphony." When Linda read it, she felt as though Bruce had known her forever.

Linda told her mother she was going out with Sue Ann, borrowed a formal dress and coat from a friend, and, on Friday night, anxiously awaited his arrival at the Kays' home. At the door she exhaled and smiled. He looked almost exactly like when she had first seen him—the black suit, purple shirt, and black tie, his hair slicked into a Clark Kent/Superman curl.

From the Eye of the Needle, the rotating restaurant atop the Space Needle, they could see the half-moon dancing on the waters below. Linda was nervous. Bruce warmed her up with a steady patter—jokes, thoughts about psychology and philosophy, stories about Hong Kong, his dreams of a chain of *gung fu* schools. After they finished dinner, he took out a gift, a Scandinavian troll whose hair he had braided into pigtails. When he dropped her off he gave her a kiss on the cheek.

"It turned out to be a very romantic evening," she recalled, "everything perfect."

Later, in his notebook, Bruce copied quotations from European and white American writers that he wanted to remember:

Fame is climbing a greasy pole for $10 and ruining trousers worth $15.

The essential thing is not to find, but to absorb what we find.

Some of us might find happiness if we would quit struggling so desperately for it.

It is always the secure who are humble.

Knowing is not enough; we must apply. Willing is not enough; we must do.

Nothing is so aggravating as calmness.

Analysis kills spontaneity. The grain once ground into flour springs and germinates no more.

At the bottom of the page, he stencilled a name in graphite: "LINDA. LINDA EMERY."

Amy had stoked Bruce's inner perfectionist and his fear of failure. Linda brought out his gentility and spontaneity. She didn't judge him.

"Meet me in fifteen minutes," he'd tell her.

"I can't keep up with you!" she would protest.

They developed a routine. "When school got out, when we finished in the afternoon, must have been about two thirty or something, we would race home to his place in the University District to watch *General Hospital*," Linda said. "That was the only time in my or his life that we ever watched a soap opera. But we said, 'We gotta get there!'"

But when they went out after dark, he still had to pick Linda up and drop her off down the street, out of her parents' sight. Doug returned for the Christmas break, and he and his Japanese American girlfriend provided them cover. Bruce could finally stop by the house, but only with Linda posing as Doug's date, and Doug's girlfriend as Bruce's. In the car they laughed about it, but Bruce disliked the charade. He had hoped to meet Linda's mom directly, the way he had Amy's. Sometimes he longed for the days when he, Leroy, and Jesse could mix their dates up just to piss off the racists in the street.

At the end of 1963, Bruce and Linda were on the road to California. Linda told her mom that she and her friends had gotten tickets for the Rose Bowl, which pitted the University of Washington against the University of Illinois. They were actually going to visit James Yimm Lee, who had received the first copies of Bruce's book from his printer in Berkeley, and then the three of them would drive to Pasadena to stay with Ed Parker and his wife. Bruce was excited to have the finished book in his hands, and boxes more to take back to Seattle. But what transpired on their visit would soon render the book a relic.

In March 1961, *Time* magazine had featured Ed Parker in an article that introduced *karate* to the American masses, calling the sport—"with more than 50 schools across the U.S. [teaching] an estimated 50,000 practitioners"—"the latest fad in craze-crazy filmland," and Parker the "high priest of Hollywood's fast-growing karate sect." Ed counted not just Elvis Presley but Frank Sinatra, Blake Edwards, Warren Beatty, and Natalie Wood as students.

James Yimm Lee had first tried to interest Ed in meeting Bruce by telling him that the young man might be well suited for the movie screen. But after they met, Ed was less struck by Bruce's looks and charisma than his outsized personality, brash opinions, and astonishing gifts.

"He was a cocky kid, very cocky," Ed recalled. "There were a lot of things he didn't know, but all you had to do was let him watch you one time and that was it. He was such a natural athlete."

Ed invited Bruce to give a presentation at his *dojo*. Later he revealed his real intentions for hosting Bruce and James. He wanted to talk to them about his plans for a major event he was calling the International Karate Championship.

Previous national *karate* contests had been amateurish and underwhelming. But Ed was now the most famous *karate* man in the country. He had won the respect of not only Hollywood, but the most important fighters and martial arts schools. He had secured the Long Beach Municipal Auditorium, an art deco building facing the Pacific with a capacity of eight thousand. If there was anyone who could give an event like this the quality and spotlight it deserved, it was Ed Parker.

Ed's vision was to bring together martial artists of different schools and styles in a tournament-style competition on a grand stage. He believed that sport and spectacle advanced the fighting arts. Competitions were not just proving grounds for the athletes; they could also pressure-test the effectiveness of different arts. Everyone would be able to see the best fighters and fighting practices rise to the top.

Bruce disagreed vehemently, and he was uninterested in competing in any kind of contest. Competitions were a symptom of a larger problem with martial arts schools, systems, and practices. He wrote that "most systems of martial art accumulate a 'fancy mess' that distorts and cramps their practitioners and distracts them from the actual reality of combat, which is simple and direct. Instead of going immediately to the heart of things, flowery forms (organized despair) and artificial techniques are ritualistically practiced to simulate actual combat. Thus, instead of 'being' in combat, these practitioners are 'doing' something 'about' combat."

Schools turned out students who were "factory-made, everybody looks the same." Whether a *kata* performance or a *kumite* point match, both turned a "living, expressive human being" into "merely a patternized mechanical robot." Tournaments did not pit one against another in "the total freedom of realistic combat," but "against the rules and regulations, the judges and referees." Schools, forms, competitions—they were all "dry land swimming."

It would be a risk for Ed to ask Bruce to do an exhibition. Bruce's views confronted his core audience—the instructors and students of the rapidly expanding network of martial arts schools. If Bruce was given a platform, his opinions might jeopardize the larger event, which many people wanted to succeed for the good of the arts. "You have to understand [Bruce] was a nobody," recalled George Mattson, a *karate* master who had already written a book on the art and officiated at previous national tournaments. "But he was somebody Ed Parker kept saying, 'You have to meet this guy.'"

On the cold morning of December 30, 1963, before the marine layer dissipated, Ed drove Bruce, James, Linda, and his young son across the city to see the Municipal Auditorium. As they walked through the arena, he said to Bruce, "I think if you were to come down to Long Beach from Seattle and demonstrate, the people would have a better cross-section of what lies in the martial arts world."

Bruce gazed at the three levels of empty seats and accepted.

At Wally Jay's invitation, Bruce returned to Oakland to perform at his 1964 Lei Day *luʻau*. Wally gave a lengthy interview to the *Oakland Tribune*, hyping the event as the public debut of "the previously mysterious but effective art of *gung fu*." He was making *gung fu* out to be even more powerful than the *judo* and *jujitsu* he taught.

Bruce Lee, he added, was one of the best practitioners in the United States. "It will be a revelation," he said. "You shouldn't miss it."

Wally had begun the biannual *lu'au* in 1957 to raise funds for his youth program. It was a family affair for the Jays, who gathered everyone at North Oakland's Colombo Club over steaming plates of food cooked up in their backyard and tiny kitchen—Wally's *imu*-fresh *kalua* pig, Bernice's famous chicken long rice, *lomi lomi* salmon, and *poi*—and hired top performers, like the legendary *haku mele* Aunty Lena Machado, who would sing her famous song, "Ho'onanea onanea."

These *lu'au* were the place to be for a rapidly growing island diaspora. Two economic recessions during the 1950s had pushed thousands of Locals out of Hawai'i to the continent, a migration critical to the growth of Asian fighting arts in the United States. They had also become a key hub for the North American martial arts movement, attracting up to a thousand attendees who constituted a who's who of the rising generation of fighters.

Everything was happening in California. There were five times as many Asians in the San Francisco Bay Area as in Seattle, six times as many in Los Angeles. James Yimm Lee, Ed Parker, and their networks were not just talking about doing big things, they were doing big things. The California fighters were wondering aloud, Bruce told Jesse Glover, why he was wasting his time in the Pacific Northwest. He wondered too.

He had all but given up on college. By the time the spring quarter of 1964 had begun, he was taking just Mandarin Chinese and a self-guided "undergraduate research seminar" in the Chinese department that gave him credit for writing about Asian philosophy and *gung fu*. He showed up tentatively for a class in logic that he did not complete.*

Only Linda and his Jun Fan Institute were keeping him in Seattle. But even with all he had invested in the institute, longtime students like Sue Ann were drifting away. Maintaining a business based on a transitory student population in a martial arts backwater was like building on quicksand. It was still a struggle to make the rent. Maybe something bigger awaited him in California.

Bruce bounded onto the *lu'au* stage to warm applause and executed a thrilling Mantis form. But after he finished he posed a strange question to the crowd, "How could you expect to fight like that?" He ran through a crisp Northern Shaolin form, punctuating his high kicks with hand slaps. But when he finished, he said, "Classical methods like this are a form of paralysis."

His system of martial arts, he explained, eliminated all the flash and excess. "The techniques are smooth, short, and extremely fast," he said, then unleashed a blur of punches. "They are direct, to the point, and are stripped down to their essential purpose without any wasted motions."

---

* Bruce's notebooks show him taking notes for just the first few classes of this course.

He brought a volunteer to the stage, backed up several feet, and asked the volunteer to try to block his punch. "Ready?" Bruce asked. When the volunteer nodded, Bruce flew across the floor and tapped him on the head a split second before the man could even raise his block. He called this the Closing the Gap exercise, and it hearkened back to his hayfield games with Leroy Garcia and a pistol.

Bruce had honed his speed and closing skills, his fight partners once said, to compensate for his poor eyesight. Mastering the technique was a kind of personal victory. But to the lay audience, it was an anticlimactic end to a confusing presentation. Instead of a demonstration, he had given the audience a deconstruction.

"Bruce left the stage to mixed applause," wrote the historian Charles Russo.

To the seasoned martial artists in the hall, his skills were evident, perhaps even impressive, but his words were polarizing. "With the Chinese community, he really got off on the wrong foot," recalled Leo Fong, one of James's students, who had studied with Lau Bun and T. Y. Wong, and had been in the audience. "Some of them were pissed off. They were talking bad afterward."

But with the can't-tell-me-nothing zeal of revolutionaries, Bruce and James were plotting. On one of their long-distance calls, James bluntly asked Bruce, "What are your plans?"

"What do you mean, Jimmy?"

"Well, if you want to stay in Seattle, give me a month or two, I'll sell the house and get a job in the shipyards in Seattle. And we can continue working and training. Or if you prefer, you come down. Stay here. We have a place for you and you can keep training all you want."

On the Monday after the *lu'au*, James invited Al Novak, Leo Fong, George Lee, a white student from Stockton named Bob Baker, and some other students to the house. It would be a memorable evening, marked by Bruce's demonstration of the one-inch punch on Baker—the biggest man in the room—that had left the telephone book he had been holding arcing over his head, his feet flying up over the tipping couch, and him inches from crashing through the plate-glass window. Then James let them hear what Bruce had decided: he was going to move in with the Lees in Oakland, and together the two would open a new Jun Fan Institute on Broadway later that summer.

Upon his return to Seattle in May 1964, Bruce was optimistic about his future. He had purchased an airline ticket back to Oakland for the evening of July 19. He told Linda he was not going to finish his degree. This decision had major implications for their relationship. But in the moment, it did not rise to the top of Linda's concerns. Not long before he was to leave, she quietly had a gynecology appointment.

In the doctor's office, Linda thought of her mother. "She didn't have to worry about me. She had to worry about my sister," Linda recalled. As a senior in high school, Joan had become pregnant.

"I found out about it because they didn't tell me anything. I just knew that something wasn't right—my sister was leaving town," Linda said. "My sister would write letters home and I would get home before my mother and steam open the letters. That's how I found out she was having a baby, which she gave up for adoption."

Now she wondered what she would have done in that situation.

"I was the straight and narrow one," Linda said, "except for things [my mother] didn't know about." Endless afternoons of laughter and color. The dark room at the back of the studio. The scent of sweat and hard teakwood.

When she returned from the doctor's office, she sat Bruce down.

She took a deep breath, grasped his hand, and said, "Guess what, honey?"

Bruce called Lanston to meet him at University Way. For hours, they talked about what Bruce had begun calling The Situation.

"In those days, you know, abortion really wasn't an option," Lanston recalled. "He would speak in a sort of strange rhetorical manner and say, 'Well, I'm gonna marry her. I'm gonna marry Linda.'" Then doubt set in and Bruce backtracked and asked, "What do you think?"

Bruce decided he needed to figure out "his legal options." Mr. Palmer was a lawyer, so perhaps he could explain what the law said about getting someone pregnant, and what it said about him needing to get married. He made an appointment to visit Doug Palmer Sr. for advice, and brought Lanston along with him.

Mr. Palmer listened patiently as Bruce asked him question after question. "Look, Bruce," he finally said. "It's not about what's legal or not legal. It's about what's the right thing to do."

Linda began preparing—for exactly what, she didn't know. "I could not receive letters from him at home. So I rented a PO box," Linda said. "I thought that was very clever."

Picture Bruce standing before Linda, for the first time having more to say in his silences than in his words.

"We were going back and forth and talking about getting married," Linda said. "We were stupid kids, and also had no education. My mother never went there."

Suddenly things seemed to be moving too quickly. Bruce gave Taky detailed instructions on managing the Jun Fan Institute. He ended his storefront lease, had Taky ship his furniture and books to Oakland, and sold his Ford for cash. Linda didn't know how to ask the big question: *Bruce, what is the plan?*

"When I took Bruce to the airport for his departure to Oakland, I still didn't know the answer to that question. Neither did Bruce. The idea of commitment scared him to death," Linda recalled. "He said simply, 'I'll be back,' and then he was gone."

As she and Taky watched the plane take flight, she could not help but wonder, "What if I never saw him again? What if he went on to bigger and better things and memories of me got lost in the shuffle?"

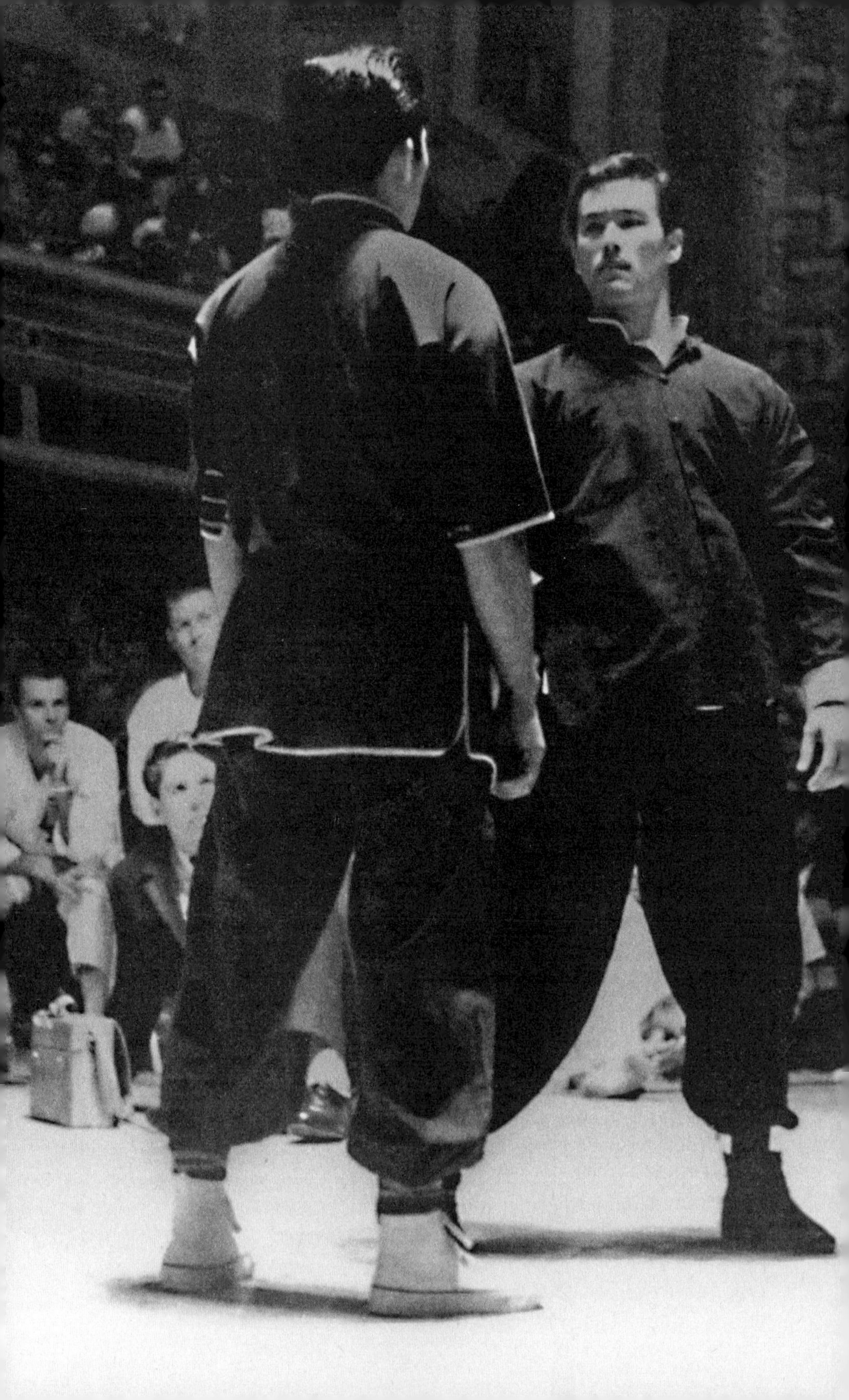

PART VI
A Bigger Stage
1964–1965

Do not press a desperate foe too hard.

—SUN TZU

Bruce and Taky in Long Beach, 1964.
Photo courtesy of the Bruce Lee Family Archive.

CHAPTER 20
Openings

On Saturday, August 1, 1964, thirteen days after he moved from Seattle to Oakland, Bruce arrived in Long Beach for Ed Parker's first International Karate Championships.

He came in like a summer storm, determined to have everyone leave that weekend knowing his name. He and Taky Kimura, who had come down from Seattle, were picked up by one of Ed Parker's most promising young black belts, a Filipino American named Dan Inosanto, who had been given a hundred dollars and instructions to show Bruce around the city. By the time Dan had driven them to a Chinese restaurant for dinner, Bruce was making another convert.

When they got out of the car, Bruce asked Dan to throw as hard a punch as he could—which Dan did, only to find himself, as countless others had before, completely trapped and immobilized. When they entered the restaurant Dan asked about the "one-inch punch" Bruce had mentioned. Before they reached their table, Bruce showed him, with one fluid snap that exploded into Dan's solar plexus like the end of a bullwhip. Dan took it better than almost anyone ever had—no pad or pillow, no flying tumble. But after dinner, he had to stop walking and sit down on the curb, so that he could grip his throbbing abdomen, stop his nausea, and vomit.

"Damn these sailors in Long Beach," one onlooker muttered, "always getting drunk!"

When Bruce wanted to show the one-inch punch in future demonstrations, Dan said, "I didn't want to do it anymore. So I was usually the guy who ran and got the phone book."

He rallied himself to deliver Bruce to the hotel for a gathering of grandmasters and star fighters in the ballroom for a showcase where masters would conduct short demonstrations. Bruce took note of the *tae kwon do* expert Jhoon Rhee executing a stunning triple combination of kicks—a roundhouse, a spinning back kick, and an arcing front kick. When the floor was his, he did the Closing the Gap demo with a volunteer and talked up the virtues of simplicity and directness. He unleashed Wing Chun punches that made Rhee think of "hyperactive electrons zipping around the nucleus of an atom."

In the audience was Barney Scollan, an eighteen-year-old white belt from Sacramento, another young American looking for the real thing. A recent high school graduate, the middle-class teen had come to the martial arts in much the same way Bruce had. "We cruised the streets downtown in hot rods and drag-raced," he recalled. "There were a lot of dances, a lot of drinking and stupid stuff. Periodically we'd get in fights for whatever reason." He had joined Al Tracy's karate school because he thought it might give him an advantage in these rumbles. But when he tried out his horse stance in a street fight, he got clobbered by the old American one-two.

After Bruce's demonstration, Barney ran to get Bruce's autograph and take a photo. Bruce invited him to the Oakland *kwoon*. Barney was excited—now he might finally learn something real. Others in the room had the same thought.

"That one," the Shotokan *karate* grandmaster Tsutomu Ohshima whispered to his senior student, "is the only one here who can do anything."

Ed Parker had gathered the most important American fighters from *karate, judo, jujitsu*, and the Filipino martial arts, including Rhee and US *karate* pioneer Robert Trias, who had both previously staged national competitions; esteemed teachers like Allen Steen, Anthony Mirakian, and Takayuki Kubota; trophy fighters Mike Stone, Joe Lewis, and Chuck Norris; and his own influential black belts, like Al and Will Tracy, who were building the largest network of *karate* schools in the country. Also in the crowd were Hollywood's most famous *karateka*, including the director Blake Edwards, the actor Robert Conrad, and the stylist Jay Sebring.

Even before the competitions started, it was already the largest, most diverse, most successful martial arts event in US history. Around the building, random encounters ignited sparks of inspiration. After Dan performed a demonstration of the Okinawan *nunchaku*, a Filipino master from Kauaʻi named Ben Largusa told him and Bruce, "You know we have that. It's called *tabak-toyok*." Then he took the sticks and showed them some basic *kali* forms as they gaped in amazement.

It was a watershed summit. For people of Asian, Native Hawaiian, and Pacific Islander descent and those devoted to their fighting arts, what would follow was like the moment between 1967 and 1972 when James Brown brought together sounds and rhythms from across the Black diaspora into what came to be called funk. A period of openness and synthesis in the martial arts had begun.

The next day three thousand people streamed into the Long Beach Municipal Auditorium. On the main floor, over eight hundred contestants competed in eight rings in point matches presided over by dozens of referees and judges.

"It was awesome. It was terrifying," recalled Barney, who was competing on a big stage for the first time. "Lots of black uniforms and white ones and green ones. It was pretty intimidating."

As the sun set over the Pacific, the contests were complete. The men from Hawaiʻi, who came from a fight culture that had been mixing martial arts for two generations, swept all the divisions. But before the final awards were announced, exhibitions would commence.

Takayuki Kubota took the floor first, inviting anyone from the audience to assault him with a knife. His demo ended early after the knife man took the mic to say it was too dangerous for *him* to continue. Jhoon Rhee's jump kicks and Tsutomu Ohshima's defense against two attackers wowed the crowd. Swinging his *kali* sticks in the style of his teacher, the grandmaster Floro Villabrille, Ben Largusa introduced Filipino martial arts to North American audiences.

But Ed Parker had placed the young no-name from Seattle who possessed knowledge of "the secret art of the Chinese," as *Black Belt* magazine put it, in the headliner slot. He loaded up three movie cameras to shoot what happened next. "I knew without a doubt," Parker later said, "that if he got on the movie screen, our industry would prosper." It was the start of a new era of Bruce on film.

Only two angles of the raw footage have surfaced—one from the stands and the other from the floor. The original sound appears lost, and key parts are missing. But the fragments are intriguing.

Bruce is in a black *jing mo* uniform. Taky Kimura appears in his blue uniform as his *uke*. We see Bruce snapping punches, and Bruce and Taky playing at *chi sao*. He is talking all the while.

Do you think you're strengthening yourself by doing all those punches? There are better ways. On the floor, he does two-finger push-ups on one arm.

What is the horse stance for? Bruce asks. *You do it for hours. How does it help you? Does it help you build your legs? Why don't you run up a hill instead?*

He leaps into the air with spinning kicks. He speeds through a Northern Shaolin form. *How do you fight with the forms you learn?* he asks.

He is gesturing firmly, as if exhorting the audience to rebel. *The individual*, he is saying, quoting Krishnamurti, *is more important than any style or system.*

You don't need a million forms and techniques. No high kicks, no twirling around, no set moves. A short kick or a straight punch can get the job done.

He calls for a volunteer—"a pretty big fellow," Barney said, "I'd say 180, 185 pounds"—and sets a chair behind him. *You don't have to throw a punch from the hip in a horse stance,* he says, *to have impact. You can create power from* right here, *from the hip to the waist to the fist.*

Bruce hits the volunteer with the one-inch punch. The man flies back into the chair, and it slides back several feet.

The faces in the audience were, like the man in the chair's, stricken with astonishment. It seemed like some sort of quantum phenomena—a leap beyond the basic physics of all the other martial arts. The young radical had introduced a different kind of equation, an uncertainty principle that might overturn all that had been thought settled.

When he was done, the crowd was quiet, then they broke into a roar of applause.

"You could see that half the people in the audience were just amazed and overcome by his skill," Barney recalled, "and the other half of the audience—faces were bright red, jaws were clenched, fists were clenched, and they had just been publicly humiliated by this young Chinese fellow in front of the masses that were gathered.

"Each instructor and each student thought his style was the best. So when Bruce got up and showed them why they weren't necessarily the best, that's what really got a lot of people upset," Barney said. "And a lot of other people rushed to become his students."

The young Filipino Puerto Rican boxer Joe Torrenueva was no stranger to the presence of stardom. As an apprentice to the Hollywood stylist Jay Sebring, he cut hair for Steve McQueen, Richard Burton, Frank Sinatra, Elvis Presley, and the Beach Boys. But Bruce left him dumbfounded.

"Everybody went home like, 'Shit! Did you see that?'" Joe said. "I went back that Monday or Tuesday to work and everybody was talking about it. I mean, the buzz was just unreal. Unreal!"

Dan Inosanto was so overwhelmed, he said, "I couldn't sleep that night."

As an athlete-scholar, Dan had packed a lot into his twenty-eight years. Raised on the wrong side of the tracks on Stockton's south side, Dan learned *jujitsu* and Okinawan *te* at the age of ten. He started boxing at eleven. At 115 pounds, he distinguished himself as his high school football team's leading rusher. At Whitworth College he won the conference title in the one-hundred-yard dash. He earned a master's degree in physical education at the University of the Pacific. He enlisted in the army and battled in bare-knuckle fight clubs at Fort Campbell. He studied *karate* under Hank Slomanski, Elvis Presley's first trainer, and become a *shodan* black belt under Ed Parker. He studied *gung fu* under Ark Wong, the Los Angeles contemporary of Lau Bun and T. Y. Wong. He trained in the Filipino martial arts under the most respected *manongs*: Johnny Lacoste, Angel Cabales, Leo Giron, and Max Sarmiento. But Bruce had turned his world upside down.

"It was like having learned an occupation for five years, and then having someone say, 'We no longer have any use for your occupation.' But in this case, I'd studied all these different arts—I won't say that they were worthless—but what he did was counter everything without really trying," Dan said. "It was very frustrating."

For Linda, the summer of '64 was "the summer of letters." Bruce wrote her daily, but she was still uncertain about his intentions. Her fears were getting the best of her. "I felt there was no need to tell my mom about Bruce now since he might never return," she said.

Bruce asked Taky what he should do. His friend was as clear as he could be: she had all the qualities that Bruce valued—"strength, honesty, purity, and loyalty." Taky said, "You've got a gem there. You'll never find anyone like her. She's got more going for her than any girl you'll find again."

Bruce finally wrote a letter to Linda proposing to her.

"There was no 'down on bended knee,'" Linda said. "It was in our letters. But Bruce wasn't a real gushy person."

"I *knew* I wanted to be with this man forever," she recalled. "Except there was the problem of my family, especially my mom." They could no longer avoid the issue of her family's racial views.

In the early years in Seattle, Bruce had carefully studied Jack Dempsey's seminal book, *Championship Fighting*, underlining passages on the falling step, the power line, ranges, feints, and footwork, using a ruler and red and blue pencils to overlay arrows and lines of balance and motion on the book's illustrations. Now he immersed himself in books about Jack Johnson, the first Black heavyweight champion of the world, seeking a different kind of instruction.*

During the height of Jim Crow, Jack Johnson's 1910 victory over the white boxer James Jeffries in the "Fight of the Century" had caused race riots in scores of cities, leaving twenty dead. The film of the fight became one of the country's first movie-theater blockbusters. Johnson had stirred controversy for his unapologetic affairs with white women in a time when Black men were being lynched for much less.

"How incongruous to think that I, a little Galveston colored boy[,] should ever become the acquaintance of kings and rulers of the old world," Johnson wrote in his autobiography. "How utterly fantastic would have been the thought that I should someday be plunged in romances and love with white women in defiance of a treasured and guarded custom."

At the same moment Bruce and Linda were discussing marriage, a woman of Rappahannock, Cherokee, Black, and Portuguese descent named Mildred Jeter Loving and her white husband, Richard Loving, were in the middle of a fight to save their marriage before the state. They had grown up together and fallen in love in Central Point, a tiny mixed-race town in rural Virginia. Knowing that Virginia was one of sixteen states that still prohibited marriage between white and "colored persons," they drove to the District of Columbia to be legally married in June 1958, then quietly returned to Central Point to live.

But within weeks of their return, local police raided their home and arrested the couple on felony charges. They pled guilty. The county judge sentenced them to a year each in jail, then suspended the sentence on the condition that they immediately leave Virginia and not return for twenty-five years. He lectured them sternly: "Almighty God created the races white, black, yellow, malay and red, and he placed them on separate continents. And, but for the interference with his arrangement, there would be no cause for such marriage. The fact that he separated the races shows that he did not intend for the races to mix."

The Lovings appealed their case through the state courts, where lawyers for Virginia argued that the state had legitimate interests "to preserve the racial integ-

---

* Bruce collected at least two different editions of Johnson's autobiography, *My Life in the Ring and Out*, as well as Finis Farr's *Black Champion* and Denzil Batchelor's *Jack Johnson and His Times*. These are all now in the collection of the Wing Luke Museum.

rity of its citizens," and to prevent "the corruption of blood," "a mongrel breed of citizens," and "the obliteration of racial pride." In June 1967, the Supreme Court unanimously gave Mildred and Richard their marriage back, overturning the state's anti-miscegenation laws.

It is difficult to overstate white antipathy for interracial marriage at the time. In 1969, two years after the *Loving v. Virginia* decision, a national Gallup poll found that only 19 percent of whites approved of marriage between a white and a non-white person.

Linda's family did not number among the enlightened.

In their letters, Bruce and Linda assembled a plan. He would return to Seattle, and they would visit the King County Courthouse to apply for a marriage license. They would have their ceremony and then fly back together to Oakland. They would inform her mother afterward.

"A friend of mine had done this a couple of months earlier and after the dust had settled, everyone had survived," Linda recalled. "It was a lousy plan, and I was scared."

Bruce wrote his family to tell them he was getting married to a Caucasian girl. Robert Chan, a close family friend, recalled, "His father, mother, and even the entire family were not happy about it." But their response to him was gratifying to Linda: "They replied that, even though they wished he would marry a Chinese, they would nevertheless welcome me to the family."

He put on a brave face and tried to reassure Linda. *Everything will be all right.* "I do think that we probably would not have gotten married at that time—but for the baby. 'Cause he really wanted his baby. So did I," Linda said.

On Tuesday, August 11, 1964, Bruce purchased two tickets on United Airlines for $122.33, a sum of money so large he likely had to borrow it from James.* He specified to the agent to list Linda's one-way ticket to Oakland under the name "Mrs. B. Lee." Early the next morning he flew out, and by the afternoon they were at the courthouse applying for their marriage license. Then they held on for a mandatory three-day waiting period. Their tickets for Oakland were booked for Monday, August 17, the day they would wed and leave Seattle.

But they had not realized that, right next to the obituaries, the newspaper printed notices of all who had applied for marriage licenses. By Friday morning her grandmother's sister Sally had called Linda's mother, Vivian, at Sears to say that she had just read in the Vital Statistics section of her paper that a certain Bruce J. F. Lee and Linda Emery who were soon to be married.

"What do you know about that?" Aunt Sally asked Vivian.

"What? Can't be!" Linda's mother screamed. "Can't be!"

---

* This is $1,237.30 in 2024 dollars.

She gathered her wits, stormed up to the third floor, and confronted Linda. "Is this you?"

Linda's worst fears had been realized. "We were going to elope and run away," she said. "But we got caught."

Vivian called a family meeting for Saturday, August 15. Everyone assembled at their new home in Capitol Hill—her stepfather, her grandmother Clara Nelson, and her uncle Harold and aunt Clara. At the center of the living room were Bruce and Linda. This was not the way she had wanted Bruce to meet the family.

"It was miserable," Linda said. "It was awful."

She confessed to her family that she and Bruce had been together for nearly a year and that she had hidden their relationship and lied to them. But through her tears, she insisted that they were in love and had every intention of getting married.

"I love Linda," Bruce said, "and I want to marry your daughter." Then he tried to lighten the mood. "I'm Chinese, by the way."

Linda's family was not going to tell her that she could not marry a Chinese man. That would have just been impolite. Instead, one by one, they made a version of the same argument. *You are only nineteen*, they said. *What difference would it make to wait a year?*

The questioning turned to Bruce. He knew how it looked—he had talked to Lanston about it—a Chinese man from Hong Kong who had dropped out of the University of Washington. *What was he going to do for a living? How was he going to support their daughter?* Bruce explained that he was setting up a chain of *gung fu* schools. But what had sounded so romantic to Linda on their first date now sounded very different in front of her family.

"They didn't know I was pregnant at the time," Linda said. "They did by the end of the day."

Her stepfather had discovered Linda's PO box and her letters from Bruce. He took them out and read their contents to the family. Then, Linda said, "The shit was flying."

Her mother fretted aloud over what it would mean for Linda to have a "yellow baby." The baby would be treated differently. *Did they really want that? Do you realize people will look down on you?* But Vivian was also seeing how determined the couple was. She tried one more appeal.

"Bruce, Linda doesn't know how to do anything," she said. "She doesn't know how to cook or iron or wash clothes."

Bruce coolly replied, "She'll learn."

Linda looked at him with pride and worry.

The intervention broke up without resolution, but there would be one last encounter. Linda's uncle Harold and aunt Claire, who were devout Christians, invited her to take a ride with them. As the half-moon rose in the darkening sky, Linda listened to her uncle say that a marriage like this was un-Christian, an abomination in the eyes of God. He told her that the family strongly believed that God had never intended for the races to mix. Her eyes widened in rage and she bit her lip.

"I heard later on," Linda said, "that my aunt and uncle were plotting to kidnap me so that I could not marry him." They thought better of it and dropped off a seething, even more resolute Linda at home.

When Sunday dawned, mother and daughter had more angry, tearful words. But then Linda told Vivian that she understood why her mother had felt betrayed. Vivian could see that her daughter would not change her mind.

"Well," she finally said, "if you're going to get married, you'd better do it in a church."

Linda's grandmother somehow secured the Congregational Church in the University District for the next day. On Monday, August 17, Bruce and Linda stood before a minister, with Taky Kimura, her mother, and her grandmother by their side. Bruce presented Linda with a ring he had borrowed from James's wife, Katherine. Vivian complained that Bruce hadn't even thought to bring flowers. But he had not even remembered to pack a suit. He and Taky had scrambled to rent one for the brief ceremony.

"Everything happened so quickly that I didn't even have a proper wedding dress," Linda recalled, "nor was there a photographer present."

As the sun disappeared behind the Olympic Mountains, Bruce and Linda were on a plane, exhaling as it banked toward Oakland.

CHAPTER 21
Training Floor

In the spring of 1963, civil rights demonstrators in Birmingham, Alabama, began a desegregation campaign with lunch counter sit-ins, marches, and boycotts. Young people in the Children's Crusade prepared themselves for confrontation by studying the theory and tactics of nonviolence. They were met with police, dogs, and water cannons. Some demonstrators held fast to the movement rule not to curse or strike back when attacked. Others threw bottles, rocks, and bricks. Self-defense took many forms.

After being arrested and placed in solitary confinement, Martin Luther King Jr. wrote a letter on whatever scraps of paper he could gather and addressed it to white moderates sitting on the fence. "Injustice anywhere is a threat to justice everywhere," he wrote. "We are caught in an inescapable network of mutuality, tied in a single garment of destiny. Whatever affects one directly, affects all indirectly."

In the fall, eighteen days after King ascended the steps of the Lincoln Memorial in the March on Washington to praise the rising tide of protest and tell the country of his dream, the Ku Klux Klan bombed Birmingham's Sixteenth Street Baptist Church, killing four young girls. On November 22, President John Kennedy was gunned down in Dallas, Texas. By the following summer, President Lyndon Johnson had signed the broadest civil rights act in history. He also escalated deployment of American "military advisers" to Vietnam. Protests against the draft and the war exploded. By the end of 1964, Barney Scollan was giving Bruce, James, and his fellow students firsthand accounts from the campus front lines in Berkeley, where students inspired by the civil rights and anti-war movements were facing off against police and sheriffs in something they called the Free Speech Movement.

But pictures of Bruce and Linda from this time show a domestic California idyll. In photos taken by Bruce, Linda poses in a brown tunic in the backyard of the Monticello home, barefoot on a freshly mowed lawn warmed by the afternoon sun, giving a hint of a smile. In another, the newlyweds sit together at the brick fireplace next to a console television, Bruce stretching his legs on a mottled shag carpet. Behind them, on the mantel above, there is a Chinese vase, a smiling Buddha, and a framed photo of him in his *jing mo* that he had used for the cover of his book.

Their world was a small one. "We didn't do much more than James Lee's house, the studio, Oakland Chinatown. We didn't really talk about current events. We didn't take a newspaper, and we hardly watched the news very much," Linda said. "It was just at that time in our lives there was a lot of other stuff going on."

Katherine Lee was in the advanced stages of breast cancer. During the day James was at his welding job, trying to earn enough to cover the mortgage and the hospital bills. His two children, Karena and Greglon, were now eleven and ten. Linda, whose mother had expressed doubts about her nineteen-year-old's ability to run a house, was pressed into caregiving duties, getting the kids fed and off to school, and making dinner for all of them from the groceries James brought home.

"I was learning how to cook now, ravaging Betty Crocker's cookbooks," Linda recalled. "When I think back, my god, the things I fed those people."

Bruce and Linda were dead broke. To bring in income, he was teaching students downstairs in the garage and building the school on Broadway. On October 5, Katherine passed away. Devastated, James often drank himself to sleep. After long days Bruce and Linda stole away late at night to the Silver Dragon Café in Oakland's Chinatown for a bit of *siu yeh* comfort.

The training floor was a release.

Bruce had written to William Cheung saying that he had enrolled at the University of California at Berkeley to complete a degree in philosophy. He was still trying to impress his *sihing*, who was securing multiple university degrees in Australia. But the truth was that Bruce had thrown himself completely into his advanced studies in the fighting arts.

When Bruce and James opened the storefront for their school on Broadway, they did not add any signage to the front. Bruce wanted control over the class. James's longtime students, including Bob Baker, Leo Fong, Ernest Benavidez, David Cox, and Al Novak, were the first to come, along with his closest friends, Allen Joe and George Lee. Bruce decided to screen and interview each new student. Once he'd vetted them, he gave them a cassette tape of himself speaking about the institute's methods and philosophy, including the ideas of *yin* and *yang*.

For over a year Bruce and James had been exchanging their respective knowledges of Wing Chun and Southern *sil lum* with each other. Now that they were together their practice accelerated. "Within the first year I had begun to realize that James and Bruce were methodically cutting away at the superficial movements and getting to the pure 'raw' essence of fighting," one student, Ernest Benavidez, recalled.

Bruce or James might discuss an idea, then jump up to test it, pulling in other students to explore possibilities, reducing and simplifying round by round. "I was amazed that two men could generate so much energy from one subject," Bob Baker recalled. "It was impossible for anyone to keep up with them."

James, Allen, and George introduced Bruce to weight training. While the older men were at work, Bruce spent his days working out. He amused them showing off his physique-building progress. They called themselves the Four Musketeers. In Oakland's Chinatown, where the rest of the guys were already notorious, Bruce became known as the jumpy new kid with a big appetite who liked high-kicking parking meters and shopkeepers' potted plants to and from the restaurant.

James had filled his garage and the new space with training contraptions he had made at home. George was also a skilled machinist, and after he gifted Bruce with a cashbox and a polished wood sculpture of the institute's logo, Bruce presented him with ideas of things he wanted—punching pads, shields, leg stretchers, and a forearm-building grip machine that Bruce could use while reading or watching television. After returning from the Long Beach tournament, he drew George a picture of two sticks connected by a chain. For the next nine years, George made and refined *nunchakus* for Bruce.

Bruce would show up at Wally Jay's doorstep in Alameda, waiting for him to return from his post office job. On the basement mats Wally drilled Bruce on grappling and throwing techniques. At night Bruce and James sometimes gathered everyone at the house to scrutinize 8mm reels of boxing fights that Bruce collected featuring Muhammad Ali, Jack Dempsey, and Sugar Ray Robinson.

"There were times where Bruce was changing so much from day to day and it was incredible that one man could grow so much in the span of three years," said Bob Baker, whom Bruce would later tap for the role of the Russian boxer in *Fist of Fury*. "We never worried about serious injury and that is probably the reason that progress was made at such a great pace."

One of the students who most intrigued Bruce was Leo Fong, a tall man with hard hands who spoke with a distinctive Southern accent. Leo had met James Yimm Lee in 1960 at T. Y. Wong's Kin Mon school. He noticed James in a corner, practicing a form. When James finished, he picked up heavy dumbbells and started the same form again. That day they became longtime friends.

Bruce was teaching the Oakland students to fight with their strong hand forward, a stance the right-handed Leo resisted. But when Bruce saw Leo turn his knockout punch—a devastating left hook—on another student, he said, "OK, Leo, you can stand however you like," and asked him to be the assistant instructor.

"I can't, Bruce," Leo told him in his molasses drawl. "I'm busy with my church on weekends."

Leo had arrived in the States from Guangdong on May 1, 1934, at the age of five. His father had purchased papers in 1918 and worked in restaurants across the Midwest before finally bringing his wife and children over. By then his father had moved to Arkansas, where his cousins had opened grocery stores that served Blacks who could not shop at white ones.

"All the Chinese had a gentleman's agreement," Leo said. "At no time can two Chinese open up a store to compete against each other." That was how his father found himself in Parkin, Arkansas, a small town in cotton country, which he didn't know was run by the Ku Klux Klan.

A few days after he opened his shop, a brick came through the window, and he looked out to see a posse of men yelling, "Get out of town, Chinaman!" For a while he slept on the porch in a rocking chair, double-barrel shotgun on his lap. But he decided instead to try again thirty miles away in a town called Widener, and sent for his wife and son.

On the first Friday after Leo arrived, the town butcher came by the store and asked the five-year-old, "Hey boy, what's your name?"

He replied with his given name, "Fung Tin Lung"—*sky dragon*.

"I can't understand you," the white man said, "I'ma call you Leo from now on." His citizenship papers would list his name as Leo Tim Fong, all necessary concessions made.

Young Leo was sent to a white school because he was not allowed to attend a Black one.* "I went to school the first day. I had a lot of attention at recess time," he remembered. "They would call me 'boy' and 'chink.' Then they would sing, 'Ching chong Chinaman!' I said, 'Damn, they like me!'"

When he got home his father asked him in Cantonese how his first day had been. "Good! They sang to me!"

"They sang to you? What did they sing to you?"

When Leo told him, his father's face turned red and he scolded the boy. "They don't like you," he said. "They're demeaning your race."

The next day Leo went to his PE class, where they were setting up a softball game using cow chips for bases. Leo was given a glove and sent to first base. A boy hit the ball and ran to first, and Leo's tag came too late. The boy laughed at him and shouted, "Chink!"

Leo punched him in the face. "That was the beginning of my boxing career," he chuckled.

The skinny Chinese kid became known for decking racists in the school hallways, on the way to school, and on the way back home: "From then on, they say, 'Hey, don't fuck around with that Chinaman. He hits you and he fights dirty!'"

As a teen he studied the Jewish boxer Barney Ross's book, *Fundamentals of Boxing*, and joined illegal fights in abandoned barns. By the time he got to Hendricks College, he was prizefighting at five foot ten and 112 pounds. Through weight training, he got up to 135 and earned twenty-five wins—eighteen by knockout—with four losses. On the brink of turning pro, he caught religion and enrolled at the seminary at Southern Methodist University. Upon graduation, he was assigned to the Chinese United Methodist Church in Sacramento.

---

* Leo's story is indicative of the strange place Chinese Americans occupied between Black and white in the South and, by extension, all of the United States. Just twelve years before, in the 1927 *Gong Lum v. Rice* decision, the Supreme Court had unanimously rejected a petition from a Chinese American family in Mississippi to have their daughter classified as white in order to attend white schools. Rather than have her attend Black schools, the Lums moved away.

"I didn't want to go. I was pissed off," he said. "I wanted to stay with all my buddies."

But in Northern California, Leo found the Asian martial arts. One weekend, after being invited to guest-preach at a Black church in San Francisco—where the congregation warmly welcomed the Chinese American who sermonized with the fire and brimstone of a real Southern preacher—he discovered Lau Bun's school.

For three years he came down from Sacramento to San Francisco to learn Choy Li Fut. He noticed that new students spent the first few months studying just the horse stance. One night after Lau Bun had left for the evening he was talking to one of the senior students. "How long you been studying here?" Leo asked.

"Ten years."

"How many sets you know?"

"I know five sets," the senior said. "Hey, you and me, let's spar."

"How do you spar with this?"

"Well, first you get in a horse stance."

Leo ended the fight quickly with simple boxing footwork and a couple of jabs. "That's when," he said, "I learned the difference between art and combat."

He joined T. Y. Wong's Kin Mon school and studied *sil lum gung fu*. But when James stormed out, Leo left too. For the next eight years, as he was reassigned across Northern California to bigger churches, Leo drove hundreds of miles each week to study at *tae kwon do, karate, judo,* and *gung fu* schools. He even sparred regularly with the Sacramento State College boxing team. After months of Friday night sessions in Oakland, Bruce asked Leo, "Hey, Leo, how come you train in so many styles?"

"I'm just trying to find the best stuff and put it together."

Bruce put his finger in Leo's chest and said, "Leo, take your boxing skill, learn to kick a little bit, learn to grapple. You don't need to pay these turkeys twenty-five dollars a month. It's all a classical mess. Effective fighting is the ability to express one's techniques like a sound and an echo."

Bruce and James, Leo recalled, freed their students. "They did not insist we punch and kick just like them," Leo recalled. "They gave us the concept, and we were to develop our own identity."

While Bruce, James, and Wally Jay were turning Oakland into a new mecca for Asian martial arts, San Francisco's Chinatown had entered a period of profound change that would not slow until the end of the century.

In November 1961, a hit movie put a new spotlight on Chinatown, seeming to pry open the neighborhood's secrets to white tourists. The success of the film adaptation of the Rodgers and Hammerstein musical *Flower Drum Song*—inspired by real Cotton Club–type establishments like Charlie Low's Forbidden City—brought Grant Avenue into white Middle America. But at the same time, the real streets of Chinatown were becoming gang battlegrounds.

Through the 1950s, youth gangs—with names like the Raiders, the 880s, the Fong-Fong Boys, and the Immortals—had been founded by disaffected American-born Chinese, who now called themselves simply ABCs. These youths flocked into the *gung fu kwoons* and changed the balance of power between *sifu* and student. The old masters no longer exerted the control they once had. Some of their students became active participants in public violence.

In 1962, a presidential directive from John F. Kennedy brought a new wave of refugees from Hong Kong to Chinatowns across the country. This migration signaled the beginning of changes that would transform Asian America. At Galileo High School, Chinese gangs had once fought with Irish, Italian, and Black gangs. Now they had split and fought between themselves, ABCs and FOBs.

The turning point came in 1964, when a powerful new gang, the Wah Ching, Cantonese for "immigrant youth," announced itself. They took over the Chinese Playground on Sacramento and Waverly, the main gathering place for local youths, and established their dominance everywhere with brutal beatdowns of ABCs in schoolyards, gambling halls, back alleys, and movie theaters.

"It used to be that the American-born would beat up on the immigrants," said Joe Louie, founder of what had once been the largest gang, the Raiders. "Now it's just the opposite." Youths on both sides swelled the ranks of the *gung fu kwoons*. All of Chinatown became their fight arena.

In 1965, the epochal passage of the Hart-Celler Act finally eliminated racist quotas against non-white immigrants. Asian American communities swelled, and in the succeeding decades, would change dramatically with new waves of migration. Until this moment, sociologists had named the primary social divide in this mostly US-born Asian population as falling along generational lines. Afterward, new schisms would also break along divides of nativity.

Between 1964 and 1969, arrests and citations of young Chinese in San Francisco increased sixfold. "This was now a different ball game," wrote Bill Lee, who would become a member of an infamous gang, the Joe Boys. "These guys grew up on the rough streets of Hong Kong and Macao where gangs were hardcore. Many had spent a good part of their youths in brutal prisons. This was now their Chinatown."

In Seattle Bruce had been the man. Even those he had defeated, like the *karateka* Yoichi Nakachi, had come around. After the bloody YMCA match that put him in the hospital, Nakachi had asked Bruce to be his teacher.

But in San Francisco's Chinatown, a much bigger stage, Bruce received no such deference. Leo Fong and Ed Parker had heard people there talking trash about him. Lau Bun and his students had not forgotten his failed challenge. T. Y. Wong was calling him "a dissident with bad manners." Chinatown was already divided against itself, and the fighters there didn't give a shit who Bruce thought he was.

The feeling was mutual. "Bruce didn't like San Francisco. He didn't like Chinatown," Linda said. "He didn't like the Chinese there."

One of Bruce's favorite conversation topics with James was how backward Chinatown's *gung fu* men were. They were anti-science, hiding behind mysticism, esoterica, supposedly ancient and unknowable secrets of *qi*. They set forth ironclad protocols and principles. They kept students busy with formal drills, exercises, techniques, and sets that did nothing but obscure the real lessons to be learned.

"The end is efficiency in fighting," Bruce complained. "But their means is making the students do all these way-out forms. As the forms become less and less real, they drift further away from the end."

"Not only that," James replied, "they focus on all these unrelated standards, like 'his horse stance is not flat,' or 'the internal energy is not flowing' or 'his hand's not on his hip.' Then if one of them gets knocked out, he'll probably say something like, 'Yeah, but he was off balance when he hit me!'"

These old men were just protecting their power and prestige. They were holding everyone back. They stood in the way of freedom. They needed to be toppled and replaced.

Young Bruce had, like Shakespeare's soldier, reached his "fourth age." He was "full of strange oaths," "jealous in honour," and "sudden and quick in quarrel." That was how he found himself facing the young Jing Wu star Wong Jack Man in his Oakland *gung fu* studio at the end of a winter's day in November 1964.

CHAPTER 22
The Boxer from Toisan

On the summer day in August 1964 when Bruce was leaving Long Beach, Dan Inosanto had come to him with a request: "I want to learn more from you." Bruce had just landed a gig that might make it possible.

He had been hired to support a tour for the Hong Kong sensation Diana Chang Chung-Wen, the curvaceous leading lady who was touring the West Coast to promote her steamy new Shaw Brothers movie, written by Chang Cheh, called *The Amorous Lotus Pan*. Bruce had been asked to be her cha-cha partner and sideman for her appearances in Los Angeles, San Francisco, and Seattle. He pitched her advance team on presenting a *gung fu* demonstration as part of the act, and they agreed.

James and Taky would be working, so Bruce told Dan, "If you dummy for me, I'll teach you all the good martial arts."

The first set of performances, held at the Sing Lee Theater in Los Angeles's Chinatown, went smoothly. The third, at the Kokusai in Seattle, was a hit with the hometown crowd. But in between, at San Francisco Chinatown's Sun Sing Theatre—the former Mandarin Theatre, the same stage on which his father had performed twenty-five years before—he would face a hostile audience.

When Bruce and Dan began their demonstration on Saturday afternoon, August 29, 1964, the matinee crowd was already warm and the theater was swathed in a cigarette haze. Diana Chang had already sung her hits and danced the cha-cha with Bruce.

Bruce's main goal was to recruit students for his institute. But many local *gung fu* adherents were in the audience, including, the journalist Charles Russo recounted, a large group of students from Bing Chan's Lup Mo studio, an offshoot of Lau Bun's Choy Li Fut school. They had already heard stories of Bruce's cockiness. They had arrived ready for something to jump off.

Bruce introduced his Jun Fan *gung fu*, which he noted they could learn more about by purchasing his book. It was direct and simple, he said, free of the confusion created by the old "classical mess." He made some arcing Northern Shaolin kicks, which Dan easily ducked and countered. "Why would you kick high and leave yourself open? Instead you can kick low and punch high," he said, demonstrating on Dan.

Bruce said, "In China, eighty percent of what they are teaching is nonsense. Here in America, it is ninety percent." The audience began to stir. Bruce punctuated the point: "These old tigers, they have no teeth."

Those were fighting words, fire-calling in a crowded theatre. The protest began with a single cigarette butt sailing through the air onto the stage, followed by a shower of them. A shout rang out: "That's not *gung fu*! That's *karate*!"

Dan, suddenly alert to the crowd, could see Bruce losing his temper.

"I will show you what *gung fu* is," Bruce yelled back. "Get up here right now!"

The shouter stood up, still jawing, but walked out. Bruce called to the audience for a volunteer. Kenneth Wong from the Lup Mo school stood up.

"We began cheering and hollering, egging him on," said Adeline Fong, one of his classmates. Kenneth ran up and made an ostentatious leap onto the stage. The Lup Mo students hooted. The rest of the crowd settled in for a show.

Bruce set up Kenneth for his Closing the Gap exercise. He stepped back. But when he lunged forward for the tap, the Lup Mo student successfully blocked him.

The crowd howled.

Bruce stepped back to try a second time. Kenneth blocked it again. They roared.

One more time. Blocked again. Mayhem. Kenneth now raised his fists and fell into a ready position.

Discomposed and backing off, Bruce said, "Thank you for participating."

Kenneth departed the stage triumphantly as a torrent of cigarettes flew toward it.

But now Bruce had to finish. He kept to the script, again pitching his new book for sale. But in the moment, and then in the many tellings and retellings afterward, his words seemed to acquire a darker intention.

"I would like to let everybody know that any time my Chinatown brothers want to try out my Wing Chun," Bruce said, "they are welcomed to come find me at my school in Oakland."

Chinatown was abuzz.

In the Sun Sing Theatre Kenneth Wong had been a hero, but Bing Chan dressed down his student for backing down from a fight with the big-talker from across the Bay. At T. Y. Wong's Kin Mon school, talk about James Yimm Lee's brash associate also ran hot. At the Gee Yau Seah Academy—the Soft Arts Academy—where *tai chi* masters and their students gathered, a group of young junior students led by a man named David Chin were even more agitated. Hadn't this guy insulted their elders and then dared them to come to Oakland? Maybe, David told his brothers, this guy should come to the Gee Yau Seah to demonstrate the effectiveness of Wing Chun.

David Chin was a twenty-one-year-old adept of Hop Gar, Fut Gar, and *tai chi*. He was known to be fight crazy. Later, after things had heated up, Leo Fong told Bruce that Chin was a "troublemaker" who had once challenged him, only to back out when the time came. He offered a distinctly un-Christian name for Chin—"Chickenshit son of a bitch." But, Wong Jack Man's biographer Rick Wing wrote, "The men at the Gee Yau Seah believed they were responding to a challenge, not instigating it."

Bing Chan helped with the wording of the challenge. Ronald "Ya Ya" Wu, David's friend, wrote it in brush calligraphy. Then they took the letter to the Jackson Café, where Chinatown's fastest rising young martial arts star worked as a waiter, a recent immigrant named Wong Jack Man.

Decades later, the story of the fight between Bruce Lee and Wong Jack Man had cohered into three overlapping but distinct narratives—Bruce's, as told by Linda; Wong's, as told by his students; and David Chin's, as reported by Charles Russo and Matthew Polly, each weighted by their narrators' fears, illusions, and aspirations.

The tale of Bruce's Sun Sing encounter was not central to these narratives until it emerged in the English-language media seven years after Bruce's death, as a passing detail in a 1980 *Inside Karate* article by Wong Jack Man's student Michael Dorgan written to resuscitate his *sifu*'s tarnished reputation. It was retold more fully in a 2013 book, *Showdown in Oakland*, by Rick Wing, one of Wong Jack Man's closest senior students. In 2016, Charles Russo wrote the definitive account in his book, *Striking Distance*.

The record they sought to correct had been set down by Linda Lee in her biography, *Bruce Lee: The Man Only I Knew*. It turned on a serious contention: that the fight between Bruce Lee and Wong Jack Man had been about whether Bruce could be allowed to teach *gung fu* to white people.

She wrote:

> Until Bruce began to teach it, kung fu was almost a secret art, cherished by the Chinese. . . .
>
> For good historical reasons, the Chinese have been always reluctant to divulge these secrets to foreigners. In the last century, Chinese immigrants to California and other Western States were often the subjects of merciless pogroms by Caucasians who saw these gentle, hard-working, pig-tailed people as the advance guard of The Yellow Peril—and, what was more to the point, cheap labor China itself was subject to increasing foreign exploitation, particularly by the British, from 1870 onwards and secret societies, practicing kung fu and other martial arts, were formed to help eject the "foreign devils" from the ancient land. . . .

To Linda, China's traumatic humiliation at the hands of the Western colonizers in the Boxer Rebellion provided a six-decade-old context for the fight. She continued:

> Since then—and the attitude is understandable—Chinese, particularly in America, have been reluctant to disclose these secrets to Caucasians. . . .
>
> Bruce considered such thinking completely outmoded. . . .

In her telling, Wong Jack Man had reluctantly challenged Bruce as a matter of racial pride:

> Wong had just recently arrived in San Francisco's Chinatown from Hong Kong and was seeking to establish himself at the time, all his pupils being strictly pure Chinese. Three other Chinese accompanied Wong Jack Man who handed Bruce an ornate scroll announcing a challenge in Chinese. Bruce read the scroll which appears to have been an ultimatum from the San Francisco martial arts community. Presumably, if Bruce lost the challenge, he was either to close down his Institute or stop teaching Caucasians.
> Bruce looked at Wong Jack Man: "Is this what you want?"
> Wong Jack Man seemed almost apologetic. "Well, no, this is not what I want—but I'm representing these people here," and he indicated his Chinese comrades.
> "OK, then," said Bruce.

Linda had not been in the Sun Sing for Bruce's failed demonstration. "I don't know exactly what he did, but there was resentment," she said years later. "But the main thing that I always knew was that they told him he was not supposed to teach non-Chinese."

A perfect contest narrative emerged—the modernist vs. the traditionalist, the maverick vs. the protector, the integrationist vs. the separatist, the fluid man vs. the classical man. It elevated an ordinary challenge into one with high stakes.

As thousands were marching across the country to racially desegregate American institutions, Bruce appeared as the hero opening Chinese martial arts to the West, liberating *gung fu* from the close-minded separatists for the good of everyone, all while pushing a backward and bigoted Chinese American community toward its inevitable assimilationist future. It was a very old narrative in the mold of Perry-in-Edo and Nixon-in-China. It would be repeated until it hardened into orthodoxy. It just wasn't true.

The sensitive, empathetic, culturally proficient Linda likely never intended for the story to be read this way. But when the fight is placed back into the history of Asians in America, it becomes clear that the challenge was just a challenge. The combatants were much more alike than they seemed, even if fate would serve them very differently.

Wong Jack Man was born in Toisan on December 1, 1941, and had immigrated to San Francisco by the early 1960s. He had distinguished himself in Hong Kong as a star student of Northern Shaolin styles in the lineage of the original Iron Palm national hero, Gu Ruzhang. He had started at the age of eight, became a senior student at the age of fifteen, and by the age of twenty-three was a master of multiple systems.

"I came to America to be united with my family," he said, "and I was asked by my teachers, Yim Sheung Mo and Ma Kin Fung, to spread the Northern Shaolin, Taijiquan and Xingyiquan to America and the world." He wanted to establish a school along the lines of the famous Jing Wu academies of China's republican era.

Wong Jack Man has been portrayed as a traditionalist, but the lineage he claimed was hardly ancient. The Jing Wu Association, called the Jing Mo Tai Yuk Woey in Cantonese communities, was birthed in revolutionary Shanghai in 1909, and after the May 4 uprising, spread to the major coastal cities, then Malaysia, Singapore, and Vietnam, and finally worldwide. It found common cause with a modernist, anti-imperialist movement led by intellectuals and cosmopolitan urbanites called the New Culture movement. They wanted to dispel the embarrassment of the Boxer Rebellion, dispose of the old, the superstitious, and the oppressive, and mobilize healthy Chinese masses to rise against the Japanese imperialists and their treasonous local warlord vassals. They renounced formal and flowery rhetoric and adopted language that was direct, authentic, and scientific.

They opposed secreting away the fighting arts. The leaders of Jing Wu—it meant "the best of martial arts"—wanted to pull *gung fu* styles and systems into the public, test and elevate the best of them, and, through a standardized curriculum, make them available to every Chinese person. (They also called for women's rights and opened their classes to women.) Northern Shaolin styles were the foundation, but instructors of different styles were welcome. The schools became incubators and training grounds for thousands of instructors and students.

The Jing Wu fighters built structure and pedagogy. They dressed in modern high-collared, long-sleeved, loop-buttoned uniforms later known in the States as *jing mo*, the Cantonese rendering of *jing wu*. The schools created a system of ranking and promotion to incentivize more learning. They produced mass publications. When students were not practicing, they studied martial arts posters and manuals.

Bruce was directly influenced by their legacy. He collected and read their books and adopted their official graduation certificates for his Jun Fan Gung Fu Institute. His mentor Siu Hon-Sang had studied at Hong Kong's Jing Wu Association, become a *sifu* there, and taught Bruce from its curriculum.

The Jing Wu hero was the Northern Shaolin martial artist Huo Yuanjia, the "yellow-faced tiger," who, according to legend, cofounded the school after using his skill, instinct, and intellect to publicly humiliate a Russian fighter who had slandered his people as "the sick men of Asia." After seeing a Japanese doctor to treat his jaundice, Huo died suddenly at the age of forty-two, leaving some of his martial arts followers to speculate that he had been poisoned. It was master Huo's death that the character played by Bruce in *Fist of Fury*, a fictional Jing Wu student Chen Zhen, sought to avenge. The film was released in Asia as *Jing Wu Men*, "The Gates of Jing Wu."

Bruce had just briefly trained in Wing Chun and, under his uncle Siu, in Northern Shaolin. To some in the Chinese martial arts community, Bruce's abbreviated *gung fu* study made him a mere autodidact whose prestige was disproportionate to his formal achievement. Wong, on the other hand, represented the best formal training in Chinese martial arts that one could receive. Word was that he knew more than fifty forms from multiple styles. Wong was pedigreed like an Ivy Leaguer. Next to him, Bruce looked like a college dropout.

When Wong Jack Man arrived in San Francisco's Chinatown, the Northern stylist was in high demand. "I was the new kid in town," Wong told Michael Dorgan. "I was the only one doing these public shows." The five-foot-ten fighter was polished, a photographer's dream. In one picture he jumps into a high kick, his right boot thrusting straight up to the sky. In another, he strikes a Crane pose in the Gee Yau Seah before a painting of Lao Tzu, his left leg perfectly counterbalancing his thrusting arms—the picture of Chinese grace and power.

To some, Bruce was an unrefined, back-alley brawler who belonged with those provincial Oakland Chinese. But when Wong Jack Man appeared in his modish *jing mo* executing one of the forms from a corpus of excellence, he looked familiar and futuristic. Modest, pious, and masterful, he was authentically, gallantly Chinese.

Wong was a regular at the Gee Yau Seah Academy. But despite the admiration he attracted, Dorgan recalled, he "had kind of a loner's personality. He didn't fit in well and he wasn't chatty." It is not clear why he entertained David Chin, Bing Chan, and Ronald "Ya Ya" Wu's proposal when they came to see him that day at the Jackson Café. None of them had been at the Sun Sing, but they told him of Bruce's "tigers with no teeth" comment and that Bruce had issued a sweeping challenge. Wong signed on to their letter. Perhaps he had been a little naïve.

David Chin told the writer Matthew Polly that he had been the one who intended to challenge Bruce and that he had only stepped aside at Wong's insistence. He said that Wong wanted to open a school and believed that winning this fight might be the best way to do it. But this telling seems out of character for the Jing Wu man. Wong's version was simpler. He told Dorgan, "The Chinatown martial arts community decided it needed to respond and that I was the best-qualified person to exchange skills with Bruce Lee."

Bruce would receive two challenge letters from David Chin. Both Wong Jack Man and David Chin would deny that either of these letters threatened Bruce to stop teaching non-Chinese. This feels credible: even if they had wanted to, an unaffiliated immigrant fighter and a junior student from a *tai chi* school had no power to make such a threat, much less back it up.

It is even harder to imagine the San Francisco Chinatown *gung fu* community, in a state of generational transition, and heightened tensions between US-born and immigrants coming together to sanction a small school on the other side of the

Bay. Nor did they have any strategic advantage—moral, physical, financial, or even cultural—to leverage Bruce. They had nothing Bruce needed or wanted. They also knew that the kinds of men who trained with Bruce and James were big, brutish, and serious.

So Bruce ignored their first letter, without any consequences. In fact, he seemed to have already scrubbed the bad parts of the Sun Sing performance from his mind. "I did not write because I was on tour," he wrote to Taky in a September 18 letter. "They flipped in Los Angeles and San Francisco after the performance."

The second time, David Chin personally came across the bridge to Oakland to present the letter to him, apparently quite motivated to make something happen. Chin found Bruce at his desk reading a novel from Jin Yong's *wuxia* series, *Legend of the Condor Heroes*. After Bruce scanned the letter, he chuckled. He scribbled a note back to Wong Jack Man accepting the challenge and thrust it in Chin's face, saying, "Okay, set the date."

Bruce had one condition. He would not go to San Francisco. Perhaps he had Sun Tzu in mind: "It is a military axiom not to advance uphill against the enemy, nor to oppose him when he comes downhill." If they were going to try to beat him, they needed to meet him on the side of the bridge where the new day began.

Ben Der had moved back to San Francisco. In the weeks before the fight, Ronald "Ya Ya" Wu asked him to teach him some Wing Chun. Ben found this strange. Ya Ya was not known for being interested in martial arts, just for hanging out.

"I'm not that good," Ben remarked.

"Not good is better than nothing!" Ya Ya said. "Show me!"

He took Ben to the Chin-Woo-Yuen Family Association building, David Chin's clan's hall. One Choy Li Fut *sifu* jumped up when Ben walked in, and after a warm greeting, asked him to demonstrate his Wing Chun. Realizing exactly what they wanted and feeling his loyalty to Bruce, Ben backed up, said his farewells, and left.

The day before the fight Ben visited another social club. There was only one topic on everyone's lips—the fighting skills of Wong Jack Man. "'Fifteen-year Northern Shaolin, Iron Palm, the guy was supposed to be very good at kicking,'" Ben recalled them saying. "'How exciting, Bruce Lee will be beat up by Wong Jack Man!'"

At the end of a cold day in November 1964, Wong Jack Man arrived at the Broadway studio in Oakland. The streets were empty in the gathering dark. Wong had ridden shotgun in David Chin's new Pontiac Tempest muscle car, with Chin behind the wheel and four of his friends squeezed in the back—Ya Ya, Chan "Baldhead" Keung, a Gee Yau Seah *tai chi* practitioner who was twice Chin's age, and two other friends eager for a show.

Before this lonely stretch of Broadway was overtaken by car dealerships, the modest Jun Fan Gung Fu Institute studio had been an upholstery shop. It was long, perhaps fifteen feet by thirty, with two showcase windows facing the street, and a door in between that opened to a step down into the main room. The room was mostly bare, just a few stools. Barre railings had been mounted on the walls for stretching. The floorboards were uneven. Toward the back was a desk and two doors on the far wall—one that led to a cloakroom, another opening to an outdoor staircase that descended into a yard area.

Waiting inside were a "very pregnant" Linda, James, and Bruce. A second group of Chin's friends arrived shortly after Wong and Chin. Wong Jack Man would only remember the Lees and the people he had driven in with. Linda recalled thirteen people in attendance, though she did not learn the names of any of those who had come from San Francisco. Other accounts placed George Lee on-site, but Linda did not recall him being there. Bruce had asked Leo Fong to be there, and Chin's presence gave him a strong incentive, but church duties kept him in Stockton. Another man, William Chen, who claimed to be part of the second Chinatown group, recalled fifteen people. David Chin insisted Chen had never been there and would complain about the many people who had inserted themselves into the story long after the fact.

James bolted the door. Linda took a seat near the desk. James went to stand by Linda's side. The Chinatown group gathered near the doorway. Wong Jack Man was dressed in his dark *jing mo*, Bruce in a white tank top and jeans. David Chin began to formally announce their arrival and introduce Wong Jack Man.

Linda recalled, "They had a scroll that said, 'We're challenging you.'" In it, she said, was an ultimatum laid out in Chinese: if Bruce lost he was to stop teaching. But hers is the only account that mentions such a scroll. David Chin would deny it ever existed.

In Wong's version of the story, he asked Bruce if he had called for a challenge on the stage at the Sun Sing. Bruce denied that he had. "At that point," Wong said, "I thought he did not really want to spar or exchange skills with me. Our group all started to leave but then the person who let us in locked the door." James had ensured they would not be able to leave without disgracing themselves.

In Bruce's version, he asked Wong if he had personally heard Bruce issue a challenge at the Sun Sing. Wong replied that he had not been there but had heard Bruce said something similar, and "therefore had to punish [him]."

The accounts *do* agree on what happened next. David Chin began enumerating rules in English—no finger jabs, no shots to the groin.

"Shut your mouth!" Bruce said. "You have already gotten your friend killed." He turned to Wong and said, "He is going to ruin your life."

Bruce then shouted, "You came here to challenge me in my school and now you want to set the rules? There's no rules. It's all out!"

CHAPTER 23
The Fight

Afterward, Wong Jack Man would say that he had come only for a friendly comparison. He had told friends he would not even use his most devastating weapon—his Northern Shaolin kicks. Perhaps Wong was thinking mercifully and Bruce's rage was a surprise to him. But he had also put on wristbands studded with metal rivets and hidden them under his long sleeves.

"It was *not* a friendly atmosphere," David Chin told Charles Russo. "The challenge was real."

Chin asked them to shake hands. When Wong bowed and reached out his hand to Bruce, Bruce gestured as if he would return the courtesy, but then quickly threw either a punch or finger-spear jab straight at Wong's eyes. Wong lunged back and felt pain and blood on his temple. He had been put on the defensive, he thought, unfairly.

"He really wanted to kill me," Wong said. "He would never say he lost until you killed him. I remember thinking, 'If he injures me, if he really hurts me, I'll have to kill him.'"

Bruce had always shared Leo Fong's feeling about what the Southern white boys had called his "dirty fighting"—it was the excuse of losers. "Speed is the essence of war," Sun Tzu had counseled. "Take advantage of the enemy's unreadiness, make your way by unexpected routes, and attack unguarded spots."

Wong's Northern Leg style made him most dangerous from middle range, where his long kicks and punches could do damage. Bruce's Southern Fist style of Wing Chun required him to fight close. Wong's style was of arcs and circles, Bruce's arrow-straight lines.

Bruce attacked with flurries of straight punches to Wong's chest and jabs at his eyes and throat. Wong backed up in a zigzag way, trying to sidestep Bruce's attacks. He parried Bruce's kicks with his knees, Bruce's punches with windmill blocks. Then he switched to trying to clinch up Bruce.

Wong told Michael Dorgan that he locked Bruce's head with his left arm. "I could have finished him off with my right fist or choked him out but did not since I feared the consequences if I seriously hurt him." Instead, he said, he let Bruce go. When Matthew Polly asked David Chin if he remembered this, David said, "I don't think so."

Neither was landing clean blows. But Bruce controlled the tempo and the temper of the fight. "That [opening] attack set the tone," Wong recalled. "Then he started to make these loud, horrifying sounds—like a ghost screaming is the only way I can describe it. I never heard sounds like that before in my life, and they were scaring everyone in the room."

Bruce pressed forward. Suddenly, according to Linda and David, Wong turned and ran. First he ran toward the back wall and through the cloakroom door. Then he came out through the other door back into the main room, with Bruce in pursuit. In later interviews, Wong never admitted that he had fled. Bruce bragged to his friends that his hands were swollen from punching the back of Wong's head.

But then Wong stopped, turned, and unleashed a circling bottom fist that landed hard on Bruce's neck and buckled him. Bruce regrouped and chased Wong toward the front of the room, near the showcase windows. As Wong backpedaled, he tripped and fell rearward on a step or a floorboard. Bruce leaped atop Wong and pounded him, shouting, *"Fook m-fook?"* *Do you yield?*

As Chin and his entourage moved to separate the two, Wong answered, *"Fook. Fook!"*

Linda would say that the fight had taken three minutes. David Chin said it was "not more than seven minutes." Wong Jack Man said the fight "actually lasted about twenty minutes," and that Bruce was "so winded that he could not go on."

James Lee rang up Leo Fong.

"Hey, Leo, it's over," he said.

"Who won?"

"I'll let Bruce describe it to you."

Bruce got on the phone. "That bastard ran from me," he told Leo, breathlessly. "I chased him around and around that room, and he scratched my back. I got so close to him, trying to forward-blast him, and then he stumbled and fell. I got on top of him ready to coldcock him and he yelled, 'I give up! I give up!' So I made him say to his ten lackeys that he brought that he's given up. Then, what I told them—'Get the fuck out of here!'"

Linda recalled a much different Bruce after the fight.

"Bruce went out the back door and was sitting on the steps back there, head in hands, breathing hard, and so disgusted with this fight," she recalled. "He was not fit enough to run around for three minutes like that."

Even if Bruce would never credit Wong Jack Man by name—he and James would disparage him as "the runner"—the fight proved instrumental to his development. After the fight, Bruce was relentless in his weight and cardio training, and more obsessive than ever about tracking the size of his chest, biceps, and thighs; the distance and times of his runs; the number of daily push-ups and sit-ups he did; and the weight and number of reps and sets he lifted for each of his muscles.

He knew that he had not scored a decisive blow. The worst that could be said was that he had struck before the fight had formally begun, and that he had been saved by the studio's uneven floor. At best he had been sloppy. As he went back over it in his mind, he was less and less satisfied with himself. Perhaps most shocking to him was the realization that his system did not work.

"He had been in lots of fights, especially in Hong Kong," Linda recalled, "and he was so disappointed that his style of Wing Chun was not effective enough on this guy. That was the revelation."

Wong, Chin, and the entourage piled back into their cars and returned to Chinatown. At the Chin Family Association they nursed Wong's eyes with hard-boiled eggs. Wong still didn't really know all these men who had shown up. All the anticipation had turned into uncomfortable silences. "The mood," Charles Russo wrote, "was sullen."

Ben Der returned to the Chinatown social club where everyone the day before had been talking about how badly Wong would beat Bruce. "The whole thing was dead quiet. Nobody said nothing," he recalled.

He remained friendly with Ya Ya and Baldhead and Wong, and soon he couldn't help but notice: "Wong Jack Man used to hang around with the Chinatown martial arts group. After the fight, he disconnected with all of those guys. He realized that they set him up."

David Chin told Charles Russo, "I've always felt bad for Wong Jack Man, so I would tell people it was a draw." Some have read Chin's account as a necessary bridge between Bruce's and Wong's versions. Perhaps it could also be read as the revisionism of a promoter who switches sides after his fighter has lost.

But the fight was not yet over.

After they had clashed, Bruce had said to Wong Jack Man that they should vow not to tell anyone of the details of the fight. Wong agreed. Silence might allow the furor to dissipate and give them each space to process what had just gone down. But then the Chinese-language press intervened.

In late November, Hong Kong's *Ming Pao Daily* ran a tabloid-style story about Bruce Lee coming to the aid of Diana Chang Chung-Wen against an unnamed suitor. *Ming Pao* was a rising newspaper bankrolled by Louis Cha—better known by his pen name, Jin Yong, the most popular novelist in Southeast Asia. The story checked all the boxes for *Ming Pao* audiences: Sex! Violence! *Gung fu!* Entitled "Chang Chung-Wen Attracts Swarms of Butterflies, Bruce Lee Fights and Suffers Light Injury," it told the fanciful tale of an unnamed suitor, an "overseas brother"—Wong Jack Man, clearly—who had stalked Diana "without regard for death, like the shadow follows the form." Into the breach Bruce had stepped to challenge him, "with a look in his eyes and *qi* in his heart."

The article quoted an alleged letter from Chung-Wen stating that while the two had been "evenly matched," "both losing and suffering injury," the fight had ended with "Bruce Lee being knocked down in the last encounter." Reprinting the *Ming*

Pao story verbatim, San Francisco's *Chinese Pacific Weekly* ran a story in its November 26 edition with additional commentary under the headline, "The Course of Bruce Lee's Oakland Fight." By the end of the Thanksgiving weekend, everyone in Chinatown was again buzzing about the Bruce Lee–Wong Jack Man fight.

The *Weekly* had never covered Bruce when he had been "The Orphan," but now it noted his acting career, his famous actor-father, his teacher Yip Man, and rumors that he had dated Pak Yan. It also included this sarcastic jab at Bruce's sifu practices:

> After finishing his schooling [in Hong Kong] he visited the West to study as a foreign student, attending school and teaching (*gung fu*), accepting foreign devils in his national art until his students were like peaches and plums, all blue-eyed youth and foreign babbling. Any excess money from tuition and teaching he used to honor his teacher and father until Yip Man's and Li Hoi Chuen's pockets were bursting green.

The story concluded, "After the incident the overseas brother realized his victory over Bruce Lee was only due to luck and he ran off to hide somewhere the next day, not daring to again bother [Diana] Chang Chung-Wen."

Wong looked like a sociopath. Bruce appeared accomplished, filial, and chivalrous, but also traitorous. He seemed to be selling out *gung fu* to the *gweilo*. But Bruce took the most offense at the charge that he had lost the fight.

Shortly after the fight Bruce, James, and Linda had visited Wong at the Jackson Café. According to Wong, Bruce had come to make peace, emphasizing that they shared a Jing Wu genealogy—Siu Hon-Sang had learned from Sun Yuk Fung, who was also the teacher of Wong Jack Man's *sifu*—and were brothers in the art. Wong said Bruce told him he had only wanted to promote his institute, not make enemies.

But when Bruce and James read the *Pacific Weekly* article, they were certain that Wong was somehow responsible. He had broken their pact of silence and made himself the winner. So now the private fight was going to be refought in the tabloids. In Linda's later retelling of the Jackson Café visit, it "was just like a scene from a movie," with Wong cast in the role of the sucker. At their mere appearance he was spilling tea and shaking in his boots.

Bruce took the media offensive. On December 17, alongside a photo of him and Diana smiling proudly at the Sun Sing, the front-page headline of the *Chinese Pacific Weekly* read, "Bruce Lee Says He Beat His Opponent Until He Surrendered." In this interview Bruce dismissed the contention that the fight had been about Diana Chang—"the overseas brother" had never even seen her in the Sun Sing. "According to Lee," the story read, "it was not he who invited this overseas brother to test skills, but in fact it was the overseas brother who wrote to him to set up the fight (and he took out two sheets of paper as proof)."

Bruce gave his account of the fight. He never went down, he said. Instead he cornered his opponent against the wall. "Lee said normally he would have stopped there, but that night he was extremely angry, and leapt forward a few paces to feed him more punches," the story continued, "but the opponent was startled and took off running." Bruce forced him to the ground, got him to yield, and held him until "the twelve people who came with his opponent stepped up to separate them.

"His opponent, because his face was black and blue, rested at home three days at work but did not leave town," the article concluded. "And what about Chang Chung-wen? She had already left for New York, and at the time of the fight, was not even in the area."

On January 7, 1965, the *Weekly* published a letter composed by Bing Chan and signed by "David," none other than David Chin. The letter stated that, because the door had been locked, "the overseas brother Mr. Wong had no choice but to meet his attacks. Very impolitely, Lee opened up with fists and kicks immediately, including several dozen kicks to the groin. It probably lasted about twenty minutes without a winner or loser, and they were separated by the bystanders so as to avoid any injuries or hurt feelings."

Wong Jack Man read these articles with mounting discontent, and sought out a reporter to give his story. Three weeks later, his interview hit the front page, accompanied by a picture of him wielding double sabers while in full splits on two chairs.

"According to Wong, Lee made it clear that this was not an exercise in creating friendship and that he 'wanted an ending,'" the article read. At 6:05 p.m., Bruce Lee asked him to step forward, ignored his "hand of friendship," and attacked. The article stated, "According to Wong's estimate, Lee punched at him about sixty times, using eye-poking hand techniques, and kicked at him about twenty-five times. He also defended and counter-attacked (he will not say how many times he punched) and altogether the fight lasted until 6:25, using Mr. Chin's introduction as the beginning."

Wong said he had caught Lee's neck and chosen not to "use his right hand to deliver a serious injury." He called Bruce's claims—that he was "forced to plead 'mercy,'" hadn't returned to work for three days, and had been forced to the ground—flat-out lies.

Finally, Wong made his intentions clear. For two months after their meeting, the fight had continued in public. No more. The story concluded: "He says that in the future he will not argue his case again in the newspaper, and if he is made to fight again, he will instead hold a public exhibition so that everyone can see with their own eyes."

Chinatown was talking again.

Into the 1970s, there were Chinese who were unhappy about *gung fu* being taught to "foreigners." Bruce's European blood had riled Yip Man's senior students. Doug

Palmer had felt hostility on *gung fu* floors in Hong Kong and Honolulu. Linda cited the experience of Al Dacascos, a Filipino American *kajukenbo sifu* from Honolulu who, upon moving to the Bay Area, was confronted by *gung fu* men who came to his school with a challenge letter.

But there is little evidence to suggest that chauvinism motivated this fight. Aside from the *Weekly*'s mocking note about Bruce "accepting foreign devils into his national art," none of the Chinese-language press articles mentioned his teaching of *gung fu* to whites. None of them mentioned a scroll. None of them mentioned a threat that he cease teaching if he lost. Any such details would have been irresistible for the gossipy Chinatown press. It seems just as significant that Bruce never mentioned any of these details in the post-fight war of words.

If a scroll or a threat had been real, is it plausible that the always strategic Bruce—as media savvy as he was fight ready—would have stayed silent about it? In Seattle, when Yoichi Nakachi had escalated his challenge into a test of Japanese vs. Chinese styles, Bruce had not sided with those urging him to fight for ethnic pride. Here, on a much bigger stage, it certainly would have been tactical to talk it up in the press, either as a way to shame bigoted aggressors or to win back the public's goodwill in a story in which he had been painted as the villain.

Over the years, when Linda was asked to clarify what she knew of the particulars of the demand, she would say that she did not know if Bruce had been told to stop instructing whites or to close the school altogether if he lost the fight. Nor was it ever clear who might enforce such an edict or how. Bruce and James were not the type to seek permission to do anything, nor were they the kind to worry that anyone might force them to close their school.

For their part, Wong Jack Man and David Chin denied that the fight had been over Bruce's "right to teach foreigners." They maintained that nothing of the sort had ever been mentioned in any of the letters, phone calls, or other exchanges over the fight. Even some of Bruce's closest friends agreed.

"That had nothing to do with it," Leo Fong said. The fight was the result of "gossipy small-town politics." Al Dacascos himself believed Wong Jack Man's side of the story and later asked Wong to be a *sifu* to him and his part-Hawaiian wife.

How might Linda have come to hear of such a threat? Perhaps some Chinatown aggressors had issued Bruce or James verbal exchanges. Perhaps after the first *Chinese Pacific Weekly* article, teaching *gweilo* became a heated topic in the Lee household. Perhaps it was a half-truth Bruce told to divert attention from the Sun Sing incident. We may never know.

The fact is that the desegregation of the *gung fu kwoons* in the sixties came without court orders, street protests, or a death match overseen by a council of grim white-bearded elders, as depicted in the fantastical 1993 biopic *Dragon*. It was voluntary and came with no significant resistance. Lau Bun and T. Y. Wong had long been training non-Chinese, as had Ark Wong in Los Angeles, Buck Sam Kong in Honolulu, and Lau Bun's senior student, Doc Fai Wong. Not long after the fight, Bing Chan and Wong Jack Man opened their schools welcoming people of all backgrounds to train. As Charles Russo wrote, "The Chinese code had run parallel to the American policy of exclusion. The two had mirrored each other for a long time and then wound down in unison." Racial exclusion—and the self-defense necessitated by it—had been a reason for the *gung fu* schools, not the result of them.

Every good fight narrative must be reduced to the elemental. But the prevailing narrative of this secret fight has less to say about Chinese American attitudes toward whites in the latter part of the twentieth century than about white attitudes toward Asians.

The American wars in Asia had fueled a countercultural vogue for Asian martial arts, not unlike the way the entry of Commodore Matthew C. Perry's battleships into the waters of Tokugawa-era Edo ignited a vogue for Japanese visual arts. The ascent of Asian martial arts in North America followed the postwar Americanization of Japan, and subsequent US interventions in Korea, Vietnam, and Southeast Asia. Bruce's appearance on American movie screens after Nixon's 1972 visit to China only magnified the curiosity. If Linda's narrative of this fight—published in 1975, the year the war in Vietnam ended—had not captured the white imagination, perhaps another story of "how *gung fu* became American" might have.

But in that moment, for those in Chinatown, the fight between Bruce Lee and Wong Jack Man crystallized a moment of transition. On the eve of the 1965 Hart-Celler Act, the conversation on the street was not about who could study *gung fu* and who could not. They were talking about the good immigrant taking on the bad one, a passing topic that would soon be forgotten. A far more important question loomed: Against the backdrop of the struggle for racial desegregation, how might Asians rise from a self-defensive crouch to a new standing in America?

Leaders like Ruby Chow had articulated a strategy: *If whites want to know more about our culture, we owe it to ourselves to educate them.* But Bruce and other young Asians would need to puzzle out what integration really meant. They would have to shake off the reflex to obliterate themselves in the presence of whites, overcome the barriers that held them back, and learn how to move forward in a new world.

The day after the fight, Leo Fong drove from Stockton to the Lees' home in Oakland. Bruce was down in the garage working out. From the door, Leo saw Bruce in the full heat of it, hitting a leather glove hanging from a chain, dancing and jabbing.

"He was moving like I had never seen him before, bouncing around like Muhammad Ali, going at angles, hitting from angles," Leo remembered.

He told Bruce, "You would have had better luck if you did that against Wong Jack Man."

Wing Chun had taught Bruce to find the shortest distance to the target. But in a wide-open fight, he needed angles and mobility.

On the drive down Leo had thought about what Bruce had told him of his fight with Yoichi Nakachi. Now Bruce listened as Leo told him, "Your Wing Chun worked against that Japanese guy in Seattle because he comes charging in like a bull. But this [Wong Jack Man] guy ran the other way. Instead of going chasing after him straight like that, you go lateral and then cut him off, like a linebacker cutting off a runner." Bruce began to explore what different systems had to teach about the types and angles of attack. He incorporated Western boxing techniques and fencing footwork. He thought about the cadence of a fight and the necessity of being unpredictable, of adopting a "broken rhythm," like Thelonious Sphere Monk cutting up a pop standard.

To Bruce, Wong presented a thesis on the stability, wisdom, and effectiveness of established ways. He had been the antithesis. He had argued that moving the fighting arts forward meant destroying everything everyone had been taught—the forms, protocols, pedagogies, and rewards that the schools and systems were built upon—and centering the individual over the institution.

But the fight had tested his burn-it-all-down beliefs, and shaken his belief in his own system. All he had left were his openness to diversity, his focus on efficiency, and faith in his process. Now he needed to create a synthesis.

He wrote to Taky:

My mind is made up to start a system of my own—I mean a system of totality, embracing all but yet guided with simplicity. It will concentrate on the root of things—rhythm, timing, distance—and embrace the five ways of attack. . . . Above all, this system is not confined to straight line or curved line, but is content to stand in the middle of the circle without attachment. . . .

Wait till I assemble everything.

Despite Wong's challenge to Bruce in the pages of the *Chinese Pacific Weekly* on the eve of the Lunar New Year in 1965, the two never met face-to-face again.

Three years later Wong organized a *gung fu* exhibition at the San Francisco Civic Auditorium and invited Bruce, James, and their students to participate. Bruce joked to George Lee, "I will show up to scare hell out of them." He flew from Los Angeles to attend what he had termed in his Day-Timer the "phony demonstration." But he dressed down so as not to be recognized and took a seat with James and his students high up in the stands. He quipped to them that he was waiting for the right time to go down and show them the right way to do it. But he left without engaging Wong or any of his students.

After the publication of Linda's biography, the fight was again on everyone's lips, making fresh headlines in the martial arts magazines. Wong Jack Man felt dishonored, Michael Dorgan wrote, "not only as a loser but a villain." The implication of bigotry particularly vexed Wong. He sued Linda and the estate for defamation.

The case was dismissed in court and he retreated from the public. Over three decades, he quietly taught hundreds of women and men of all backgrounds at his Jing Mo Athletic Association in San Francisco and Oakland, including Kam Yuen, who in 1972 became the fight choreographer for a TV show called *Kung Fu*. As he aged his students protected him and his privacy.

Michael Dorgan conducted the only public interviews Wong gave after 1965. He maintained his silence until the year before he died, when a movie about the fight, *The Birth of the Dragon*, was released and he was asked to retell his story. Even his wife was surprised to hear he had once fought Bruce Lee. In 2018, he passed away quietly. Though he had been as influential a *gung fu* teacher as any in the United States, there would be no public memorial for him. Of the fight, he had told Dorgan, "If I had to do it over, I wouldn't."

Amid the 1965 Lunar New Year celebrations, Bruce's life lurched in a different direction—with a birth, a death, and a new beginning.

BOOK II
MIRROR

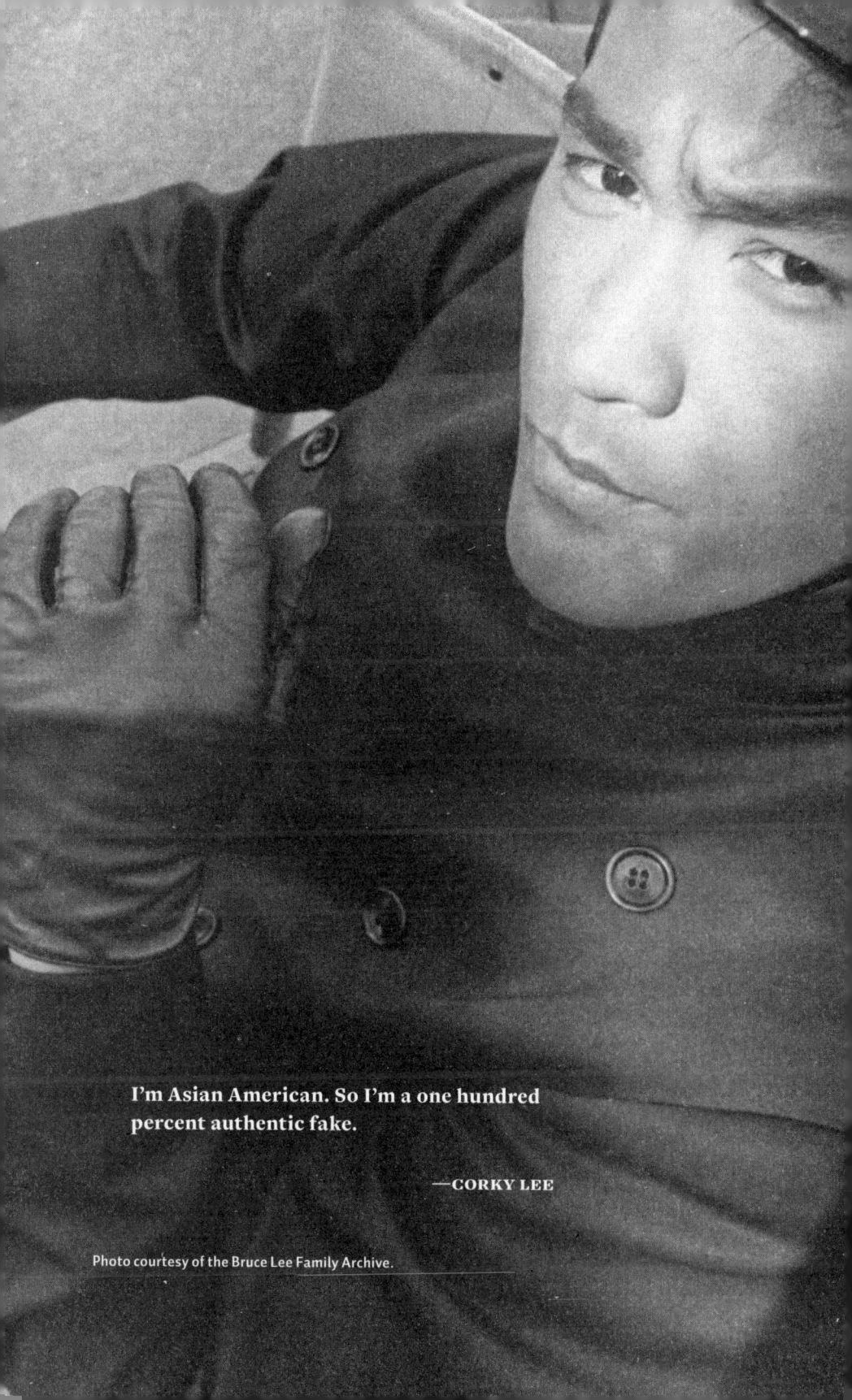

I'm Asian American. So I'm a one hundred percent authentic fake.

—CORKY LEE

Photo courtesy of the Bruce Lee Family Archive.

THE GREEN HORNET
PREMIERE EPISODE - ONE HOUR
BEAUTIFUL DREAMER

PART VII
Broken Mirrors
1966–1967

"You are minor character, always," he explains. "No major feelings, please. The background is your province—keep as far back as is humanly possible."

—EARL DERR BIGGERS

Bruce at home, 1966.
Photo courtesy of the Bruce Lee Family Archive.

CHAPTER 24
The Screen Test

In 1965, only one in two hundred Americans were of Asian descent. Because of racial segregation, it was very unlikely that the average white person in America might actually *know* an Asian. Yet, after nearly a century of imperial, military, and cultural engagement across the Pacific, the image of the Asian—more specifically, the misrepresentation of the Asian—had come to occupy a disproportionate part of the national imagination. By the end of the year, the passage of the Hart-Celler Act would swing open the gates to immigration and change the math forever. But changing the *picture* of the Asian in America remained as unthinkable as securing an act of Congress had once seemed.

Years after he had come to Hollywood to begin the second part of his acting career, Bruce reflected on it as if it had been a dream. "Maybe when I was hired to play Kato in *The Green Hornet*," he said, "it was an accident."

Contingency, wrote the literary theorist Stanley Fish, who hated the genre of biography in general, is the thing that makes celebrity biographies different from the other kinds. Most bios justify themselves by making big claims, he argued. Celebrity ones are more honest. They begin with "the accident of 'discovery,'" followed by "the big break," then "the even bigger accident of the 'role of a lifetime.'" In the celebrity bio, it is harder for the writer to pretend that the subject's skill, vision, and design are more important than timing, improvisation, and dumb luck.

What Stanley Fish never said is that oftimes all that the unrepresented and misrepresented have is contingency.

Sometime late in 1964 or early in 1965, Linda received what she would name "the call that changed everything." It came, of course, at exactly the right moment.

After the Wong Jack Man fight, Bruce and James realized they would not be able to make the rent on the studio much longer. Bruce's insistence on quality over quantity had made it unsustainable. They simply did not have enough students. About six months after they had opened, they quietly closed the storefront and relocated sessions back to James's garage.

When they weren't driving each other on the practice floor, James worked by day and mourned his wife at night, the pregnant Linda filled Katherine's household duties, and Bruce tried to figure out what to do next. Taky, who had full-time work running his family's supermarket, was sending him all the dues he was collecting from the Seattle Jun Fan Gung Fu students. But if the schools were going to be Bruce's primary source of income, he needed a new plan.

The call came one quiet afternoon when everyone was out but Linda. It was from the office of William Dozier, a fifty-six-year-old producer who had a deal with 20th Century-Fox for his new company, Greenway Productions, and was developing several action-hero TV shows. Dozier told Linda that he wanted Bruce to come test for a role in a show he had in development.

"I was surprised and so was [Bruce]," she recalled. "This was out of the blue. When he came to the States, he never considered going into acting because he thought his whole career was in martial arts schools."

Stunned—"here I am, a Chinese," he recalled, "but really in realistic thinking, how many times on film is a Chinese required?"—Bruce returned the call. It was arranged for him to fly to Los Angeles to audition on Friday, February 5, 1965.

But before that, on February 1, the eve of the Lunar New Year and the last day of the Year of the Dragon, Linda gave birth to Brandon Bruce Gwok Ho Lee at 5:48 a.m., at Oakland Hospital on East Fourteenth Street. In the delivery room Bruce's heart had been pounding, and when Brandon was born he exclaimed, "I just knew it was going to be a boy!" His Chinese name, "Gwok Ho" (國豪), could be translated as "national hero," as if Bruce's models for Brandon were Huo Yianjia or Wong Fei-Hung. He was born with black hair, but after three months it would fall out. When it grew back Bruce would brag to his friends about his little "blond, gray-eyed Chinaman."

On the other side of the Pacific, the family erupted in cheers when they got the news of the family's first grandson. But Bruce's call was tinged with sadness. His father, they told him, was dying. Bruce assured his mother they would be visiting as soon as they could. Three days later he took Linda home to settle in with the new baby and begin the joyful, sleepless nights of new parenthood.

The next morning he flew to Los Angeles for his screen test, and out of one line of history into another.

Bruce sits in a chair, tilting back just a little, in a finely cut dark suit and skinny tie. His hair is perfect. He affects a mask of cool. He puts one leg over the other and rests his hands on his knee. But his eyes betray his excitement.

He had ended up in this audition chair in the most clichéd of Hollywood ways. In the audience at Ed Parker's tournament, seated next to Joe Torrenueva, was his mentor in men's hair styling and a fellow *karate* student, Jay Sebring. It was Jay with whom Little Joe was raving about Bruce Lee's jaw-dropping performance as they cut hair at their salon on Monday. Bruce had been "discovered."

Sebring had parlayed his infallible taste and his skill with the scissors into becoming the most important men's stylist of the mid-1960s. Steve McQueen, Paul Newman, and Frank Sinatra entrusted him with their locks. Sebring had joined their rarefied circles, stepping out of his Porsche 911 or Shelby Cobra at all Hollywood's parties with beautiful actresses and models on his arm. Warren Beatty, another client, would model his womanizing hairdresser in *Shampoo* after Sebring. If Ruby Chow had turned the dinner seat into political power, Jay Sebring converted the barber's chair into cultural power.

One day he was giving a haircut to William Dozier, who was telling Sebring about a show he was having great difficulty casting—a Charlie Chan spinoff called *Number One Son*, in which Charlie Chan was dead and his Americanized son in San Francisco was stepping into his crime-solving shoes. Dozier was willing to consider an Asian male lead. In American television, there had only been one Asian lead before—Anna May Wong as an art-dealing detective in 1951's short-lived *The Gallery of Madame Liu-Tsong*. Dozier understood that an Asian male lead could be a Jackie Robinson–level breakthrough, and he a network TV Branch Rickey. But first of all, Dozier told Sebring, he needed someone who could command the screen like a true action hero. He needed "a Chinese James Bond."

"I have your guy," Sebring said.

After the haircut, he called Ed Parker and arranged to have Dozier see the footage of Bruce's presentation at the tournament. Soon Sebring would be personally picking Bruce up at the airport in his Cobra to meet Dozier at Fox Studios.

"Now Bruce, just look into the camera right here and tell us your name, your age, and where you were born," a director says to him off-screen.

Since the call with Dozier, he and Linda had been going over this moment endlessly, anticipating possible questions, practicing how he might present himself. He had waited restlessly through seven long hours for the director and his crew to secure and prep a studio to shoot the audition. Now it was finally happening.

He sits up stiffly and sucks in a deep breath.

"My last name is Lee. Bruce Lee. I was born in San Francisco. Nineteen forty. I am twenty-four right now."

It had been two generations since an Asian had set Hollywood afire. In the early days, before films became one of America's leading exports, there had been not just one, but two Asian stars in Hollywood—Sessue Hayakawa and Anna May Wong. During the silent-film era, both became icons of forbidden love for white moviegoers.

In 1915, Hayakawa's performance as the dangerously seductive villain in Cecil B. DeMille's *The Cheat* made him Hollywood's leading lothario. Hayakawa moved with the ease and agility of the *jujitsu* man he was. While his peers gestured broadly and theatrically as if they were still on a proscenium stage, he affected a Zen-inspired restraint, modeling the kind of ready-for-a-close-up cool one could later see in Bogart, Mifune, and McQueen.

With her smoldering beauty and barbed elegance, Anna May Wong defined the femme fatale. She starred in her first feature film at seventeen, as the doomed young Chinese lover of a white castaway in *The Toll of the Sea*. By nineteen, she had vaulted into international prominence, stealing the screen as a Mongol handmaiden in Douglas Fairbanks's *The Thief of Bagdad*.

Over a century later it is clear how grotesquely narrow the roles available to Hayakawa and Wong were—the rapey Oriental rogue, the tragic Butterfly. Asian activists on both sides of the Pacific denounced the actors as perpetuating destructive stereotypes. But Hayakawa and Wong were also unsatisfied with the roles on offer.

Anna May Wong told a journalist, "I was so tired of the parts I had to play. Why is it that the screen Chinese is nearly always the villain of the piece and so cruel a villain—murderous, treacherous, a snake in the grass? We are not like that."

At the peak of their success, they each formed independent production companies, a business answer to the artistic and existential problem of racist typecasting.* But both companies failed in the face of larger social forces.

In the 1920s, politicians like US Senator James Duval Phelan campaigned for office under the slogan "Keep California White." Alien land laws were passed to dispossess Asians of their land and prevent further land ownership. Under such pressures, Sessue Hayakawa left the country in the early 1920s.

Hollywood entered an era of moral hysteria. State and municipal censorship boards decried the film industry and called upon it to establish standards of "decency and Christian morality." To placate conservatives from pushing for federal regulation, the industry moved to censor itself with the Production Code, a set of self-imposed rules against "any licentious or suggestive nudity," "any inference of sex perversion," and "miscegenation."

Fights over the law are about the government's powers of enforcement and punishment. They are about where society draws the line between what is and is not *permissible*. The war over culture is fought over the unspoken standards that ground a society, about determining what is and is not *acceptable*. The fights that led to Hollywood's Production Code were about setting social norms and defining Americanness. The libertine Anna May Wong was constantly testing the limits of what society allowed of Asian women. She was therefore doomed to pay a narrative price by "dying a thousand deaths" on-screen. By 1928, she left the United States too, for the stages of Berlin, London, and Paris.

As the advent of sound in film ended the careers of many immigrant actors, including non-British European ones, the brief window for Asian stars in America slammed shut. Hollywood was by then the pop culture center of the world, and

---

* The first Asian American production company may have been the Japanese American Film Company, formed around 1914, which produced *The Oath of the Sword*, perhaps the first Asian American film ever made. It was found by Denise Khor and restored in 2023.

it knew exactly what it wanted. Leading roles for Asian characters could never be entrusted to actual Asians. They were reserved for those whom the Chinese American cinematographer James Wong Howe called "adhesive tape actors," white men and women who taped their eyelids to mimic epicanthal folds. Makeup was an expensive and arduous but efficient method to preserve the fictions of whiteness.

In the 1930s Anna May Wong returned to the United States a fashion icon, declared by the international media, "The Most Beautiful Chinese Girl in the World." But she yearned for a real Hollywood breakthrough. MGM Studios announced it was making a film based on Pearl Buck's Pulitzer-winning novel about a family of rural Chinese farmers, The Good Earth. Pundits and fans implored the studio to offer her the lead role of O-Lan.

But the casting exec wrote that she did "not seem beautiful enough." She looked too Oriental. Instead she was offered the role of Lotus, a scheming temptress. She rejected the offer as beneath her. The lead was given to Luise Rainer, who played O-Lan in yellowface and won that year's Oscar for Best Actress.

And so Anna May Wong began an extraordinary protest. Just before the Lunar New Year in January 1936, she boarded a ship from Los Angeles bound for Shanghai. She had been given a column in the New York Herald-Tribune to document her journey. She intended to make a documentary of herself touring China. She had launched a kind of proto–social media campaign to appeal directly to her fans.

Along the Huangpu River in Shanghai, thousands gathered to catch a glimpse of her. Dressed in lush dark furs and what she called a "tiger hat" of her design, she descended the gangway to greet well-wishers and reporters with an imperturbable cool. The photojournalist H. S. "Newsreel" Wong followed her, filming her visiting open-air markets, movie sets, and diplomatic quarters, and greeting large, excited crowds in Shanghai, Chang'an, and Beijing.

She filled the dailies, tabloids, and theater newsreels from the Pacific to the Atlantic with images of herself in the light she had desired—an American-born Chinese woman of glamour and grace, fully in control, beloved by farmers, hawkers, scholars, shopkeepers, aristocrats, and diplomats alike.

But when she returned to Hollywood, she was largely cast aside. She never recovered the heights she had known. After she succumbed to cirrhosis and troubles of the heart, Time magazine memorialized her as "the screen's foremost Oriental villainess." Perhaps that was even meant to be a compliment.

After World War II, roles for Asians and Pacific Islanders opened up a bit. A surprise hit in 1951, Go for Broke!, told the story of the 442nd Regimental Combat Team's dramatic rescue of the Lost Battalion deep in Nazi-occupied France. South Pacific memorialized "the good war" in Asia and the Pacific and signaled a new global American hegemony. Asian women, in particular, became the broken-English-speaking objects of desire and salvation for white men,* the necessary foil to America's view of itself as muscular, attractive, and heroic.

In 1958, *The World of Suzie Wong* opened on Broadway, with France Nuyen originating the starring role. "That was a first, because there had never been a person of color in the title role on Broadway before," she recalled. "Later on came *Raisin in the Sun*, *Flower Drum Song*, *A Majority of One*, and *West Side Story*. So all of a sudden it became a fad. It was a trend for exotic people."

While Bruce was settling into Seattle, learning about race in America, another young actor from Hong Kong had her big break.

Nancy Kwan Ka-shen was the freckled daughter of a Chinese architect and a British model, born a year and a half before Bruce. In the summer of 1959, when she was home from London's Royal Ballet School, she visited the Cathay Studios— which her architect father had designed and her granduncle owned—to watch actresses audition for an important overseas production. Securing the role would grant the winner a ticket to America.

Invited by a producer to step before the camera, she was "discovered." When it was time to return to school in London, she was flying to Los Angeles instead for more screen tests. In one of them, she stands in high heels in a high-necked red *cheongsam*, her hair pulled back. She is relaxed before the camera, confident and coquettish.

"Uh, Miss Kwan, how do you pronounce your name?"

She looks up from the floor with bright eyes.

"Kwan," she says on beat, tilting her head and giving a crushing smile.

"And your first name?"

"Nancy," she says, her gaze softening.

"What nationality are you?"

"I'm Eurasian," she says, eyes drifting up to the ceiling, then dropping her chin to punctuate the point: "I'm half Chinese and half English."

"Are you?" She smiles. "How old are you?"

"I'm just twenty years old."

A year later, Nancy was on the covers of *Esquire* and *Life* magazines, hailed as "A New Star." In November 1960 she debuted in the big-screen version of *The World of Suzie Wong*, three months before Anna May Wong's heart gave out.

The story was adapted from a novel by Richard Mason, a Britisher inspired by his time frequenting a brothel in Hong Kong's Wan Chai district, where white sailors cavorted with "yum yum girls." Nancy's sex worker Suzie Wong is not unlike

---

* Some of the movies from this period include *China Doll*, *The Geisha Boy*, and *Japanese War Bride*.

Bruce's Kid Cheung—illiterate and abandoned as a child, streetwise but purehearted, dreaming of the good life in America. William Holden plays Robert Lomax, an American artist-*cum*-savior. Nancy's wide-eyed directness, soft-sheathed worldliness, and mixed-race features made her perfect for the role.

She quickly followed that film's runaway success with another star turn in the screen adaptation of Rodgers and Hammerstein's musical *Flower Drum Song*, the first major studio movie to feature a nearly all-Asian American cast,* with actors of Chinese, Japanese, and Filipino descent. The musty old plot pivoted around an arranged marriage. But the cast performed with an undeniable exuberance, turning their full-throated production numbers into small wonders, Asian Americans singing and moving in joy and freedom.

A half-century after Chinese Americans had secured their hood by letting white architects build "Oriental City," Hollywood was reimagining Chinatown again. In Flower Drum Song, it was a lively enclave of nightclubs, street parades, households of wealth and morality, and frothy romantic intrigue. No vicious tongs and sleazy brothels, savage highbinders and irredeemable aliens, just the tourist trap the white builders intended. Mass media, ignoring rising youth violence, heralded segregated Chinatowns as "havens of law and order," trailheads from which exceptional Orientals started their climb to proper assimilation.

Nancy was getting a crash course on how to become a superstar, and another on what it meant to be an Asian in America. In San Francisco's Chinatown for *Flower Drum Song*'s premiere, she received a rapturous reception. But while on tour for *The World of Suzie Wong*, she and the other Asian cast members could not stay in whites-only hotels, even in northern cities like Chicago and Detroit.

For a time at the beginning of the sixties, she seemed to have brought down decades of exclusion with a song and a smile. But after that explosive start to her career, Nancy hit a ceiling. "After [*Flower Drum Song*] she was never really offered any films with great essence," her friend the actor James Hong recalled. "There were no more leading men or leading women roles for those leading people."

"It was a very difficult time," Nancy recalled. "Very few Asians were working and hardly any good roles were being written—I mean roles that could advance your career. They had little roles like a laundry person or a cook or something else, but not substantial roles [with which] an Asian actor can sustain their career. I think that actually the Asian men got it even worse than the actresses."

The image of the Asian male had long petrified into an awful binary: Fu Manchu or Charlie Chan.

---

* Anna May Wong was slated to play the grand matriarch Madame Liang, but when she died, the role was given to Juanita Hall, a Black American.

In a 1911 serial called *The Mystery of Dr. Fu-Manchu*, Arthur Henry Ward, writing under the Anglo-heroic pen name of Sax Rohmer, conjured Oriental evil:

Imagine a person, tall, lean, and feline, high-shouldered, with a brow like Shakespeare and a face like Satan, a close-shaven skull, and long, magnetic eyes of the true cat-green. Invest him with all the cruel cunning of an entire Eastern race, accumulated in one giant intellect, with all the resources of science past and present, with all the resources, if you will, of a wealthy government—which, however, has denied all knowledge of his existence. Imagine that awful being and you have a mental picture of Dr. Fu-Manchu, the yellow peril incarnate in one man.

The image of the Yellow Peril had sprung from a nightmare of Prussian Kaiser Wilhelm II in which he saw the Buddha unleashing the dragons of the East upon the lands and peoples of the West. The image spread across Europe and America through a Hermann Knackfuss illustration of Archangel Michael calling out to white Christian warriors, "Join in the defence of your faith and your homes!"* In popular cartoons, the Yellow Peril was an octopus whose arms stretched around the face of the earth, an Asian invasion from all directions. These images spoke to Western aggression in Asia: *if we don't get them first, we will be destroyed.*

The fiction of Fu Manchu arose from a failed magazine assignment. Rohmer was commissioned to write about a criminal tong leader in London's Chinatown, but he learned nothing because no one would speak to him. Instead he invented a fantastic villain and bragged, "I made my name on Fu Manchu because I know nothing about the Chinese!

"I know something about Chinatown," he added. "But that is a different matter."

Rohmer's pulps were followed by many movies. Fu Manchu would always be played in yellowface—feminized, sadistic, a strawman Other with taped eyes, thin mustache, and long fingernails. He had been born to fail. He was the Yellow Peril contained, never a worthy enemy, simply a mirror to the abidance of white supremacy.

When Anna May Wong and Sessue Hayakawa finally shared the screen, it was in 1931's *Daughter of the Dragon*, a film that forecloses all Asian and Asian American futures. Anna May Wong plays Ling Moy, an orphaned burlesque dancer in London, who longs to meet the father who has abandoned her. He will, predictably, turn out to be Fu Manchu. Sessue Hayakawa plays Ah Kee, diligent Chinese detective and guardian of whiteness, obsessed—in revulsion and attraction—with Ling Moy.

Ah Kee kills Fu Manchu, because he must. But having discovered her parentage, Ling Moy transforms herself into the number-one son that Fu never had, accepting

---

* See illustration on page 16.

her world-conquering inheritance. Ah Kee dies, because he must, in a three-story fall he inexplicably survives long enough to shoot and kill Ling Moy. Over her dead body, he declares his love for her and then perishes.

THE END.

In the sixties, as Western fears escalated over a Red East stretching from the Great Wall to the Java Sea, the Yellow Peril returned.

"The bad guys are taking on a new complexion. On television and in the movies, more and more of the guys in the black hats have a definite Oriental look," the *Wall Street Journal* reported. "Sometimes, even the Russians—for many years the screen's heavies—are cast as good guys helping the American heroes outwit the Orientals."

Fu Manchu returned to the screen with the British actor Christopher Lee in yellowface. Tsai Chin assumed Anna May Wong's role as his daughter. "I'm not particularly proud that I did these films," she told the film historian Arthur Dong. "Every time I do it I get all upset with all my friends: 'How could I do something that is against my race?' This kind of thing I think about all the time, okay?"

Fu Manchu embodied the fear of invasion and a panic for containment. But not far behind the Fu Manchu revival was a Charlie Chan revival. Charlie Chan was what America wanted from minorities—affirmation, exertion, pliability, and a comforting goofiness.

Invented by the novelist Earl Derr Biggers in the early 1920s, Charlie Chan was

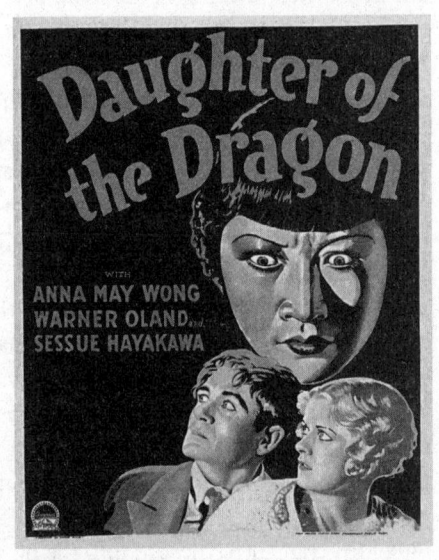

Daughter of the Dragon, 1931. Public Domain.

Drums of Fu Manchu, 1940. Image from Everett Collection, Inc./Alamy Stock Photo.

inspired by a Honolulu detective, Chang Apana, a wiry, explosive, real-life action hero who rode around town on a horse with a fearsome facial scar and a bullwhip for the criminals. But Charlie Chan looked more like the author himself. He was "very fat indeed, yet he walked with the light dainty steps of a woman." Biggers, Jill Lepore wrote, "knew very little about Hawai'i and less about China."

But he argued that he was different from Rohmer. "I had seen movies depicting and read stories about Chinatown and wicked Chinese villains," he said, "and it struck me that a Chinese hero, trustworthy, benevolent, and philosophical, would come nearer to presenting a correct portrayal of the race."

He wrote six novels before he died. Over fifty Charlie Chan movies, and many more radio, television, cartoon, and comic book serials followed. In the hands of white writers, Charlie Chan solved crimes while dispensing what Elaine Kim called "fortune-cookie English":

Tongue often hang man quicker than rope.

Hasty deduction, like ancient egg, look good from outside.

At night all cats are black.

Better for Oriental to lose life than lose face.

Confucius say, "No man is poor who have worthy son."

When Chan first appeared on-screen in 1926, he was played by Japanese and Chinese American actors—George Kuwa, Sôjin Kamiyama, and Edward L. Park. But when 20th Century-Fox invested in Charlie Chan for a full-length film in 1931, they brought in the Swedish immigrant actor Warner Oland. Two years before, Oland had played Fu Manchu in the character's first US adaptation and, fifty years before that, had had the good fortune to be born with the cost-saving advantage of not needing to have his eyes taped. With Oland as the lead for sixteen films, Charlie Chan movies became a blockbuster franchise. After he died in 1938, other yellow-face actors continued the franchise into the 1980s.*

Charlie Chan was so popular that the franchise expanded through family lines. In 1935, Keye Luke, from Seattle's Central District, took the role of Lee Chan, Charlie's "Number One Son," sparring verbally with dad across the cultural and generational divides. Charlie's second-generation ABC sons were college educated and bilingual. At the University of Chicago, Robert Ezra Park and his team of sociologists were studying the "Oriental Problem": *Would they ever assimilate?* The Chan clan provided a reassuring image of an Americanizing nuclear family.

---

* In 1981, massive Asian American protests forced the six-million-dollar film *Charlie Chan and the Curse of the Dragon Queen* to shut down its production in San Francisco's Chinatown and move elsewhere.

In 1966, the year that Stokely Carmichael declared Black Power, the American mass media trumpeted Japanese and Chinese in the United States as "success stories," ideal ethnics "pulling [themselves] up from hardship and discrimination to become a model of self-respect and achievement in today's America." They were like generations of bootstrapping European immigrants, whites by proxy, conscripts in the attack on Blackness.

The image of the insipid, grinning, "gentle Oriental" and the image of the cunning, grasping Yellow Peril—it made sense to many young Asians in America that these contradictory images were recirculating at the same time. Frank Chin and Jeffery Paul Chan wrote:

> For Fu Manchu and the Yellow Peril, there is Charlie Chan and his Number One Son. The unacceptable model is unacceptable because he cannot be controlled by whites. The acceptable model is acceptable because he is tractable. There is racist hate and racist love.
>
> ... The successful operation of the stereotype results in the neutralization of the subject race as a social, creative, and cultural force. The race poses no threat to white supremacy. It is now a guardian of white supremacy, dependent on it and grateful to it.

Frank Chin told a sociologist, "The only Chinese that appear in American culture are as a kind of debris: playing Number One Son in Charlie Chan movies while Charlie Chan, who is the teacher, is played by a white man. A white man teaches us how to be Chinese."

When Keye Luke and Frank Chin finally met, the "Number One Son" actor ad-

Keye Luke as Number One Son with Warner Oland in *Charlie Chan in Shanghai*, 1935. Image from Masheter Movie Archive/Alamy Stock Photo.

mitted to the angry young writer, "In those days, and we always used to kill about it, you know—a white actor can play anything, Blackface, the Oriental, anything. A colored actor, so to speak, any pigment other than white, has to play exactly what he is."

Chin asked Luke about his big break. Before acting, Luke had been a successful young graphic designer and commercial artist. He had created and painted the murals in Grauman's Chinese Theatre. When an exec needed a love interest for an Anna May Wong feature, he auditioned. The movie was never made, but with his stage-ready American accent and commanding presence he received some attention.

"They sent me down to Fox," he told Chin. "And they said, 'Well, we've got a solid contract that is coming up. We're introducing the part of the Number One Son. There's no reason you shouldn't play it.' That's how it got started, a series of coincidences."

After Warner Oland died, in 1938, Luke quit the Number One Son role out of respect for "the old man" and became Kato, the sidekick of the radio serial hero the Green Hornet. That year he landed the lead in another Chinese American detective franchise, playing Jimmy Lee Wong in *Phantom of Chinatown*, a role once reserved for Boris Karloff to play in yellowface. But the movie failed at the box office, killing the franchise, and Luke played number two at best for the rest of his life.

And so here is Bruce in the winter of 1965, after hours on a Friday night on a Fox soundstage, another accidental Asian under the lights, facing a small crowd behind the camera in his screen test. Unaware of the history resting upon his shoulders, he exhales his nervousness and begins.

First, the director* asks Bruce to establish his bona fides for execs watching this footage later. "And you worked in motion pictures in Hong Kong?"

"Yes, since I was around six years old."

Bruce's eyes shift anxiously. To stop his wandering gaze, the director asks Bruce to look only at him as they talk. Twenty-year-old Nancy Kwan had been in full control of the camera in her screen test—relaxed and flirtatious. But Bruce is stiff, nervous, out of practice. The director throws a softball.

"I understand you just had a baby boy."

Bruce exhales and chuckles, shaking his head over his lack of sleep. The director asks Bruce what he studied in college. Bruce hesitates and says, "Uh, philosophy,"

---

* The man is unidentified in the original screen test video. He has been identified as William Dozier in the supplemental materials to the *I Am Bruce Lee* video and in other books. But when the man who is speaking comes on-screen to readjust Bruce, he looks distinctly younger. His voice is also lower and doesn't have Dozier's unique cadence. For comparison, see the 1966 CBC *Telescope* interview with Fletcher Markle, posted on YouTube under the title "Batman and William Dozier," youtube.com/watch?v=rkvR4PGqBhA. I don't believe the voice in the screen test is Dozier, so I am identifying him here as "the director."

before his eyes dart away. In interrogations, this would be a tell. In Hollywood—which is to say, in America—it is mythmaking.

"Now you told me earlier today that *karate* and *jujitsu* are not the most powerful or best forms of Oriental fighting. What is the most powerful or best form?"

"Well—ahem." Bruce clears his throat, calculating just how far to take this on camera. "It's bad to say the best, but, um . . ." His eyes wrinkle with mirth, a small grin forms, and he laughs.

Then he recovers and delivers it straight. "In my opinion, *gung fu* is *pretty good*."

"Tell us a little bit about *gung fu*."

Finally he warms up, punctuating his points with his hands. But the director still needs a clip of Bruce that shows he can hold the screen and be directed.

"Would you look right in the camera lens and explain the principle of the glass of water as it applies to *gung fu*?"

He focuses directly on us now, his audience. The pitch of his voice rises. The studio set is now Roethke's classroom, Skip's fraternity, his Broadway *kwoon*.

"Well, *gung fu*, the best example would be a glass of water. Why? Because water is the softest substance in the world, but yet it can penetrate the hardest rock or anything, granite, you name it."

He pronounces it "grie-NIGHT." But he has found a minister's Sunday rhythm.

"Water also is insubstantial. By that I mean you cannot grasp hold of it. You cannot punch it and hurt it. So, every *gung fu* man is trying to do that, to be soft like water, and flexible, and adapt itself to the opponent."

In the next cut, the director asks Bruce, now standing, to turn this way and that to capture profiles. The camera pulls back, and he asks Bruce to show him how actors in the Chinese opera would walk. He becomes a warrior, kicking up a leg crossways, then straight out, then stomping. He becomes a scholar, pattering forward in minced steps, shoulders back—"Like a girl," he snorts.

"Now show us some *gung fu* movements."

"Well, it's hard to show it alone," Bruce says, hands beseeching.

The silence is broken by the young crew members volunteering each other, until the assistant director, an old white-haired gentleman in thick black glasses and a suit, lumbers from stage left toward Bruce.

Bruce giggles, covering his mouth like a tittering co-ed. "Although accidents do happen!"

Then he snaps back into arena mode. He speaks even louder now. The studio set, with its Persian rug, sensible chaise, and columned fireplace, is now Vancouver's Majestic Theatre, Oakland's Colombo Club, the Long Beach Municipal Auditorium.

"There are various kinds of strikes," he says. "To the eyes, you would use fingers."

He jabs, and the man rolls back like a rocking horse.

Bruce smiles. "Don't worry!"

He throws a straight, a hook, and another hook—his jacket sleeve snapping crisply, his fist a blur. Bruce demonstrates a back fist—"using the waist, again"—noting the technical detail.

The old man feels the wind of each punch on his cheek.

"And, uh, let's have the assistant director back up just a bit," the director says. The room bursts into laughter. "OK. Go ahead. Continue."

"And then of course, *gung fu* is very sneaky," Bruce says. "You know the Chinese . . ."

He lets the comment hang out there for a second, the better to land his punchline. "They always hit low."

He raises a fist into the assistant director's face—"From *high* . . ."—then snaps it down at the gentleman's balls—". . . go back to the groin!" The man folds forward like he is bowing to Bruce.

Bruce smiles and pats him on the shoulder. "Don't worry."

The old man says, "These are just natural reactions." He repeats shakily, "Natural reactions."

"Right, right," Bruce says, back in dead serious *sifu* mode.

The cameraman finally has Bruce in the proper viewing position. Bruce repeats the strikes. We see them as cleanly as we hear them.

"There is the finger jab." Snap!

"There is the punch." Snap!

"There is the back fist." Snap! "And then low." Snap!

"Of course, then they use the leg, straight at the groin." A front kick. Snap!

"Or then come up." A roundhouse kick. Snap!

The old man is jerking back and forth.

"Or if I can back up a little bit—they start from back here . . . and then come back!"

A high side kick to the assistant director's eyes. Snap!

Bruce slaps the old man on the shoulder, turns to the crew, and grins. "He's kind of worried."

The director asks him to demonstrate the difference between *gung fu* and *jujitsu*. Bruce gives a lengthy discourse on "what we mean by simplicity," not exactly what the director needed.

"Okay. Show me once again just a few movements there."

Bruce drops his chin, raises an explaining hand, and falls back into demonstration mode. "Well, *gung fu* can be practiced alone or with a partner. Practicing alone there involves forms. Some imitate a crane. A monkey. A praying mantis. This is a crane form."

He turns to his right and extends his arms wide. "Start off . . ."

Then he's crouching, whirling his arms, dropping back into a Northern Shaolin pose, his right hand over his head, his left arm stretched back into a crane's beak.

A swift circling kick with the crack of a hand slap, a hop back onto his left foot, his right hand extended and probing, probing. A final dramatic side kick and a scream.

"Hooooooiiiii!!!!!"

He drops back into a left horse stance, chin down, eyes sharp, drawing out his hands to mark an imaginary opponent. Then softly he steps forward to stand chin high and chest out, fists turned back like a *karateka*'s, and exhales.

The crew is gaping.

Bruce adjusts his jacket sleeves. He tidies himself in his Western suit.

The spell is broken. He is suddenly self-conscious. He mutters, "This is one of the movements involved."

"Show us one more and then we'll be over."

"Okay, I—I'm glad to hear that," he says, laughing nervously.

Then he is dropping down into another horse stance, pants legs rising above his ankles. He forms his hands into claws and waves them like clouds. He scratches with the claw hand, then stabs with it, then swings each of them one after the other in figure eights.

The film can only capture the trails of these movements.

He thrusts back up to full height, as if breaking the surface of the water, and exhales.

"Thank you very much," the director says.

Bruce returned to Oakland satisfied with the way the audition had gone.

In Kowloon, amid the first weekend of the Lunar New Year, his father—the one man Bruce had always wanted the most to impress—passed away just after sunrise, in the hour of the Dragon.

CHAPTER 25
Number One

Bruce arranged to return to Hong Kong, where he would be needed for at least a few weeks. In Oakland, Linda was a new mom with a colicky infant.

"Bruce had this idea about giving birth. He said, 'You know, Chinese women would just give birth in a field and carry on cooking,'" Linda said. "Before I had Brandon I wouldn't know any different. But that was kind of his attitude."

James had his own two children to look after, and his older stepson, Dickie, had returned. Linda decided to ask her mother if she could return to Seattle to stay while Bruce was away. It was the first time Linda had asked her mother for anything since the newlyweds had fled Seattle. Her mother agreed to take her in, but when Linda arrived, Vivian could not help but harp on their shotgun wedding.

"Here I was, a babe in arms," Linda recalled, "and my mother was saying, 'How could you have done this?'"

Bruce was unable to book a flight in time to attend his father's funeral ceremony. By the time he had arrived at Kai Tak airport on February 15, his brother Robert could see he was distraught and ashamed. "To Chinese, to come late to your father's funeral is like being unfilial," Robert said. He then described an agonizing scene that Bruce would later draw upon for the beginning of *Fist of Fury*.

"When we got to the funeral parlor, he walked on his knees all the way from the elevator to the cassock in front of the coffin," Robert said.

Sobbing and wailing loudly as he crawled to the casket, Bruce was fulfilling the expectations of his family and community. But the emotions were real. Just after Brandon was born, Bruce had sent his father a photo of the baby to raise his spirits. His family felt they were racing the clock. Hoi Chuen's birthday was not until March, but by the traditional calendar, if he lived to the sixth day following the Lunar New Year—the seventh of February—he would have reached his sixty-fourth year, the year a fortune teller had said he would die.

"Dad held up the photo and said that if he could only make it through the seventh, then he'd be all right," Robert said. On the seventh, Hoi Chuen had a heart attack and passed away. Bruce had only just begun to reconcile with his father, and now Hoi Chuen would never meet his first grandson.

William Dozier wrote to Bruce in Hong Kong to express his condolences and added, "The film you shot here looks very good, and when you return to San Francisco, please let me know. There is no hurry about it."

Dozier was a three-decade industry veteran, with executive stints at Paramount, RKO, and CBS TV. He had produced films like Alfred Hitchcock's *Notorious* before moving to television, overseeing shows like *Gunsmoke*, *Have Gun Will Travel*, and *Playhouse 90*. "His finest training for life in the Hollywood jungle," he once wrote of himself in the third-person, "was one year of preparation for the Catholic priesthood in a Jesuit novitiate in his teens and two years in a Federal prison in his early twenties." He had been pardoned for that mail fraud conviction, he liked to add, by President Harry Truman.

Network television is, by nature, an exceedingly conservative medium, mostly in the business of selling diversions as if they are canned goods. It is where bold ideas sometimes, rarely, ignite the masses, but more often simply go to die. The American Broadcasting Company was a distant third among the three networks and most in need of bold ideas. That was why they had set Dozier up with swanky offices on the 20th Century-Fox lot. Dozier's bold idea—three years after the explosion of pop art and one since the civil rights confrontations in Birmingham and the assassination of President Kennedy—was that the masses wanted "pure escapism" and "unreality."

He commissioned a young writer named Lorenzo Semple Jr. to write the treatment for *Number One Son* and sent him a stack of Charlie Chan novels to read. In late April, Semple delivered a sixteen-page "presentation" for "a slam-bang, one-hour action-adventure series." Bruce began reading with excitement and dread. He admitted later, "I wanted to make sure before I signed that there wouldn't be any 'ah-so's' and 'chop-chops' in the dialogue and that I would not be required to go bouncing around with a pigtail."

Semple's treatment opens on contemporary Grant Avenue, where Charlie Jr. lives. "Old Charlie Chan is now in heaven," Semple writes, "quoting Confucius to Sherlock Holmes." Inside Junior's apartment we find a second-gen Chinese American who is thoroughly modern—a University of California, Berkeley grad from Honolulu, an aficionado of cool jazz, an aesthete who drives a Morgan and can hold forth on Terry Southern and Mason Hoffenberg's 1958 ironic pulp sex novel, *Candy*.

Reluctant to follow in his father's footsteps, Junior is pulled into the family business by relatives, including Aunt Anna May in Hong Kong, "a delicious old dowager who is proprietress of a high-class *fan-tan* parlor," and all kinds of pretty girls. On the wall is a large portrait of Charlie Chan Sr. In each episode, Number One Son demonstrates his filial piety by staring at the portrait and asking the question, "What would Pop have done?" But unlike dear old sedentary dad, Junior also possesses the fearsome skills that come with the "Badge of the North Wind" of "A'zu-taki . . . that ancient, almost forgotten Oriental school of weaponless mayhem."

Picture Bruce frowning.

In red ink,* Bruce underlines the qualities that Dozier and Semple seem to be asking of him: "respect for age," "good manners," "loyalty," the belief that "wisdom and serenity are life's ends." Number One Son is "a very hip fellow, much given to the deadpan sort of crack," "lithe and pantherlike . . . He thinks cool. Above all, he moves cool."

Picture Bruce smiling.

Semple adds, "In his relations with women, as with everything else, we'll look on Charlie as 100% American and entirely eligible. Despite his ancestry, there will not be a shadow of a race problem in any episode."

Picture Bruce now flipping back to the section on "A'zu-taki," Semple's fake martial art that sounds like an item from an *izakaya* menu. He crosses it out with a pencil, writes something in with his red pen, thinks better of it, blots it out with Liquid Paper, goes back, reads some more, and underlines the qualities of the art: "Misdirection. Deception. Innocent surprise."

He reads, "A'zu-taki depends instead on the infinite precision, incredibly fine timing, obscure vectors of leverage undreamt of by the mere Black Belt adept of karate. It doesn't even require much exertion. After Charlie refrigerates an adversary with a single thunderbolt chop, he has to merely strengthen his lapels and walk blithely off."

Picture him adding a red check mark beside this section.

"There will be the strongest and most calculated accent on the BIZARRE in all our hero's adventures," Semple writes. For instance, Charlie Jr. will stop a Communist Fu Manchu villain from accomplishing evil schemes involving mind control and murder. "From beginning to end, it will be plain that this series is not merely about a private investigator who happens to be Chinese-American. He is and always will be NUMBER ONE SON of the fabled Charlie Chan."

Dozier wrote back immediately, praising Semple's work as "excellent," "exactly the right content and esprit," and "excitingly commercial." He had only one major note. "I am all for anything bizarre but I think the test of the efficacy of anything containing a bizarre quality is whether or not it could happen," Dozier wrote. "For example, your suggestion of the brainwashed ape climbing into the window of an Embassy in Washington D.C. etc. is indeed bizarre but I doubt that it could happen or that an audience would ever believe that it could happen."

At the same time, Bruce responded to Dozier, exercising restraint. "After reading the 'presentation' I'm very enthused on the whole project and have added several ideas of my own to add more 'coolness' and 'subtleness' to the character of Charlie Chan's son," he wrote. "This project does have tremendous potential and its uniqueness lies in the *interfusion* of the best of both the Oriental and American qualities plus the never before seen Gung Fu fighting techniques.

---

* All of these sections are marked in Bruce's draft with his precise ruler-aided underlining.

"I have a feeling that this Charlie Chan can be another James Bond success if handled properly," he said.

Back in Seattle in March 1965, Bruce suddenly had a lot of time to think. The year before, he and Linda were hanging out carefree in the U-Dub Hub. Now he was a married father without a real job. In Oakland, James was having a hard time adjusting to single fatherhood. Bruce and Linda were unsure about whether to return.

Bruce invited Lanston Chinn to visit him at Linda's family's household, where he was pumping iron in the basement. "He was kind of fried, a little bit," Lanston said. "He didn't know what to do exactly." Hollywood wasn't happening yet. The martial arts schools weren't coming along the way he had wanted. With the McCullochs he was the stranger in the house.

Bruce focused on something he could control, beginning a charm offensive on Linda's mother with all the old tricks—the jokes, the coin tricks, the stories. On their best days, he might catch her in the kitchen and murmur lasciviously, "You know, Mom, you've got the greatest legs of any woman of your age I've ever seen!"

"She came around to love Bruce very much," Linda recalled. "I thought, 'Oh, this is wonderful. My mother is not as prejudiced as she has always expressed herself.' I reasoned later that she wasn't exactly *color-blind*-blind. She just liked Bruce."

By May, Bruce's new agent, William Belasco, and 20th Century-Fox were finally nearing a deal. Bruce decided to splurge the advance he had not yet received and give Linda a version of the "honeymoon trip"—at least the Hong Kong part—that he had promised her. He, Linda, and Brandon took an American President Lines ship back across the Pacific. For the next four months, they lived at Nathan Road.

Bruce hoped that having Brandon there would cheer up his depressed mother and excite the family. The number-one grandson soon became, in Linda's words, "the number-one spoiled child." The family gave them a crib and one of the two bedrooms. During the day, when Brandon cried, all the women—remembering the wartime sickliness of the Lee boys—came running. At night, Linda recalled, "Brandon was hell on wheels.

"I basically picked him up every second he made a noise and walked him, walked him around the house. And I'd get up at the first light of dawn and put him in the stroller and take him down the street—yeah!—while Bruce was sleeping. He was not a participating parent at that time. That's a woman's work!" Linda recalled. "I have never been as tired in my life as when I was twenty years old."

Bruce visited Yip Man to show off Brandon and learn more dummy techniques. Master Yip posed for a picture with Brandon, but refused to allow Bruce to film the techniques. Bruce also learned more Jing Wu and Northern Shaolin forms from Uncle Siu Hon-Sang. He taught a small group of his brothers and friends *gung fu* at Nathan Road. He wrote Taky that he was developing the concept of "no limit limitation."

It was Linda's turn to feel like an outsider. "Hong Kong was crowded. You couldn't walk down the street in a straight line," she recalled. "I remember we went up into the hills where the poor people lived in huts and there was a guy who was making shoes for Bruce. So I was seeing everything, how the real people lived there.

"His family were all really nice to me," she recalled. "I didn't know what they were saying."

Bruce told them she was an amazing cook and that she made one American dish they would find especially delicious—spaghetti. He told her he had invited all the relatives. She went panic shopping and realized she could not find her secret ingredient in Hong Kong—Lawry's spaghetti seasoning. On the two-burner gas stove, which she had never used before, she burned the tomato sauce. When she served the food, the family took bites and began talking all at once.

"One thing I could understand in Chinese—'Even a dog won't eat this!'" she recalled. "It was awful." Linda worried that Bruce's family was talking behind her back, feeling sorry for him.

"But guess what? I never had to cook again!"

On June 8, Bruce signed an option agreement with 20th Century-Fox and received eighteen hundred dollars, the largest check he had ever cashed. He was to receive four hundred dollars per episode in the first year, with escalations through the fourth year, if the show reached that point. If the show was successful, the network could offer him a term contract that would pay four hundred dollars per week for forty weeks.[*] For a series lead, the deal was awful. But his agent, William Belasco, who had been suggested by William Dozier, assured him it was the best he could get, and Bruce felt nothing but gratitude.

On July 2, William Dozier wrote to Bruce in Hong Kong, "I'm delighted we worked out our deal. I hope you are watching as many English language television programs as you can and speaking English as much as you can so you will continue to progress with your ability to speak English clearly."

When he did not hear back from Dozier for three weeks, Bruce became anxious that the option would lapse in September. William Belasco wrote to tell him not to worry. But on August 10, Bruce sent a note to Dozier directly.

He assured Dozier that he was "watching as many English television programs as I can to improve my clarity in speaking." He promised to return to the United States soon, after "settling my father's estate." Most important—in that Asian way of giving gifts when one wanted to nudge someone toward getting something done—he sent a hand-carved seal, a "chop," of Dozier's name in Chinese.

---

[*] In 2024 dollars, eighteen hundred dollars would be about eighteen thousand dollars, and four hundred dollars would be almost four thousand dollars.

He wrote, "Could you let me know of the progress of 'Number One Son' as I am anxious to know. Thank you!"

In September the Lees returned to Seattle. With the option contract set to lapse on the twenty-first, Belasco and Dozier hastily drew up an extension. On September 20, Dozier wrote Bruce: "How very kind and thoughtful of you to send me the hard carved seal!" He added, "As Bill Belasco has doubtless told you by now, all our plans are delayed. But rest assured we are still very Bruce Lee conscious."

A week later, Dozier sent a one-sentence letter: "Just a note to demonstrate to you that everything here is under control." He signed it with the chop Bruce had sent.

But behind the scenes, Dozier was scrambling. ABC had initially green-lit *Number One Son*. But by the summer the network had gotten cold feet. Dozier soon found out why.

"Bill got a call from the network," Lorenzo Semple Jr. recalled. "Unfortunately for 'Number One Son,' the powers had decreed they would not air any show featuring a Chinese person. In fact, no ethnic heroes whosoever. Period."

ABC needed high-risk, high-reward ideas from Dozier. But a prime-time Chinese American lead was far too risky. "We owe you one," the ABC execs told him. Not long afterward Dozier flew to Spain to see Semple at his villa. Semple recalled that Dozier had just come from network meetings: "'This,' he said, with a look of humiliation bordering on shame, 'is what ABC has given us.'"

He pulled out a *Batman* comic book. But if Dozier felt humiliated, Semple was excited.

Months before, Susan Sontag had written an essay, "Notes on 'Camp,'" describing the return of an old aesthetic after the shocks of pop art and the Kennedy assassination. It was a sensibility familiar to urban, queer, and minority communities. "Camp," Sontag wrote, "is a vision of the world in terms of style—but a particular kind of style. It is the love of the exaggerated, the 'off,' of things-being-what-they-are-not." Camp was *King Kong*, the *National Enquirer*, La Lupe, and Flash Gordon. Camp was so bad it was good. "It is the farthest extension in sensibility," she wrote, "of the metaphor of life as theater."

Semple and Dozier agreed that a grown man and his young male sidekick running around in brightly colored tights fighting similarly costumed villains was an idea so outlandish it had to be played as camp. "The fairly obvious idea," Dozier recalled, "[was] to make it so square and so serious and so cliché ridden and so overdone, and yet do it with a certain elegance and style that it would be funny, that it would be so corny and so bad that it would be funny."

ABC's execs had commissioned audience research to discover the comic book

---

* As we shall see, Semple's *Number One Son* treatment would still prove to be very influential on Bruce's future projects.

properties most ready for prime time. In order, they were *Superman*, *Dick Tracy*, *Batman*, *The Green Hornet*, and *Little Orphan Annie*. *Superman* and *Dick Tracy* were already off the table. Dozier locked up the rights to *The Green Hornet* for 20th Century-Fox and Greenway Productions. When he presented Semple's *Wham! Zap! Pow!* treatment of Batman to the network in the middle of 1965, ABC fast-tracked the show.

William Dozier likely never told Bruce Lee the real reason *Number One Son* had been torpedoed. He still needed an Asian.

Two days before Thanksgiving, as Dozier was rushing to have *Batman* ready for its prime-time debut in January 1966, he wrote Bruce:

> As Bill Belasco may have told you, my thinking is to feature you as Kato, the Oriental-ish righthand man of the Green Hornet in the series of that name which was on radio and in comic books for many years and which we have just bought to put into production for next season.
>
> More about this later, but it is a very important property, and if it is put together as I visualize it, it will provide an auspicious launching pad for you.

By the end of the year, Dozier had offered Bruce another twelve hundred dollars to extend his contract. He was promising Bruce an article in *Life* magazine. Everyone just needed to wait another few months until *Batman* debuted. If it did well, Dozier said, and already it appeared to be testing very well, *The Green Hornet* would follow. Bruce would not have to do any more tests, Dozier assured him; the role of Kato was already his.

The Green Hornet had been a Depression-era creation of radio mogul George Washington Trendle and serials writer Fran Striker. Just before Black Tuesday, Trendle had cashed out of the movie theater business and bought radio stations across Michigan. Looking to distinguish his stations, he and Striker created a program called *The Lone Ranger Show* in 1933, and struck the pop culture mother lode.

It was a western about a Texas Ranger who had survived an outlaw's ambush through the devoted efforts of an Indian named Tonto. The white man becomes a masked vigilante, working to restore order. The Lone Ranger lives by a creed: "that all men are created equal and that everyone has within himself the power to make this a better world; that God put the firewood there, but every man must gather and light it himself . . . that 'this Government, of the people, by the people, and for the people,' shall live always."

"The point," Trendle said, "was to teach the youngsters respect for the law." The uniquely American twist was that the Lone Ranger always worked outside the law, so that he could circumvent the most inconvenient ones. By the end of the decade, the show's listening audience numbered twenty million, mostly kids. During the worst of the Depression, the show satisfied a desire for order and a nostalgia for stability.

Trendle conceived *The Green Hornet*, he said, "to appeal to a little older group—the young people about to become voters. I wanted to show that racketeers and crooked politicians could succeed unless they were stopped." It was built from the same template: the Lone Ranger became the Green Hornet, Silver his trusty horse became the Chrysler Imperial Black Beauty, the silver-bullet six-shooter became the Hornet's deadly technology, and Tonto became Kato.

Britt Reid is a playboy millionaire distantly related to the Lone Ranger who inherits a media empire.* Reid also masks himself to work outside the law. Other American superheroes were regular people bestowed with extraordinary powers. Clark Kent was a working bullpen journalist, Superman a nearly omnipotent interplanetary migrant; Peter Parker, a depressive orphan, Spider-Man a wisecracking, high-flying media star. But Batman and the Green Hornet came from a different archetype. Bruce Wayne and Britt Reid were scions fueled by their wealth and rage to avenge the heinous violence done to their parents, endlessly descending into the depths of society to reverse the original crime in confrontations with evildoers.

Kato inherited Tonto's subordination, sense of duty, and Otherness. While adventuring in Asia, Britt Reid had saved his life in an unnamed incident. Kato had pledged his life to serving Reid because, according to the Hollywood writers, this was "a custom in some parts of the Orient." Before the first *Green Hornet* show aired in 1936, Cato—as he was originally named—was made Japanese. But while his name was changed to begin with the letter K, no one would ever pronounce it in the Japanese way. Trendle had another instruction for his staff—to present "a Kato who shows intelligence, affability, servility, alertness, and a certain sparkle that removes all traces of the usual Japanese immobility and austereness."

A Japanese American man, Tokutaro Hayashi, whose stage name was Raymond Toyo, originated the role of Kato. But by July 1939, after the Imperial Japanese Army had taken parts of China, the writers changed Kato to a Filipino, reflecting US interests in the Pacific.** The next year, Hayashi disappeared, presumably to the concentration camps. In the theatrical serials which premiered in 1940, Keye Luke played a Kato who described himself as Korean, the Asian ethnicity Universal Studios execs felt at the time was the least controversial.

As Dozier prepared the role for television a quarter-century later, he imagined Kato as pan-Oriental, a human conflation. He told Trendle that Bruce was "actually an American-born Chinese, but can play any sort of Oriental or Filipino. I don't

---

* In the 1960s version of *The Green Hornet*, this empire includes not just the newspaper his father had founded, the *Daily Sentinel*, but also a radio station and a television station.

** Radio publicists in 1938 took photos of Kato from a distance. Later, the role was filled by white men in yellowvoice.

think we should ever say what sort of nationality Kato is: just let him be what he looks like—an Oriental."

That was the point of Orientality: it was fungible.

Misrecognition had led Asians into cycles of shame, fear, and retreat. During World War II, when Japanese Americans were targeted, some Chinese and Filipino Americans put up signs on their homes and businesses: WE ARE CHINESE. Or WE ARE FILIPINOS. WE ARE NOT JAPANESE. Throughout history, Asian and Pacific Islander groups in America vied for favored status against each other and other racialized minorities, to be seen and individuated by whites in a winner-takes-nothing game. In 1965, the idea of the "Asian American" was still three years away.

In the meantime, the roles were clear. The Green Hornet was an Information Age boss, more brainpower than fist power, relying on capital, access, and technology. He did his work from the back seat, commanding Kato to "prepare the Black Beauty," "drive faster," or to simply *"gung fu!"* Kato was a skilled mechanic, weapons inventor, driver, and fighter, the sidekick whose labor made it possible for Britt Reid to wear the mask.

Bruce Lee, the Hong Kong boy who had been waited upon, cooked for, and driven around most of his young life, had grown up to play a manservant, cook, chauffeur, and an all-purpose yellow savior in America. It was a steep drop from Number One Son to the Green Hornet's number two.

By the end of 1965, Bruce had grown impatient over the delays, unhappy about the lack of details he had received, and disenchanted with the uncommunicative William Belasco. *Life* magazine had not yet called. Belasco was a "good for nothing sucker." The concept for *Batman* made him anxious. *Gung fu* wasn't camp to him. It was the furthest extension in sensibility of the metaphor of life as struggle. He poured out his frustrations in a letter to Taky.

"The Twentieth Century Fox deal is further postponed to next year. They have to wait for rating of 'Batman,'" he wrote. "As far as I'm concerned the Batman got to go, but I heard the rating is good though, probably 99% from children and imbeciles."

He was contemplating whether to move his family to Hollywood or Hong Kong. He had demanded eighteen hundred dollars from Belasco for round-trip tickets to Hong Kong so he could work with a film company he was speaking to there. He thought he might leave in March 1966. He listed some fencing and boxing books for Taky to read for teaching at the Seattle institute. But his focus was on restarting his acting career. In the meantime, he concluded, he was "just sitting around doing nothing!"

There was nothing he could do but wait.

CHAPTER 26
The Sum of All Projections

On Wednesday, January 12, 1966, *Batman* became the surprise TV hit of the season. An astonishing 52 percent of all televisions tuned in that night in America, to the bafflement of TV critics everywhere.

In the morning paper, behind the news of President Johnson's gloomy State of the Union address, which was preoccupied with the war in Vietnam, a *New York Times* reviewer wrote, "The show is amusing in spots, though the avant-campists might contend it wasn't really bad enough to be excellent." But, he noted, *Batman*'s merchandising would be "a full-fledged craze with a multimillion-dollar business potential."

ABC was all-in on *Batman*. It would air two half-hour shows a week, on Wednesday and Thursday nights, and added an unprecedented fourth commercial minute on each show. Bette Davis, Liberace, and Tallulah Bankhead were vying to fill the role of Special Guest Villain of the Week against the Caped Crusader, whose painted eyebrows were arched in permanent irony. It was the first year that television was broadcast completely in color, and *Batman*'s lurid pop colors were made for the moment. Dozier himself provided the cliffhanger narration—"Tune in tomorrow, same bat time, same bat channel!"

All this was good news for *The Green Hornet*. Bruce signed a second extension of his contract, and he and Linda packed up and moved out of James's home in Oakland into a small apartment on the busy corner of Wilshire Boulevard and Gayley Avenue, near the campus of the University of California at Los Angeles.

But Bruce still had concerns about Kato.

He had seen what happened with one of television's biggest shows, the long-running Western called *Bonanza*. Its writers had taken the name of the once-feared Chinatown tong, Hop Sing, given it to a cooking-and-grinning servant, and put the great character actor Victor Sen Yung in a pigtail and a baby blue Manchu suit to mouth lines like, "Good mo'ning, Meesta Cotlight, you take 'nuff food along?"

Bruce wondered if he was being set up to play a Chinese Tonto. "[The role of Kato] sounded at first like typical houseboy stuff," he recalled. "I tell Dozier, 'Look if you sign me up with all that pigtail and hopping around jazz, forget it. In the past the typical casting has been that kind of stereotype. Like with the Indians. You never see a human-being Indian on television."

Bruce requested a meeting with Dozier and the screenwriter so he could convey his ideas for Kato. Dozier parried, writing, "Later on before we start shooting, you may be sure we shall sit down and talk with you about various little things you can bring to the show, and I am sure we will profit greatly by your suggestions." Dozier now signed all his letters to Bruce with his chop.

By the end of April, Dozier had a pilot script and set the calendar. They would begin shooting on June 6. The premiere was set for September 9. The show was slated for the Friday night death slot, but everyone hoped excitement for *Batman* from Wednesdays and Thursdays might carry over.

Dozier rounded out the cast, selecting Van Williams as Britt Reid/the Green Hornet, Wende Wagner as his secretary Lenore "Casey" Case, Lloyd Gough as the police reporter Mike Axford, and Walter Brooke as District Attorney Frank Scanlon. Bruce was billed second on the show. He would shoulder the media advance work with Williams. He would appear on-screen an average of seven minutes for each twenty-six-minute episode, much more than any other actor but Williams.

But his pay stub would never reflect it. He received $400 per half-hour episode, the same terms he had signed on for *Number One Son*. Van Williams received $2,000. Supporting actor Lloyd Gough was paid $1,000, Wende Wagner $850, and Walter Brooke $750 per episode. In December, he received a small bump to $550 per episode. Bruce was receiving less than some of the stuntmen, a Chinaman's wages.

But Bruce and Linda felt their luck had finally turned. He wrote Fred Sato in Seattle, "I'll be playing Kato (doesn't sound like a Chinaman, does it), the right hand man of the Green Hornet. Instead of carrying all kinds of weapons, this fellow is to *gung fu* all his opponents.

"It will be a lot of fun and this job will take care of raising a family. Financially wise, this job is most satisfying."

Two weeks later, Bruce wrote Taky to tell him that they were moving into the Barrington Plaza, high-rise towers in West Los Angeles which, upon its opening, the *New York Times* had called "the largest privately built apartment development west of Chicago." Bruce crowed that the apartment came with "doormen and attendant parking, laundry & dry cleaning valet service, Olympic-size pool, all-wool carpeting, all electric kitchen (dishwasher, built-in range and oven, etc.), electronic huge elevators." The Lees settled into a twenty-third-floor apartment—"The higher, the more expensive," Bruce wrote—with a stunning view of downtown, installed a kiddie gate to keep Brandon off the balcony, and marveled at their fortune every morning when the sun rose over the San Gabriel Mountains. Burt Ward, who played Robin, lived on the twelfth floor.

Bruce cut a deal with the building manager to pay less than half the market rate in exchange for private *gung fu* lessons. Bruce had also begun lessons for Jay Sebring, in part because, his friend Peter Chin joked, "The most important thing that Bruce cared about was his hair." Sebring took Bruce to shop at Fred Segal, let him drive around in his Cobra, invited him to the right parties, and promised to introduce him to the right people as possible clients—Paul Newman, James Garner, and Vic Damone. One night Sebring brought Bruce to a show at Whisky a Go Go on Sunset and introduced him to Steve McQueen. Bruce told Taky he might fly to Vegas to meet Frank Sinatra, then he splurged some of his future earnings on a brand new sky-blue Chevy Nova.

Linda wrote, "Within a few months of Bruce's dazzling success, I found it almost impossible to remember how low we had been."

Dozier enrolled Bruce in twice-a-week acting classes with the legendary coach Jeff Corey, whose list of students had included James Dean, Jane Fonda, and Jack Nicholson. Corey's approach to acting was consonant with Bruce's approach to martial arts. "Engage your own intuition, use your own frames of reference and give something which is uniquely yours," Corey would tell his students. "Simplicity is the cherished quality."

Bruce told Taky, "This cat is very Zen-ish," and began buying books on the Stanislavski method. He offered to give Corey *gung fu* lessons, which the middle-aged coach politely declined. But when the scripts came in, the two of them realized that Kato had been given almost no lines.

In the pilot, he had seven lines—mostly of the "Look!" or "Are you all right?" variety. In the second episode, he had just one: "Over there!" For the first several episodes, most of his screen time came in the stock scene where Kato and the Hornet dash to the underground garage, he punches some wall buttons, and the two wait for the Black Beauty to rotate into position so that they can drive off. His most frequent speaking scene found him dressed in a white waiter's jacket and a black bow tie—looking like Warner Oland's Charlie Chan or a busboy at Ruby Chow's—picking up the phone to say, "Mr. Reid's residence." Keye Luke had been given more lines in the fifteen-minute theatrical serials of the 1940s.

Corey put him through nonverbal improvisation exercises. But as Bruce worked through them, he realized the character was a black box. Kato had no past, no future; there was literally nothing there. No one had ever bothered to imagine the stock "inscrutable Oriental" character beyond the labor he provided—driving Mr. Hornet, affirming Mr. Hornet, kicking ass to save Mr. Hornet and the city, then returning to the house to serve Mr. Britt Reid.

Even after shooting and press interviews had begun, Bruce felt like an impostor on the set. By day he told journalists that he was playing Kato as the strong, silent type. "They are going to portray me as The Weapon," he said. By night he was composing an impassioned letter to Dozier:

Dear Mr. Dozier,

Simplicity—to express the utmost in the minimum of lines and energy—is the goal of *Gung Fu*, and acting is not too much different.

Since the first episode, I've gained actual experience. I've learned to be "simply human" without unnecessary striving. I believe in Kato and am truthfully justifying the physical action economically. . . .

True that Kato is a house boy of Britt, but as the crime fighter, Kato is an "active partner" of the Green Hornet and not a "mute follower." Jeff Corey agrees and I myself feel that at least an occasional dialogue would certainly make me "feel" more at home with the fellow players. . . .

I'm not complaining, but I feel that an "active partnership" with the Green Hornet will definitely bring out a more effective and efficient Kato. My aim is for the betterment of the show and I bother you with this because you have been most understanding.

Thank you very much.

Sincerely,
Bruce Lee

Dozier responded quickly. "We think there is great value in presenting Kato as a somewhat taciturn and enigmatic 'man of action' rather than a talker," he wrote. "We have no intention of never having him say *anything*. He will have some dialogue now and then, but when he does, it will count for something.

"I think you are coming off very well on screen. Carry on."

At ABC's May upfronts, the gala events networks staged for media and advertisers to introduce their fall schedule, Bruce met Van Williams for the first time.

The two entered the packed banquet room, each wearing flower boutonnieres, to be introduced by Adam West, the star of *Batman*. Van introduced himself in his native Texas accent, though he would affect a bland mid-Atlantic one for Britt Reid. When he first met Bruce he could not understand his Hong Kong accent.

"I kind of said, 'Say that a little slower or something, I'm not getting it.' And he tried to say it a little slower. I still couldn't understand," Williams said. "Bruce had a very thick accent when I first met him. I mean, really thick, and he was hard to understand."

When it was Bruce's turn at the mic, he exclaimed with a broad smile, "Well, I'll say it the Chinese way, *Do jeh saai!* Thank you very much!" He bowed his head, chuckled nervously, and stepped back behind Williams. Of the many Cantonese ways to say thanks, Bruce had chosen the most formal, the one used to express deep gratitude for a gift bestowed.

Then the pro forma meeting threatened to go off the rails. A reporter asked about Kato's ethnicity, noting that the character had once been Japanese, then changed to Filipino.

Bruce stiffened. "Speaking for myself," he said, "I am Chinese."

The reporter pressed further, "Would some knowing Oriental protest since Kato, after all, was a Japanese name?"

Stern-faced, Bruce explained he was the equal of any black belt in *karate*. "Anyone object—I put them on their back," he said.

Dozier quickly grabbed the mic. It didn't matter if Kato was Japanese, Filipino, or Chinese because the show, he explained, "was not exactly striving for reality."

Williams recalled, "I felt like he was pushing himself a little bit for the affiliates, and I didn't think that was really him. A little bit of arrogance came through, which I didn't think was exactly the thing to do at that time.

"But after all of that was done and we're backstage and everything else, we kind of got to talking. He kind of relaxed in a little bit. Now I can understand him a little bit better," Williams added, "and he just seemed like a nice guy."

ABC's press flacks quickly realized they were in uncharted territory. There was no precedent for a campaign around an Asian costar of any ethnicity.

In July, two months before the show's premiere, they sent Bruce to a low-stakes personal appearance in Minneapolis. Bruce left the *Saint Paul Dispatch*'s TV columnist, P. M. Clepper, effusive: "I can tell the producers of *The Green Hornet* how to improve their show—even before it's on the air. What they should do is let the Hornet's sidekick, Kato, write his own dialogue. If they did that, I predict they'd have another duo as entertaining as Bob Culp and Bill Cosby on *I Spy*."

Clepper called Bruce "bright and funny, as well as an expert in Oriental fighting." Half the column quoted Bruce's excited *gung fu* patter, including his disdain for "fancy jazz" and "land swimming." ABC could not have hoped for anything better, and Clepper's comparison of Bruce's Kato to Bill Cosby's cool, smart, ultramodern Scotty on *I Spy*, rather than the old Tonto, was exactly the kind of press Bruce wanted.

Clepper called Kato's limited speaking "a shame" because the actor told hilarious jokes, like the one Bruce said he had told his producer: "How lucky can you get—you've got a Chinaman from Hong Kong who can say 'Britt Reid.'" After this point, Bruce's Kato interviews were a steady stream of old Oriental one-liners. "I don't smoke, don't drink, and don't gamble, but that's as far as I go," Bruce said. "I do chew gum. After all, many men smoke, but Fu Manchu." He told the same joke a dissipated Anna May Wong repeated in her latter days to fans who visited her at an LA dive called the Dragon's Den: "700 million Chinese can't all be Wong."

But jokes he had told friends at a post-workout *dim sum* table hit differently on the pages of the nation's biggest magazines and newspapers. Bruce told Clepper he had been in show business since childhood, but came off disingenuous in discussing his father's opera career: "Gongs and the whole bit—I had a heck of a time understanding what was going on."

Under the hot lamplights of the world's biggest dream factory, the proud Chinese man and teacher of the Asian fighting arts turned into a fledgling star a little too eager to please, as if he worried his black Kato suit was an invisibility cloak he could not control, and that at any moment he might disappear.

But a buzz for Bruce came from an unexpected source: white middle-class housewives.

An early article in a magazine called *TV/Radio Show* signaled the shift. Written by a pseudonymous "Sara," it began, "There's only one thing wrong with Bruce

Lee—he's perfect. He's a perfect husband, a perfect father, and perfectly cast in the role of Kato."

Grocery checkout stand tabloids like *TV/Radio Show*, *TV/Radio Mirror*, and *TV and Movie Screen* were crucial for the networks. Housewives were arguably television's most coveted demographic. *TV and Movie Screen*'s certified circulation was four hundred thousand. *The Green Hornet* would begin airing as the Supreme Court deliberated over the *Loving* decision. ABC publicists pitched a new angle—Bruce's marriage to Linda and their mixed-race son, Brandon.

In articles bylined by white women, the Lees generated headlines like "I Want My Son to Be a Mixed-Up Kid!" and "What's It REALLY Like to Live a Mixed Marriage!" Photo spreads featured the beaming family and artsy black-and-whites of Bruce performing *gung fu*. "Marriage is a friendship," Bruce told a reporter. "Marriage is breakfast in the morning, work during the day—the husband at his work, the wife at hers—dinner at night and quiet evenings together talking, reading, or watching television."

Bruce was just the Oriental next door. He said he might teach Brandon martial arts before he taught him baseball, but he would let his son decide if he wanted to be Taoist or Baptist. Linda was "more Oriental than some of the Chinese I know," Bruce said. "She's quiet. Calm. She doesn't yak-yak-yak all the time like some women."

ABC's publicists scheduled solo interviews for Linda, and she was highly quotable. "A lot of people, especially here, where I guess mixed marriages aren't as common as in Seattle or San Francisco, have asked me, 'What's it really like?'" she told a reporter. "Well, I'll tell you something: the biggest 'adjustment' *I've* had to make is learning how to eat *rice* instead of *potatoes*!"

Movies like *Japanese War Bride*, *Sayonara*, and *South Pacific* had sentimentalized the "good war" in Asia and the Pacific and its radioactive fallout by focusing on interracial love. These films gently called out racist attitudes. Sidney Poitier's *Guess Who's Coming to Dinner* was a year away, closely following the *Loving* decision. Linda and Bruce had agreed not to speak ill about her family, all the better to protect her mother and maintain a narrative much bigger than themselves. Their story fit the Cold War ideal of a colorblind nation united against communism in Asia.

"Basically," Bruce said, "human traits are the same everywhere."

Peak coverage came in a piece in *TV Picture Life*, one of the nation's largest tabloids, entitled "Love Knows No Geography." Its author, Fredda Dudley Balling, had interviewed Bruce and Linda and filed a straightforward piece for *TV and Movie Screen* under the headline, "Our Mixed Marriage Brought Us a Miracle of Love." But in a second piece for *TV Picture Life*, she would spin a delirious kind of fan fiction.

"How does it happen," her piece begins, "that two people from opposite ends of the earth meet, fall in love, establish a true and contented union, and bring up their children as a triumph of human grace? Let the story of Bruce Lee (Kato in Twentieth Century Fox's 'The Green Hornet') and his wife, Linda Emery Lee, explain it."

In this story Linda is the star. The lovely blonde enrolls in a Mandarin class Bruce is teaching at the University of Washington, and becomes his top pupil and the most popular girl in a cohort of international students. By summer, she and Bruce are partying at a classmate's beachside pool. In the winter, they sit together in a car at the same beach speaking quietly. As rain softly pelts the roof, Linda asks herself, "Might the very differences between us solve problems? Might each of us have more to bring one another because we are, in some ways, half a world apart?"

Linda's mother gently counsels her to think carefully about her future and discuss it with Bruce. In the next scene, he slides a platinum wedding band on her finger. They visit Hong Kong, where Bruce presents her with a pair of velvet boxes: "One held a white gold wedding set and five generous diamonds, and the other revealed a brilliant solitaire."

The rapturous couple enjoys an enchanting sunset at Repulse Bay. But then Linda hears a round of loud gunfire-like pops, a premonition of war, and bursts into fearful tears.

"The Red hordes must have landed," Dudley Balling writes. But no, it is simply the opening of a new Chinese restaurant. The red firecrackers are warding off evil spirits, bringing auspicious luck for the marriage. The strings swell. A denouement:

When the Lees returned to Hollywood, one of Linda's friends observed, "Do you realize that you have an accent? You sound exactly like Bruce."

"Why not?" asked Mrs. Lee. "We're a family."

FADE TO BLACK.

A yellow-fever fantasy inspired by a masked Oriental who says little, high-kicks bad guys, and outfits himself so alluringly in black-on-black.

On the set, Bruce was struggling to find his place, both on the set and in front of the camera. He was fighting the feeling that he didn't deserve to be there. "As I looked around," he later recalled, "I saw a lot of human beings. And as I looked at myself, I was the only robot there. I was not being myself."

Long days that began before sunrise and ended after midnight were routine. Bored between takes, he tried to entertain the crew by flashing his muscles and kicking dimes off six-foot-high camera gimbals. He gave *gung fu* seminars to his costars for as long as he could hold their attention.

"I knew what he was doing," said Van Williams. "He really wanted to show off what he could do. He didn't have the time to do that on-screen, because when he'd go in, he'd do one shot and it was all over."

Bruce invented a new game: sneaking up behind a crew member and throwing a back fist or a jump kick over their shoulder, leaving them with only a swoosh of air and a tap of their earlobe to marvel that they hadn't just had their head knocked off.

"He was just so fast and accurate with the tip of his toe," Williams said.

Until he wasn't. One day a grip talking with Williams turned his face just as

Bruce's kick was coming in and had his jaw dislocated. "The executive producer comes roaring down, 'That's it!'" Williams recalled. "'No more of that stuff, Bruce!'"

Bruce awaited the last five minutes of each episode, because after the Hornet had solved the crime, the only thing left was for Kato to kick some criminal ass. But as Bruce shot these scenes, he found himself in conflict with the white stuntmen.

Most of these fall guys had come up on the old Westerns. They were used to staging fights, veteran stuntman "Judo" Gene LeBell recalled, in "the old John Wayne method where you'd reach from left field, tell a story, and hit the man." Hollywood's Production Code was fading, but most American fight scenes were still big, dull, and lumbering.

"The fights I had seen on-screen back in those days weren't very good," said Stirling Silliphant, a leading screenwriter.

Kicking was verboten, he said, because censors believed it was "not good sportsmanship." As late as 1972, a film rep trying to sell kung fu movies to American distributors was told, "When somebody throws a punch, they want to see John Wayne throw a roundhouse. They don't want someone leaping up and kicking you in the head. That's un-American."

Bruce wanted his on-screen fights to look realistic. At first he simply did what he did on the fight floor. "He'd hit you in ten different spots," said LeBell. But the stuntmen were unsure of how to receive his punch or kick. Benny Dobbins, Van Williams's longtime double and *The Green Hornet*'s lead stunt coordinator, tried to explain to Bruce that he needed to move more slowly and give the stuntmen more distance so that they could react. Bruce would not listen. Constantly, if often unintentionally, he clocked the stuntmen with full force. They marked Bruce as a "tagger," an actor who didn't pull his punches, and they started quitting. "The tension grew and it grew," said Williams. Bruce and Benny Dobbins nearly came to blows over all of it, until Williams intervened.

Dobbins backed up and took another tack. First he asked LeBell to break the young colt. LeBell was a redheaded, five-foot-ten, 185-pound former national *judo* champion. In 1963, LeBell had taken offense when he was told that *judo* was fraudulent and that no *judoka* could ever beat a respectable middleweight boxer. He accepted a challenge to disprove it in the ring. In the fourth round LeBell took the pro boxer Milo Savage to the ground and choked him out in a landmark fight that presaged the rise of mixed martial arts.

LeBell had a locker-room alpha dog style and was loved by the blue-collar stuntmen. He wore Bruce down with a showman's timing and racial gibes.

"I'd tell him, 'You're so great you could be a world-class stuntman. We'd have you double all the kids,'" LeBell said. "I'd tell him he put too much starch in my shirt."

As Bruce seethed, the white guys guffawed. One day when the stuntmen felt the kid was being particularly much, LeBell hoisted Bruce over his shoulder in a wrestler's crouching nelson hold—one arm between the legs and the other around his neck—and carried him around the soundstage as Bruce screamed, "Put me down! I'm going to kill you!"

"I can't put you down, Bruce. You'd kill me," LeBell retorted, as the stuntmen roared with laughter.

After the *chanbara* and *Game of Death*–loving director Quentin Tarantino read Matthew Polly's account of these stories, he decided that Bruce had "nothing but disrespect" for "American stuntmen." He wrote a cinematic vengeance into his novel-turned-MAGA-era-movie, *Once Upon a Time . . . in Hollywood*. His hero Cliff Booth, a fall guy modeled partly on LeBell, fights an insufferable Bruce Lee character and puts the Chinaman back in his place. But Tarantino had taken offense where LeBell had not. LeBell and Bruce became close friends—the locker-room ribbing never stopped—and training partners.

On the *Green Hornet* set, Dobbins and Williams executed the second part of their plan. Television directors usually refused to show an actor the raw footage known as dailies. It brought out an actor's perfectionism, setting off a domino effect of reshoots that messed with continuity, schedules, and good sense. But after securing the buy-in of the cameraman, the director, and the executive producer, Dobbins and Williams appointed a delighted Bruce the stunt coordinator for the day. They wanted to show him how he actually looked on film.

The scene involved four men in low lighting, and Kato breaking down a door to free a captive Green Hornet. After the shoot, a proud Bruce joined the crew and the stuntmen in the playback room. "It was hilarious," Williams remembered. "The scene opens up. It's pitch black. It's yelling and screaming. People fly through the air. You don't ever see Bruce at all."

"Somebody on the first row started to laugh, and then it went back all the way up to where we were," Williams said. Soon the entire crew was howling.

It was all too much for the twenty-five-year-old. "Somebody's laughing at him?" Williams said. "Oh, that just killed him." Bruce fled to his dressing room, slammed the door, and refused to speak to anyone. Hours later, he emerged and asked to speak with Williams and Dobbins.

"I don't know a damn thing about this business," he told them. "You guys know what you're doing. I don't want to do it anymore."

The three sat down. Bruce needed to understand some basics. The camera flattened space. The frame-rate technology could not match his speed. The stuntmen required physical distance and personal respect. The experienced crew needed his trust.

Picture Bruce, humbled, nodding.

Perhaps he left that night feeling for the first time like he belonged.

CHAPTER 27
Mirrors and Smoke

After Jack Dempsey's career was over, he began wondering what he might pass on to the next generation of boxers. He thought about his entire career, from his early days in Manassa, Colorado, to his last prizefight against Gentleman Gene Tunney in Chicago, and everything he had been taught by trainers, managers, and other fighters along the way.

"Like a blotter on legs," he recalled, "I absorbed all that information in those days, and then discarded what seemed wrong."

In longhand, he filled 384 pages with all that he had learned. In the end he was satisfied that he had written "a clear panorama of self-defense." The book he published in 1950, *Championship Fighting*, became one of Bruce's favorites.

At the twilight of his own career, to amuse his students and friends, William Dozier wrote something he called "A Hollywood Glossary." Under "T," he wrote:

Television—Once the scourge and then the savior of Hollywood, it has never lived down Frank Lloyd Wright's unforgettable description, "chewing gum for the eyes." Hundreds of little and a few big men scrambling and falling all over one another trying desperately to pretend their primary purpose is something other than to sell merchandise.

He had been one of those "few big men."

From a merchandising point of view, Batmania was a historic and rare piece of good news for the network in distant third. As *The Green Hornet* neared its premiere, ABC had landed sponsorship from General Mills, Bristol Myers, and Lehn & Fink beauty products. Its merchandising department boasted of deals with seventy-five licensors to create two hundred separate *Green Hornet* products, including "trading cards, buttons, playing cards, board games, puzzles, comic books, coloring books, paint-by-number sets, slot cards, hats, masks, T-shirts, sweatshirts, baby bibs, greeting cards, candy, bedspreads, glass ware, hosiery, slippers, jewelry, towels, quilts, rugs, and peanut butter!"

But *The Green Hornet* was not to be *Batman*. Dozier had wanted to position *The Green Hornet* like *Batman* in 1966—bright colors and outrageous villains for the kids, happy nostalgia and clever irony for the adults, a necessary escape for an awful age in America. But George Trendle—who found *Batman* insultingly dumb—wanted his show played like the interwar moral drama he had created.

Dozier came to think of Trendle's notes as being like the pompous dolor of the funeral priest who opens the *Green Hornet* pilot, zapping the fun before it even got started. There would be no irony, no eccentric camera angles, no *Biff! Bam! Crash!* The mood would be dark, the palette shadowy, the crimes more violent. But adults found *The Green Hornet* too cheesy for noir, too serious for distraction.

Up against *The Wild Wild West* and *Tarzan* in Friday prime time, *The Green Hornet*'s premiere came nowhere near *Batman*'s 52 share. To his friends, Bruce expressed excitement about the show. With Taky, he was real: "The first national rating of 'Green Hornet' was indeed not good; however ABC and Greenway Production are not too worried about it.

"However one thing is lousy," he wrote. "*Tarzan* beat us."

The Hornet's ratings never turned around. Dozier and the cast made a belated push at the network to extend the show to an hour. At a sitcom's length, they argued, they had no room to develop any drama. Bruce was still averaging only a few lines per episode, mostly of the "What do we do now, boss?" variety. When he continued to press for a meatier role, Dozier blamed Trendle for backgrounding Kato.

But out in America something was happening.

Like many in his generation, Jeff Chinn was a child raised on television. For him and his Chinese American family, it was a constant source of disheartenment. "Whenever an Asian person came on the TV screen, we would all drop everything that we were doing and go, 'Hey look, there's a Chinese on the screen!'" he said. "But about ninety-nine percent of the time we would be disappointed because it would be some stereotypical Asian guy talking funny.

"When I first saw *The Green Hornet* I thought it was really cool because I saw not only a Chinese guy on the TV screen, but he portrayed a superhero," Jeff said. "The show was called *The Green Hornet*, but everyone knew that Kato was the one that did all the fighting."

Bruce finally received a concession. "The Preying Mantis" was the tenth episode of the season and the first in which he appeared for more than two-thirds of the screen time. It was scheduled for the week before the Thanksgiving holiday.

The Green Hornet and Kato are called to prevent an imminent tong attack on a Chinese restaurant. To extend its extortion racket into Chinatown, the Italian mob has hired a tong run by Low Sing, played by the Japanese American actor Makoto "Mako" Iwamatsu, who practices a very strange style of Mantis *gung fu*. In their first fight, Low Sing leaves Kato upside down in a trash can.

"You know," Kato says to Britt Reid in his most consequential line yet, "if we ever meet up with that masked *gung fu* man again, I want him."

At the climax, the Green Hornet and the mob boss stand united in wanting to shut down Low Sing's rogue operations. But Low Sing refuses, saying he no longer will take orders from the mob or anyone else.

"How would you stop us?" Low Sing sneers at the Green Hornet. "*Gung fu?*"

"Isn't that the traditional way?" the Hornet answers. He gives Kato a look. "What do you say, Low Sing? Man against man."

Kato and Low Sing formally bow toward each other. (For the next couple of years, this strange formality becomes commonplace in Bruce's on-screen fights and choreography.) Soon they are circling and tumbling around each other. Kato leaps into a double front jump kick and steps in with Wing Chun punches. Low Sing slashes at Kato's face, drawing blood. But then, inexplicably, he keels over stiffly. Kato's *dim mak* fists apparently have had a deadly effect.

George Trendle had insisted that the fight "not be overdone." He got his wish. What was likely the first staged *gung fu* fight in American television history was forgettable. But, encouraged by Benny Dobbins, Bruce had choreographed the scene with Dan Inosanto, who served as Mako's body double. "The Preying Mantis" marked the first time in his career Bruce drew from his repertoire of jump kicks, which he knew were ineffectual in the street but spellbinding on-screen.

And the episode sealed the legend of Kato. Bruce was invited to serve as grand marshal of the Los Angeles Chinese New Year's parade. Personal appearance offers poured in. Bruce sent letters to his friends telling them to watch. Still, he confided to Taky:

> The show is doing bad, rating wise. Dozier is trying to make it go by changing it into an hour show. Whether or not we can change it remains to be seen. For our sake, we better....
>
> You know, whether or not this show will go, the show will last at least until March. So Gung Fu will have enough exposure and so is Kato, Bruce Lee.

The fan mail was telling a clear story. Merchandisers knew it too. "Right in the beginning, toys came out with just the image of Van Williams. Slowly, as Bruce became more popular, they put his image next to Van Williams," the collector and historian Perry Lee said. "In the end, he became more popular than Van Williams. He stood alone."

Just after shooting "The Preying Mantis," Bruce submitted a thirteen-page episode treatment he had written to Dozier. "The Cobra from the East" finds the Green Hornet protecting a drug trafficker from an assassin named the Cobra, who keeps an arsenal of deadly snakes in a walking stick. For most of the episode, Britt Reid is immobilized by a poisonous snakebite, allowing Kato three fight scenes and a chance to reshoot the stock Black Beauty underground garage scene without the Green Hornet.

"Future episodes might need such a shot," Bruce wrote.

At the climax, Kato neutralizes the Cobra's henchman with a two-section *gung fu* staff. The Green Hornet's only action is to knock the Cobra onto his stick, whereupon the villain is bitten by one of his own snakes. The Cobra himself inexplicably bites his henchman, and both of them perish from the poison. Bruce had written the quiet stuff loudly: the Hornet cannot stop villains without gadgets, dumb luck, and Kato.

Dozier accepted the treatment with thanks and wondered if Bruce had been right all along—that there was much more to Kato. Had he made a mistake in having Kato "be what he looks like—an Oriental"? Perhaps Kato was a South Korean or a Chinese ally whom Britt Reid had met in Korea in a "police action."*

"Where and how did their relationship come into being?" Dozier asked. "What does Kato do in his off hours?" In a long letter he appealed to top network execs, arguing that the show needed a half-hour more and a second season to reveal the characters: "If we could know more about [Kato] as a human being we would be more interested in his exploits as a crime fighter.

"Further," Dozier concluded, "the merchandising on *Green Hornet* is an important item for everyone concerned, and has proved very lucrative so far."

Bruce told Taky he was meeting with other producers and directors, but he saw the Jun Fan Gung Fu Institute as a hedge against his uncertain fortunes. "I'm preparing for it," he wrote. "Let's make use of this opportunity, buddy."

In January Bruce flew to Oakland to surprise James Yimm Lee at a banquet hall for his birthday. For a night, the crew was all back together, joking and feasting. James stood and raised his glass for a toast, shouting, "*Tin haa yut gaa!* 天下一家! Under the heavens, there is one family!"

The old friends roared and laughed and downed their drinks together.

At the end of 1966 *The Green Hornet* approached its mid-season break. Shooting for all of the season's episodes was nearly completed, and the cast anxiously awaited their second-season fate. Dozier scheduled an appearance of the Green Hornet and Kato on *Batman*. The two-episode special crossover would air on March 2 and 3, 1967, during the high-stakes sweeps week that would set ad rates and determine which shows would be canceled.

Bruce was guaranteed more visibility and good bonus money. But when he got the script, he was so upset that he stomped off the soundstage, slammed his car door, and screeched off the lot. The *Batman* writers had concocted a scene in which Robin, played by Burt Ward, kicked Kato's ass.

Bruce certainly must have objected to showing *gung fu* defeated by *karate*. He definitely objected to being defeated by Burt Ward. Bruce's downstairs neighbor at the Barrington Plaza claimed to be a black belt in *karate*. But Bruce had trained with him, and didn't think much of Burt's claim.

---

* This euphemistic language is President Harry Truman's, who used it to describe to the American public what we now call the Korean War.

When he returned, Bruce told Dozier, Williams, and everyone else in earshot, "I refuse to do it. That makes me look like an idiot." Dozier asked Williams what he thought of the scene. He supported Bruce. Dozier instructed the writers to have the scene end in a draw, "a Mexican stand-off."

But it wasn't over. In the lead-up, Bruce treated Kato vs. Robin as if it were a prizefight. He rallied his *Green Hornet* cast and crew members, and fired himself up. "We'll see how great a black belt you are, boy!" he shouted across the set.

As cameras rolled, Bruce stalked him across the stage. "But boy, he came swaggering on that set! And he was staring [Burt] down and everything else," Williams recalled. "I'm telling you he had him scared to death!"

"Bruce, remember this is not for real," Burt stammered. "It's just a show."

"I started to crowd Burt and he started to flap his elbows, jumping around me," Bruce told *Black Belt* editor Mito Uyehara. "I was really scaring him until I heard someone in the back whisper, 'the black panther and the yellow chicken.'

"At that instant, I burst out laughing. I couldn't keep a straight face anymore."

By then, he, Linda, and Brandon had been evicted from the Barrington Plaza. "The owners of these buildings found out that the manager was giving deals to everybody for their services," Linda said. "Yeah, 'You're out of here!'" They hastily found a spot in Inglewood, fifteen miles away.

ABC decided to complete airing the full twenty-six episodes. On January 17, 1967, William Self, 20th Century-Fox's executive vice president, wrote Bruce, "In spite of some unfavorable publicity, I want to reassure that ABC has not yet dropped its option on the series and there is still some hope for next year."

But he concluded ominously, "At any rate, it was nice to have you with Twentieth Century-Fox."

On March 7, days after the *Batman* crossover episodes were broadcast and with some *Green Hornet* episodes still to air, William Dozier wrote Bruce to inform him of ABC's final decision:

Dear Bruce:

Confucius say: "Green Hornet buzz no more."
    I'm sorry, too, as I know you must be. You worked very hard, and very well, and I believe you made a lot of friends for yourself, as well as respectful admirers.
    It has been a great joy for me, both personally and professionally, to work with you.

My best, always,
Bill

This time he did not sign his letter with Bruce's chop.

•••

The Green Hornet show had been canceled before it even had a chance to showcase much true *gung fu*. But Bruce's presence had introduced the Asian martial arts to national audiences and ushered in a new era for the movement in the US. After months of letters pouring into the *Black Belt* magazine offices, Mitoshi Uyehara finally decided to run his first Bruce Lee cover story in the October 1967 issue.

Mito, as he was known, was born in 1928 and raised in Lahaina, Maui. During the 1955 recession he moved to Los Angeles to work as an accountant for a Japanese bank. He was studying the Japanese art of *aikido*, then still new to the United States. His writing career began when he was asked by the influential Japanese American newspaper *Rafu Shimpo* to write about it. In 1962, Uyehara launched *Black Belt* as a national publication, overseeing almost all aspects of the magazine, from publishing and editing to its minimalist design.

At first Uyehara focused on what he knew—*aikido*, *judo*, *kendo*, and *karate*. But soon the self-titled "magazine of self-defense" was exploring other arts—*tai chi*, *pukulan*, Okinawan *te*, *arnis*, and *gung fu*. But his curiosity mirrored that of Bruce, Ed Parker, and the rising new generation, and his magazine tracked and boosted the rise of Asian martial arts in the United States.

But featuring Bruce and *gung fu* marked a shift for the magazine, which had until then focused on contest coverage, technique tutorials, interviews with fighters and masters, and retellings of history and legends. "Is *The Green Hornet*'s Version of Gung Fu Genuine?" was the magazine's first celebrity profile. The writer Maxwell Pollard presented Bruce as a modern martial arts man—pedigreed but progressive, physical and philosophical, a bicultural family man who also happened to be regularly mobbed by autograph seekers.

Three years after Ed Parker's Long Beach breakthrough, Bruce was commanding up to three thousand dollars to appear as a guest at fight tournaments across the country.* Whether at a Fresno auditorium, Long Beach Municipal Auditorium, or Madison Square Garden, he needed security to guide him through throngs of fans. "I couldn't protect myself," he admitted.

The martial arts world had found its first true star. "People ask me as an actor, 'How good are you really in *gung fu*?'" Bruce said. "I always kid them about that. If I tell them I'm good, probably they'll say I'm boasting, but if I tell them I'm no good, you know I'm lying."

In Washington, DC, for Jhoon Rhee's National Karate Championships, Bruce entertained a lunch crowd of reporters. He admitted that he thought the *Green Hornet* scripts "were lousy," and that the show had been doomed. He said he was considering two different starring roles, one for CBS and the other for Dozier and

---

* This is the equivalent of twenty-nine thousand dollars in 2024 dollars.

Greenway Productions—the first a "one-hour fantasy" about which he could give no more details, the other "a kind of *I Spy* thing called *Charlie and Chan*. I'd be Charlie, a kung fu teacher, and Chan would be a ski instructor."

He was still feeding the white writers a constant patter of Oriental one-liners. In *gung fu*, he told them, "I possess the yellow belt. It signifies that I can run pretty damn fast."

Such performances already seemed to belong to another time.

The United States had been at war in Asia and the Pacific for a quarter-century. At home, even the passage of civil rights legislation had not reduced the violence that Black people daily faced. In 1964, Malcolm X invoked the Chinese revolution as a model of how "the people rose up against their oppressors." He told a New York crowd, "So today, when the Black man starts reaching out for what America says are his rights, the Black man feels that he is within his rights—when he becomes the victim of brutality by those who are depriving him of his rights—to do whatever is necessary to protect himself."

When he was murdered the following year in Harlem's Audubon Ballroom before a packed house, the concept of self-defense no longer felt academic. By the fall of 1966, Stokely Carmichael and his comrades had moved the Student Nonviolent Coordinating Committee away from integration marches toward what he called "Black Power," with the goals of dismantling white supremacy and building political institutions that functioned for the good of all.

Through the Black freedom struggle, Asians in America were finding the words and actions for their own struggles. Speaking to a conference of Black organizers in San Francisco, Richard Aoki, a Japanese American activist, called the Vietnam War a "double genocide": "If the Black soldier kills an Oriental Viet Cong, that's one less Oriental running loose. If the Oriental Viet Cong kills the Black soldier, one Black soldier ain't coming back."

Asians were finding purpose in solidarity work. In Harlem, Yuri Kochiyama was active with the Congress of Racial Equality and the Organization of Afro-American Unity. In Detroit, Grace Lee Boggs was organizing Black autoworkers. Richard Aoki was the most contradictory of his generation of warriors, a dynamic street-hardened radical—the kind some admiringly called an "organic intellectual"—who was discovered later to have also been an FBI informant. Born in 1938, he had grown up in the Topaz concentration camp and served in the US Army. When he killed himself with a gun at the age of seventy, Aoki laid out his army uniform and his Black Panther uniform on his bed beside each other.

In the fall of 1966, Aoki was invited by his friends Huey Newton and Bobby Seale to become one of the first members of the Black Panther Party for Self-Defense. He took Newton and Seale to a book distributor with direct ties to China to obtain copies of the book *Quotations from Chairman Mao Tse-Tung*, known as the Little

Red Book, which the Panthers used to educate cadres and to sell to the white students to raise funds. Newton and Seale wanted to purchase weapons. They asked Aoki to procure some for the party, Seale recalled, "to defend ourselves as Malcolm X said we must."

Aoki gave the Black Panthers a 9mm handgun and an M-1 carbine, and sold them a .357 Magnum. He helped set up its chapter on the Berkeley campus, attracting several Asians before the party closed itself to non-Blacks. He was there when Newton and Seale outlined the party's Ten-Point Program. It began: "We Want Freedom. We Want Power to Determine the Destiny of Our Black Community."

Freedom meant "Land, Bread, Housing, Education, Clothing, Justice and Peace." The platform called for "An Immediate End to Police Brutality and the Murder of Black People." It also called for an end to the draft: "We will not fight and kill other people of color in the world who, like Black people, are being victimized by the white racist government of America."

Much of the party's appeal to Black residents lay in its efforts to deliver a broad array of badly needed community services, which included food, health, clothing, education, and martial arts programs. But it was sealed by their audacious stand against authorities. The party's cop-watch groups were "dedicated to defending our Black community from racist police oppression and brutality."

Named a field marshal, Aoki trained select members in weapons for their cop-watch patrols. He said, "I remember several times, some person was being arrested, might have been a traffic stop, couple of cops busting him. We roll up, surround the cops. They'd radio out and they surround us. And the next thing you know the community is surrounding them. That was awesome."

In the spring of 1967, alarmed by the Panther patrols, a Republican assemblyman from Oakland named Don Mulford sponsored a bill banning the carrying of loaded weapons in California. On May 2, Huey, Bobby, the Panthers' first recruit, a seventeen-year-old named Bobby Hutton, and twenty-eight other men and women marched up the steps of the state capitol in Sacramento, packing loaded guns and rifles, to protest Mulford's bill. Seale read a statement calling on people to "take full note of the racist California legislature aimed at keeping the Black people disarmed and powerless at the very same time that racist police agencies throughout the country are intensifying the terror and repression of Black people."

History had shown, he said—from the wars on American Indians to the lynchings of Black people, the bombing of Hiroshima and Nagasaki to the incarceration of Japanese Americans—"that towards people of color, the racist power structure of America has but one policy: repression, genocide, terror, and the big stick."

He concluded, "The Black Panther Party for Self-Defense believes that the time has come for Black people to arm themselves against this terror before it is too late."

The Republican-led assembly passed this gun control bill with the National Rifle

Association's vocal support. It was quickly signed by Governor Ronald Reagan. The following spring, two nights after the assassination of Martin Luther King Jr., the police and the Black Panthers entered into a shootout in North Oakland. As the house where the Panthers had been cornered caught fire, Bobby Hutton dropped his gun, put his hands up, and stepped through the smoke to surrender. Police shot him to death.

Seale was devastated. He took the guns away from party members and instructed the marshals to retreat from the city for their weapons training, the better to promote focus and discipline. "You're in the Black Panther Party," he said. "People are going to get killed for nothing. We have to learn to defend ourselves."

One day Bruce told Dan Inosanto he had been studying Mao Zedong and Ho Chi Minh. He wanted to understand how they thought about war and strategy.

Dan was not an ideologue. He had volunteered for the army and served as a paratrooper in the 101st Airborne Division. He also felt fortunate to have been discharged just before the massive deployments to Vietnam.* But Bruce's talk of Mao and Ho Chi Minh intrigued him.

Bruce gave Dan copies of two books that he had heavily underlined—the Little Red Book and Samuel Griffith's 1963 translation of Sun Tzu's *Art of War*. Dan took note of one passage in the latter that Bruce loved. At the People's Liberation Army stronghold in the remote Jinggang Mountains, Griffith wrote, Mao had adapted Sun Tzu's teachings into four slogans to prepare for battle against the Japanese:

When the enemy advances, we retreat!
When the enemy halts, we harass!
When the enemy seeks to avoid battle, we attack!
When the enemy retreats, we pursue!

There was another quote from Mao, too, that would be forever seared into Bruce's and Dan's minds, one that harmonized with Jack Dempsey: "We should carefully study the lessons which were learned in past wars at the cost of blood and which have been bequeathed to us. . . . We must put conclusions thus reached to the test of our own experiences and absorb what is useful, reject what is useless, and add what is specifically our own."

---

* Dan recalled, "The life expectancy of a second lieutenant in Vietnam is like, they say, twenty minutes once they hit the drop zone." Interview with Dan Inosanto, Sept. 26, 2023.

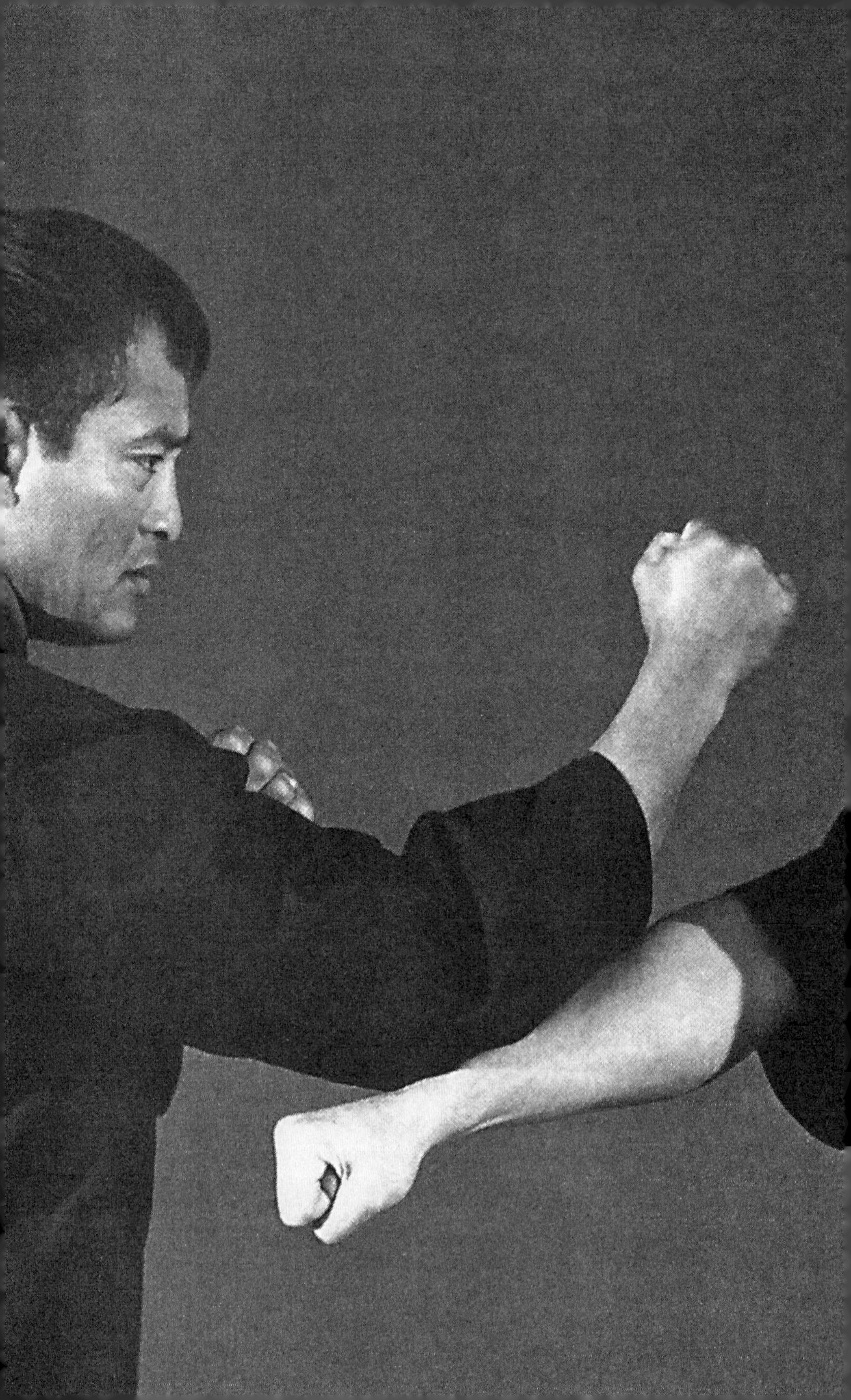

PART VIII
Warrior State of Mind
1967–1969

All art is martial art. Writing is fighting.

The individual in the Asian moral universe trains to fight. Living is fighting. Life is war.

—FRANK CHIN

Bruce and Dan Inosanto, 1969.
Photo courtesy of the Bruce Lee Family Archive.

CHAPTER 28
The Names, Part 1

As Bruce and Dan drove down a Los Angeles highway one bright day, they fell into the kind of charged discussion in which each could almost feel what the other would say next.

"We were talking about fencing, Western fencing," Dan recalled. "Bruce said the most efficient means of countering in fencing was the stop-hit. A stop-hit is when you do not parry and then counter, it's all done in one step. When the opponent attacks, you intercept his move with a thrust or hit of your own."

Bruce told him, "We should name our method the 'stop-hitting fist-style' or 'the intercepting fist style.'"

The name had come to Bruce at the beginning of 1967. He wrote it in small precise strokes in his Day-Timer under January 6— "截拳道"—then again even more decisively on the next page, across the entries for January 8, 9, and 10.

In Los Angeles, Bruce was reconciling the philosophical aspirations of his time in Seattle, where he had emphasized self-defense, with the physical intensity of his time in Oakland, where he had focused on attacks. He explained, "截 means 'to stop, to stalk, to intercept,' while 拳 means 'fist or style' and 道 means 'the Way or the ultimate reality.'" The idea of 截拳, "the intercepting fist," captured the efficiency and directness of the stop-hit. It was an established concept captured in two *gung fu* sayings—敵不動, 我不動, 敵一動, 我先動, "When the enemy does not move, I do not move, when the enemy moves, I move first"; and 後發先至, "Strike second but land first."

Philosophers and statesmen had long debated the ethics of warfare. Could a person or a state justly attack first if they felt threatened? Was the use of force only justifiable when defending oneself against an attack? "The way of the intercepting fist" suggested a third way for a warrior to be—neither an aggressor nor a passive casualty, not in offense or defense but both at the same time, a counterforce meeting force, an engaged resistance.

As *The Green Hornet* wound down, Bruce was working out on weekends in a Los Angeles Chinatown community rec room with Dan, Tony Hum, and Wayne Chan and considering his future. He was at a crossroads. As Kato, he had brought *gung fu* to millions of viewers weekly and elevated Asian martial arts in the United States. It had taken almost two decades for *karate* to enter the American mainstream.* But less than two years had passed between Bruce presenting *gung fu* at Ed Parker's Long Beach tournament and performing it on *The Green Hornet*. He was being approached by investors who would back him if he opened a chain of licensed Kung Fu Kato schools. He was on the verge of achieving his dream.

But what did he want now? To go bigger than even Ed Parker had with *karate*, bringing *gung fu* to the American masses and making a fortune? Or to continue to focus on testing, teaching, and practicing hand-to-hand as he was doing in his Jun Fan Gung Fu Institutes? How would he harmonize his ambitions in martial arts with the taste he had acquired of a much larger fame?

Bruce held serious discussions with the renowned fighters George Dillman and Daniel K. Pai about managing satellite schools across the country. But in the end, he told his friend Peter Chin, he didn't want to prostitute himself. "If money was what I wanted then," he mused later, "I'd have put up signs saying, 'Kato—Mothers, bring your little boys.'"

Instead, on February 5, 1967, he and Dan quietly opened the third Jun Fan Gung Fu Institute, in a modest white two-story building at 628 West College Street in Chinatown. As in Oakland, Bruce asked Dan to identify only committed students for the *kwoon*. There would again be no signage on the front. After a grand opening on a Thursday night, February 9, attended by a rapt audience of two dozen men and women, and at which Bruce and Dan explained the school, its philosophy, and their plans, and did some brief demonstrations, there would be no more public events.

Bruce had written in his notes: "No sign—Door locked—No Affiliation With." One had to know the secret knock to be admitted. If the Seattle *kwoon* had been earthy and earnest, and Oakland's intense and contentious, the LA school would be exclusive, hip, and ferocious.

Dan Lee, who was a student of Ed Parker's at the time, remembered that when Dan Inosanto called to invite him to join the school, "I was overjoyed!" In the first classes, he would be joined by students like Jerry Poteet, Steve Golden, Bob Bremer, Pete Jacobs, and Larry Hartsell, all of whom also had already earned advanced belts with Ed Parker.

From the two dozen who had been at the open house, Richard Bustillo recalled, "There were only twelve of us that he selected."

For warm-ups, Little Joe Torrenueva, who drummed in an Afro-Cuban band when he wasn't cutting hair, played his congas and they got loose and limber to the rhythms. Then they really got down.

"During the first few months of training, Bruce stressed the importance of physical conditioning: fitness, flexibility exercises, and basic punching and kicking

---

* One could use any number of dates. Here are two. Robert Trias formed the first national *karate* association in the States in 1948. Elvis Presley started taking *karate* in 1958.

drills. We trained four times a week, and they were always grueling sessions," Dan Lee said. "As a result, quite a few quit after a few weeks."

Those who remained became the class. After warm-ups, they practiced footwork, kicking, trapping, punching, asked a lot of questions of Bruce, then sparred.

"When we were working out, we were damn serious. Bruce told me that he was going to kick me and that I should get back as fast as I can. I've never moved back so fast in my life," recalled Steve Golden. "Fat lot of good it did. His kick still knocked me back across the room, into a concrete wall, and I thought he broke my ribs. And that was while moving away from him and wearing two chest protectors."

The classes used the same Jun Fan Gung Fu curriculum he had Taky and James teaching in Seattle and Oakland. But Bruce was clarifying the core ideas that would define the new art whose name was still known only to Dan Inosanto. He commissioned George Lee to create pieces of art for the new space that crystallized these ideas. The first was a small sculpture, a black gravestone over a black coffin ringed with chains and laden with flowers, which read IN MEMORY OF A ONCE FLUID MAN CRAMMED AND DISTORTED BY THE CLASSICAL MESS. He placed it on a table at the front of the school.

The second was a set of three aluminum-on-wood wall plaques. Over the years Bruce had encouraged his students to see themselves progressing on a journey in threes—three acts, three steps, three stages. In Seattle, inspired by lines from the Tang dynasty–era Buddhist monk Ch'ing-yüan Wei-hsin, a favorite of Alan Watts and D. T. Suzuki, he had told his students: "Before I studied the art, a punch was just a punch, a kick was just a kick. After I'd studied the art, a punch was no longer a punch, a kick no longer a kick. Now that I understand the art, a punch is just a punch, a kick is just a kick."

After Bruce had named his art Jun Fan Gung Fu, he told his students, "First, learn the center, second, keep the center, and finally, dissolve the center." But as he moved past both Wing Chun and Jun Fan Gung Fu, he began speaking of the "three stages of cultivation": Partiality, Fluidity, and Emptiness.

Partiality, "the Primitive Stage," was illustrated by a *yin* in gold and *yang* in red, divided and without their dots. Bruce called this stage "the Running to Extreme." Fluidity, "the Stage of Art," was illustrated by the symbol he was already using for the institute—the *tai chi* symbol of *yin* and *yang*, the sign of the Grand Terminus, with its rotating arrows, what he called "the Two Halves of One Whole."

The final stage, Emptiness, the level of full maturity, the "Stage of Artlessness" or "cultivated ignorance," was a simple, undecorated board of black. It marked a return to "original freedom," Bruce wrote, where a punch was a punch, a kick was a kick, and a fighter's techniques "are performed on an almost unconscious level without any interference from his mind. Instead of 'I hit,' it becomes 'It hits!'" He called this stage the Formless Form.

He devised a similar ranking system. "The first rank is a blank circle," he would explain. A student then proceeded up through six more color combinations of a yin-yang symbol until they reached the highest, "a blank circle, the return to the beginning stage."

"In other words, all the previous rank certificates are useful for cleaning up messes," he joked. It was "a ranking system of no ranking."

At the *kwoon*, Dan Inosanto served as Bruce's second, teaching most of the classes while Bruce went to local auditions and traveled to national appearances.

They were perfectly matched. Dan's daughter Diana Inosanto recalled, "When they would spar, my dad was so fast it could give him a challenge." They also shared an insatiable curiosity, an openness to the world. For Dan, that quality had been forged in the Little Manila community in the California Central Valley farming hub of Stockton.

Into the 1950s, Stockton had been a sundown town. Dan recalled, "You had to be back on the south side of Stockton by five p.m. or the police paddy just comes out and starts hauling people." Segregated South Stockton was home to the city's Chinese, Japanese, Black, and Mexican American communities, and to Little Manila, which, until the post-1965 immigration, was the heart of Filipino America.

Dan Inosanto was born on July 24, 1936, the second of Sebastian and Mary Arca Inosanto's two children. His parents were pioneers. His mother had moved to Stockton from Kauaʻi and won a full scholarship to Stanford University, but turned it down to work in the fields. Instead she used her earnings to support her sister, Flora Arca, to become one of the first Filipino Americans to graduate from the University of California at Los Angeles. His immigrant father, Sebastian, helped start the Filipino Agricultural Laborers Association, a forerunner union to the United Farm Workers. While Dan was still in diapers, the elder Inosanto had helped organize Filipinos to win a historic asparagus strike. The Inosantos cofounded a local Presbyterian church and ran a transition home and food bank for migrant farmworkers.

One day after school, Dan came home upset over a US history lesson. "I don't want to be Filipino," he told his father. "We killed Magellan. How could we kill Magellan?

"How come we're not like the Chinese and the Japanese and the Koreans? They have characters in their language, and we don't even have an alphabet."

His father shook his head and said, "We had eleven or twelve different alphabets. They destroyed it."

So began his parents' efforts to decolonize Dan. Sebastian Inosanto took Dan back to the asparagus fields, where the *manongs* harvested crops with long iron knives. Dan watched the workers on their lunch breaks as the men paired off, hearing their clanging and shouting as they turned their tools of labor into weapons and practiced the art of *kali*.

As Dan grew older, he distinguished himself in South Stockton athletics, playing alongside youths of all backgrounds. But when he and his cousin competed against the North Stockton football teams, he recalled, "We don't know if they're tackling this hard because of the color of the jersey or the color of our skin."

When Dan came home from the army, he and his mother enrolled at the University of the Pacific together. She finished her bachelor's degree and joined her sister teaching in South Stockton. Dan completed his master's in physical education and moved to Los Angeles, where his sister, Lilia, was trying to break into Hollywood as an actor. He met Ed Parker, and then Bruce. He taught physical education during the day, moonlighted as a driver's ed instructor, and sometimes ran Bible classes. In Dan, Bruce had found a perfect teacher for the school.

In Peter Chin and Ted Wong, he found the perfect pupils.

Peter was born on August 16, 1947. When he arrived at St. Francis Xavier a couple of years after Bruce had left for America, the students who gathered after school on the rooftops for *beimo* matches still invoked his name with awe and reverence. Eager to learn *gung fu* and join in the action, Peter felt compelled to choose a side.

"Those years it's between Wing Chun and Choy Li Fut," he recalled. "So when I heard about Bruce—he only studied Wing Chun a short time and he ran around and kicked everybody's ass—that's what I signed up for."

But his time studying with Chu Shong Tin was not to last. As political instability overtook Hong Kong, the family moved to Australia. In 1963, Peter met his older brother in San Francisco with two hundred dollars in his pocket. His older brother was close friends with Pearl Tso's older brother, Howard, who informed them that Bruce was living and teaching in Oakland. They went to meet Bruce and James at their house.

When Bruce heard of their connection to his Aunty Eva, he warmed to them, entertaining them with dirty jokes. Their friendship through the years, Peter said, would always be full of "locker room talk." Peter was planning to move to Los Angeles, so Bruce told him to come see his exhibition in Long Beach. As Peter watched Bruce in August of 1964, he could not help but thinking, *he is the one!*

Peter worked as a busboy at Madame Wu's, studied fashion design and frequented the rock and roll clubs. He soon found himself in small parts in *The Sand Pebbles* and other film and TV productions. One day at Paramount Studios, where he was an extra on the set of *Star Trek*, he ran into Bruce again, taping one of his last episodes of *The Green Hornet*. He told Bruce, "I've been trying to contact you. I want to study with you. But I don't think I can afford you."

Bruce smiled and said, "Don't worry. I am starting a private class at my house on Wednesday nights. Come by, I'll teach you as a friend."

Ted Wong's life, like Bruce's, had been shaped by war. His father had been born in San Francisco in 1906, the year of the earthquake, and returned to southern

China to marry. When war broke out, the family was unable to leave. Born on November 5, 1937, in Hong Kong, Ted spent his first ten years on the move. When the family lived in Guangdong, the young Ted had thrilled to the *gung fu* street performers who roamed the city. But after his mother passed away and the Communists gained ground, they fled again for Hong Kong. When he was fifteen, he immigrated to San Francisco.

He lived in Chinatown with his aunt, who, he recalled, "was just a boxing nut," tuning in to the Wednesday and Friday night TV fights to see Sugar Ray Robinson, Archie Moore, and Rocky Marciano. Ted got hooked, too. After work at a Chinese newspaper, where he read about the Bruce Lee–Wong Jack Man fight, he often stopped by the *gung fu* schools to watch the students train, but never mustered the courage to join. He moved to Los Angeles, and his roommate told him that there was a Chinese guy on *The Green Hornet*. Ted watched "The Preying Mantis" and became obsessed with the young fighter in black.

His roommate learned where Bruce worked out in Chinatown. "So I went there on a couple of occasions but just sort of stayed in the background and watched him," Ted recalled. "I was a little too intimidated to just walk up and introduce myself." On the Jun Fan Gung Fu Institute's opening night, Ted slipped in and sat in the rear, then slid back out, unsure of himself. A few days later, he came by, noticed the door was cracked open, and stepped inside.

Bruce was with some students. After he gave them their instructions, he came over and grilled Ted. His heart pounding, Ted blurted out in Cantonese that he was from Hong Kong, had been following Bruce, and wanted to learn *gung fu*. Bruce allowed him to stay.

"I was terrible. Really, at one point I was being laughed at because I was so bad. He must feel kind of sorry for me," Ted recalled. "At the same time I'm really in it, I really wanted to do it."

In Bruce's Inglewood backyard, they spent hours talking about American boxing in their native language. Ted began seeing Bruce four times a week—Tuesday and Thursday nights and Saturday afternoons in classes at the school, Wednesday nights in backyard sessions with Peter Chin, Mito Uyehara, and Herb Jackson, a military vet with a few years of *karate* under his belt. To Bruce, Ted was the perfect blank slate. He didn't have the experience or the physical skills of the others, so he compensated by studying the physics of Bruce's movements.

One day, Bruce took Ted aside and said, "You need to work on your basic requirements."

"What's that?"

"Well, first you need some muscle," Bruce said. "Why don't you come over to my house and I'll get you fixed up in that department."

Bruce took him to get protein supplements and a barbell set, then wrote him a training program. In three months he gained fifteen pounds, looked swole, and was shedding the feeling that he did not belong. Bruce took Ted to get new clothes and to Little Joe for a new haircut.

"A complete makeover!" Ted laughed. "He gave me confidence."

Bruce wanted a photographer to capture someone receiving the full impact of his side kick. He invited Ted to come with him to the *Black Belt* magazine offices, and asked Ted to stand on the other side of a heavy bag, with his back to the bag. In the photo, Bruce's right leg is fully extended into one side of the bag. On the other side is Ted, his hair shooting skyward as if electrified, his heels and knees shooting upward, his arms an involuntary blur, his body about to be flung into the wall.

"It was just like getting hit by a freight train," Ted remembered. He was in a neck brace for weeks. Years later, a chiropractor frowned at his X-rays and asked him if he had been hit from behind by a car. For Ted, it had all been worth it, like Krazy Kat receiving an Ignatz Mouse brick of love to his head.

One summer day as they relaxed in a parking lot across from the institute, Bruce told Ted that all his fighting tactics and philosophies had evolved into something new, something big, and that he was going to give this *thing*—it wasn't a school, it wasn't a style—a new name. It would be called, he told Ted, "截拳道."

The two went to meet a linguistics professor at UCLA to learn how to formally Anglicize the name. In his Day-Timer entry for Monday, July 9, 1967, Bruce wrote the new name in bold letters: JEET KUNE DO.

CHAPTER 29
The Names, Part 2

"The Negro" had become "Black," "the Mexican American" had become "Chicano." But "the Oriental" remained "the Oriental"—the sign of an East that was far away, the antonym of what was real and right here, everything the West ridiculed, desired, and feared.

The media critic and futurist Marshall McLuhan was convinced that the wars in Korea and Vietnam were signs of rapidly accelerating change, a "total revolution and the reversal of roles" in which "the Western world is going Oriental, the Oriental world is going Western." The West—once focused on "outer exploration"—was now on an "inner trip," while the East was on "an outer trip, aided by Western technology."

When Duke Ellington introduced one of his last musical masterpieces, *The Afro-Eurasian Eclipse*, inspired by his friendship with McLuhan, he extracted from this upside down state of things a reason for optimism. "Mr. McLuhan says that the whole world is going Oriental and that no one will be able to retain his or her identity, not even the Orientals," he said. But Ellington suggested that some marvelous globally minded identity might emerge from the exchanges in McLuhan's "global village."

Yet if the world was split between East and West, "Oriental" and "Western," what did that mean to the one and a half million people of Asian descent living in the United States? They were a small fraction, less than 1 percent, of the US population. They were urban, concentrated especially in the San Francisco Bay Area, Los Angeles, Honolulu, New York City, and Chicago. They were younger than the rest of a country at the peak of its Baby Boom. Because of historic exclusion, they were overwhelmingly American-born.

For many restless young Asians in America, "Oriental" signified the rug everyone walked on or the dark peal of thunder from the other side of the world. It was easy for them to bomb someone—some *thing*—that was abstract and distant. When they called you "gook," from a Korean hillside, in a Vietnamese jungle, or even on an American street, they were saying you could be removed too.

There were others. They praised you for keeping quiet and to yourselves. They asked you to tally your American traits and your Oriental traits, as if you could divide yourself into asset and liability columns like a balance sheet, as if you added up to the sum of the American ones minus the Oriental ones. At certain times of the year they wanted to put your difference on parade, but most of the time they expected you to leave it at the door. They meant well, or at least they cared that you thought they did. They wanted you to become like them, except that you never could become them. These were the kinds of things people like Ruby and Taky and Amy and James and Dan had known in their bones and spent their lives trying to catharize. They were the things Bruce had to learn in Seattle and Oakland and Hollywood.

"Chinese-Americans," wrote Maxine Hong Kingston, the hyphen sitting there like a vestigial organ ready to burst later, "when you try to understand what things in you are Chinese, how do you separate what is peculiar to childhood, to poverty, insanities, one family, your mother who marked your growing with stories, from what is Chinese? What is Chinese tradition and what is the movies?"

Was there a way to escape this crushing binary, a new name with which to make a world of possibility?

By the spring of 1968, two American-born Asian organizers from the Peace and Freedom Party—which had recently formed around an anti-war agenda with strong ties to the Black Panther Party and the Chicano movement—had noticed something new at the demonstrations: the growing presence of young people who looked like them. Asians were there in the jails during Stop the Draft Week. They were at the "Free Huey" rallies at San Quentin. They were marching with SNCC and the United Farm Workers.

Yuji Ichioka and Emma Gee were a couple living near the University of California at Berkeley. They had met as graduate students at Columbia University who were against the war, and were drawn to the pivotal 1965 anti-war demonstration in Washington, DC. White demonstrators were calling for the troops to be brought home. But Yuji and Emma saw pictures of those who were being bombed and thought of their friends and families. Maybe, they thought, there were other Asians out there in America who felt the same way.

The two pored over the party's voter registration rolls, looking for surnames that sounded Asian, to invite them to meet and form a party caucus. In May 1968, they held their first meeting at their wood-shingle-sided, barn-shaped apartment building at 2005 Hearst Avenue. Only four other people showed up. But what happened that night would echo down the ages.

Victoria Wong had been born to an immigrant father from Toisan and a mother from Fresno's Chinatown. She grew up in the fields of Salinas, picking green onions with her second-generation Filipina American classmate Lillian Fabros. While still high school students, they joined a group that supported conscientious objectors. They signed up with SNCC and invited Dolores Huerta to help them start a chapter of the United Farm Workers. In the fall of 1967, both of them moved to

Berkeley and enrolled at the University of California. People accosted Vicci in the streets, calling her a "gook" and telling her to go back to Vietnam. It was far from the first time she had been called racial slurs, but now they raised an existential question—who did she belong with?

She and Lillian joined the Stop the Draft Week protests, one of the first major anti-war events in the country. They went to San Quentin to demand the release of the prisoners, and were arrested themselves. Vicci was struck by the fact that although the war was in Asia, most of the demonstrators were white. Only the Black Panthers seemed to be talking about Asian lives, racism, and imperialism. Vicci cooked dinner for Sam Napier, the editor of the Panthers' newspaper, so that she could ask him if she could join.

"I'm sorry, sister," he told her, "but you can't join because you're not Black. You have to find your own group."

She was still puzzling over what that meant when she received the call from Emma inviting her and Lillian to the meeting. Lillian could not make it, so on a clear spring evening, Vicci went alone and knocked on the door. Inside were Richard Aoki, already a celebrity in radical circles, Victor Ichioka, a graphic artist and Yuji's younger brother, and Floyd Huen, a premed student involved in student government and the Chinese Student Club. Vicci knew none of them. When it was apparent no one else would be showing up, Yuji began the meeting, explaining that they intended to talk about forming an Asian caucus of the Peace and Freedom Party.

But all of them were already wearing "Peace" and "Free Huey" buttons. Mobilizing Asians to vote was so basic. They all agreed that ending the war was more important than just bringing the troops home. The real issue was ending the West's capitalist and imperialist ambitions in Asia, the reason they were American in the first place.

Suddenly they were in a conversation that, in retrospect, seemed like it had already happened. Every one of them—not just Vicci—had been asking themselves: *Where do we belong?* Maybe they belonged with each other.

"I've been thinking about what we should call ourselves," Yuji said, "and I think we should call ourselves 'Asian American.'"

Like dammed waters bursting free, the discussion rushed forward.

"The Orient" was a foreign place, not here. "Oriental" was a thing, an object, not a human being. It was a past that had been stolen, a present that was predetermined, a future already foreclosed. But "Asia" was an ancient term for the area east of the Aegean Sea. It did not center a white West. "Asian" was someone from the vast area America had once excluded. "Asian American" was capacious—a place to belong, a cup to be filled, a home.

In Vicci's memory, acceptance was instant.

"Asian American—no debate. It was like we didn't even have to say it," she said. "I went into the meeting an Oriental and came out an Asian American."

That night, they formed a group they called the Asian American Political Alliance. It was meant to be bigger than a student organization or a political party. It was a way to intervene in the politics of the time and change people's consciousness. They adopted the Chinese character 東, for "East," as their symbol. They drew up a "General Philosophy" statement that doubled as a declaration of identity:

> We Asian-Americans believe that American society has been, and still is fundamentally a racist society, and that historically we have accommodated ourselves to this society in order to survive.
>
> We Asian-Americans believe that heretofore we have been relating to white standards of acceptability, and affirm the right of self-definition and self-determination.
>
> We Asian-Americans support all non-white liberation movements and believe that all minorities in order to be truly liberated must have control over the political, economic, and educational institutions within their respective communities.
>
> We Asian-Americans oppose the imperialistic policies being pursued by the American government.

Nineteen-year-old Jeffrey Leong was searching for himself. He was a conscientious objector, an aspiring English major, and a folksinger. He hung out in the hippie scene, writing and singing until someone told him Orientals could not play American folk music. In his literature classes he felt like an outsider.

He enrolled in a controversial class taught by the Black Panther Party's Minister of Information Eldridge Cleaver as one of two students of color, both of whom were Asian. Cleaver's racial analysis set his mind on fire, but also threw him into an identity crisis. Meeting Vicci Wong and her network of draft-resistance activists drew him into the Asian American Political Alliance. Declaring himself Asian American, he recalled, "opened up a whole different way of inhabiting your body, your face—literally—and also to be able to declare a kind of a position that was sympathetic to the Black struggle and also sympathetic to other people struggling against war."

At Berkeley the organization exploded in membership, and within months, there were AAPA chapters at San Francisco State, UCLA, UC Davis, Cal State Hayward, and Columbia University, as well as in San Jose, Oakland, Chicago, Hawai'i, and New Hampshire. Similar Asian American organizations formed at Yale, Oberlin, the University of Michigan, the University of Illinois, and many other campuses.

On a fall day in 1968 in New York City, two middle-aged Nisei women, Kazu

Iijima and Minn Matsuda, longtime political activists who had been agitating since their time in the concentration camps, met for lunch on a park bench. They got to talking about how the Black Panthers had brought pride back to the Black community. They vowed to organize something their children could proudly join.

Kazu spoke to her son, Chris, a musician. He told them it should not be a strictly Japanese American effort, but a pan-Asian one. At anti-war rallies, they approached anyone they saw who looked Asian and invited them to a meeting. In the spring of 1969, Asian Americans for Action launched as a radical multigenerational group, a mix of young students and accomplished organizers like Malcolm X's close confidant Yuri Kochiyama.

In Seattle, clergy, professionals, and community leaders joined with students and alumni activists like Larry Matsuda to form the Asian Council for Equality. They backed student demands that the University of Washington expand recruitment of impoverished Asian American students. After winning that battle, they joined with Black activists to press for the desegregation of the construction industry and private social clubs.

This new vanguard began calling itself the Asian American Movement, a name cohering from the depths of a shared unconscious into a mass awakening. "It seemed like all of us came to the same threshold in history and stepped over it simultaneously," said Warren Furutani, a member of the San Jose Asian American Political Alliance who would become a leading voice of the movement. "Whether it was L.A., the Bay Area, Seattle, New York or the Midwest, people we ran into all over the country had the same epiphany at the same time."

The idea of the Asian American, Viet Thanh Nguyen would later write, met the urgent need for self-defense, made a claim for representation and inclusion, and centered the necessity of solidarity. Alone Asian Americans would be weak and vulnerable. Together they could celebrate the joy of belonging. They might even be able to imagine what students from San Francisco State's Philippine American Collegiate Endeavor (PACE) were audaciously calling "a new humanity, a new humanism, a New World Consciousness."

The movement soon had a national organ in a newsprint monthly called *Gidra*, assembled by a collective at UCLA, where Yuji and Emma had moved to help launch the new Asian American Studies Center. *Gidra*'s voice was bracing, often skeptical and critical of the same movement it was helping build.

Chinese and Japanese Americans "have become white in every respect but color," wrote Amy Uyematsu in a much-discussed piece entitled "The Emergence of Yellow Power in America." They had given up "their languages, customs, histories, and cultural values." They mutilated themselves to meet white standards of beauty. They were "silent," "frightened," and "passive." To Blacks, she wrote, it seemed that Asians "just want more of the money pie."

"Unless Asian Americans are willing to confront and challenge the traditional

Hundreds of Asian Americans, Native Hawaiians, and Pacific Islanders march in an anti-war protest in Los Angeles, April 22, 1972. Courtesy of *Gidra*, 1972.

American system they will always be racially oppressed," she wrote. "The yellow power movement cannot begin to move forward until the yellow people in America have reached the primary stage of yellow consciousness."

In *Gidra*'s inaugural April 1969 edition, under an image of a *samurai* charging forward with his *katana*, Larry Kubota wrote that "the dawn of a new era" was underway. It was time for "the birth of a new Asian—one who will recognize and deal with injustices." Kubota wrote:

> Yellow Power is a call for all Asian Americans to end the silence that has condemned us to suffer in this racist society and to unite with our Black, Brown, and Red brothers of the Third World for survival, self-determination and the creation of a more humanistic society.
>
> We must search our souls for the flame of the Asian warriors who fought for their people and their pride without fear of death.

He concluded with a quote that D. T. Suzuki had plucked from an early commentary on the *bushido* classic the *Hagakure*: "Let the enemy touch your skin and you cut into his flesh; let him cut into your flesh and you pierce into his bones; let him pierce into your bones and you take his life."

Bruce Lee regarded this passage with the same kind of reverence as the young Asian Americans. When he transcribed these lines into his own notes, he added: "Approach Jeet Kune Do with the idea of mastering the will. Forget about winning and losing; forget about pride and pain."

Like the activists' call to build an Asian America, Bruce hoped that the rise of Jeet Kune Do would mark the return of a true warrior consciousness.

The first media mention of Jeet Kune Do came in the November 1967 issue of *Black Belt*. "Jeet Kune Do is simply the direct expression of one's feelings with the minimum of movements and energy," Bruce explained. "My movements are *simple, direct*, and *non-classical*." He continued,

> Art is really the expression of the self. The more complicated and restricted the method, the less the opportunity for the expression of one's original sense of freedom.
>
> Though they play an important role in the early stage, the techniques should not be too mechanical, complex or restrictive. If we blindly cling to them, we will eventually become bound by their limitations.
>
> Remember, you are expressing the techniques and not doing the techniques. If somebody attacks you, your response is not Technique No. 1, Stance No. 2, Section 4, Paragraph 5. Instead, you simply move in like sound and echo, without any deliberation.
>
> It is as though, when I call you, you answer me, or when I throw something at you, you catch it. It's as simple as that, no fuss, no muss.

Bruce felt he had left the stasis of other styles and systems behind. He focused his students on conditioning, which in turn supported mobility, dynamism, and responsiveness. He drilled them in fencing footwork and worked on maximizing body alignment and coordination for power and speed. He elaborated on five different kinds of attacks—an idea that he had been thinking about since his days with Fred Sato in Seattle—and had his students test different kinds of execution as well as counters. He sought competitive fighters like Chuck Norris, Mike Stone, and Joe Lewis to train with him.

In a time when fighters still distinguished themselves by the styles they had trained in, Bruce was cross-pollinating Chinese, Japanese, Korean, Okinawan, and Filipino martial arts with Western boxing and fencing. He would explore French *savate*, *muay Thai*, Indonesian *pencak silat*, Burmese boxing, and Western wrestling.

"Bruce's concept was to put as many styles as possible together in the beginning," Dan recalled. But then, he said, Bruce realized "it was the roots we were seeking and not the particular style—and he changed the system in his classes after that. It started as a gradual change, although there was an abruptness around the winter of 1967. All of a sudden he said, 'This is not right,' and he went after the essentials rather than the styles."

Jun Fan Gung Fu was still the institute's official name and curriculum. Jeet Kune Do was, like Asian American identity, quickly evolving. Bruce told the *Black Belt* editors he was writing a book he would call *Tao of Jeet Kune Do*. But privately he told his students that Jeet Kune Do was not to be thought of as a style or a system. It was *anti-style* and *anti-system*. It was a process that would constantly remain in process.

By 1968, Bruce was telling Dan, "What Jeet Kune Do is now will be different in 1969."

"But this is really good stuff I'm doing right now," Dan protested.

"No, Jeet Kune Do will be different in 1969. It's going to be different in 1970."

Perhaps because Dan Inosanto was one of the few who shared Bruce's ability to ingest and metabolize new ideas, it would not be long before the two had moved past even this name. One day Dan called it "JKD," and Bruce thought the acronym was hilarious. JKD became their in-joke.

"In our personal conversations, we used 'JKD' as a term for something very good, out of this world, unique, or very fast," Dan recalled. "'Yeah, the food at that place is JKD!' Or, 'That movie I saw last night was JKD!' Or, 'Mmmmmm, his singing is JKD.'"

For all the rest who were still trying to follow, Bruce said, "JKD is just a name, don't fuss over it."

CHAPTER 30

Stand!

When Bruce met Kareem Abdul-Jabbar, a month after the 1968 national college basketball championship, he was still known as Lew Alcindor, the most hyped young basketball star in history.

Lew was seven feet two and, for his whole life, had been unable to hide. He disarmed reporters with a fierce intelligence masked by a laconic intensity. He was just completing his junior year at UCLA, and after indulging in two years of partying, drugs, and women, he wanted something different. "All sophomore and junior years I'd been looking for something to believe in," he would later write.

During those two years, he had been in the eye of the storm. In the "Game of the Century," witnessed by fifty-two thousand in the Houston Astrodome and millions more on television on January 20, 1968, he brought men's college basketball to new heights. That night he played with blurred vision after having his cornea scratched. UCLA lost by a basket to the University of Houston, breaking their forty-seven-game winning streak, and the team melted down in its aftermath. Lew's closest friend, a Black man from South Central Los Angeles, quit the team in a dispute with coach John Wooden, and racial tensions simmered in the locker room the rest of the season.

By the end of the season, Lew had led UCLA to its second consecutive national championship and was voted Most Outstanding Player for the second year in a row. It was the year that began the "March Madness" era. But after the season, he retreated.

Born Ferdinand Lewis Alcindor in 1947, the day after Jackie Robinson desegregated pro sports, he had grown up in an integrated housing project in uptown Manhattan. In third grade he stared at a Polaroid of his class: "There I was, freakishly towering over all the other kids, with skin much darker than everyone else's." When he was twelve, his white friends abandoned him. His former best friend picked a fight with him one day, calling him a "jungle bunny" and "big jungle n——r."

At seventeen, Lew stepped out of the subway in Harlem and was caught in the first hours of six days of rioting that followed the police shooting of a Black teen. As bottles and bullets whizzed by and buildings went up in flames, he ran home. "Right then and there I knew who I was and who I was going to be. I was going to be Black rage personified, Black power in the flesh," he later wrote. He led his team to a 79-2 record and two national high school championships. But once, to motivate him in a game, his coach had called him a "n——r," and he never forgot it.

In his sophomore year at UCLA, in 1967, he was traveling with extra security because of death threats. He took comfort in listening to hard bop and reading about African and Asian history and religion. He was particularly captivated by *The Autobiography of Malcolm X* and the late Black leader's journey into Sunni Islam, and sought out young Black Muslims in Los Angeles.

That summer he was the only college athlete among a group of prominent Black athletes invited by Jim Brown to meet with Muhammad Ali to try to change the boxer's mind about his anti-war stance. Ali had asked, "Why should they ask me to put on a uniform and go ten thousand miles from home and drop bombs and bullets on brown people in Vietnam while so-called Negro people in Louisville are treated like dogs and denied simple human rights?" After declaring, "I don't have no personal quarrel with those Vietcong," he saw his heavyweight boxing title revoked, and faced a prison sentence for draft evasion. The men spent hours grilling Ali on his position, then emerged to face the press. Alcindor sat beside Brown, Ali, and Bill Russell as the athletes joined together in a historic show of solidarity for Ali.

Invited to a Black Youth conference by a young San Jose State College professor named Harry Edwards, who was organizing a Black athletes' boycott of the 1968 Olympics, Alcindor spoke with conviction:

> I'm the big basketball star, the weekend hero, everybody's All American. Well, I was almost killed by a racist cop shooting at a black cat in Harlem. He was shooting on the street—where masses of people were standing around or just taking a walk. But he didn't care. After all we were just n——rs. I found out that we don't catch hell because we aren't basketball stars or because we don't have money. We catch hell because we are black. Somewhere each of us has got to make a stand against this kind of thing.

But in the media, an explosion of racist invective followed him and other Black athletes as they were accused by white writers of being ungrateful, unpatriotic, uppity "Black Hitlers."

Weeks after the 1967 championship, the NCAA banned the dunk—in what became known as the "Alcindor rule"—an effort he believed was racist. Forced to improvise, he contemplated how to deal with triple-team defenses and worked on a new offensive weapon: the skyhook. One night after watching a Zatoichi flick, he was struck by the idea that the blind swordsman's grace, control, and precision might be exactly what he needed. Instead of brute force, he thought, I will slide and roll and slip by them without fouling. In New York City, Alcindor started training in *aikido*.

"A victory [in martial arts] is your mind over someone else's mind, as much as, if not more than, a simple physical mastery," he later wrote. "The discipline also becomes a means of staying in shape mentally and keeping your entire inner self trained."

That fall Alcindor visited the *Black Belt* offices to meet a fellow *aikido* adept, Mito Uyehara, and ask him if he knew someone with whom he could continue his martial arts training. Alcindor had become especially curious about *tai chi*. "This guy Bruce Lee—he's really good at it," Mito told him. "He knows more about those things than I do."

"Who's Bruce Lee?" Alcindor asked.

"He was Kato in *The Green Hornet*."

Alcindor was skeptical he could learn anything from an actor.

"No, no! He's the real deal."

That night Mito drove to see Bruce and said he was sending Lew Alcindor over.

"Who's Lew Alcindor?" Bruce asked.

Mito explained that he was the tallest and most famous college basketball player in the country.

"I don't watch basketball."

Bruce asked Linda to bring a tape measure, stood on a chair, and dropped it down, to visualize Alcindor's height. Then he thought aloud, "I wonder how fast he is." Mito assured Bruce he was very fast, one of the best athletes in the world.

"He would have no chance with me," Bruce said with a chuckle. "I would break his legs before he could do anything else."

They met for the first time at Bruce and Linda's house on a comfortable Los Angeles afternoon.

"He greeted me with a broad smile and friendly demeanor and right away I knew this was not a scowling teacher from Japanese films demanding bowing obedience," Alcindor recalled. "We talked UCLA basketball for a while and then got down to business."

Bruce first had Lew punch and kick the heavy bag, so he could gauge the big man's power. Then he called Linda over, asked Lew to hold a pad to his chest, and told Linda to kick it. Linda grinned and got up from the patio seat where she had been watching.

"Bruce, I don't think this will work," Alcindor said. "I'm two feet taller and a hundred pounds heavier than Linda."

"Just hold it up to your chest, Lew," Linda said.

He lowered the pad so that it would be below her head.

"Your chest," Linda said, frowning and pointing at the pad. "Do you want Bruce to show you where that is?"

He moved the pad up. Bruce nodded at Linda. Kareem would never forget what happened next.

"Suddenly Linda fired off a kick that not only reached the pad, but the impact rocked me backward a few feet, readjusted my spine, and possibly rearranged the order of my teeth," he remembered. "They stood there smiling at the shocked expression on my face."

Linda—Bruce's longest-running student except for Taky—had just done what Bill Walton, Happy Hairston, Kent Benson, and Robert Parish never would.

"Okay," Alcindor said, still sore where she had kicked him. "Teach me that."

Bruce was just as intrigued. Not long afterward, he told Leo Fong, "You know why I'm getting him to train with me? I want to learn how to beat a tall guy!"

"Big Lew," as Bruce called him, came to his backyard every Tuesday during the off-season, and sometimes Thursdays as well. Bruce taught him Jeet Kune Do footwork, the *mook jong* dummy, and punches and kicks on the bag. At first, Bruce told Mito that Big Lew was slow, his arms were weak, and he wasn't good at *chi sao*. A reporter who witnessed one of their workouts was more impressed with Bruce than Big Lew. He wrote that Bruce could "leap and kick over Alcindor's head, and says he can defeat him by taking advantage of his shin and thigh with a kick."

But Bruce soon realized all that was irrelevant. Even if he could get inside Big Lew's reach, it wasn't easy. And with his front kick, Big Lew could rattle the rim of the basket. Bruce's Wing Chun skills were all but useless. He joked with Doug Palmer, "Try doing *chi sao* with someone when you're staring at his belly button." Bruce called Taky and told him not to focus on *chi sao* in the school anymore.

"Bruce and I sparred regularly," Kareem remembered. "But we didn't compete; I was like a drawing board on which he could work out his theories and he was instructing me how to deal with people and attack him."

Kareem came to appreciate Bruce's approach. "Nothing was for art's sake. Everything he taught was to achieve an end in doing damage to an opponent," he recalled. "After studying for a little while, you learn a lot about how easy it is to hurt someone, and how easily you can get hurt. That makes you really respect what you're involved in. With violence, you learn to respect it and see how easily you can become victimized by it."

To him, Bruce was as effective a teacher as John Wooden. Both were focused on fundamentals, preparation, and what worked. "Bruce used to say, 'I fear not the man who has practiced 10,000 kicks once, but I fear the man who has practiced one kick 10,000 times.' In sports, we call this concept 'muscle memory,'" he said. "For me, my hook shot was the one kick practiced 10,000 times."

Bruce helped the young athlete understand his movements in a way that seemed to decelerate time. "Bruce showed me how to harness some of what was raging inside me and summon it completely at my will. The Chinese call it *chi*; the Japanese, *ki*; the Indians, *prana*—it is the life force," he said. "I was quite amazed to find, after working with Bruce, that when I really had my presence of mind, when I did control my life force, that's what I saw, things coming at me in slow motion with plenty of time to get out of the way.

"It sounded mystical when he first told me, but I was becoming increasingly involved in matters of faith, and besides, Bruce grounded his philosophies in a good fight, which I could relate to."

These sessions were a refuge from the media, who were painting Lew Alcindor as a coddled, ungrateful, unpatriotic athlete. In July 1968 he had agreed to an interview on the *Today* show to highlight the summer program for Black youths where he was working. But sports announcer Joe Garagiola ambushed him, asking Alcindor why he had declined to play in the Olympics. "You live here," Garagiola said.

"Yeah, I live here, but it's not really my country," Alcindor answered.

"Well then, there's only one solution: maybe you should move."

"Well, you see," Alcindor responded, heating up, "that would be fine with me, you know, it all depends on where we are going to move?"

The producers cut away to a commercial.

"I felt no part of the country and had no desire to help it look good," he later recalled. "I had better things to do."

That summer he joined a mosque, declared *shahada*, became a Sunni Muslim, and received a new name: Abdul-Kareem, later Kareem Abdul-Jabbar, "noble, generous servant, powerful spirit." He kept his name to himself and his closest friends until he asked the media two years later to call him by it. He recalled, "I was still Lew to almost everybody, as if I knew them but they didn't know me. . . .

"The heat I'd taken about the Olympics, and the absolute unwillingness I'd found in the press, and by extension the general public, to accept what to me seemed so obvious—that the country was run by white people for white people, and that even the most powerful Black men were still operating at a handicap—made me suspicious of strangers and even more jealous of my privacy."

But with Bruce, everything was easy. The two talked philosophy and religion. They went to see *Zatoichi* flicks. Kareem even babysat sometimes, lifting Brandon up to give the five-year-old a view of the roof. They shared an understanding of fame and privacy. From youth, both of them had been under the spotlight.

In Chinatown they never paid for meals—everyone was a UCLA fan—and they often ate in the kitchen. Bruce joked to their companions that it would guarantee they weren't getting the garbage served to the *gweilo*. But Bruce was also shielding the big man from the rabid autograph seekers.

"Bruce and I had something else in common," Kareem recalled. "We both had experienced discrimination."

Kareem talked about the Black liberation movement and his role in what Harry Edwards had come to call "the revolt of the Black athlete." Bruce shared his frustrations with Hollywood, saying he sometimes felt like a "valet to the stars." They swapped books. Bruce gave Kareem Miyamoto Musashi's *Book of Five Rings*. Kareem gave him books to read on Islam and imperialism. He told a shocked Bruce that Europeans had barred Chinese from parks in their own cities.

"I recommended certain books about the British occupation of China," Kareem said. "He didn't know anything about that, and he'd gone to school in Hong Kong."

Before his twenty-second birthday, in April 1969, Kareem declined a million-dollar offer to play with the Harlem Globetrotters. He became the number-one pick in both the NBA and ABA drafts. Before the drafts, he and his advisers had given the leagues and teams the rules—one bid only. The New York Nets and the ABA had lowballed him the first time, then tried to subvert the process with a second, eleventh-hour offer worth three times what the NBA team, the Milwaukee Bucks, offered him. He chose to sign with the Bucks.

None of this made any sense to the pundits. Most Americans would have just taken the money. One sportswriter warned another, "He can be very difficult. Says very little. Gets into fights. Not very cooperative." But Kareem lived by his code. With a hook shot for a slingshot, he was a skywalking David meeting the Goliath of white supremacy.

One day Kareem wondered aloud to Bruce how he might fit in with the white players on the Bucks. The question genuinely perplexed Bruce. "But one day," Bruce told Mito, "he came to me and said that some of the white guys on his team are alright. I looked at him a little surprised and said, 'Hey, there's good and bad guys in all races.'" Kareem had been shaped by race from childhood. Bruce thought he was the more enlightened one, but some of his biggest lessons lay ahead.

Kareem asked Bruce how he might put on thirty pounds. He had the Los Angeles Lakers' 275-pound Wilt Chamberlain, his friend and now rival, on his mind. Bruce wrote up a weight training and cardio program. He got Kareem jumping on his trampoline to improve his strength and balance. Mito couldn't believe it.

"What would happen if you had fallen off and got hurt?" he exclaimed.

"Contract already signed," Kareem said, "so I'd still get paid."

Bruce couldn't stop laughing.

Kareem thought of Bruce as similar to himself, a loner who stood apart. "Bruce wished he had more friends," he said, "but he didn't want to be that vulnerable. He had to keep up a kind of mystique." But between them, he said, "There wasn't any real competition, no clash of egos, and Bruce needed friends."

One moment stood out for Kareem:

I was over at his house one afternoon. We'd just finished working out; it was sunny and warm, and Bruce said, "Hey, I have to go drop something off at a friend of mine's house."

"I might go with you," I offered.

"You want a ride?"

"Yeah," I said, "where is it? Is it far away?"

"No," he said, "it's near Lobertson."

He meant Robertson, an avenue off Venice Boulevard, but maybe two or three times a year his Chinese accent would sneak through.

Bruce's face went cold...

He thought I was going to mock him, and friend or no friend, he wanted to fight me. I saw him begin to coil, and I grabbed him, and hugged him, and we began to laugh. I couldn't tell anybody, of course; it was the kind of confidence that cements a friendship, but as I let go he punched me on the arm, real hard, just to let me know he was still Bruce Lee.

Cities were on fire—Prague, Paris, Mexico City, Chicago. Martin Luther King Jr. and Robert Kennedy were dead. The gangs had returned to the Bronx. Some believed the revolutionary horizon was nearing. Others thought it another illusion. In the San Francisco Bay Area, the song of the moment was Sly and the Family Stone's "Stand!"—in which Sly sang, "There's a midget standing tall, and a giant beside him about to fall."

Between 1968 and 1969, Asian student organizations had undergone a major transformation. In their newsletter, UC Berkeley's Chinese Student Club promoted their annual spring break ski trip to Lake Tahoe, but also "a community exchange on the Third World College," a proposal that the university create a dedicated school for ethnic studies. At San Francisco State, three different Asian groups—Philippine American Collegiate Endeavor (PACE), the Intercollegiate Chinese for Social Action (ICSA), and a new chapter of AAPA, led primarily by *sansei* women—were joining the uprising.

The students articulated exactly what they wanted: colleges of ethnic studies, the hiring of faculty of color, and the expansion of admissions and financial aid for students of color. They met day and night among themselves, with other Asian student organizations, and with other student-of-color organizations to hammer out strategies and tactics. Navigating and maintaining coalitions along multiple lines at once would become a permanent feature of Asian American politics and culture.

During the San Francisco State Third World Strike, a conversation. 1969. Photo by Stephen Shames/Polaris.

Under the banner of the Third World Liberation Front—first at San Francisco State College, then at UC Berkeley—they joined Black, Chicano, and Native American student organizations. On November 6, 1968, San Francisco State's TWLF launched the longest campus strike in US history. That year two student occupations at Columbia University were quickly broken up by authorities. But the night before the Third World Strike began at San Francisco State, Black Student Union leader Benny Stewart told a crowd of student activists to prepare for "a prolonged struggle."

"We call it the war of the flea," Stewart said. "What does the flea do? He bites the dog, he slowly sucks the blood from it.

"We are the people. We are the majority," he said, "and the pigs cannot be everywhere, every place all the time. And where they are not, we are." They had been reading Mao, *The Art of War*, and the *Tao Te Ching*.

Stewart laid out the scenario. "Something is always happening all the time. Toilets are stopped up. Pipes is out. Water in the bathroom is just runnin' all over the place.

"When the pigs come runnin' on campus, ain't nothing happening. When he leaves it starts all over again. On and on and on."

The next day, students executed this exact scenario, plunging the campus into chaos for the next several months. George Murray, the Black Panther–affiliated lecturer whose firing had precipitated the strike, told the media, "This is the first time in this country that barriers have been dissolved between Black, brown and yellow people."

Over the next week, half the classes were canceled, the faculty voted to cease instruction altogether, and police and students clashed daily. Governor Ronald Reagan called the campus a "domestic Vietnam," and pressed Chancellor Glenn

Dumke and the board of trustees to appoint a new campus president, its third in six months. Three weeks into the strike, the job was offered to a Japanese American linguist named Samuel Ichiye Hayakawa. The young Asian American radicals now had a common enemy.

S. I. Hayakawa was a *nisei*, born in 1906 in Vancouver, Canada. During World War II he had not been incarcerated because he had been born Canadian and lived outside of the area covered by Executive Order 9066. Instead he gained fame for authoring a bestselling book on semantics and writing for the Black newspaper the *Chicago Defender*, where he took a strong assimilationist stance. While most Japanese Americans were locked in incarceration camps, he wrote in *The Defender*, "The trouble with most whites is not cruelty or viciousness, but simply thoughtlessness." In this sense, he aligned with many *nisei* who had come through the war eager to prove their value and loyalty to white America, and even some of his other Asian American contemporaries like Ruby Chow, who would not agree with him on much else.

In 1955, shortly after Hayakawa began teaching at San Francisco State, he had been invited by a national Japanese American student organization to speak. Hayakawa declined, telling them, "*Nisei* social groups should cease to exist." Incarceration—what he once called "the adventure of relocation," as if the concentration camps had been summer camps—had been a good thing for Japanese Americans: "The relocation forced them out of their segregated existence to discover the rest of America." He opposed Asian American Studies but agreed with the student demand for Black Studies because he believed it could help Negroes assimilate quicker.

Hayakawa had no administrative experience and barely taught anymore. But he had won the admiration of Reagan, Chancellor Dumke, and the board of trustees when he spoke at a campus emergency convocation on behalf of a group of professors who advocated strong punishment of student organizers of the strike and their faculty supporters. Claiming to speak also for the "silent majority of Negro students," Hayakawa proposed the university agree to a Black Studies program if the college's Black deans would pressure students to end the strike by December 2.

"If he'll take the job," Ronald Reagan was heard to joke, "we'll forgive him for Pearl Harbor."

In his first press conference, Hayakawa called upon Asian Americans to stake out a moral high ground in a race war between whites and Blacks. "In a profound sense I stand in the middle," he told the media. I'm not white and I'm not Black. I'm appealing to my Oriental friends that I might be a channel to bring Black and white together."

He declared a state of emergency and made a massive show of police force. On

December 2, he imposed emergency protocols limiting free speech and interrupted a demonstration at the edge of campus. He stormed a sound truck, tussled with protesters over the microphone, then climbed atop the truck and pulled the cables from the speakers, yelling, "Don't touch me. I'm the college president!" Editorialists called it a "bravura performance."

Hayakawa called the student strikers "a gang of goons, gangsters, con men, neo-Nazis, and common thieves." Overnight he became the man who kept the university open in the dark days of student protest, a national hero, and the most famous Oriental in America. San Francisco's *Hokubei Mainichi* named him "Nisei of the Year."

Hayakawa was now accepting invitations to Japanese American events. At them he called Asian American activists "hippies," and dismissed the terms "racism" and "institutional racism" as "absurd abstractions." He argued, "The Sansei should not be imitating the Negro. He should be urging the Negro to imitate the Sansei." He seemed to support racial segregation, praising Chinese Americans for staying in Chinatown where they could manage a neighborhood they could display to the *hakujin* with pride. Students and community members disrupted his appearances and called Hayakawa a "puppet," a "running dog," a "yellow Uncle Tom," a "banana," and "really white."

As a writer for the *Pacific Citizen*, another Japanese American newspaper, wrote, "Isn't Hayakawa doing exactly what a certain segment of the White Establishment always wished they could do except that a White person could never have gotten away with it?"

In 1969, daily demonstrations swelled to thousands of protesters, met by hundreds of police. On one day in January, 453 were arrested. The strike at San Francisco State continued until March 21, 1969, when administrators agreed to the creation of a School of Ethnic Studies. Hayakawa had delegated the final negotiations to a committee and left town.

In Berkeley, where Reagan sent in National Guard troops in a failed effort to stop the strike there, students won a Department of Ethnic Studies. In the 1969–70 school year, Black Studies, Chicano Studies, Native American Studies, and Asian American Studies programs began at both universities. Across California alone, fifteen other colleges and universities would offer Asian American Studies courses that year.

"We wanted the college to become a place in which Asian American history, culture, and communities would be accepted as legitimate areas of study at the university level," wrote Malcolm Collier and Dan Gonzales, Chinese American and Filipino American strikers at San Francisco State. "We wanted Asian Americans to be seen as Americans, not at the price of assimilation, but through a change in the conception of America that was broader and more varied in its character."

To be Asian in America meant being in between white and Black, in between assimilation and freedom. At its inception, the name "Asian American" was an invitation to join a narrative of solidarity. It was a provocation, a fight one picked with the world against its condescension and hostility.

One had to face the questions: Who are you and what do you fight for? To sidestep them was also a form of answer. As the new decade neared, Bruce would be increasingly unable to avoid these questions.

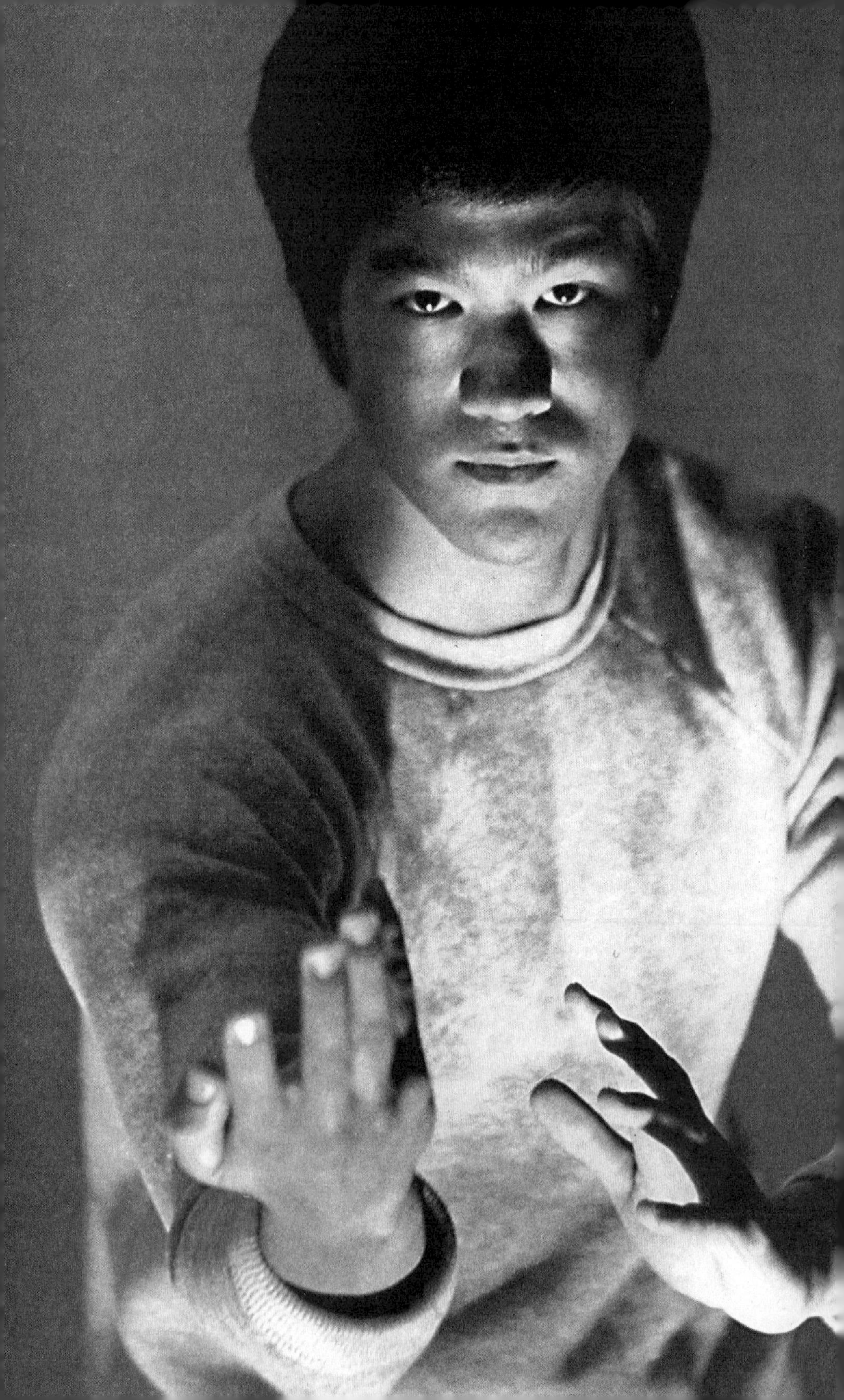

PART IX
Above and Below Sunset

1968–1970

> Marginalization is a sword with two edges: as we use it to attack racism, we wound our villain downstroke, but each time we raise the sword for ourselves, we wound ourselves ... and there is no possible victory, for to be marginal is to be in the battle.
>
> —CHARLES GAINES

In a Wing Chun stance, 1969.
Photo courtesy of the Bruce Lee Family Archive.

CHAPTER 31
Plateaus

The world's biggest stars were looking to the East. George Harrison led the Beatles into Indian classical music and spirituality. John Lennon and Yoko Ono became icons of the global peace movement and the world's most famous interracial couple. *Karate* and *judo* had become signifiers of cool. "During the late Sixties and early Seventies, there was hardly a movie tycoon or actor who did not try to become a black belt," recalled one jet-setting socialite. But *gung fu* had the additional allure of secrecy and exclusivity. Retaining a personal *sifu* signaled a higher status lifestyle.

Not long after *The Green Hornet* was canceled, Bruce had lunch at the 20th Century-Fox lot with Charles FitzSimons, William Dozier's assistant executive producer at Greenway Productions, an Irish immigrant whose sister was Maureen O'Hara and who had, in the early fifties, also been an actor. Bruce needed advice and FitzSimons had taken a strong liking to him.

Bruce said that he had opened a *gung fu* school and was charging twenty-two dollars a month per student. He added that Jay Sebring had introduced him to Steve McQueen and was helping him secure clients. He figured he might charge them twenty-five dollars an hour.

Charles scoffed. "You're crazy. If you sell a hot dog for $2, nobody will think it is special, but if you charge $8.50, people are going to think there is something special about it," he said. "You should be charging these actors $50 an hour.[*] They can afford it." All these guys, FitzSimons said, had "middle-aged macho syndrome." The premium price would just make them want it more.

Soon Bruce was training members of Hollywood's A-list elite, including Tom Tannenbaum, a former talent agent who was now running Paramount TV; Joe Hyams, the celebrity columnist and publicist; Sy Weintraub, the film and television producer who had revived *Tarzan*; Vic Damone, the famed crooner; Roman Polanski, the movie director rolling high with *Rosemary's Baby*, who would later direct *Chinatown*; Blake Edwards, who had directed *Breakfast at Tiffany's* and the *Pink Panther* series;[**] and Ted Ashley, the chairman of Warner Bros. studios. In less than

---

[*] In 2024 dollars, this would be about $478 an hour.

[**] Blake Edwards had directed scenes featuring egregious Oriental stereotypes in *Breakfast at Tiffany's* and the Pink Panther series. He had also been an enthusiastic *kenpo karate* student under Ed Parker before coming to learn from Bruce.

two years, Bruce would be charging up to ten times what FitzSimons had first suggested, and calling himself "the highest-priced martial artist in the United States."

As he started with each of them, he retold a story he had read when he was a young *sifu* dreaming of opening *gung fu* schools across the United States. It was from a little paperback called *Zen Flesh, Zen Bones*:

> A learned man once went to a Zen teacher to inquire about Zen. As the Zen teacher explained, the learned man would frequently interrupt him with remarks like, "Oh, yes, we have that too . . ." and so on.
>
> Finally the Zen teacher stopped talking and began to serve tea to the learned man. He poured the cup full, then kept pouring until the cup overflowed.
>
> "Enough!" the learned man once more interrupted. "No more can go into the cup!"
>
> "Indeed, I see," answered the Zen teacher. "If you do not first empty your cup, how can you taste my cup of tea?"

In his copy of the book, he had penciled above this passage his own stunning, concise rendering of that same idea: "The usefulness of a cup is in its emptiness." Two of his most important vessels would be the actor Steve McQueen and the screenwriter Stirling Silliphant.

Bruce started training Steve McQueen in August 1967 and the two began an intense and complicated friendship.

For a decade, McQueen had been a bankable draw. He was on a very good run that was about to get much better. He entered 1967 nominated for an Oscar for his role in *The Sand Pebbles* and was about to shoot a pair of blockbusters, *The Thomas Crown Affair* and *Bullitt*, that would rocket him into global superstardom.

McQueen was becoming "The King of Cool," reaching the apex of American male star power. Even as the world burned he remained stoic, impregnable, untouchable. While his contemporary Clint Eastwood affected a scowl that promised to face chaos with a cleansing vengeance, McQueen faced it with a Sessue Hayakawa–level mask of detachment.

But he was rapidly approaching forty, and his life was a shambles. As a child he had been abandoned by his father, shunned by his mother, and beaten by his stepfather. He became a juvenile delinquent and a drifter until a stint in the marines straightened him out. He returned to New York and stage acting and, armed with the Stanislavski method, found his way to the screen.

By the late sixties, a long run at the top had separated him from reality. He was ruled by his impulses for cars and racing, women and control, and by deep insecurities over his desirability and physicality. On-screen he stalked purposefully like a panther. Off-screen he routinely berated everyone on set, from producers and directors on down. At home he drove loved ones away with impetuous, unaccountable behavior. He was, one of his handlers said, "a very spoiled brat. He got everything he wanted."

When Steve was shooting *The Thomas Crown Affair*, he wanted more than anything else to learn Asian martial arts, which he had come to think of as the avant-garde of manliness. After he started training with Bruce, Steve once slashed his toe on a granite step and bled profusely. Yet he insisted on continuing the workout until he was drained. "That guy," an impressed Bruce told Mito Uyehara, "doesn't know the meaning of quitting."

After another session, an exhausted McQueen had his shirt soaked through. But McQueen invited him to his offices, and Bruce saw the actor's aura of supreme power on full display. "It was kind of funny," Bruce told Mito. "Steve looked like a bum off the street and everyone looking up at him and kept calling him, 'Mr. McQueen.'" After visiting McQueen's stone home at the top of a Brentwood hill, dubbed "The Castle," Bruce told Mito, "Just to get to his front door is a hassle."

Bruce brought Steve to Ed Parker's 1968 International Karate Championships in Long Beach and introduced him to Chuck Norris before Norris's championship bout. "[Steve] had a hat and sunglasses on and slouched down in his seat," recalled Pat Johnson, a student of Norris's who became McQueen's trainer. "Just before the final bell of the last fight, he and Bruce literally got up and ran from the place. After they started running, people from the stands jumped up and started running after them."

As with Kareem, Bruce had been afforded another front-row seat to see a star accelerating into superstardom. Stardom is one thing, superstardom something much more consuming. Steve's risky stunts, his womanizing, even his passion for martial arts were meant to maintain his alpha edge and postpone the moment everything went away.

On Bruce's twenty-eighth birthday Steve phoned the house from Palm Springs, over a hundred miles away. Bruce told them he, Peter, Ted, and Herb were about to have a workout. "I'll be there in an hour," Steve said. He pulled up at the house an hour later. The men went out to see Steve in his new racing-green Porsche. When Bruce said he was nearly ready to buy his dream car, Steve promised to take him out first. "It's not a toy and you've really got to know what you're doing," he said.

McQueen headed up to Mulholland Drive with Bruce in the passenger seat and told him, "Hold on, I'm going to take it through its paces." Then the world-class racer—in 1971 he would do all his auto stunts for his movie *Le Mans*—roared out at top speed, fishtailing around the bends. Bruce cringed in his seat and hung on.

"Now, watch how this baby can do a beautiful one-eighty," Steve said, as he whipped the car into a sideshow doughnut, then gunned it again. "Well, Bruce, what do you think?"

He pulled the car over. Bruce had slumped to the footwell.

"McQueen! You crazy motherfucker!" he yelled. "I'll kill you!"

McQueen laughed and put his foot back on the accelerator. "Bruce, I'm going to drive as fast as I can until you calm down."

"Okay, okay," Bruce said, throwing his hands up. "I'm calm, Steve."

Steve invited him to the set of *Bullitt*. He asked Bruce to get him in shape for his media appearances, invited him over for dinner with his Filipino American wife, Neile, and to exclusive screenings of his films. When the lights came down Bruce carefully studied how Steve moved on-screen.

Sometimes they met or talked several times a week.[*] In his Day-Timers Bruce noted all of Steve's calls and visits, sometimes just referring to him admiringly as "Bullitt." He was taking mental notes of everything—Steve's clothes, his car, the control he had over his art and career.

"Both men had what the other wanted," James Coburn recalled. "It was two giant egos vying for something: stardom for Lee and street-fighting technique for Steve."

Bruce admitted as much to Mito: "I teach Steve *jeet kune do* and he gives me advice on acting."

One afternoon, Bruce wondered aloud why Asian actors weren't being given a shot at leading roles in Hollywood.

"Bruce," Steve said, laughing, "no American woman would ever go to bed dreaming of an Oriental lover."

The fifty-year-old Stirling Silliphant was one of the most successful and celebrated screenwriters in Hollywood, the rare millionaire writer, according to *Time* magazine. But the former boxer and champion fencer felt he had gotten soft. When he had been a student at USC, Stirling was a champion fencer. Now he was feeling his middle age.

Stirling had long been fascinated by Sufism and Zen Buddhism. He studied Asian martial arts books so that he could write *karate* scenes into his scripts. It was finally time to try it out. He arranged a set of private lessons for himself and other top executives, including Jim Aubrey, the head of MGM Studios, and Richard Zanuck, the head of 20th Century-Fox. But he quickly realized that the black belts were starstruck and not teaching them anything, so he quit.

At a Hollywood party he heard someone tell a tale about a Vegas encounter Frank Sinatra had with a Chinese martial artist, who had—after hearing Sinatra say that *gung fu* was useless—knocked his hotel door down, flattened one of his bodyguards, and kicked the cigarette out of another bodyguard's mouth. It turned

---

[*] In the first month alone, they met seven times and talked on the phone as well. Some weeks in 1968 they spoke and worked out almost every day. That Bruce had carefully documented these encounters in his Day-Timers gives a sense of how large Steve loomed in his mind.

out not to be true, but Stirling believed it could be. He soon found that everyone in town seemed to have heard of the story and of Bruce Lee. But no one seemed to actually know him. A three-month search led him to William Dozier, a call to Bruce, and an invitation to meet at his office at Columbia Pictures.

"I don't know if I want to teach anyone that old," Bruce told Stirling. "It seems pointless." But he had Stirling kick a cushion and punch his mitt anyway.

"I will say that you've got speed and your reflexes are good," Bruce said. "But I have to tell you, you could hit someone and he wouldn't even know it. I can tell we have a lot of work with you."

Beginning in March 1968, Stirling trained with Bruce as often as three times a week, at the rate of $275 an hour. He wouldn't be learning any *katas*, Bruce told him, because they were "vertical death." He started with basic kicks. "When you can kick so you aren't jarred but the tree is jarred," Bruce said, "then you will begin to understand a kick."

After Silliphant had made progress, Bruce inducted him into the basics of Jeet Kune Do. He explained that a kick had as much power and more length than a jab and was the best way to close the gap. He then showed Stirling one of his favorite targets, the kneecap, and described the effectiveness of aiming a proper kick there.

He routinely pushed Stirling past the point of exhaustion. One day as they ran three miles at a strong pace, he told Stirling they were going to do five.

"If I run any more," Stirling protested, "I'm liable to have a heart attack and die."

"Then die," Bruce replied, and ran on.

Silliphant finished the five miles enraged. But in the showers afterward, he confronted Bruce, demanding to know why he had said that.

"Because you might as well be dead," Bruce said. "Seriously, if you always put limits on what you can do, physical or anything else, it'll spread into the rest of your life. It'll spread into your work, into your morality, into your entire being.

"There are no limits. There are plateaus, but you must not stay there, you must go beyond them. If it kills you, it kills you."

As Stirling got into better shape, Bruce taught him defense and attacks, often relating it to fencing theory. But Stirling soon reached another plateau. In sparring, Bruce told him, his defensive moves were sharp, but his attacks were weak. Stirling told Bruce that when he was fencing, the way he won was through counterattacks. It was just who he was.

"Bullshit. That's a technical rationalization. There's something in *you*, something deep in your psyche, that stops you from attacking," Bruce said. "You don't have the killer instinct."

For weeks Bruce pressed Stirling. Finally Stirling burst out with the admission that his father had never hugged him or shown him physical signs of love. "In fact,

I had never touched a man or had any body contact with another male," he recalled. "No, I was not homophobic. I just—hadn't—ever—done it."

Stirling continued:

> I remember that afternoon so vividly. Bruce and I were sweating—we were naked from the waist up, wearing those black Chinese bloomer pajama pants only. Bruce moved in closer.
>
> "Put your arms around me," he ordered.
>
> "Hey, Bruce," I said, "you're all sweaty, man."
>
> "Do it!" he demanded.
>
> So I put my arms around him.
>
> "Pull me closer," he said.
>
> "Jesus, Bruce!"
>
> "Closer!"
>
> I pulled him closer, I could feel the *chi* in his body—a vibrant force which literally throbbed from his muscles. His vitality passed between us—and it was as though a steel wall had just been blown away. He felt good. He felt alive. When I opened my arms and he stepped back, he was studying me.
>
> "You have to love everyone," he said, "not only women, but men as well. You don't have to have sex with a man, but you have to be able to relate to his separate physicality. If you don't, you will never be able to fight him, to drive your fist through his chest, to snap his neck, to gouge out his eyes."

In later years, Stirling would say, "I never met another man who was even remotely at his level of consciousness."

Bruce had been reading Fritz Perls's books on Gestalt therapy, which Leo Fong had sent after studying them in his graduate psychology classes at Sacramento State. "Don't let other people impose their egos on you," he told Stirling. "At the same time, of course, don't impose your ego on others. Just have your ego. Period."

"Because of Bruce," Stirling said, "I opened all my windows." He had found exactly the kind of Asian teacher he had been seeking.

In his career, Bruce had also reached a plateau. Hollywood wanted him as a teacher, but did it want him as an actor?

Perhaps because he had been raised in the colony of Hong Kong in a majority-Chinese society, or perhaps because he was full of youthful disdain for the old, he had drawn a line about the kind of work he would not take. "Most of those shows want me to wear a queue and I won't do that. I don't give a damn how much they pay me," Bruce told Mito. "When the Manchus ruled China, they forced the Chinese natives to wear those damn pigtails to mark them as women."

Bruce auditioned for a role on *Hawaii Five-O* as detective Chin Ho Kelly but lost the job to a Local entertainer, Kam Fong Chun. He landed small roles playing Japanese martial arts instructors on the detective procedural *Ironside* and family sitcom *Blondie*. The minor indignity of playing a *karate/aikido/judo sensei* in *Ironside* was offset by the joy of staging fight scenes with Gene LeBell.

On *Here Come the Brides*, ABC's answer to *Bonanza*, Bruce costarred in an episode called "Marriage Chinese Style," playing a young bachelor in early-twentieth-century Seattle. San Francisco–born *pinay* Linda Dangcil was Toy Quan, a prostitute who is saved by a white man from being assaulted and—following the Hollywood fake book of Oriental customs—begins following him everywhere, pledging to marry him. Bruce's character, Lin Sung, must save the day by marrying the prostitute so that the white Christian man won't have to. Lin Sung and Toy Quan dress and speak like Westernized Orientals, a small grace. But the script still revealed the limit of Hollywood's imagination. If Bruce wasn't going to wear the queue, he still couldn't expect much better work than this.

He accepted a job as a fight coordinator for *The Wrecking Crew*, a movie starring Dean Martin and Sharon Tate, who had once dated Jay Sebring and had introduced Bruce to her fiancé, Roman Polanski. He leveraged his position to get acting parts for Ed Parker and Chuck Norris, and a job for Mike Stone doubling for Dean Martin. He choreographed and taught Sharon and Nancy Kwan their fight sequence.

In the very small world of working Asian Americans in Hollywood, Nancy and Bruce had been bound to meet. They hit it off famously. Although she was a year older and a star, they had so much in common as biracial actors from Hong Kong, Catholic school alumni, and students of Jeff Corey that they could talk about anything. They developed a sibling-like relationship. Around her, Bruce turned into an energetic chatterbox. Sometimes he would phone her at two in the morning, Nancy recalled, "and go on and on and on. I said, 'You know, there are some people who like to sleep.'"

Acting while yellow was their recurring topic. After *The World of Suzie Wong* and *Flower Drum Song*, Nancy had realized that the only way for actors like them to go was sideways or down. The few agents who did represent Asian actors mostly sent them out as extras or to fill stereotypical two-line roles. She understood Bruce's frustration: "He played Kato and it didn't get him anywhere." Bruce often told her he thought about going back to Hong Kong to restart his career.

Stirling Silliphant reciprocated his gratitude to Bruce by writing him into his film adaptation of Raymond Chandler's 1949 Philip Marlowe mystery, *The Little Sister*. On August 1, 1968, they began shooting the retitled movie, *Marlowe*, with one of Bruce's *gung fu* students, James Garner, as the star. Bruce played a character named Winslow Wong, a mob enforcer in a Brioni suit sent to bribe the detective.

"I had seen so many parodies of a thin guy with a weasel face and a fat guy with a black suit come into the offices to threaten people," Silliphant recalled, "I thought, let's send in one of the world's greatest martial artists and have him demolish Marlowe's office."

Upon entering Marlowe's office a smiling Wong kicks a hole in the wall and chops down a coat rack. Marlowe pulls out a pistol. "You won't need that," Wong says, still grinning, and offers him a bribe to stop his sleuthing.

When Marlowe refuses, Wong storms across the set, breaking bookshelves, rearranging furniture with his feet, kicking out wood panels, and punching out the glass door. As a coup de grâce, he takes two steps and launches into a spectacular flying kick that brings down the ceiling light fixture with a thunderous crash. He does this all in a single continuous motion.

Silliphant's instinct was right: nothing like this had ever been seen on American screens. For first-time viewers, the scene still elicits big gasps—but also big laughs. He and Bruce had compressed as much camp into Winslow Wong's three-minute showcase as Kato's entire twenty-six-episode run.

Wong returns later to assassinate Marlowe at a rooftop restaurant, intending to push him off the edge of the building. With spinning kicks, he backs Marlowe into the corner of the roof. The detective continues to crack wise, "You're light on your feet, Winslow. Are you just a little gay?"

Wong is so outraged by this insult to his manhood that he leaps into a flying kick, which misses, and he soars over the balcony to his death. Hard-boiled, not so much. Believable, not at all. If Silliphant hoped the movie might make *gung fu* look serious, and Bruce look like a serious actor, he had failed. The power of the Asian fighting arts had been crushed by the laughter of the American masses.

Sharon Farrell, who played the little sister in *Marlowe*, thought that Bruce was a little crude in front of the camera. "He tried too hard," she said. Yet she had her eyes on him for other reasons.

"When the day's shooting had finished, he followed me to where I had parked my car on the lot. He just stood there grinning at me like a little kid," she wrote in her autobiography. "I just thought he was cute and harmless enough to flirt with."

A few months later, Steve McQueen invited Bruce to join him in Mississippi on the set of his movie *The Reivers*. He was there to keep Steve occupied with *gung fu* training. On set Bruce played court jester to Steve's king. Another martial artist there thought Bruce "couldn't stand to be second banana, so he would do tricks in front of Steve to impress him." But Bruce believed he was helping his friend.

"The public thinks acting is a lot of fun or exciting. It's not," Bruce told Mito. "A star like Steve had to work extremely hard. That's why so many actors turn to the bottle and become alcoholics.

"Steve flies me in because he wants to talk to somebody else besides the same guys he works with all day long," he added. "We usually talk about life, philosophy, and work out a little."

Soon Sharon Farrell arrived on set to be McQueen's costar and his character's love interest. Years later, she would remember her brief fling with Bruce fondly. But at that moment she had her eye on McQueen. That was just how Hollywood worked. They were all climbers in the talus and scree.

By the end of 1968, Bruce had seen enough to know how steep it was from his ledge to the summit, and how he was just one step away from falling into oblivion.

CHAPTER 32
The Seeker

On letterhead stamped "SECRET" at the top and bottom in red, and dated January 7, 1969, Bruce wrote the final draft of something he called his "Definite Chief Aim" in florid blue marker script:

> I, Bruce Lee, will be the first highest paid Oriental super star in the United States. In return, I will give the most exciting performances and render the best of quality in the capacity of an actor. Starting 1970 I will achieve world fame and from then onward till the end of 1980 I will have in my possession $10,000,000. I will live the way I please and achieve inner harmony and happiness.

He had first encountered Napoleon Hill's motivational ideas when his belief was flagging in Seattle, and as uncertainty set in again, he had returned to them.

"Success," the historian Richard Lingeman once wrote of Hill's career, "is the great American secular religion." An American self-help pioneer and a serial fabulist whom some thought a fraud, Napoleon Hill had come to prominence during the Great Depression, selling millions of books touting the idea that anyone could "think and grow rich."

"Whatever the mind of man can conceive and believe it can achieve," Hill had written. "You are what you are because of the dominating thoughts you allow to occupy your mind."

Autosuggestion, Hill argued, could make one's dreams of prosperity real. All one needed to do was eliminate negative feelings and cultivate faith. This idea—which the Reverend Norman Vincent Peale later called "the power of positive thinking"—would influence Tony Robbins, the preachers of the Prosperity Gospel, and Donald J. Trump to try to make people believe they could soar.

To focus his followers' energies on their life purpose, what he called a "Definite Chief Aim," Hill directed them to daily repeat his creed and affirmations "until these vibrations of sound have reached your subconscious mind." Bruce had carefully transcribed Hill's "Creed for Self-Discipline" into his 1968 and 1969 Day-Timers. From *Think and Grow Rich*, he also copied an affirmation: "I know that I have the ability to achieve the object of my definite purpose in life; therefore I demand of myself persistent, continuous action toward its attainment, and I here and now promise to render such action." He was focusing himself on his aim: becoming not just a star, but a superstar.

Bruce's schedule was wide open, so he threw himself into his workout regimens. In the mornings, he jogged several miles with his brawny but dumb Great Dane, Bobo. A typical day might then include four hundred finger jabs, one thousand punches, hundreds of high kicks, side kicks, and hook kicks, multiple sets of jump rope, isometrics, weights, stretches, and cycling. He documented his physical exercise plans alongside the amount of time he had spent listening to Hill's cassettes. Hill had given him a mental workout plan.

By then, he and Linda had a mortgage to pay. During their first two years in Los Angeles, Bruce, Linda, and Brandon had moved five times, even staying for a short while in Ted Wong's small Chinatown apartment. They decided to buy a house. "And that was Bruce and I in 1968," Linda later wrote, "young, foolish, and with grand visions."

Steve McQueen asked his finance team and his manager to provide them with advice and support. In Upper Bel Air, they found a three-bedroom fixer-upper at 2551 Roscomare Road, which was then considered the tract-home section of town, "the poor man's Bel Air," Linda joked. With some help from her mother, who had just sold her Seattle house, they purchased it for forty-seven thousand dollars. At the end of September 1968, with the help of Dan Inosanto, Dan Lee, Ted Wong, Herb Jackson, and Peter Chin, they moved in their belongings.

In the living room, Bruce set up shelves to house his large book collection. But Linda remembered, "We couldn't afford a couch." Instead, they used Hoi Chuen's old teakwood bed for a sofa, the same one upon which he had smoked his opium.

He set up his growing stash of training gear and equipment in the backyard and the garage. He had a hanging bag, a hitting pad, a *mook jong*, a squat machine, and many other devices to increase his power, speed, and flexibility. Dan Inosanto's expertise, Mito Uyehara's Japanese manufacturing connections, George Lee's craftsmanship, and Herb Jackson's workshop skills had produced an innovative collection of fingerless punching gloves, focus gloves, air shields, forearm grips, shin, arm, and chest guards, and kicking dummies, all future equipment standards for mixed martial arts training.

The spacious backyard became his fight lab. On Wednesday nights he did regular private sessions with Ted, Herb, and Peter, sometimes also Mito Uyehara. Other afternoons champion athletes like Mike Stone, Chuck Norris, Joe Lewis, Louis Delgado, and Big Lew stopped by to work out. It was where Bruce felt freest.

That fall, they learned that Linda was pregnant again. Perhaps buying the house had been exactly the right decision. After practices Bruce gazed at the dramatic smog-tinged violet-and-orange sunsets over a small green gulch and the indigo Pacific, and contemplated Jeet Kune Do.

Doctors had told Bruce and Linda that his cryptorchidism might cause cancer. In March 1969, they found the money to get Bruce testicular surgery. But while small *Green Hornet* residual checks were still coming in, his paid appearances had peaked. He had also pulled back from the school. He disliked the Hollywood party scene, so he was not picking up new clients quickly. Since he had decided against opening the Kato schools, his world had been shrinking. With a new mortgage, a child on the way, and Hollywood work hard to come by, money had become a constant worry.

One day Bruce called Nancy Kwan. "Nancy, I have no money," he told her. "I can't even buy a new pair of glasses." He had worn them until the bridge snapped, then taped it up so he could still read with them.

In the spring of 1969, Stirling Silliphant got Bruce work on *A Walk in the Spring Rain*, an Ingrid Bergman–Anthony Quinn drama he was writing and producing. In this story set in Appalachia, there was no role for an Asian actor, so Stirling hired Bruce to direct the climactic fight scene and paid him extra for in-person JKD sessions.

While Bruce was on set in the Great Smoky Mountains or at the Howard Johnson's in Gatlinburg, Tennessee, Linda was with her mother at Santa Monica General Hospital. Just as his father had missed his, he would be absent for his daughter's birth. Instead, when he got the news of her birth on April 19, he spoke to Linda three times, and then later rang Dan Inosanto to tell him the good news.

Proudly, he wrote in his Day-Timer: "4:30pm—Shannon E. Lee 6 lbs., 6 oz. 19 inches."

A month later, his mother and Robert left Hong Kong for good and moved in with Bruce and Linda at their Bel Air home. Despite their cashflow troubles, Linda recalled these days as happy ones.

They received a welcome surprise when they learned that Grace had sold a building the family owned in Hong Kong and they were owed a share. Bruce took the seven-thousand-dollar windfall and bought a cherry-red Porsche 911S Targa like the kind Steve McQueen and Jay Sebring owned so that he could roar around the curves of Mulholland Drive as they did.

"It was an extravagance, but it made Bruce happy," Linda recalled. "He had to do everything faster and faster."

On a clear Sunday, he took Jhoon Rhee out for a spin in the hills. "I was experiencing white-knuckled, teeth-clenching, chest-tightening fear," Rhee recalled. "I could barely talk, I was so nerve-wracked."

It would not be long before Bruce received a speeding ticket. Not long afterward he got into an accident. He was still fixed on reaching the heights of his Hollywood friends. But perhaps he had seen something else too, something much more mundane and profound—that his youth was fading.

Then, on August 9, 1969, an unfathomable darkness descended upon Los Angeles. Five gruesomely mutilated bodies were discovered in a Beverly Hills mansion whose front door had been painted in blood with the word "PIG." The West Coast version of the sixties—with its fist-raising rebellion and free-love counterculture—had abruptly ended. Bruce's friends Jay Sebring and Sharon Tate were among the dead. The next day a couple in a Los Feliz home were found murdered in a similarly horrifying fashion. "WAR" had been carved into one of the bodies, and "RISE," "PIG," and "HELTER SKELTER" were written in blood on the walls.

The killers came from a death cult led by Charles Manson, a white supremacist with a god complex and a Revelation worldview who had slipped between the seams of the counterculture and insinuated himself into the Los Angeles party scene. He had allegedly exhorted his followers to begin killings across the city's most exclusive neighborhoods to spark a race war between whites and Blacks. The killers would not be captured for two more months.

When Bruce received the news, he called Steve McQueen right away. He knew Jay had been one of Steve's best friends, and that Steve had partied a lot with Sharon. Steve was to have been at the mansion that evening but had left for another tryst. Now, the distraught Steve said, he was going to carry a handgun everywhere. Bruce came home from Jay's and Sharon's joint funeral shaken. He admitted to Mito, "It scares the hell out of you, especially when you have a family."

Sharon had been pregnant, just two weeks away from giving birth. She had been stabbed sixteen times. Jay's body was nearby. A rope hanging over the rafters was wound twice around Sharon's neck at one end, and twice around Jay's neck at the other. He too had been stabbed several times then shot. A bloody towel covered his face, which had been beaten beyond recognition. He appeared to have died, Vincent Bugliosi and Curt Gentry wrote, with "his hands up near his head as if still warding off blows."

Mito wondered aloud if Jay could have used what Bruce had taught him to defend them that night. "Sebring could never get out of a situation like that," Bruce said at first. But then perhaps he too wondered if he might have been able to stop such a horrifying massacre.

"[Jay] was still too green and he wasn't the type of guy who would fight back," Bruce told Mito. "He was a small man and far from being a fighter."

It was a harsh thing to say about his friend. But self-defense had become very real.

Bruce was hypervigilant, tense all the time, always checking the doors, wanting to know where the kids were every moment of the day. The assassinations of Martin Luther King Jr. and Robert Kennedy, Linda said, had "made us feel less safe in the world." These killings were even closer to home. "It was just a couple of canyons away," Linda recalled. "You thought, 'Oh my god, these murderers are roaming around at random.'"

Panic and paranoia descended on the hills of Los Angeles. Tate's mourning husband, Roman Polanski—who had been away filming when the murders happened—

stepped up his self-defense classes with Bruce. Polanski also knew that a pair of horn-rimmed glasses had been found at the bloody mansion. One day Bruce—unaware of this detail—mentioned that he had lost his glasses. To Polanski, that made him a suspect. Polanski offered to take Bruce to his optometrist to buy a new pair. Pinched as he was, Bruce was happy to accept. Only after he saw that Bruce's prescription did not match the lenses from the mansion did Polanski breathe more easily.

By the time Charles Manson was arrested, in Death Valley, in October 1969, Bruce and Linda's bank account balance had dwindled to $85.12.

Bruce had been having a recurring dream about a man he had come to call the Seeker. The man was being called by a "silent flute," a sound played by a mysterious blind man that only he could hear. Both the Seeker and the blind flutist represented to him a kind of purity. The Seeker is committed to discovering truth through physicality. The blind man is a Musashi-style stoic who has won his wisdom through bloody experience. Excited, Bruce sketched out some notes.

A highly skilled martial artist, the Seeker is bound by society's constraints and shackled by his indoctrination. Through a series of fights and a worldwide martial arts competition, he proceeds toward his awakening. But he can only fulfill his destiny through the interventions of the blind man, a *sifu* who leads the Seeker away from the "classical mess."

Bruce realized he had an idea that could put him back in the game. It would be Hollywood's first martial arts movie, the broadest way to show the world the beauty of Asian philosophy and fight, and to achieve his chief aim. But he was also aware that, like his Seeker, he would need lots of help. His notes were thin, and he had never written a complete screenplay before.

He also realized that in *this* Hollywood he could never play the lead. He comforted himself a little with the thought that instead he could play the blind teacher, and—just to make sure audiences saw him and everything he could do—*all* three of the opponents the Seeker needed to face.

He codenamed the movie "Project Leng." "Leng," he later told Jhoon Rhee, "is a Chinese word meaning 'beautiful.'"

Then, with fresh energy, he brought the idea to the two friends who might be able to help him make it happen—Steve and Stirling, respectively the biggest actor and the biggest screenwriter in the world.* In his 1968 Day-Timer, he would mark dozens of dates on which he had called or met with either of them.

---

* In an undated letter from this period, Bruce expressed to Silliphant, "The character of the blind martial artist will be in the company of Bond, Flint, Helm, etc." He added, "Of course right now I am in no position to say anything especially before the film is made, However, do forgive my faith, for I KNOW I will be a credit to you and add on to your 'already' string of success list." This letter is reprinted in Steve Kerridge and Darren Chua's excellent *Bruce Lee: Mandarin Superstar* (On the Fly Productions, 2018), unpaginated.

They did not exactly jump at his idea. Stirling was encouraging but told Bruce he was too busy. Steve was more circumspect. But he finally convinced Steve and Stirling to meet with him. On September 25, 1968, three days before Bruce was to move into his new home in Bel Air, he and Stirling went up to the Castle.

"We met with Steve in his study and laid [Project Leng] on him as a potential film project," Silliphant recalled. "Bruce had some idea that it would be a film starring Steve and him and that I would write it."

After Bruce introduced his project, Stirling said that he would write the script if Steve would agree to come aboard. Bruce turned the question to Steve.

"Nah," Steve said. He was too busy.

Bruce pressed harder. At that point, Stirling recalled Steve's demeanor was courteous, but his words were clear and cruel.

"Let's face it, Bruce, this is a vehicle to make a big star out of you," Steve said, "and I gotta be honest with you. I'm not in this business to make stars out of other people. I love you, buddy, but you're just going to be hanging on my coattails and I'm just not going to do that. I'm not going to carry you on my back."

As they left, Bruce stopped and waved his fist at the exterior of the Castle. He turned to Stirling and said, "I'll be bigger than Steve McQueen! Who is he to tell me he won't do this film with me?"

Years later, Stirling expressed sympathy for Bruce. "He'd lost face in front of me," Silliphant said, "because he had brought me to a superstar with the hope that he would come out of the meeting with a deal."

But another part of Stirling was also still in disbelief at how presumptuous his young Asian martial arts teacher had been—the same one who had once cautioned him about ego: "He thought Steve would simply say, 'OK, go write the script; we'll do it.'

"Can you imagine," Stirling said, "how gigantic Bruce's self-belief was?"

After his death, a certain narrative about Bruce would be amplified by his most vociferous critics, from Albert Goldman to Quentin Tarantino—that he was a narcissistic little Asian who didn't know his place and needed to be knocked down a few pegs.

But one can also picture Bruce arriving at a despairing realization in that moment. His house in Bel-Air was, in many ways, a gift of Steve's. His ability to pay the mortgage rested on the work Steve and Stirling and others provided him, even while, as he had told Kareem, he served as a "valet to the stars." And what they had given, they could take away. If it had not been so clear to him before, it was now inescapable how much of his presence in Hollywood depended on the benevolence—and the capriciousness—of his powerful white male friends.

Two weeks later, Bruce left for the Tennessee set of *The Reivers* to serve as Steve's personal trainer and entertainer. After Steve's rejection, Bruce had not given up. He pitched Steve's longtime producer and business partner Robert Relyea until the man finally erupted: "Stop bothering me, Kato, and forget this crap about starring in movies. Just concentrate on keeping our star in shape."

Stirling wanted to help his *sifu*, even if he would do so in ways that indicated he was unsure about how seriously he should take Bruce's ambitions.

He sent Bruce to meet with his nephew, Mark Silliphant, a recent UCLA film school graduate, whom he hired at $150 per week to help Bruce turn his ideas into something script-ready. Mark later reported to his uncle that he was in the university library reading books with names like *Bits of Old China*, *The Magic Flowery Land*, and *A Chinese Mirror: Being Reflections of the Reality Beyond Appearance*. It was immediately clear to Bruce that Stirling's nephew was in way over his head.

For his part, Stirling continued to send Steve updates on Project Leng, who showed no apparent interest. But at a Hollywood party, Stirling met James Coburn and decided to flex. He complimented Coburn on his *karate* performance in *Our Man Flint*. Coburn confessed he had been faking it. Stirling said he knew someone Coburn should meet, and on Halloween, connected the two.

Coburn had risen to fame in a Zen-like role as Britt in *The Magnificent Seven*, John Sturges's 1960 remake of the Kurosawa classic *Seven Samurai*, and became a star with the James Bond parody that Stirling had cited. He was in his forties, but at home with the young generation. He experimented with psychedelics and collected rugs, antiques, books of erotica, and gongs from West and East Asia. His house smelled of incense and patchouli oil. He and his wife were known to throw spontaneous parties for a Dennis Hopper movie cast or an entourage of visiting Tibetan Buddhist monks.

He was soon working out with Bruce at three hundred dollars an hour. Coburn was fascinated by what he called the "esoteric" aspects of Asian martial arts. He was delighted to find in Bruce "a person who relates everything to martial arts or the martial arts to everything." Sometimes when the two met they just sat down and talked Eastern philosophy for hours.

On the same day in 1969 that Bruce had composed his "Definite Chief Aim," he had also written in his Day-Timer, "WILL MAKE GOAL—SERIES [OR] MOVIE."

Six days later, on Monday, January 13, he had lunch with Stirling Silliphant. That night he wrote, "FORMATION OF STIRLING AND ME ON MOVIE IDEA." The two of them approached Coburn about starring in *The Silent Flute*. He loved the idea. The next day Bruce wrote, "COBURN'S INVOLVEMENT." On Saturday, January 18, capping a week of positive developments, he copied a Napoleon Hill affirmation into his Day-Timer: "Keep your mind on the things you want and off the things you don't want. 'ATTITUDE.'" By the end of January, Stirling, his nephew Mark, James, and Bruce were meeting regularly to break the script.

Bruce had poured his ideas into eighteen handwritten pages of notes. Set in the near future, a totalitarian government has, in the name of peace, banned all martial arts and driven warriors underground. Two factions of fighters—those who are mechanical, "no-soul" classicists and those who "crave to be individualistic under oppression"—battle to determine the future of humanity. At this point, Bruce had less plot than pugilism and philosophy. He filled most of the pages with details for fight scenes. Alluding to Suzuki, Zhuangzi, and *The Huainanzi*, he discussed the martial artist's struggle to confront the "problem of psychical stoppage."

"Basically this is a story of man's quest for his liberation," he wrote, "the returning to his original sense of freedom."

On May 5, 1969, Mark Silliphant delivered a film treatment in which the Seeker, temporarily renamed Coburn in this draft, leaves an oppressive society behind to search for the blind flutist, an ideal of elevated consciousness. By July, Mark had written a fuller story presentation for the movie now named *The Silent Flute*.

In this draft, the government controls the populace through brutally enforced "violence control" measures, a state-run prostitution agency, and the mandated use of tranquilizing narcotics. Democracy has been reduced to voting on the fate of alleged violators of anti-violence laws. The choice offered is always punishment or death.

Coburn comes to his personal awakening in a *dojo*, then enters the anarchic subculture of martial arts fighters. In the World Championship of Fight, staged to pacify the public's need for spectacles of aggression, Coburn makes the finals, but breaks the rules by unleashing his full combat skills and leaving his defeated opponent unconscious. He is sentenced to death and killed with a bullet to the head in a scene recalling Eddie Adams's infamous 1968 war photo, "Saigon Execution." In a final dreamlike sequence, Coburn is shown clashing with the Blind Man on the mountain peak.

But though the treatment reflected Bruce's views on the "classical mess" of the martial arts scene, he felt something essential was still missing from the script—the resplendence of Asian philosophy and fighting. He had been underwhelmed by Stirling's nephew anyway, and convinced Stirling and James to let him go. By September, Stirling and James had kicked in seventy-five hundred dollars to hire a more experienced writer named Shelly Burton.

To teach Burton more about the deeper ideas underlying the martial arts and the movie, Bruce invited the screenwriter to train with him, but Burton missed half their scheduled meetings. When he sent his draft back to them at the end of 1969, the script was unrecognizable. Burton had leaned into the Orwellian sci-fi dystopia part, and reduced the martial arts to violent ambience, less Tao than THX-1138.

"In your personal apocalypse you appear to have been far more intrigued with sex and computer loopholes than martial arts," Silliphant wrote in an angry letter to Burton. "Martial arts is not an affirmation of the Animal, but of the Spirit.

"We will have to begin all over again with another writer," he wrote.

Bruce had gone all in on the movie to rescue himself and Linda from their financial situation. But now any possible payday had been pushed beyond the horizon. With Jay Sebring gone, Stirling had become Bruce's primary patron. He was trying to get a *samurai* movie off the ground, and promised Bruce he would be associate producer and technical adviser. But he also knew that the one thing that Bruce really wanted—for him to take over the writing duties—would also increase *The Silent Flute*'s chances of getting made.

"Seeing that he was in terrible financial condition and because I loved him, and because of his teaching me to be a better person spiritually and physically," Stirling recalled, "I said, 'I'll write the goddamn thing.'"

To Bruce, the project now felt destined to happen. Stirling could cut loose to write the freakiest script he'd ever written, James had the countercultural antihero starring role he had always wanted, and here was Bruce, the muse, the source of authenticity, and the third brother once again, holding the project together and driving it forward.

After Stirling had shown him some early drafts, Bruce wrote him to say, "Script is definitely of Jeet Kune Do quality, and your skill in writing is a special art, the art of the soul."

Stirling recalled, "It was evident to me that the thing I cared most about at that particular point in time was martial arts and advocating Bruce Lee."

But looking back later, he admitted that even *he* had underestimated Bruce.

Stirling's impression was that Bruce "was beginning to accept what we kept telling him, which was, 'You'll never be a superstar here. But stick around anyway. We'll keep working you into things. Who knows?'" His attitude about his *sifu* had been: maybe a fight choreographer job here, a TV or movie appearance there—and then maybe something might catch fire for him. Then again, maybe not.

"Even though we loved him," he said, "I guess we all secretly believed that was about as far or as high as Bruce could aspire."

But at home, Bruce had put up a black-light poster by Art Bevacqua, a lurid cartoon of two starving vultures perched high above a scorching desert empty of anything to eat.

"Patience my ass!" one says to the other. "I'm gonna kill something."

CHAPTER 33
What Is Freedom?

"JKD is unbound. JKD is freedom," Bruce once told Dan Inosanto. "It possesses everything, yet in itself is possessed by nothing."

He may have been speaking of himself. "He was like the beacon, the source of the energy that everybody got something from," James Coburn said. But to his closest friends, it sometimes seemed that he lived life in a ready position, on guard, behind a mask. "Bruce kept a lot of things to himself," Dan said.

In their backyard sessions Mito Uyehara, who had taken up *aikido* because he was attracted to the idea of *qi*—*ki* in Japanese—noticed that when they did sticking hands together Bruce seemed to possess a powerful internal energy. He asked Bruce about how he had built such powerful *qi*.

"Ah, Mito," he said with a laugh, "there's no such thing as *qi*."

But one day in the office, Mito threw a surprise punch at Bruce's stomach and he blocked it with shockingly concentrated force. "You son of a gun!" Mito shouted. "You told me there's no such thing as *qi*!"

Bruce smiled and said, "Everyone makes it mystical using that word. It's just flowing energy."

Each day, Dan recalled, "the first thing on his schedule was meditation. He was heavily into what I call 'esoteric studies' . . .

"What I'm trying to say," Dan said, "is that he sort of pointed his students in one direction and pointed himself in another."

As 1970 dawned, Bruce felt far from free. He had not been teaching much at the school. Thinking about Jeet Kune Do as a process of evolution had been exciting to him, but thinking of it as something to be propagated took the joy out of it.

"You can't organize truth," he told a reporter. "That's like putting a pound of water into wrapping paper and shaping it."

For years, he had written copiously detailed programs and curricula for Taky, James, and Dan to teach in the Jun Fan Gung Fu Institutes. He had written and rewritten these almost obsessively—sometimes, as his interests shifted, every three months. In the fall of 1967, for example, Bruce had issued new guidelines called a "Six Week Lesson Plan for Jeet Kune Do." He emphasized teaching fewer techniques.

"It's not how much you've learned, but how much you have absorbed in what you have learned," he told them to tell the students. "The best techniques are the simple ones executed right."

Bruce urged them not to let their students become passive. As teachers, they needed to infuse reps of basic techniques with surprise—varying the speed, partners, distance, or cadence "so they will not become a bore and a chore." He encouraged them to embody their teaching: "Let's *be* broken rhythm . . .

"The best you can do is to ask questions and provoke the students to think and solve their own training problems," he wrote. "They have to be involved."

But by 1970, he seemed to have finally buried his decade-long dream of becoming America's *sifu*. Wiliam Cheung had written Bruce telling him he was developing an "abstract field of self-defense" in Australia, involving "operational research." Bruce congratulated him but also cautioned William.

"Really, martial art is not for the masses," Bruce wrote. "Keep it to yourself and close friends."

Bruce had begun writing a piece for Mito for *Black Belt* magazine, and he was talking of freedom again.

"True observation begins when one sheds set patterns and true freedom of expression occurs when one is beyond systems," he wrote. "Truth cannot be perceived until we come to fully understand ourselves and our potentials. After all, *knowledge in the martial arts ultimately means self-knowledge.*"

In one sense, his thinking was converging with that of the Asian American activists who were advocating a liberatory education. Almost as soon as the young radicals had named themselves Asian American, they realized that. Americanization had erased their communities' histories, leaving them abject. They needed to recover their stories and learn each other's.

"That was a moment of discovery that Asian Americans had a history that was dark—really, really dark," recalled Third World Liberation Front activist Jeffrey Thomas Leong. "We want to have a present and a future, and we can't have any of that unless we have a knowledge of our past."

The exiled Brazilian thinker Paulo Freire, who thought of education as the grounds on which to sow a freedom consciousness, and whose book *Pedagogy of the Oppressed* would prove influential on the movement, echoed Frederick Douglass: "Freedom is acquired by conquest, not gift. It must be pursued constantly and responsibly." The Asian Americans set out to write themselves a new past. When they launched classes to teach this new narrative of themselves, they found a huge demand from peers on their campuses and from members of the community. They were encouraged in their goal of building new schools of liberated studies. Self-knowledge would free them to fight for themselves.

But here Bruce and the young radicals departed from each other. Bruce thought of self-knowledge as more of a personal quest than a collective one, and of freedom as something to be unlocked from within. "We do not have to 'gain' freedom because freedom has always been with us," Bruce wrote in his notes.

"Freedom is not an ideal, an end to be desired; we do not 'become,' we simply 'are.'"

"At this point you may ask, 'How do I gain this (self-)knowledge?'" he wrote in his piece for *Black Belt*. "That you will have to find out by yourself. You must accept the fact there is no help but self-help. For the same reason I cannot tell you how to 'gain' freedom, since freedom exists within you, I cannot tell you how to 'gain' self-knowledge . . .

"There is no standard in total combat, and expression must be free," he wrote. "This liberating truth is a reality only in so far as it is *experienced and lived* by the individual himself; it is a truth that transcends styles or disciplines."

This logic led Bruce in a different direction than the Asian Americans. Schools were efficient in teaching the arts to large numbers of people. But Bruce was coming to the conclusion that schools did not teach students to become efficient or artful in combat. They were just sources of toxic dogma and empty technique. He wrote:

> It is conceivable that a long time ago a certain martial artist discovered some partial truth. During his lifetime, the man resisted the temptation to organize this partial truth, although this is a common tendency in a man's search for security and certainty in life. After his death, his students took "his" hypothesis, "his" postulates, "his" inclination, and "his" method and turned them into law. . . . In so doing, the well-meaning, loyal followers have not only made this knowledge a holy shrine, but also a tomb in which they have buried the founder's wisdom.

After Bruce's death, when disputes broke out among his students over the nature and teaching of Jeet Kune Do, these words would read differently. In the moment, when George Lee's coffin for "A Once Fluid Man" still greeted all those entering the Los Angeles *kwoon*, his critique of martial arts schooling stood. He continued:

> But the distortion does not necessarily end there. In reaction to "the other's truth," another martial artist, or possibly a dissatisfied disciple, organizes an opposite approach. . . . Soon this opposite faction also becomes a large organization, with its own laws and patterns. A rivalry begins, with each style claiming to possess the "truth" to the exclusion of others.
>
> At best, styles are merely parts dissected from a unitary whole. All styles require adjustment, partiality, denials, condemnation and a lot of self-justification. The solutions they purport to prove are the very cause of the problem, because they limit and interfere with our natural growth and obstruct the way to genuine understanding. Divisive by nature, styles keep men apart from each other rather than unite them.

His piece would be published in the September 1971 issue of *Black Belt* under the provocative title "Liberate Yourself from Classical Karate." It marked a culmination of a journey that had taken him from the streets of Seattle to a partnership with James Yimm Lee, into battle with Wong Jack Man, onto the big stage in Long Beach, and now into the role of the premier renegade of the martial arts.

No one would ever fill the *Black Belt* mailbox as Bruce did. Readers wrote in to defend *katas* and *karate*, to call his one-inch punch demonstrations a farce, to say that they heard he had been defeated—twice!—by a white guy in Connecticut, to assert that he was "probably all mouth and no action—except when he shows on television." Even readers who wanted to agree with him had doubts.

One wrote, "I don't think [he] could absolutely hold to his statement '. . . beyond systems,' since he himself has his own system." Another wrote, "I appreciate the [Taoist] saying, 'He who knows does not speak. He who speaks does not know.' What do you think?"

Bruce had returned—or retreated—to his core contradictions: How could one really create an anti-system system? What did it mean to have a style of no style? Have no rules as rules? Have no limit as a limit? These questions were not just philosophical and polemical. They had concrete implications. If schools by design were bound to lead the sheep astray, then what was the point of having his own?

Jeet Kune Do could not be useful to anyone unless it was something different to each one. "I think the art has to be a personal experience," he told Dan. "You can't have a curriculum that will fit everybody." He added, "A good instructor functions as a pointer of truth, exposing the student's vulnerability, forcing him to explore himself both internally and externally, and finally integrating himself with his being."

From his Seattle days through the opening of his Los Angeles *kwoon* in 1967, he had thought of personal training and a generalized curriculum as opposites in a dynamic relationship. The process of teaching was also the process of learning. A set curriculum could generate discovery. But by 1970, his deconstruction of the martial arts was approaching its terminus. There was only one thing left to do.

Closing the schools would hardly be a sensible thing to do. They organized the lives of his students. They offered him and his family a steady income. They lent legitimacy to his personal-trainer business and gave him a platform to air his opinions. But where had they gotten him? Here he was, stuck in a stuffy space in Chinatown, tied to a stagnant business, arguing on the letters page of *Black Belt* with the same old small-minded conformists.

By the end of January 1970, he had shuttered the Jun Fan Gung Fu Institute. "Money comes second. That's why I've disbanded all the schools of Jeet Kune Do," he told Dan Lee, one of his first LA Chinatown students, "because it is very easy for a member to come in and take the agenda as 'the truth' and the schedule as 'the Way,' you know what I mean?"

He found affirmation in the words of Jiddu Krishnamurti: "Death is a renewal, a mutation, in which thought does not function at all because thought is old. When there is death there is something totally new. Freedom from the known is death, and then you are living."

In his notes, he paraphrased another Krishnamurti line: "To express yourself in freedom, you must die to everything of yesterday."

He had closed his *gung fu* schools in the name of liberation. But whose liberation?

"At the time I was with him, I didn't fully understand," Dan Inosanto recalled. "But he says, 'I'm going to make movie pictures, and from these movie pictures, people are going to appreciate martial arts. When they start to appreciate martial arts, they are going to appreciate the Chinese culture. If they can appreciate what the Chinese have, then they will be able to appreciate what other Asians have. If they appreciate what other Asians have, then they are going to appreciate things from other cultures. It serves as a universal vehicle for all of us to understand each other.'"

Bruce told Taky and James they could continue teaching as they wished, but in private. He asked Dan Inosanto to promise never to open a commercial Jeet Kune Do school. "You would probably make some money out of it," he told Dan. "But I would be very disappointed if you did." He urged Dan to begin teaching women because he felt they would be less inclined to all the regressive tendencies of the men: the competition, the codification of standards, the creation of a false meritocracy. They might be more ready to pour out their cups.

Then he left for trips around the world, in search of himself.

Bruce had been helping his friend Jhoon Rhee develop a TV program on self-defense for women. Rhee was also expanding his enterprise in the Dominican Republic and invited Bruce to be his guest of honor. Bruce was pleased to learn there were a lot of Kato fans on the island. He broke boards in Santo Domingo, La Vega, and Santiago, and appeared on national television, where he was interviewed about his *Green Hornet* days and his fight choreography.

"We both bought long African evening gowns, kaftans," Rhee remembered. "We spent all day walking through downtown San Juan wearing them."

A couple of weeks later, Bruce was in the alpine ski resort of Gstaad, Switzerland. Roman Polanski had been suffering from writer's block, so he invited Bruce for an all-expenses-paid two-week trip to his mountain retreat, throwing in an additional one thousand dollars a week for martial arts lessons. Upon arrival, Polanski spirited him up to the slopes.

"I started showing Bruce how to ski but he always seemed that he wanted to learn for himself and wouldn't listen to my advice," Polanski recalled.

That first night Bruce wrote Linda, "Though I had a few falls, everybody thought I adapted to it great."

But the winter getaway was already a bust for him. He was not taking to the skis and abruptly quit, telling Polanski, "I hate skiing."

Bruce was not adjusting well to the social altitude either, feeling a little like James Baldwin's stranger in the village. "Gstaad is the resort for the very rich," he wrote to Linda. "They, the few friends of Roman who stay at the same house, are the so-called jet set, and they are stoned practically all the time, and they are kind of silly. Roman, if not skiing, is always after some girls.

"All in all the group is not my type," he wrote, "and for once I'm looking at the jet set from the inside out."

It only got worse. Roman was dragging Bruce around to all the nightclubs, and he couldn't get any sleep. Everyone he met seemed to own "a couple of houses, or chalets as they called them." He and Formula One racer Jackie Stewart got to talking about the excellent performance standard of Porsches. But he knew that when he returned to Los Angeles, he was going to have to put his Targa up for sale. When he caught the flu, he was almost relieved. He was offered five thousand dollars from one of the millionaire guests to stay on and teach another week. But he declined and made plans to escape early so that he could visit his childhood friend Wu Ngan in London.

Years later, an interviewer asked Bruce, "Why do people want to become students?"

Picture Bruce weighing his words, thinking carefully of what he will *not* say.

"Some want to lose weight. Some say they want to defend themselves," Bruce answered. "But I would say that the majority are there for one reason—vanity. It is exotic."

When he returned to Los Angeles he sold his Porsche to a neighbor, and set aside some money for the mortgage and bills. He told Linda he needed to take a trip back to Hong Kong. April 1970 would mark the fifth Ching Ming since his father's death—the day Chinese return to sweep the tombs of their ancestors—and he wanted to be there for it. With the rest of the money from the car sale, he purchased tickets for himself and Brandon and left Linda and Shannon with his mother and Robert.

Before he left, he received a phone call early one morning from Hong Kong. It was a radio announcer who wanted to do a live on-the-spot interview with him. Later he told Mito about the strange call.

"First," Bruce told Mito, "he asked me if I'm gonna go back to Hong Kong and I said, 'Soon.' Then he asked me if I'm doing any movie right now, and if I ever plan to do one in Hong Kong . . .

"I told him that I would if the price was right. You know we talked for an hour about nothing important . . .

"Boy," he added, "that call must have cost them a mint."

Only later did he realize that Hong Kong's brand-new TVB network had been showing reruns of *The Green Hornet*, which had taken the colony by storm. People were calling it "The Kato Show." As TVB producer Robert Chua Wah-Peng recalled, "What he achieved in Hollywood is something that made all of the Chinese proud, especially the people in Hong Kong."

Perhaps his destiny really was back across the Pacific.

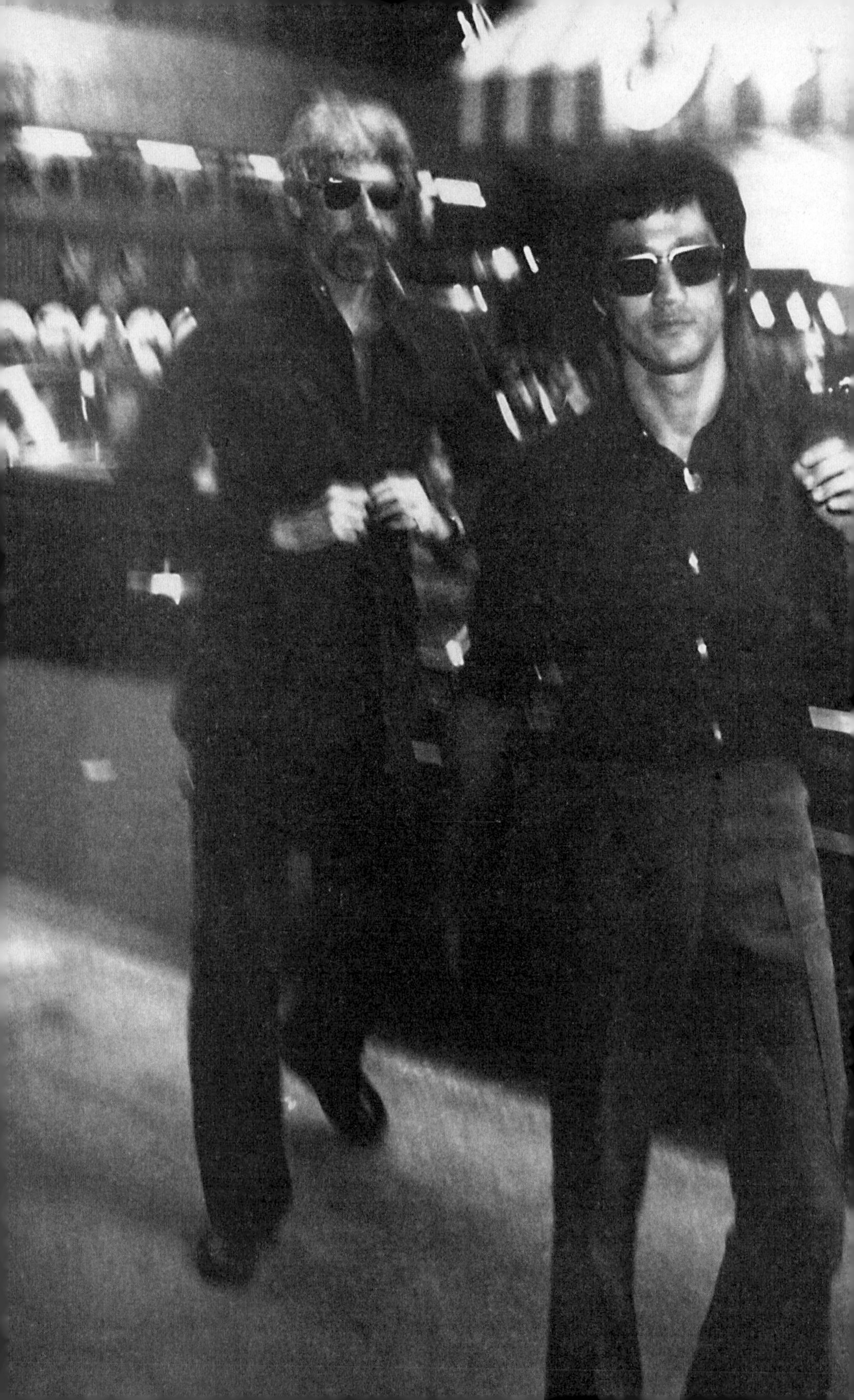

PART X
Action Action

1970–1972

Hexagram 39: 蹇 *gin*—Hardship Following Hardship, Difficulty in Walking

Line 6: Going forward: hardship

Coming back: a great achievement.

Good fortune.

Favorable to see a great person.

—*I CHING*

With James Coburn, 1971.
Photo courtesy of the Bruce Lee Family Archive.

CHAPTER 34
Water Above, Mountain Below

Hong Kong in 1970 was a far different place than the one Bruce had left five years before.

While Bruce had been preparing for *The Green Hornet* in 1966, a solitary young man's hunger strike in Hong Kong against a proposal to double the Star Ferry fare escalated into days of rioting. For four days in April, pitched battles roared up and down Nathan Road past the Lis' flat. After the midnight cinemas let out, clashes between youths and Gurkha soldiers peaked, filling the Kowloon air with ashes, acrid smoke, and tear gas. Nearly fifteen hundred arrests were made.

Colony authorities spoke of a "youth problem." Only one in eight ten- to fourteen-year-olds was in school. But as one high-ranking British official was heard to say, "We have built housing for the underprivileged. Do you expect us to give them education too?" An investigation found broad and deep disgust at government corruption—firemen expected gifts for putting out building fires, public officials regularly took bribes, police brutality was widespread.

By May 1967, as youths were rising up across China in Mao Zedong's Cultural Revolution to root out the "Four Olds": Old Ideas, Old Culture, Old Customs, and Old Habits, the anger was boiling over in Hong Kong. A series of labor strikes, beginning at an artificial flower factory owned by the mogul Li Ka-Shing, grew into anti-colonial protests—often led by youths chanting Maoist slogans—and were followed by general strikes. When the British authorities violently cracked down on unions and pro-China groups, leftists began a bloody guerrilla bombing campaign in retaliation. Eight months of unrest transformed Hong Kong into a police state.

Across Southeast Asia, in Singapore, Malaysia, and even nearby Macao, young people filled the vanguard of anti-colonial movements. Hong Kong threatened to become a new front of the Cold War. When a Chinese Communist militia attacked a border town at the edge of the colony, the British army was quickly dispatched. Colonial authorities updated an emergency evacuation plan for a quarter-million British people. By the time the tide of violence had receded at the end of 1967, fifty-one were dead, including seventeen shot by police and fifteen killed by guerrilla bombs.

The naïve entertainments of Bruce's teen years felt distant. Since he had left Hong Kong, the moviegoing audience had grown by 36 percent. The Orphan Generation had arrived, forging a common identity as Hong Kongers, and these children of war desired stories of heroism, action, and blood loyalty. With shrewd timing, the Shaw Brothers company had begun sinicizing the popular Japanese *samurai chanbara* genre in 1965, putting several Chinese swordplay movies into production, and announcing a "new *wuxia* century."

Martial arts films—*wuxia* and kung fu—had long been a cornerstone genre of Chinese cinema, beginning with Zhang Shichuan's epic *The Burning of the Red Lotus Temple*, an eighteen-film series that first screened in 1928, projecting a New Heroism to overturn "sick men of Asia" tropes. The genre provoked fear in the authorities. The Nationalist government quickly banned all martial arts films; their anarchic spirit was deemed counterproductive to the discipline needed for the building of China. During the war, the Japanese melted down celluloid to extract the silver, destroying the vast library of China's early films. But in the 1950s, the Wong Fei-Hung kung fu movies recaptured the glory of a pre-war hit, *The Adventures of Fong Sai Yuk*, and and defined a fair part of the colony's popular culture in the decade after the war.

By the mid-1950s, these action films had given way to escapism—sweeping costume epics, opera adaptations, and sentimental musicals increasingly dubbed in Mandarin for sale to a rising Southeast Asian market, whose core audiences were overseas Chinese in the Philippines, Malaysia, and Singapore, a potential market even bigger than Japan's. The Shaw Brothers became the industry leader, triumphing with the massive success of 1963's *The Love Eterne*, a musical adaptation of the popular Chinese folktale, the Butterfly Lovers tragedy. But in 1966, *wuxia*'s return marked a new era of Chinese martial arts movies. Set in an imagined Chinese past, they built on the opera's penchant for sword-fighting and Northern *gung fu* movements. These tales of "young swordsmen, assassins, martyrs, and death-defying fanatics"—all of them "tragic men who defy authority and the establishment," as the critic Law Kar put it—also spoke to the modern wave of anti-colonial protests and youth uprisings.

The director King Hu established himself as martial arts cinema's auteur with 1966's *Come Drink with Me*, which opened in theatres at the height of the Star Ferry riots, and followed with 1967's *Dragon Inn*, and 1971's influential masterpiece, *A Touch of Zen*. Chang Cheh pioneered the genre of "heroic bloodshed" in 1967's *The One-Armed Swordsman* and *The Assassin*. The director quickly found himself in the middle of a media controversy over the violence in his films. But, he said, moralists and cultural conservatives were missing the point. His movies simply reflected the realities of society. His heroes were compelling to young Hong Kongers because they were angered by the injustices around them. Violence was their last resort.

Chang Cheh had never forgotten Bruce's performance in *The Orphan*. In 1968, after his early *wuxia* triumphs, he had an opportunity to connect with Bruce. In Los Angeles, a mutual friend, Victor Lam, told Bruce of Chang's desire to work with him, and offered to arrange a meeting. Bruce asked his friend Peter Chin, who had attended St. Francis Xavier with Chang Cheh's wife's younger brother and was returning back to Hong Kong for a family visit, to take the meeting with the director. Chang was enthusiastic. He said that while he did not want to get involved in any negotiations, the Shaw Brothers' standard star rate was five thousand Hong Kong dollars.* When Peter told Bruce, he shook his head and said, "That's too low."

At the end of March 1970, Bruce was back in Hong Kong again, and he could see that cinema had shifted in his direction. Audiences were packing theatres for Chang Tseng-Chai's big-budget Cathay Organization movie, *From the Highway*, which marked a turn in action from *wuxia* swordplay back to "fist and leg" kung fu combat. Anticipation was building for Chang Cheh's *Vengeance!*, starring David Chiang and Ti Lung, former stuntmen who were real *gung fu* fighters. By the end of the year, both movies would claim box office success and sweep the industry awards.

In this context, Hong Kongers saw Bruce in a better light than he saw himself. He was not a struggling Hollywood Asian uncertain where his next dollar was coming from. Just three days into his trip, Bruce wrote to Linda: "I'm recognized everywhere as Lee Siu Loong, 'Kato,' especially with my clothing and Brandon." In the Dominican Republic, he had enjoyed being received as a fellow non-white Hollywood star. In Hong Kong, he was *their* Hollywood star.

There was just one problem, he wrote, "everyone is asking for favors nowadays, getting them into U.S. show business or getting over to the States, or appearing on shows."

Bruce threw himself into family activities. He helped his mother with her US visa application. She was planning her permanent move to the States, where all of her children, except Peter, now lived. He spent time with Peter and his bride, Eunice Lam, and the Tso family. He took Brandon to an amusement park. On the day of Ching Ming he went with the family to his father's grave at St. Rafael Cemetery and showed his son how to kneel, hold the joss sticks, and perform the rituals that ensured Brandon's grandfather was comfortable in the afterlife and raining down blessings upon them.

Bruce enjoyed tea with Unicorn Chan and other friends. He trained with his mentor, Uncle Siu Son-Hang, and Larry Lee Gam-Kwan, from an Okinawan *karate dojo*. But word was getting around town that Kato had returned. His mother was a major source, proudly boasting to her friends about her son, and now the phone would not stop ringing. Front-page articles appeared in the tabloids. Next to a picture of him high-kicking Unicorn's raised hand, the English-language *Star* ran the headline, "Bruce Quitting Boxing for Acting."

Bruce fed the reporter a story that he was forming a company with James Co-

---

* In 1968, this sum would have been about $830 in US dollars, or about $7,600 in 2024 US dollars.

burn and Stirling Silliphant to make *The Silent Flute*, possibly with Roman Polanski as director. He said he would not teach any students in Hong Kong. "Besides," he said, "I am too expensive." The article mentioned that rumors were circulating that he had been killed. "They all came," Bruce said, "from boxing instructors who are jealous of my success."

Uncle Walter Tso Tat-Wah organized a special dinner for Bruce. Uncle Tso had invited Choy Li Fut *sifu* Chan Tat Fu and White Crane *sifu* Au Wing Nien. He had also invited Uncle Siu and another friend of Hoi Chuen with whom he had worked on the Wong Fei Hung movies—Shek Kin, a Jing Wu adept whose thick brows and distinctive mane combed back from a spectacular widow's peak had made him one of the most unforgettable villains. Uncle Shek had known Bruce since he was thirteen. "When I was over at the house, Bruce would come home and want to spar with me," he recalled.

Journalists captured the men discussing film and martial arts, and duly noted *The Silent Flute*. They snapped pictures of Bruce wearing a kaftan, jeans, and sandals, throwing a sidekick at his business-suited Uncle Tso. The night was meant to mark a ceremonial passing of the torch. His elders were clearing a path for Bruce to step into his inheritance.

During the time Bruce had been gone, Hong Kong's media landscape had also changed dramatically.

With Run Run Shaw as a co-owner, TVB went on the air as the colony's first free over-the-air network, ushering in the TV age in Hong Kong. Its only competition was the cable subscription-only network Rediffusion TV (RTV). TVB's evening variety show, *Enjoy Yourself Tonight*, instantly became the center of Hong Kong's pop culture.

On April 8 Bruce showed up for an appearance on *Enjoy Yourself Tonight* as if the moment had been prepared just for him. Backstage, Leung Sing Por, Hoi Chuen's opera star friend and Margaret Leung Man Lan's father, welcomed him. For the first time, Bruce met his brother Robert's girlfriend and future wife, Sylvia Lai, one of the show's newest-signed talents as the pop singer "Sum Sum." He sat opposite the turtlenecked and dark-suited host Michael Hui, the older brother of his friend, the Cantopop star Sam Hui. Dressed casually in a brown leather jacket, a knit crewneck sweater, white pants, and sandals, it was as if Bruce had shown up to a family party, one that much of the colony just happened to be watching.

After some bantering, Michael encouraged Bruce to demonstrate some *gung fu* for the studio audience. He started with two-finger push-ups. Then two *karate* black belts stepped in. One of them held up five boards, and Bruce destroyed them with a back kick. He asked one black belt to hold an air shield and the other to stand behind him on the small five-foot-long stage. The two took their positions casually.

"I kicked the mother perfectly, lifting that guy off his feet, driving him back hard. The second guy didn't expect the guy to fly at him and didn't brace himself," he told Mito. The two knocked over the props, nearly brought down the stage, and looked up in astonishment.

"The next day, when he walked on the street everybody noticed him," Sylvia Lai said, laughing. "Every single person knew about him! Everyone!"

RTV, where another childhood friend, Michael Cheng Ching, was an executive, booked him to appear on their variety show two days later. Bruce came with Unicorn Chan and a special guest, Brandon, and delivered another memorable performance. He spoke about Jeet Kune Do with cohosts Gou Leung and comedian David Lo Dai-Wai, the son of a famed Shaw Brothers director named Lo Wei. He brought Brandon onstage to punch his hand and abs. Taking off his shirt, Bruce chopped a dangling board in half and split five more with a side kick. A picture taken after the show shows audience members encircling Bruce and Brandon at an almost bashful distance.

Tabloids reported that Bruce was the *sifu* of Steve McQueen and making the foreigners pay seventeen hundred Hong Kong dollars an hour for lessons. They also printed that he had been ambushed by ten *karatekas*, defeating them all but breaking his leg in the process. On days the gossip was thin, they ran stories stating that Bruce had been assassinated.

As Bruce and Brandon left for California, a large entourage came to see them off. Long afterward Bruce was still receiving calls and letters of congratulations. When Bruce had first arrived, he thought people wanted him to take them back to America. Now he realized that people wanted him to return to Hong Kong.

Back in Los Angeles, Linda was shopping for groceries with a list in one hand and a tally clicker in the other. She was thinking, "I only have twenty dollars each week, so I have to add it up." One weekend she and Bruce drove from Bel Air to Chinatown to treat themselves to an inexpensive dim sum brunch.

"I must have opened my wallet, maybe when I was getting money out to pay. We get back home and there's twenty dollars missing from my wallet," she said. "We call the restaurant. We drive all the way back to Chinatown to get the twenty dollars and drive all the way back. That's how broke we were."

Bruce booked as many private lessons as he could—including with Roman Polanski, Sy Weintraub, Blake Edwards and his wife, Julie Andrews, and Kareem, who was back in Pacific Palisades for the off-season. He scheduled meetings with Stirling, James, and his lawyer Adrian Marshall around *The Silent Flute*.

Stirling had agreed to take on the screenwriting duties on one condition—that James and Bruce were going to work with him on it together. In intensive meetings at Stirling's house during the spring of 1970—eight of them in the last two weeks of May—the three hammered out the outline for a new script. After a full day of work on Friday, May 29, Stirling promised to have a new script ready to read within two months. Bruce drove home, his mind and body afire with excitement.

But, on Sunday morning, his life screeched to a halt.

Bruce had skipped his warm-up, gone straight to his workout, and placed a 125-pound barbell on his shoulders for what he called his "Good Morning" exercise. The object was to bend forward at the waist as far as he could, keeping his back and legs straight. But as he returned to an upright position, he felt his back pop. By evening he was feeling excruciating pain. Warm compresses, cold compresses, topical solutions, soaking in the bathtub—nothing brought relief.

In his Day-Timer under May 31, Bruce wrote, "BACK PROBLEM." For much of the rest of the year, the daily entries dwindled, until most of what remained were doctor's appointments and canceled meetings. He and Linda visited a doctor and he submitted himself to a battery of tests. "They said he had injured his fourth sacral nerve," Linda recalled, "and that he was never going to do *gung fu* again."

At first, Bruce simply ignored the doctor's warnings. "When friends visited him, he became overly enthusiastic, throwing high kicks or hard punches and only quitting when he felt the pain in his back," Mito Uyehara recalled. He quickly—and badly—reinjured himself. On September 18, he wrote in his Day-Timer, "Back set back." He was prescribed Delaxin for his muscle spasms and Darvon for his pain and sent home to bed rest.

"I did not know for many decades later that [Darvon] was an opioid," Linda said. "The fact that he kept taking them was indicative of how bad his back was."

For most of the next three months, Bruce would be mostly confined to his bedroom. His world had shrunk to just his desk, his chair, and his bed. Brandon and Shannon adjusted to playing with him gently.

No one could help him now, not Stirling Silliphant or James Coburn, not all the folks who had been so solicitous in Hong Kong. He had lost his livelihood and his ability to express himself. He felt he had fallen into a state beyond his worst imaginings. He told friends he did not want to be seen.

Peter Chin called weekly to check in. Bruce was disconsolate and terse. It was the first time in his life, he told Peter, that he was really scared.

"Quite a few times in the summer when we talked," Peter recalled, "Bruce always felt he's not going to have a long life."

Weeks before he had injured himself, their checking account had dwindled to $2.73.

Mito offered to publish the *Tao of Jeet Kune Do* book that Bruce had promised years before. But Bruce declined. He had resolved to bury it when he closed the Jun Fan Gung Fu Institutes, and he would not go back on his word now.

Linda told Bruce she needed to get a job. But, she recalled, "Bruce was adamant in his opposition. My main job was to be wife and mother and to Bruce, it was a disgrace for his wife to work." Linda reluctantly agreed to stay home with him, at least until he could move around again.

Bruce read as voraciously as he had in his Seattle days: Norman Vincent Peale, Eric Hoffer, and Jiddu Krishnamurti; *Sources of Chinese Tradition* and *A Source Book in Chinese Philosophy*; Edwin Haislet's *Boxing*, Laurence Morehouse and Philip Rasch's *Sports Medicine for Trainers*, John Dobson Lawther's *Psychology of Coaching*, Roger Crosnier's *Fencing with the Sabre* and *Fencing with the Foil*, and Herman Hesse's *Steppenwolf*.

Linda brought him binders and three-hole-punched paper in different colors. He filled the pages with precisely detailed writings and illustrations of punching, kicking, and defending. He listed types of ripostes and how to execute each of them. He diagrammed angles of kicks, parts of the body to target, the sections of the foot and their comparative effectiveness in "relaying destructive force." He made comprehensive lists of attack combinations, defenses to those attacks, and counterattacks.

Now that he was immobile, the man who had once said that one could not think his way through a fight could only think about fighting. He wrote like he was Jack Dempsey, compelled to pour out all he knew for Taky, James, Dan, and other close friends. Eventually, he compiled seven binders full of meticulously organized pages. He called these his *Commentaries on the Martial Way*, a nod to the Chinese classics.

Picture him in his room surrounded by books, papers spread across his bed, writing furiously, his mind finally calmed, his emotional anguish eased at the moment of his highest physical pain.

Linda took a swing-shift job at an after-hours medical answering service, leaving home in the midafternoon. Bruce could no longer object, but Linda recalled, "We never told anyone that I was working and had an elaborate scheme of reasons for why I was not at home if anyone called or came over." Each night, he fed the kids dinner and put them to sleep. Each night, Linda returned after midnight to find Bruce asleep, sometimes finding a note of gratitude he had written to her.

Weeks passed before he could regularly move around. In his Day-Timer, under each day for the week of September 7, he wrote, "Walk." But after a doctor's visit on September 14, the Day-Timer remained empty until the end of the week, where he had written, "Back set back."

The doctors scheduled him for cortisone injections. They were still uniformly pessimistic about his prospects of returning to martial arts. They told him and Linda that he would be lucky if he could ever walk properly again.

"Walk on," Bruce wrote to himself.

He wrote it on the back of his business card and made a little stand for it so he could see it when he sat at his desk. He wrote it on tiny cards that he placed around the house and in his wallet. He taped the words to his mirror so that they would be the last thing he saw before settling down for another night of comfortless sleep.

CHAPTER 35
A Journey from the West

"In my fifteenth year, I set my heart to learning," Confucius had recalled, as he looked back over his long life. "In my thirtieth year, I took my stand."

After the cortisone shots, Bruce recovered slowly, stretching and working through his pain. By his thirtieth birthday, he felt strong enough to resume training sessions with Stirling Silliphant, Sy Weintraub, and James Coburn. He began morning runs with Coburn. The two had much to discuss.

On October 19, 1970, Stirling Silliphant had delivered his script for *The Silent Flute*. Their ambition had been to make what Silliphant called "the definitive and classical martial arts film," and the screenplay seemed to vindicate two years of hard work, financial stress, and heartache. Everything was becoming finally real, and the downtime had given Bruce clarity.

"I was determined then to be an actor," he told Mito. "Not just an actor, but a star."

In Washington, DC, for an appearance with Jhoon Rhee, he spoke to a reporter about *The Silent Flute*, mustering the same kind of bravado he had brought to his 1966 interviews, but with a new conviction. "It's about time we had an Oriental hero," he said. "Never mind some guy bouncing around the country in a pigtail or something. I have to be a real human being. No cook. No laundryman."

He told Mito he had seen an astrologer. "She had predicted 1971 would be my year. But I've already had this feeling that my time for success is here. I can just about taste it."

Still, as the year began, Bruce wrote two lines of Chinese across his Day-Timer entries for January 1 and 2, words of caution to steel himself against disappointment: "If one becomes wealthy, one is filled with anxiety. If one loses the opportunity one can have peace of mind."

In the script, the Seeker was now named Cord. Bruce had named the blind martial artist Ah Sahm. The name, he had written in his notes, represented "number 3, the dynamic number representing Jupiter, ruler of the sign Sagittarius, also a catchy sound." Cord would meet fighters representing *yang* power, *yin* power, and fighters from the "Animal & Insect" schools—Praying Mantis, Eagle Claw, Snake. His weapons would include throwing stars, an iron fan, a three-sectional staff, and a *nunchaku*. The finale would feature Cord and Ah Sahm atop a mountain in a blinding sunset, representing "the fulfillment of the dead and the carry on of the living."

Silliphant's script seemed to point to *Zatoichi* and Chang Cheh's films, Dennis Hopper's *Easy Rider*, and Richard Sarafian's *Vanishing Point*. He presented it in an unusual form, using a European narrative format. It opened with a two-page foreword Bruce had written, a keynote meant to make clear Bruce's lofty intentions, and set a high bar for Hollywood's first martial arts film:

> To the Westerner the finger jabs, the side kicks, the back fist, etc., are tools of destruction and violence which is, indeed, one of their functions. But the Oriental believes that the primary function of such tools is revealed when they are self-directed and destroy greed, fear, anger, and folly. . . .
>
> True mastery transcends any particular art. It stems from mastery of oneself—the ability, developed through self-discipline, to be calm, fully aware, and completely in tune with oneself and the surroundings. Then, and only then, can a person know himself.

Stirling wove together James's countercultural interests in psychedelia, Vedic ritual, and Tantric sex with Bruce's Zen, Taoist, and Jeet Kune Do ideas into a classic hero's journey.

The movie begins by literally summoning the New Age, with Ah Sahm playing the silent flute at sunrise atop a mountain peak. Cord is on a quest to obtain the Book, "the bible of martial art" which "supposedly contains the innermost secret doctrines of empty-hand combat." He joins a worldwide contest held every ten years to determine the best candidate to face the Three Trials and become "the Keeper of the Book." No one has ever returned from these Trials.

In the contest, Cord's opponent is Shabani, the Mechanical Man, a character meant to represent institutionalized martial arts. Cord beats him, but the contest judges decide he has broken the rules, so the Mechanical Man is sent on the quest. Inadequate to the task, he is brutally killed in the First Trial. Cord must complete his quest and face the Three Trials: Ego, Love, and Death. Ah Sahm—the blind player of a silent flute that only Cord can hear—shadows his journey and prepares him for the Trials with perplexing riddles.

In the First Trial, Cord confronts the frantic, noisy Monkey Man, the embodiment of Ego. "The way of the monkey is to play the fool. While you laugh at his antics—he bites you from behind," Ah Sahm counsels Cord. "Unmask his ego—you expose a coward disguised as a monkey."

After vanquishing the Monkey Man, Cord ventures to a desert, where Changsha, the Rhythm Man, has erected a world party under caravan tents, and constant drums play seductive polyrhythms. Guests speak all the languages of the world while enjoying abundant food, orgiastic sex, and gory gladiatorial death fights. Cord meets Tara, one of the Rhythm Man's wives, who leads him through a night of

Orientalized rituals that climax in sensual intercourse. He awakes the next morning to find the caravan leaving and Tara beheaded and crucified. This is the Second Trial—Love. Cord must learn about releasing attachments. With this horrifying violence, perhaps Silliphant was referencing the Manson family murders.

Ah Sahm has now earned Cord's trust. But then the blind man stuns his pupil with two devastating acts. A destitute old ferryman lends them his boat to cross a river. But when they get to the other side, Ah Sahm destroys the boat and, seemingly, the peasant's livelihood.

They escape a band of *samurai* pursuing them on horseback and come to a fishing village where they are surrounded by children who beg them for alms. Ah Sahm takes an interest in a handsome dark-skinned boy, then picks him up and kills him by hurling him against a wall. The villagers take the body away, wash the wall, and continue with their lives.

A shocked Cord confronts Ah Sahm, first asking why he destroyed the old man's boat. Ah Sahm replies, "The boat I damaged could be repaired. If it had not been damaged, it would have been confiscated by the war party of horsemen and the old man killed. Thus I saved his life."

"How then can a man of such charity seize a child and brain him against a wall?"

"He was too beautiful. He would have grown up to be a tyrant," Ah Sahm says.

With this direct reference to the war in Vietnam, *The Silent Flute* plied the same stereotype that had informed disastrous American decision making there, a misguided idea that the writer Viet Thanh Nguyen once mocked as "The Oriental Mode of Destruction." As General William Westmoreland said in a 1974 interview for the documentary *Hearts and Minds*, "The Oriental doesn't put the same high price on life as does a Westerner. Life is plentiful. Life is cheap in the Orient, and as the philosophy of the Orient expresses it, life is not important." *The Silent Flute*—which contained more of Bruce's philosophical ideas than any film he would make—was still a representation of a certain American imagination of the Orient.

In his Third Trial Cord is attacked by the Panther Man, a shadowy figure who pounces on him from the jungle trees and disappears back into them, like a Vietcong guerrilla. The Panther Man represents Death, and unable to overcome his foe, Cord must retreat. He looks at himself in a pool of water, which at first mirrors his face Narcissus-like, but then reveals his teacher Ah Sahm's image saying to him, "Of the two of us, you are the blind one. Blinded by the things you see. You *think*—therefore you stand apart from the things you try to understand."

Cord understands. "The truth I have been seeking—this truth is Death. Yet Death is also a seeker. Forever seeking me." Once at peace with his mortality, he triumphs over the Panther Man.

He comes to a beach where Changsha's world party caravan entertains martial artists who have survived the Three Trials. Cord learns he must now defeat Changsha, the Rhythm Man, to get to the Book.

The Rhythm Man, who has the power to split into the Monkey Man and the Panther Man, and is activated by the sound of the drummers, represents a man living for the power of the collective. Cord, who fights in broken rhythm and is animated by Ah Sahm's silent flute, represents the individual actualizing himself. Here the movie poses an existential question, one that still troubled Bruce—is the best fighter one who fights for his community or for himself? The two fight to a draw—achieving a unity of opposites—and Changsha releases Cord to seek the Keeper of the Book.

Cord ascends to the top of the mountain, where Yamaguchi, the Keeper of the Book, presides over a version of heaven described in the Chinese classics. It is "the seat of harmony," whose denizens keep busy by "studying the perfecting of perfection." Yamaguchi tells Cord, "You have evolved out of struggle into the sweet and timeless spirit of everlasting peace."

Cord is stunned to find that he and Yamaguchi will not fight for the Book. Yamaguchi, after all, has transcended earthly coils. But he admits to Cord that he wants one last time to "feel pain, know suffering—to be confused and uncertain—to experience. In short, to live again."

Hearing this, Cord decides he no longer wants the Book. "I wish neither to possess nor to be possessed. I no longer covet paradise. More important, I no longer fear hell," Cord says. "The medicine for my suffering I had within me from the very beginning but I did not take it."

Cord is free. "Now I see that I will never find the light unless, like the candle, I am my own fuel, consuming myself."

He meets Ah Sahm on the mountain peak, and warrior and teacher rush toward each other "until both are blended by and lost within a golden flash of light." Perhaps they are clashing in battle. Perhaps they are merging in limitless communion, a secular nirvana achieved through the American idea of freedom through self-actualization.

"You must believe me," Stirling said years later, "if you had read the original script, and knowing what Bruce and Jimmy would have done acting together in it, it would have been something to remember."

From the first page, he had declared it "a shooting script," with Coburn as director, coproducer, and star, himself as writer and coproducer, and Bruce as fight director and actor playing four costarring roles: Ah Sahm, the Monkey Man, the Rhythm Man, and the Panther Man. The movie was to be shot in Thailand, Japan, and Morocco. It would require a multilingual cast, speaking Cantonese, Japanese, Urdu, Thai, and Arabic.

They were tendering the studios a full-package flex without compromise, offering a brash invitation to sign a check or be left behind.

The Silent Flute had always been a long-shot project in a town of miserable odds. But to Bruce, it still looked like the safest bet to address his stalled career and mounting financial problems.

A week before his thirtieth birthday, the three met with Warner Bros. executives, who would green-light the film if they could shoot in India. The corporation had a million rupees* that the government would only let them spend within the country. They could use this money to begin *The Silent Flute* project.

They left on January 29, 1971, for London, where they would stay overnight at Stirling's expense before traveling on to India. Bruce was excited about what he thought was to be a preproduction visit and location survey. But, Stirling remembered, "Jim and I went, I must say, with some trepidation and grave reservations.

"I didn't really think that subcontinent was the right location for our film," said Stirling, who had visited three times before. "India is a too-much, walked-over, lived- and died-in tragic mess. And there was just no place within its borders I knew we could find to work. Jimmy knew this, too. We couldn't say this to Bruce, [because] you never know, maybe we might have found the place to shoot somewhere in the country."

Upon arrival James used his contacts to release the rupees from the proper government official. "We had to get him laid," he recalled. Over the next ten days, a local team took them across the subcontinent to scout locations—from Bombay to New Delhi to Jaipur to Madras to Goa and back to Bombay. It was a brutal schedule, and tensions reared up between Bruce and James. On one of the flights the two sat beside each other in first class, and Bruce kept punching a pad he held atop the tray table.

"Bruce," an exasperated James finally said, "will you cut it out, man? You're shaking the whole airplane."

"See, it helps me condition my knuckles."

"I know, but it's pissing me off!"

On an all-day drive to the Thar Desert near the Pakistan/India border, Bruce sat in the back seat, complained about his back, and constantly hummed the melody of the Beatles' "Yesterday." James turned around and shouted, "For Christ's sake, will you stop that? You're driving me crazy!"

"I will never forget," Stirling said, "when Jimmy turned back, Bruce shook his fist at the back of Jimmy's head."

Coburn had confirmed his hunch: the film could not be shot in India. There were no locations for the jungle shots. On the beaches and in the cities, even in the

---

* This amount would have come to about $130,000 USD in 1971, which is a little over $1 million in 2024 USD.

desert, he said, "We didn't have a 360 degree anywhere, where you didn't see thousands of people or villages or camels or buses coming over."

As they flew across the country, Bruce looked out the window and said, "Hey, it's beautiful down there. We can shoot down there."

Stirling wondered how to explain to Bruce what it would take to get crews, equipment, and generators into the jungles. "He had no idea of the production problems involved," Stirling said. "And because Bruce had never traveled, he didn't know the difference."

In one village, they met with a group of Indian martial artists to see if they might be able to cast them. The fighters seemed excited to beat up on each other, but Bruce thought them beginners. Children gathered around the entourage to beg, and Bruce amused them with coin tricks and *gung fu* forms. They stopped for lunch, and Bruce was so displeased with the food, he tossed it to the dogs. Three men ran out of the kitchen and began to beat the dogs, tearing the food away. Bruce moved to stop them, but James held him back.

"Pardon me, sahib," the cook told Bruce, "but you don't understand. Our children have no food, and to give it to a dog is wrong." Stunned into silence, Bruce was overcome with emotion.

"I thought I saw poverty in Hong Kong when I was growing up," he told Mito later, "but poverty in Hong Kong is nothing compared to what I saw in India."

The three found the beaches of Goa full of white hippies from the United States and Europe. Bruce fit right in, and was welcomed into their communes. James and Stirling were feeling their age. But when they returned to their hotel, Bruce was frustrated, his back was throbbing, and his mood was foul. He knew the trip was coming to an end soon. Stirling noticed that Bruce had also become resentful. Coburn was checking into opulent sea-view suites large enough to sleep a whole crew. Meanwhile Bruce and Stirling were tossing and turning on lumpy beds in tiny rooms. Bruce asked Stirling why Coburn deserved such royal treatment.

"*I'm* the star, not him," Bruce said. "I'm going to be the biggest star in the world, bigger than Coburn or McQueen."

When Bruce had made comments like this at Steve McQueen's Castle, Stirling had brushed them off. Maybe it was just Steve and Bruce's weird competitive friendship, the on-court shit-talking that continued after a tough practice. But now the Hollywood veteran was looking at Bruce with new eyes, seeing desires that were familiar, even banal.

"For the first time," Stirling recalled, "I realized my *guru* wasn't just a great martial artist. He was also an actor filled with ego."

And so the guru's unhyphenated American student, who also happened to be a Tinseltown power-player, summoned the courage to finally speak his truth.

"No way," Stirling told Bruce. "You're a Chinese in a white man's world."

• • •

The three returned to Los Angeles broken.

Neither Coburn or Silliphant wanted to continue the project in India. Coburn's enthusiasm for the project had cooled. Silliphant sent legal papers to recover costs from Coburn's production company. Less than two weeks after they had returned, the trio met with Warner Bros. The Warner execs confirmed that if *The Silent Flute* could not be shot in India with those rupees, they would not move ahead.

Bruce blamed Coburn for the project's collapse and abruptly canceled his martial arts appointments with him. Silliphant quietly directed his agent to send the script around town. He knew that Bruce and Linda had gone months with no income. But when he and Coburn offered to help them financially, Bruce was offended, even outraged. He thought they had been equals. He did not want their charity.

Privately he was dejected. "I was counting so heavily on that movie," he told Mito. "It was my one chance of a lifetime."

Perhaps Bruce had been fooling himself. Playing four supporting roles—three of them alien villains destined for defeat, the last one a new Oriental stereotype born of the sixties, the *guru/maharishi/sensei/sifu* to the stars—was not the same as being the star.

Perhaps Bruce was thinking of his proud voiceless grandfather when he told his brother Robert, "I'm not going to beg anyone to give me a part. I'd rather be a security guard if I have to."

CHAPTER 36
The Teacher and the Warrior

Stirling Silliphant soon had another part for Bruce, an apology of sorts and a gift. "I want you to play yourself, in a sense. Call it a personal monument," he told Bruce. "But I want the public to know what the spirit of your Jeet Kune Do truly is."

At Paramount Studios, he was creating a new series for ABC, based on Baynard Kendrick's novels about a blind public investigator, called *Longstreet*. A New Orleans insurance investigator named Mike Longstreet, played by James Franciscus, is blinded by a bomb that kills his wife. While mourning and learning to deal with his loss of sight, he returns to his job to find his wife's killers. The night after Stirling, James, and Bruce received the bad news from Warner Bros. about *The Silent Flute*, the *Longstreet* pilot did well enough for ABC to pick it up for a season.

Writing quickly in the spring of 1971, Stirling put Bruce into the very first episode and titled it "The Way of the Intercepting Fist." When he brought it to Paramount, execs nearly balked. "What? Martial arts? A Chinese? Are you insane?" they told him.

By 1970, more recurring Asian and Pacific Islander actors had joined Victor Sen Yung's Hop Sing on NBC's *Bonanza*. ABC's *The Courtship of Eddie's Father* cast Miyoshi Umeki as Mrs. Livingston, a housekeeper. CBS's *Hawaii Five-O* alone added seven Asian and Native Hawaiian actors in supporting roles. But to the Paramount TV execs, even if a fighting Chinaman had worked on *The Green Hornet*—and a one-season show was a terrible comp—times had changed. People wanted reality and resolution, not costume and camp.

Bruce probably didn't do himself any favors when, before his first meeting with *Longstreet* producer Joel Rogosin, he hid behind Rogosin's office door and then jumped from behind and locked the producer in a bear hug. But word had gotten around Paramount Studios that Warner Bros. had seriously considered *The Silent Flute* and was still angling to make the first American *gung fu* movie. Stirling assured everyone he had written something very much of the moment, and prevailed. Shooting was set for June, sorely needed financial relief for Bruce and Linda.

"The Way of the Intercepting Fist" is notable for the faithfulness Stirling accords Bruce's words and teachings. In their earliest private sessions, Bruce had blindfolded Stirling and Joe Hyams to train them in building sensitivity. "Everything that I had gone through as Bruce's student, I had Franciscus go through," he said. "Franciscus was playing a blind man. But I had felt blind as Bruce's student in the early months."

Bruce plays Li Tsung, an Asian antiques dealer who saves Mike Longstreet from a group of thugs who want to stop his investigation of theft at a port warehouse. Longstreet enlists Li Tsung to teach him Jeet Kune Do so that he can fight the gang boss. "I'm willing to empty my cup in order to taste your tea," Longstreet says.

"I don't believe in systems, Mr. Longstreet, nor in method," Li Tsung replies. "And without systems, without method, what's to teach?"

But soon the men are meeting in Longstreet's courtyard, Li in a red tracksuit, Longstreet in blue. Li asks Longstreet to kick his air shield, then he kicks it in turn, knocking Longstreet back a few feet. He demonstrates the logic of a good side kick to the kneecap, a finger jab to the eyes, or a bite on the arm. He tells Longstreet not to think, to cease his "quarrelsome mind," to make his "mind and body one."

LONGSTREET:
. . . so much to remember.

LI TSUNG:
If you try to remember you will lose! Empty your
mind. Be formless, shapeless, like water. Now you
put water into a cup, it becomes the cup. Put it into
a teapot, it becomes the teapot. Now water can flow
or creep or drip or *crash*! Be water, my friend.

Of all Bruce's students, Stirling Silliphant had done the most to put his ideas into the world. Li prepares Longstreet to confront the gang boss by saying, "Like everyone else you want to learn the way to win, but never to accept the way to lose. To accept defeat—to learn to die—is to be liberated from it. So when tomorrow comes you must free your ambitious mind and learn the art of dying." This was the way Stirling Silliphant wanted to think of Bruce—as a wise, flawed, but giving guru who had changed his life.

But does the student ever consider the teacher? What it means for the teacher to bear the responsibility of honing another's potential? What it means to be left behind, even forgotten, when the student reaches that potential? The teacher's job is to actualize, not become actualized. The teacher is a mirror, an echo.

In Hollywood, Bruce could remain the teacher. But the success of the Shaw Brothers' martial arts bet presented Bruce with an alternative. Their swordplay films were filling movie houses with rowdy, young, working-class Asians in Southeast Asia and Chinatowns across the United States. Perhaps he could finally play the role he had wanted since childhood—the warrior.

But who would offer it to him on his terms? He had to visualize it, manifest it. Bruce immersed himself in Elia Kazan interviews, *Hitchcock/Truffaut*, and other books on acting and moviemaking. He thought of movies and TV shows he could create.

One day, perhaps around 1969, he had written notes for himself: "Western, Modern, Others?" Next to "Western," he scribbled "San Francisco," and next to "Modern," he listed "1) Bounty Hunter, 2) Agent?, 3) Detective, 4) Embassy intrigue?" In several more pages of notes, he added more ideas: "H.K. police chief (interpol)," "a social worker in rough slums area." Under the heading "gimmicks," he wrote "fantastic art," "manual weapons," "'soul movement.'" He titled another page, "What Bruce Lee has for this part":

1. Champion caliber skill
2. Grace & agility
3. Realistic speed & power
4. Top-shape physique
5. Cool "aura gestures"
6. Personality?

Underneath these, he wrote and underlined the word: "Define." Then he decided to set aside the "Modern" ideas to focus on what he knew. He began working on the idea of a Western set in San Francisco's Chinatown.

He had read Richard Dillon's book *The Hatchet Men*, an account of the rise of the outlaw highbinders, or *fu tow doy* who—between the 1882 Exclusion Act and the 1906 San Francisco earthquake, while horrifying Chinese purges erupted across the West—had plunged Chinatown into an era of tong wars. He filled a dozen pages of a bright yellow spiral notebook on whose cover he had scribbled a provisional title: *Here Comes the Warrior*.

He visualized opening credits displaying documentary photos of Chinese migrants, alongside an ironic Mark Twain quote: "The Chinese are quiet, peaceable, tractable, free from drunkenness and they are as industrious as the day is long. A disorderly Chinaman is rare and a lazy one does not exist."

He composed a scene: A white sheriff visits the docks where a ship is discharging a group of highbinders. One stands out from the rest. He wears no Manchu queue, but instead has the dress and mien of a Ming dynasty royal, with eighteen kill notches on his belt. "That guy is known as the scientific killer," the sheriff tells one of his men. As Bruce developed the idea, he gave the martial artist a name—Ah Sahm, naturally—a flaw, and a backstory.

A war is raging in Chinatown. A shadowy man enters a laundry and tosses a hatchet into the owner's back. The killer goes back onto the street, where he is handed money. Later, people gather around a reward poster for the killer. The tong meets and decides to recruit a top highbinder from China to find the murderer, while keeping an Irish American police sergeant and his Chinatown squad at bay. When Ah Sahm arrives, the tong members are shocked to discover he is blind.

Sometime, perhaps as early as 1969, but no later than the spring of 1971—the papers are undated—Bruce used Lorenzo Semple's *Number One Son* treatment as his template to write "a presentation" for "Ah Sahm, a new one-hour television series." He asked Stirling Silliphant to help him edit it. The result was a seven-page presentation—copying Semple's phrasing—for "a slam-bang, half-hour Western ACTION adventure series," featuring a Chinese hero who is a "champion of the oppressed and a helper of the weak."

The first page is worth quoting at length:

> The plot evolves around two persons, a "fantastically" skilled Chinese martial artist Ah Sahm and his friend and guide Big Bill Walker as they journey across the U.S.
>
> Originally Ah Sahm arrived in the States as a hired Fu Tow Doy (hatchet man), salaried soldier of one of the rival Tongs. However, Ah Sahm comes not to help in the struggle for power among the fighting Tongs (1880–1906) with the good people of Chinatown the pawns and the prey.
>
> On the contrary, and much to the miseries of the Tongs all over the States, Ah Sahm's mission is to eradicate them, to awaken the long-abused Chinese people to abandon the wrong idea of "self-preservation" and make "freedom and progress" the keystone of their philosophy. So with the help of a guide named Big Bill Walker, Ah Sahm begins the long journey across the U.S.

The treatment goes on to describe Ah Sahm as "a very cool customer," carrying not a gun but a bamboo staff, not very tall but "lithe and pantherlike," and "a master of Jeet Kune Do, the Oriental unarmed hand-to-hand combat." With his JKD and flashy weapons—a mace and chains or a three-sectional-staff—Ah Sahm takes on *karate* men, *judo* men, *gung fu* men, and everyone else.

"Then," the proposal continues, "he merely has to straighten his Chinese jacket and walk blithely off."

Ah Sahm speaks in oak-and-bamboo Taoist quotations: "My friend, rigidity is the companion of death; pliability is the companion of life." He attempts "to be discreet and stay anonymous as possible." But his white sidekick, Big Bill Walker, is a ham-fisted drunk whom Ah Sahm must constantly save—the *Green Hornet* formula flipped.

"The under dog image is very apparent in this series. However, unlike most under dogs, the viewers know this one is a tiger in disguise," he wrote. "Of course, a Chinese traveling in the days of the West has to be an under dog." Of course, Ah Sahm was Bruce.

Like the Asian American activists, Ah Sahm rejects his elders' fearful, self-defensive crouch and exhorts his people instead toward pride, liberation, and unity. He disdains segregation, "separation of the races," or "partiality." "Under the heaven," Bruce wrote, "there is but one family."

Then he closed his presentation by making the best case he could for an Asian-led series:

> There has not been one show done with martial art as the theme, and definitely not by an Oriental actor (which is such a natural), who in this case will also be a capable martial artist as well. But most important still, he will come across on the screen because that is his life, his character....
>
> [T]his is the right time to have an Oriental "do his thing"... to really do it like it is. This is a revolutionary idea and definitely very commercial.

In 1970, there actually were other writers who shared the outlandish belief that a white Hollywood executive might risk their neck to back a prime-time Western in which the hero metes out justice gunless and hand-to-hand in the Oriental style of animals or insects. But only Bruce could imagine such an explicitly Asian American show—one featuring a Chinese American hero with a drunken bumbling white sidekick, who strides proudly through a multiracial West dispensing *koans* and calling for Asian people to be free.

After five years of having all his color washed out in the Hollywood machine, Bruce had reached the "fuck it" stage of cultivation. It was time to actualize his muscular dreams. He no longer wanted to be the teacher. He wanted to be the warrior.

On the warm summer night of July 26, 1970, Bruce Lee met Fred Weintraub, a garrulous six-foot-two executive vice president at Warner Bros., over dinner at the home of Weintraub's boss and close friend, Ted Ashley, and his photographer wife, Linda. One of Bruce's students, the film producer Sy Weintraub—no relation—had arranged the meeting. Ted Ashley had met Bruce through Sy also, and become a sometime student. Linda Ashley already knew Bruce and Linda Lee well, after shooting photos of the family and of him sparring with Dan Inosanto.

"These men have enormous power," Bruce told Mito. "That kind of party is what every actor hopes to be invited to."

Fred was seeking a lead for a screenplay he had just purchased, a Western about a fugitive Shaolin monk who had fled China to the American West to escape an imperial death sentence. It had been written by two young Jewish American writers from New York and was called *The Way of the Tiger, the Sign of the Dragon*, but they would soon change the name to something simpler: *Kung Fu*.

Fred had two of the most coveted qualities in the culture industry: an eye for emerging talent and a skill for converting long shots into big money. In the early sixties he had opened a club in Greenwich Village called the Bitter End and championed the careers of Bob Dylan, Nina Simone, Joni Mitchell, and others. When

Ted Ashley took over at Warner Bros. in 1969, he hired Fred with one charge: win the young Baby Boomer demographic. Fred placed his bets on a film of a music festival called *Woodstock*, and it became a defining movie of the time, grossing hundreds of millions on an investment of six hundred thousand dollars.

Fred's assistant Bennett Sims had brought him a strange screenplay by two writers named Ed Spielman and Howard Friedlander. At a young age, Ed Spielman's life had been turned upside down by Kurosawa's *Seven Samurai*. He learned Mandarin, *karate*, and *gung fu*, and became one of the few non-Chinese frequenting New York Chinatown's Canal Street theaters for Shaw Brothers kung fu flicks. He thought the West desperately needed some of the East, and he knew it could be conveyed through film.

His friend Howard Friedlander was good at breaking stories. Spielman said he wanted to write a story about Miyamoto Musashi visiting the Shaolin temple. Friendlander wasn't sure he understood all the philosophy stuff but was happy to follow his friend's enthusiasms. He also thought it might be better if the fighter were coming to the West—then it could be an "eastern western."

Together they invented a character they named Kwai Chang Caine, the child of a white American man and a Chinese woman. (They were tapping into the postwar, pro-miscegenation themes of *South Pacific* and *Love Is a Many-Splendored Thing* amid a crisis of abandoned Amerasian babies in Korea and Vietnam.) When the child is left at the steps of the Shaolin temple, the secretive monks break all their rules by taking him in and training him in kung fu.

One day when Caine is older, the nephew of the emperor kills his *sifu*. In a fit of rage, Caine murders the royal and must flee to the United States. Tailed by Manchu government agents, he tries to disappear, but when provoked he becomes a hero of the weak and oppressed. Spielman would later say this was their version of the Superman story, which had also been created by a pair of young Jewish American men—the mild-mannered interplanetary migrant outsider who, when called, steps forth to put things right.

"There were some people who thought, 'Who's going to be interested in a bunch of Chinese guys?'" Spielman recalled. "*Those* Chinese guys were *us*."

Fred Weintraub had come to dinner convinced that martial arts movies were going to be the next big thing. He had been watching the Shaw Brothers flicks, wasn't a fan, but understood something was happening in these inner-city theaters. As they spoke that night, Fred found himself intrigued by Bruce's vast knowledge of boxing, martial arts, and Chinese film. After a few months of hanging out with him, studying his work on TV, and seeing him in action training Sy and Ted, Fred knew he wanted to be in business with Bruce Lee.

Here is where the story needs to be separated from the myth.

Linda wrote in her biography, "Bruce himself had been working on the idea of a Shaolin priest, a master of kung fu, who would roam America and find himself involved in various exploits. The studio contacted him and he was soon deeply involved. He gave them numerous ideas, many of which were eventually incorporated in the resulting TV success, *Kung Fu*."

Over time, this passage has been distorted into the idea that the writers of *Kung Fu* stole their idea from Bruce. But neither the facts or a basic understanding of how screenwriting works support this reading. Ed Spielman and Howard Friedlander had created *The Way of the Tiger, the Sign of the Dragon* on their own. When they had sold their idea, they surrendered all creative control over their work. After they submitted their last rewrite, studio executives and the creatives hired to handle the project would take over.

What is likely true is that the two ideas—*Kung Fu* and *Ah Sahm*—were similar, if distinct, projects floating in Hollywood at the same time. That was how the machine worked. Ideas are always cohering in the deep waters of the mass unconscious, waiting to be surfaced by the dreamers and the telephone screamers. The artist is percipient, angler, and chef. The star-maker is seducer, psychologist, and barker. When it comes to the business of art, the creator needs timing, position, and surprise. The capitalist needs divination, charm, and force. Those who do it best make contingency seem like magic, an inevitability, a thing whose time has come.

In that moment, kung fu—lower case—looked like that thing.

Fred Weintraub commissioned a rewrite from Spielman and Friedlander for Warner Bros., and they submitted it on April 30, 1970, three months before Weintraub met Bruce. On September 8, 1970, they delivered a revised draft, under the new title *Kung Fu—The Way of the Tiger, the Sign of the Dragon*.[*]

It was not until March 12, 1971, that Fred and Bruce began meeting formally about the project. In that time, Bruce became very familiar with Spielman and Friedlander's script. Weintraub said, "We talked about it a lot."

It is not clear when Bruce Lee wrote the treatment for *Ah Sahm*, which at some point he renamed *The Warrior*. The documents in Lee's archives are undated. But it is safe to guess that he may have started around his lean year of 1969, and accelerated his process after the collapse of *The Silent Flute*. It was likely near presentation-ready shape by the time Bruce met with Fred. Two weeks later, on March 26, 1971, Bruce wrote in his Day-Timer, "Freddie Weintraub," "Sy called," and four more words: "Submit script to Warner."[**] That script was very likely Bruce's treatment for *Ah Sahm* or *The Warrior*.

---

[*] Another way to read this is that, by the time Weintraub met Bruce, Spielman and Friedlander had completed most of their contracted work. When Weintraub began pushing for Bruce to be given the role of Kwai Chang Caine, they were out of the picture. Friedlander did not even know the project had been greenlit until he read about it in the trade press.

[**] The entry for the day before, March 25, had read, "Bring treatment to Sy."

Someone at Warner Bros. had given Bruce the opportunity to pitch it there, probably Fred himself, with his fellow dinner guests Ted Ashley and Sy Weintraub taking a close interest. It is not clear why Bruce might have been asked to pitch a TV series that might conflict with an existing movie project, which at this point *Kung Fu* still was. But as a wise woman once said, players only love you when they're playing.

Bruce wrote to Jhoon Rhee, who had recently experienced a series of business setbacks. "Greetings from Los Angeles where, like many places in the States, business is not too good," he wrote. "Remember my friend to enjoy your planning as well as your accomplishment, for life is too short for negative energy."

He told Jhoon that he was awaiting a guest appearance on a new TV show called *Longstreet*, another movie project (probably Stirling's *chanbara* film), and a new budget and a second trip to India for *The Silent Flute*. He said he was writing a movie for Hong Kong. "Of course the damn thing is I want to do something now!" he wrote. "So I have created a T.V. series idea and I should know within a couple of weeks . . .

"So action! Action!" he told Rhee. "I mean who has the most insecure job as I have? What do I live on? My faith in my ability that I'll make it. Sure, my back screwed me up good for a year but with every adversity comes a blessing because a shock acts as a reminder to oneself that we must not get stale in routine. Look at a rainstorm; after its departure everything grows!"

Jhoon would recall that Bruce had, in high spirits, signed his letter, "李大龍. [Lee *Big* Dragon.]"

But less than two weeks later, on April 2, Bruce wrote in his Day-Timer, "Warner deal fell." His script had been rejected.

On the next line of his Day-Timer, Bruce wrote, "Call Hong Kong."

CHAPTER 37
The Fighter's Instant

Stirling Silliphant remembered another lesson that he had learned from his teacher—this one about time and opportunity.

"Bruce taught me to dissect time into infinite degrees. It's what he called 'playing between the keys' of the piano," he said. "It's the understanding that you actually have worlds of time within split seconds to do something else unanticipated while your opponent is committed to his already announced action."

If you had prepared your body well and your mind was free, you might—in between the before and after, in that slow-motion expanse of the fighter's instant—be able to feel not only how many options you had but exactly which one to choose. That is where Bruce found himself in his career by the summer of 1971.

Kung fu movies were driving a Hong Kong film industry boom. They now made up 70 percent of the industry's output across the Asian market, which included Taiwan, the Philippines, Indonesia, Singapore, Malaysia, Vietnam, Laos, Burma, Thailand, South Korea, and Japan. At the top was the Shaw Brothers empire, run by the Shao family from Shanghai.

With five thousand employees in Singapore and two thousand more in Hong Kong, the Shaw Brothers had up to twenty-five movies in production on any given day at their Movietown studios in Clearwater Bay. Sets were being built and torn down so fast that the entire place always seemed covered in sawdust and drywall powder.

Actors were trained in an academy so exclusive that the odds of being accepted were lower than those of getting into Harvard. They were housed in gender-segregated dormitories, governed by strict house rules that resembled, the journalist Don Atyeo wrote, "military boarding schools." Sex, booze, or drugs brought immediate expulsion, which meant the end of a career. Only one in fifty graduates became a regular Shaw actor, and those chosen received a standard five- to seven-year contract that paid them the equivalent of US $250 a month.

After the movies were dubbed and subtitled, outfitted with soundtracks and credits, and finished, they were sent to the hundreds of theaters the Shaws owned from Asia to the United States. Their model was Warner Bros., down to their logo, and other vertically integrated studios of yore.

"We were like the Hollywood of the 1930s," said Run Run Shaw, whom Atyeo called the "Cecil B. DeMille of the Orient." "We controlled everything: the talent, the production, the distribution and the exhibition."

Shaw Brothers could churn out entertainment for Asia's masses the way Ford did automobiles. After a plane crash in 1965 took the lives of the leadership of the Cathay Organization, the Shaw Brothers' main competition, they had nearly complete dominance over the Mandarin film market. But cracks were appearing in their stronghold.

Raymond Chow was a native Hong Konger and a former journalist whose résumé had included a stint at the Voice of America. In 1958, Chow joined the Shaw Brothers as their director of publicity just as Run Run Shaw was expanding the business in Hong Kong. He soon threatened to leave because he hated the sentimental pablum the company was releasing. Run Run countered by offering him the position of director of production as well. Over the next decade Chow was at Run Run's side in building the Shaw Brothers dominance, bringing in Chang Cheh and other talent. He and Run Run developed a relationship that Andre Morgan, who would later work closely with Chow, characterized as "like father and son."

By the end of the sixties, Raymond believed the future of film was in kung fu movies. As one of his last major creative decisions at Shaw Brothers, he green-lit an idea from the Shaw star Jimmy Wang Yu for a movie called *The Chinese Boxer*. After the 1967 riots, even the bloodiest of the costume swordplay *wuxia* epics no longer felt urgent enough. Their villains and concerns were too distant. *The Chinese Boxer* shifted the action back to fist and leg combat and the setting to the republican era before the Chinese Civil War. The fighting was visceral and the enemy was clear. Wang's kung fu hero dealt sweet justice to twentieth-century Japanese oppressors with Iron Palm fists calloused by being thrust into wok-fired coals. *The Chinese Boxer* joined King Hu's *Come Drink with Me* as one of Hong Kong's top-grossing films to date.

But Run Run had decided the future of media was in color television and turned his focus to TVB, which controlled more than 80 percent of the colony's TV market. He intended to retool Movietown into TV Town. Raymond Chow proposed that Run Run let him form a film production company that would make six to eight movies a year and share profits with Shaw Brothers. It was a good deal for both. Run Run could reduce his exposure while still taking a share of the film and theatre revenues. Raymond could have financial and creative control, and sales and distribution muscle. With a handshake, Shaw agreed, and Raymond formed Golden Harvest Pictures with his lieutenants, Leonard Ho and Leung Fung.

The split between Shaw and Chow came swiftly. Raymond had learned from angry directors—who, like the actors, were bound by contracts that paid flat monthly rates—that assistant directors and other contract workers could negotiate higher rates. Raymond instead proposed a system of directors' bonuses. Run Run refused.

If Shaw Brothers had been built in the centralized way of the old American studios, history also offered Raymond a blueprint for bringing it down. Golden Harvest began offering directors and actors what Shaw Brothers would not—profit-sharing deals. It also wooed away directors and actors whose contracts were expiring. Run Run was outraged. Poaching his talent was bad enough, but the fact that Golden Harvest had given those directors and actors bargaining power was even worse. He swiftly purged Chow and his staff. Although he still had much of the colony's talent locked up, he would never stop nursing his feeling of betrayal.

By April 1970, Chow had no alternative but to go all in with Golden Harvest. He secured lines of credit from Bangkok Bank and others, then went around the world to shore up distribution deals, from Manila and Saigon to London and Rome. What he needed now was talent. He lured some away from Shaw, including the actors James Tien Chuen, Nora Miao Ker Hsiu, Maria Yi, and Angela Mao Ying, and two directors, Huang Feng and a cigar-chomping, diamond-pinky-ringed former actor from Shanghai named Lo Wei.

All this was happening when Bruce Lee had come to town in the spring of 1970 and appeared on TVB's *Enjoy Yourself Tonight* and RTV's *Golden Hour* show. "His charisma stuck in my mind. I kept thinking of a screen vehicle for him," Raymond Chow recalled. But he had been unsuccessful in tracking Bruce down. For his part, Bruce had stayed in contact with *Enjoy Yourself Tonight*'s producer Robert Chua and approached Chua to produce his movies. Chua demurred, "You need a real film producer like Raymond Chow who knows how to put things together."

Raymond decided to send one of his producers, Gladys Liu Liang Hua, a fluent English speaker and Lo Wei's wife, to Los Angeles to try to woo the *Come Drink with Me* star Cheng Pei-Pei out of retirement. Pei-Pei had recently married a Taiwanese businessman, moved with him to the States, and quit the business while still in her mid-twenties. Gladys's son, David Lo, who had hosted Bruce on the RTV *Golden Hour* show, urged her to speak to him as well. Raymond enthusiastically agreed.

By then, Bruce was also being actively courted by Law Chi, whose mutual friendship dated back to when they had played street kids together in *Infancy*. Law had been directing *wuxia* pictures for independent companies in Hong Kong and Taiwan and wanted Bruce to star in a kung fu epic in which the triads unite to fight off the Japanese army. But he had been slow in getting his funding together.

For years, Bruce had been trying to reach Run Run Shaw, and now, through Unicorn Chan and others, they were speaking.* Bruce relayed his terms: ten thousand US dollars per movie, script approval, and control over fight choreography. The Shaw Brothers staff fixated on the money. "That was too much," Lawrence Wong, a producer, said, "because if we paid him, we would then have to upgrade all of our other contract stars accordingly." Shaw's deputy Mona Fong told Unicorn to pres-

---

* In his 1971 Day-Timer, Bruce also lists calls with someone named 寶珠, likely the actor Connie Chan Po-Chu, who worked with the Shaw Brothers and also Bruce's old friend Chor Yuen. Connie was living in San Francisco at the time.

ent Bruce with their best offer—five thousand US dollars per movie, an upgrade from what Chang Cheh had discussed with Peter but still not enough.

"Bruce laughed it off," Linda recalled. "At one stage, Bruce did go so far as to wire Shaw asking about script details and other matters. Shaw's reply was a paternalistic, 'Just tell him to come back here and everything will be all right.'"

Bruce was no longer in the mood to play any game that seemed rigged. As Bruce prepared for his *Longstreet* shoot, he felt like maybe he finally had some tail winds. On Sunday, June 6, he returned from a prep meeting at Stirling Silliphant's house and wrote in his Day-Timer, "WILL MAKE T.V. SERIES."

Gladys Liu Liang Hua arrived in Los Angeles the same week, and she invited Bruce and Linda to attend a reception that the Chinese American actor Benson Fong was hosting for her at his Ah Fong restaurant in Beverly Hills. There, she took Bruce aside, told him about Golden Harvest, and invited him to meet her at Cheng Pei-Pei's house to talk about working together. A patchouli-scented Bruce arrived at the house looking and smelling, the actress would recall, like "a bit of a hippy!"

Their conversations fast turned serious. Gladys connected Bruce with Raymond on a call, and the two were soon talking action movies. Bruce had seen *The Chinese Boxer* in Los Angeles's Chinatown with Steve McQueen, Kareem Abdul-Jabbar, and Victor Lam, the producer who had once tried to pair Bruce with Chang Cheh. He had a strong opinion about it.

"Is that the best you could do?" he asked Raymond.

Raymond admitted that it was.

"I could do much better," Bruce said, launching into a detailed critique.

"Yes, yes," Raymond interrupted, "but if you help me, together I am sure we can build something."

After the call, Raymond instructed Gladys, "Sign Bruce to a two-picture deal, three-picture deal, any number of pictures you can get!"

At the end of June, after Bruce shot the *Longstreet* episode, "The Way of the Intercepting Fist," everyone at the studio seemed excited about it. Paramount head Tom Tannenbaum—who had also been a student of Bruce—called him over to his office and told him the studio wanted to develop a series for him. Ted Ashley caught wind of Tannenbaum's moves and plotted with Fred Weintraub on how they might lock in Bruce for Warner Bros. Suddenly two of his students looked like they might be competing for his services.

Bruce wrote to Leo Fong, "This happens so fast I don't know what to think—must have done a good job!?"

Gladys Liu Liang Hua came back to Bruce with an offer for three movies with Golden Harvest. She told him Raymond had no problem with giving him script review or fight choreography. Bruce countered with two movies. She quickly returned with a two-page offer—$15,000 for two movies, tentatively to be entitled *The Big Boss* and *The King of Chinese Boxers*, at the rate of $7,500 per picture, with $10,000 to be delivered when he began work on the first and $5,000 upon the completion of the second.

They would fly him to Thailand to begin shooting in July. All he had to do was sign.

Golden Harvest was an undercapitalized start-up that shot its films in tiny run-down studios on a hillside surrounded by squatter settlements. It had released several movies in 1971 and none of them were creating much buzz. But Anna May Wong had gone to Germany. Jimi Hendrix had gone to London. And, as Bruce was telling family and friends, Clint Eastwood and Charles Bronson had gone to Italy.

"There is just no other way," Bruce told Linda. "I can't get in the front door here."

If he left, that meant Linda would be caring for the kids and his family, his mother, and his brother, Robert, in Bel Air, by herself. "It was a real risk," Linda recalled, "especially with the state of moviemaking in Hong Kong not being as sophisticated as in the United States."

Bruce went to his Hollywood patrons Fred Weintraub, Stirling Silliphant, and James Coburn, with whom he had reconciled, to seek their advice. Weintraub surprised him. "Do it!" Fred said. Bruce said he was worried about the money and worse—that going to Hong Kong might rule out a future in Hollywood.

"I would be giving up," Bruce told him. "I'll be stuck in Hong Kong forever."

But Weintraub assured him that if he came back with a strong reel, the door would remain open.

After a training session at Coburn's house with Stirling and James, Bruce sat down with them to talk about his future.

Stirling had just heard from his onetime *karate* partner, Jim Aubrey at MGM, that they were passing on *The Silent Flute*. But he thought Bruce should still pursue his prospects in America. *Longstreet* was just a beginning. If he kept at it, he might get his own series, and then the opportunities would cascade down.

"Bruce, don't take this offer. Don't go," Stirling said. "Stay here. You're just starting to get hot."

Coburn disagreed. "Man, you go into TV and you're going to burn out your show in a season," he said. "Television chews up genius—it can chew a man up in a series of thirteen episodes. It's a waste of time. Set your sights on Hong Kong instead."

"Raymond Chow is not going to pay you enough money," Stirling countered. "My god! I can get you that much for a TV show. You're not going to fly all the way to Hong Kong for a lousy ten grand, are you? Has he given you a round-trip first-class air ticket? What if you get over there and he doesn't pay your hotel bill?

"Bruce," Stirling continued, "no one knows the Chinese better than you. You know they can be slightly tricky when it comes to these long-distance deals. These fellas can teach Arabian horse traders tricks. So how do you propose to protect yourself? What happens if you get over there and it's a lousy script and they won't pay your fare back?"

For a long moment, Bruce looked at Stirling. Finally, he responded, "They won't do that to me."

It came down to Linda. This was his big break, she reasoned. "You go do it," she said. "Send for us when you can."

By July 12, 1971, Bruce had signed the Golden Harvest contract and was boarding a flight across the Pacific.

"Well, what more can I say," he wrote to Leo Fong, "but that things are swinging my way."

Bruce had been in the United States for twelve years, a full Chinese cycle. In the first six years he had learned what it meant to be an Asian in America. In the last six he had contorted himself to fit into Hollywood. He was thirty now, and more driven to win than ever.

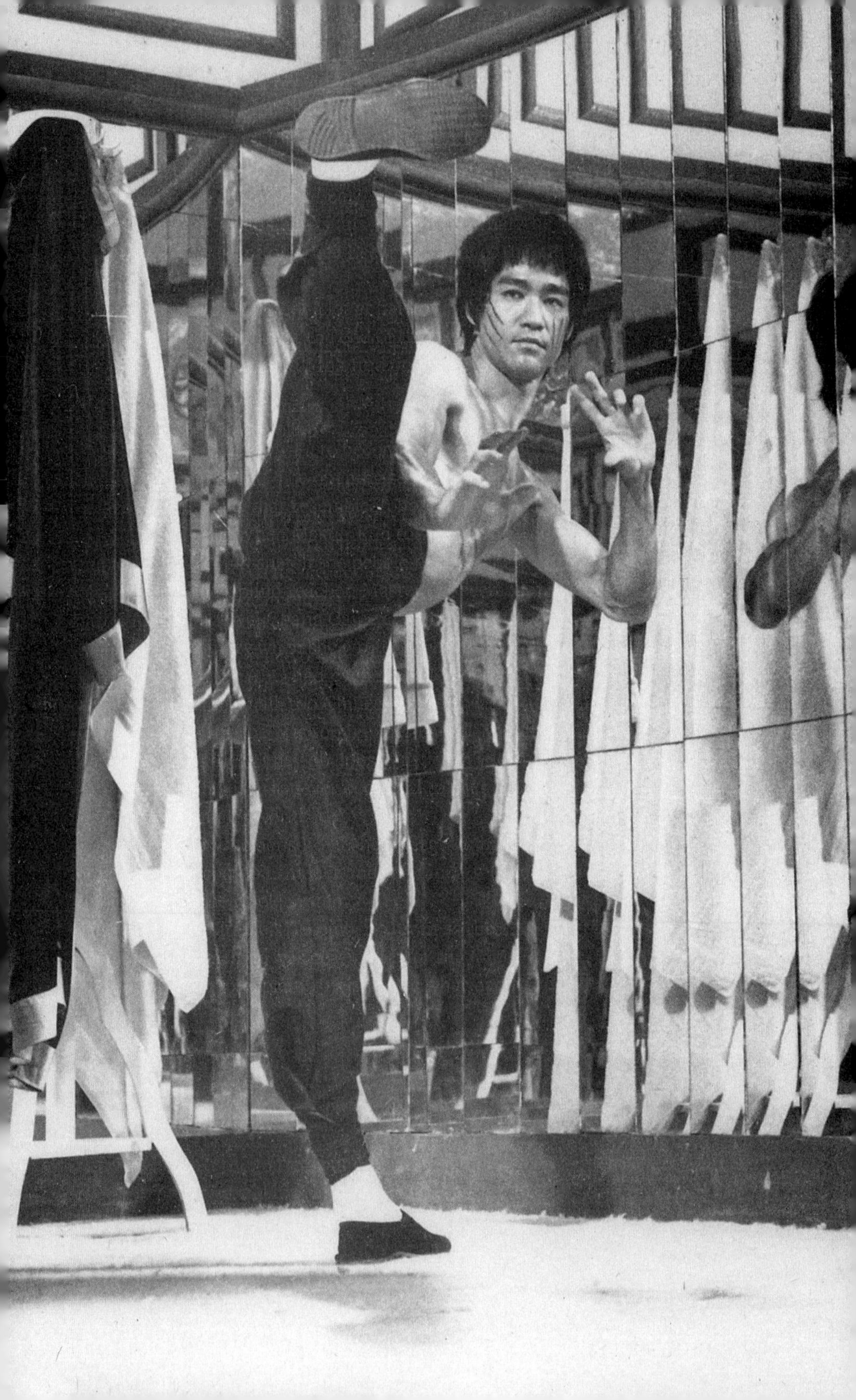

BOOK III
ECHO

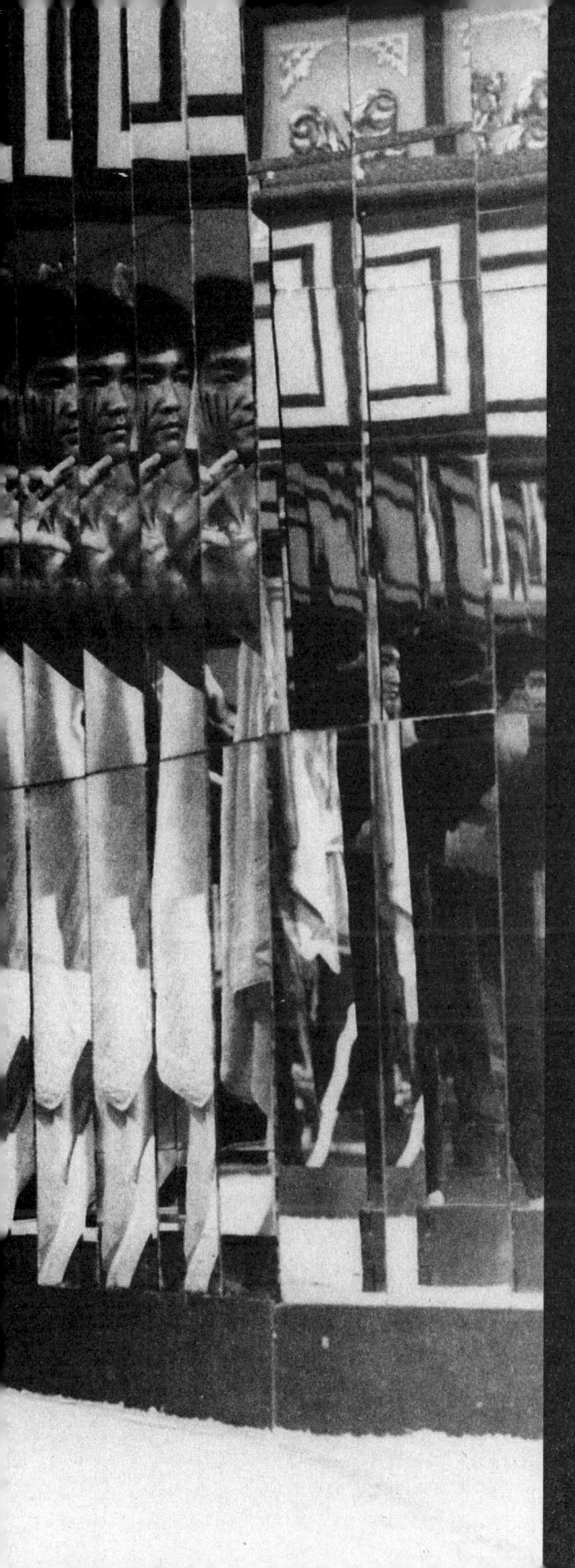

Heaven produces the teeming multitude.

—BOOK OF ODES

In the hall of mirrors.
Photo courtesy of the Bruce
Lee Family Archive.

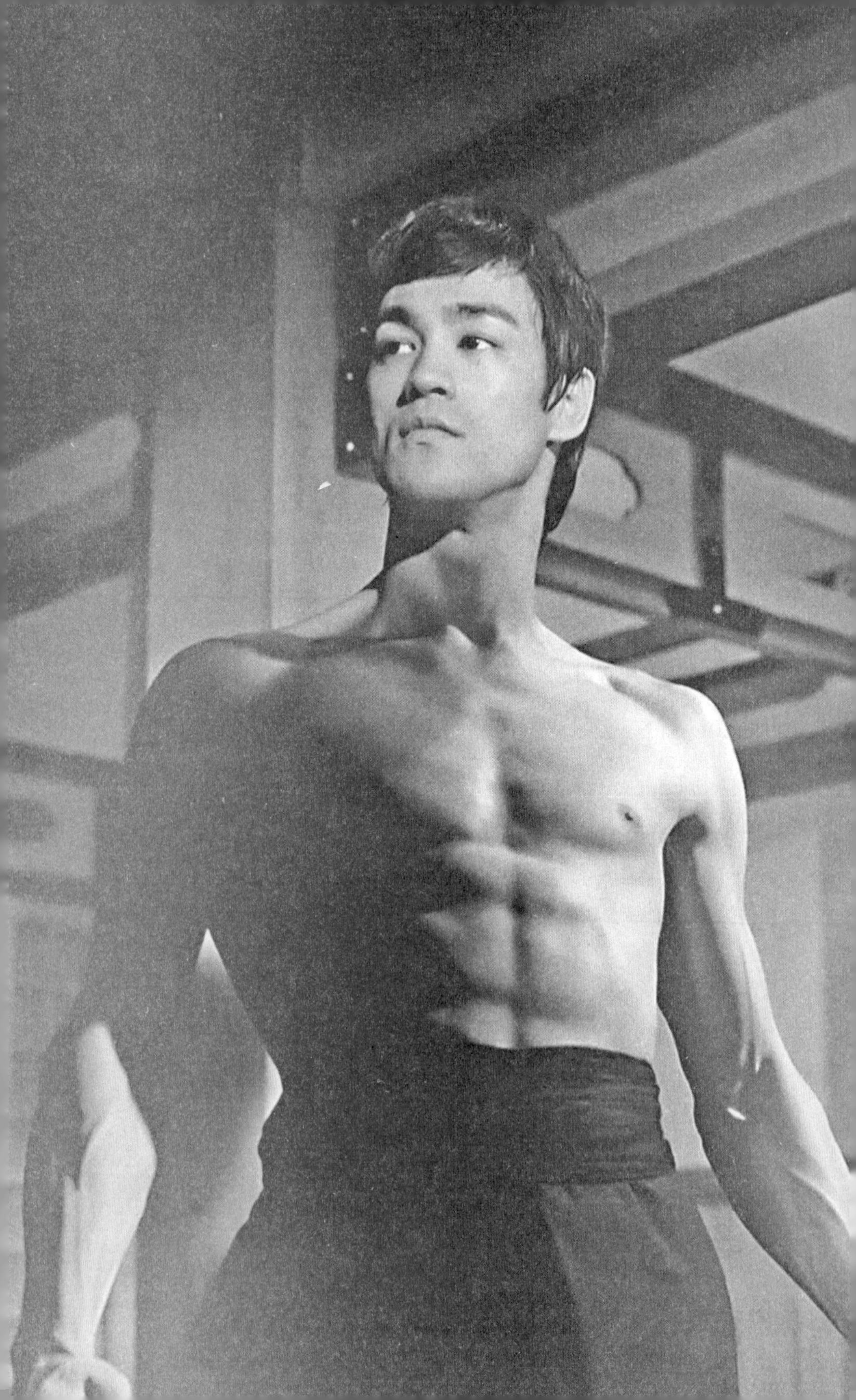

PART XI
The New Hero

1971–1972

Therefore the wise say:

If you take on the humiliation of the people, you are fit to rule them.

If you take upon yourself the country's disasters,

You deserve to be ruler of the universe.

The truth often sounds paradoxical.

—LAOZI

Fist of Fury, 1972.
Photo courtesy of the Bruce Lee Family Archive.

CHAPTER 38
Us Against the World

Raymond Chow was paranoid that Run Run Shaw might send representatives to intercept Bruce Lee at Kai Tak airport. He wanted Bruce to fly directly to Bangkok, where his employees would spirit their talent to the set farther north in Pak Chong. Run Run's people *were* frantically trying to reach Bruce, saying that Shaw Brothers was prepared to make a new deal—perhaps up to triple the money—if he would break his agreement with Golden Harvest.

But Bruce made a point to fly first to Hong Kong, just to show Raymond who was boss, the way he had seen Steve McQueen do things. Then he sent word to Run Run that he was too late and just wrong, the way he had seen Kareem Abdul-Jabaar deal with the New York Nets. At Kai Tak, Bruce met the aides Raymond had sent to shadow him, saw some friends, made some calls, and finally boarded the connecting flight to Bangkok.

He had emerged from Hollywood's isle of the flies into a young world in revolt. Everywhere in Asia and the Pacific, it was *us against the world*.

In Honolulu and Tokyo, students left the campuses to stand with farmers fighting to keep their lands in Kalama Valley and Sanrizuka. In Calcutta, they took up arms with rural peasants in the Naxalite movement. In Manila, they filled the streets to decry the corruption and authoritarianism of President Ferdinand Marcos. In a Seoul marketplace, a twenty-two-year-old garment worker set himself on fire to protest sweatshop conditions, launching a broad labor movement.

In the States, Asian Americans were following the words of Mao and the example of the Black Panther Party. Their movement's new cry was "Serve the People." In cities like Minneapolis, Madison, and New Haven, and from coast to coast, organizers focused on securing basic needs for their communities, including housing, health care, and legal aid. A new militancy cohered against establishment leaders, whom the young radicals called "Uncle Tongs." Some students in San Francisco launched a youth program called the Free University for Chinatown Kids, Unincorporated—F.U.C.K.U. "In Chinatown," recalled Bryant Fong, a former AAPA leader from UC Berkeley, "it was ripe for rebellion."

The heart of Asian America—and the pulse of its warrior consciousness—was a city block on San Francisco's Kearny Street, at the border of Chinatown and Manilatown, home to a three-story red-brick single-room-occupancy hotel called the International Hotel, affectionately called the I-Hotel.

One of the young warriors there was Harvey Dong, a born fighter drawn to other fighters. He had come from Sacramento—where he had studied *gung fu* with Leo Fong—to UC Berkeley in 1966 as an ROTC student. His roommate took classes with James Yimm Lee and introduced him to Bruce Lee, high in the stands at Wong Jack Man's 1968 *gung fu* convention.

But as American atrocities in Vietnam came to light, Harvey grew disillusioned. He attended anti-war and pro-Panther demonstrations, and after Martin and Bobby and My Lai, he left ROTC for the AAPA and the TWLF. In Chinatown he volunteered to help seniors, and began hanging out at a space across from the Jackson Café called Leways—short for "Legitimate Ways"—a gathering place for youth gang members where the men shot pool and pinball and the women talked about the struggle. They smoked cigarettes, listened to soul music, read Mao, hung out with Black Panthers, ate ice cream, and practiced martial arts.

Down the block, the I-Hotel was home to more than a hundred elderly men—mostly Filipino *manongs*, as well as Chinese bachelors, and some Blacks and Latinos, all workingmen who had labored in agriculture, factory, service, domestic, or military jobs. "Urban renewal"—what Calvin Trillin called "the Manifest Destiny of the Financial District"—was underway. The I-Hotel and the adjacent Victory Building occupied the last block of what was once a flourishing Manilatown of thirty thousand Filipino workers, the kind of real estate that San Francisco Redevelopment Agency head Justin Herman now said was "too valuable to permit poor people to park on it."

Developers instead targeted the land to build a parking lot for rich people, and served the tenants eviction notices. Harvey and his comrades rallied to their defense. Soon after, a suspicious fire took the lives of three residents and forced everyone to leave. An army of volunteers—most, like Harvey, veterans of the Third World student strikes—came to repair the hotel and help the elders move back in.

The revolution moved in too. Joining Tino's Barber Shop, the Lucky M pool hall, and the Bataan Lunch Counter were organizations like the Asian Community Center, which offered a free food program, after-school services, and art classes; Asian Legal Services, which provided draft support; and Eastwind, which acclimated new immigrants. There was a cooperative garment factory that produced jeans and Mao jackets, and the offices for competing sectarian groups, Wei Min She and I Wor Kuen.

The Chinese Progressive Association occupied the space that had been the Hungry I nightclub, where the Beat poets once gathered. Al Robles, the I-Hotel's grizzled bard, held court at the Kearny Street Workshop, which attracted artists like Nancy Hom and Leland Wong, and writers like Jessica Hagedorn, Janice Mirikitani, Russell Leong, and Luis and Serafin Syquia, pioneers of the grand flowering of Asian American arts.

At the end of 1969, as one of UC Berkeley AAPA's last grand acts, Harvey and three others collected donations from members to start a bookshop in the I-Hotel. With six hundred dollars they opened Everybody's Bookstore, the first self-proclaimed Asian American bookstore in the country. It became the block's primary magnet.

The windows at Everybody's were plastered with flyers for protests, concerts, and plays. It was the only place to find classics like *Journey to the West*, *Romance of the Three Kingdoms*, and *Outlaws of the Marsh*, and rediscovered works of Asian American literature, like Toshio Mori's *Yokohama, California*, Jade Snow Wong's *Fifth Chinese Daughter*, and Carlos Bulosan's *America Is in the Heart*. The racks were stuffed with martial arts manuals, Maoist pamphlets, and movement zines—*Gidra*, *Rodan*, *Bridge*, *Kalayaan*, *Hawai'i Pono Journal*, *Asian Women's Journal*, *Black Panther Party News*, *Palante*, *Getting Together*, *Wei Min Bao*—all breathing the fire of the moment.

"China was called the 'sick man of Asia,'" read a manifesto in *Wei Min Bao*'s first issue. "But the 'sick men' were willing to struggle, because they knew it was only through struggle that victory could be won."

At any given hour, the I-Hotel hummed with the noise of elderly tenants, labor organizers, law students, seamstresses, filmmakers, poets, painters, *kai doy* gangbangers, single mothers, and *bolero* dancers. "Now, the people have asserted themselves before this repressive society," wrote International Hotel Tenants Association president Emil De Guzman. "They stand as a symbol—for Asian community control, Asian self-determination, and Asian self-reliance."

But soon the downtown cops were hounding the Leways youths until they closed their storefront. When the young radicals began screening revolutionary movies from China before huge crowds, Kuomintang Nationalist thugs began issuing threats. "Some of the old men were old-time activists who had been suppressed during the McCarthy era and they were worried about us," Harvey said. During the screenings, the old men packed guns and guarded the door. "One of the elders suggested that we actually prepare for the possibility of violence and that we should all be learning *gung fu*."

Soon the basement was filled with multiple generations of I-Hotel activists being led by a Black male expert in White Crane *gung fu*. Wong Jack Man's Jing Mo followers—some of whom had also joined the revolution—came by to teach, practice, and spar. Slowly displacing the Asian Americans' revolutionary ardor were fears that a violent reckoning might be around the bend. The pure zeal of any collective awakening cannot last.

When Bruce arrived in Pak Chong, a rural town a hundred miles north of Bangkok, it was monsoon season, humid and gray. He slashed his hand when he crumbled a thin glass he was washing, requiring ten stitches, and would wear a bandage on his hand through the entire shoot of the movie. He wrote to Linda, "The mosquitoes are terrible and cockroaches are all over the place." The food was terrible—it was hard to get decently cooked meat—and he was down to 128 pounds.

He was back in the Third World, farther from the comforts of empire but closer to the fires of emergence.

As the cast arrived, he was happy to find that a family friend Tony Lau Wing had been cast as one of the villains. Lau told Bruce he had been practicing and teaching *karate* in Hong Kong and Macau. "Forget your classical *karate!*" Bruce said. The two met each morning to jog together. Bruce taught him Jeet Kune Do, and Lau introduced Bruce to the Chinese and Thai stuntmen.

Many of the Hong Kong fall guys had come up together in Kowloon's China Drama Academy and other schools that had succeeded the opera companies of Bruce's father's generation. Most had grown up poor, often the children of migrants, and some had street-fighting bona fides. When martial arts films exploded in the seventies, this tight-knit community would produce the likes of Jackie Chan, Sammo Hung, and Corey Yuen. The ones who weren't from Hong Kong were locals who had come up in *muay Thai* fight circles.

As in Hollywood, the Asian stuntmen were a brotherhood with their own codes of honor and conduct. Everyone already knew that Bruce had received a fat sum from Raymond for the movie, and that made him immediately suspect. One of the men in the group Lau brought to Bruce's hotel suite was a bony seventeen-year-old named Lam Ching-ying, who loudly demanded that Bruce demonstrate his qualifications for the role. Bruce was happy to oblige. First he knocked the kid back with a solid punch. But Lam kept yapping. So Bruce had the stuntmen fix him with a pillow and, in one swift side kick, knocked him into the wall.

After Bruce had passed this test, Lau recalled, "A lot of people looked up to him." Lam became Bruce's personal assistant. Lau became Bruce's wingman.

Bruce was right back where he wanted to be, entertaining everyone on the set with coin tricks and filthy jokes. He was showing the guys Jeet Kune Do and learning *muay Thai* from the local stuntmen. Bruce knew whom he wanted to align himself with.

"When he saw Raymond Chow, he would order Raymond to come over. When he saw those of us who were playing the supporting roles, he would come over and talk to us like good friends, like, 'Hey Anthony!'" Lau recalled. "He treated others that were lower than him very well. He treated those above him with indifference."

This us-versus-everybody attitude would soon play out with the movie's director, Wu Chia Hsiang.

The Big Boss—its Chinese title would be *The Big Brother of Tangshan*—was a movie about Chinese migrant workers at a Thai ice factory who discover the owner controls not just their labor, but the area's gambling dens, brothels, and, most critically, its underground heroin trade.

The conventionally handsome James Tien had originally been cast as the film's hero, Hsu Chien, a dauntless and beloved worker who always wins justice with his *gung fu*. Bruce is Cheng Chao-An, a country boy from Tangshan fleeing a shadowy past as a deadly martial artist. He wears a jade pendant around his neck to remind himself of a promise he has made to his mother that he will never fight again. As he joins Brother Hsu and the migrant workers, no one knows what he is capable of, emotionally or physically. When Bruce arrived on set, his character was similarly unformed.

Raymond Chow had lured away James Tien and the director Lo Wei from the Shaw Brothers, and the pair had just completed their last movie for Run Run. His coup had been the talk of the town. James had already shot scenes for Wu Chia Hsiang as the star. But now Raymond was pushing Wu to expand the role for Bruce, his latest big investment. The reluctant director decided to size up Bruce by putting him in a fight scene against the Big Boss's Pinkertons. But an argument broke out between Wu and Bruce over how to stage the fight.

On-screen kung fu fights at that time used the grammar of the Chinese opera's weapons-centered choreography and the big moves of Northern Shaolin fist styles. Wu's action director, Han Ying-Chieh—who was also playing the titular villain, the Big Boss Hsiao Mi—was considered one of the most innovative martial arts directors of his time. A veteran of the opera and the Shaw Brothers system, he had pioneered the use of trampolines, while his colleague Chan Siu-Pang introduced the use of wires, which they had brought from their work in the circus. Han had elevated *wuxia* swordplay into high art in King Hu's *Come Drink with Me* and *A Touch of Zen*.

In 1970, Jimmy Wang Yu's Iron Palm thriller *The Chinese Boxer* and David Chiang and Ti Lung's knives-out *Vengeance!*—which opens on an opera stage—had set the standard for fist-and-leg choreography. But these film fights still owed much to *wuxia*'s staginess. They built tension through blow-meets-blow repetition until a fighter erupted with a decisive punch or high-flying kick.

"They were awful," Bruce told a journalist. "What really bothered me was that everybody fought exactly the same way." Aside from the lack of personality—fight was supposed to be about human expression, after all—he deplored all the excess flash and wasted motion. These fights were inauthentic and interminable, and belonged to his father's generation. Now that he was free of ignorant American directors and zealous television censors, he wanted fighters who revealed themselves by the signature of their movements, through action that resembled the swift unmannered chaos of a real street fight. Wu wanted prog rock. Bruce wanted punk rock.

Wu was not going to let an inexperienced Chinese American tell him what worked in a Hong Kong film. He disdained Bruce's lack of a formal opera and *gung fu* pedigree, telling Raymond Chow that Bruce knew nothing but three kicks. He belittled Bruce as "Three Leg Lee." Bruce knew that those three kicks—the crescent kick, spinning hook kick, and roundhouse kick—were battle tested and, when executed in combination the way he did, sensational to watch. After all that overly mannered choreography, he was certain audiences would be thrilled to see a fight that looked like the real thing, especially the young generation raised on war and *beimo* culture.

Lau and the stuntmen sided with him. "With Bruce's way, you could feel the power of his moves," Lau, who was playing the Big Boss's son Hsiao Chun, said. "You could sense what the fighting was like." But the argument threatened to derail the entire production.

Raymond was hearing complaints over Wu's treatment of cast and crew. "His attitude was wrong," Lau said of Wu. "He didn't care much about the film. He wasn't keen to push boundaries and he didn't do much homework. It was Bruce who did a lot of the research. He was treating it like it was his own project." Lau remembered seeing Bruce tell Raymond, "We mustn't be sloppy in our effort!"

After the Golden Harvest staff in Hong Kong watched the dailies they knew that Bruce was right. "I saw the rushes and they were just terrible," Raymond said. "The director had no feeling for it at all." Raymond consulted with Gladys Liu Liang Hua, who was the production manager. She told him that Wu Chia Hsiang had lost the trust of the cast and crew. He decided to fire the director. Gladys suggested that her husband, Lo Wei, replace him.

With the remit of saving the movie, Lo arrived, just weeks after production had started, into a troubled project. He found Wu's script histrionic, a problem compounded by its focus on James Tien's impossibly virtuous, dramatically dull Brother Hsu. Nothing was wrong with Tien's performance. It was simply that Bruce was the star.

Writing late into the night after day shoots were complete, Lo Wei saved the movie. In his revised script, Hsu Chien was killed off at the end of Act I. Lo intensified the brutality of the Big Boss Hsiao Mi, his son, and their band of thugs. The new story pivoted around Cheng Chao-An's efforts to avenge their bloody crimes. It was, the movie critic Walter Chaw wrote, "an anti-capitalist/anti-colonialist screed," a mirror to a time of uprisings.

The movie still starts slowly. Brother Hsu is the protector of the ice factory workers and the poor villagers in a company town. The workers have formed a chosen family, which includes bright-eyed Maria Yi as Chow Mei, everyone's "little sister" and a potential love interest for Chao-An. They welcome the secretive newcomer from Tangshan warmly.

The workers discover that the ice factory is a front for heroin trafficking, and Brother Hsu disappears after confronting the Big Boss. Fearing he has been murdered, the workers organize. Forty-five minutes in, when Cheng Chao-An lets out his wildcat scream and intervenes to help the workers, the movie finally takes off.

Chao-An triumphs and leads the workers in a joyous parade around the factory town. But the Big Boss and his cronies decide to sever Chao-An's relationship with them by plying him with a promotion, women, and many bottles of wine. The Big Boss orders the slaughter of the Chinese workers, including Chow Mei and the children. Haunted by his complicity in their deaths, Chao-An kills Hsiao Chun in the ice factory, his trembling fists disclosing his guilt-fueled rage. At the bloody climax, Cheng Chao-An tracks and kills the Big Boss, before keeling over onto his enemy's dead body in a bloody embrace.

Lo Wei shared his predecessor's taste for long, operatic fighting, and resumed the argument over fight choreography with Bruce. "Right now if I say Bruce Lee can't fight, for sure no one would believe me," Lo recalled later. "That's what I said—he didn't know how to fight in movies. Maybe his martial arts is really incredible, because I don't know anything about that anyway...

"I told him, 'We're shooting a movie, if you can only strike those few times, that's only two, three seconds on the screen. What do we do with the film? The audience won't feel satisfied!'"

But Bruce questioned why fights needed to be so long, especially the ones early in the movie. An action movie was supposed to build in intensity over the film's arc. If the early fights were drawn out, he reasoned, what would be left for the finale?

Lo told Bruce to watch as he directed James Tien fighting with flips, falls, and trampoline shots. "[Bruce] thought, 'Wait a minute, [Tien] is doing so many fight scenes, once it's released, he will become the main character, I will become a side character.'

"So then he started behaving more."

The director was taking too much credit. As the shooting proceeded, Han Ying-Chieh came to see Bruce's point of view, and the action director and the young star warmed to each other. Chao-An's final outdoor fight with the Big Boss features the stylistic clash of Bruce and Han's choreographies as subtext and text. Han accommodates Bruce's preferences with snappy confrontations that include *chin-na* grappling rolls. Bruce's concessions include a trampoline shot that produces his iconic flying kick silhouette.

But Lo and Bruce's relationship deteriorated. In the beginning, Bruce had visited Lo's room after hours to pepper him with questions about how to approach specific scenes. "He seemed obsessed with acting," Lo recalled.

As shooting continued for another month in Pak Chong, Bangkok, and Hong Kong, delayed by monsoon rains, they argued over staging, lighting, and other issues small and big. In most Mandarin movies, there was never quiet on the set. Sound and

The Big Boss, 1971. Photo courtesy of the Bruce Lee Family Archive.

multilingual dubs were added in postproduction. But Lo Wei's set was extreme. Crew members conversed, ice machines buzzed, and the director, an inveterate gambler, kept a radio tuned to the reports from the horse and greyhound tracks back in Hong Kong. All this drove Bruce mad.

After filming was complete, Lo and Bruce fought over specific scenes all the way to the editing room. In one of them, Chao-An kicks a villain through an icehouse wall, leaving a man-shaped hole more suitable for a kiddy cartoon than a bloody fight film. Over Lee's loud objections, Lo insisted upon keeping it.

Bruce never shook his impression that the famous old pinky-ringed director Lo Wei was an amateur.

The Shaw Brothers scheduled Lo Wei and James Tien's last movie for the Shaw Brothers, *Vengeance of a Snow Girl*,* for a late October release. Golden Harvest

---

* Tien had been the action director for that movie as well. He had been thrice eclipsed by Bruce.

moved its Saturday midnight premiere of *The Big Boss* up by a week to October 23, 1971, to set up a historic duel. In Hong Kong's gossipy trade press, the main storyline might have been about Chow and Shaw's proxy war with Lo and Tien's two movies going head-to-head. But for the first time, and not the last, Bruce would take over the entire narrative.

As the premiere date approached, Bruce grew anxious. He wanted Linda there, as well as Bob Baker—an old Oakland student of his whom he had invited to come work with him on a new movie he was calling *The Intercepting Fist*. After a return to Los Angeles in September, he brought Linda, the kids, and Bob to Hong Kong with him on October 16. The family moved into a new apartment Golden Harvest provided for them. He told the press that he and Baker were starting work on the new movie.

On opening night, the three sat near the back of the Queen's Theatre in Central Hong Kong, unrecognized amid the sold-out crowd of nearly a thousand. "Hong Kong moviegoers, they're really tough critics," he told Linda. "If they don't like it, I mean, they'll slit the seats with a knife."

When the movie came to its sudden, shocking conclusion, there was silence. Bruce whispered to Linda, "Oh my god. They hate it. They hate it. They hate it!"

"All of a sudden," Linda recalled, "just a *roar*. Everyone standing up, clapping, yelling, turning around. 'Find Bruce.' 'Where's Bruce?'" As they were caught in the surging tide of people in the lobby, Linda was separated from him. She stepped outside to find they had lifted him upon their shoulders and were carrying him through the street.

The Big Boss not only outearned the Shaw Brothers' *Vengeance of a Snow Girl* by nearly fourfold in its first week, it became the highest-grossing film in Hong Kong history, surpassing the Julie Andrews movie, *The Sound of Music*. The Von Trapp family saga had taken nine weeks to gross HKD $2.3 million. *The Big Boss* topped that in nine days. By the time its local run ended ten days later, it had grossed HKD $3.2 million, and had been seen by 1.2 million people, one in four of all Hong Kongers. It went on to shatter records across Asia.

If *The Chinese Boxer* had signaled a turn for Hong Kong cinema, *The Big Boss* ushered in a new era. At the end of the fifties, Bruce had played The Orphan, beset by circumstances and seeking redemption. At the start of the seventies, as change-hungry Asians from Southeast Asia to America were in revolt, he was The New Hero, a symbol of the tidal energies of a generation finding its level.

"Only one person predicted the success of the film," Lau Wing recalled, "and that was Bruce Lee."

When people on the set were talking about how good David Chiang, Ti Lung, or Jimmy Wang Yu were, Bruce smirked and told Lau Wing, "Good? You will know what's good after watching me. We will educate the audiences what really is good. They will disappear after the audiences watch *me*."

"Wing," Bruce told him between shoots, "sitting here we see how a movie is made. If we observe the set from a higher place, the set will be very small. We must aim higher. We must take the American market."

Lau Wing said, "Yes! That's it!"

And yet he could not imagine how it could ever happen.

"I thought he might be popular in Hong Kong," he said, "but how could he make it in America?"

CHAPTER 39
The Mid-Pacific Man

When Li Hoi Chuen and Grace Li first crossed the Pacific in 1939, it took them twenty-one days to make the passage. Bruce's exile journey two decades later took nineteen days. By 1971, he could cross the Pacific in less than two.

Li Hoi Chuen's occupation as an artist allowed him to experience the global mobility of the Asian elite. After the 1965 Hart-Celler Act, the barriers to immigration were no longer as daunting and discouraging for common people, and traffic across the Pacific was no longer expected to move mainly in one direction. Like his father, Bruce would have most of his travel fares paid by those desiring his services. He had become part of a growing class of immigrants whose lives straddled Asia and America.

"I was once asked where I spent most of my time," Bruce told a journalist, "and my answer was 'over the Pacific.'"

In English-speaking Hong Kong, some were reaching for the language to describe this very old, perennially new phenomenon. One of the terms was "Mid-Pacific Man," applied prominently in articles by a white Canadian expat writer named Jack Moore to describe Bruce Lee. It was a loaded term with a long history.

"The Mid-Pacific" was a notion first advanced in Hawai'i at the turn of the 20th century after the United States' forcible takeover of the islands. An American migrant named Alexander Hume Ford began publishing a travel magazine, *The Mid-Pacific*, to promote the idea of Hawai'i as "the Crossroads of the Pacific," and entice other white Americans to settle the islands. In this imagining, the Mid-Pacific was a space of appropriation. The Mid-Pacific Man would Americanize the islands, especially its Oriental populations, and extend the nation's sphere of influence to the Far East, "half the population of the world," all while enjoying the native fruits of paradise.

A half-century later, the cultural traffic had reversed, and the Mid-Pacific was a more fluid space. Moore had reappropriated the term to describe Bruce as an Asian living between two worlds. "His background and training has been acquired in both the Far East and the Far West, and he has even managed to have a couple of really international children," Moore wrote. "Not that Bruce is suffering from any kind of identity crisis, as any Mid-Pacific Man might be expected to do."

The Bruce who had left Hollywood did his best to sound less confused or conflicted about his identity than self-aware and ironic. "Sometimes I feel a little schizophrenic about it," he told Moore. "When I wake up in the morning, I have to remember which side of the ocean I'm on, and whether I'm the superstar or the exotic Oriental support player."

On September 3, 1971, after shooting for *The Big Boss* had wrapped, a thousand fans greeted Bruce and the cast at Kai Tak when they arrived from Bangkok. He departed for Hollywood two days later. He was more busy than he had ever been.

While in Thailand, he had negotiated long-distance with Paramount to shoot an additional three episodes of *Longstreet*. He had demanded they double their offer to two thousand dollars per episode, and he received it. He was on set less than twenty-four hours after touching down at LAX.

Two weeks later, on the eve of the premiere of "The Way of the Intercepting Fist," a review came in from *New York Times* TV writer John J. O'Connor, who praised the "spectacular demonstration of super karate" from "a disciplined superboy, providing a Robin for Longstreet's Batman." "Inner peace is Li's secret weapon," O'Connor wrote. "The Chinaman (who emerges impressively enough to justify a series) lends a deft touch of exotica with advice on how to 'learn the art of dying.'"

The day after the *Times* review, Paramount's Tom Tannenbaum met with Bruce for lunch. He congratulated Bruce and they spoke about an *A-Team*–style action series they were developing called *Tiger Force*. After the episode aired, fan letters poured into the Paramount offices, asking for more Asian philosophy and more of the Asian man. At *Black Belt*, which had published Bruce's article on Jeet Kune Do in the same month, readers passionately debated Bruce's views on classical *karate*.

Demand was building for "the exotic Oriental support player," and Paramount had him locked for more episodes of *Longstreet*. But Stirling Silliphant was unavailable, and none of the other writers knew what to do with Bruce's character. In the three episodes he shot that fall, he was still the guy in the tracksuit who kept the white male star in shape. His acting consisted of trying to look interested as all the white people talked.

On his off days, Bruce took meetings with Blake Edwards at MGM and Rick Rosner at Screen Gems. All this made Ted Ashley and Fred Weintraub nervous. They couldn't stand the idea of losing Bruce. Hadn't they discovered him? But the problem, Ashley knew, was of his own making. Just weeks before, he had nixed Fred Weintraub's *Kung Fu* movie project, worried the concept was still too big a risk.

"The general consensus was that the public would not be willing to accept a Chinese hero," Weintraub recalled. "But I was convinced of the viability of the genre and believed in the script itself so I wasn't about to give up."

To keep Bruce in his orbit, Weintraub tried to hype him up about a Western he was working on called *Kelsey*, in which Bruce would play a third supporting character behind a white and a Black star. As his last act for *Kung Fu*, Weintraub vowed to encourage the Warner Bros. TV division to pick up both the screenplay and Bruce.

One day he stormed past the secretary into the office of Warner Bros. vice president of TV production, Tom Kuhn, and tossed the *Kung Fu* screenplay on his desk.

"What's a kung fu?" Kuhn joked, looking at the title. "I think I got some on my tie at lunch in Chinatown today."

Weintraub grunted, "Just read it."

Impressed by Weintraub's imposing introduction, Kuhn read it that evening. He called the next day to say he loved it, but it couldn't be made for TV. It was too long and too expensive. Weintraub thought for a second, then said, "Tear out every other page."

Kuhn and his boss, president of television Jerry Leider, soon sold the screenplay to ABC's Barry Diller for the network's new *Movie of the Week* slot. All that remained was to find a lead. Weintraub arranged for Bruce to meet with Kuhn and Leider on September 21. To underscore the importance of the meeting, Ashley called Kuhn, explaining that they were trying to find something for this young Chinese man everyone was buzzing about and that Paramount was breathing down their necks.

The afternoon after his lunch with Tannenbaum, Bruce politely introduced himself to the secretary and was escorted into Kuhn's office. He had a gym bag in one hand and a *nunchaku* in the other. Kuhn put his hand out to shake Bruce's, but the actor slammed the door shut with his foot, stepped back, and shouted, "Don't move!" Then he whipped his *nunchakus* around in front of Kuhn's nose.

Kuhn shouted, "Put down that goddamn thing and sit down!"

Bruce dropped his gym bag and said, "Feel my arm."

"It was like touching a rock, and I couldn't believe it," Tom Kuhn recalled. "The room was exploding."

The conversation that followed was much quieter. Bruce showed Kuhn his actor's portfolio and told him about his roles on *Longstreet* and *The Big Boss*. Kuhn brought up the role of Kwai Chang Caine, and Bruce affirmed how much he would love to do it.

"I kind of tried to explain—probably not successfully—to him that Caine was a very peaceful guy. This was a guy who didn't want to fight, he wanted to pull his hat down over his face. He basically wanted to disappear and just do good where he could do good," Kuhn said. "I guess I honestly never knew whether or not Bruce accepted that, whether he bought into it."

Kuhn recalled, "We talked about everything—the world situation, the role of Asians in film, American television . . ."

"In the television world, there were only three clients," Kuhn said. "No one of them could take a chance on going too far out to get out of the mainstream, because you lose that giant television audience and you're screwed."

When the meeting concluded, Kuhn had the impression that Bruce understood the difficulties he faced: "He knew it was a long haul before there was going to be an American television series with an Asian as the leading role. Supporting? Maybe."

But Bruce had left the meeting feeling confident. A Eurasian walking through the Old West armed with the deadliest hand skills imaginable—who else in Hollywood or even Hong Kong was anywhere near as qualified as he to play the part? Warner Bros. had rejected his treatment for *The Warrior*, but perhaps *Kung Fu* would still allow him to become The Warrior.

The signs were positive. Bruce took additional meetings with Warner execs, including one with Ted Ashley, Jerry Leider, and Tom Kuhn all in the room. Kuhn's assistant producer Harvey Frand followed up by soliciting Bruce's notes for revisions of the *Kung Fu* screenplay, and on October 12, Bruce met with Frand to discuss them.

Two days later, Ted Ashley and Jerry Leider moved to lock in Bruce for Warner Bros. Television, perhaps an indication of their confidence in his ability to secure the *Kung Fu* role, and at the very least, a hedge against him fleeing to Paramount or another studio. They offered him a development contract that would advance him twenty-five thousand dollars against fees of ten to seventeen thousand dollars for a pilot and three to four thousand dollars per show telecast. Above the Day-Timer entry for October 14, 1971, he scribbled a Chinese character and decorated it with exclamation points: "勝!!!!! WIN!!!!!"

Nancy Kwan recalled, "We were in a restaurant and Bruce comes to me and he says, 'Hey, I'm going to star in a TV series.' And I said, 'Yeah?' He said, 'Mm-hm.'" I said, 'I don't know, Bruce.' I said, 'I don't know if they are ready in Hollywood to accept an Asian as a lead in a TV series.' 'You want to bet?' I says, 'Yeah. Okay.' So we made a bet."

Bruce and Linda packed their things to move the family to Kowloon. He told her he wasn't going to sign the Warner Bros. contract until he knew how well *The Big Boss* was going to do. When he, Linda, the kids, and Bob Baker arrived at Kai Tak airport on Saturday, October 16, the week before the midnight premiere of *The Big Boss*, they were greeted by Raymond Chow, Maria Yi, Han Ying Chieh, the TVB staff and crew, a large contingent of journalists and photographers, and dozens of outfitted Boy and Girl Scouts standing in formation in front of massive welcome banners. It was loud, crowded, and bright, and Linda and Bob were stunned. As a sleepy Shannon squirmed on her arm, and Brandon held her hand, nonplussed, Linda was trying to comprehend all the pandemonium her husband was causing.

"It was my first exposure to what it was going to be like to be the wife of a movie star, and it filled me with pride," she recalled, "as well as some trepidation about how our lives were changing."

Bruce had become the most sought-after interview in Southeast Asia, and in these early days of stardom he was a willing subject.

A theme developed quickly among the pundits: Will Bruce stay in Hong Kong or seek his fortune in the United States? *The Big Boss* had set off powerful stirrings of recognition among Chinese and working-class communities across Southeast Asia. The press was gauging how much to invest in the actor, but also reflecting the insecurities their readers had about their status in the world. Would Bruce leave them behind to embrace his American destiny? Or would he truly represent them?

At first, Bruce came off as tone deaf. In interviews he chose to talk up his prospects in the States, highlighting his Warner Bros. development deal and the *Kung Fu* TV series. "What I am trying to do is start a whole trend of martial arts films in the U.S. To me they are much more interesting than the gun-slinging sagas of the West," he told a reporter. "In the Westerns you are dealing solely with guns. Here we deal with everything. It is an expression of the human body."

"I should find out within a week whether this thing is on," he told Jack Moore. "If so I will hustle back to Hollywood to make a pilot for a series called *The Warrior*, which is a really freaky adventure series. It's about a Chinese guy who has to leave China because he manage to kill the wrong person, and winds up in the American West in 1860. Can you dig that? All these cowboys on horse with guns and me with a long, green hunk of bamboo. Far out."

In all his Hong Kong interviews that winter, he had never referred to the project by its true name, *Kung Fu*, but by *The Warrior*, his failed pitch. It's not that he didn't know the name of the project. He had met with Tom Kuhn for the role of Kwai Chang Caine, not Ah Sahm. He had met with Ashley, Leider, and other Warner Bros. execs to talk about *Kung Fu*. He had titled his October 12 script notes for them "*Kung Fu* Notes By Bruce Lee." Even in his Hong Kong interviews, Bruce was describing the plot of *Kung Fu*, not *The Warrior*.*

But during this period, it is clear that he was publicly conflating *The Warrior* with *Kung Fu*, and we can only speculate as to why. Perhaps he refused to call the show *Kung Fu* because in Hong Kong he knew the name itself could be misinterpreted and provoke the easy-to-rouse martial arts community, making him countless enemies he didn't want. Perhaps he thought that after securing the starring role he could begin to turn *Kung Fu* into *The Warrior*. Maybe, per Napoleon Hill, he was naming his ambition to manifest it into existence. Perhaps this was simply the way he thought of his projects—as evolving things whose title was whatever he needed to remember them by until they were eternally fixed on-screen—with no regard for things like intellectual property litigation or the satisfaction of future fans and documentarians.

Whatever the case, sometime around his thirty-first birthday, Bruce seemed to have come to a realization of how it would all end. He began lowering expecta-

---

* Among the many differences between the two scripts: In *Warrior*, Ah Sahm is brought to the States by a tong. In *Kung Fu*, Caine is a fugitive from the Manchu government. *The Warrior* is largely set in the tong wars after the Chinese Exclusion Act, while *Kung Fu* is set two decades before it.

tions about the project for everyone in Hong Kong, perhaps even himself. "What's holding things up now is that a lot of people are sitting around Hollywood trying to decide if the American television audience is ready for an Oriental hero," he told Moore. "We could get some really peculiar reactions from places like the Deep South."

All this talk about *The Warrior* made Southeast Asian fans anxious. They wanted him to affirm he really was one of them, that he was not going to desert them for America like some jet-setting transnational Mid-Pacific Man. Bruce was coming to understand that he needed to address concerns that he had become "too Western" for audiences in Asia.

"There are some scenes in *The Big Boss* where I really didn't think I was being Chinese enough," he admitted to Jack Moore. "You have to do a lot of adjusting."

From Hong Kong, Bruce wrote Ted Ashley to propose amendments to the Warner Bros. offer. He wanted participation in any TV series and merchandising and four-month breaks each year to shoot films in Hong Kong. He also remained in communication with Stirling Silliphant, Tom Tannenbaum, and the Paramount staff.

Tannenbaum's team had scrapped *Tiger Force* but engaged Silliphant to entice Bruce with a proposal for a series set in an inner-city school in San Francisco called *The Concrete Children*, in which he would play a tough-as-nails principal dealing with problem kids. It was just a half-step up from playing a teacher. It was also in line with the new rhetoric of Asian Americans as a "model minority," disciplining inner-city children through example and force. The project died quietly.

In the meantime, Bruce decided to renew with Raymond Chow for two more films at twenty thousand dollars apiece. But they were also continuing discussions about forming a joint venture company that Bruce wanted to call Concord Productions. Raymond would finance the movies, Bruce would make them, and they would split the profits. All that remained was for them to figure out how to split the profits. Raymond wanted Bruce to exclusively shoot for Concord, and he wanted 51 percent of the profits while offering Bruce 49 percent. Bruce wanted equal shares and non-exclusivity. If they completed such a deal, it would mark a turning point for actors' bargaining power in the Hong Kong film industry.

Yet negotiations were taking a toll on their partnership. "Raymond's trying to con me," Bruce told Peter Chin. "He needs me more than I need him!"

The Hong Kong tabloids were focused on whether Southeast Asia would be losing Bruce to the States. As one headline put it: "Will Bruce Lee Stay in Hong Kong or Return to the U.S.? Audiences Have Taken a Deep Interest in the Development of the Matter."

An article in an English-language newspaper, the *China Mail*, speculated on how much he might be paid—sixty thousand Hong Kong dollars a week in the United States for *The Warrior*—versus what he might receive for a Hong Kong movie—Jimmy Wang Yu was reportedly getting two hundred thousand Hong Kong dollars per film.

When a journalist caught up with Bruce, he now offered mixed messages about returning to the United States. Perhaps he was beginning to be tactful. Perhaps he was truly torn:

> I am leaving all things to them. To me, it doesn't really matter whether or not *The Warrior* is made. It has its advantages and disadvantages.
>
> Naturally, I am proud to be the first Chinese star on American TV. But I find filming for TV dull and monotonous.

More pointedly, the article noted that *The Warrior* was scheduled to commence shooting on December 1 in Los Angeles, and that Bruce had not yet been informed if he was to be its star. Bruce told the reporter the shoot date had instead become their deadline to tell him of their decision.

By December 2, the question was trending. With his oblique answers, Bruce had invited them not just to speculate about his future, but make claims on his identity.

"In the U.S., it's unheard of for a Chinese person to play the starring role. Bruce Lee wants to fight on behalf of Chinese people for this point of 'pride.' He wants the people in the American film industry to understand that a film starring a Chinese man can also appeal to audiences there," wrote one pundit. "This is why he's caught in a dilemma."

"Bruce Lee said that if he cannot be the male lead in *The Warrior*, then he will lose interest in productions in the U.S.," another wrote. "With the compensation he is getting right now, there would be no point for him to fly back and forth anymore."

Still another pundit articulated the hope of his fans in Southeast Asia: "In the American South, racism is still very common. Under these circumstances, ABC needs to investigate whether using a colored man to play the lead would be well received by the audience there. If they find it is not, then Bruce Lee can use that as an excuse to get out of his contract for his show and would no longer need to go back to the U.S."

In the second week of December, a tiny item appeared on the international page of *Variety*, the American movie industry magazine of record. It was entitled "'Big Boss' Hong Kong's New Boxoffice Champ," and it noted that Bruce Lee's movie had outearned *The Sound of Music* in the colony by eight hundred thousand Hong Kong dollars. "Meanwhile," it concluded, "Lee is now in Hong Kong filming his second

Golden Harvest film, 'The Intercepting Fists.' He is due to return to Los Angeles this month for a top role in Warners' full-length TV feature, 'The Warrior.'" The wording of the item, particularly the titles of the film and TV projects, suggests the authorship of Bruce or one of his friends. If he wanted to return to Hollywood now, perhaps this was his last card to play—a strategic leak to the American media.

The item ran in the December 8 edition of *Variety* in the United States. But by the time it hit the newsstands it was already outdated, its last line untrue. In Hong Kong two days before, Bruce had received a hurried cable from Jerry Leider at the Warner Bros. Television offices in Burbank.*

AM TERRIBLY SORRY TO TELL YOU THAT I WAS UNABLE TO WORK OUT THE KUNGFU PICTURE FOR YOUR [sic] DUE TO ENORMOUS DIFFERENCES OF OPINION AND PRESSURES FROM THE NETWORK REGARDING CASTING OF THIS PICTURE

HOWEVER AM PERSONALLY COMMITTED TO DEVELOP ANOTHER PROJECT FOR YOU AND LOOK FORWARD TO MEETING YOU WHEN YOU RETURN TO THE STATES

---

* Hong Kong is sixteen hours ahead of Hollywood. The cable is dated Tuesday, December 7, Hong Kong time, and appears to have been sent from Hollywood on Monday, December 6, at 12:46 p.m. It was sent nearly a week past the deadline Bruce had publicly noted.

The item in *Variety* was datelined December 7, meaning it had to have come from Hong Kong on or before December 6, Hollywood time. It ran on December 8, which would have been December 9 in Hong Kong.

It is possible to ask now: Was Leider's cable intended to belatedly quell any further speculation about Bruce's participation in *Kung Fu* or to short-circuit a lobbying campaign like the one a generation before to get Anna May Wong to star in *The Good Earth*?

Oddly enough, December 8, 1971, was the day that Hong Kong marked the 30th anniversary of Japan's World War II attack.

CHAPTER 40
Yellow-Faced Chinese

It had been six years since ABC had killed *Number One Son* and three years since the emergence of the Asian American. In *Kung Fu* the network had a second chance to make history. But they reverted to form. Hollywood was racist because America was racist, and around it went.

In September 1971, hours after Bruce Lee's audition meeting for *Kung Fu*, Fred Weintraub had called Tom Kuhn to ask how the kid had done. "He's amazing," Kuhn told him. "I've never seen anything like that. But getting him the lead is still going to be a long shot. He might be too authentic."

Perhaps Kuhn had made up his mind as soon as Bruce opened his mouth. There were other reasons for Kuhn to reject Bruce—lack of charisma, acting experience, fitness for the role—for which Weintraub or Ashley might have found ready rebuttals. But as Kuhn told the Bruce Lee documentarian Bao Nguyen nearly fifty years later, "The bottom line at the end of the half-hour was, and it killed me to even think this, but Bruce's accent was going to be a little tough on the American television audiences."

Shortly afterward, Kuhn called Ted Ashley to tell him the same. According to Kuhn, Ashley responded, "You know what, I understand that. I'm going to try to find something else for him."

Even Weintraub would recall, "To my continued frustration, Tom was right."

On a linguistic level, all English is accented, no matter who is speaking it. We recognize this fact when we hear someone talk and think, Oh, they must be from Brooklyn, Canada, the South. Hollywood had forced Asian Americans like Keye Luke and Victor Sen Yung—who both spoke in the Mid-Atlantic accent that has come to be accepted as the standard of American English—to deliver their lines in an exaggerated inauthentic singsong pidgin, a Hollywood Chinese accent. These actors, and all who would follow them, knew what Kuhn knew: the question was never about accent, it was about the social value of an accent.

And yet, in order to capitalize on the growing fascination with China, ABC scheduled the *Kung Fu* pilot movie to premiere the same week that President Nixon was making his historic trip to meet with Mao Zedong in Beijing. Shooting began in December 1971, a week after Jerry Leider informed Bruce he had been rejected. Instead, standing before the camera was David Carradine, born of Western European descent to the famed American character actor John Carradine.

"They put a little tiny corner at the inside of my eyes. It made my eyes look slightly more Oriental, and they painted me yellow," Carradine said. "And also I bent my legs a little bit most of the time so I didn't look so tall."

"That's where I first heard the term 'epicanthic fold,'" Tom Kuhn said, "and our brilliant makeup people did a little job on his eyelids, very minor but enough to give the Asian look some kind of authenticity."

Over the years, Kuhn insisted he had auditioned every Asian he could find. "It was not a very large talent pool, and when it came to a starring role, it was *really* not a very big pool, which caused us a lot of difficulties because the Asian acting community in Hollywood got on their horses about it," Kuhn said. "George Takei, as I recall, led the charge."

The actor and activist George Takei first saw—"Didn't meet," he said—Bruce Lee at Paramount Studios while he was shooting the pilot for a TV show called *Star Trek* as Lieutenant Hikaru Sulu, working alongside Nichelle Nichols, who played Officer Uhura, a major breakthrough for actors of color.

At an adjacent soundstage, Bruce was dressed in his black Kato suit shooting the pilot for *The Green Hornet*. Takei had stepped out for a smoke break with Jimmy Doohan, who played Scotty. Having spotted another Asian in the house, Bruce walked over.

Without a word, Takei said, "He made some martial arts movement at superspeed, the arms and the leg kicking and all, and suddenly our conversation stopped. We were stunned, astounded. He just moved like a whirlwind. Then he'd stop and he'd think, and he'd do another one real fast. Then the assistant came out and said, 'Bruce, we're ready for you now.' And he went back in."

Five years later, George heard from his agent that ABC was casting for the role of Kwai Chang Caine, a potential starring role for an Asian male. But Takei recalled his agent also telling him, "They're interviewing people who have martial arts background." Takei did not and chose not to audition. He knew most of the Asian American actors in Hollywood at the time, and did not know of anyone who had auditioned.

"I thought the obvious person to play it was Bruce," he said.

Takei was part of a generation of artists organizing to tell Asian American stories. In 1965, Mako, James Hong, Beulah Quo, and four other actors formed the East West Players theater company. At UCLA, the EthnoCommunications program and the Black collective called LA Uprising produced an influential cohort of filmmakers of color. In 1971, Bob Nakamura and three others from UCLA started the film organization Visual Communications. These institutions became cornerstones of the emerging Asian American arts movement.

Takei became the cultural affairs chair of the Japanese American Citizens League, leading the organization to call out racist content and casting. Their agitation forced ABC-TV to change the title of a movie of the week, a World War II interracial love story set in the camps originally called *My Husband, the Enemy*. They made a list of what they believed were anti-Asian movies, like the Fu Manchu films, and pressured stations and networks to stop airing them.

When the trade magazines announced that Carradine had been given the *Kung Fu* lead, a group of activists led by Alan Nishio, the director of UCLA's Asian American Studies Center, staged a picket at ABC's offices. The network refused to replace Carradine but agreed to hire Asian actors and advisers, a partial victory. Over three seasons, *Kung Fu* provided work for so many actors that *Variety* magazine called them "the cream of Hollywood's Oriental actor colony"—including Keye Luke, Nancy Kwan, Victor Sen Yung, Benson Fong, Philip Ahn, James Hong, and even George. But all of them also knew that nothing had changed since Anna May Wong had protested *The Good Earth*.

"Casting Caucasians as Asians—that was what the initial fuss was about," George said. "The case of Bruce Lee is a failure of the movement to get representation."

Tom Kuhn said, "ABC got a lot of flak for it, I got a lot of flak for it, Warner Bros. got a lot of flak for it, but at the end of the day you have to be able to sell what you are out there selling, and I didn't find one Asian actor that I thought I could sell to ABC."

Linda saw enough of *Kung Fu* to become outraged over how much of it seemed stolen directly from Bruce. The opening sequence featured Caine wandering through the desert, in scenes that resembled photos James Coburn had snapped of Bruce in the Thar Desert. When Master Kan told Caine he would not be able to leave the temple until he could snatch the pebble from his hand, it reminded her of Bruce's coin tricks. Caine's blind teacher, Master Po, seemed modeled after Bruce's blind master Ah Sahm. Kwai Chang Caine even played a flute.

She was still angry when she wrote in her biography, "I understand that neither Warner Brothers or ABC had even considered starring Bruce in the series; they thought he was too small; too Chinese; that he wasn't a big enough name to sustain a weekly series; that he was too inexperienced. I doubt if they ever really tried to rationalize their ideas; they obviously just didn't see him as the right heavyweight material. Probably it just never occurred to them that a Chinese could become a hero in a white man's world. . . ."

Privately, Jerry Leider's bombshell telegram had left Bruce somber and devastated. "He just couldn't understand it," Linda recalled. "He was so hurt and just disgusted with the whole system."

But two days later, on December 9, even as the *Variety* article was still circulating and ABC's machine was gearing up for the *Kung Fu* pilot, Bruce needed to pull himself together to explain to his public what had happened. He did so for a live interview with the Canadian television journalist Pierre Berton, an extraordinary session that stands as the best representation of his maturing views ever captured on video.

Not knowing that Warner Bros. and ABC had already made its decision, Berton had hoped to frame the Hong Kong media's persistent question—"Will he stay or will he go?"—as an existential one, the Mandarin Superstar and Mid-Pacific Man facing a choice between East and West. Bruce knew that there was no choice for him to make, and that no one who looked like him had ever really had that choice.

The two sit together on a darkened set, Pierre in his trademark bow tie, Bruce in a sporty suede jacket.

"You set up a school in Hollywood, didn't you? For people like James Garner and Steve McQueen and the others. Why would they want to learn Chinese martial art? Because of a movie role?"

"When I teach, you know, all type of knowledge ultimately means self-knowledge," Bruce says. "They want to learn to express themselves through some movement—be it anger, be it determination or whatsoever.

"Ultimately martial art means honestly expressing yourself. Now, it is very difficult to do. I mean, it is easy for me to put on a show and be cocky and be flooded with a cocky feeling and then feel, like, pretty cool and all that," he continues. "But to express oneself honestly, not lying to oneself, and to express myself in this? *That*, my friend, is very hard to do."

Pierre asks him to recite his "Be water" monologue from *Longstreet*, and Bruce obliges. Then Berton says, "There's a pretty good chance that you'll get a TV series in the States called *The Warrior*."

"That was the original idea," Bruce says. "Paramount wants me to be in a television series. On the other hand, Warner Bros. wants me to be in another one. But both of them, I think, they want to do a modernized type of thing and they think the western idea is out."

Pierre circles through other questions before returning to the one he wants to ask. "You came back to Hong Kong on the verge of success in Hollywood and full of it. And suddenly, on the strength of one picture, you become a superstar," he says. "Now what are you going to do? Are you going to be able to live in both worlds? Are you going to be a superstar here or one in the States or both?"

Bruce smiles and dodges. "Well, let me say this. First of all, the word 'superstar' really turn me off, and I'll tell you why. Because the word 'star,' man, it's an illusion, it's something what the public calls you. You should look upon oneself as an actor."

"Let's get back to the question. Are you going to stay in Hong Kong and be famous? Are you going to go to the United States to be famous? Or are you going to try and have your cake and eat it too?"

"I am going to do both, because, you see, I have already made up my mind that in the United States, I think something about the Oriental, I mean, *the true* Oriental should be shown."

"Hollywood sure as heck hasn't."

"You better believe it, man. I mean, it's always that pigtail and bouncing around and Chop Chop, you know, with the eyes slanted and all that.* And I think that's very out of date."

Pierre asks whether Bruce was supposed to have played Charlie Chan's number-one son. Bruce responds that the role was for "a new Chinese James Bond," but also admits about his performance as Kato: "I did a really terrible job in that, I have to say."

"Let me ask you, however, about the problems that you face as a Chinese hero in an American series. Have people come up in the industry and said, 'Well, we don't know how the audience are going to take a "non-American"'?"

If Bruce notices the category error—after all, he is more "American" than the Canadian Berton—he does not pause to correct the host.

"Well, such question has been raised. In fact, it is being discussed. And that is why *The Warrior* is probably not going to be on."

The camera pulls in tightly.

"You see, because unfortunately, such thing does exist in this world. You see, like, I don't know, certain part of the country, right? Where they think that business-wise it's a risk. And I don't blame them," he says, in a syntax as tangled as his thoughts. "It's like in Hong Kong, if a foreigner come and became a star—if I were the man with the money, I probably would have my own worry of whether or not the acceptance would be there."

"But that's all right." Bruce is nodding now at Berton. "Because if you honestly express yourself, it doesn't matter."

"Are you too Western for Oriental audiences?"

Bruce is smiling now and wagging his finger. "I have been criticized for that." He pauses.

"Well, let me say this. When I do the Chinese film, I'll try my best not to be as American, as I have been adjusting to for the last twelve years in the States. But when I go back to the States, it seems to be the other way around."

"You're too exotic, eh?"

"Yeah, man. I mean, they trying to get me to do too many things that are really for the sake of being exotic. Do you understand what I'm trying to say?"

---

* Chop Chop was a cartoon character created by Will Eisner and Chuck Cuidera in 1941. Written and illustrated as a bucktoothed, queue-wearing, ukulele-playing idiot cook, the character persisted in the DC Comic Universe until the mid-fifties.

Bruce frowns, like he has a lot more to say but knows that he shouldn't. Pierre saves him with a commercial break.

Nineteen seventy-one had been a thunder ride of a year—from the failure of *The Silent Flute* to the triumph of *The Big Boss* and, after Raymond finally agreed to Bruce's demands for equal profit splits and non-exclusivity, the formation of Concord Productions. But after the *Kung Fu* rejection, he was as uncertain of his future as he had been in 1969. To bolster himself he carefully recopied Napoleon Hill's "Creed for Self-Discipline" into his 1972 Day-Timer for the new year, and added some additional maxims:

We live, not live for.

Beware of illusion.

Be flexible so you can change with change.

When I listened to my mistakes I have grown.

On Golden Harvest letterhead, he prepared a formal letter to Ted Ashley, his last of the year. "Dear Ted," he typed, mistakes and all, "I am sorry to hear about the outcome of 'The Warrior.' Well, you cannot win them all, but damn it, I am goint [sic] to win one of these days."

Then he listed bullet points for "Several things I like to talk with you":

(A) Knowing my capability as an actor, plus the ever-increasing mentioning of martial art—which I always feel such "unique" and exciting action film has universal appeal—as well as the China situation, I feel Warner can definitely create a script, preferably for feature, tailored for me.

(B) I have started a film company (Concord) with a trusted friend of mine, and am looking very much to work with Warner on some future projects, or maybe Warner can help in releasing our future pictures in the States—like 'A Fistful of Dollar' from Italy.

He asked for his advance of twenty-five thousand dollars to be paid. But in a tone that echoed the boyish agreeability of his early letters to William Dozier and hinted at how much the *Kung Fu* snub still stung, he concluded,

Enclosed you will find some clippings which may or may not interest you, but more important still is the fact that I am daily improving in my acting and as a human being, and my dedication will definitely lead me to my goal. Any fair and rightful assistance from you will be deeply appreciated. Again, thank you kindly for your kind participation on the initial stage of *The Warrior*.

But this self-effacement feels like an act, perhaps even the beginning of a new strategy. For now he fully understood the gap between how he was seen in Asia and in America. More specifically, he had come to see himself in the way Asians from America saw themselves. He could review the entire arc of his acting journey in a different light.

The question had been inescapable—not just Pierre Berton, but other reporters and friends in Hong Kong and Southeast Asia had asked it of him: Why had he given up working in America to shoot Chinese films in Hong Kong? Why would he walk away from Hollywood, the pinnacle of global popular culture?

Picture him vexed at first by the question. Were they asking him if he thought he was incapable of making it on the biggest stage? No, they had assumed his future in America was as bright as it was in Asia.

Picture him, then, confused. Didn't they understand how things *really were* for Asians in America?

He wrote a piece for a Taiwanese newspaper to explain his dawning realization: "The truth is, I am an American-born Chinese. My identity is Chinese beyond all doubts. At least I have always looked upon myself as a Chinese during all my years in the States, and in the eyes of the Westerners I am of course a Chinese."

He bluntly assessed how he had appeared in the broken mirror of Hollywood:

[T]he producers in Hollywood, thinking that my martial arts could be an attraction, invited me to play a role in their films. The television series *The Green Hornet* is an example. At this moment, I found it was meaningless to go on shooting movies like that because I did not fit in with my roles.

This is not to say that I could not play my roles well. The truth is I am a yellow-faced Chinese. I cannot possibly become an idol for Caucasians, not to mention rousing the emotions of my countrymen. Because of this, I decided to come back to serve the Chinese film industry.

He was not merely flattering his fans. In this moment, only *here*, he was saying, can I really be *seen*.

Unlike his activist Asian American contemporaries, Bruce did not yet have the language to name himself outside of the received binary of American versus Oriental. He was unable to imagine himself into the third space Asian Americans had begun to make. But he certainly shared a powerful feeling with them: that the Oriental would always be a "non-American," a nonbeing, until this form of unseeing was confronted at the source.

• • •

When Pierre Berton returns from the break, he asks Bruce, "Let me ask you whether the change in attitude on the part of the Nixon administration towards China has helped your chances of starring in an American TV series."

Bruce laughs. "Well, first of all, this happened before that. But I do think that things of Chinese will be quite interesting for the next few years.

"I mean, not that I'm politically inclined toward anything," he says, "it's a very rich period to be in. Like if I were born, let's say—forty years ago? If I have a thought in my mind, I said, 'Boy, I'm going to star in a movie or star in a television series in America.' Well, that might be a vague dream. But I think right now—*maybe*?"

"Do you still think of yourself as Chinese? Or do you ever think of yourself as North American?"

"You know what? I want to think of myself as a human being, because, I mean, I don't want to sound like, you know, 'As Confucius say,' but, 'Under the sky, under the heaven, man, is but one family.' It just so happen, man, that people are different."

He had transformed the joyous old toast that he, James Yimm Lee, and his friends had often lifted to each other into a universal call for respect, solidarity, and equality. It would become one of his signature sayings in the decades hence, as misunderstood as Martin Luther King Jr.'s dream for his four children, that they might "one day live in a nation where they will not be judged by the color of their skin but by the content of their character."

In that moment, Bruce had offered a call to colorblindness, but also a strong rebuke to Hollywood's racism, and a deeply felt plea for people to see him—and others like him—in all their humanity.

With that, Pierre Berton thanked him.

CHAPTER 41
Fists and Mayhem

After *The Big Boss*, Bruce needed to make a second movie to fulfill his Golden Harvest contract. The placeholder title in his original contract had been *King of the Chinese Boxers*. In the press, Bruce had called his next project *The Intercepting Fist*, but all that was hype. Now Golden Harvest needed something real.

Raymond Chow and Leonard Ho decided to take a Ni Kuang script idea that they had been holding for Lo Wei and Jimmy Wang Yu and give it to Bruce. The idea centered on the republican-era Chinese hero Huo Yuanjia, the famed cofounder of the Jing Wu Association, who had died at the relatively young age of forty-two. But then they learned that a Taiwanese company was about to release a similar biopic on Huo.

Lo Wei instead proposed a character named Chen Zhen, Huo Yuanjia's fictional first son, who would avenge his father's death at the hands of the Japanese imperialists. Bruce and Raymond liked the idea. When Bruce left for Los Angeles in September 1971, he could mark his six years of progress from being recruited to play Charlie Chan's number-one son to playing Huo Yuanjia's.

Set designer Chan King-Sam constructed a set for a Japanese *dojo* with a dramatic backdrop of the painted character "武"—*mo* in Cantonese, for "martial," as in *beimo*; *wu* in Mandarin, as in "Jing Wu"; or *bū* in Japanese, as in *bushido*. Bruce returned to join the cast for a promotional photo shoot at Golden Harvest's new studios on Hammer Hill Road to publicize his still unnamed next film.*

These photos are some of the most striking of his career. Bruce kicked and tossed sword-wielding Japanese villains. He flexed like the warriors in the old Jing Wu Association photos in the book Uncle Siu had gifted him when he was eighteen. The highlight of the marketing package would be an extended trailer featuring Bob Baker as the Russian fighter Petrov, concluding in a face-to-face ready-to-rumble pose that would be replicated in countless MMA fight posters decades later. It would be shown in theaters still screening *The Big Boss*.

But Lo had barely written a word of the new movie. And Bruce refused to proceed until there was an actual script to consider.

The family had settled into a two-room flat on the thirteenth floor in an upscale Kowloon neighborhood called Waterloo Hill, just a mile from La Salle College.

---

* Golden Harvest had recently purchased Yung Hwa Studios from the Cathay Organization, and this movie would be one of the first to be shot on the new campus.

Linda was adjusting to a downsized Third World life. The elevators often broke down, so she and Bruce took to running the staircases for exercise. The kitchen was Hong Kong sized, narrow and small, and the clothes needed to be hand-washed and hung outside the window on a bamboo pole to dry. The first time she tried to hang her clothes, the pole collapsed from the weight and her day's wash fell thirteen floors to the street. Bruce invited his childhood friend Wu Ngan and his new bride to move in to spare Linda the household chores. It made him happy, and her uncomfortable.

Bruce enlisted Raymond Chow to accompany him to La Salle to seek admission for Brandon, nervous that the brothers might remember his reputation. They enrolled Shannon in an elite preschool. It was the life he had dreamed of before he had met Linda. For Linda, who was learning Cantonese so she could communicate with Ngan Jai and his wife, and whose only acquaintances came from Bruce's circle, it was a life she never could have imagined.

Ravenous tabloid writers had begun showing up at the door of his flat. They published his apartment address. They disclosed the route and time of his daily runs. They gave ample column inches to *gung fu* men issuing challenges to Bruce.

"I find this sort of thing really annoying," he told one of them. "I'm not going to fight with anybody."

He called his Chinese American friend Dan Lee in Los Angeles to vent his frustration. "I haven't as yet been able to control my anger," he said.

But didn't his decision not to respond, Dan replied, mark "a process of maturity"?

"Not *maturity*," Bruce said, calmer and becoming philosophical. "There is no such word as 'maturity.' Rather, 'matur*ing*.' Because when there is a maturity, there is a conclusion and a cessation, man. That's the end. That's when the coffin is closed. I mean, you might be deteriorating physically in the long process of aging, but man, in your daily discovery—it's still the same every day."

Bruce grew a beard and, when he appeared in public, wore hats and dark glasses. He started doing his morning and evening runs with Tony Lau Wing and an entourage of stuntmen, who could serve as security if they were confronted in the streets. Over the phone, he commiserated with Nancy Kwan, who had recently returned to the city to care for her ailing father.

"Hong Kong's a small place and they love to gossip, the Chinese press. They're going to write whatever sells newspapers," said Nancy. "You couldn't avoid it."

Golden Harvest had Hong Kong's hottest star, someone so big that the company had become a real threat to Shaw Brothers' domination. Shintaro Katsu, the actor who played Zatoichi, had personally arranged for two of his actors to appear in Bruce's next movie. But tensions between Bruce and Lo Wei again threatened the project.

This time, Raymond and Leonard Ho themselves stepped in to rewrite the script, turning it over in just seventy-two hours and making changes that would free Bruce from the burden of the myth of Huo and the Jing Wu. Chen Zhen would not be Huo's son but instead his fifth disciple, a rebellious loner seeking vengeance for his master at all costs. Raymond promised Bruce more control over the fight choreography—even though Han Ying-Chieh was again scheduled to be the action director. Bruce finally agreed to participate and he and Bob Baker left to join the cast and crew in Macao. The production team burned the final title—*Fist of Fury*, or *Jing Wu Men*—into the marketing trailer and sent it off to theaters.

As soon as shooting began Bruce took control of his fights. When the actors and stuntmen gathered to shoot the first fight scenes in the *dojo*, the stuntman Zebra Pan recalled, "Han Ying-Chieh says, 'Okay Bruce, let's try this.' And Bruce goes, 'No, how about this?' And for the first time started to really *do* Bruce Lee, to do all the stuff with the multiple kicks and the nunchaku and everything. We were just knocked out by it and after that Han Ying-Chieh just kept quiet." Step by step, Bruce walked the entire room through the fight. He and the stuntmen were united in a new mission. Lau Wing recalled, "Each fight scene had to be something fresh and new for the audience."

But his relationship with Lo Wei continued to worsen. Bruce brought books on acting and cinematography to the set to study. Nora Miao recalled, "I noticed he was learning other things, like how the cameras were set up, how to position the lighting. He was learning everything about films." Bruce felt he was demonstrating his commitment to the movie's success while Lo Wei was off gambling.

Bruce and Nora prepared to shoot the midnight love scene. They were both nervous. They had brushed their teeth, and Bruce was dipping into a pack of chewing gum to keep his breath fresh. Bruce asked Lo for advice on how he and Nora should approach the scene, and the two rehearsed. But when the time came to shoot, the director was not to be found, until they heard the unmistakable sound of the greyhound reports on the radio.

One day Bruce finally threatened Lo Wei with a walkout. The director had given instructions to everyone, then left the set. Minutes later he could be heard yelling for his horses above the sound of the radio announcer. Bruce screamed at the director, "What are you doing?" Then to the cast and crew he shouted, "Everybody go home!"

Lam Ching-Ying recalled, "In fact we didn't wrap, but he made his point."

"They probably both resented each other a bit," Nora Miao recalled, "and those feelings accumulated over time."

If *The Big Boss* marked Bruce's return, *Fist of Fury* signals his true arrival. In the opening scene, Chen hurries into the Jing Wu school in a monsoonal downpour dressed in a Sun Yat-sen suit, colored white in the Chinese sign of mourning. He throws himself into the grave hysterically and must be stopped with a spade to the head. Bruce plays the scene with all the emotion of his return to his own father's funeral. Elsewhere in the film, he also demonstrates some comic range, disguised as a rickshaw driver, a newspaper hawker, and a phone repairman.

Fist of Fury is set in Shanghai, an early-twentieth-century metropolis beset by foreign aggression, where the Japanese and European imperial powers have divided the city into their own concessions and displaced and disenfranchised the native Chinese. Chen Zhen is an anti-colonial hero, patriotic to the core, taking down the *dojo* with a *nunchaku*, kicking down a park sign that says "No Dogs and Chinese Allowed," and finally slaying Chinese collaborators and Russian and Japanese aggressors on the soil they have taken from the Chinese.

When Chen Zhen fights Bob Baker's Petrov, he conjures the legend of Huo Yuanjia, who supposedly had defeated a Russian aggressor who had blustered about his mastery over the sick men of Asia. Scholars say the fight never happened, because the Russian fighter actually punked out. They also debate whether signs hung in Shanghai's Hongkou Park had ever explicitly banned Chinese. But such debates were beside the point.

"Why did people like *Fist of Fury* so much?" Nora Miao said. "The fact it was about fighting the Japanese added a nationalistic aspect to the film. But the main thing is, that sense of good and evil was so unambiguous."

Like Cheng Chao-An in *The Big Boss*, Chen Zhen in *Fist of Fury* is propelled forward by a losing battle between his impulses and a discipline that might better serve the good of the collective. "Chen Zhen is a headstrong, impulsive, and heroic personality with a sense of 'Yang' masculinity," Bruce told a reporter. "That's why he is reckless, dares to take risks, and is full of excitement."

In *The Big Boss*, Cheng Chao-An bumbles into losing his community's trust and then, disastrously, the community itself. In *Fist of Fury*, Chen Zhen is so consumed by his desire for vengeance that he brings violence upon his *gung fu* schoolmates and everything his master has built. He is blinded by his rage, and everyone else must suffer for it. These tensions—and the body count they create—rush him toward the tragic conclusion.

Where *The Big Boss* was meandering, *Fist of Fury* is focused and propulsive. In the first fight in the *dojo*, Chen Ching-Chu's camera swirls, darts, then swirls again to follow Chen Zhen's every movement. After he disposes of the entire *dojo*, he strikes a hero's pose. When he kills the Japanese collaborators in the kitchen of the Jing Wu building, the frames slow to emphasize Chen Zhen's deadly power.[*]

Bruce had wanted to include Bob Baker specifically for the climactic fight in the

---

[*] Here, too, is another symbolic killing of Han Ying-Chieh.

garden. Together the two old friends finally broke free of kung fu movie conventions. Bruce had asked Baker to fight in the style of Jimmy Wang Yu. But as Baker recalled, he was too nervous in front of the camera to act.

"I had a hard time because I wasn't an actor," he said. "He had to really fight me."

In most of their fight scenes, they kicked and punched each other as hard as they would have in the Oakland *kwoon* or James Yimm Lee's garage. At one point when Bruce and Bob were on the ground Bruce bit him, just as he had always recommended his students do if they were locked up. "I just about pulled his tooth out," Bob said.

Lo Wei played the police investigator who betrays Chen Zhen, escorting him to face a firing squad of policemen awaiting him at the gates of the Jing Wu school. Off-screen, the two would have a final fight over the film's ending. Lo Wei argued that the virtuous hero could not die. Golden Harvest had to reserve the prerogative of Chen Zhen sequels. But to Bruce, Chen Zhen was less like Wong Fei-Hung than William Goldman's and George Roy Hill's antiheroes, Butch Cassidy and the Sundance Kid. Chen needed to pay for all the blood he had shed.

"We argued for a long time," said Lo Wei. "Bruce's self-conceitedness and arrogance had emerged, and his attitude upset me."

Raymond Chow stepped in again to mediate. Golden Harvest execs landed on the ambiguity of a freeze frame, preserving Chen Zhen's scream and flying kick. Lo Wei and Golden Harvest had given themselves room to figure out a sequel later.

"At the end I died from the gunfire," Bruce told Dan Lee, a line he would repeat to journalists. "It's a very worthwhile death."

To satisfy demand, Golden Harvest set up several premiere showings across Hong Kong and Kowloon in advance of the general release on March 22, 1972. Bruce and Bob Baker slipped into a screening and sat in the front row. In the end, when the audience roared its approval, Bob turned to Bruce with tears in his eyes and shook his hand, exclaiming, "Boy am I happy for you!"

Fist of Fury did even better than *The Big Boss*, grossing HKD $4.4 million and millions more across Asia. Even in Japan—where Raymond Chow had made some strategic edits and line changes but left the storyline intact—*Fist of Fury* became one of the top-grossing movies of the year.

The anti-war activist and folk singer Phil Ochs finished a tour of Southeast Asia and on his last day in Manila stepped into a theater to kill some time. A double feature of *The Big Boss* and *Fist of Fury* was playing. With a San Miguel beer and a bag of peanuts, he sat dumbfounded at Bruce's electric gestures—his lip-quivering stare, his thumb wipe, the leer with which he fingered his own wounds and licked his own blood.

"I could hardly believe my eyes," he recalled. "When he gets to the major villains it becomes a dance of extraordinary beauty." He was just as astonished by the alchemic reaction in the dark theater: "The audience is hysterical: clapping, cheering, sometimes leaping to their feet."

Across Southeast Asia *Fist of Fury* was causing mayhem. In the Philippines, the film packed houses for over six months, causing panicked national economists and politicians to intervene. Mito Uyehara wrote, "The government finally had to limit the amount of foreign film imports to protect their domestic film producers." In Singapore, scalpers sold two-dollar tickets for forty-five dollars, and traffic jams near theaters clogged the city streets so badly that authorities shut down the movie to clear the roads.

Back home, Nancy Kwan received a call from a friend telling her that after the screening, the audience had torn out the seats in anarchic ecstasy, an echo of the youth protests in the streets. "Good for Bruce!" she exclaimed. "He's invoking these riots going on now!"

All across Asia Bruce's screams were now the war cry of the unheard, and he the embodiment of their uprisings, avenging their suffering and delivering them—at least for a moment in a darkened theater—a feeling of freedom.

He was ready to win over the world—if he could survive success.

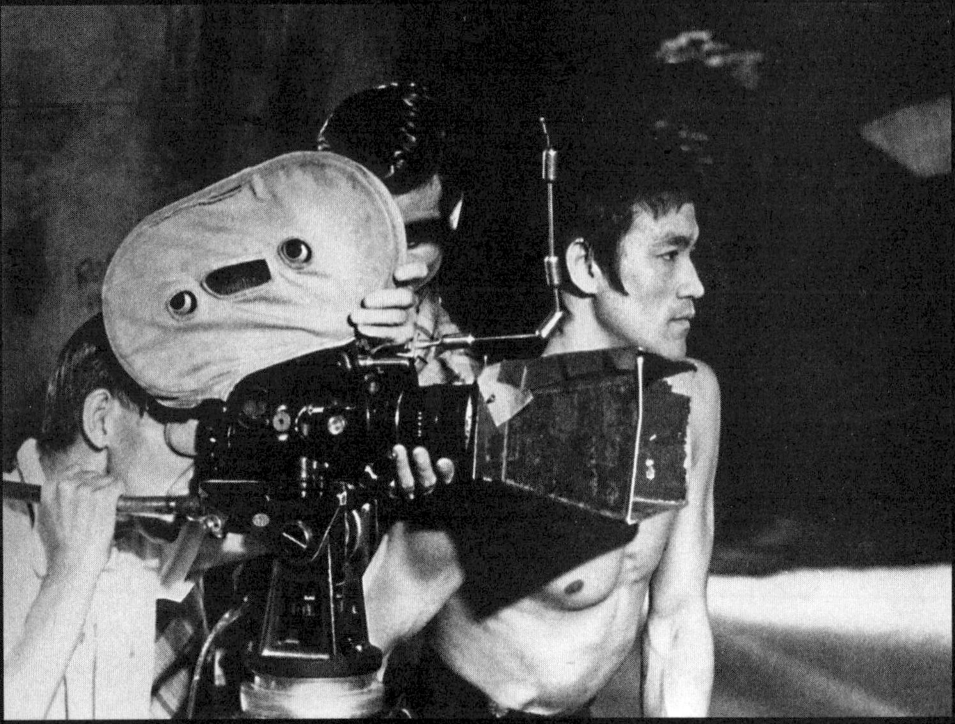

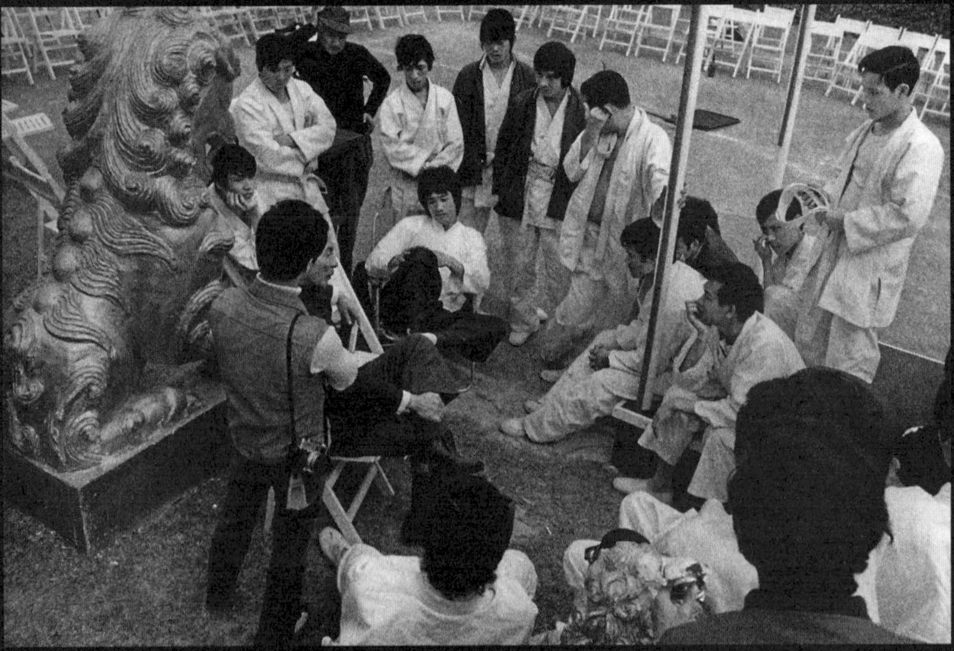

PART XII
Watch Me Now

1972–1973

> Such disfiguring of senses engenders the minor feelings of paranoia, shame, irritation, and melancholy.
>
> —CATHY PARK HONG

On set, *Way of the Dragon*, 1972. Photo courtesy of the Bruce Lee Family Archive.

On set with Shek Kin and the stuntmen, *Enter the Dragon*, 1973. Photo courtesy of the Bruce Lee Family Archive.

CHAPTER 42
The World Stage

The strategist, the person of experience, knows this: for those who hold power in times of upheaval, change is an acceptable, even necessary risk. War opens social mobility to the excluded. Economic decline expands representation to the unseen.* For those without power, the right things often happen for the wrong reasons.

At the beginning of the 1970s, the old Hollywood studio system was in a state of collapse. After years of being weakened by antitrust legislation, challenged by television, and undermined by its reliance on expensive blockbusters out of step with the new generation, the major studios were struggling to stay afloat. In 1971, Hollywood's weekly box office take was less than a third of what it was at its peak in 1946.

During this downturn, Black audiences were "discovered." Trade magazines reported that while Blacks were only about 11 percent of the US population, they made up more than 30 percent of filmgoers in the most important first-run theaters. This discovery followed years of pressure from Black artists and activists that had resulted in the Justice Department pushing six studios and two networks to desegregate their hiring practices.

At the same time, forgotten audiences in the dead center of American cities would become the unlikely source of industry renewal.

In 1970, Ossie Davis's *Cotton Comes to Harlem* earned $15 million for United Artists on a $2.2 million budget. The following year, Melvin Van Peebles's *Sweet Sweetback's Baadasssss Song* established the market for what would come to be called Blaxploitation. Van Peebles had financed his film independently for far less than a million dollars, but when it hit the theaters—announcing it was "dedicated to all Brothers and Sisters who had enough of the Man"—it made over $15 million.

MGM hired acclaimed director and photographer Gordon Parks Sr. to adapt a story of a streetwise Black private investigator entangled with Black revolutionaries, the Harlem drug syndicate, and the Mafia. But he had to fight executives who wanted a white lead to cast the Black actor Richard Roundtree and fully realize his vision.** The movie he made—*Shaft*—allowed audiences, Black audiences espe-

---

* On American television, fringe shows like *The Green Hornet* and *Kung Fu* had reached the airwaves on ABC because the perennially third-place network had little other choice but to roll the dice. In the 1990s, Fox, the emerging fourth network, would target Black and youth audiences with shows like *In Living Color*, *Martin*, and *The Simpsons*. Ambition and contingency sometimes favors the excluded.

** Stirling Silliphant was an executive producer of the movie. He was not one of those MGM execs.

cially, to "see the Black guy winning," and saved MGM from bankruptcy. His son, Gordon Parks Jr., followed by making *Super Fly*, which took in more than $30 million, a total larger than *Sweetback* and *Shaft* put together, and rescued Warner Bros. from collapse.

It was "a turning point in representation," the Black British fashion designer Grace Wales Bonner would say a half-century later. "The men seemed very free and openly sensual and beautiful and elegant and sexy." The status quo no longer seemed preferable. Following Blaxploitation, an even less likely genre—kung fu movies from Hong Kong dubbed in English and displaying a proud Asian masculinity—would sweep across America and Europe. But first there would need to be a plan and a superstar ready to meet the swirling, unstable moment.

At the start of 1972, Raymond Chow took a trip around the world with his wife, part victory lap and part strategic sortie to ensure Golden Harvest's growth. He met with the heads of some of the biggest independent studios in Europe—Goffredo Lombardo at Titanus in Italy, and the heads of Gaumont in France and Rank in England. All of them told Chow they were shrinking production.

"When he got back to Hong Kong," Andre Morgan recalled, "he felt very confident that there was a future for the Chinese film industry. Because his takeaway was there would be less foreign movies to import to the theaters of Singapore, Malaysia, Hong Kong, and Taiwan."

Andre had arrived in Hong Kong that year as a fresh-faced twenty-year-old graduate of the University of Kansas. Born in French Morocco to an American military man of white and Osage descent and an English nurse, he entered and graduated from college early. Whip-smart and pragmatic, he majored in Oriental languages and literature because he needed a scholarship to cover his tuition, and the ones on offer in science, engineering, and Romance languages were too competitive. He found himself following his father's craft, studying to be a China watcher for the CIA. Then Nixon went to China and much of the knowledge he had acquired was instantly outdated.

Andre met Raymond Chow through his professor—an old friend from their Voice of America days—and was offered a job if he could pay his way to Hong Kong. He found the money, moved to the colony, and joined the small Golden Harvest office of less than a dozen employees. There was no way he could have known that his spook training would be perfect for the film biz.

"I was the first foreigner into the company," Andre said with a chuckle. "The Chinese kept saying, 'What do you do?' 'I don't know. I'll be an office boy. That's what Mr. Chow told me.'"

Raymond first had him watch all the company's films. Andre was fluent in Mandarin, so he was dispatched to fix the Hanyu and English subtitles and compose ads for the English-language newspapers. Soon Raymond called him in and asked, "What do you think of the movies? Do you think we can sell them to the world?"

Andre had seen Tom Laughlin's landmark 1971 American indie hit, *Billy Jack*—which featured a half-Navajo *hapkido*-practicing hero fighting racial injustice and sexual predation in a small Southwestern town—win over a crowded, raucous theater in the States. He was sure that the same hip urbanites would embrace kung fu movies as the real thing. But the films needed some work.

"Frankly, Mr. Chow," Andre said, "the scripts are pretty awful and the dialogue and the acting is kind of corny by American standards. But the action is amazing. If we can make the scripts better and make the acting better, I think we can."

"What would you do with the ones we already have?"

"I would dub them in English. I would do a little bit of reediting," he said.*

"Okay," Raymond said. "You go work with the editor, show me how you'd recut it, then go find some people to dub it."

Andre recalled later, "What I didn't say to him, but I felt in my own heart, was that if we were going to dub them, we couldn't dub them seriously." His first projects would be Bruce Lee's two movies. With translated scripts that used American idioms and voice actors who imbued the characters with campy brio, the dubbed movies might close the cultural gap with young Americans.

Satisfied with Morgan's work and his work ethic, Raymond gave him an expense account and told him to take Bruce's white American costars to restaurants, nightclubs, and wherever else they wanted to go. The twenty-year-old had fast made himself indispensable. One night Raymond invited Andre to dinner. As they crossed the harbor on the Star Ferry, Chow told the office boy he wanted to promote him, and offered the choice of production or distribution.

"I'd better go into distribution, because I don't speak Cantonese," Andre said.

"Fine, we'll start you as the assistant manager of Golden Harvest International Division on Monday."

"Who is the manager?"

"Me."

Andre volunteered to shave his beard and mustache and cut his hair, admitting he had let himself get scraggly while partying in Hawai'i. "I think you better keep the beard and mustache," Raymond said. "You will be giving orders to people older than you. It will be very helpful if you start to age."

One morning Bruce strode into the Golden Harvest offices, gladhanding and greeting everyone loudly by name. But when he got to Andre's desk, he was as

---

* Andre added in his interview with me, "Chinese cinema tradition—I didn't know it then and realize now—came from Chinese opera. The master gestures were theatrical onstage, which was a throwback to Hollywood in the twenties and thirties."

startled to see a young blond with a mustache and beard as Andre had been transfixed by his grand entrance.

"Who are you?" Bruce asked. "What are you doing here?"

"I am the assistant manager of the foreign division."

"Golden Harvest has a foreign department? Who's the manager?"

"Raymond."

Bruce laughed. He asked, "Are you American?"

Andre nodded.

"So am I. Let's get coffee."

So began an intense thirteen-month relationship. Day and night, Andre would be mediating between Raymond and foreign movie men, between Raymond and Bruce, and between one or both and a rapidly expanding group of investors, executives, staffers, technicians, extras, and publicists. After hours Bruce and Andre might light up a joint and talk about films, directors, and actors they loved—*Bonnie and Clyde*, Sergio Leone, Terence Hill, and Bud Spencer.

Years later, Andre admitted, "If somebody said, 'This is how you'll get in the film business,' you'd say, 'Come on, that's a bad Hollywood script.'"

For Concord's first production, Raymond wanted Bruce to work with Lo Wei on a film called *The Yellow-Faced Tiger*, a prequel to *Fist of Fury* in which Bruce would play the teacher of Chen Zhen, Huo Yianjia. It was old territory, embarrassingly obvious, but most important, Bruce had no intention of ever working with Lo Wei again.

He told the press he had rejected the script. He told Raymond that Lo Wei just didn't understand what young working-class audiences in Hong Kong wanted. There was another reason, one that he and Raymond Chow agreed on. "He felt that just being stuck in Hong Kong, doing movies in Southeast Asia, you could never internationalize," Andre Morgan said.

Bruce wanted to step it up—to write, direct, and star in his own film, and set it overseas. He had written a one-page treatment for a project he was calling *Enter the Dragon* about a "young Chinese peasant from Hong Kong" named Tang Lung. This name was a layered bit of mythmaking. Bruce had paired Lung (or Loong), "Dragon," with a claim to the artistic glory of the Tang dynasty, which had been founded and led by warriors from the Li clan. The name would be equally legible to Chinese in the diaspora who referred to themselves as "the Tang people" and their Chinatowns as "the streets of the Tang people."

Tang Lung is sent to Rome's Chinese Quarter to help Chen Ching Hua, the daughter of a family friend whose restaurant has been targeted by an Italian gangster with designs on gentrifying the neighborhood. Lung saves her from a kidnapping and takes on an escalating series of fights that culminate in a grand clash with a *karate* champion in the Colosseum. Later, when it seemed Bruce might fulfill his dream of starring in an American-funded production, he would set the original title aside and change this movie's title to *The Way of the Dragon*.*

The story had developed from fragments, ambitions, and constraints. The core story of the migrant guardian Tang Lung echoed Ah Sahm's heroic arc in *The Warrior*. The European setting disclosed Raymond's international aspirations and Bruce's desire not just to exceed the imagination of his Hong Kong peers but to return to Hollywood. The choice of Rome—and the team's plan to shoot almost verité style there—spoke to Raymond's Italian connections and Concord's budgetary limits. Bruce's creative process revealed how deeply he was thinking about his persona in relation to his different audiences in Asia, America, and even Asian America.

Each day Bruce had broken the story at the table in his apartment with pots of *pu-erh* and chrysanthemum tea in animated Cantonese discussions with his assistant director, Ricky Chik Yiu-Cheong. They riffed on extensive daily notes that were written, transcribed, and assembled in Chinese by Golden Harvest staffers. When Chik left for the day, Bruce recounted everything over again to Linda in English to seek her feedback. Then he would refine the notes some more for the next day's session.

"I tried writing in English at first and to have somebody translate into Chinese, but it didn't work. The translation inevitably loses some of the original ideas. So I decided to write in Chinese with the help of a dictionary," he recalled. "It is quite funny, really. I bought this English-Chinese dictionary originally to help me find the suitable English words when I first went to the United States when I was 18. Now I find that I have to use it to find the Chinese words which I have in mind."

Hong Kong, South Korea, Singapore, and Taiwan were beginning their ascent as the "Asian Tigers," and Raymond was consolidating the Asian market. At Bruce's urging, Golden Harvest would soon be working on a South Korean production starring his friend Jhoon Rhee. In *Zatoichi versus the One-Armed Swordsman*, Jimmy Wang Yu starred opposite Shintaro Katsu. The movie bridged Chinese and Japanese audiences, but required a different ending for each audience, an incomplete reconciliation in the new Asia.

But no Hong Kong production had yet dared to set itself in Europe. *The Way of the Dragon*'s Mandarin title was "Powerful Dragon Crosses the River," and the opening sequence depicted a stylized dragon boat journeying to the West. The Concord production was a power move that reflected optimism about a rising Asia.

Yet they were still a Third World company working with a Third World budget.

---

* *The Way of the Dragon* would later be officially released in the United States in 1974, after *Enter the Dragon*, as *The Return of the Dragon*.

Bruce, Raymond, and Nora Miao, who had been signed to costar as Chen Ching Hua, the immigrant restaurant owner in Rome, departed from Kai Tak before the photographers' flashbulbs. But they slipped into Italy like guerrillas from the hills. The cast and crew quickly shot their scenes in Navona Square, Tivoli Gardens, and the Colosseum without permits. Sometimes they posed as tourists; other times they depended on their local Italian production company to ward off trouble by paying fixers and off-duty police.

Bruce opens his fighting in the film by having Lung declare he is an actual Chinese boxer, then performing the same Mantis form he had done in his *Number One Son* audition in 1965. His choice of opponents was deliberate. It would not be lost on his audiences, whatever side of the Pacific they were on, that he was one of the first Asians to triumph over a white criminal boss and a globalized gang of multiracial goons. Nor would it go unnoticed that those goons—Bob Wall, Hwang In-Shik, and especially Chuck Norris—weren't actors, but actual champion titleholders. Golden Harvest publicity boosted Norris as the "seven-time American karate champion."

Here the transition to his style of action choreography is complete. He eludes his attackers with Ali dodges, whips them one by one with staff or *nunchakus*, gives his reverse spinning kick the name of "Dragon Whips Its Tail," and previews the neck-breaker he will use in *Enter the Dragon*.

The seven-and-a-half-minute climax between Bruce Lee and Chuck Norris stands as the best fight scene of his career. Although Bruce had composed dozens of pages of written instructions for the fight, the characters of Lung and Colt—Chuck Norris has no lines in this, his first movie—dissolve into the performance. *The Way of the Dragon*'s glorious last twenty-five minutes feature combat at its most naked—intimate, primal, an irreducible physical dialogue.

Chuck and Bruce trade kicks along a straight line in three regular beats. Chuck picks up on Bruce's rhythm, anticipates Bruce's spin kick, and counters, knocking him to the ground. In the beginning Bruce's attacks are direct, rigid, and predictable, so Chuck simply waits and counters.

After being knocked down three times, Bruce adapts and breaks into Jeet Kune Do, signaling the shift with an Ali-style shuffle, feints, and broken rhythm. Chuck can't locate Bruce anymore; now he has become the rigid, impatient one. The fight turns. Chuck refuses to bow, but Bruce finishes him with speed, purpose, and mercy. He covers his opponent's body out of deference, softly whispering a Buddhist prayer.

The Way of the Dragon was Grace Li's favorite of his movies. Bruce had joked, "Mom, I'm an Oriental person, therefore I have to defeat all the whites in the film."

But if Bruce was going to be seen by different audiences around the world, he was increasingly aware he needed to bridge the cultural gaps between them.

At the start of the movie, a starving Tang Lung is on display, spending a long, awkward moment in the Rome airport as the object of gaping Europeans. Confounded by the language barrier Lung orders five different kinds of soup. His lactose intolerance causes him to suffer bowel-snarling consequences.

To audiences in Asia, these early airport scenes played to howls of recognition and laughter.* But the same scenes might have discomforted Asian American and other minority audiences in the United States. The way the Italians gawk at Tang Lung could be read as racist, and Tang Lung's hick ignorance as replaying Hop Sing/Chop Chop stereotypes. They would be trimmed later for screenings in the States.

A surprising debate was sparked by scenes of the shirtless Tang Lung warming up, stretching himself, cracking his knuckles and spreading his lats like a menacing cobra. All this stuff was distasteful, British critic Tony Rayns argued; the preening Bruce Lee was "taking pleasure and pride in his own body" in a way that was "all but onanistic."

Rayns wrote, "This narcissism blooms fully in the film's action scenes, where everything from Tang's fighting stance to the barrage of wails, shrieks, and cries he emits to taunt his opponents bespeaks a profound satisfaction in the self."

The Hong Kong critic Stephen Teo responded that Bruce Lee was not a narcissist, but a nationalist, a self-made representation of Chinese power and pride. He wrote, "Lee shows himself to be a specimen of thorough training, a true-to-life fighter and not the imaginary creation of an action movie director." He was *gung fu* in its original meaning of "hard work."

"To the West, Lee is a narcissistic hero who makes Asian culture more accessible. To the East, he is a nationalistic hero who has internationalised some aspects of Asian culture," Teo wrote. "When the dragon looks in the mirror, it sees not Narcissus but the Chinese masses looking back."

Yet both perspectives refuse Bruce Lee—much less Tang Lung—an inner life. For that, one must turn to a third place: the diaspora. *The Way of the Dragon* is attuned to the experience of migrants and immigrants, and deeply informed by Bruce's American immigrant experience. As he had in Seattle, the on-screen Bruce aligns himself with the migrant workers.

The kitchen crew, like the ice workers in *The Big Boss*, create in their Chinese Quarter restaurant a world contained by differences in language and culture, but warmly felt and richly lived. The presence of Ho, a bootlicking collaborator,** and Uncle Wang, a betraying patriarch, point to other themes present in *The Big Boss*:

---

* On the commentary track for the 2023 British Blu-Ray version of *The Way of the Dragon*, Frank Djeng cites many other examples of uniquely Hong Kong–centric humor.

** The characters Paul Wei-Ping Ao plays in *Fist of Fury* and *The Way of the Dragon* are problematically, distressingly queered. They are explicitly made to be gay and treasonous, the opposite of a heroic masculine nationalism.

The Way of the Dragon, 1972.
Photo courtesy of the Bruce Lee Family Archive.

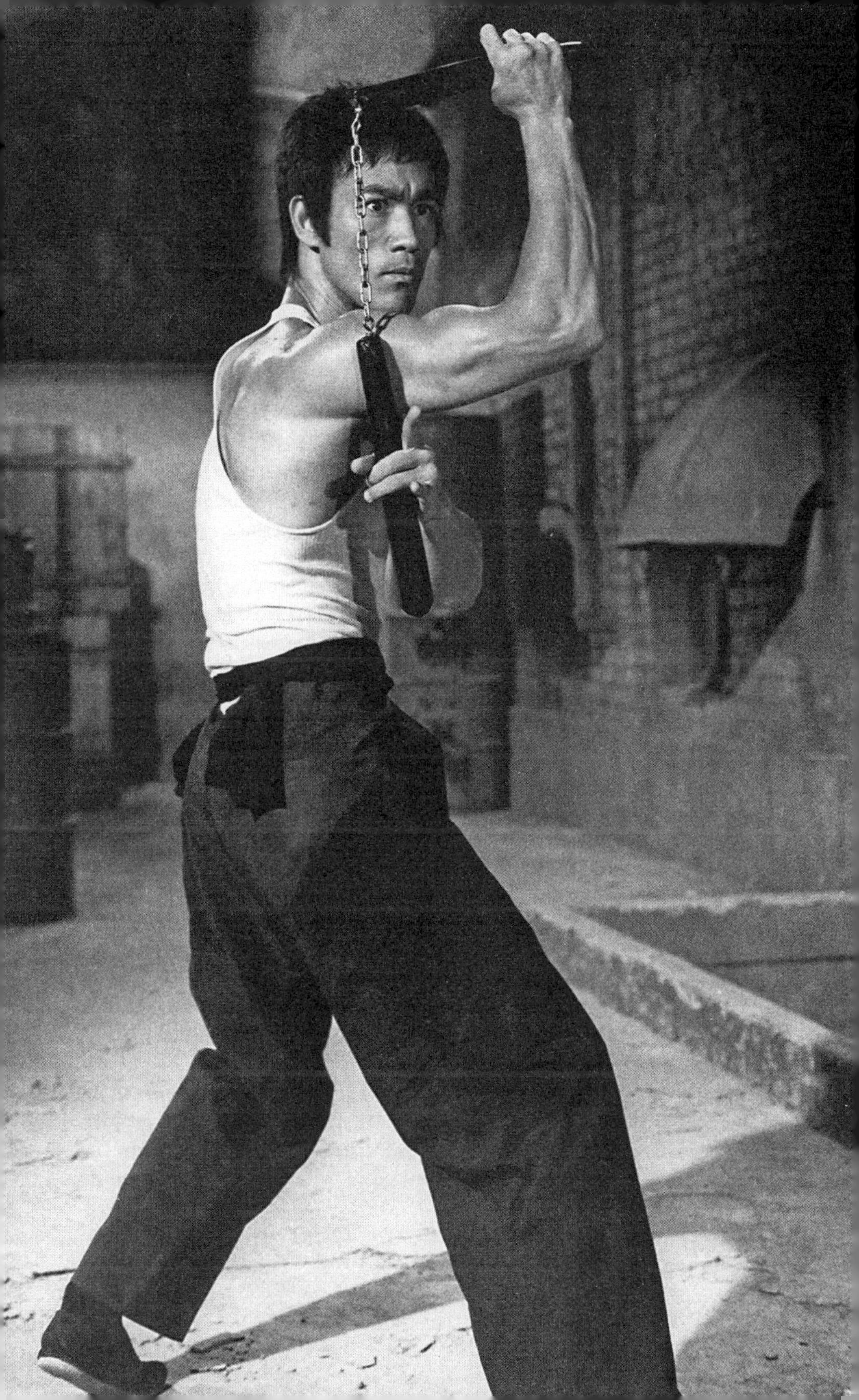

assimilation versus pride, submission versus self-defense, the corruptibility of aging versus the purity of youth. Here Tang Lung infuses the workers with self-respect by teaching them *gung fu*, defeats everyone the Boss throws at him, and secures their tenuous space in the Chinese Quarter. The migrant workers are never forced to assimilate. They can build their own form of belonging. The restaurant becomes a symbol of migrant precarity, the movie an anti-displacement tale with a hopeful resolution.

Unlike in *The Big Boss* or *Fist of Fury*, *The Way of the Dragon* lets its hero escape a tragic end. Tang Lung's violence is liberating. He returns to wandering the world like Ah Sahm in *The Warrior*, a forever migrant—or perhaps an Asian American—still searching for a place to call home.

After hours in the Golden Harvest offices, the weed smoke wafting into the air, Bruce told Andre he had a new goal—to be able to move freely back and forth across the Pacific, making a movie in Asia and then one in America each year. It would be the best way to satisfy his audiences and his ambitions.

In Hong Kong and across Southeast Asia, an outcry was growing over what some called "the cult of violence" in popular culture. Bruce had noted the ancient taste for death sport in *The Way of the Dragon*, invoking in Jon Benn's character of the mafia boss the Roman elites who drank, feasted, and cheered gladiators—always the enslaved, the poor, and the outcast—to their very slaughter.

He was also aware how turbulent a half-decade it had been across Asia, marked by race riots between natives and ethnic Chinese in Indonesia, Burma, Malaysia, and Singapore. This violence paled in comparison to the ongoing American-backed wars in Vietnam, Laos, and Cambodia, where millions of tons of bombs had been dropped. But Bruce understood that he had still become the face of national debates over on-screen mayhem.

On November 16, six weeks before the movie was scheduled to open, Golden Harvest submitted *The Way of the Dragon* to the Hong Kong Film Censorship Authority for what everyone believed would be a routine approval. But the authority ruled that several scenes needed to be cut, including portions of the alley fight where the gang member pulls a knife and Bruce responds by bringing out his *nunchaku*, as well as a clip from the Colosseum fight in which Bruce delivers several kicks at Chuck Norris into the camera.

The authority's explanation was outrageous: "A foreigner being beaten by a Chinese in such brutal fashion would make the foreigners lose their sense of superiority." Bruce took his case directly to the press, arguing he'd rather not release the movie if it were to be censored. The outcry forced the authority to let the movie open uncut.

Released on December 30, 1972, *The Way of the Dragon* exceeded everyone's expectations, grossing a new record in Hong Kong—HKD $5.3 million, nearly three-quarters more than *The Big Boss*. In less than eighteen months, Bruce had become Asia's biggest star.

But amid a reactionary hysteria, Singapore's primarily ethnic Chinese leaders quickly moved to censor and ban kung fu movies. Arguing that the films were responsible for a rise in gang and street crime, politicians also established a national body to restrict martial arts schools.

"I think it is unhealthy to play up violence," Bruce told Pang Cheng Lian of Singapore's *New Nation*. That was why, he said, he had insisted Chen Zhen needed to pay the price at the end of *Fist of Fury*. "But it should be remembered," he added, "that violence and aggression is part of everyday life now. You see it over the TV and in Vietnam. You can't just pretend it does not exist."

In an interview with the *Hong Kong Standard*'s Piera Kwan, he was more personal. "An action film borders somewhere between reality and fantasy," he told her. "See, I have this intensity in me that the audience believes in what I do because I do believe in what I do."

He removed his sunglasses to underscore his point to her. "As long as what I do is credible and as long as I have this intensity in me then all is well," he said.

But he also knew, *if only it were so simple.*

CHAPTER 43
The Cost

The Icarus flight from stardom to superstardom is treacherous—the fans, the paparazzi, the feeling of always having a tsunami ready to break on the other side of the door, knowing that outside are many who have no investment in your best interests, only their own. Surviving superstardom is the loneliest task. It requires a sufficient distance from the clamoring world.

Some can separate themselves from the image the public has claimed. They are able to tease, baffle, and deflect the vampires and parasites that make the machine run. They can delegate the care and feeding of the image to those skilled in managing the public's consuming hunger. Perhaps they even learn how to vanish.

Bruce was not this type. He was the kind to engage. His was the art of interception. He would represent himself the way he wanted, and fight his own fights.

In order to ground himself, Bruce was writing drafts of a manifesto that he called "What Is An Actor?":

> ... I have to take responsibility for myself and to do whatever is right. The script has to be right, the director has to be right, my time devoted toward preparation of the role. After that comes the money.
>
> Now, to the business people in films (and I have to say cinema is a marriage of art and business), the actor is not a human being, but a product, a commodity. However, you, as a human being, have the right to be the best goddamn product that ever walked and work so hard that the business people have to listen to you. You have that personal obligation to yourself to make yourself the best product possible according to your own terms. Not the biggest or the most successful, but the best quality—with that achieved, comes everything else.

It was a crystallization of his *gung fu* ethic applied to show business—what his friend Peter Chin called "the dirtiest business."

But Bruce had expended so much of his energy trying to close the gap, and he did not know yet how to build in a distance.

Black Belt magazine had named Bruce to its 1972 Hall of Fame, an honor that, just two years before, when he had been bedridden and depressed, might have been gratifying. But now it left him in a whirl of complex emotions. He wrote a passionate letter to Mito Uyehara, apologizing for his ambivalence but explaining he was also in need of "letting it out."

"To many, the word 'success' seems to be a paradise, but now that I'm in the midst of it, it is nothing but circumstances that seem to complicate my innate feeling toward simplicity and privacy," he wrote. "Fame and fortune are illusive creations and impostors."

A part of Bruce longed to be anonymous and unseen again in America. He wrote, "I miss you and our once simple lunches together and our many joyful communications. Take care and have fun—hope you are still jogging, which is the only form of relaxation to me nowadays."

Dan Inosanto also got a glimpse of his friend's new life when Bruce invited him to Hong Kong. They went out to lunch, and he was surrounded by autograph-seekers. Gawkers stared at them from the street through the windows. They went to Japanese restaurants with private rooms enclosed by screen doors. But the waiters hovered over them, competing to serve them.

Dan heard sadness in his old friend's voice when Bruce said, "I'm glad you showed up. I don't know who's my friend. People are going to ask me something to get a job in the movie. They will say, 'Hey, Lee Siu Long, remember me when I was in high school? You think you can use me as a stuntman or maybe an actor?'"

Golden Harvest moved Bruce, Linda, and the kids to a five-thousand-square-foot, eleven-room mansion with a Japanese garden and a koi pond behind eight-foot-high walls and bright yellow gates at 41 Cumberland Road in Kowloon Tong, a property formerly owned by an indie movie producer, Andy Vajna. Bruce set up his library and study in one room and a complete Marcy gym system in another. He had complained to Dan that he had not been working out as much as he wanted.

But though the security had been increased—the high outer stone walls were spiked with sharp glass, in Third World fashion—an intruder still managed to get onto the property before Bruce chased him back over the fence. He had still more unwanted visitors.

"Strangers would stop at my door and just hand me checks for thousands of dollars. When I would ask them what the money was for, they'd reply, 'Don't worry about it; it's just a gift to you,'" Bruce told Mito. The lesson, Linda said, was that "in Hong Kong, everybody knows where to find you."

By a stroke of luck, Doug Palmer, now a lawyer practicing in Tokyo, reconnected with Bruce while on a trip with his wife, Noriko, to Hong Kong in October 1972. Palmer had not seen Bruce in years and had no idea what a superstar he had become. When Bruce got the call, Linda rushed over to pick up the Palmers at their hotel in Bruce's scarlet Mercedes 350 SL. Over the next couple of days, they entertained their old Seattle friends, screened *The Big Boss* for them at the Golden

Harvest studio—Bruce thought Noriko might be offended by *Fist of Fury*—and caught up for hours, a homecoming that neither couple wanted to end.

But as happy as they were for Bruce's success, Doug and Noriko could also see how things had changed. "He made the comment that there were a lot of sharks," Doug recalled. "He didn't know who to trust and said it'd be nice having an old friend who could have his back doing his deals."

"When Noriko had to use the toilet," Doug wrote, "Bruce produced a chain of keys to unlock the bathroom door. The house was then being renovated, and apparently he had to keep almost every room in the house locked to guard against theft by the workmen."

Most troubling, Doug added, "He was very conscious about when his kids were taken to school and picked up. They were very conscious of the possibility of them being kidnapped."

Publicly Bruce signaled a new distancing. "I don't feel like social gatherings," he told a journalist. "Nor am I interested in publicizing myself. But such things are simply unavoidable in a star's life, particularly in a small place like Hong Kong." A more confrontational stage in his relationship with the media had begun.

"I think he loved it, being famous," Nancy Kwan recalled. "You become famous but then you have to sustain it. Does fame cost? Yeah, it's very costly."

After shooting ended for *The Way of the Dragon* in the summer of 1972, Bruce was sketching out ideas for a new movie called *The Game of Death* when he learned that Kareem Abdul-Jabbar was visiting Hong Kong.

Bruce had been doing a public dance with Run Run Shaw, visiting Movietown for high-profile meetings. For Run Run, it was a way to continue harassing his sworn enemy and inflate Raymond's costs of doing business. For Bruce, it was a way to keep Raymond prioritizing him and Concord.

"To stop Bruce getting too focused on Run Run, quickly the set was built for *The Game of Death*," Andre Morgan said. "We had no idea what the movie was going to be. But if you got twenty or thirty minutes in the can and he's directing, you know damn well he's going to finish it."

As with *The Warrior* and *The Silent Flute*, Bruce started with an image: a rigid oak breaking in a winter blizzard, a willow bending with the wind and snow. He developed a rough story about a retired martial artist named Hai Tien traveling with his sister and young brother. On the plane, Hai encounters a passenger who accuses him of having thrown his last tournament fight. When the plane stops in Korea, Hai's siblings are kidnapped, and in order to free his loved ones, he must complete a mission for a criminal boss.

It is not hard to read Bruce writing his real-life weariness with fame and his fears for his family into this plot.

Hai Tien must join a group of fighters to attack a pagoda called the Temple of the Leopard and recover a treasure at the top of this tower of death. But each level of the pagoda is a hall governed by formidable fighters expert in different arts. No one who has tried to recover the treasure has returned.

The rest of the movie and even the actors could come later. For now, Bruce was excited to reunite with old friends, if only to experience some of that old fun and brotherhood again. He booked Kareem and contacted Taky, Dan, Peter, and James to invite them to Hong Kong. He had roles for Taky, Peter, and Dan. With James, whom he knew was sick, he just wanted a chance to spend time together. But James said he could not travel, and Taky told Bruce he didn't feel comfortable in the role. Kareem came to shoot in the first week of September. Dan arrived in Hong Kong a week later.

The fight scenes—shot between September and late October 1972 and now recovered in reconstructed films like *The Warrior's Journey*, *Bruce Lee in G.O.D.*, *The Game of Death Redux*, and *The Final Game of Death*—would also include James Tien and Chieh Yuan as his fellow fighters, and *hapkido* experts Hwang In-Shik, who would double Chieh and defend the first hall, and Ji Han-Jae, who would defend the fourth hall, the Hall of the Dragon.

For Bruce's costume, the wardrobe people had sourced a yellow jumpsuit with black stripes and a black jumpsuit with yellow stripes. Bruce preferred the black at first, but he wanted Kareem's first move to be a kick to his chest, leaving a footprint. When the crew showed him how the imprint would look on the yellow suit, he sent Andre and the team to procure three more.

Taken together, the fights are meant to demonstrate Jeet Kune Do's superiority over all other systems. Each illustrates aspects of Bruce's theories. Dan plays Pasqual, a Moro Muslim in a red headband protecting the third hall, the Hall of the Tiger. They are physically matched for each other, going head-to-head with *kali* sticks, open hands, and finally blinding displays of *nunchaku* prowess, until Hai Tien recognizes his only advantage is psychological. At the peak of the fight, he shuffles and backs around the floor, strutting and swaggering and bouncing around in a hyperactive dance that would inspire b-boys and b-girls for decades to come. When Dan's character finally loses his cool, Hai rushes in with a series of kicks and finishes him.

Kareem is Hakim, the keeper of the final hall, the Hall of the Unknown, resting in a blue shirt in a rocking chair, cool and deadly behind dark glasses. He represents the warrior of an unknown style, who practices the way of no way. He mirrors Hai Tien as an enlightened ideal of Jeet Kune Do. In a dialogue echoing Krishnamurti's "Freedom from the Known," the characters affirm to each other that because they do not fear death, they are able to fight free. Hakim's intimidating size makes him seem unbeatable. Hai can only triumph by learning his opponent's weaknesses, which include an ironic sensitivity to light, and adapting his strategy.

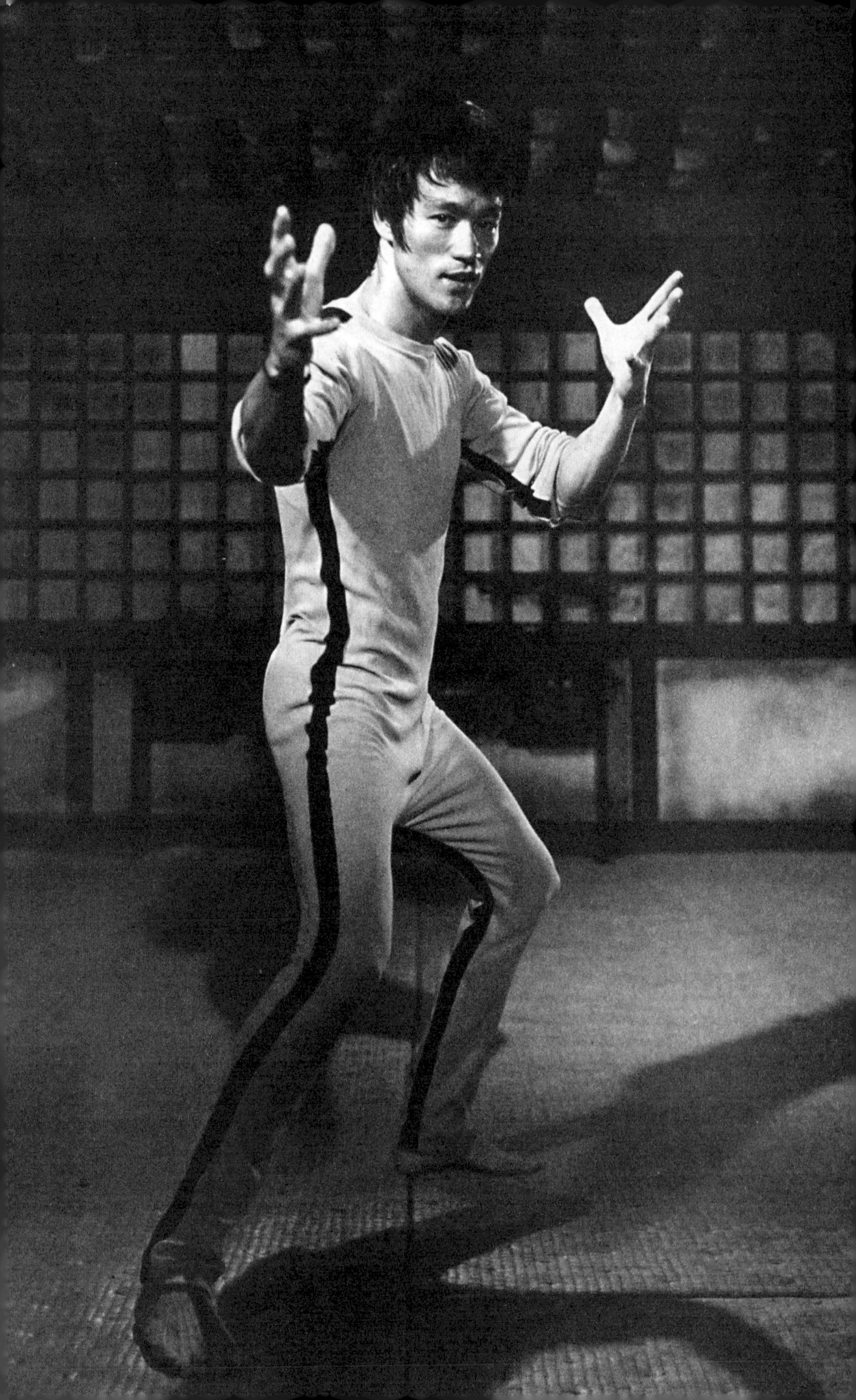

Most of these fight scenes—including a less compelling face-off with Ji Han-Jae's character, and some outdoor footage shot in the New Territories—were shot from a wide angle to highlight the fighters' full-body realism and Bruce's theatricality. They remain tantalizingly suggestive of what *The Game of Death* might have become. "It was never guaranteed that the pagoda would be the end of the movie," said Andre Morgan. "The pagoda was the end of the movie we were making in 1972."

By the end of October, Bruce had shot two hours of footage for four scenes, of which perhaps fifteen or twenty minutes were usable. About twenty-five minutes were appropriated for Golden Harvest's Bruceploitation release of *The Game of Death* in 1978. The fight footage would have constituted only a small portion of a feature-length film. Perhaps the movie was always destined to be transitional.

Bruce increasingly felt further from freedom, straitjacketed by his public and private lives, and contained even by his exploding career.

He admitted to a journalist, "I would like to evolve into different roles, but I cannot do so in Southeast Asia. I am already type-cast. I am supposed to be the good guy. I can't even be a bit gray, because no producer would let me. I can't even express myself fully on film here, or the audience wouldn't understand what I am talking about half the time. That's why I can't stay in Southeast Asia all the time."

But in the United States he was known only to niche audiences: martial arts enthusiasts, fans of *The Green Hornet*, devotees of kung fu films, and young Asian Americans. It was especially uncomfortable for him to see the *Kung Fu* TV series igniting unprecedented interest in Asian martial arts. It certainly seemed like the right thing had happened for the wrong reason.

On the cover of the October 1972 issue of *Black Belt Yearbook*, the same issue that had announced Bruce's Hall of Fame honor, was David Carradine. The headline read, MARTIAL ARTS: THE COMING RAGE IN ENTERTAINMENT! The accompanying story announced a number of kung fu TV shows in production, including a pilot for *Number One Son*, starring a Chinese American named Rocky Gunn. Bruce was being honored as one of the best fighters of all time, but the yellowface poseur had become the world's biggest kung fu superstar, and a host of no-name pretenders waited in the wings.

In one of their after-hours sessions, Bruce admitted to Andre that even after he had chosen to come back to Hong Kong, he had remained obsessed with what it would take to get a starring role in Hollywood. "I had to prove not only that I could do the part, but that people would pay to see me," he explained to Andre. "Hong Kong was that avenue."

By now, Fred Weintraub had left Warner Bros. But on his way out, he had secured a three-movie production deal. Bruce sent him reels of *The Big Boss* and *Fist of*

The Game of Death, 1972.
Photo courtesy of the Bruce Lee Family Archive.

Fury, which he screened for Dick Ma, the Chinese American executive at Warner Bros. who oversaw international distribution, and Ted Ashley, who, Weintraub recalled, "was amazed also at how Bruce was in the fights."

Ashley phoned Bruce in Hong Kong to reconnect. When they got off the phone, Bruce asked Linda to help him compose a follow-up letter to Ashley. He wrote:

> Presently, Hong Kong will be my base of operation as my films are enjoying "unbelievable" success, breaking all-time records one after another....
>
> ... Ted, I have gone through the interesting experience of being Number One in Mandarin films. Fame and fortune, and I mean by any standards, are mine. I would like to feel you would not interpret this as an ego trip, for after this swift unexpected adjustment, I have found, after much soul searching, that deep down what I honestly value more than anything else is quality: doing one's best in the manner of the responsibility and craftsmanship of a Number One.
>
> ... The way I look at it, and honestly feel it, is that this Chinaman will definitely invade the states in a big way, one or another. I am sure, if you give this matter a fair and serious thought, something will be worked out to our mutual benefit. Should this project come through, we, as good friends, will enjoy it that much more.

"By this time, Bruce was a phenomenon already," Fred Weintraub recalled. "So I went to Hong Kong."

CHAPTER 44
Representations

In the summer of 1971, when Bruce Lee was arriving in Thailand to begin shooting *The Big Boss*, Henry Kissinger was returning to the United States from China, having just completed a secret set of meetings that would culminate the following February with the shocking image shown around the world of Mao Zedong and Richard Nixon smiling and shaking hands, East and West, Red China and white America, in a thawing of the Cold War. In his limousine to the airport, Kissinger was accompanied by Mao's close adviser Marshal Ye Jianying, who told him a story.

As a strong and resolute young man four decades before, Marshal Ye said, he had ably served the Nationalists against the Westerners. Then he heard of Mao and his army of two thousand in the mountains, and he left to join the Communists. His comrades were dignified, proud, and committed, their cause irreproachable. But while they were on the Long March, suffering major casualties in their retreat from the Nationalists, none of them believed they would achieve victory in their lifetimes. They comforted themselves with the thought that they were fighting for future generations.

"And yet, here we are," he said to Kissinger, "and here you are."

In early October 1972, Fred Weintraub landed in Hong Kong, towering over nearly everyone, to close a deal for Bruce's services. He felt a sense of urgency.

When *Fist of Fury* opened at the Pagoda Theater in New York's Chinatown, *Variety* wrote of Bruce: "His balletic grace, curled mouth, arched eyebrows and clenched fists make his demonstrations of this athletic sport highly entertaining, but an exuberant novelty act remains a tenuous basis for a film hoping to find an Occidental audience." But the movie was one of the theater's biggest ticket-sellers ever. "For the first time in the Pagoda Theater's history," owner Lucas Liang crowed, "half the audiences were non-Chinese." By the end of 1972, inner-city theaters in Seattle, Oakland, Los Angeles, and Honolulu were packed with mixed crowds for Shaw Brothers films like *The Boxer from Shantung* and Bruce's first two movies.

As theater chains and studios faltered, indie movie distributors were filling inner-city theaters with entertainment for the riotous diversity that mainstream America disparaged—Black movies, Spanish-language movies, foreign art films, grindhouse cinema, X-rated porno, and kung fu flicks. Pundits would wonder why Black audiences had become such big fans of kung fu movies. The answer was hardly a secret, even if no one wanted to name it. These movies were opening in the Village, the Deuce, or Chinatown because of white flight, the politics of abandonment, and American segregation.

Some of the Asian American radicals had dismissed Bruce as a sellout when he was Kato. But now many of them were seeing him in a new light. Third World Strike veterans Vicci Wong and Lillian Fabros were taking martial arts classes while organizing in the Chinese and Filipino American communities. After hours they joined the multiracial crowds in San Francisco's Chinatown for the kung fu flicks.

Lillian Fabros saw in Bruce's movies an affirmation of her community's warrior consciousness: "We're not going to show it until we're really pushed. It's simmering underneath the surface. Don't push us too far because when you push, you're going to get smashed."

Vicci Wong recalled, "When Bruce kicked that sign—'No dogs and Chinese allowed'—the audience whooped. Cheering, standing up, everybody's jumping up and down!"

Pagoda Theater proprietor Lucas Liang declared, "I think the United States and the rest of the world is now ready for the explosion of Chinese made films." Weintraub and his business partner, Paul Heller, agreed. They had lined up the proper backing at Warner Bros. Dick Ma was closing a deal with Run Run Shaw to release a dubbed version of a new kung fu film from Shaw Brothers in the United States. Ted Ashley was ready to consider a distribution deal along the lines of what he had done for *Super Fly* and *Billy Jack*. He was even willing to look at a production deal. He told Weintraub that if Dick Ma thought that they could make $250,000 in foreign sales, he would commit to spend that amount. Dick was certain they could. They just needed Golden Harvest to match the rest.

So here was Fred in Hong Kong, saying all the right things to Bruce and Raymond. The men had some history. When Fred was still at Warner Bros., Raymond had offered him distribution rights for *The Big Boss* and *Fist of Fury* at the price of $25,000. But Weintraub had balked, a decision he regretted and was hoping to put behind him.

Ten days of negotiations brought them to the outline of an agreement. Warner Bros.—through Weintraub and Heller's company, Sequoia Pictures—would pick up above the line costs for producer, director, screenplay, talent (except Bruce), and other preproduction expenses. Concord would cover below the line costs for production, postproduction, location, and support expenses. But then, according to Weintraub, negotiations bogged down over territories and profit-sharing. Weintraub believed he needed to control Hong Kong, Singapore, and Thailand to make back Warner Bros.' $250,000 investment. But Raymond, he wrote in his memoir, "asked for the world," and "kept insisting on more and more key foreign territories, knowing that I couldn't give them up."

Weintraub was also frustrated he could not get Bruce and Raymond in the same room at the same time. "[Raymond] didn't want to alienate his star, so he kept up the pretense of bargaining in good faith," Weintraub wrote. "When the deal fell through, he could assure Bruce that it was the Americans' fault." He believed Chow was "very protective of his cash cow—his very lithe and agile cash cow," and fearful that Bruce would jet to America if the film was a success.

Weintraub's breaking point came, he said, when he offered Raymond Hong Kong, Singapore, Thailand, Malaysia, Laos, and Taiwan, and Raymond still declined to sign. The night before he was to leave, he, Chow, and Bruce had dinner at a Japanese restaurant. As Weintraub described the scene,

> "Bruce," I said, "I'm leaving tomorrow because we couldn't strike a deal. I'm sorry things didn't work out. It's too bad Raymond doesn't want you to be an international star." Bruce looked at the growing throng outside, while Raymond—dropping his facade of cordiality—stared at me with a sudden, all-consuming hatred. In that instant he knew he had lost. It seemed like a mere formality when Bruce said, "Sign the contract, Raymond."

It's a dramatic story—made even better by Weintraub's shout-out to a "tactic passed down by generations of Jewish mothers, guilt"—but it appears less plausible than the old one about American muscle. Chow's reluctance to close, Andre Morgan said, was "because he wasn't sure how the economics would really work." And in fact the final contract was more favorable to Warner Bros. and Sequoia. Concord ponied up half of the budget, but retained the rights of distribution and the profits for only the territories Weintraub had originally offered. Warner Bros. received the rest of the world, even a portion of Asia: the Philippines, Vietnam, and Indonesia.

The contract was executed on November 3, 1972. Raymond sold the US rights for *The Big Boss* and *Fist of Fury* to National General Pictures, an independent distributor where Sy Weintraub was an officer, which began preparing them for release in 1973. The new year was shaping up to be a big one for Hong Kong film and for Bruce Lee.

When Fred Weintraub had come to Hong Kong he already had a vehicle for Bruce in hand. He and Paul Heller had banged out a story idea and commissioned a young screenwriter named Michael Allin to deliver a treatment they named *Blood and Steel*. "It was wonderful," Allin said, "because I didn't know anything about martial arts. I didn't know anything about Hong Kong."

Heller had something specific in mind, a script that gave him the same feeling of wonder he had gotten as a kid from reading Milt Caniff's mid-century Orientalist adventure comic strip, *Terry and the Pirates*. He wanted "the mystery and the Dragon Lady," he said, "high chroma reds, golds, and blues." Allin delivered a nineteen-page treatment with a James Bond flavor.

The treatment introduces Lee, a "lithe, flawless"* Oriental spy; Roper, a Caucasian fighter "without eastern humility"; Mei Ling, a Chinese woman working as an undercover Interpol spy; Bolo, "a silent, black giant" who is the villain's primary fighter; and Okata, the villain's Japanese enforcer. The villain is Khan, who rules an island state from which he "controls white-slavery and drug traffic throughout Indo-China"—a textbook Fu Manchu, flanked by comely prostitutes and swarthy fighting hordes.

Lee, Roper, and Bolo are participating in Khan's martial arts tournament, a premise familiar to American audiences nearly a decade after Ed Parker's Long Beach event, and an obvious echo of *The Silent Flute*. Lee is an Interpol agent sent to capture Khan, but is captured instead. Roper is a rakish American gambler who has come to Hong Kong to escape debts to the mob. He remains neutral about Khan's criminality until the third act, when he beds Mei Ling and frees Lee from Khan's clutches. Roper is a composite of American Cold War archetypes—the rebel without a cause, the rough-hewn yet irresistible alpha male, the world's reluctant but reliable white savior. Lee is a dutiful, only somewhat effective foil, barely an upgrade from sidekick.

As the Interpol helicopters descend, Lee deals the villain a crippling punch, but he is not even allowed to fulfill his mission. In the final scene, Khan commits suicide Mishima style.

At the end of October, Bruce and Raymond flew to Beverly Hills to close the deal.

Bruce had wanted to work with Arthur Penn, but the director of *Bonnie and Clyde* scoffed at the tiny budget. Instead he was meeting Robert Clouse, a director whom Weintraub and Heller had selected in part because he was inexpensive.

Robert had started out as a still photographer in the 1950s, and funded his own Oscar-nominated short, *The Legend of Jimmy Blue Eyes*, about a blue-eyed Black jazzman who sells his soul to the devil to reach the perfect note and perishes at the climax of a cutting contest. His first full-length, which he had also written, was 1968's *Dreams of Glass*, an interracial love story of an Italian American fisherman and a Japanese American woman who must confront the bigotry of their parents and everyone around them. But Bruce was sold by the unfettered fight scenes in his 1970 movie, *Darker than Amber*, that had left its bloodied stars with real-life broken bones.

Bruce introduced himself by throwing a kick that ended at the tip of Robert's nose. "Extremely intense. Enormous ego," were the director's first impressions—

---

* Here again are direct echoes of Lorenzo Semple's *Number One Son* treatment.

but also, "very dedicated." Bruce was fixated on how to clean up the mess of a script.

The story had been revised and rebalanced with three protagonists—the Deadly Three, Warner's marketing would call them—by adding Williams, a Black *karateka* who had served in Vietnam with Roper and was escaping police brutality. After the breakthrough success of *Super Fly*, the addition seemed necessary. Williams is killed by Khan, which precipitates the penitent Roper into confronting Khan. But Lee is still Roper's Oriental second, there to offer pointless parables and set up the white guy's locker room cracks about the prostitutes.

Blood and Steel was the product of ignorance as much as imagination. To lend the script authenticity, Allin seemed to have nicked details from *The Warrior* (the description of Lee), *The Silent Flute* (an old master catching flies with his chopsticks), and *The Chinese Boxer* (fighters hardening their hands in woks of steaming sand). At some point, someone made the decision to rename the evil Khan as Han, the name of China's majority ethnic group.

Bruce must have wondered if they understood why Asians and Asian Americans wouldn't buy this bullshit, that this kind of stuff could bring pickets and protests, or much worse, complete apathy at the box office. When Hollywood had been offering him close to nothing, it had been easier to refuse racist representations. Now he had to confront the entire canon of misrepresentations. He was heading for a massive payday. If he completed the film he would receive one hundred thousand dollars, by far the biggest portion of the production budget, multiples higher than any check he had ever received. But would it be worth the price?

He told Weintraub, Heller, the Warner Bros. execs, and anyone else who would listen that he wanted to make sure that the movie treated Asian martial arts and Asian philosophy seriously. Doing so would mark the difference between success and failure, a film that would be embraced and one that would be dismissed and forgotten. If Warner Bros. and Sequoia failed, they would be out a quarter million. If he failed, he might lose the trust of everyone in Hong Kong, Southeast Asia, and the United States who wanted for once to win. He might never recover from it.

Now it was his turn to make contractual demands. He asked for his usual—fight choreography, script approval—and one more thing. He wanted the title changed from the one that bore the Orientalist imprint of its creators—*Blood and Steel*—to the one he had saved for this moment of emergence for him and all those to whom he felt he had to answer—*Enter the Dragon*.

Then he headed back to Hong Kong without signing a contract.

CHAPTER 45
The Proud Dragon

Bruce was playing the game he had wanted to play.

But he told Mito Uyehara, "I didn't know whom to trust and I even grew suspicious of my old pals. I was in a period when I didn't know who was trying to take advantage of me."

Now he was heading back into turbulent waters in Hong Kong.

To support his childhood friend Unicorn Chan, he had cast Chan in *The Way of the Dragon* and credited him as an assistant fight choreographer. An opportunity had come Unicorn's way because of it, a film to be called *Fist of Unicorn*. Bruce agreed to help with fight sequences and promotion. But the producers and director filmed him on set and at the presser, included the footage in the film, and tried to promote it as a new Bruce Lee film. Feeling betrayed, Bruce sued the production company and distanced himself from his longtime friend.

Stirling Silliphant visited Bruce in Hong Kong. Bruce took his former student to meet Raymond and then to see *Fist of Fury*. He was stunned to see the hysteria Bruce caused in the streets. "He was wearing a white, form-fitting three-piece Brioni suit, walking like a king and smiling," Stirling recalled. "It was beautiful to see." It reminded him of when he had worked with Marilyn Monroe.

Stirling told him he had taken up Shotokan *karate* and promised to get *The Silent Flute* going again. But later, after he had received a verbal commitment from 20th Century-Fox and called to tell Bruce the good news, Bruce said, "I don't think you can afford me anymore."

Then he told Stirling that studying *karate* was "an act of betrayal." "How could you do that?" he asked.

"You left me," Stirling cried. "What was I supposed to do?"

"He had many faults. He became very arrogant as he became successful," Stirling recalled later. "But on the other hand, he had a rough time, so what the hell.

"I think in another year or two he would have mellowed and become one of the most incredible human beings who ever existed. He was . . ." Stirling paused. "He was a very special person. He meant a great deal to me."

When Bruce was not working at Golden Harvest, he was increasingly withdrawing from the world and isolating himself.

One night he called Nora Miao, someone with whom he had once been linked in the media. Nora knew she was being considered for *Enter the Dragon* but was reluctant to do a fourth movie with Bruce. She didn't want to be seen as having relied upon him to become a star, and had taken the lead in a romantic film called *The Story of Daisy*. But he wanted to talk about something else. He told her he felt all alone.

"The reason why you feel lonely is no one dares get close to you," she told him.

"Why do I feel that I don't have a real friend?"

"It is nothing strange. You've become an idol that no one dares to touch. When they see you they only flatter you. However, when they do this you despise them. On the other hand, if they criticize you, you resent it," she said. "You are implicated by your fame."

Bruce invited Tony Lau Wing, Lam Ching-ying, and the other stuntmen over to Kowloon Tong to work out with him. They passed the time lifting weights, monkeying around, and bullshitting. But after they left he was back in his shrinking world.

On December 2, Yip Man passed away. He was given a grand funeral and buried in Fanling. No one informed Bruce. The tabloids filled with angry quotes from Wing Chun students about the indecorum of their *sifu*'s most famous student. Even Wong Shun Leung publicly criticized him: "People shouldn't forget their roots." He added, "It is certainly very difficult for a person not to let fame get to him!"

"You know, those son of bitches, they live right in the city and they never called me," Bruce fumed to Mito. "Shit, I felt real bad and disappointed." He quietly visited Yip Man's grave site to pay his respects and went to Yip's family home to apologize.

Later, after the furor had died down, Bruce reached out to Wong Shun Leung to ask if he might come to see him at the studio to take some pictures. Ah Leung refused to participate in the photo shoot but visited Cumberland Road with his wife, son, and top student, Wan Kam Leung. Bruce proudly showed them his training equipment—his leg guards, punching devices, and electric-shock muscle-stimulation machines. In his garden, he had a spring-loaded ball for punching. The two began playing with it, and although Ah Leung was nearing forty and had never tried it before, he was destroying the ball.

After they compared kicks and punches and did some sparring, they sat down to talk. The teacher was still trying to lead his pupil. "If you do not take yourself as a superman," Wong said to Bruce, "you will have a better and meaningful life. Otherwise you will feel lonely and cold."

Bruce thought for a moment. Then he exhaled and said, "Ah Leung, I am different now. I have had my life insured. I am ready to face any accident. My family need not worry about their future lives. I don't have any worry too. If anybody disturbs me, he should be careful. I am not afraid of death. I can kill any attacker at any time."

"You should not think in this way," said Wong. "To be a father is more than just leaving behind some money. If this is correct, then every millionaire would be a model father. I think if you have time you should try to care more about your wife and children. Don't spend all your time on making money."

Bruce looked again at Wong Shun Leung. He shook his head and smiled.

Linda said, "When he was home, he was in his study and he would be writing and reading, and that was his great getaway time from all of the stardom business."

Quietly, she was suffering. She took some Cantonese lessons. She had developed a strong friendship with Sam Hui's Filipino American wife, Rebecca, whom she called Rebu and often had over to the house. But that was about it. "I did not socialize much," Linda said. "I had one Caucasian family that had kids Brandon and Shannon's ages that they used to play with sometimes. But basically I stayed home quite a bit with the kids."

She wanted to go back to college to finish her degree. "We had Wu Ngan's wife who could look after the kids," Linda sighed. "Bruce didn't like that idea at all. He wanted me to stay home with the kids. He was pretty kind of old-fashioned Chinese in many ways."

Feeling trapped in the confines of the Kowloon Tong house, she was still reluctant to step out. "I didn't feel like I had a good reception in Hong Kong at all after Bruce was a big star. The people didn't warm up to me. I think they always thought he should have married a Chinese," she recalled. "I would go in a store and I could understand what they were saying. They would say, 'She's ugly' in Chinese and words like that. I didn't like it too much in that way. Another reason to stay home more."

In a 1975 interview, she recalled, "Sometimes the wife of someone would call me up and ask me out to lunch. I figured out pretty soon that certain people would try and get around me just to get to know Bruce. I tend to accept people at face value and get slapped later on. I think Bruce sometimes got a little carried away with the feeling [of distrust,] but at the same time it was justified. Everybody was trying to get at Bruce for their own reasons."

She just wanted to go home.

On the afternoon of December 31, 1972, a month after his thirty-second birthday, Bruce picked up the telephone to hear the trembling voice of James Yimm Lee's nineteen-year-old son, Greglon, calling from Oakland. A half hour before, Greglon had found his father dead in the bathtub. James Yimm Lee had succumbed to lung cancer a month before his fifty-third birthday.

Bruce was stunned. He had just opened a birthday card on which James had written, "Friends like you, comes once in a blue moon."

Bruce had known for a while that James was not well. Before he had left for Hong Kong in 1971 he had asked Mito to resurrect a book he once helped James write on Wing Chun, but—in his JKD fervor—had subsequently mothballed. Mito published *Wing Chun Kung Fu* early the next year, listing Bruce as a "technical editor" on the cover, and, at Bruce's request, gave all the proceeds to James. But no one had ever told him that James had lung cancer. James had insisted to everyone that he did not want to burden Bruce with the knowledge. The tickets to Hong Kong Bruce had sent to James were still lying on a table in his Oakland home.

Bruce gathered himself to ask, "Was anybody there with him when he died?"

"No," Greglon said. Bruce promised to support the family with anything they would need for the funeral.

When they were alone, Bruce assured Linda that they would move back to the States. "I don't want to live here forever," he said.

But they both understood that first he needed to meet his fate. Bruce received word back from Ted Ashley on his contract demands. Warner Bros. would not grant him script approval, would not use the title of *Enter the Dragon*, and were keeping the title of *Blood and Steel*. Just as in Raymond's negotiations with Fred, he had won exactly nothing, but he signed the contract anyway. Shooting would commence right after the turn of the year. Still, the game was not yet over.

The Warner publicists scheduled Bruce for an interview with *Newsweek*, a piece he knew would be his most important in America to date. Published in the magazine's January 29, 1973, edition, the unbylined article heralded Bruce as "Asia's first superstar—the epitome of high living, the heartthrob of thousands of adoring girls and the idol of adoring young overseas Chinese from New York to Taipei," and called his movies "a new wave in Chinese cinema." It noted he had a Rolls-Royce on order, which would be equipped with a gold plaque "attesting to the fact it was designed especially for him."

There was a picture of Bruce in his garden, flexing a bodybuilder's front lat spread. "Lee relies heavily for his success on a formula of rippling muscles and a sort of 'yellow power,'" the article continued. "While the villains he tangles with—and always defeats—are usually stock bad guys, they are also invariably dim-witted *kwei lo* (foreign devils)."

The piece's kicker announced that the Warner Bros. coproduction was underway, concluding: "It is scheduled for release this summer to *kwei lo* audiences around the world. Its title: '*Enter the Dragon*.'"

Newsweek had even made Bruce's preferred title its headline. It didn't matter what Ted Ashley or anyone was going to tell him. He had intercepted the studio's opening attack.

But often at night when she was going to bed, Linda saw the light on in Bruce's study and him at his desk, worried. His vigilance over every detail of his Hollywood debut—his true global debut—was swallowing him.

When Bruce had still been living under Ruby Chow's roof, dreaming of teaching *gung fu* to the American masses, he had written to Pearl Tso about *yin* and *yang*:

"Extremes, though contrary, have the like effects, as extreme heat kills, and so does extreme coldness. Truth lies between these extremes and only a sober moderation seems secure."

He had also composed an essay in Chinese to teach students how to position themselves and allocate their power when facing an opponent. "Let's say that the strength of both hands together equates to a total of 100 points," he wrote. "When it's split between the left and right hands, each with 50 points, the split is even, and this is called Double Weight. When these 100 points are completely to the left or the right hand, with one hand with strength and one hand without strength, then this is called Single Weight.

"For self-defense, one must eliminate the randomness of Single Weight, and for attack, one should change the sluggishness of Double Weight. That's why the power held in the two hands and feet should consist of hard and soft, divided into ratios such as two-and-eight, three-and-seven, four-and-six.

"You cannot have a ratio of ninety-and-ten," he wrote. "This would cause the kind of collapse that happens when you go too far to an extreme." To underscore his point, he cited the top line of the I Ching's first hexagram, "Initiation," the only *gua* that is pure *yang*: "亢龍有悔"—"The proud dragon has regrets."

Eight years before, Bruce had sat in his audition seat unaware of the history of Asian Americans in Hollywood. Now he wore his knowing like a drowning stone.

"He had so many problems in his head he could not sleep," Linda recalled. "The pressures at the time made him especially moody.

"Once or twice he talked about 'in case anything happens to me' for he was aware that everything depended on a fragile foundation; his continued physical fitness."

One day Bruce told her, "I won't live as long as you."

"Why would you think that?" Linda scoffed. "You're a lot healthier than I am and in far better condition, for heaven's sake."

He shrugged. "I don't really know," he said. "The fact is I don't know how long I can keep this up."

CHAPTER 46
The Weight

It was 1973 and it was time.

This film was still very far from perfect, especially the script. The assistant director, Chaplin Chang, had privately warned Raymond Chow that its Orientalist stereotypes would make it unsuitable for Asian audiences. Even Robert Clouse thought it "juvenile."

But Bruce also recognized the tiger symmetries.

He would finally be playing a Chinese James Bond. His character, carrying his own surname, would be fighting in the only kind of competition he claimed to respect—the pure fight, without bounds, where the death of the self or the Other was a possibility. Acting as a warrior in a film—where death was but an entertainment to be enjoyed in the dark—was one of the few socially acceptable places to reconcile the arts of war with performance art.

The production, the deal, even he himself in his own body, marked a unity, a temporal and tentative concord between East and West. His job now was to imbue the work with dignity. He needed to be a man who, once seen, could never again be unseen. Perhaps his success could even redeem the image of Asians in the Western world.

Only one other person knew how serious he was about all these notions. "It wasn't just, oh, this is the next project," Linda recalled. "It was his dream."

Late at night, Bruce was free-writing page after page of a new manifesto that he was calling "In My Own Process," his handwriting growing less distinct as the hours wore on, but his desires never dimming:

> Ever since I was a kid I have this instinctive urge to craze for expansion and growth. To me the function and duty of a human being is the sincere and honest development of one's potential and "self-actualization." Not self-image actualization.
>
> ... I have done a lot during these years of my process. Well, in my process I have changed from self-image actualization to self-actualization, from blindly following propaganda, organized truths, etc., to search internally for the cause of my ignorance.
>
> I am a hard-working man. . . .
>
> I am doing my thing because I have been training, physically & mentally, for this minute all my life.
>
> All my life.

He was a fuel, a flame consuming himself, his last line scrawled messily at the very edge between clarity and dissipation.

As far as Warner Bros. execs were concerned, 1973 was to be the year of *The Exorcist*. They had sunk eleven million dollars into William Friedkin's movie, so much of the corporation's cash flow that at one point execs froze the budgets of every other film in production.

Blood and Steel—the fight over the name had just begun—invited, by contrast, little attention at first. There were no other major stars attached. Its biggest was John Saxon, an Italian American who had taken an Anglo stage name and often played Latinos in a long career as a character actor. Fred Weintraub had lured him with a forty-thousand-dollar contract and a promise that he might be the lead. He left it to Robert Clouse to shut down Saxon's script rewrite requests and tell him the real star was not the one playing Roper.

The other American actors came in much cheaper. Ahna Capri, who played Tania, had been in Robert Clouse's *Darker than Amber*. After Chuck Norris declined, Bob Wall returned to play Han's chief gang enforcer, and the character Michael Allin had originally written as a Japanese man was renamed Ohara. The gloriously afroed Jim Kelly was the last hired when Rockne Tarkington, the studio's first choice to play the Black protagonist Williams, told Fred the low fee was "exploiting" him.

Kelly had won the middleweight title at the 1971 Long Beach International Karate Championship. Not unlike Bruce, he had maintained designs on acting while running a *dojo* on Crenshaw Boulevard. His introductory scenes would be shot nearby at the red-black-and-green cobra-decorated Black Karate Federation *dojo*, a legendary Black martial arts organization that had branched from Ed Parker's school, and was home to the world's top Black martial artists.

Bruce had recommended Hong Kong bodybuilding champion Yeung Sze for the role of Han's most powerful warrior, Bolo,* changing the villain Allin had originally written as Black to Asian. Bruce had also asked that his Uncle Shek Kin be cast as Han. He wanted to work with the old friend of his father's, but he also knew that working opposite the villain of the Wong Fei Hung movies would signify to Hong Kong audiences a new generation replacing the old. Uncle Shek could not deliver his lines in English, so, in another poetic turn, Keye Luke—the Seattle Central District native and pioneering Asian American actor who had played Charlie Chan's number-one son and Kato in the early *Green Hornet* serial—was signed to be the voice of Han.

There was one important casting choice left—Su Lin, the sister of Lee who commits suicide rather than be violated by Ohara and Han's henchmen. Some

---

* Yeung would permanently adopt this stage name as his own.

wanted Nora Miao, who could be the "delicate" flower described in Allin's original script. Bruce wanted Angela Mao Ying, Golden Harvest's Lady Whirlwind, who could play the part as a woman warrior, a symbol of resistance.

Relative to *The Exorcist*, this production problem seemed solvable. Warner Bros. was only in for a quarter million on this movie. Dick Ma reassured everyone they could make their money back. To satisfy the many executives who still didn't think an Asian male lead could carry a movie, they had brought in a white and a Black costar. Most of the risk had been mitigated on paper.

But by the middle of January, Fred Weintraub and Paul Heller were distressed over their production. On January 15, the day shooting was to commence, Bruce had decided to boycott his own movie.

"He was so mad about that script," Linda recalled.

"This is not going to be worthwhile," Bruce had told her. "I don't want any part of it."

When Bruce had met Fred, Paul, and the Warner Bros. execs in Beverly Hills, he had said that he wanted a movie that was more than just escapism. He wanted to include additional scenes that might, as he had put it to Pierre Berton, reveal something of the true Asian.

One scene Allin had written in the original screenplay, a nod to Stirling Silliphant's *Longstreet* episode, had hit that mark. It took place after Bolo killed the guards on the fighting ground for failing to prevent Lee and Williams from leaving their quarters overnight:

Khan looks from face to face, coming last to Williams.

KHAN:
You are shocked, Mr. Williams?

WILLIAMS:
(*lying cool*)
Only at how sloppy your man works.

Khan stands.

KHAN:
As martial artists, we live with death. Every moment of our lives is lived in the light of that final dignity. Ours is the art of dying. And because we embrace death, we are the kings of this life.

But for the most part, Allin's screenplay left Bruce disturbed, and Allin's personality left him irritated. When the two had met in Los Angeles, Allin argued with Bruce over the smallest of the script's details. Bruce returned to Hong Kong convinced that they would be unable to work together. He told Weintraub to fire Allin. Weintraub promised to do it.

Bruce had given Fred and Paul extensive notes on the script and new scenes he had written. He added a scene demonstrating the rigors of Shaolin training. He introduced an abbot who questions Lee about the uses of violence and the spiritual dimensions of fight, then sends him on his mission. He had Lee preparing a student for combat with Zen ideas. In another scene, Lee cleverly one-upped another contestant—an aggressive white *pākehā* New Zealander—by demonstrating the "art of fighting without fighting," in a nod to the *Tao Te Ching* and *The Art of War*.

But the revised screenplay included only this last scene. Fred and Paul also slashed Allin's monologue on the art of dying.

"I'd seen all the old Japanese pictures," Fred told a journalist. "It was only in the last twenty minutes after three hours of preaching and philosophy that the hero would face off against a dozen men and emerge victorious. That was the exciting part—if you were still awake by that time."

Worst of all for Bruce, the script still had Lee playing Roper's Kato. "The main thing," he had written on the back of the last page in large cursive letters, "is LEE!"

Michael Allin arrived in Hong Kong just after the New Year on a ticket that Weintraub had bought him in lieu of proper compensation. Although he had told Bruce that he would, Weintraub had never fired Allin. He had Allin in a room at the Hyatt Regency doing rewrites, and warned him to lay low.

But one morning Bruce had gone to the Star Ferry terminal to see the new posters for *The Way of the Dragon* and walked in at exactly the same time Allin was heading to catch the ferry to Macau. The two awkwardly acknowledged each other. Then Bruce rushed over to the Golden Harvest offices.

The cast and crew were already in town. Sets had been built. It was go time. But at Golden Harvest, Bruce was raging at Fred, Raymond, Andre, and everyone else, telling them that he had quit the movie.

When the day for the start of shooting arrived, Robert Clouse busied the crew with shooting b roll of street scenes around Hong Kong Island and Kowloon. Warner Bros. execs called to check in, and Weintraub assured them they were getting amazing footage that they would send along as soon as they could. Fred, Paul, and Robert delayed the start of principal photography two weeks, to the end of January. But they had no idea if they were going to have a movie. At night, they met in the hotel bar and glumly downed shot after shot.

At home with Linda, Bruce complained that Warner Bros. was treating him like he should be kissing their asses, but he was not going to work until they listened to him. Linda began to understand the role she needed to play. "It was testy because he could have blown the whole thing," Linda later recalled. "They could have up and left."

"Linda was the peacemaker," Andre Morgan said. "She understood how important this movie was for Bruce. Also, objectively speaking, as you can imagine, he was under tremendous pressure—the weight of his dreams, the weight of being the star of the movie, the reason everybody was showing up and wanting to put the right foot forward—knowing as much as he knew about how Hollywood worked."

Another Warner Bros. exec in the States, not knowing any better, had sent Bruce a script for another martial arts movie. He discussed a new plan with Linda. Late one night, Linda called Robert Clouse at the hotel to ask if he would meet with Bruce at a nearby restaurant. When they sat down, Bruce told Robert about this new script and asked if he would direct it. The director was flabbergasted.

"I told him this was madness," Robert recalled. "Too much money and effort had already been spent to be thrown aside at this late hour."

The late-night meeting led to a thaw. Linda called Fred and patiently but firmly explained the changes Bruce wanted to see in the script. "It's going to work out if you guys will listen to him. You're not even listening to him," she told Fred. "It's got to be a two-way thing. You don't just get your way. This is a coproduction."

None of the changes Bruce asked for were going to break the budget. Fred and

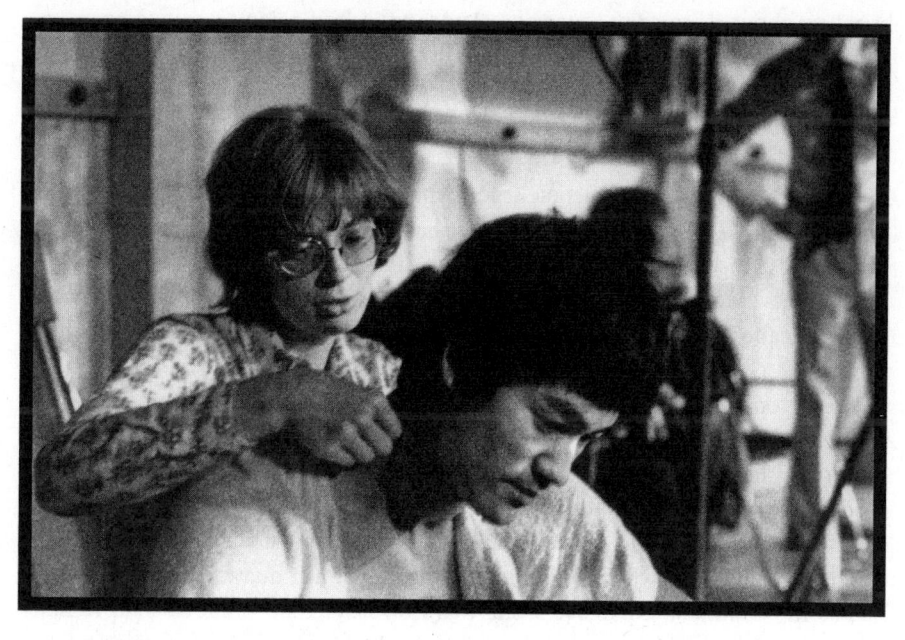

Linda and Bruce on the *Enter the Dragon* set, 1973. Photo courtesy of the Bruce Lee Family Archive.

Paul caved. By January 22, after speaking with Ted Ashley, Weintraub delivered Bruce a new script with all the changes that Bruce had asked for.

There was one last casting question to resolve—the role of Su Lin. "Hollywood was looking for *The World of Suzie Wong*. 'Can't we have a girl in a cheongsam running down?'" Andre recalled. "And Bruce is looking more for, 'This is my sister!' He wanted an honorable statement about Chinese, about his family, and about his sister." In the end, the producers acceded to Bruce and cast Angela Mao Ying.

"In looking back on it," Andre Morgan said, "yes, it was systemic racism. It was the stereotypes that Hollywood had in those days. It was *lazy*. It was just, *what else did they know?*

"But to Bruce," he said, "it was very important because that was what was going to be in *his* movie, and he still had to deal with the audiences who would be criticizing him and scrutinizing him. And so that weight was on *him*."

On the first day of shooting, the plan had been to ease Bruce in by having him shoot the scene in which he first meets Mei Ling. But after Fred, Paul, Raymond, Andre, and others had gathered on the soundstage, the director and the crew had finished their preparations, and Bruce and the actress Betty Chung were in place, everyone noticed Bruce had developed a twitch in his cheek that would not stop. Nobody wanted to tell Bruce. Everybody knew that he knew. They waited. They brought tea. They made light jokes. But Bruce's tic would not go away.

"It was not a small problem," Andre Morgan recalled. "It was all nerves."

After countless takes, Robert dismissed everyone for lunch. Fred was upset, babbling about doomsday scenarios. Andre took him aside to calm him down. Raymond went with Bruce. After lunch, Bruce, Betty, Robert, and everyone else returned to their places.

"They got it in one," Andre said. "And then there was no looking back."

When Fred and Paul had screened Bruce's three kung fu movies for Robert Clouse, the director told them, "The first thing we have to do is kick the strut out of Bruce Lee. We're going to Westernize him to some degree."

"He'd have a strut and he would do this thing with the thumb across the nose," Robert recalled. "And I said, 'Bruce we're not going to do that.' He said, 'What do you mean? That's my trademark, everyone expects me to do that.' I said, 'No, no. You're beyond that now. A Western audience doesn't like the obvious strut. Let's play it straight here.'"

On set, the white Americans were bewildered by the Chinese. Some days hundreds of extras showed up, and then the next, only half of them. They did not understand why the local actresses did not want to play prostitutes or junkies. They could not understand why the Hong Kongers did not just do what they said.

The movie's most expensive scene was Han's welcome banquet. Paul Heller's yellow-fever, high-chroma circus was to include birdcages, lobster tanks, large plates of fried fish and crispy suckling pig, lion dancers, jugglers, tumblers, musicians, courtesans, sumo wrestlers, and a big gong. Robert and Fred also wanted bamboo birdcages, a hundred of them hanging from the rafters, each with two birds inside.

On day one of the banquet shoot, Fred was pleased the Chinese prop master had produced the cages and the birds. On day two the Chinese crew returned to the set to find the birds had broken free and shit on everything. Part of the crew was dispatched to clean up the mess. The others tried to catch the birds and return them to the cages. Watching the hapless prop master using a weathered stepladder to place the birds back into their cages, Fred lost it and unleashed a torrent of curses at him and the crew. As the shoot proceeded, the food spoiled. The heat and incense killed many of the birds. The prop master disappeared—"so humiliated he didn't come back for weeks," Fred wrote.

And then the Chinese went from strange to difficult. If an actor was filmed sitting on a green couch, the next day the couch would be red. The white *gis* for hundreds of extras disappeared on one shoot day because the wardrobe woman had sent them to be cleaned.

Fred came to believe that yelling at the Chinese crew and then storming off to get the couches or the clothing by himself was the only way to solve such problems. When Paul Heller took over Fred's duties, he yelled and cursed and stormed off too. For years afterward, Fred told interviewers, "The Chinese say yes to everything, but they don't mean yes," as if completing the film had been a triumph of American leadership and resourcefulness over Chinese indolence and inscrutability.

But the Chinese crew had been talking about the white Americans the entire time. Andre Morgan said, "The Chinese hated their guts and thought they were imbeciles."

As they were trying to complete a difficult shoot of Bruce, John, and Jim arriving on their sampans in Aberdeen Harbor, Robert Clouse described becoming upset with one recalcitrant woman who had stopped rowing her boat. He was getting a great shot. Why was she screwing with him? He later learned she was upset she might be fined and lose her boat because he had steered her into Communist Chinese waters.

Another time, Robert and the crew were perched on the rooftop of a twenty-story building to capture a wide-angle shot of a sampan moving through the harbor. But as they started shooting a Chinese crew member poked his head out of the boat to light his pipe. Robert called, "Cut!" But the crew could not hear him. Frustrated that it might take another forty-five minutes to set up the shot again, he exclaimed, "Fucking Chinese."

Andre Morgan recalled, "The continuity guy, who's this little old man, says in Cantonese, 'That's the last insult I'm going to take from these fucking foreigners.'

With that, he takes his clipboard and he's coming over to hit Clouse from behind." Andre and assistant director Chaplin Chang tackled the old man before he could push the director off the roof.

The white Americans came to lean on Bruce to solve their problems. "The Chinese crew were his slaves," Paul Heller said. "I mean, they were his willing, eager slaves—as were the stunt guys that he worked with. Whenever we came to sort of an impasse, all you had to do is mention something to Bruce, and Bruce would say two words and whatever the problem was disappeared." To them it seemed Bruce had built some kind of cult of personality.

While shooting his climactic fight scene with Bob Wall, Bruce suffered a bloody accident involving real glass bottles.* They had practiced the scene: Wall was to confront Bruce with two broken bottles; Bruce was to reverse-spin-kick the first bottle, which Wall was to drop, then spin again and punch him. But as cameras rolled, Wall did not drop the bottle; Bruce slashed his hand on it and was soon in a car heading to the hospital to receive twelve stitches.

The stuntmen were outraged, believing Wall had sabotaged the scene on purpose. Tabloids published accounts that insinuated Bruce and Bob Wall now had a blood beef, further inflaming the stuntmen. Bruce's on-screen role as their avenger had crossed into real life. In reshoots, Bruce felt compelled to kick Bob without holding back. Even with a protective pad, Bob took twelve takes' worth of a beating that day.

But the Chinese cast and crew's loyalty to Bruce had less to do with their racial animus against the *gweilo* or his nose-wiping charisma than his comparatively enlightened authority.

"Whenever you advise rulers in the way of the Tao, counsel them not to use force to conquer the universe for this would only cause resistance," Laozi had said. "Force is followed by loss of strength."

Bruce was patient with the elderly caterers and young personal assistants. He took time to recognize the carpenters and plasterers. He ate with the crew members, stuntmen, and extras. He made sure that they received the same kind of box meal as him. They marveled over how Bruce called them "brother."

"When they saw his car coming, they'd jump up. He's the boss, right?" Bolo Yeung recalled.

But Bruce was telling the workers, "Everybody sit down, I want to talk."

"So they all squatted down on the ground and talked," said Bolo. "You never saw Raymond Chow squat down on the ground and talk."

At the end of days in which the stuntmen had endured difficult shoots, Bruce instructed Golden Harvest officials to double their pay. He pushed Raymond to better compensate Angela Mao and other actors. He paid for them to see doctors

---

* At the time, Hong Kongers did not use Hollywood-style stunt-glass props made of sugar.

for their injuries or to cover family emergencies. This kind of treatment inspired protectiveness and pride.

"It's a Chinese thing," Angela said. "Be gentle to people below you."

New problems arose when the production moved to the final tournament scenes. Many more extras were needed, sometimes as many as four hundred. In the wild closing fight scenes, street rivals sometimes met each other face-to-face on the grass tennis courts that served as the tourney's battlefield and tore each other up.

Bruce found himself the regular target of challenges. He laughed off most of them. But at the end of one long day, he was talking with cameraman Henry Wong when a kid emerged from a crowd of extras and asked Bruce to show him how to execute a specific kick. Bruce got up to demonstrate and Henry began rolling film. Once he was satisfied that the extra got it, Bruce said he had to go.

But then the extra said he wanted to show Bruce what he had learned. Bruce chuckled, said no, and turned to leave.

"My *sifu* thinks your martial arts are inferior," the extra said. "Your *gung fu* isn't real."

"If I don't have real *gung fu*, I don't think you will have it," Bruce said with a laugh. "You're stupid!"

The extra called him a coward. His mother was there, trying to pull him away, telling him it was time to go. But then the extra got in Bruce's face. "How shall we play?" he demanded.

"This after Bruce help him, right?" Henry recalled. "Everybody watching what Bruce do."

It wasn't the first challenge Bruce had on set, nor would it be the last. Bruce had left a couple of extras bloodied and toothless. But this kid had not just challenged Bruce's skills, he had maligned Bruce's generosity.

All benevolence and patience gone, all the frustration and rage of the past year welling inside him, Bruce's entire body changed.

"Fight," Bruce snarled. "This is how we play."

He let out a scream and kicked the extra above his groin, sending him flying back into a pile of lumber. The extra got back up and charged Bruce with flailing arms. Bruce plunged another kick into his solar plexus. The stuntmen circled the boy, ready to continue the beat-down. Who did this nobody think he was?

All the challenges Bruce had faced on set had been minor squabbles that he had dealt with quickly. But this fight lingered with him. He later recounted it to Wong Shun Leung: "[The boy] was hurt. His look was bad. He did not make any sound."

The extra got up shakily, apologized, and said his *sifu* had been wrong.

"Seeing his appearance," Bruce told Ah Leung, "I did not want to hurt him again." He waved off the stuntmen.

But the extra was badly injured. After crew members examined the boy, they told Bruce he had broken the boy's rib. Bruce gave his mother twenty thousand

Hong Kong dollars and advised her to take him to the hospital right away. Then he turned to Henry and asked for the footage so that he could destroy it.

Bruce had come through these on-set challenges physically unscathed. But Ah Leung could see that Bruce's choice to take every fight alone, big or small, had taken a lot out of him. "He was like a wounded beast," he said.

As the shooting stretched into March, well past its original deadline, the film still did not have a beginning or ending anyone felt good about.

The script had opened with Williams at his *dojo* and Roper playing golf. The climax took up just a quarter of a page. After Lee declares to Han, "You have offended my family and you have offended the Shaolin temple," the script reads: "With a cry the two of them rush together and the fight begins. This is to be the smashingest, fuckingest fight ever put on Eastman Kodak #5254 color stock."

At the Repulse Bay Hotel, where the producers, as well as Robert Clause and his wife, Anna, were staying, was a clothing boutique whose entryway contained thin recessed vertical mirrors. Robert watched Anna's reflection as she walked in one day. He remembered seeing the mirrors "shatter her image as she walked by them."

Paul Heller had been intrigued by the effect as well. Whether they knew it or not—Robert Clouse would insist he had never seen the movie—Orson Welles had used a similar idea for a fun-house shootout at the climax of his 1947 noir, *The Lady from Shanghai*. The two attempted to convince Bruce to stage the final fight in a hall of mirrors. He was skeptical at first, but agreed to try it.

The crew built a round room and a box in the center to house the cameras, and installed eight thousand dollars' worth of mirrors. Robert Clouse, assistant director Chaplin Chang, and cinematographer Gil Hubbs spent days figuring out angles. Then they put in Shek Kin and Bruce Lee to begin shooting, which was made more difficult by the excessive heat in the studio.* Paul asked the Chinese crew to move the fans, but was told it was "somebody else's rice bowl." Bruce intervened.

Everyone was exhausted. But when Bruce saw the dailies, he was blown away. "There are only two people who give a damn what this picture looks like," Bruce told Robert Clouse. "That's you and me."

On March 4, 1973, with the scheduled shooting done, the cast and crew presented a cake and sang "Happy Birthday" to Andre Morgan. Andre flew that afternoon to South Korea to shoot Golden Harvest's new movie with Jhoon Rhee, *When Tae Kwon Do Strikes*. Most of the other white Americans were relieved to finally be heading home.

Bruce still needed to shoot the scenes that he had won through his protest. He directed and choreographed the scenes at the Shaolin temple by himself, including

---

* One story has Shek punching Bruce in the face during their practice sessions by accident. Another has Bruce reacting with kicks, causing Shek to tell him, "Hey, son, it's just a movie!"

the opening temple match with Sammo Hung, as well as the scenes with Roy Chiao as the abbot and Stephen Tung Wai as Lee's young student. These scenes would finally provide the movie's beginning.

By mid-April, all the filming was complete, and excitement for the film was growing on both sides of the Pacific. In his large, newly finished office at Golden Harvest studios, with its wallpaper of naked women and a large oak desk featuring a hand-carved dragon on its exterior and a secret compartment for his hashish underneath, Bruce had reserved a special place for his old pair of broken eyeglasses, a reminder of his days of struggle in Hollywood. On the wall, he had hung his black-light poster of the impatient vultures. He was spent, but still hungry.

CHAPTER 47
The Names, Part 3

On March 7, 1973, under a headline that screamed, "KUNG FU: INSTANT BOX-OFFICE," *Variety* announced that "the biggest explosion of violence in the Orient since the Boxer Rebellion" had begun.

The catalyst for all the hype was the first fruit of the distribution deal that Warner Bros. international head Dick Ma had brokered with Run Run Shaw to introduce the United States to kung fu movies—Chung Chang-Wha's *King Boxer*. When he had first screened it for his execs, one of them recalled, "It was a ludicrous, awful film. We all sat in the projection room and laughed at it." Then *King Boxer* was released in Europe as *The Invincible Boxer* to stunning success, topping the box office in Italy and outearning *The Godfather* in England.

On the eve of its US premiere, skittish Warner Bros. execs changed the movie's title five more times. When they released it on March 21 under a final name, *Five Fingers of Death*, Dick Ma's gamble paid off beyond anyone's expectations. In its second week, it became the number-one movie in the country, despite, or perhaps because of, what one reviewer called its "battering savagery," which eclipsed "the roughest Hollywood western" and inaugurated "a whole new era of bruising." By the end of May, the same Warner Bros. execs who had dismissed the film were crowing that it had taken in ten million dollars worldwide.

Suddenly all eyes were on Bruce and the unprecedented transpacific coproduction between Concord and Warner Bros. he and the media were calling *Enter the Dragon*.

Behind the scenes, Bruce was furious with Raymond Chow. In a press release, Golden Harvest, not Concord, had been credited as the coproducer of the movie. The PR flacks had also run an article in Golden Harvest's in-house magazine saying that Raymond was "like a babysitter" to him. Bruce wanted it clear: Concord was a partnership, and he was Raymond's equal, not his little child savant.

He decided he could no longer trust Chow. He believed Chow was withholding large sums of money from *The Way of the Dragon*. He was outraged by Raymond's US distribution deal with National General Pictures for *The Big Boss* and *Fist of Fury*. He had wanted *Enter the Dragon* to be his US debut and believed Chow, hastily trying to cash in on his good name, had been lowballed by a second-rate company.

National General soon proved him right. They told Chow they would give *The Big Boss* a new title, *The Chinese Connection*, to tie it to William Friedkin's *French Connection*, 1971's smash hit on the heroin-smuggling trade. But when they brought the movies to market, *The Big Boss* became *Fists of Fury*—including the inexplicable plural—and *Fist of Fury* became *The Chinese Connection*. Legend has it that a hapless staffer mixed up the film cans when they received the shipment. Within the year, National General would be defunct.

Seizing his opportunity, Run Run Shaw sent Bruce a stack of fresh scripts to review and a promise that he could do his next movie with his childhood friend, the director Chor Yuen. Bruce paid a visit to Movietown to take pictures in period costume wielding axes and swords as the Qing dynasty general Nian Gengyao. On March 2, 1973, the *China Mail* ran the headline, "Who Will Get Superstar Li?" The cover of the *Star* the next morning trumpeted, "Bruce Will Make Film for Shaws." Reports had Run Run Shaw tendering him a blank contract, asking him to fill in the number, to which Bruce had demanded the record amount of HKD $2.5 million, half a million in US dollars. It was the art of fighting by keeping Run Run and Raymond fighting.

On May 2, as *Fists of Fury* opened in big American markets, *Variety* declared that Bruce was generating "torrid box office . . . from Lebanon to South America, and from Malaysia to Italy," and that martial arts films were set to become the "klondike fad-of-the-moment." The United States Catholic Conference condemned kung fu films, singling out Bruce, who, they wrote, "shows his stuff here in a manner that is simply too realistic, too savage to be either cleverly amusing or comfortably entertaining." But at Cannes, everyone was buzzing about the stunning rise of what *Variety* had named the "Hong Kong–made 'chop-socky.'" Before May was out, *Fists of Fury* was at number one in the States. Rounding out the top three were *Five Fingers of Death* and Angela Mao's *Deep Thrust: The Hand of Death*—originally released by Golden Harvest as *Lady Whirlwind* and retitled to link it with the hit porn movie *Deep Throat*.

After Bruce's power move in *Newsweek* to secure the name *Enter the Dragon*, Fred Weintraub and Ted Ashley had tentatively agreed to support his title. But now everyone at Warners wanted to weigh in. Weintraub sent a memo to Ashley:

> As we know, Chinese films will be flooding the market. I believe it is important to immediately differentiate ENTER THE DRAGON from the Mandarin pictures. We must let theatre owners and the public become aware that this is the first International Martial Arts Film starring a Chinese actor, a Caucasian/American and a Black/American actor.

Weintraub did not want their film stigmatized by the campy foreignness of the dubbed imports. He also wanted to reopen debate on the name:

> There have been rumblings about changing the title. Can this be clarified quickly so we can continue to send out publicity and advertising as soon as possible?

Weintraub thought *Enter the Dragon* sounded like a kids' flick. Ashley agreed, thinking it sounded like a monster movie. To them, a dragon was a fairy-tale creature, at best a sacrificial beast for a young boy of the old legends to slay on his way to knighthood, not, as it was for Asians and Pacific Islanders, a god of mysterious, destructive, and transformative powers.

On April 19, Ashley asked Dick Lederer, his executive vice president of worldwide advertising and publicity, to send a list of all their alternative titles.

Names mattered. They reflected world views. When you named something, you defined it—all its powers, all its relations, all its potential.

Asian Americans who wanted to see the opening of *The Chinese Connection* at double-feature drive-ins in Oakland or Hayward in June still had to sit through a Fu Manchu flick starring Christopher Lee first. But at another theater nearby, the name BRUCE LEE took up the entirety of the marquee, with the movie title in smaller letters below it.

After the film critic Michele Lomax saw the movie at a San Francisco theatre, she wrote, "The (predominantly black) kung fu audiences beat any I've seen, including the group at a Berkeley theater showing *Shaft* who gave Moses Gunn's fedora and double-breasted camel's hair coat an ovation . . .

"Bruce Lee strikes some responsive chord that is not to be believed," she continued. "The first sight of him draws the shouts and screams usually heard calling on Jesus Christ, Willie Mays, or B. B. King."

From the doorstep of Everybody's Bookstore in the I-Hotel in San Francisco, Harvey Dong could see crowds of Asians, Blacks, Chicanos, and whites lining up for Bruce Lee movies across the street at the Bella Union Theatre. The owner let the gang kids Harvey was trying to organize in for free. A little respect went a long way.

Afterward, they poured back onto Kearny Street, imitating the moves they had seen. Some of them headed up the hill to the *gung fu kwoons*, which were now packed with students of all races, ages, and political lines. "It seemed," Harvey recalled, "like everybody was into some kind of *gung fu*."

One film critic found all this kung fu fighting a little bit frightening. Aljean Harmetz's feature in the influential *Los Angeles Times* on the rise of martial arts film detoured into an account of her fears of their inner-city audiences:

Black adolescents wandered the aisles announcing their antagonism toward the whites in the audience, using the crudest language they could muster.

Although four armed security guards patrolled the Los Angeles Theater, my 10-year-old son—who has been to two matinees at this theater in the last few weeks—whispered that he did not want to come here again . . . he was intimidated by the hostility of the 10-year olds, frightened by the antagonism with which the thin boy in the camel's hair coat planted himself on the arm of a seat in front of an elderly white man and asked, "Honky, what you going to do about it?"

But Asian Americans were seeing something different. "That black youth was not mimicking Bruce Lee, or trying to do Kung Fu, but dealing with his own real anger *in the same manner* as the films," wrote Jeff Furumura in *Gidra*.

These movies were for "people who have no actual control over the course of their daily lives," he added. "So isn't it neat to go down to the local theater and see Bruce Lee, for example, in *Fists of Fury*, wipe out his racketeer bosses?"

Furumura interviewed Asian American filmgoers after a Los Angeles screening. "Even though [these movies] stress ethnic chauvinism, sexism, and paint a world where 'good' always overcomes 'evil,'" one audience member told him, "just maybe, if you're a young Asian male, maybe you'd come walking out of the theater feeling just a bit more proud, self-confident, and secure. And that's a step up from Hop Sing and Chop-Chop."

Wally Jay's son, Leon, who had come of age fighting his way around multiracial East Oakland, felt the shift through the names he was being called in the streets.

"I was being called 'chink' by the whites and the Blacks," he recalled. "When Bruce came out, next thing you know, it was 'brother.' Last week I was a 'chink,' this week, I'm 'brother.' Boom!"

But as Bruce's profile was building in Europe and America, he was in Hong Kong slowly losing control of his image and himself.

Linda said, "Bruce would go outside our door in the morning with me, and one day two girls were walking by. They asked him could they take a picture with him. So he puts his arm round each girl and takes a picture like that. The next day the picture's in the paper, reporting that Bruce is having an affair with these two women. It just gets to a point where it's ridiculous."

Tabloids regularly linked Bruce to other women. "I considered them rumors because I know what the press does with anyone who is a celebrity," Linda said. "So I was ready for that."

She did not know that Bruce was seeing a former Shaw siren, Betty Ting Pei, whom Raymond Chow had brought into the Golden Harvest fold. Bruce, Betty, and Linda had met the year before, introduced by Raymond, after a birthday dinner for Linda at the Hyatt Regency. Tabloids were suggesting that Bruce had somehow been responsible for Betty's alleged suicide attempt at the end of 1972. "That dumb girl," he told Mito, "took several pills and said that she's in love with me and gonna kill herself if she can't have me. Shit, I can't do much in that kind of situation."

Instead Bruce absorbed himself in upgrading from Raymond Chow and Golden Harvest to Ted Ashley and Warner Bros. With Linda's assistance he composed a letter to Ashley that he sent on April 22. He wrote:

Nowadays, my offers for doing a film have reached to the point which I guarantee you will both surprise as well as shock you. . . .

I have had a bad experience doing a picture with some person or organization in Hong Kong. In other words, I was burned once, and didn't like it. . . .

My twenty years of experience, both in martial arts and acting, has apparently led to the successful harmony of appropriateness of showmanship and genuine, efficient, artful expression. In short, this is it and ain't nobody knows it like I know it. . . .

Under such circumstances, I sincerely hope that you will open up the genuineness within you and be absolutely fair and square in our transactions. Because of our friendship, I am holding up my money-making time—like ten offers from hungry producers—to look forward to this meeting. You see, Ted, my obsession is to make, pardon the expression, the fuckingest action motion picture that has ever been made.

From May through August, traditionally the high period of Hollywood blockbusters, kung fu films from Hong Kong stormed *Variety*'s chart of highest-grossing movies. Bruce's bargaining power had never been higher.

But, once again, everything stopped.

On the hot, humid afternoon of May 10, Bruce was in a sound studio at Golden Harvest to dub his lines for *Enter the Dragon*. The air conditioner had been shut off so that they could record. But after working a little in the steaming room, Bruce excused himself to go to the bathroom. When he got there, his legs gave way and he crumpled to the floor. Noticing he hadn't returned after twenty minutes, the sound engineer dispatched a studio assistant to check on him.

When Bruce came to, he was on his knees. He heard the assistant's steps and began fumbling around, acting as if he had dropped his glasses. The two walked back to the studio. But as soon as he stepped into the room again, he fainted and blacked out. He vomited and went into convulsions.

The assistant rushed across the lot to alert Raymond Chow, who asked staffers to call a doctor and ran back to the studio with the assistant. Chow was horrified at Bruce's state: "I saw Lee was having difficulty in breathing. He was making a loud noise and was shaking." When Bruce was admitted to Baptist Hospital, he was unconscious, unresponsive, drenched in sweat, and suffering from a high fever. He went into convulsions again and the hospital staff struggled to control him—his body was strong.

Dr. Charles Langford received him and brought in a neurosurgeon, Dr. Peter Woo. Bruce was experiencing brain swelling, and the doctors administered a dose of the diuretic mannitol to reduce it. Linda had arrived and saw her husband gasping for air. "His eyes were open at this stage, but they were not focusing," she recalled.

"Is he going to be all right?" she asked Dr. Langford.

"He's very sick," he told her.

Dr. Langford had downplayed the gravity of the situation to Linda.

"He had very irregular respiration. He was perspiring profusely. His color was not good. He was alternatingly flaccidly unresponsive and then some rigidity," the doctor later recalled. "He literally looked like a dead person."

It took two and a half hours for Bruce to regain complete consciousness. At first, his speech was slurred. But slowly his memory returned, and he was joking with the hospital staff.

In her biography Linda wrote, "Almost the first words Bruce had said to me after he recovered consciousness were that he felt very close to death—but that he could still exert his will and he had told himself, 'I'm going to fight it—I'm going to make it—I'm not going to give up' because he knew that if he thought any other way, he would die."

Bruce and Linda decided to return to Los Angeles, where they could see the best doctors in state-of-the-art facilities. He could also visit his mother, his brother Robert, and his old friends. Perhaps, Linda thought, Bruce could relax.

When he got there, he called Taky.

"You never write, you never call me!" Bruce protested.

Taky laughed. "I'm enjoying what you're doing. You don't need me."

"You're still my number one friend and don't you forget that. Let me know what you need. Anything you want," Bruce said. "I haven't changed. I'm still the same guy."

But in some important ways he had changed.

"I had tried to tell him that there was no longer any need for him to work so hard; that his career was now running along the right lines and the future was assured," Linda wrote. "Besides, the most important thing was that the four of us should be together, that as long as we had each other, everything was fine."

But Bruce did not want to stop. As he arrived at the UCLA Medical Center, with its red-brick exteriors and its palm trees, and walked down its antiseptic fluorescent halls past all the orderly bustle, he knew one thing. He wanted to work. He had additional sound looping to do. He had meetings to take with Robert Clouse, Fred Weintraub, Paul Heller, and Warner execs. Everything he did now was setting up his bright future.

At UCLA, Bruce received a brain scan and brain flow study, an electroencephalogram, and a complete physical. But Dr. David Reisbord and his team could not figure out what had gone wrong. His brain functions seemed to be working fine, they told him, and he had "the body of an eighteen-year-old," a comment that delighted Bruce. He was told he had suffered an idiopathic grand mal seizure—a seizure without a known cause—and prescribed an anti-epileptic drug called Dilantin.

From their bungalow at the Beverly Hills Wilshire, Bruce and Linda received family and friends. Bruce invited Mito Uyehara and Peter Chin to join him at leisurely lunches with Fred Weintraub, Raymond Chow, Warners execs, and the Argentine composer Lalo Schifrin. Bruce boasted to everyone that the doctors had told him he had the body of an eighteen-year-old. He repeated this line over and over, laughing the same way every time.

When Mito saw Bruce, he exclaimed, "Bruce, you're too skinny!"

Bruce smiled. "Yeah, OK. Hold this cushion."

Later, when Bruce and Linda were alone with Mito, Bruce boasted that Brandon too had become a published journalist. He took out a clipping of a piece Brandon had written that had run in a Hong Kong newspaper. But Mito was surprised when Linda seemed triggered.

"I hope we can return to Los Angeles as soon as possible," she said sharply to Bruce. "The kids can't have a normal life."

He went to see Dan Inosanto. "You almost lost your *sifu*," he told Dan.

They waxed nostalgic about the old days, and the subject turned to getting old, a topic they had often discussed. Bruce had long mocked the idea of the elderly fighter. Only in the Asian martial arts, he had once told *Black Belt* magazine, were there so-called champions who were ninety-nine years old. "You don't get better with age," he said. "You only get wiser." Bruce knew that for every fighter, time was the final enemy and the outcome was certain.

He joked with Dan, "I'm going to make sure when I'm fifty that no fifty-year-old man is going to push me around!" Decades later, Dan remembered that, for Bruce, "fifty was already really old."

Back at the hotel, Robert saw his brother staring at a hunchbacked old man struggling to walk with his cane. "You know, Robert," he said, "I don't think I can be like this gentleman when I get old. I don't think I would like that at all."

Robert said, "He saw people all around him growing weak with age, and he finally realized he might get old himself one of these days. He never wanted to wake up, look at himself in the mirror, and feel weak. He really dreaded that."

One evening, Peter Chin picked up Chinese takeout and they ate and talked. Bruce seemed unusually depleted. Peter worried he had become *zau fo jap mo*, that he was burning in the fires of his own bodily obsessions. They watched a TV show that featured an old man in a wheelchair and another in a walker. "Peter," Bruce declared, "I'm never going to be like that."

When Bruce visited his mother, she was shocked at how he looked. His face appeared drawn, his bones lived in. Seven months before, when he had returned to Los Angeles after finishing *The Way of the Dragon*, she had scolded him about his weight and told him to rest and take care of his health. He seemed even more parched and worn now.

"I couldn't believe the person before me was my son," she recalled. "He told me he would not live long because doctors in Hong Kong had told him that there was serious disease in his head."

Bruce had already quietly obtained life insurance policies, including a $1.35 million policy with Lloyds of London, not long before the May incident. He told her, "Mom, don't worry. I'll be all right. Even if I die, you needn't worry about your living. There will be no financial problem."

"Don't talk like that," she said. "It's unlucky."

Bruce was scarred and battle-worn, but he had done his job on the movie. He met Robert Clouse in a Warner Bros. screening room to see the assembled work print, grease pencil marks and all, without sound effects or a score. As the lights rose, Bruce looked at the director, nodded, and smiled broadly: "We've got it."

After screening the same rough cut for the Warner Bros. execs, Paul Heller announced their reaction: "They went bananas."

Distribution, sales, and publicity mobilized. Ted Ashley prepared to authorize hundreds of thousands of dollars more to hire the composer Lalo Schifrin, who had scored *Mission Impossible*, *Dirty Harry*, and *Bullitt*, for the soundtrack, and to ensure that the marketing would be massive.

He began talking to Bruce about a long-term deal. There could be sequels, a franchise. Ashley was reportedly offering Bruce one hundred thousand US dollars a year for life if he agreed to make five movies for Warner Bros. The long shot from Asian America had begun to receive *Exorcist*-level attention.

But there was still another battle to fight—over the movie's name. In Hollywood, it had been a constant topic of discussion. On June 7, shortly after he had returned to Hong Kong, Ashley telegrammed him:

AFTER SPENDING A FULL TWO HOURS WITH DICK LEDERER VICE PRESIDENT OF OUR ADVERTISING DEPARTMENT IT HAS BEEN RESOLVED THAT THE TITLE WHICH WILL GIVE THE PICTURE THE BROADEST DIMENSIONS IS HANS ISLAND

THIS HAS MANY OF THE PLUS FACTORS OF THE TITLE ENTER THE DRAGON AND NONE OF THE NEGATIVES I AM TOLD THAT (WEST COAST PRESIDENT) FRANK WELLS AGREES AS WELL

Hours later, Dick Lederer telegrammed Bruce:

FOLLOWING UP ON TED ASHLEY'S CABLE TO YOU IN WHICH WE INDICATED WE WERE PLANNING TO USE THE TITLE "HAN'S ISLAND" IN PLACE OF "ENTER THE DRAGON" WE HAVE NOW GONE ONE STEP FURTHER AND CHANGED IT TO "THE ISLAND OF HAN".

WE'VE DONE THIS TO AVOID CONFUSION WITH OTHER NEW TITLES AND BECAUSE ON FINAL ANALYSIS WE FEEL THAT THIS WORDING OF WHAT IS ESSENTIALLY THE SAME IDEA

PROMISES SOMEHOW A MORE IMPORTANT FILM AND LENDS ITSELF MORE DRAMATICALLY TO OUR ADVERTISING MATERIALS IN PARTICULAR OUR RADIO COMMERCIALS.

As if the significance of a dragon was beyond the comprehension of the average American moviegoer. As if the only Oriental who mattered in a Hollywood film was the one who died. As if an Asian hero was less imaginable than an ocean rock, a piece of real estate.

Picture Bruce screaming, *Han's Island? The Island of Han? What the fuck!*

The next day, on Hyatt Regency letterhead, he handwrote a letter to Ashley:

Dear Ted,

Just a note to let you know that this "18 year old" has arrived safely.

Do consider carefully in regard to the title of Enter the Dragon.

1. This "unique" dragon (the Chinese, the spiritual, etc.) is not one of those Won Ton Kung Fu flicks from H.K.

2. With the rightful publicity we can tell on the screen as well as outside that this dragon has broken the all-time record consecutively—like you said, "it comes across."

I really think this is a good title and like I said, do think it over carefully because "Enter the Dragon" suggests the emergence (the entrance) of someone (a personality) that is of quality.

Time is pressing, Ted.

Do please send me the two scripts so I can work it over.

Warmest personal regards,
Bruce Lee

Under his English signature, he signed the character "龍" and drew an arrow to it: "The Dragon in Chinese, by the way." If Ashley wanted a franchise, he would not get it from Han or his island, only from the Dragon.

Five days later, the Warner Bros. chief telegrammed Bruce again, all the typos suggestive of great worry and haste:

AS REQUESTED WE HAVE GIVEN HE TITLE [sic] STILL FURTHER THOUGHT

AND HAVE TAKEN GREATLY INTO ACCOUNT YOUR PREFERENCE AS WELL

THE TITLE WILL THEREFORE BE ENTERED [sic] THE DRAGON

He signed off, "Love to you and Linda."

Bruce telexed Ted the next morning, June 16. "I am so relieved and impressed with your final preference," he wrote. "Toward inner peace to both of us."

CHAPTER 48
The Light of Stars

As Bruce and Ted were ending their war of the names, *The Chinese Connection* was rush-released by National General Pictures in the United States. In its second week, it hit number one. On June 20, with *The Chinese Connection* at the top, five kung fu films from Hong Kong were in the top fifty.

Offers were pouring in from around the world. The producer Carlo Ponti—who had produced Fellini's *La Strada*, Antonioni's *Blowup*, and Lean's *Dr. Zhivago*—wanted Bruce to star opposite his wife, Sophia Loren. MGM wanted to pair him with Elvis Presley. His friend the producer Andy Vajna and the director Ivan Nagy wanted him to make a period movie called *Journey to the East* with Nagy's wife, the Chinese American actress Irene Tsu. The giant Roman movie studio Titanus was eager to talk. Hanna-Barbera was interested in doing a Saturday morning cartoon. Clothing, sponsorship, and endorsement proposals piled up on his desk. Sy Weintraub was coming to Hong Kong to present him with "a super plan."

James Coburn had already flown out, with Elmo Williams, Twentieth Century-Fox's Vice President of Worldwide Production in tow, to meet Bruce about reviving *The Silent Flute*. Now Bruce was circumspect. Jim didn't take Bruce's reticence as a no, and left Hong Kong ready to tell Stirling to make plans to return in late July. But Bruce had already spoken to Stirling, and told him he couldn't see himself playing four supporting Oriental roles to Coburn's lead anymore. "I won't carry Jim on my shoulders," he said. Stirling decided not to repeat this to Coburn.

Preparations were being made for a marketing blitz for *Enter the Dragon*, including an appearance on Johnny Carson's *Tonight Show*. Bruce had returned to work on *The Game of Death*, attempting to mold his canned scenes, fight drawings, and concept notes into a complete script. He was continuing to cast the movie, with Taky Kimura, Peter Chin, and Wong Shun Leung still on his list for the Tower of Death, Nancy Kwan for the female lead, and George Lazenby, a former James Bond, as the villain. He was still considering whether to include Betty Ting Pei, whom he had begun seeing again.

Bruce sent word to Run Run that he was holding the fall months to shoot a movie for Shaw Brothers. Raymond wanted to meet about the future of Concord. Bruce agreed he would "hear him out."

But success had only put him more on guard. "I must be very, very careful," he told a friend. When Mito Uyehara called to discuss business, he was happy to hear his old friend's voice.

Bruce was scheduled to headline *Black Belt* magazine's first "Oriental Fighting Arts Expo" in Hollywood in August, what Mito was billing as the largest showcase yet for Asian martial arts. The two were forming a company to sell posters, photos, and Bruce Lee–branded products. One of the items was a biography Mito would write, and they spoke about meeting when he got to Los Angeles.

Bruce seemed to be searching for a way back home. He told Mito he wanted to buy homes in Europe, Hong Kong, and the United States. He said he also wanted to open a new school in Los Angeles. Maybe he could have someone teach *aikido* and ask Hayward Nishioka to teach *judo*. Perhaps he might even teach Jeet Kune Do again.

He called Peter Chin and asked him to join him for his *Enter the Dragon* media tour. Only after *Enter the Dragon* opened would he rest. But he was beyond tired. He still wasn't sleeping. He was having severe headaches. He was short with friends. They told him to try to relax. He snapped back, *"Trying to relax? That's a contradiction."* Although Bruce was perched at the biggest success he had ever experienced, Peter recalled, "He was kind of down, depressed, like very lonely. Extremely lonely."

One July afternoon, Bruce ran into Lo Wei and Gladys Liu Liang Hua in the Golden Harvest screening room. Lo had been claiming credit in the tabloids for Bruce's success, and the sight of him set Bruce off. As he and Lo Wei screamed at each other, the police were called, trailed by an infantry of reporters. Headlines about Bruce's turbulent behavior filled the newsstands.

His old friends were increasingly worried about him. Upon finishing his film in Korea, Jhoon Rhee had come to see Bruce in Hong Kong. He was hearing that Bruce had become "nervous, suspicious, and hard to get along with." After visiting with Bruce in Kowloon Tong, Jhoon confirmed to Taky Kimura, "He's not the same person he used to be."

On Thursday, July 19, as Hong Kong cleaned up after the ravages of Typhoon Dot, Nancy Kwan joined Bruce and Raymond Chow for lunch to discuss *The Game of Death*. Bruce began an expletive-laden tirade at Raymond, whom he accused of ripping him off. Exasperated, Nancy interrupted, "What are *you* doing, Bruce? What about all these stories about you and Ting Pei?"

"It doesn't mean anything," Bruce shot back.

"Everyone's talking. Hong Kong's a small place and they love to gossip," she said. "You're giving them this!"

"Disregard it. It doesn't mean anything!"

"Well, unfortunately for Linda and your children and your mother, they have to read this."

Maria Yi ran into Bruce at the Golden Harvest offices. "He often took out from his handbag the picture of his beloved car and asked me to comment on it," she recalled. "He repeated this action four or five times a day without knowing that he had done it before."

Bruce's last datebook is small, marbled, and white—the color of mourning—with a single gold line wrapping around the face of the leather cover.

Its first entry is on Thursday, July 19, as if he had only picked up the planner the day before: "SIGNED GEORGE TO DO THE FILM."

A handful of entries follow—a trip to Seattle at the end of July, a meeting on August 3 with his lawyer Adrian Marshall to discuss pending deals, a publicity tour beginning in Los Angeles on Monday, August 13, and finishing in New York on Friday, August 24, then a flight back to Los Angeles to meet Linda and on to Hong Kong, before the big one for Wednesday, August 29: "ENTER THE DRAGON OPENS IN L.A."

The last entry in the planner is for Thursday, September 20: "'GAME OF DEATH.'"
The book's final pages stick at the edges, as if they have never been opened.

On Friday, July 20, 1973, Bruce, Andre, Raymond Chow, and Betty Ting Pei were scheduled to meet with George Lazenby to discuss *The Game of Death*.

What happened before then on that day—who was where with whom at what time and what they were doing—has by now been pored over endlessly, with the players playing their parts in countless variations, given new lines, reassigned motives and arcs. New characters appear, others disappear. Different versions yield different meanings, different sympathies. A thousand stories bloom—of scandal, sex, drugs, bombs, triads, the Mafia, Japanese ninjas, contract assassins, killer cannabis, bad *feng shui*, *dim mak* death touches, jealous dragon spirits; some stories partial to science and history, others to memory and myth, some reaching for truth and finding it difficult to grasp, some leaping into fantasy and legend.

The facts remain. In the morning, Bruce typed a letter to Adrian Marshall to preview the deals he was being offered. As Linda was leaving for lunch with a friend, he told her he would be meeting Raymond and George Lazenby about the film. Later that afternoon, he went to Betty Ting Pei's apartment, at 67 Beacon Hill Road. Raymond came by and Bruce acted out his ideas for scenes from the film for them. They made plans to meet for dinner with Lazenby.

Bruce complained of a headache. Betty gave him an over-the-counter aspirin and tranquilizer called Equagesic. He went to take a nap, and Raymond left to meet Lazenby at his hotel. When Bruce and Betty did not show up, Raymond called Betty's apartment at about 9:30 p.m. But when checking on him, Betty found that Bruce could not be awakened. She panicked. Raymond rushed over. Betty called her doctor, who came but could not revive Bruce. The doctor then called an ambulance, which arrived at around 10:30 p.m., a full hour after Raymond's call.

The result is always the same: Bruce arrives at Queen Elizabeth Hospital. He is dead on arrival from severe cerebral edema, a massive swelling of the brain.

Linda said, "I was called by Raymond Chow, who said to come to the hospital. And I said, 'Why? What happened? What happened?' He said, 'Something like the time before.' And so I went to the hospital."

She arrived at the hospital fifteen minutes before the ambulance. They wheeled Bruce past her into the emergency room.

"This can't be true," she said to herself. "But I was there, I saw him."

In Los Angeles, Robert Lee was walking into the apartment where he lived with his mother, a newly purchased stereo under his arm.

"The phone rang. And I noticed my mom started to cry as it was going on. A friend of hers called her, saying that Bruce passed in Hong Kong," he recalled. "I said, 'No, come on. It's a joke, right?' The friend asked her to turn on the four o'clock news."

Kareem Abdul-Jabbar was in an airport in Singapore, about to catch a connecting flight to Hong Kong to see Bruce and Linda. As he passed by a newsstand, he saw the headlines. For a long while he stood there amid the passing travelers, solitary and stunned.

In Seattle, Leroy Garcia brought the morning paper by Jesse Glover's house. Together they read it over and over again and sat in silent disbelief. When Taky Kimura arrived at his grocery store, one of his employees told him, "Bruce Lee is dead. It's all in the papers." Over the years, he had heard so many rumors like this that he just brushed the worker off.

"Then," Taky recalled, "Linda's mother rang me."

"My dad just burst through the doors and he could not believe it," Dan Inosanto's then-seven-year-old daughter, Diana Lee Inosanto, recalled. "He was just inconsolable, and my mother just came up to me and said, 'Let him have his moment to cry.'"

On July 25, tens of thousands of mourners filled the sidewalks near the Kowloon Funeral Parlour in Tai Kok Tsui. Some had been gathering overnight for a last glimpse of their hero's body. Barricades kept them off the blacktop. Hundreds of riot police pressed back against the swelling lines.

There were so many people in the mortuary hall that friends linked arms to create a pathway for Linda, the children, their caregivers, and the Lee family. Linda entered on Raymond Chow's arm, her grief hidden behind sunglasses, the most disconcerted and devastated of all. The Lees had dressed her in the ceremonial white linen and brown jute garments of bereavement. If her best friend, Rebu Hui, had not stayed by her side, arm hooked into hers, she might not have been able to remain standing.

Thousands gather in Kowloon for Bruce Lee's funeral, July 25, 1973. Photo courtesy of the Bruce Lee Family Archive.

Waves of mourners—including many of the biggest names in the Hong Kong film industry—walked toward an altar for Bruce, and bowed their respects to the family three times, which Linda and Bruce's siblings—Peter, Agnes, Phoebe, and Robert—reciprocated. Eight-year-old Brandon and four-year-old Shannon, also outfitted in white and brown, were brought in by family friend Robert Chan and a circle of adults. Shannon seemed bewildered. Brandon mustered the courage to make his three bows.

When the pallbearers brought forth the bronze coffin, dozens of photographers raised their cameras above their heads and filled the room with blinding flashes, as if it were a red carpet event. Linda, Brandon, and Shannon came forward to view the body, rigid under glass in a white suit. There would be the long, snaking viewing line, and more ceremonial exchanges of sympathy and bereavement. By the time the family departed the parlour, Linda was ready to collapse.

For hours more outside, the crowds and the police did their tidal dance at the barricades, women and children being plucked from the cresting surge, ambulances removing the fallen to the hospital. "Long after the coffin was gone," Felix Dennis and Don Atyeo wrote, "police with loudspeakers were still patrolling the streets, urging people to return to their homes." The grief was oceanic.

Under rainy skies, the family left the next day for Seattle to take Bruce to his final resting place. Golden Harvest cameramen tailed closely behind. They captured a bereft Linda gazing out the first-class cabin window at the setting sun, sitting next to Rebu in seats Andre Morgan had purchased to transport Bruce and the family to America for the *Enter the Dragon* publicity tour.

Seattle was even brighter and more beautiful than the autumn day in 1959 when Bruce had first arrived. At the airport, flanked by Ruby Chow, Grace and Linda embraced and cried. Finally she could exhale, feeling safe among family and friends again. In the days before the service, she visited the Sylvan Grove Theater and Columns at the University of Washington, and the Congregational Church. She was twenty-eight, a shy single mother now in the spotlight's glare.

At Linda's request, Andre Morgan met with the funeral director to arrange for a burial at Lake View Cemetery in Capitol Hill, near where Linda had grown up. The director asked Andre, "Do you want him buried with his kind?" When the director clarified that the cemetery had a "Chinese section," Andre demurred and selected two plots under shade trees on a hillside. Even in death, Bruce's body was still doing the work of desegregation.

The burial on July 30 would be intimate. Steve McQueen arrived in a Canadian tuxedo to serve as a pallbearer. Taky Kimura, Dan Inosanto, Robert Lee, Peter Chin, and James Coburn also put on the white gloves. Taky Kimura and Ted Ashley gave eulogies. Then Linda stepped to the podium and began to speak:

> I am not standing here to tell you about the kind of person Bruce was, how great he was, and the things he did, because I believe all of you are here because you know the kind of man he was and loved and respected him. I want to share a bit of Bruce with you, certain feelings he had about life and about death.
>
> . . .
>
> Bruce believed that the individual represents the whole of mankind, whether he lives in the Orient or the Occident. He was able to bridge the gap between people, and not regard them as representatives of a particular nation, race, religion, or class. He crossed the barriers of prejudice and accepted individuals for what they are.
>
> . . .

Bruce lived every day as a day of discovery, a renewal of creation. The new cannot be where there is continuity—the new being the creative, the unknown, the eternal. Only in ending, in dying, in that coming to an end, is there renewal, that creation which is eternal. His thirty-two years were full of living, and he had a fuller life than many who live twice as long. And we are the privileged ones because he shared his life with us.

. . .

The light of stars that were extinguished years ago still reaches us. So it is with great men who died centuries ago, but still reach us with the radiation of their personalities. So it will be with Bruce.

. . .

Bruce would not want us to weep after him, but to take joy in the wisdom he gave to us.

When Jesse Glover came to the casket, his emotions exploded.

"I broke down and cried like a baby," he recalled. "When I looked at the coffin and saw the pale imitation of what used to be Bruce I felt a wild anger and the need to strike out at something. On my way out the door I struck out at a base of flowers."

But after the coffin had been lowered, and everyone else had left, he lingered. He stood beside the open grave with some of the old Seattle crew—his brother Mike, Skip Ellsworth, Ed Hart, and Fook Yeung. Soon Skip and Ed said their goodbyes. But something still felt unfinished.

"When the workmen came to fill the grave," Jesse recalled, "we took over the shovels because it didn't seem right that Bruce should be covered by strange hands."

Fook Yeung dropped a handful of dirt onto the coffin. The brothers finished their labor and rested their hands on their shovels. Having completed this last rite of honor and protection together, they wept.

A burning summer sun beat down upon them. The birds were silent. After dark, no moon would rise to brighten the sky. Bruce Lee was gone.

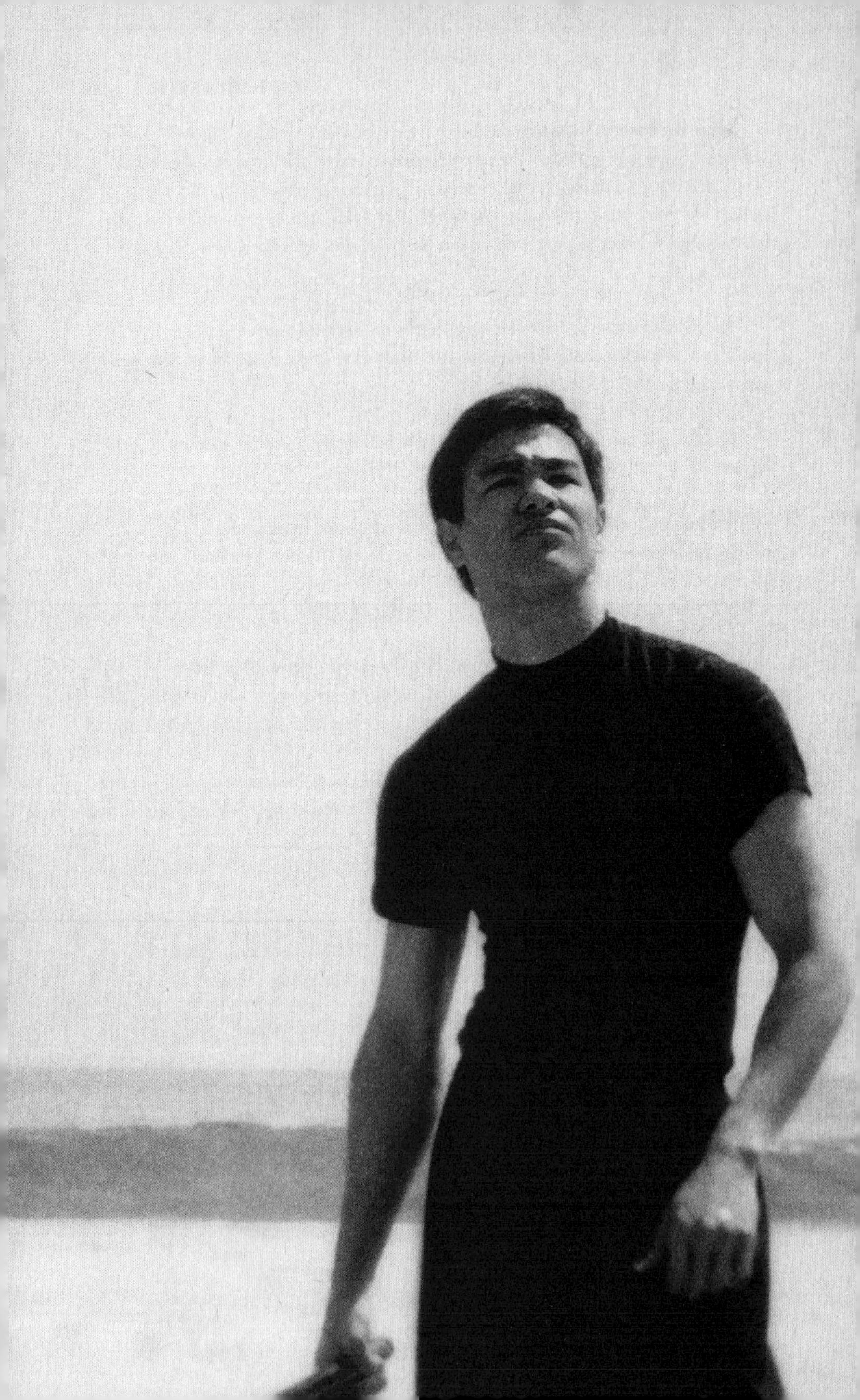

PART XIII
Afterlives
1973–now

Death is a return to where we set out from when we were born. So how do I know that when I die here I shall not be born somewhere else? How do I know that life and death are not as good as each other?

—LIN LEI IN THE *LIEZI*

Photo courtesy of the Bruce Lee Family Archive.

CHAPTER 49
The World Is a Ghetto

In 1973, kung fu movies took in more than eleven million dollars in the United States. Bruce's three movies—*Fists of Fury*, *The Chinese Connection*, and *Enter the Dragon*—accounted for more than two-thirds of the entire kung fu film market. Added together, these films would have ranked seventh among the top year-end American grosses, well ahead of Steve McQueen's *The Getaway*.

Yet *Enter the Dragon* was not especially well received in Hong Kong and throughout Southeast Asia, grossing little more than *The Big Boss* had at HKD $3.3 million. By most standards that was a hit. But after Bruce's two-year run of breaking records, it was a disappointing take.

Perhaps the anti-violence political hysteria across Southeast Asia had affected receipts. But the movie had also failed the high expectations of its audience. The fight scenes were not as imaginative as those in *Fist of Fury* or as electrifying as those in *The Way of the Dragon*. Perhaps the tournament conceit—a concession to the American experience of Asian martial arts as sport, not self-defense—bored them. Fans noticed that after his opening match with Sammo Hung, Bruce didn't fight again until an hour into the movie. Only his underground fight scenes provided new thrills.

They were also appalled at the Orientalisms. The banquet scene and Han's museum—an orgiastic collection of stereotypes staged in settings of excess and plunder—were an unwelcome reminder: *this is how they see us*. From his seat in Hong Kong, the film critic Stephen Teo saw Bruce silenced by the movie's Eurocentrism.

"[*Enter the Dragon*] conveys the West's antipathy towards Lee's nationalism, and it shows a sullen and sulking Lee forced to submit to the West's perception of him as a mere action hero," he wrote. "Clearly Lee could not fully express himself, finding satisfaction only in action—his shrieks, wails and cries are his most eloquent among all his movies."

But many Asian Americans felt—finally—seen. Jim Kelly's last quip before Williams's final battle with Han—"Man, you come right out of a comic book"—wasn't just a punch line that brought the house down, it exposed the villain's genealogy in Yellow Peril cartoons and Fu Manchu flicks. After Williams has escaped the Vietnam War and racist inner-city police only to gaze upon a city of sampans in Aberdeen Harbor, he utters the timeless line: "They don't live so big over there. Ghettos are the same all over the world. They stink."

It was the equivalent of calling an Asian person "brother," but it had not been in any of the scripts. This note of solidarity may have been improvised between Jim Kelly and Robert Clouse. If so, it was an unforeseen effect of the "Deadly Three" format that Warner Bros. had adopted to hedge its bets against a single Asian American lead. Racism often unwittingly plants the seeds of its destruction.

Despite the cool reception for it in Hong Kong and Southeast Asia, *Enter the Dragon* was part of a profound and enduring world-cultural shift that can be traced directly to 1973.

At the beginning of the year, one of the fastest-selling albums in the country was a moody, streetwise statement by a Black, brown, and white funk band from South Los Angeles named War. It was called *The World Is A Ghetto*.

On April 13, Bob Marley and the Wailers released *Catch a Fire*, their first album for the major label Island Records. Chris Blackwell had overdubbed solo lines from American rock musicians over their Jamaican riddims in hopes of propelling the keening voices of the former rude boys from Kingston 12 to international attention.

On August 11, DJ Kool Herc and his sister Cindy Campbell threw a house party in their humble West Bronx apartment building, launching a new movement that would come to be known as hip-hop.

Eight days later,* *Enter the Dragon* premiered at Grauman's Chinese Theatre in Los Angeles with one of the biggest lion parades Hollywood had ever seen. Lines of moviegoers curled through the courtyard and wound down the boulevard.

That opening week, Andre Morgan stood with Fred Weintraub and Paul Heller on a Westwood corner near the UCLA campus. The year before, Morgan had stood on the same corner gaping at the lines for the American immigrant epic *The Godfather*. He remembered, "I'm looking at this fucking line around the block, and I'm saying to Freddie, 'That's as big as the line was for *The Godfather*.' And he says, 'Shut up, *bubbe*, let's see if they like it.'

"We sneak into the back and we're watching and watching the movie and then we're waiting outside as they come out to see if they're smiling and if they're laughing, if they're talking about it—because that's how you knew you had a hit movie," Andre said. "They're smiling! It's a good movie! They didn't throw the popcorn at the screen. They didn't rip up the seats. It must be a hit!"

And yet it wasn't *just a hit*. Jim Kelly understood that Bruce's impact went far beyond film grosses. He talked about it in that backhanded way fighters talk about their rivals and friends. "Lee had an ego as big as Muhammad Ali's. Most people couldn't dig it," Jim said. "But I could appreciate what he had done for himself, his family and his people. Those Chinese movies have done more than Henry Kissinger could ever do."

---

* The release date had been moved up from Wednesday, August 29, to Sunday, August 19.

The long decolonization of global pop culture had begun. It would be increasingly impossible to unsee or unhear the Third World. American whiteness was being decentered toward something as yet unnamed, more open and fluid, brimming with the ecstasy of exchange.

Muhammad Ali had taken on a new name, nearly lost everything for standing in solidarity against the war in Vietnam, then returned to become a global icon of Black pride. Bob Marley had risen from Trenchtown to reveal the view from the tenement yard, broker peace in his country's political war, and invite the world to sing his songs of freedom.

Watching Bruce Lee in that dark Manila theater, as everyone around him lost their minds, the American folksinger Phil Ochs was sure he had seen the future. Bruce's bare, fluid movements were challenging images of Western muscularity.

"It is not the vulgarity of James Arness pistol-whipping a stubbled, drunken stage robber; it is not the ingenious devices of James Bond coming to the rescue, nor the ham-fisted John Wayne slugging it out in the saloon over crumbling tables and paper-thin imitation glass," Ochs wrote. "It is the science of the body taken to its highest form—and the violence, no matter how outrageous, is always strangely purifying." He had come to represent the downtrodden's right to self-defense and their fight for self-determination.

Some of what makes *Enter the Dragon* feel so enduring was accidental. The movie's themes—captivity, corruption, freedom—were boilerplate Cold War spy film tropes. It was just that Hollywood had never staged such a movie with a man of color as the star.

Bruce's image was also cleansing because it asserted that the underdog, armed with pride, focus, and hard work—*gung fu*, in other words—could overcome the orchestrated brutality of the mighty. These qualities also lent the warrior, to borrow a phrase from the movie, a "spiritual insight" that everyone could witness in the purity of action.

Bruce had remained a teacher, drawing on his own life and inspirations to present his perspective of how to live as a warrior. And so, even after his death, there would be more fights. Fred Weintraub and Paul Heller readied their razors to slash the very scenes that Bruce had fought so hard to include.

Bruce had added one for Lee and his pupil, Lau. When the boy kicks at Lee the way he thinks his teacher wants, Lee presses his student, like Wong Shun Leung in Bruce's teenage rooftop fight, toward *wu hsin—do not think, feel*. Drawing on Zen wisdom popularized by Alan Watts, Lee admonishes the boy not to focus on "the finger pointing to the moon," but the moon itself: *act not to satisfy someone else's picture of you, but to find yourself.*

Weintraub and Heller kept this scene, but scrutinized another.

When Lee and the Shaolin abbot meet at the temple, the elder asks, "What is the highest technique you hope to achieve?"

"To have no technique," he replies. He has dissolved his "I," his ego—his only opponent remains himself. Bruce was restaging his early *wing chun* lessons with Ah Leung and Yip Man.

"A good martial artist does not become tense, but ready, not thinking yet not dreaming, ready for whatever may come," Lee continues. "When the opponent expands, I contract. When he contracts, I expand." These were lines influenced by Musashi Miyamoto that he had written in his 1962 letter to Pearl Tso.

"Now you must remember," the abbot cautions Lee, "the enemy has only images and illusions behind which he hides his true motives. Destroy the image and you will break the enemy."

Weintraub and Heller cut this last scene and a later portion in the hall of mirrors scene that referenced it. "With regards to the philosophy," Weintraub said, "a little of it goes a long way with American audiences."

"I think we were all a little bit afraid of it," Heller admitted years later.

The scenes remained in versions released everywhere but the United States. After fan protests, they were restored. They seem indispensable now.

For Asian Americans, the references are clear. The "images and illusions" are stereotypes and misrepresentations, the hall of mirrors an allegory for how racism fragments their public identities, the climactic battle a staging of their fight for visual sovereignty. Caught in a claustrophobic, disorienting space, where foreground and background flatten, Lee and Han stalk each other through the maze, asymmetrically matched, open hand against weaponed hand, two slashed brown bodies whose flesh and actions are replicated, riven, and sharded into infinite pieces that can never become whole.

Only after Lee hears the voice of the abbot telling him to destroy the image can the battle rush to its conclusion. He breaks the mirrors and forces Han to emerge. Lee finally impales his enemy—the image of the Yellow Peril—on a spear from his own museum of imperial spoils and looted weapons of war.

An exhausted thumbs-up, a look to the sky as death-from-above helicopters descend, a final image of Han's animal claw, and a bone-weary Lee—Bruce Lee—descends the stairs, out of focus and out of the picture. His fight is over.

CHAPTER 50
Melancholia and Memory

Premature death admits no closure. For the living, there is a wound that cannot heal, an endless mourning, a melancholia.

Outside of Bruce's family and friends there was mass disbelief. Too swift even for the camera, too fluid to be stopped, unconquerable—how could a man this alive die?

Before Linda left for Seattle to bury Bruce, she had made a statement to the press, a plea to the public:

> Although we do not have the final autopsy report, I have no suspicion of anything other than natural death. I myself do not hold any person or people responsible for his death. Fate has ways we cannot change. The only thing of importance is that Bruce is gone and will not return.

She continued, "I appeal to you to please let him rest and do not disturb his soul."

But in her biography, she concluded, sadly, ironically: "No one, I'm sorry to say, seemed to be listening."

For Linda, Bruce's sudden passing began a turbulent, disorienting period. She was back in the States with her mother and two devastated young children, with no income. The funds generated by Bruce's sudden fame would be locked up for years in a complex web involving lawyers, government officials, insurance companies, and Raymond Chow.

Theories of Bruce's death proliferated. Soon Linda would be returning to Hong Kong to testify at an inquest that the tabloid press covered with the sordid glee of vultures circling a kill. The demand for news, rumors, and salacious details about his death filled thousands of tabloid column inches.

On September 24, 1973, after a week of extensive testimony that included Linda, Raymond, the attending doctors involved in Bruce's May 10 episode, and those who had treated him on July 20, a three-man jury returned an official verdict of "death by misadventure." It had been an accident, a hypersensitivity to the over-the-counter Equagesic pill Betty Ting Pei had given Bruce for his headache.

The disbelief did not dissipate. Even now, decades later, the thoughtful and the sober still gamely try to explain the unexplainable—offering conflicting theories of death by epilepsy, dehydration, and heatstroke, or even hyponatremia, the condition of having drunk *too much* water.

"Personalities and narratives projected onto the screen of our imaginations are far more haunting—and far more likely to be the stuff of conspiracies and conjecture—if they have not been allowed to play themselves out to their logical or illogical ends," Gloria Steinem once wrote of Marilyn Monroe. "When the past dies there is mourning, but when the future dies, our imaginations are compelled to carry it on."

In 1975, two years after his death, the editor of *Fighting Stars* magazine—a spinoff of *Black Belt* magazine that had been financed with a large marketing check from Warner Bros. for *Enter the Dragon*—lamented "The Cult of Bruce Lee." "We felt it wouldn't last," Charles Lucas wrote. But by his own admission, 70 percent of the magazine's mail was still about Bruce. One of these fans wrote, "I loved Bruce Lee as if he were part of my family and would have gladly taken his place in death."

That year, Linda published her partly ghostwritten biography, *Bruce Lee: The Man Only I Knew*, which began with her wrenching account of his last minutes.* Along with Alex Ben Block's 1974 biography *The Legend of Bruce Lee*, her book established the narrative commonplace of foregrounding Bruce's death before speaking of his life.

The reenactments of his life were just beginning. On a rain-lashed April day in Burbank, she found herself, a bit bewildered, sitting alongside Robert Clouse, Chuck Norris, Pat Johnson, *Black Belt* publisher Dick Hennessy, and Barbra Streisand as hundreds of *gi*-wearing Bruce clones auditioned for a proposed Warner Bros. and First Artists biopic. That movie, thankfully, would never be made. But dozens more would.

Just months after Bruce's passing, Raymond Chow had rush-released the first Bruceploitation movie—a documentary called *Bruce Lee: The Man, the Legend*, which began unsubtly: "Bruce Lee, recognized king of kung fu, is dead." Interspersing footage of his Hong Kong and Seattle funeral ceremonies with clips from *Enter the Dragon* and teasers of what would eventually become *The Game of Death*, it betrayed the naked desperation of a cash grab.

The film could be defended as Concord's attempt—*if they didn't, someone else would*—to feed a Bruce Lee economy that had sprung up to meet the unquenched

---

* In 1989, Linda revised the book as *The Bruce Lee Story*. In 1975, Linda also commissioned a *Black Belt* magazine editor named Gilbert Johnson to assemble Bruce's notes into a book. *Tao of Jeet Kune Do*—a book that mixes his notes with quotes he had copied from fighters, philosophers, and scholars who go uncited, and the book most associated with his thinking—was published in October 1975 by Mito Uyehara's Ohara Publications. Two decades after its publication, there were nearly half a million copies in print. See James Bishop, *Who Wrote The Tao? The Literary Sourcebook of the Tao of Jeet Kune Do* (Promethean Press, 2022), p. 110.

demand of a vast and passionate fandom, who, in ways bathetic, fractious, and profoundly heartfelt, were making him immortal. Followers of Bruce filled martial arts schools. They argued over his techniques, movements, and ideas. Aching just to see him once again, they filled the grindhouse theaters.

Those films introduced an army of clones named Bruce Li, Bruce Le, Bruce Ly, Bruce Lo, Bruce Liang, Bruce Chi, Bruce Ali, Dragon Lee, and even Lee Bruce. They dressed in clothes like the ones he had worn, moved in the way he had moved, talked in the way he had talked, everything but the real. Flicks like *Brucefinger*, *Bruce Lee Against Supermen*, *Bruce Lee Fights Back from the Grave*, *Bruce Has Risen*, *Bruce Is Loose*, and *Bruce Lee in New Guinea* placed their hero—mostly degraded copies without the original—in simulations novel and familiar.

In *The Dragon Dies Hard*, a "biopic" that caused Linda, Raymond, and Betty Ting Pei to sue its producers, young Bruce begins learning martial arts only after thugs strong-arm him for his *Washington Post* newspaper delivery route. The Shaw Brothers released a double exploitation flick starring Betty Ting Pei—who later disavowed it—telling an outlandish version of his last day. It was called *Bruce Lee and I* in some territories and *Sex Life of Bruce Lee* in others. The desolation and anguish of public mourning had passed into the ridiculous and morbid.

Despite more complaints from Linda, Raymond, Betty, and even organized groups of angry fans, Bruceploitation[*] persisted longer than Bruce's adult movie career. In these D-movies, he not only lived on, he lived a hundred more lives, each less satisfying than the last.

Quietly, Linda returned to college and obtained a political science degree from California State University at Long Beach. She finally settled the family in Rolling Hills Estates, where she raised Brandon and Shannon with her mom at her side. She welcomed the regular routines of an elementary school teacher and mother. She deliberately did not encourage her children to study martial arts or to go into acting. But her son seemed to take after his father.

"Not only did he walk and talk like him," Ted Wong said, "he told jokes and had everyone laughing like his father used to do."

By the time Brandon had reached his teens he was fighting in the schoolyard. "I moved around a lot and attended a lot of different schools," Brandon recalled, "and sometimes when I'd go to a different school there would be somebody there who would want to prove they were tough by beating up Bruce Lee's son." He and Shannon began studying with Dan Inosanto, Richard Bustillo, and Ted Wong.

---

[*] By the official Golden Harvest release of 1978's *Game of Death*, the increasing schlock and parody of Bruceploitation finally cleared the way for kung fu film to transition into a new era with Jackie Chan as its leading light. Chan restored Bruce's *Way of the Dragon* formula of balancing vengeance and comedy, accelerated the fight choreography, and amped the stunts into jaw-droppingly dangerous territory.

For his senior year, at Chadwick School in Palos Verdes, Brandon was elected student body president by his classmates. But not long before graduation, the school's administration asked him to leave. Brandon had organized his classmates to protest what he was calling the school's outmoded curriculum. Like his father, he earned his GED elsewhere, then enrolled at Emerson College in Boston. He studied drama.

"My father was a martial artist first and an actor second," he told a journalist. "I'm sure you have read and heard of his fanaticism for the martial arts. That's how I am with acting."

In 1986, while working as a gofer for Andre Morgan's production company, he was asked to audition for a TV-movie reboot of the *Kung Fu* franchise and won the part opposite the star, David Carradine. The role in *Kung Fu: The Movie* he took on was as problematic as his father's television parts had been.

Photo courtesy of the Bruce Lee Family Archive.

Brandon plays Kwai Chang Caine's son, Chung Wang, whom Caine had abandoned in China after killing the emperor's nephew. Chung is an orphan—not unlike Anna May Wong's Ling Moy in *Daughter of the Dragon*—who has no idea who his real father is. He has been raised as an assassin by the father of the man Caine had killed. This villain, played by Mako, has the on-the-nose name of the Manchu, everything but the Fu. Even during Brandon's lifetime, a full generation after his father, very little had changed for Asian American actors in Hollywood.

Chung and the Manchu cross the Pacific to capture Caine. In the end, the Manchu and his migrant hordes are defeated and Chung Wang is reunited with Caine. This assimilationist fantasy folds back on itself several times: the actual son of Bruce Lee plays The Orphan/the Number One Son, who learns he is the child not of an evil Oriental man but a benevolent half-white father, who is played by Carradine, a white actor in yellowface who had once told a kung fu magazine, "I feel almost possessed by the spirit of Bruce."

Over the next several years, Brandon continued to act in the theater and minor films. He was a celebrated regular on the youthful Sunset Strip/Echo Park club scene. His career slowly advanced, enough for him to purchase a motorcycle that he used to tear around Mulholland Drive at top speeds. His other vehicle—the one he used to drive to the supermarket—was a hearse. He got a kick out of the reactions he got. But with some of his most intimate friends late at night, he would share dark premonitions about dying young that echoed his father's.

Rob Cohen's *Dragon: The Bruce Lee Story*, a biopic centered on Bruce and Linda's love story, went into production. *Dragon* burnishes a certain version of the Bruce Lee mythos, reducing his real-life struggles against racism to individual acts of discrimination (or even less) in thoroughly fictive scenes. In Seattle, a college gym brawl pits him against racist football players. In Hollywood, his manager steals his idea for *Kung Fu*.

The movie also thrusts Bruce into the role of yellow savior. Like Sessue Hayakawa's Ah Kee in *Daughter of the Dragon*, this Bruce must protect the white world from bad Orientals, whether jealous kung fu guys, bigoted Chinatown elders, or child-slaughtering ghosts. Despite charming performances from Jason Scott Lee and Lauren Holly, *Dragon* becomes *Model Minority Bruce Against Yellow Peril*, and remains a source of persistent fictions about Bruce.

Brandon would take on yet another *Kung Fu* reboot and more unmemorable flicks. Marvel Comics head Stan Lee reportedly wanted him to play Shang Chi, the Master of Kung Fu. Then in 1992, he finally broke through with the successful neo-noir *Rapid Fire*, in which he was marketed as "the action hero of the 90s." He was cast as the lead in Alex Proyas's big-budget take on the beloved Goth graphic novel *The Crow*, playing Eric Draven, a rock musician who returns from the dead to avenge the vicious gang murder of his fiancée and himself. It was the role Brandon had been preparing for his whole life—big, action-oriented, and perfectly befitting his dark humor and sense of the macabre.

After working as Brandon's assistant on the set of *Rapid Fire*, Shannon had also caught the movie bug. She finished her music degree from Tulane University and took a small part in *Dragon*, singing "California Dreaming." She was planning to move back to Los Angeles to follow her brother into the biz.

On April 8, Brandon was scheduled to finish the movie in Wilmington, North Carolina. He and his real-life fiancée, Eliza Hutton, were set to be married on April 17. *The Crow* would premiere not long after the spring release of *Dragon*. Nineteen ninety-three was going to be a great year for the Lees.

But on March 31, Linda and Shannon received horrifying news. While filming the scene for *The Crow* in which Eric Draven is murdered, Brandon had been accidentally shot in the abdomen by a faulty blank. Doctors were trying to resuscitate him in a hospital in Wilmington.

As they flew to North Carolina, Shannon recalled, "Suddenly I felt this bolt shoot through me, like a beam of energy that passed through the plane, through my body and out the top. It was powerful and completely disconcerting. I burst into tears because in that moment I knew that my brother had died."

Once more, Linda and Shannon had been plunged into an unwanted public spectacle. The media spoke of "The Curse of the Dragon." But to the grieving Lees, Brandon's death—less than four months before the twentieth anniversary of Bruce's death—was simply unfathomable.

When her father had died, Shannon was a toddler. She wrote,

> What I remember of that was a much more vague confusion and chaos, the imprint of a sea of grieving humanity in Hong Kong as thousands lined the streets for his funeral. The grief of my mother and my brother. And the turn inward on myself. But that's all. . . . I had unconsciously and mercifully cordoned that off from my memory.
>
> But here I was twenty years later and grief was thrust upon me like a wild animal.

She returned to New Orleans and took a job painting dorm rooms at Tulane, spending most days by herself with her boom box, paint cans, and a roller. But one day she collapsed and had a long, wretched cry. She returned to Los Angeles and took up martial arts training with Ted Wong and Benny Urquidez. Some part of her felt that acting was what her father and brother might have wanted. But her heart was barely in it.

"I was in constant pain, sometimes unable to get up in the morning, get dressed, or move off my couch for hours at a time. I would cry as I drove around LA in my car," she wrote in her memoir, *Be Water, My Friend*. "I existed in this way for years."

Caught in a boundless melancholia, she began to reach again for her father's presence. Her mother had been organizing her father's papers, and bit by bit she went through them, not knowing what she was looking for, only knowing that she needed to. She stumbled upon lines from *The Silent Flute*: "The medicine for my suffering I had within me from the very beginning, but I did not take it. The ailment came from within myself, but I did not observe it until this moment. Now I see that I will never find the light unless, like the candle, I am my own fuel, consuming myself."

Then she came upon another piece of paper, on which her father had written, in a wisdom older than trauma, these words: "We are always in a process of becoming and nothing is fixed. Have no rigid system in you, and you'll be flexible to change with the ever changing. Open yourself and flow, my friend. Flow in the total openness of the living moment. If nothing within you stays rigid, outward things will disclose themselves. Moving, be like water. Still, be like a mirror. Respond like an echo."

In life, Bruce had plumbed what it meant to be like water. In his last year, he believed he was working toward his own freedom. But he was also tethered to what the writer Cathy Park Hong would name "minor feelings"—paranoia, shame, irritation, and melancholy. "At the end," Shannon said, "he was not at peace."

It would be human nature to point out all the ways that, consumed by his desires, Bruce Lee failed himself. But that would be beside the point. Among the most profound tragedies of his premature death is that he never had a chance to fully explore in life what it meant to be still, like a mirror, what it meant to respond like an echo.

And yet, decades afterward, with these same lines he had shown his daughter the moon. Her healing began.

Linda lives a quiet life with her husband, Bruce Cadwell, in an oasis-like setting near a river in Idaho. Behind her house, water flows in a burbling tributary creek. Each morning she steps onto her red-brick patio to look at it, the sun reflecting off the sparkling ripples, lighting her face. Hearing the songbirds, she turns to her right and looks up. A beautiful white birch rises thirty-five feet above the garden, its branches gesturing broadly, shading her as if in an affectionate deference. She smiles.

She tells guests a story about her favorite tree. "It started out as a five-inch sapling when it was gifted to us by the homeowners in our community on the event of Brandon's passing," she says. "It is called a 'Heavenly Birch' and, reportedly, is a species that does not do well in Idaho."

"Hah!" She suddenly laughs, then looks up again. "It is thriving."

CHAPTER 51
How We Use Our Hands

In death Bruce had succeeded and failed in ways broader than he could have ever imagined.

He was not only the most recognizable Asian American who had ever lived. To those of us who came of age in the After Bruce era, which was also the era following the Asian American awakening, he was an image of power transcending the scrum of our everyday, a renewable resource of pride, a light that never goes out, the premier icon of Asian America.

But he also became an unaccountable source of shame. Bruce's image was so pervasive, it became a stereotype that saddled future generations of Asian Americans. I was fortunate enough to experience my childhood in Honolulu, where on the playground—like the kids in Southeast Asia—we could fill a field with screaming Bruces. But for my sons who came of age on the American continent among kids of many cultures not Asian or Pacific Islander, only *they* could be Bruce Lee, and Bruce Lee was the *only* thing they could be. And that was among friends. Still others remained so hostile to us that they would never call us by any name we would want to answer.

One summer night in 1992, not long after the Rodney King uprising in Los Angeles seemed to have left the rainbow dreams of the Third World Liberation Front in ashes, I went with a group of friends, both immigrant and American-born, to a multiplex in a Sacramento exurb newly risen from the farmlands in triumphant stucco conformity. We were going to see Brandon Lee in *Rapid Fire*.

After the movie, we were hyped. That slow-mo Jeet Kune Do intro. The legit fighting. The way he wiped his nose before attacking. The fact that he even got the girl, a smart, tough one at that. We were talking about how proud Bruce would have been. We were savoring how Brandon had made his own moment. We lingered by our cars on the cool moonless night in the vast empty parking lot, young, Asian American, and free.

From across the lot a white pickup turned and accelerated in our direction. It was gumball-machine full of drunken white guys, and as it pulled near us it slowed. From the flatbed one of them called out to us, "Hey! Hey! Fuck you, chinks!" The others were making slant-eyes. Then the truck screeched off into the distance.

I remember the sound of their laughter. I remember being frozen, as if my feet were stuck to the asphalt. One of us was reaching for his car door, ready to chase after them. Another was grabbing his hand. *Not tonight, man. Life is not an action movie.*

Silence fell over us like a shroud. We were turning away from each other, disassembling, retreating into our aloneness.

What are we, cowards? We could've taken them. Fucking rednecks. Running off scared. What if we had followed? This is not where we're from. Maybe they have guns. What the fuck. How can we let them get away with this? Come back, you fucking assholes.

I remember my face hot, my thoughts fast and loud, my fists clenched. I was turning slowly in circles.

In 2017, when Phil Yu and Jeff Yang shrewdly chose to name their popular Asian American podcast *They Call Us Bruce*, they were not only referencing the 1982 Bruceploitation film but also the painful memory of schoolyard bullying and mundane everyday microaggressions.

What did anyone else know about people who looked like us except Bruce Lee—if they would even call us by a name we would want to answer?

"And so I am in my room chasing Bruce Lee," the poet Beau Sia once said, "until I am *me*."

In the decade after Bruce Lee's death the necessary fiction of Asian America became true and real, a headlong leap into the flow of history.

The idea of the Asian American spread beyond the cloistered ambit of the campus. Religious organizations, community leaders, and the media embraced it. Activists built community organizations, decentering the work from the old ethnic associations. There would be many more leaders like Wing Luke and Ruby Chow. Scholars, historians, and culture bearers recovered and constructed an Asian American past. Writers, poets, artists, filmmakers, dancers, and musicians expanded an Asian American imaginary.

Then the first era of the Asian American awakening came to an end, sometime after 10:00 p.m. on August 3, 1977, on Kearny Street in San Francisco. At that hour, a red alert went out to hundreds of organizations and activists across the Bay Area—*the police are moving, get to the I-Hotel as soon as possible*. The long night of evictions had arrived.

Dozens of elderly tenants who had remained in the hotel were securing their belongings, assisted by young supporters who boarded up the front doorway from the inside, filled the staircases with bedsprings, mattresses, and boards, and then stayed with the elders as they locked themselves in their rooms and waited.

Police and deputies had blocked the freeway offramps to cut off demonstrators arriving from Oakland and Berkeley. They shut down Kearny Street all the way up to North Beach. Hundreds of helmeted riot cops outfitted for war, many on horseback, were proceeding from Market Street up the hill in formation.

Through the 1970s, this block on Kearny Street had illustrated the grassroots rise of Asian America. But what warriors are best at is fighting, and as more people were drawn to the hotel, it became an *alcázar* divided by intrigue. Organizations separated into factions, bickering over thin ideological differences.

"Feeling power, wielding power, demonstrating power," Karen Tei Yamashita had written in her epic novel *I Hotel*. "A group could act as a single fist or an open handshake. Well, handshakes were not the tenor of our times."

As eviction day drew near, Felix Ayson, a seventy-nine-year-old disabled *manong* leader who was a veteran of both world wars, had been a migrant laborer and farmworker organizer, and had lived in the I-Hotel off and on since 1926, articulated the stakes. "By saving the Hotel we are saving the respect for human dignity," he said. "By saving the respect for human dignity, we are helping to save the human race."

So that night, the warriors returned and set aside their squabbles to take one last stand to protect the I-Hotel, a home these elders were fighting to keep and an imperiled symbol of the "new consciousness" that had once united them.

Outside, police mounted spotlights that made parts of the block as bright as a movie set. Thousands of supporters locked arms, forming a human barricade several bodies deep, blocking the hotel's entrance.

They shouted, "Stop the eviction!"

They sang "We Shall Not Be Moved."

After midnight the police attacked, attempting to pry apart the demonstrators, driving their horses into the lines, and swinging their truncheons wildly down upon them. For a while the barricade held.

The cops ascended the fire ladder and bludgeoned the protesters assembled on the roof. They penetrated the hotel by descending a fire escape and smashing through a boarded-up window, shattering the glass on a *manong* in his bed.

On the ground the demonstrators hoped to hold the lines until sunrise, when the city would come back to life and see what the authorities were doing to them, the old men, and the I-Hotel. But after hours of bloody confrontation the tenant leaders, fearful the carnage would only become more bloody, asked the demonstrators at the door to yield.

With the entrance finally breached a few hours before dawn, police and sheriffs moved room by room to evict the tenants, smashing down their blockaded doors with sledgehammers to find frail old bachelors on the other side, crying.

One of the last to be removed from the hotel, Felix Ayson emerged on the arms of two young activists. "I am crippled. I am deaf. I am very old. I'm alone and they put me out on the street," he said. "I want freedom, the principle of American democracy, the richest country in the world."

A year later, he passed away. For two more decades, what was left of the memory of the revolution was a gaping block-long hole in the ground, a community's open wound.

● ● ●

In the next era of Asian America, the revolution would be institutionalized. Thousands built a vast architecture of social service providers, civil rights and legal organizations, and arts groups, forming a bridgehead in society. Leaders from different Asian and Pacific Islander ethnic groups came together to lobby for a consolidated census category. They succeeded in winning the category of "Asian American/Pacific Islander" for the 1980 census.

But while securing the formal recognition of the census category was historic and had consequential policy implications, by itself it would not move people to forge a shared destiny. To convince people of the valence of Asian America, to engage them in building an Asian American future, would require a broad structure of feeling. That would come from a shocking act of violence.

On June 19, 1982, in Detroit, a city hard hit by economic competition from Japanese car companies, a twenty-seven-year-old Chinese American went out with some of his white and Asian friends for a bachelor party at the Fancy Pants Lounge to celebrate his imminent wedding.

Seated at a strip bar next to a table of white men, Vincent Chin and his friends overheard a man named Ronald Ebens calling them "chink," "Nip," and "fucker."

Ebens was employed as a superintendent at a Chrysler plant. He was there with his stepson, Michael Nitz, who had recently been laid off by Chrysler.

"Don't call me a fucker," Vincent shouted.

"It's because of motherfuckers like you that we're out of work," one of them yelled back.

Vincent clocked Ebens in the face. When Nitz grabbed a chair to throw at him, he bloodied Nitz's face as well. They were all thrown out.

In the parking lot, the shouting continued. Nitz went to his car and pulled a Louisville Slugger baseball bat out of his trunk. Vincent and his friends fled. Still steaming, Ebens and Nitz resolved to find the "Chinaman." They drove by a McDonald's and saw him sitting outside with one of his friends.

They snuck up from behind. Nitz caught and held Vincent Chin. Ebens swung the bat at his arms, legs, and body, then, with a big wind-up, brought the bat down on his head.

By the time two off-duty police officers ordered them at gunpoint to stop, Vincent was slumped on the ground, unconscious, his skull covered in blood. The jade pendant he had worn around his neck had been shattered.

He fell into a coma and, four days later, succumbed to his wounds.

"Instead of attending Vincent's wedding, his four hundred wedding guests went to his funeral," recalled Helen Zia, a journalist who played a central role in the organizing that followed.

Ebens and Nitz pled guilty, but a white judge let them off with probation and less than four thousand dollars in fines. "These aren't the kind of men you send to jail," the judge said. "You fit the punishment to the criminal, not the crime."

As if Ebens and Nitz were good Americans who just had a bad night. As if the Chinaman was just another Jap. As if Vincent Chin was not an American, not in any moral, legal, or common sense. As if he was *just what he looked like.*

A family friend told Helen Zia that Vincent's life had been worth less than a used car.

She and others formed a pan-Asian group called American Citizens for Justice. Other groups, similarly encompassing a diversity of ethnicities, generations, and cultures, sprung up across the country to track, defend against, and seek justice for acts of anti-Asian violence in America.

Violence had made the idea of the Asian American real.

By the end of the 1980s, "Asian American" was a national idea—the banner under which all kinds of activity were underway. But as its usage spread some of its meaning was lost. "Asian American" was now less a subject than a modifier: Asian American politics, Asian American culture, Asian American identity.

Perhaps the idea was descending into meaninglessness, leaving us back in our aloneness.

After the 1965 Hart-Celler Act, also known as the Immigration and Nationality Act, finally banished racist quotas against non-European immigrants, a new wave of migrants from the former Asiatic Barred Zone transformed Asian America, turning the idea of the Asian American back into a collective question.

Asian and Pacific Islander populations skyrocketed. Census counts revealed that for the first time since the turn of the twentieth century, most Asian Americans were foreign-born. After 9/11, as the United States again narrowed legal paths to immigration, the newcomers increasingly skewed toward the wealthy, educated classes, making the Model Minority Myth a state-enforced prophecy.

In the first two decades of the millennium, the Asian American population grew by 81 percent, becoming the fastest-growing racial group in the country. We are now the most diverse of all racial groups, a confounding pluralism of ethnicities, languages, and religions. We are engineers, software developers, and doctors, and also farmers, manicurists, and casino workers. We are ahead of the national average in receiving college degrees, but 45 percent of us do not have one. We have the widest income inequality. Those with college degrees earn a median income 25 percent higher than whites of the same class, but those without one earn the same as comparable Black and Latinx workers, less than 87 percent of the median income of whites without a degree.

Because of this head-spinning diversity, many—even those sympathetic to the idea—have questioned the coherence of an Asian America. In times of crisis, these questions return, become urgent, even existential. What truly unites the descendants of people from Asia and the Pacific in America?

The minimal answer—and the oldest one—remains hatred and violence.

During the pandemic, anti-Asian violence spiked. Two teens attacked an eighty-nine-year-old Chinese American grandmother and set her on fire. A knife-wielding man in a Sam's Club slashed and stabbed a Burmese American father and his two young sons, ages six and two. The assailant told investigators he was certain the family "was Chinese and infecting people with the coronavirus." In January 2021, an elderly Thai American man was killed in San Francisco while on his daily walk. And on and on until the violence reached a horrific climax. On March 16, six Korean American women and two others were massacred in Atlanta. On April 15, four Sikh Americans and four others were killed in a mass shooting at an Indianapolis FedEx facility.

It was a time of danger and death, but also organizing and renewal. The image of Bruce Lee returned, a symbol of action and agency, appearing on city walls and across social media. To be in action is to make oneself an agent of one's destiny—to self-actualize, as Bruce put it. His image seemed to be holding together a physical, virtual, and mental geography.

In a sense, Asian America was—and always will be—in a process of becoming. But must violence—suffering it, inflicting it, or preparing for either—always be the source of identity?

One way to index a people's becoming is through the tracking of representation, the mirror to their emergence.

In the early 1990s, as Brandon Lee and *Dragon* were hitting the big screen, Margaret Cho's *All-American Girl* and Wayne Wang's *The Joy Luck Club* signaled a possible inflection point. But it was not to be. Even as indie filmmakers like Stephen Okazaki, Greg Araki, Justin Lin, and Renee Tajima-Peña made groundbreaking work, Asian Americans faded again into the background for a generation. In the 2000s, cable channels like MTV Asia and AZN TV presented a rapidly evolving globally connected Asian American aesthetic. But not until the late-2010s, a generation after Brandon had passed, would there be the twin popular successes of Eddie Huang's *Fresh Off the Boat*, which ran for six seasons on ABC, and Jon Chu's *Crazy Rich Asians*, which became the highest grossing romantic comedy of the decade.

By 2023, a half-century after *Enter the Dragon* and Bruce's death, Asian Americans were celebrating on-screen breakthroughs. There was the Oscar-sweeping *Everything Everywhere All at Once*, starring a former Golden Harvest star, the ass-kicking Michelle Yeoh, as well as tonally varied offerings like Celine Song's *Past Lives*, Randall Park's *Shortcomings*, and Adele Lim's *Joy Ride*. On television there was Dwayne Johnson and Nahnatchka Khan's *Young Rock*, Bisha Ali's *Ms. Marvel*, Gene Luen Yang and Kelvin Yu's *American Born Chinese*, and Bruce's own creation, finally brought to the screen by Shannon Lee, Justin Lin, and Jonathan Tropper, with a strong dose of historical realism—*Warrior*. At least in that moment, there were truer images for everyone to see.

This renaissance in Asian American arts was in part an industry concession—the right thing happening for the wrong reasons, amid the Black Lives Matter movement and Asian American, Native Hawaiian, and Pacific Islander organizing. But this creative uprising, a collective effort to build a shared identity and culture, also marked the arrival of a new generation finding their voices and images, whose excellence could not be denied.

Writing in this moment of recension, Viet Thanh Nguyen argued that Asian Americans had always organized their politics, their culture, and themselves for self-defense, representation, and solidarity.[*] He wrote:

> Self-defense is needed to ward off efforts to kill or subjugate us, to reduce us to the bare life of a human animal. In defending ourselves, we also become the authors of our own stories. But the danger in self-defense lies in our becoming absorbed by our own victimization, and through insisting so strenuously on our humanity, becoming incapable of acknowledging our inhumanity—or the humanity of our adversaries.
>
> Through self-defense, we seek inclusion into a larger community that has excluded us, such as the nation. But if we succeed in gaining entry, we may forget who still remains excluded as an Other, and whether we, the included, now participate in and profit from the mistreatment of others.
>
> Inclusion requires solidarity, as those who have excluded others now extend hospitality to the excluded. The excluded also need solidarity as they seek kinship with one another. But how far does solidarity extend?

With his provocative question, Nguyen was building upon the insight of James Baldwin, who spoke about the struggle that compels an artist to create, which in turn is "a metaphor for the struggle, which is universal and daily, of all human beings to get to become human beings." The artist, Baldwin said, is compelled to create by a hurt they once suffered, one that isolates them from others in a world in which most people hide their wounds and cannot bear to look at one who has not.

"And what is crucial here," he said, "is that if it hurt you, that is not what is important." He said:

> Everybody's hurt. What is important, what corrals you, what bullwhips you, what drives you, torments you, is that you must find some way of using this to connect you with everyone else alive. . . .

---

[*] Viet uses the term "inclusion," not just in the numerical sense, I think, but in the affective sense of belonging. I choose "representation" here to specifically highlight both symbolic and institutional inclusion.

Activists join arms to stop the eviction of the I-Hotel residents, August 3, 1977. Photo by Chris Fujimoto. With deep gratitude to the Manilatown Heritage Foundation.

You must understand that your pain is trivial except insofar as you can use it to connect with other people's pain; and insofar as you can do that with your pain, you can be released from it, and then hopefully it works the other way around too; insofar as I can tell you what it is to suffer, perhaps I can help you to suffer less.

The difference between the hero and the mere celebrity, the teacher of myth Joseph Campbell once said, is that one life is lived for the self, and the other for the redemption of society.

Looking back on her son's life, Grace Li said, "During the pre- and post-war periods, there was no safe place in the world. Under such circumstances, everyone worried about his security. Thus Bruce began to practice *gung fu*."

He lived as a warrior. He began fighting as a way to defend himself. But he only took the stage of history when he rose from the In-Betweens—that space Asian

Americans inhabit between self-victimization and self-actualization, between complicity and freedom, between retreating and reaching—to connect to the struggle of becoming more human. At that point his journey became everyone's.

To picture Bruce now, lowering himself into a fighting stance, cocking his neck and fixing his gaze on his opponent, is to recall our countless hours in child's play, moments of laughter and joy in which we are also unwittingly preparing ourselves to face the unjust injuries of life. It is also to remember the microdramas of bullying and bullied, to feel the ways we have trained our minds and bodies to preserve ourselves. To watch him as he springs from ready position into action is to consider our daily labor, in all its strains and contentions, and wonder whether we, too, can move with such grace, power, and purpose.

The first line of Bruce's favorite aphorism—"Moving, be like water"—has inspired athletes to superhuman feats, and activists to acts of stunning resistance. When masses of Hong Kongers took to the streets in 2019 to fight China's antidemocratic lurch, "Be Water" informed their strategy of improvisational, adaptable protest. Activists in Catalonia soon took up the idea to advance their own movement for independence. In the summer of 2020, after the brutal murder of George Floyd at the hands of Minneapolis police, Hong Kong organizers connected with Black Lives Matter demonstrators to share tactics and lessons.

Bruce Lee, the recurring sign of Asian America, has come now to represent the necessity of solidarity and the fight for freedom everywhere. Andre Morgan said, "Bruce was giving dignity to Asians all over the world. And what I didn't realize then, but I've come to realize in the years since then—it resonated with Filipinos. It resonated with Blacks. It resonated with Hispanics. It resonated with everyone non-white. And the truth was, it actually resonated with a lot of white folk, too. He was a hero for all seasons, all colors."

Picture him now, nodding before he turns to leave. He has roused us to see what we may accomplish with our own hands.

When James Wong Jim—Bruce's onetime schoolboy nemesis who became a good friend—was asked to compose lyrics to Joseph Koo's theme song for *Fist of Fury*, his thoughts turned to how Bruce had used his hands. *He used his hands to help and hold others. He used his hands to form fists and fight for justice.*

And so we are left to ask ourselves: Who are we and what do we fight for? What can we build together? What would it look like if we all were free?

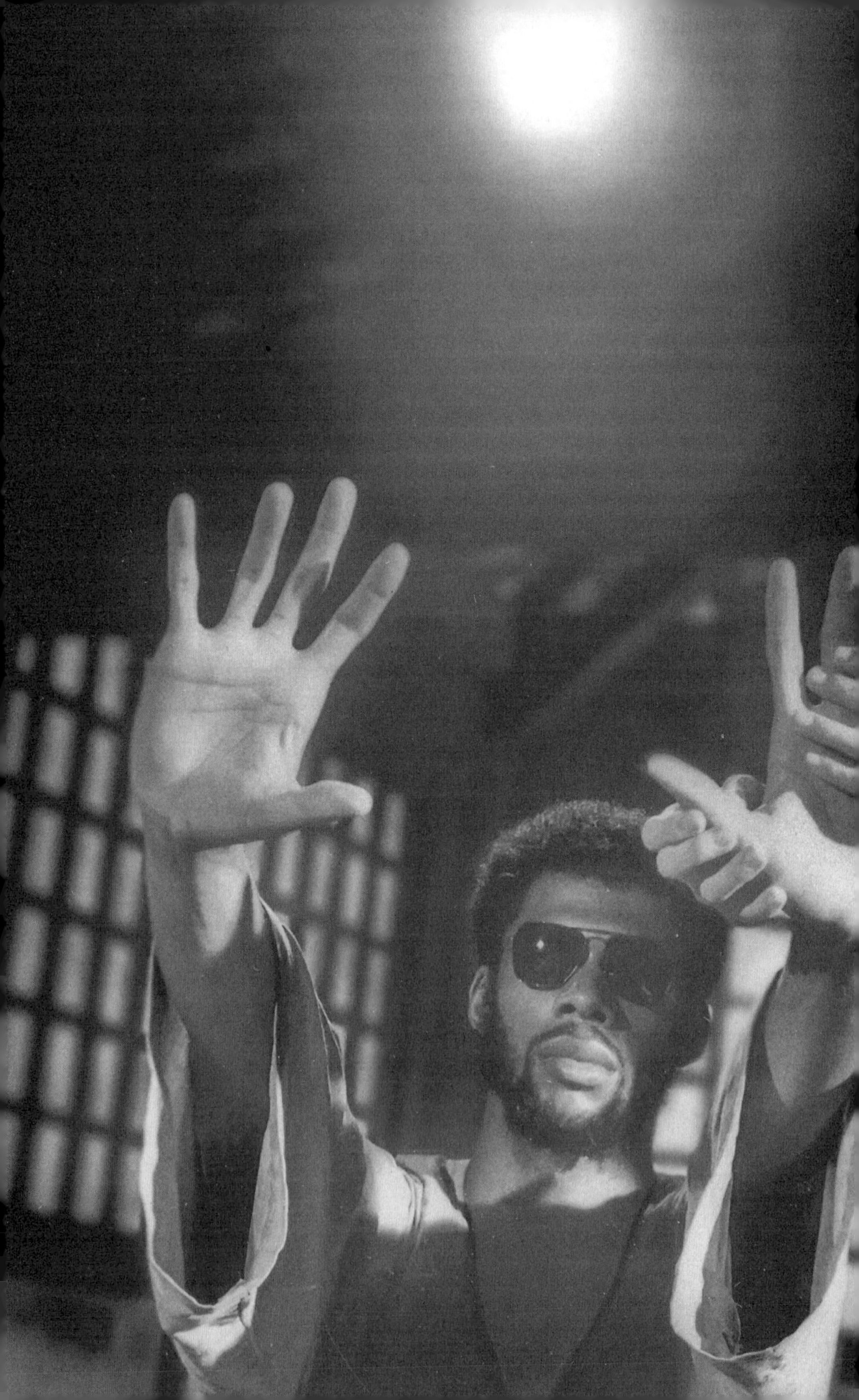

Photo courtesy of the Bruce Lee Family Archive.

Acknowledgments

When drinking water, consider the source indeed.

This book originated with a then-young Korean American editor named Junie Dahn, who approached me after he had read my first book, *Can't Stop Won't Stop*, and asked me to consider writing a biography of Bruce Lee. How could I turn down an offer to write about the most famous Asian American ever? It didn't take long to say yes.

But Junie soon left the publishing industry. There were a lot less Asian American and Pacific Islander editors around then, and his loss was felt. I had three other book contracts to complete, which I did, and this one was put on hold. The years passed, talented and patient editors came and went, and other books about Bruce Lee were published. I was ready to give up.

But a group of people—angels, honestly—intervened.

Lourdes Chang, best known as my alpha and my omega, walked me briskly to a park in Honolulu, and, as the cool tradewinds blew around us, proceeded to issue me an impassioned, expletive-laced declaration, the exact content of which I cannot and will not disclose. Needless to say, I take such things very seriously.

The marvelous Joy Yoon had already introduced me to Bao Nguyen, a superb director who was working on what would become *Be Water*. In his very Zen-ish way he always reminded me why the Bruce Lee story was so important, and left me freshly inspired.

W. Kamau Bell—who calls himself "the biggest Bruce Lee Expert in the World, Non-Asian Division," but I think he's talking about his height—propped me up, dusted me off, and reconnected me with Shannon Lee.

I got going again.

Then at the bottom of the pandemic, amidst all the violence in the country, when I was feeling that the book was more necessary than ever, its fourth editor canceled it.

My wise and compassionate agents Victoria Sanders and Bernadette Baker-Baughman saved the day in so many ways I can't even begin to list them. They told me that this setback would turn out to be the best thing to ever happen to the book. And then they worked tirelessly to make it real.

My new editor, the wonderful Rakia Clark, came on board in 2021 and guided me toward what *Water Mirror Echo* finally became. She grasped what the book needed to be before I did, and then, with all the skill and sensitivity of a veteran trainer, whispered this horse home. She became the most dedicated advocate for the book any writer could ever ask for.

For all of these people my gratitude knows no bounds.

I am also profoundly thankful for the many people who brought me along this blessed journey.

I did most of the writing for this book in a fellowship granted to me by the Lucas Artists Residency Program, on the grounds of the Montalvo Arts Center, a beautiful Bay Area hillside retreat on a parcel of land once owned by the racist San Francisco politician James Duval Phelan (a model for the conniving Mayor Samuel Blake in *Warrior*). Thank you to Kelly Sicat, Judy Dennis, Emily Borchers, Christina Von, Patrick Ip, Jose Ortiz, and Lori

Wood, and to all my brilliant peer fellows, the Montalvo Arts Center staff, and the board members. They made me feel like my time there was a small bit of reparations, and, even more, that the spirit of reparations is about the joy of experiencing and sharing the kind of creativity that frees everyone.

I am thankful to all the people who agreed to be interviewed. They shared their stories and their lives, sometimes their food and sometimes even their fighting techniques: Brad Burgo, William Cheung, Peter Chin, Lanston Chinn, Mark Chow, Ben Der, Anthony DiMaria, Arthur Dong, Harvey Dong, Michael Dorgan, Lillian Fabros Bando, Leo Fong, Leroy Garcia, Trevor Griffey, the Inosanto family, the Jay family, the Kay family, Steve Kerridge, Denise Khor, Andy Kimura, Nancy Kwan, Greglon Lee, Perry Lee, Phoebe Lee, Robert Lee, Linda Lee Cadwell, Jeffrey Thomas Leong, Lawrence Matsuda, Andre Morgan, James Muro, James Mussels, Doug Palmer, Amy Sanbo and Lisa Yamamoto, Abe Santos, Barney Scollan, Patty and Yoshi Takahashi, George Takei, Joe Torrenueva, Irene Tsu, Mito Uyehara, and Vicci Wong.

I am grateful to those who granted us permission to reprint their images: Chris Fujimoto for the Manilatown Heritage Foundation, Mike Murase for GIDRA, and Stephen Shames/Polaris, and the Bruce Lee Family Archive.

Many people came out of the woodwork along the way to guide me, procure an essential film, document, or person, commission a piece, invite me to a podcast, event, or shoot, or otherwise make an indispensable contribution to pushing me forward: Hanif Abdurraqib, H. Samy Alim, Freddy Anzures, Katy Baker, Marc Ball, Rehema Barber and the Kalamazoo Institute of Arts staff, Richard Bermack, Alex Brisland, Angela Bronner Helm, Cynthia Brothers, Vivian Chan, Kaliko and Aoi Chang, Aunty Charlian Wright, and Delene Osorio, Sophia Chang, Ken Chen, Uncle Al Cheng, Ava Chin, Cassie Chinn, Olivia Cheng, Trudi Cheung, S. Leo Chiang, Ava Chin, Jane Chin, Jeff and Julie Chinn, Sonya Childress, Cynthia Choi, Yvonne Chow, Michael Cohen and Leigh Raiford, Brian Cross, Gabriel De La Cruz and Mandeep Sethi from Stacks, Henry Der, Sik Lee Dennig, Chris Fong, J.K. Fowler and the Bay Area Book Festival and Litquake community, Shin Futatsugi, Kate Goldstein-Breyer and Holly Mulder-Wollan, David Henry Hwang, A-lan Holt, Ellen Oh, and the staffs of the Stanford Institute for Diversity in the Arts past and present, Justin Hoover, Idris Goodwin, Karen Ishizuka, Taichi Iwamoto, Steve Jang, DJ 2-Tone Jones and Shaolin Jazz, Jay Katelansky, Jungwon Kim, Kimmie Kim, Hoon Lee, Janice Lee, Pam Tau Lee, Tom Lee, Evan Jackson Leong, Annabeth Leow, Yinshi Lerman-Tan and the Huntington Library, James Leventhal, Zoë Latzer and the San Jose Institute for Contemporary Art team, Lisa Ling, Marian Liu, Colleen Lye, Sean McDonald, Mike Madden, Krishna Mann, Carolyn Mao, Michelle Meow, Elizabeth Mendez Berry, Ben Mercer, Sarah Mizes-Tan, Maureen Moore, Steffi Morrison, the MUA crew-ah of Amy Choi and Becca Lehrer, Pooja Nansi and the Singapore Writers Festival team, Janis Newman and the Page Street writing community, Julia Nottingham, Caleb Heller, Carolyn Mao, Jim Choi and everyone involved with *Be Water*, Motoko Oshino, Vincent Pan and the staffs of Chinese for Affirmative Action and AACRE, Janice Pettey, Vijay Prashad, William Ramirez, Susan Rogers, Charles Russo, the RZA, Tom Shimura, Samantha Spellman, Beth Takekawa, Joël Barraquiel Tan, Maeley Tom, Karen Umemoto, Melany De La Cruz, and the staff of the UCLA Asian American Center, Ling-chi Wang, Ted Widmer, Oliver Wang, Rick Wing, Casey Wong, Jeff Yang, Nina Yang Bongiovi,

Charles Yao, Tom, Gagnon, and the entire Lavin Agency staff past and present, Don Young and the staff at the Center for Asian American Media, Mark Young, Phil Yu, Perry Yung, and Helen Zia.

I am thankful to *sifu* Kate Hobbs, *sifu* Lynn Keslar, *guro* Allan Duncan, and all my friends past and present at Oakland Kajukenbo Kwoon, and to *tai chi* instructors Nathan Ng and Yan Li.

I am thankful to my friends Dave Lin, Andy Yang, Manuel Cruz, and P.J. Matubang for their constant grooves and encouragement. I am somewhat thankful to my old friends Michael Vann, Matt Teho, Ben Ignacio—who have known me since I weighed in at a small fraction of what I do now—for constantly interrupting my concentration with questionably appropriate texts and memes.

Thankful is not exactly the word I want to use for my good friend Davey D's nonstop trolling. But the mixes and jokes were always on time. I am thankful for Lasana Hotep's encouragement and reverse trolling and his close early read. I am thankful to the great music DJs at KALW and KEXP who kept me moving through the writing process with more fire (and water) music, especially Larry Mizell, Jr., Prometheus Brown, and Wonway Posibul.

I am thankful to Winnie Fu and Nina Tabios for their indispensable research and support. I am thankful to all the talented translators I had the privilege to work with: Calif Chong, Monica Ying, Weikuen Tang, and especially Sze Kwan Chan, who was the perfect *Wing Chun*-practicing, literary-degreed, bone-and-*qi* healing, tea-drinking, fascist-fighting comrade I didn't know I needed.

I am thankful for Renee Tajima-Peña, who invited me to participate in the *Asian Americans* documentary series, and agreed to collaborate with me on the May 19th Project. She helped me better understand the many dimensions and meanings of Asian American solidarity. I am also thankful to the dozens of amazing creatives we worked with on the Project, including Kana Hammon, Teja Smith, Eurie Chung, Annie To, Janet Chen, Victoria Chalk, and Bo Mirhosseni, who produced the Bruce Lee episode. I am thankful for Sheila Marcelo and The Asian American Foundation, who funded us and platformed our work.

I am thankful for the moral presence of the Kochiyama family and all those maintaining the legacy of Grace Lee Boggs and James Boggs.

I am thankful for Sydnie Wilson at the Bruce Lee Foundation/Bruce Lee Enterprises, who always met me at the Archives with a warm smile and deftly facilitated all of our requests, and also Chris Husband, Sharon Ann Lee, and Kris Storti, for their many kindnesses.

I am thankful for Evan Jackson Leong, who took me through the interiors of San Francisco Chinatown through his eyes, then invited the irrepressible Phoebe Lee and me to lunch at Dragon Beaux. Robert Lee kindly sent me a copy of his out-of-print biography from Hong Kong, and suffered all my questions.

I am thankful to the entire Mariner team for welcoming me with their abundant enthusiasm, conscientiousness, and craft, including Peter Hubbard, Mumtaz Mustafa, and Maureen Cole. Thank you to Ivy Givens for keeping all the trains running on time, Amanda Hong for putting it all together, Trina Hunn for the legal advice, Jen Overstreet for the gorgeous interiors, Megan Wilson and Allison Carney and Jillian Perez for letting the world know, and Julianna Lee for the sensitive, exuberant, and powerful art direction.

Thank you to Lily Qian for the beautiful illustrations.

Thank you to Greg Villepique for the excellent copy read.

The works of Hua Hsu, Viet Thanh Nguyen, and Cathy Park Hong—all of whom I have been lucky to call friends—gave me the language to explore the idea of friendship as central to biography, and the notion of war and migration as foundational conditions of Asian America, and the importance of Bruce's interiority, his minor events, and his minor feelings.

In a public conversation that Viet and Cathy had in San Jose on the release of *A Man Of Two Faces*, Viet disclosed a terrifying method of improving one's manuscript: assemble the toughest readers you know and allow them to tear your shit all the way up. Intrigued and a little fearful, I tried to put together a similar team, and I am eternally grateful they all said yes. Dubbed the Firing Squad, it consisted of Bao Nguyen, W. Kamau Bell, Cathy Park Hong, and the undisputed blurb champ of all time, Adam Mansbach.

The team did their job very well, on time and under budget. (I tried to buy them lunch and they wouldn't take my money. Do you know how shameful this is? If not, go to a *dim sum* restaurant on a Sunday.) This book is so much the better for their uncut and loving critique. All faults you may find are all mine.

I could not have written this book without the singular efforts of Gabrielle Zucker. She did difficult research, tracked down hard-to-reach folks, read all the bad drafts, kept me on calendar, and efficiently handled countless other things crucial to making this book happen. She did it all. Most of all, she believed in the book with a fervor that was contagious. She, too, ranks in my pantheon of angels. Thank you, Gab.

I would not have been able to start or finish this book without the big-hearted support of the Lee family. One of the many joys of working on this book has been to be able to get to know them better. Linda Lee Cadwell welcomed me into her home, took me with Bruce Cadwell to the best dinner in Boise, and patiently sat for a day and countless emails more of my questions.

Shannon opened up the Family Archives and provided responsive and gracious access to her resources in a spirit of trust and respect. Like her father, she was a thoughtful and close reader. I asked for and received from them complete editorial independence, and they granted it while also opening their doors to me.

Through their grace and dignity, Shannon and Linda—as well as Robert, Agnes, and Phoebe Lee, and Wren Lee Keasler—reminded me of something that Bao had said. A biography may be for the world, he said, but there are people for whom this story is their life. As writers and as readers, we are always well advised to remember this and to hold it with the requisite care.

Most of all, I am thankful for the mighty and ever sprawling Chang, Chai, Pagaduan, and Andaya clans, who probably doubted I would ever finish this book but still fed me and let me cha-cha at their parties anyway.

I am especially thankful for Jonathan Makanaonalani Chang, Solomon Keali'iho'omalu Chang, who are each beacons in their own way, and Lourdes Kahi'ilani Pagaduan Chang, the most impressive and very best warrior I know.

Jeff Ponokanaka Chang
鄭 金華
Berkeley and Honolulu, January 2025, The Year of the Dragon

Author's Note

In *Water Mirror Echo*, I have tried to harness, chronologize, and contextualize actual facts in order to make a portrait of Bruce Lee and Asian America that feels materially and psychologically true. I came to this work unhappy with the often sensational coverage of Bruce's life, and by contrast, the broad lack of comprehension of Asian and Asian American history. I tried here, as I always do, to approach my work with probity, proportionality, and transparency.

This book was shaped by primary documents, and interviews with many of Bruce's closest surviving family and friends, and others with stories about how Bruce Lee and Asian America intersected.

I read many thousands of pages of his original handwritten and typed papers in the Bruce Lee Family Archive, to which Shannon Lee and Sydnie Wilson entrusted me with full access. Shannon also generously shared with me other resources not previously made public. She encouraged me, corrected me, and sometimes disagreed with what I wrote, but always gave me all the support and autonomy I needed. She never asked for editorial input, even for passages that must have been very difficult for her to read.

I will add that this book was never "authorized" or "approved" by the Lee estate. It is a work of scholarly independence, for which I accept all accountability.

I focused on speaking with Bruce's most intimate family and friends, and others who might provide important context. What I could not achieve in the quantity of interviews—many whom I wished I could have spoken to have sadly passed away—was matched by their quality, nuance, and depth. My subjects were unfailingly generous. They opened their homes, fed me, and plied me with many more primary documents and sources. Nearly all of them offered me an open door to follow up. After clocking well over a hundred fifty hours of interviews, I did not want this portion of the work to end. Some of my sources related information that they did not want on the record, and I honor their wishes.

I want to express deep gratitude to Bao Nguyen, who shared ideas, resources, and transcripts from his documentary, *Be Water*, in which I was also honored to participate. If *Water Mirror Echo* feels a bit like a written companion to *Be Water*, perhaps it is a reflection of how profoundly his work and our collaboration and friendship has influenced this book.

I humbly submit *Water Mirror Echo* as an offering of what might be called a third wave of Bruce Lee scholarship. The first wave consisted of those who knew Bruce during his lifetime, the second wave of those who continued the work after Bruce passed away. I am deeply indebted to the work of these giants—in the first, people like Linda Lee Cadwell, Robert Lee, Mitoshi Uyehara, Chaplin Chang, Jesse Glover, Jhoon Rhee, Eunice Lam, and many others who documented Bruce's life and words; in the second, people like John Little, Charles Russo, Steve Kerridge, Darren Chua, the Bruce Lee Jeet-Kune-Do Club, Bruce Thomas, Tommy Gong, Teri Tom, Paul Bax, Jose Fraguas, Fiaz Rafiq, Bey Logan, David Tadman, Matthew Polly, Tom Bleecker, and scores of others who documented Bruce's friends and contemporaries.

This community of family, friends, and enthusiasts created a corpus—a large, public (if not always easily accessible) English-language archive of interviews, images, documents, and books—that forms the canon for the serious Bruce Lee fan. It was not made by academic professionals. Much of the work was done for magazines, newsletters, websites, and books geared for fans, not scholars, and rightly so. But the ephemerality of these forms and the lack of traditional documentation have sometimes allowed myth and legend to take up where fact should be. Unfortunately we now live in a world where, more than ever, information and misinformation float around together, without anchoring in context. For this reason, I made the choice to be copious and thorough in my documentation. You may track my sourcing in the footnotes and endnotes here, and access a bibliography at watermirrorecho.net, watermirrorecho.com, and jeffchang.net.

It is not that I have a preference for an academic approach. I defend hip-hop, Asian, Asian American, and kānaka maoli historiographies, which depend upon orality, story, and many other forms of knowing that parts of the academy often look down upon. But I also believe that Bruce Lee and Asian America are subjects that should be taken seriously. In *Water Mirror Echo*—which is for everyone—I applied organic and academic methodologies to try to paint a full and veracious portrait.

While a fair portion of Bruce Lee's papers have been published, I worked as often as I could from the primary documents, including notes, diaries, scripts, letters, videos, films, archival footage, audio recordings, photographs, school papers, bank records, promotional flyers, immigration papers, inquest documents, witness testimony, and much more.

Some of these sources were in Chinese. For these texts, I sought fresh translations from an amazing team of Hong Kong and Cantonese American scholars, which yielded new insights into Bruce's thinking and actions at key points in his life. I chose to mostly refrain from imagining dialogue, and instead sought quotations directly from Bruce or those who quoted him. As far as contemporary coverage went, I tried to source the original interviews and articles as much as I could. I fastened all the bits of information I collected to a robust timeline in order to build a solid foundation for interpretation and analysis.

Some of what I learned recontextualized long-accepted notions about Bruce's ideas and motives or challenged long-standing myths that have become part of his legend. I have tried throughout the text and also, in far more detail, in the notes to explain my positions and have documented the sources that led me there. I have also tried to be clear about areas where I may be wading into speculation. Here, again, I both assert my independence and accept accountability.

Allow me a slight digression for a note on Chinese names and phrases. I have chosen not to standardize them wholly in either *pinyin* or *jyutping*, but to write them as I received them. My preference was always to use the more common rendering—the Cantonese rendering of Li Hoi Chuen, rather than Mandarin of Li Haiquan, say, or the Mandarin rendering of Huo Yianjia rather than the Cantonese of Fok Yuen-Gap. Of course, this process was complicated by the lack of a universal standard for romanizing Cantonese. At any rate, the choices here are mine and not of my extremely meticulous translators.

My task, of course, has not been solely to write about Bruce Lee's life, but also his times. In this regard, I am thankful for having long been in community with some of the most heroic Asian American, Native Hawaiian, Pacific Islander thinkers and organizers to ever do it. For decades they have mentored me, opened up their personal archives, and graciously granted me time to ask them lots of small and big, often impertinent questions. They have made me the student of Asia, the Pacific, and America that I am. If this book has been able to evoke for you a picture of the world that Bruce Lee walked through, it is undoubtedly due to the investment my community has put into me. I bear my *kuleana* with gratitude and humility.

Stanford's Green Library and UC Berkeley's Doe Library provided me with access to countless rare monographs and academic, news, and trade magazine articles. At the UC Berkeley Art Museum & Pacific Film Archive, Jason Sanders patiently dug up hard-to-find volumes on and about the Hong Kong film industry. My writing about Bruce's early film work was informed by the meticulous research and translations of the inestimably wise and patient Winnie Fu in Hong Kong. My thanks also to the Hong Kong Film Archive for their stellar reference work.

I thank the staffs of UCLA's Charles E. Young Research Library, where I accessed the papers of Stirling Silliphant, and of the American Heritage Center at the University of Wyoming, where I accessed the papers of William Dozier. I want to send special shout-outs to Sine Hwang Jensen at the UC Berkeley Ethnic Studies Library, who provided me with documents on the Asian American Political Alliance and the Third World Liberation Front, and many other important leads; to the generous staff of the Wing Luke Museum, which holds much of Bruce Lee's voluminous book collection, and has mounted an ongoing set of phenomenal Bruce Lee exhibitions; and to the team behind the "We Are Bruce" Lee exhibition at the Chinese Historical Society of America in San Francisco Chinatown. These shows, not to mention a large continuing exhibition at the Hong Kong Heritage Museum, join with the vast Bruce Lee fandom—his Instagram account has more than 12 million followers in this moment—to paint a picture of the ongoing significance of the man and his life.

Every generation seems to finally find the Bruce it needs. I am hopeful that this book may continue to speak to future generations chasing Bruce Lee and making Asian America.

Notes

You may find a selected bibliography online at watermirrorecho.net.

Epigraph

ix   "I'm writing you all this": Chris Marker, director. *San Soleil*. 1983; Criterion Collection, 2012. Blu-Ray DVD.

Book I: Water

xv   "A monk asked Chao Chou": The translators note that the sixth consciousness is called "Wondrous Observing Knowledge," and they describe it as "conceptual thinking" beyond the five senses, which together comprise the "Knowledge of Accomplishment." Thomas J. Cleary and J. C. Cleary, trans. and ed., *The Blue Cliff Record (Pi Yen Lu)* (Shambhala Press, 2005), pp. 437–42.

The Lives of Bruce Lee

1   "The first thing the colonial subject learns": Frantz Fanon, *The Wretched of the Earth* (Grove Press, 1963), translated by Richard Philcox, 2004, p. 15.

3   "one thing we all have in common": "Bosnia Unveils Bruce Lee Bronze," BBC News, Nov. 26, 2005, news.bbc.co.uk/2/hi/entertainment/4474316.stm.

3   "our idea of universal justice": Alexander Zaitchek, "Mostar's Little Dragon," *Reason*, Apr. 2006, reason.com/2006/04/01/mostars-little-dragon-2/.

5   a study found: Eleven percent of respondents named Jackie Chan, and 9 percent named Bruce Lee. Leading Asian Americans to United for Change (LAAUNCH), *STAATUS Index Report 2021* (LAAUNCH, 2021), 30, uploads-ssl.webflow.com/5f629e7e013d961943d5cec9/6098a7be3d627168e03054da_staatus-index-2021.pdf.

Three years later, after ample media coverage and community organizing around violence against Asian Americans, there was little indication that things may have improved. In a poll taken by Savanta Research in early 2024, 52 percent of Americans in a "nationally representative survey" said they "can't think of a famous Asian American." Again Jackie Chan and Bruce Lee topped the poll as people whom they could name. Kamala Harris received just 2 percent. Niala Boodhoo, "Scoop: Asian Americans Fear Hate Crime Is Rising," *Axios*, May 1, 2024, axios.com/2024/05/01/asian-americans-hate-crime-fear.

7   "Under heaven nothing is more soft": "(Chapter) Seventy-Eight," in Lao Tsu, *Tao Te Ching*, trans. Gia-Fu Feng and Jane English with Toinette Lippe (Vintage Books, 1972/2000), unpaginated.

8   never learned to swim: Interview with Phoebe Lee, May 8, 2021; Robert Lee, *Bruce Lee, My Brother* (Masterpiece Films, 2010), p. 30, trans. Monica Ying; SPH Razor video, "Bruce Lee Couldn't Swim," July 9, 2013, youtube.com/watch?v=gpR67z18ucg&t=3s.

8   Water, from antiquity: "In ancient times, crossing a river represented great danger. Thus, the attribute of water was designated a situation of difficulty or danger." Alfred Huang, *The Complete I Ching. 10th Anniversary Edition* (Inner Traditions, 1998/2010), pp. 248–50.

Part I: War Child, 1940–1950

11   "You reckless monster": *The Journey to the West, Volume 1*. Revised Edition. Translated by Anthony C. Yu (The University of Chicago Press, 2012), p. 128.

See also *Monkey: Folk Novel of China*. Translated by Arthur Waley. Grove Press, 1943. p. 29. *Monkey King: Journey to the West*. Translated by Julia Lovell (Penguin Classics, 2021), p. 20.

Chapter 1: Anchor Baby

12   "That I should be": Bruce Lee, "Me and Jeet Kune Do," in John Little, ed., *Bruce Lee: Words of the Dragon, Interviews, 1958–1973* (Tuttle, 1997), p. 124. Published in English in *Bruce Lee: Studies on Jeet-Kune-Do* (Bruce Lee Jeet-kune-do Club, 1976), pp. 21–22. It is published in transcript form as "The Knowing Is Not Enough Interview: Bruce Lee on the Role of Philosophy in Martial Art," in *"Knowing Is Not Enough": The Official Newsletter of Jun Fan Jeet Kune Do* 1, no. 1 (Spring 1997), pp. 2–4. All attribute the article to an unnamed Taiwanese newspaper in June 1972, after the release of *Fist of Fury*.

12   a hospital built: Claire Wang, "When Chinese Americans Were Blamed for 19th-Century Epidemics, They Built Their Own Hospital," *Atlas Obscura*, Apr. 13, 2020, atlasobscura.com/articles/chinese-blamed-19th-century-epidemics.

12   the sixth child of eight: See family tree by Robert Lee in Robert Lee, *Bruce Lee, My Brother*. Hong Kong:

462 NOTES

Masterpiece Films Ltd. 2010, p. 64-5. Judging by the nicknames listed for each of the siblings, Hoi Chuen's third-born sibling seems not to be accounted for in this tree.

12 most likely on March 27, 1902: Different accounts list Li Hoi Chuen's birth year as 1898, 1902, or 1904. The Hong Kong Film Archive lists Hoi Chuen's birth year as 1898, based on newspaper clippings and the work of Cantonese opera experts, including the film producer and documentarian Manfred Wong. Li's gravestone lists his birth as occurring in the year 1902. (It also includes information on his hour of birth and death.) Robert Lee's family tree lists 1902, also. In Bruce's diaries, he lists his father's birthday as the 18th day of the second lunar month. This corresponds to Li Hoi Chuen's gravestone also. Converting from the Chinese calendar to the Gregorian calendar, this would be March 27, 1902. Robert Lee, *Bruce Lee, My Brother* (Masterpiece Films, 2010), trans. Weikuen Tang.

12 the Four Arts: Yung Sai-shing. "Moving Body: The Interactions Between Chinese Opera and Action Cinema," in Meaghan Morris, Si Keung Li, and Stephen Chan Ching-kiu, eds., *Hong Kong Connections: Transnational Imagination in Action Cinema* (Duke University Press/Hong Kong University Press, 2005), 27-28.

13 "the golden age of Guangdong's martial arts": Benjamin Judkins and Jon Nielson, *The Creation of Wing Chun: A Social History of the Southern Chinese Martial Arts* (State University of New York Press, 2015), 111.

13 Family lore: Robert Lee, *Bruce Lee, My Brother*, p. 53, trans. Monica Ying.

13 "rusty voice": "Lee Hoi-Chuen," Hong Kong Film Archive, no date, filmarchive.gov.hk/documents/6.-Research-and-Publication/06-02-Filmmakers-Search/English/LEE-Hoi-chuen_e.pdf.

13 December 12, 1907: The year of Grace Ho's birth is taken from Robert Lee's family tree in *Bruce Lee, My Brother*. In his diary, Bruce lists his mother's birthday in Chinese as the eighth day of the eleventh month. Assuming this is the lunar calendar rather than the Gregorian, as in the other similar entries on the same page, her birthday would be December 12.

13 shrouded in mystery: Charles Russo discusses the question in depth, including a theory that Grace may have been adopted. Charles Russo, "Was Bruce Lee of English Descent? Just Ask His Mother," *Medium*, Sept. 23, 2018, medium.com/@charlierusso23/was-bruce-lee-of-english-descent-just-ask-his-mother-c1f080d83a57.

13 deserted the family: Matthew Polly, *Bruce Lee: A Life* (Simon & Schuster, 2018), pp. 13-14.

13 remarried a Chinese businessman: Hotung was the blue-eyed blood son of Bosman. But after Bosman disappeared, Sze Tai married a Chinese businessman named Kwok Hing Yin, who likely fathered Ho Kom Tong. Maggie Farley, "A Family's 'Priceless' Legacy," *Los Angeles Times*, June 15, 1997; May Holdsworth, *Sir Robert Ho Tung: Public Figure, Private Man* (Hong Kong University Press, 2022), pp. 43-44.

13 tell US immigration officials: "Bruce Lee (Lee Jun Fon)," Return Certificate Application Case Files of Chinese Departing (12017), 1912-1943, ARC Identifier 296477, Mar. 7, 1941, US Department of Justice, Immigration and Naturalization Service, San Francisco, California; Russo, "Was Bruce Lee of English Descent?"

14 Cheung King-sin: Russo's article cites Eric Peter Ho's genealogy, which suggests the Eurasian mistress Cheung King-sin was Grace's blood mother. Russo, "Was Bruce Lee of English Descent?"

14 "She liked drinking beer": Robert Lee, *Bruce Lee, My Brother*, p. 41, trans. Monica Ying.

14 horse-drawn carriage: Bao Nguyen interview with Sylvia Lai, May 25, 2019.

14 less than two years: "Bruce Lee (Lee Jun Fon)," Return Certificate Application Case Files of Chinese Departing (12017), 1912-1943.

14 refugees in China: Robert Lee, *Bruce Lee, My Brother*, p. 27.

14 saw the couple off: Interview with Phoebe Lee, May 8, 2021.

15 "Asia, with her numberless millions": Leland Stanford, "Inaugural Address," Jan. 10, 1862, Governor's Library, governors.library.ca.gov/addresses/08-Stanford.html.

15 nation's biggest recruiter of Chinese workers: Gordon Chang, *Ghosts of Gold Mountain: The Epic Story of the Chinese Who Built the Transcontinental Railroad* (Houghton Mifflin Harcourt, 2019), p. 62. Chang also describes Stanford's personal relationships with the Chinese who served him in his household.

15 die in the process: Iris Chang, *The Chinese in America* (Penguin, 2004), pp. 63-64.

15 Tabloids ran cartoons: See the 1881 cartoon from Ambrose Bierce's *The Wasp* in Philip Choy, Lorraine Dong, and Marlon Hom, eds., *The Coming Man: Nineteenth-Century American Perceptions of the Chinese* (University of Washington Press, 1994), p. 91.

15 the "Yellow Peril": Judy Yung, *The Chinese Exclusion Act and Angel Island* (Bedford/St. Martins, 2019), p. 31.

16 "any Black person, mulatto, Indian, or Chinese": Rachel J. Anderson, "Timeline of African-American History in Nevada (1861-2011)," Scholarly Commons @ UNLV Boyd Law, Feb. 2012, scholars.law.unlv.edu/cgi/viewcontent.cgi?article=1706&context=facpub. For more, see "Anti-Miscegenation in California," *Foundations of Law and Society* blog, Dec. 9, 2016, foundationsoflawandsociety.wordpress.com/2016/12/09/anti-miscegenation-in-california/.

16 "few of whom": Ulysses S. Grant, "Seventh Annual Message," Dec. 7. 1875, The American Presidency Project. University of California at Santa Barbara, presidency.ucsb.edu/documents/seventh-annual-message-3.

NOTES 463

17 killed twenty-eight: Tom Rea, "The Rock Springs Massacre," WyoHistory.org, Nov. 8, 2014, wyohistory.org/encyclopedia/rock-springs-massacre.

17 their slaughter: Gordon Chang, *Ghosts of Gold Mountain*, p. 232.

17 leave or be lynched: See Erika Lee, *The Making of Asian America: A History*; Jean Pfaelzer, *Driven Out: The Forgotten War Against Chinese Americans* (University of California Press, 2007); Howard A. DeWitt, *Anti-Filipino Movements in California: A History, Bibliography, and Study Guide*; Patricia E. Roy, *The Oriental Question*; and Paul Engelsberg, "The 1907 Bellingham Riot and Anti-Asian Hostilities in the Pacific Northwest."

17 Between 1850 and 1906: Jean Pfaelzer, "The Chinese Rewrite the Letter of the Law," *The California Supreme Court Historical Society Newsletter*, Spring/Summer 2009, p. 22, cschs.org/wp-content/uploads/2014/03/CSCHS-2009-Newsletter-Spring-Summer.pdf. See Pfaelzer, *Driven Out*.

17 "America's first undocumented immigrants": Erika Lee, *At America's Gates: Chinese Immigration During the Exclusion Era, 1882–1943* (University of North Carolina Press, 2003), pp. 41–43. *Backstory* podcast, "Border Patrols: Policing Immigration in America," Nov. 12, 2018, transcript and audio, backstory.newamericanhistory.org/episodes/border-patrols/1.

17 "Chinese catchers": Erika Lee, *At America's Gates*, p. 186. Mae Ngai, "The 100-Year-Old Racist Law That Broke America's Immigration System," *Public Books*, May 28, 2024, publicbooks.org/the-100-year-old-racist-law-that-broke-americas-immigration-system/.

By the early twentieth century, the Border Patrol would turn its focus to migrants of color and indigenous migrants from Mexico and Central America.

17 "America must be kept American": A. Naomi Paik & Catherine S. Ramírez. "The Border Is The Crisis: Reflections on the Centenary of the Immigration Act of 1924." PublicBooks.org. May 27, 2024. Accessed at: https://www.publicbooks.org/the-border-is-the-crisis-reflections-on-the-centenary-of-the-immigration-act-of-1924/.

17 "perfected Asiatic exclusion": Ngai, "The 100-Year-Old Racist Law."

17 only 2 percent of immigrants: Ngai, "The 100-Year-Old Racist Law."

17 "proxies for foreign troops": In 1893, in the case of *Fong Yue Ting v. United States*, the US Supreme Court upheld the certificate requirement. The majority opinion held, "If, therefore, the Government of the United States, through its Legislative Department, considers the presence of foreigners of a different race in this country, who will not assimilate with us, to be dangerous to its peace and security, their exclusion is not to be stayed because at the time there are no actual hostilities with the nation of which the foreigners are subjects. The existence of war would render the necessity of the proceeding only more obvious and pressing." "In truth," Mae Ngai wrote, "immigrants have historically pursued not the political interests of states but individual and family improvement. Even when politically motivated, migration is more often a matter of escape than one of conquest." Cited in Mae Ngai, *Impossible Subjects: Illegal Aliens and the Making of Modern America* (Princeton University Press, 2004), p. 18.

18 On Angel Island: Interview with Robert Lee, December 9, 2021. For the description of immigration procedures, see Him Mark Lai, Genny Lim, and Judy Yung, eds., *Island: Poetry and History of Chinese Immigrants on Angel Island, 1910–1940* (University of Washington Press, 2014), pp. 11–16, 341.

18 "America has power": Lai, Lim, and Yung, eds., *Island*, p. 72. See also Jeffrey Thomas Leong, trans., *Wild Geese Sorrow: The Chinese Wall Inscriptions at Angel Island* (Calypso Books, 2018), p. 121.

18 carefully prepared papers: "Bruce Lee (Lee Jun Fon)," Return Certificate Application Case Files of Chinese Departing (12017), 1912–1943.

18 Immigration and Naturalization Service. "Immigration Arrival Investigation Case File no. 39707/8-25. (Ho Oi Yee)." The National Archives at San Francisco. Papers are from November 22, 1939 to April 11, 1941.

18 how unfree the Chinese: Interview with Robert Lee, Dec. 9, 2021.

18 "Heartland Asian America": Bonnie Tsui. *American Chinatown: A People's History of Five Neighborhoods* (Free Press, 2010), pp. 27–28.

19 "At that time": Bruce Lee, "Me and Jeet Kune Do."

19 full of appreciative white spectators: Philip P. Choy, *San Francisco Chinatown: A Guide to Its History & Architecture* (City Lights Books, 2012), pp. 150–51.

19 the Chinese audience rioted: Nancy Yunhwa Rao, *Chinatown Opera Theater in North America* (University of Illinois Press, 2017), p. 44.

19 "The opera": Frank Chin, "The Three Kingdoms: Ruby Chow," in David Brewster and David M. Buerge, eds., *Washingtonians: A Biographical Portrait of the State* (Sasquatch Books, 1989), p. 373.

19 near midnight: Rao, *Chinatown Opera Theater in North America*, p. 8; Choy, *San Francisco Chinatown*, p. 150.

19 Chivalry in Red: Robert Lee, *Bruce Lee, My Brother*, p. 25, trans. Monica Ying.

19 Seattle and New York City: Rao, *Chinatown Opera Theater in North America*, p. 228. These cities were among the most generous in the defense of China.

464 NOTES

19 "across the street": Russo, "Was Bruce Lee of English Descent?," p. 33.

19 the English name of "Bruce": Robert Lee, *Bruce Lee, My Brother*, p. 26, trans. Weikuen Tang and Monica Ying.

20 Jun Piu: Jun Piu—震彪—could be literally translated as "thunder of the tiger" or "the rousing of the tiger." I'm deeply indebted to Winnie Fu, Monica Ying, and Weikuen Tang for help with this section. Robert Lee, *Bruce Lee, My Brother*, p. 26. Translated by Monica Ying.

20 hopes for his son: Robert Lee, *Bruce Lee, My Brother*, p. 26. Translation assistance by Monica Ying, Weikuen Tang, and Winnie Fu.

20 the 1906 catastrophe: Robert Lee, *Bruce Lee, My Brother*, p. 26. Translation assistance by Monica Ying, Weikuen Tang, and Winnie Fu.

20 "They will cross the mountains": Frederick Douglass, "'Composite Nation,' Lecture in the Parker Fraternity Course, Boston, 1867," p. 12, loc.gov/resource/mss11879.22017/?st=gallery.

20 "birthright citizenship": See Martha S. Jones, *Birthright Citizens: A History of Race and Rights in Antebellum America* (Cambridge University Press, 2018); Martha Jones, "Citizenship," in Nikole Hannah-Jones, Caitlin Roper, Ilena Silverman, and Jake Silverstein, eds., *The 1619 Project: A New Origin Story* (One World, 2021), pp. 220-229.

20 "I want a home here": Frederick Douglass, "Composite Nation," p. 16, loc.gov/resource/mfd.22016/?sp=1.

20 South and East Asia: These are the numbers of legal admissions. "Modern Immigration Wave Brings 59 Million to U.S., Driving Population Growth and Change Through 2065." Pew Research Center, Sept. 28, 2015, pewresearch.org/race-and-ethnicity/2015/09/28/modern-immigration-wave-brings-59-million-to-u-s-driving-population-growth-and-change-through-2065/.

21 "anchor baby": Carol Nackenoff and Julie Novkov, *American by Birth: Wong Kim Ark and the Battle for Citizenship* (University of Kansas Press, 2021), pp. 71-77.

21 denied him birthright citizenship: Erika Lee, *At America's Gates*, p. 52. Nackenoff and Novkov, *American by Birth*, pp. 98-100.

21 A US attorney questioned: Erika Lee, *At America's Gates*, p. 105.

21 "enter fully into a birthright": Charles Caldwell Dobie, *San Francisco's Chinatown* (Appleton-Century, 1936), pp. 325, 327-28.

21 But he was jailed there: Amanda Frost, "Birthright Citizens and Paper Sons," *American Scholar*, January 18, 2021. theamericanscholar.org/birthright-citizens-and-paper-sons/

21 "a barrage of humiliating interrogations": Erika Lee on *Constitutional* podcast, *Washington Post*, Aug. 24, 2017, washingtonpost.com/news/on-leadership/wp/2017/08/14/episode-3-of-the-constitutional-podcast-nationality/.

22 submitted himself to deportation: Erika Lee, *Constitutional* podcast. See also Bethany R. Berger, "Birthright Citizenship on Trial: *Elk v. Wilkins* and *United States v. Wong Kim Ark*," *Cardozo Law Review* 37, no. 4 (2016), pp. 1253-54.

22 "I thought it would": "Bruce Lee (Lee Jun Fon)," Return Certificate Application Case Files of Chinese Departing (12017), 1912-1943.

23 At the age of twenty-one: When she passed away, the *New York Times* eulogized her and her extraordinary Chinatown restaurants: "Esther Eng Owned Restaurants Here," *New York Times*, Jan. 27, 1970. See also S. Louisa Wei's 2013 documentary *Golden Gate Girls* and S. Louisa Wei, "Esther Eng," in Jane Gaines, Radha Vatsal, and Monica Dall'Asta, eds., *Women Film Pioneers Project* (Columbia University Libraries, 2014), doi.org/10.7916/d8-rhpq-0f69.

23 Grandview studio in San Francisco's Chinatown: Wei, *Golden Gate Girls* documentary. Law Kar, "In Search of Esther Eng: Border-Crossing in Chinese-Language Filmmaking," trans. Chris Tong, in Linzheng Wang, ed., *Chinese Women's Cinema: Transnational Contexts* (Columbia University Press, 2011).

Joseph Sunn Jue actually opened the first movie theater in the United States for Chinese-language films the week before Bruce was born. The Grandview was located at 756 Jackson Street. Arthur Dong, *Hollywood Chinese* (Angel City Press, 2019), pp. 243-44.

Chapter 2: The Dead and the Diseased

24 "I think I spoiled him": Mitoshi Uyehara, *Bruce Lee: The Incomparable Fighter* (Ohara Publications, 1988), p. 7.

24 Their first son, Li Jung Teung: "Bruce Lee (Lee Jun Fon)," Return Certificate Application Case Files of Chinese Departing (12017), 1912-1943, ARC Identifier 296477, Mar. 7, 1941, US Department of Justice, Immigration and Naturalization Service, San Francisco, California.

24 "When we were young": Interview with Robert Lee, Dec. 9, 2021.

24 "Bruce almost didn't make it": Linda Lee, *Bruce Lee: The Man Only I Knew* (Warner Paperback Library, 1975), p. 33.
24 "He believed": Interview with Robert Lee, Dec. 9, 2021.
24 "Hong Kong was on the verge": Robert Lee, *Bruce Lee, My Brother* (Masterpiece Films, 2010), p. 27, trans. Monica Ying.
24 infant mortality stalked China: Some reports have as many as 35 percent of children in China dying before their fifth birthday in the latter part of the 1930s. Ian Christopher Petrie, "The Problem of Infant Mortality in Hong Kong, 1886-1937," Master of Arts Thesis, University of British Columbia, Aug. 1996, p. 53.
25 "soaked in blood": John Faber, *Great News Photos and the Stories Behind Them* (Faber, 1978), p. 74.
25 gathered up the baby: Faber, *Great News Photos*, p. 74. See also "The Camera Overseas: 136,000,000 People See This Picture of Shanghai's South Station," *Life*, Oct. 4, 1937, pp. 102-103, books.google.com/books?id=wkQEAAAAMBAJ&lpg=PA102&pg=PA102#v=onepage&q&f=false.
26 doubled Hong Kong's population to over 1.6 million: Steve Tsang, *A Modern History of Hong Kong* (I. B. Tauris, 2007), p. 109.
26 thousands of rape victims: Frank Welsh, *A History of Hong Kong* (HarperCollins, 1993), pp. 417, 433. The Kempeitai, the Japanese military police, took over the local structures of crime, deputizing local gangsters as neighborhood police while siphoning off their underworld gambling proceeds.
26 After dark fell: Interview with Phoebe Lee, May 8, 2021.
26 two surviving sisters: His two eldest brothers likely had passed away before the war.
27 "The question of color is dead": Welsh, *A History of Hong Kong*, p. 421. See "Cultural Activities in the New Hong Kong, a Special Article from the Hong Kong Broadcasting Office," originally published in *The New East Asia*, Sept. 1942, in David Faure, ed., *A Documentary History of Hong Kong: Society* (Hong Kong University Press, 1997), p. 225.
27 "an illusion of peace": Robert Lee, *Bruce Lee, My Brother*, p. 56, trans. Monica Ying.
27 "My father never received": Interview with Phoebe Lee, May 8, 2021.
27 "after the war as collaborators": Matthew Polly, *Bruce Lee: A Life* (Simon & Schuster, 2018), p. 31.
27 losing a million people: Tsang, *Modern History of Hong Kong*, p. 127.
27 feed everyone for a day: Interview with Phoebe Lee, May 8, 2021.
27 seen by hundreds of millions: "The Camera Overseas: 136,000,000 People See This Picture of Shanghai's South Station," *Life*, Oct. 4, 1937, books.google.com/books?id=wkQEAAAAMBAJ&lpg=PA102&pg=PA102#v=onepage&q&f=false.
28 dirty, disease-ridden people: Larissa N. Heinrich, *The Afterlife of Images* (Duke University Press, 2008), pp. 19, 25.
28 "moral lepers": Charles McClain, "Of Medicine, Race, and American Law: The Bubonic Plague Outbreak of 1900," *Law and Social Inquiry* 13, no. 3 (1988), p. 453.
28 "concealing their cases of smallpox": Joan B. Trauner, "Chinese as Medical Scapegoats, 1870-1905," *California History*, 1978, foundsf.org/index.php?title=Chinese_as_Medical_Scapegoats,_1870-1905.
28 "a public nuisance": Guenter B. Risse, "San Francisco's Chinatown: A Chronology of Conditions and Disinfection," pp. 5, 6, academia.edu/3817790/Plague_Fear_and_Politics_in_San_Franciscos_Chinatown.
28 one in five of the city's residents: David K. Randall, *Black Death at the Golden Gate: The Race to Save America from the Bubonic Plague* (W. W. Norton, 2019), p. 43.
29 "did not trust or understand": Randall, *Black Death at the Golden Gate*, pp. 45-47.

Chapter 3: The One Who Can't Be Stopped

30 a couple of dozen housing units: Interview with Robert Chan in Chaplin Chang and Roger Lo, *The Bruce Lee They Knew* (Infolink Publishing, 2003), p. 32. Translated by Sze K. Chan.
30 The other room: Interview with Doug Palmer, Oct. 12, 2018. Doug Palmer, *Bruce Lee: Sifu, Friend and Big Brother* (Chin Music Press, 2020), pp. 98-99.
30 "I suppose I was spoiled": Bruce Lee interview with Helen Hendricks, from a partial article in Bruce Lee archive, undated (likely 1966).
31 He tortured his siblings: Interview with Robert Lee, Dec. 9, 2021; interview with Phoebe Lee, May 8, 2021; Agnes Lee, Grace Lee, and Robert Lee, *The Untold Story: Bruce Lee's Life Story as Told by His Mother, Family, and Friends* (Unique Publications, 1986), pp. 4-5, 11.
31 demented mischief: Agnes Lee, Grace Lee, and Robert Lee, *The Untold Story*, p. 11.

466 NOTES

31 "go strolling off": Agnes Lee, Grace Lee, and Robert Lee, *The Untold Story*, p. 5.
32 He had been out cold: Interview with Phoebe Lee, May 8, 2021.
32 *tai chi* heroes: "Bruce Lee Had Ten Masters," in Wong Shun Leung, *Bruce Lee: His Unknowns in Martial Arts Learning* (Bruce Lee Jeet-kune-do Club, 1977), pp. 14–15.
32 "Show some moves to your uncles!": Bao Nguyen interview with Tony Lau Wing, May 27, 2019. Robert Lee believes that this initial training gave Bruce a foundation for his interests in wing chun and his later *gung fu* experimentation. Robert Lee, *Bruce Lee, My Brother* (Masterpiece Films, 2010), p. 109. Translated by Sze K. Chan.
32 off the stage by company members: Interview with Phoebe Lee, May 8, 2021.
32 "generals, magistrates, and fools": Stephen Teo. *Hong Kong Cinema: The Extra Dimensions* (British Film Institute, 1997), p. 42.
33 *Wealth Is Like a Dream*: Previous biographies in English have listed *Birth of Mankind* as his first movie. But an article in *Kung Sheung Evening News* from July 2, 1971, notes that his 1951 movie, *Infancy*, was also known as *The Birth of Mankind*. See "Law Chi Has Pre-Affinity with Lee Siu Loong," in *Lee Siu Loong, The Rise of the Mandarin Superstar: Old Hong Kong Newspaper Collection (Volume 1: 1970–71)*, trans. Sai Loong, Kindle edition, 2006, loc. 274. The most complete record of Bruce Lee's films is in the Hong Kong Film Archive database. *Wealth Is Like a Dream* is listed there as the movie's international title. Its original Chinese title was 富貴浮雲. The Hong Kong Cinemagic database lists the movie as shot in 1946, and the Hong Kong Film Archive lists the release date as Nov. 24, 1948, days before his eighth birthday. He did meet Unicorn Chan on the set of this movie. Special thanks to archivist Winnie Fu for all of her research.
33 "At two o'clock in the morning": Linda Lee, *The Bruce Lee Story* (Ohara Publications, 1989), p. 21.
33 "I want to make some money!": Connie Schimpf, "A Mother Remembers," *Fighting Stars*, Summer 1977, p. 12.
33 "just see": Interview with Phoebe Lee, May 8, 2021.
33 "They were the minority": Mito Uyehara, *Bruce Lee: The Incomparable Fighter* (Ohara Publications, 1988), p. 9.
33 to await crossing: Fujio Mizuoka, *Contrived Laissez-Faireism: The Politico-Economic Structure of British Colonialism in Hong Kong* (Springer, 2018), p. 73.
33 from 600,000 to 2,237,000: Alvin Rabushka, *Hong Kong: A Study in Economic Freedom* (University of Chicago Press, 1979), pp. 11–12.
33 "Hong Kong also has no future": Jamie Peck, "Milton's Paradise: Situating Hong Kong in Neoliberal Lore," *Journal of Law and Political Economy* 1, no. 2 (2021), p. 195.
33 The first people of Hong Kong: This section owes much to Louisa Lim's magisterial *Indelible City: Dispossession and Defiance in Hong Kong* (Riverhead Books, 2022), pp. 41, 65.
34 sentimental and moralistic: See chapters 1 and 5 in Teo, *Hong Kong Cinema*.
34 "They either went off": Robert Lee, *Bruce Lee, My Brother*, p. 80, trans. Sze K. Chan.
34 In *Wealth Is Like a Dream*: My deepest thanks to Winnie Fu for her research.
36 "the ultimate fear of Hong Kongers": Lim, *Indelible City*, p. 33.
37 "child genius actor": Robert Lee, *Bruce Lee, My Brother*, p. 75, trans. Sze K. Chan; Lee Chui Mei, "The Missing Pages in the Bruce Lee Legend," in *Bruce Lee: Kung Fu, Art, Life* (Leisure and Cultural Services Department, 2013), p. 40.

Part II: The Orphan, 1950–1959

39 "The smaller man": George F. Jowett, *The Modern Commando Science: Guerilla Self-Defense for The Home Front* (The Abell Press, 1943). Reproduced on the internet: www.scribd.com/document/58574941/32119551-Guerilla-Self-Defense-for-the-Home-Front-Jowett

Chapter 4: The Kung Fu Guy

40 "Li Yum": Robert Lee, *Bruce Lee, My Brother* (Masterpiece Films, 2010), p. 28, trans. Monica Ying.
40 "Genius Child Star": Robert Lee, *Bruce Lee, My Brother*, p. 45, trans. Monica Ying. Bruce's cousin Li Fat was also an actor and called "New Hoi Chuen." My thanks to Winnie Fu for this research.
40 observes how the boy's presence: Interviews with William Cheung, Feb. 2, 2022 and Feb. 14, 2022. He has also told this story in William Cheung, *Mystery of Bruce Lee* (Bruce Lee Jeet-kune-do Club, 1980); William Cheung, *My Life with Wing Chun*, 2nd ed. (World Wing Chun Kung Fu Association, 1996); William Cheung, *City of Dragons: Ah Hing—The Dragon Warrior* (Healthworld Enterprises, 2005); as well as in countless other interviews.

Over the years, while the substance of Cheung's story has stayed the same, he has changed some of the details—he once said that Bruce came out at the party in a girl's outfit, and has also said that Bruce was attending

NOTES 467

a nearly all-girls school, which is inaccurate. I've tried to report here the substance and the details that have stayed consistent over the last forty-plus years.

41 *Infancy*: Information compiled by Hong Kong Film Archive. The Cantonese name for the film is 人之初 *The Birth of Mankind*. My thanks to Winnie Fu.

41 "Their lives are abnormal": "An Interview with Bruce Lee's Mother," in Bruce Thomas, *Bruce Lee: Fighting Spirit* (Bruce Lee Jeet-kune-do Club, 1979), p. 63.

41 Bruce lets Robert tag along: Robert Wang, *Walking the Tycoon's Rope* (Blacksmith Books, 2013), pp. 109–10.

41 To Michael Lai: Michael Lai in Chaplin Chang and Roger Lo, *The Bruce Lee They Knew* (Infolink Publishing, 2003), p. 68, trans. Sze K. Chan.

42 "a Teddy Boy from head to toe": James Wong Jim, "Days When I Fought with Bruce Lee," *Next Magazine* 41 (1990), trans. Winnie Fu.

42 They turn to throw stones: Jim, "Days When I Fought with Bruce Lee"; Wan Xiao Dao, "James Wong: Fist Fight with Bruce Lee; Marriage with the Singer and the Pretty Writer; Checking Out Nightclub Scenes with Ni Kuang and Cai Lan," *KK News*, Feb. 16, 2021, kknews.cc/zh-hk/news/6rjeqom.html, trans. Monica Ying.

42 until all are prey: See Elsa Dorlin, *Self-Defense: A Philosophy of Violence*, trans. Kieran Aarons (Verso, 2022), pp. 177–79.

42 slash the tires: Wang, *Walking the Tycoon's Rope*, p. 109.

42 Leading him into the bathroom: Interview with William Cheung, February 14, 2022.

42 a ban from acting: Interview with Phoebe Lee, May 8, 2021.

43 Half of Hong Kong's population: See Poshek Fu, "The 1960s: Modernity. Youth Culture. and Hong Kong Cantonese Cinema," in Poshek Fu and David Desser, eds., *Hong Kong Cinema: History, Arts, Identity* (Cambridge University Press, 2000), p. 73.

43 middle of its Baby Boom: US data from 1960 Census. See also Pew Research Center, "Population Change in the U.S. and the World from 1950 to 2050," Jan. 2014, pewresearch.org/global/2014/01/30/chapter-4-population-change-in-the-u-s-and-the-world-from-1950-to-2050/.

43 45,000 to 300,000: Alan Smart, *The Shek Kip Mei Myth: Squatters, Fires and Colonial Rule, 1950–1963* (Hong Kong University Press, 2006), p. 48. Before the end of the decade, the estimated number of squatters was at half a million.

43 "a glorified soup kitchen": Laura Madokoro, *Elusive Refuge: Chinese Migrants in the Cold War* (Harvard University Press, 2016), pp. 41–42. See also Chi-Kwan Mark, "The 'Problem of People': British Colonials, Cold War Powers, and the Chinese Refugees in Hong Kong, 1949–1962," *Modern Asian Studies* 41, no. 6 (2007), 1149. The same year, the British administration also refused official Chinese aid missions to help the Tung Tau squatters, causing a riot.

43 the margins of a treaty: Louisa Lim, *Indelible City: Dispossession and Defiance in Hong Kong.* (Riverhead Books, 2022), 74.

43 "a barren rock": Frank Welsh, *History of Hong Kong*, p. 1.

43 "It is just one big bazaar": Alvin Rabushka, *Hong Kong: A Study in Economic Freedom* (University of Chicago Press, 1979), p. 27.

44 "They recruited young people": Robert Young, "William Cheung: Hong Kong Bullies, Wing Chun Kung Fu, and Bruce Lee," *Black Belt*, May 2013.

44 In Macao, a real-life showdown: See John Christopher Hamm, *Paper Swordsman: Jin Yong and the Modern Chinese Martial Arts Novel* (University of Hawai'i Press, 2005), pp. 3–11; Benjamin Judkins and Jon Nielson, *The Creation of Wing Chun: A Social History of the Southern Chinese Martial Arts* (State University of New York Press, 2015), 234–37; and Matthew Scott, "Bruce Lee and the Hong Kong Fights That Helped Shape Modern MMA," *South China Morning Post*, May 22, 2019, scmp.com/sport/mixed-martial-arts/article/3011171/fights-brought-hong-kong-halt-three-contests-helped-shape#.

45 "I had ways of controlling": Robert Clouse, *Bruce Lee: The Biography* (Unique Publications, 1988), pp. 9–10.

45 odds turned against him: Linda Lee, *Bruce Lee: The Man Only I Knew* (Warner Paperback Library, 1975), p. 43.

45 "Please watch over him!": Robert Lee, *Bruce Lee, My Brother*, p. 33, trans. Monica Ying.

45 "He was always talking": Felix Dennis and Don Atyeo, *Bruce Lee: King of Kung Fu* (Straight Arrow Books, 1974), p. 11.

45 "who wouldn't fight?": Bao Nguyen interview with Steve Lee Ka Tai, May 30, 2019.

45 "In the end, we": Jim, "Days When I Fought with Bruce Lee."

45 "Where's Bruce?": Steve Rubenstein, "In the Shadow of a Legend," *Black Belt*, Aug. 1974, p. 19.

45 "needed a mentor": Linda Lee, *The Bruce Lee Story* (Ohara Publications, 1989), p. 22.

468 NOTES

45 ten movies a year: See the Li Hoi-Chuen entry at Hong Kong Movie Database, hkmdb.com/db/people/view.mhtml?id=944&display_set=eng.

45 "We did not know much": Robert Lee, *Bruce Lee, My Brother*, p. 39, trans. Monica Ying.

46 before they were allowed to eat: Robert Lee, *Bruce Lee, My Brother*, p. 54, trans. Monica Ying.

46 "He would sort of toke": Interview with Robert Lee, Dec. 9, 2021.

46 "Only rich people": Matthew Polly, *Bruce Lee: A Life* (Simon & Schuster, 2018), p. 40.

46 "I told Bruce": "An Interview with Bruce Lee's Mother," in Bruce Thomas, *Bruce Lee: Fighting Spirit*, pp. 62–63.

46 ran things: Clouse, *Bruce Lee: The Biography*, p. 13. Brother Henry recalled, "They owned Perth Street."

46 "We had what we call": Clouse, *Bruce Lee: The Biography*, p. 13.

46 "The white kids have all the best jobs": Linda Lee, *The Bruce Lee Story*, p. 26.

47 William was protected: They shared Chiuchow ancestral ties. Interview with William Cheung, Feb. 14, 2022.

48 tossed money boxes in the air: Interviews with William Cheung, Feb. 9, 2022, and Feb. 14, 2022; Wong Shun Leung, *Reminiscence of Bruce Lee* (Bruce Lee Jeet-kune-do Club, 1978), pp. 41–42.

48 two fights a day: Robert Lee as told to Tony Page, "My Brother, Bruce: Reminiscences by Robert Lee," *Fighting Stars*, Aug. 1983, p. 45.

48 "Those days, kids": M. Uyehara, "Bruce Lee: The Man, the Fighter, the Superstar," in Editors of *Black Belt* magazine, eds., *The Legendary Bruce Lee* (Ohara Publications, 1986), p. 10.

48 Bruce believed it could be: Jesse Glover, *Bruce Lee Between Wing Chun and Jeet Kune Do* (self-published, 1976), p. 15.

48 junior *gung fu* student: Paul Maslak, "The William Cheung Story: Bruce Lee in the Early Years," *Martial Arts Legends*, Jan. 1993, p. 7; Robert Chan in Chang and Lo, *The Bruce Lee They Knew*, p. 42, trans. Sze K. Chan.

48 *I will talk to your father*: Linda Lee, *Bruce Lee: The Man Only I Knew*, p. 37; Connie Schimpf, "A Mother Remembers," *Fighting Stars*, Summer 1977, p. 12.

Chapter 5: Talk with Your Hands

49 "angry . . . young men": Benjamin Judkins and Jon Nielson, *The Creation of Wing Chun: A Social History of the Southern Chinese Martial Arts* (State University of New York Press, 2015), p. 212.

49 Challenges were issued: For this section, I relied on interviews with William Cheung and accounts like those included in Eric Lilleør, *Gong Sau Wong: A Tribute* (Mui Fa Publishing, 2021), and Wong Shun Leung, *Reminiscence of Bruce Lee* (Bruce Lee Jeet-kune-do Club, 1978).

49 "throwing punches first": Interview with William Cheung, Feb. 14, 2022.

50 Yip Man had been born: For this section, I relied upon accounts from Judkins and Nielson, as well as Yip Chun, *116 Wing Tsun Dummy Techniques As Demonstrated by Grandmaster Yip Man* (Hong Kong: Leung's Publications, 1981); Ip Ching and Ron Heimberger. *Ip Man: Portrait of a Kung Fu Master* (King Dragon Press, 2001); and Leung Ting, *Roots and Branches of Wing Tsun. Second Edition* (Hong Kong: Leung's Publications, 2003).

50 "play at martial arts": Danny Xuan and John Little, *The Tao of Wing Chun* (Skyhorse Publishing, 2015), p. 23.

50 accept during his lifetime: Yip Chun, *116 Wing Tsun Dummy Techniques As Demonstrated by Grandmaster Yip Man*, p. 101.

51 Communist kill list: Yip Chun, *116 Wing Tsun Dummy Techniques*, p. 102; Leung Ting, *Roots and Branches of Wing Tsun*, p. 70; Judkins and Nielson, *The Creation of Wing Chun*, p. 207.

51 he fled: Ip Ching and Ron Heimberger. *Ip Man: Portrait of a Kung Fu Master* (King Dragon Press, 2001), p. 107. One story has it that the entire family migrated with Yip but that his wife, Cheung Wing-sit, took a son back to Fatshan to retrieve their identity cards and was locked in when the borders closed. She passed away shortly after, reportedly because of cancer.

51 Yip Man told them a story: Leung Ting, *Roots and Branches of Wing Tsun*, pp. 31–35.

52 *restore the Ming Dynasty*: Leung Ting, *Roots and Branches of Wing Tsun*, pp. 31–35.

52 that now included them as well: This is Bruce's genealogy as he wrote it in a letter to Taky Kimura on May 23, 1966. Taky Kimura, *Regards from the Dragon: Seattle*, rev. ed., compiled by David Tadman (Empire Books, 2009), pp. 12–13.

Depending on the different branches of Wing Chun, different genealogies have been cited. In a letter from Yip Man called "A Brief Statement for the Purpose of Organizing the Wing Tsun Fellowship Union," which purportedly dates to 1965 or 1966, reprinted in Leung Ting's *Roots and Branches of Wing Tsun*, Yip Man lays out a genealogy that additionally mentions Leung Lan Kwai and Leung Jan (whom Bruce may be calling Leung Teong here). Leung, p. 31–35.

52　taught widely, strategically, and scientifically: Judkins and Nielson, *The Creation of Wing Chun*, pp. 111–14, 130–34.

53　"In a short time": Interview with Ben Der, January 27, 2022.

53　"How can a woman": Interview with William Cheung, February 9, 2022.

53　"not be technicians": Hawkins Cheung, as told to Robert Chu, "Bruce's Classical Mess: Cleaning Up the Mess the 'Little Dragon' Left Behind," originally published in *Inside Kung Fu*, Feb. 1991, hawkinscheung.com/html/hcarticle4.htm.

53　refine his basics: Also romanized as Tsui Sheung-tin (commonly pronounced "Choy Shee-oong-tin"). William Cheung cited Chu as Bruce's initial teacher in an interview. In an interview posted on YouTube, Chu said Bruce came to study with him three times and then he never saw him again: youtube.com/watch?v=R6DCJbp5FPs.

54　"His devotion to *gung fu*": Linda Lee, *The Bruce Lee Story* (Ohara Publications, 1989), p. 27.

54　"I never thought he was serious": Interviews with William Cheung, Feb, 9, 2022, and Feb. 14, 2022.

54　"I've been learning Wing Chun": Linda Lee, *Bruce Lee: The Man Only I Knew* (Warner Paperback Library, 1975), p. 42.

54　red, black, and blue bruises: Jesse Glover, *Bruce Lee Between Wing Chun and Jeet Kune Do* (self-published, 1976), p. 22.

54　"When he started doing *chi sao*": Interviews with William Cheung, Feb. 9, 2022, and Feb. 14, 2022.

54　"Those bastards enjoyed": M. Uyehara, "Bruce Lee: The Man, the Fighter, the Superstar," in Editors of *Black Belt* magazine, eds., *The Legendary Bruce Lee* (Ohara Publications, 1986), p. 12.

Chapter 6: Days of Being Wild

55　blackmail Hoi Chuen: Robert Lee, *Bruce Lee, My Brother* (Masterpiece Films, 2010), p. 46, trans. Monica Ying.

55　"He wanted Mom": Robert Lee, *Bruce Lee, My Brother*, pp. 44–45, trans. Monica Ying.

55　Ticket sales doubled during the 1950s: I. C. Jarvie, *Window on Hong Kong: A Sociological Study of the Hong Kong Film Industry and Its Audience* (University of Hong Kong Centre of Asian Studies, 1977), pp. 61, 75.

55　*The Guiding Light*: The movie was released in Hong Kong as *A Son Is Born*. Information from the Hong Kong Film Archive.

56　"All for one and one for all!": Information on the movie from the Hong Kong Film Archive. Stephen Teo, *Hong Kong Cinema: The Extra Dimensions* (British Film Institute, 1997), p. 46; Jing Jing Chang, *Screening Communities: Negotiating Narratives of Empire, Nation, and the Cold War in Hong Kong Cinema* (Hong Kong University Press, 2019), p. 81.

56　"like stormtroopers": Phoebe Lee, Robert Lee, Agnes Lee, and Peter Lee, *Lee Siu Loong: Memories of the Dragon*, compiled by David Tadman (Bruce Lee Club, 2004), p. 48.

56　"enough to feed our family": Robert Lee, *Bruce Lee, My Brother*, p. 46, trans. Monica Ying.

56　"as a courtesy": Robert Lee, *Bruce Lee, My Brother*, p. 32, trans. Monica Ying.

56　disarmed and disciplined: Matthew Polly, *Bruce Lee: A Life* (Simon & Schuster, 2018), pp. 46–47.

56　"He was trouble": Robert Wang, *Walking the Tycoon's Rope* (Blacksmith Books, 2013), p. 112.

57　"boss of the whole school": Linda Lee, *Bruce Lee: The Man Only I Knew* (Warner Paperback Library, 1975), p. 43.

57　"Everyone wanted to be top dog": Hawkins Cheung, as told to Robert Chu, "Bruce Lee's Hong Kong Years." HawkinsCheung.com. Originally published in *Inside Kung Fu*, November 1991. https://hawkinscheung.com/html/hcarticle1.htm.

57　to Yip Man's door: Almost a decade later, St. Francis Xavier students were still talking about Bruce and his Wing Chun exploits. Interview with Peter Chin, Dec. 15, 2023.

57　convened in Mongkok: Ving Tsun Athletic Association, "The Development of Ving Tsun KungFu in Hong Kong, 1954–1960," 1990, http://www.vingtsun.org.hk/development_1954-60.htm. For more on Wong Shun Leung, see Eric Lilleør, *Gong Sau Wong: A Tribute* (Mui Fa Publishing, 2021).

58　Bruce showed up: Wong Shun Leung, *Reminiscence of Bruce Lee* (Bruce Lee Jeet-kune-do Club, 1978), p. 21; Robert Lee, *Bruce Lee, My Brother*, p. 110, trans. Sze K. Chan.

58　"I did not welcome this young man": Wong Shun Leung, *Reminiscence of Bruce Lee*, p. 21.

58　"I enjoyed practicing with him very much": Wong Shun Leung, *Reminiscence of Bruce Lee*, pp. 22–23, 42–43.

58　Peter said: Felix Dennis and Don Atyeo, *Bruce Lee: King of Kung Fu* (Straight Arrow Books, 1974), p. 14.

470 NOTES

58 "This is the guy they want to know": Interview with Ben Der, Jan. 27, 2022.
59 on a small card in his wallet: Linda Lee, *The Bruce Lee Story* (Ohara Publications, 1989), p. 30.
59 "tried to persuade him not to teach Bruce": Hawkins Cheung, as told to Robert Chu, "Bruce Lee's Hong Kong Years: Cleaning Up the Mess the 'Little Dragon' Left Behind," originally published in *Inside Kung Fu*, Nov. 1991, hawkinscheung.com/html/hcarticle1.htm.
59 "*pak sao* cha-cha, *heun sao* cha-cha!": Interviews with William Cheung, Feb. 9, 2022, and Feb. 14, 2022.
59 "beat him hard with the latch": Robert Lee, *Bruce Lee, My Brother*, p. 43, trans. Monica Ying.
59 "sincerely to the ancestors": Robert Lee, *Bruce Lee, My Brother*, p. 54, trans. Monica Ying.
59 "second mother": On the back of a picture of herself dated August 11, 1963, she wrote, "Dearest Bruce, Wishing you every future success and Happiness. Time changes many things, But not old friends. With love, Your second mother." Bruce Lee Family Archive.
59 "back to this one": Interview with Robert Lee, Dec. 9, 2021.
61 "use Wing Chun to beat you?": Interviews with William Cheung, Feb. 9, 2022, and Feb. 14, 2022.
61 to start shit: Robert Lee, *Bruce Lee, My Brother*, p. 111, trans. Sze K. Chan.
61 Robert said: Linda Lee, *The Bruce Lee Story*, p. 31.
61 amassing enemies: Robert Lee, *Bruce Lee, My Brother*, p. 113, trans. Sze K. Chan.
61 "he would not speak with them": Paul Maslak, "The William Cheung Story: Bruce Lee in the Early Years," *Martial Arts Legends*, Jan. 1993, p. 75.
61 black and blue: Jesse Glover, *Bruce Lee Between Wing Chun and Jeet Kune Do* (self-published, 1976), p. 22.
61 "He asked too much": Wong Shun Leung, *Reminiscence of Bruce Lee*, p. 23.
61 "That's why he tried so hard": "Bruce Lee in the 1980s: William Cheung and Dan Inosanto," *Fighting Stars*, Aug. 1983, p. 44.
62 recalled Robert: Robert Lee, *Bruce Lee, My Brother*, p. 114, trans. Sze K. Chan.
63 "One had to fight": Wong Shun Leung, *Reminiscence of Bruce Lee*, p. 33.
63 "do it in the street": Interview with Robert Lee, Dec. 9, 2021.
63 "couldn't hurt him": Mito Uyehara, *Bruce Lee: The Incomparable Fighter* (Ohara Publications, 1988), p. 8.
64 the teacher and his students left: Wong Shun Leung, *Reminiscence of Bruce Lee*, pp. 36–38.
64 whose students Bruce had challenged: Wong Shun Leung, *Reminiscence of Bruce Lee*, p. 34.
64 *How could he stay?*: Linda Lee, *Bruce Lee: The Man Only I Knew*, p. 47; Robert Lee, *Bruce Lee, My Brother*, pp. 120–23, trans. Sze K. Chan; Robert Clouse, *Bruce Lee: The Biography* (Unique Publications, 1988), p. 23; Alex Ben Block, *The Legend of Bruce Lee* (Dell, 1974), p. 24.

Chapter 7: Dualities

67 comparing him to James Dean: The full quote is this: "I went to see the film, mostly because of Bruce Lee. My friend praised him as the best actor in the history of Chinese film. While that might be an exaggeration, it did give me an urge to consider it a 'must-see' . . ."; "Bruce Lee's talent does not fall short of James Dean's (but he is not the 'Chinese James Dean'. This is only the 'score' we use to judge a genius). Yet where can we find Elia Kazan?" Recounted in footnote 2 in Po Fung, "From Wild Child to Superman—Bruce Lee in Films," in *Bruce Lee Kung Fu Art Life* (Hong Kong Heritage Museum, 2013), p. 73. The original quote in Chinese is in Chang Cheh, *Zhangche Huiyilu, Yingping Ji*, ed. Wong Ain-Ling (Hong Kong Film Archive, 2002), pp. 220–21. My thanks to Winnie Fu.
67 disappeared to America: Chang Cheh, *A Retrospective of Hong Kong Films over the Last Thirty Years*, 2nd ed. (Hong Kong: Commercial Press, 2019), pp. 100, 102, trans. Winnie Fu.
68 "upon a great circle of people": Flora Rand, "I Want My Son to Be a Mixed-Up Kid!," *TV Radio Mirror*, Nov. 1966. Reprinted in John Little, ed., *Bruce Lee: Words of the Dragon, Interviews, 1958–1973* (Tuttle, 1997), p 48.
68 a small collection of plants and flowers: Robert Lee, *Bruce Lee, My Brother* (Masterpiece Films, 2010), pp. 46–49, trans. Monica Ying. His last movie, *The Orphan's Adventure*—yes, another movie about an orphan!—opened in 1961.
68 "you should continue": Jesse Glover, *Bruce Lee Between Wing Chun and Jeet Kune Do* (self-published, 1976), p. 23.
68 acquired new meaning: Connie Schimpf, "A Mother Remembers," *Fighting Stars*, Summer 1977, p. 11.
68 "November 30, 1958": Linda Lee, *Bruce Lee: The Man Only I Knew* (Warner Paperback Library, 1975), p. 44.
68 "while he was at home": Robert Lee, *Bruce Lee, My Brother*, p. 124, trans. Sze K. Chan.
68 "THE BIGGER THEY ARE, THE HARDER THEY FALL": Caps in Bruce's original transcription.

George F. Jowett, *The Modern Commando Science of Guerilla Self-Defense for the Home Front* (Abell Press, 1943), scribd.com/document/58574941/32119551-Guerilla-Self-Defense-for-the-Home-Front-Jowett.

69 "I do not fear": Translated from the original documents by Sze K. Chan. Documents from the Bruce Lee Family Archive.

69 "seeks advice": Translated from the original documents by Sze K. Chan. Documents from the Bruce Lee Family Archive.

69 "You should learn it": Wong Shun Leung, *Reminiscence of Bruce Lee* (Bruce Lee Jeet-kune-do Club, 1978), p. 43.

69 "First, you must have martial arts virtue": "Meeting One of Bruce Lee's Masters: Sifu Siu Hon-San," in Wong Shun Leung, *Bruce Lee: His Unknowns in Martial Arts Learning* (Bruce Lee Jeet-kune-do Club, 1977), p. 35.

69 He gifted Bruce: Ryan Ohl, *Jun Fan Gung Fu: Origins and Evolution* (self-published, 2023), p. 341.

69 "It would take a few weeks": Wu Shih, dir., *Bruce Lee: The Man and the Legend* (Golden Harvest, 1973).

69 "our own self": Wong Shun Leung, *Reminiscence of Bruce Lee*, p. 44.

70 "Challenge him!": Bruce Lee, "Me and Jeet Kune Do," in John Little, ed., *Bruce Lee: Words of the Dragon, Interviews, 1958–1973* (Tuttle, 1997), p. 124.

70 "the hardest substance in the world": Bruce appears to have been inspired by this section of Evan S. Morgan's translation of excerpts from the *Huai Nan Tzu*, titled *Tao, The Great Luminant* (1933; repr. ed., Forgotten Books, 2008), p. 51:

"Nothing in the world is more yielding and softer than water; yet its greatness cannot be measured, nor its depths sounded. . . . It is so fine that it is impossible to grasp a handful of it; strike it, yet it does not suffer hurt: grab it, and it is not wounded: sever it and it is not divided: burn it, and it does not ignite . . . Its advantage is that it will penetrate into stone and metal; its strength consists in going to every shore bearing ships for mankind. . . ."

71 "I had become one with nature": Linda Lee, *The Bruce Lee Story* (Ohara Publications, 1989), pp. 37, 39.

71 "I am going to become famous in America": Charles Russo, *Striking Distance: Bruce Lee and the Dawn of Martial Arts in America* (University of Nebraska Press, 2016), p. 28; Chinese Kung Fu & Tai Chi Academy, "Interview: Grandmaster Vince Lacey Speaks on Training with Bruce Lee in 1959," Sept. 30, 2017, youtube.com/watch?v=jfbHYnxgNkE.

71 "the happiest moment in my life": Interview with Ben Der, Jan. 27, 2022.

71 "I don't know what it'll be like over there": Robert Lee, *Bruce Lee, My Brother*, pp. 124–25, trans. Sze K. Chan.

71 "From your loving brother, Robert": Phoebe Lee, Agnes Lee, Robert Lee, and Peter Lee, *Lee Siu Loong: Memories of the Dragon*, compiled by David Tadman (Bruce Lee Club, 2004), p. 2.

71 "I hope he makes it": Robert Lee interview in *Bruce Lee: The Curse of the Dragon* (film documentary), 1993.

71 *made something of yourself*: Linda Lee, *Bruce Lee: The Man Only I Knew*, p. 47.

71 *I really am*: Connie Schimpf, "A Mother Remembers," *Fighting Stars*, Summer 1977, p. 11.

Part III: Learning America, 1959–1961

73 "But the Chinese": James Duval Phelan, "Why The Chinese Should Be Excluded," *North American Review*. 173, No. 540 (November 1901): p. 673.

Chapter 8: A Return Passage

74 "turned out to be an Indian man": Translated from the original by Sze K. Chan. Some of these notes are included in Bruce Lee, *Letters of the Dragon: Correspondence 1958–1973*, ed. John Little (Tuttle, 1998) and are rendered as letters. However, as I encountered these notes in the archive, they are all on a single notepad. I cannot be sure if Bruce did indeed send these as letters as they are rendered in that book and if these are drafts. I chose to discuss the notes here more as if they are a personal diary, which is what they appear to me to be.

75 When the ship docked next in Honolulu: The details here come from a letter included in *Letters of the Dragon*. In that book, this letter is attributed under the title "To Melvin Dong," but while Melvin Dong's name is rendered in English in the top margin on the notepad, it appears to me to simply be an unrelated note, a contact he is to connect with. Within the letter, in my opinion, the telling detail is his direct address to "Doggie," which was Bruce's pet name for Robert: "Tell Doggie that I bought two types of trucks for him and will mail it to him once I've reached San Francisco. I'm sending this letter away when the ship arrives at San Francisco. I hope that you all can write to me more so that I don't have to worry about you so much." In *Letters of the Dragon*, pp. 23–24, trans. Sze K. Chan. Documents from the Bruce Lee Family Archive.

75 "I could not even touch him": See interview with Wu Chin-li in Louisa Lim's *Golden Gate Girl* DVD.

472 NOTES

75 "It was quite annoying": Translated by Sze K. Chan.

76 Bruce composed lists: Translated from the original traditional Chinese by Sze K. Chan. One of these is translated as part of a letter dated May 4, 1959, in *Letters of the Dragon*, but may be decontextualized.

76 an annual quota: Mae Ngai notes that the United States sometimes did not even use it for Chinese. Of the 1924 Immigration Act, she wrote, "Only by reading the fine print would one notice that China had a nominal quota of one hundred that, even so, could not be used by Chinese people. This is why, during the 1930s, European Jews who made their way to Shanghai to escape Nazi fascism were able to use the China quota to seek admission to the US." Ngai, "The 100-Year-Old Racist Law That Broke America's Immigration System," *Public Books*, May 28, 2024, publicbooks.org/the-100-year-old-racist-law-that-broke-americas-immigration-system/.

78 Chinatown was a city within a city: Bonnie Tsui, *American Chinatown: A People's History of Five Neighborhoods* (Free Press, 2010), p. 24.

78 *picture us any way you wish*: See Anthony W. Lee, *Picturing Chinatown: Art and Orientalism in San Francisco*. University of California Press, 2001.

78 "threats of infiltration": See "San Francisco, California," *Mapping Inequality: Redlining in New Deal America*, University of Richmond, dsl.richmond.edu/panorama/redlining/#loc=12/37.782/-122.491&city=san-francisco-ca.

78 Quan Ging Ho as their proxy parent: Interview with Ben Der, Jan. 27, 2022; Charles Russo, *Striking Distance: Bruce Lee and the Dawn of Martial Arts in America* (University of Nebraska Press, 2016), pp. 29–31.

79 disturbing the neighbors: Tommy Gong, *The Evolution of a Martial Artist* (Bruce Lee Enterprises, 2013), pp. 249–50.

79 to teach and perform: Russo, *Striking Distance*, pp. 48–49; Allen Joe with Svetlana Kim and Dmitri Bobkov, *The Last of the Four Musketeers* (Balboa Press, 2015), p. 62.

79 *The Oath of the Sword*: Big shout-out to Denise Khor for locating and ensuring that this pioneering Asian American film was restored in 2023.

79 By the mid-1950s: For an excellent history of this period, see John Corcoran and Emil Farkas, *Martial Arts Encyclopedia: A Century of Martial Arts Worldwide* (Trans-Euro Film Trust, 2011), pp. 212–86.

80 "Wing Chun people are all troublemakers": Interview with Ben Der, Jan. 27, 2022.

80 "He was a pure entertainer": "Harriet Lee's Reflections of the Dragon," in David Tadman and Steve Kerridge, eds., *Bruce Lee: The Little Dragon at 70* (Bruce Lee Enterprises, 2010), p. 10.

80 Praying Mantis form at top speed: "The 'Knowing Is Not Enough' Interview: Allen Joe," *"Knowing Is Not Enough": The Official Newsletter of Jun Fan Jeet Kune Do* 1, no. 4 (Winter 1998): pp. 7–8.

80 flurries of Wing Chun punches: Russo, *Striking Distance*, p. 47; Matthew Polly, *Bruce Lee: A Life* (Simon & Schuster, 2018), p. 88; interview with Greglon Lee, July 13, 2023.

80 his self-confidence: Sid Campbell and Greglon Lee, *Remembering the Master: Bruce Lee, James Yimm Lee, and the Creation of Jeet Kune Do* (Blue Snake Books, 2006), p. 30.

80 "It was hidden and unrecognized": Ying-Jen Chang, "The Rise of Martial Arts in China and America," dissertation, New School for Social Research, 1978, p. 155.

81 "from the tongs to the public": Russo, *Striking Distance*, P. 25

81 Kung Fu Club of Choy Li Fut: He later renamed it Hung Sing, in a special nod to tradition and his lineage.

81 first North American media appearance of Chinese martial arts: Russo, *Striking Distance*, p. 39.

81 among T. Y. Wong's: Roger D. Hagood, "Ming Lum, Martial Arts Ambassador," KungFuMagazine.com, Summer 1993, kungfumagazine.com/magazine/article.php?article=214; Rick Wing, *Showdown in Oakland* (2013), self-published, Kindle eBook; Gene Ching, "Great American Great Grandmaster," KungFuMagazine.com, Jan./Feb. 2010, kungfumagazine.com/magazine/article.php?article=871.

81 Lau crossed the border: This entire section owes much to Charles Russo's excellent reporting and digging. Do yourself a favor and read *Striking Distance*. Ben Judkins, "Lau Bun: A Kung Fu Pioneer," *Kung Fu Tea* blog, Oct. 8, 2017, chinesemartialstudies.com/2017/10/08/lau-bun-a-kung-fu-pioneer-in-america/.

82 anything resembling Hong Kong's anarchy: Russo, *Striking Distance*, pp. 26–27, 57–58.

82 "Wing Chun was the best": Russo, *Striking Distance*, pp. 57–58.

82 a cook named Fook Yeung: His name has variously been rendered as Fook Young, Fook Yeung, and Fook Yueng, the latter by some of his students who continue to teach his boxing and other works. The official death record shows his name as Fook Yeung. "King County Deaths," *Seattle Post-Intelligencer*, Apr. 27, 2012.

83 Red Junk Opera branch of Wing Chun: Interview with Leroy Garcia, July 8, 2022.

83 "Uncle Fook": Interview with Mark Chow, July 21, 2022.

Chapter 9: The Power Broker

84 "he hit me first": Frank Chin, "The Three Kingdoms," in David Brewster and David M. Buerge, eds., *The Washingtonians: A Biographical Portrait of the State* (Sasquatch Press, 1989), p. 364.

84 *It's wise to vote for Wing Luke*: "Wing Luke," in *The Washingtonians*, pp. 364–66.

84 sixty Chinese restaurants in town: Yong Chen, *Chop Suey, USA: The Story of Chinese Food in America* (Columbia University Press, 2014), p. 9, citing a 1946 survey by a Chinese-language newspaper, *Hua Qiao Nian Bao* (Annals of the Overseas Chinese). By 1950 census numbers, that means there was literally a Chinese restaurant for every 200 Asian residents in the city. At the time, Seattle ranked sixth in the country for the number of Chinese restaurants.

84 "People in Chinatown": "American Life: The Life and Career of Ruby Chow," C-Span, Sept. 15, 1984, c-span.org/person/?60670/RubyChow.

84 outbursts of domestic violence: Interview with Mark Chow, July 13, 2022.

85 "Why didn't you help?": Interview with Mark Chow, July 13, 2022. Much of the background for this section comes from my many interviews with Mark Chow.

85 were buzzing about: In the 1940s, New York's Chinatown was still very much a bachelor's society—men outnumbered women 6 to 1. Min Zhou, "Social Capital in Chinatown: The Role of Community-Based Organizations and Families in the Adaptation of the Younger Generation," in Min Zhou and James V. Gatewood, eds., *Contemporary Asian America: A Multidisciplinary Reader* (New York University Press, 2000), p. 316.

86 to be married: Interview with Mark Chow, July 13, 2022. Ping was suffering from blocked tear ducts.

86 "an all-present tense language": Frank Chin, "The Three Kingdoms," pp. 367–68.

86 in one of the back rooms: Interview with Mark Chow, July 13, 2022.

86 level themselves up to get there: Some writers assert that the restaurant was located in the Central District, in a predominantly Black neighborhood. This is not entirely correct. At Broadway and Jefferson, Ruby Chow's restaurant was indeed on the border between the Black and white communities. But the heart of the Black community was still more than ten blocks farther east, and even there, Blacks did not make up more than 45 percent of the population in 1950. More important, the statement misapprehends how racial segregation was felt on the ground back then. Census maps from 1950 count only four Blacks among the more than four thousand people in the neighborhood tract immediately surrounding the restaurant. The invisible boundary between white and non-white at Broadway was very real for people of color, and the Chows' restaurant/residence was on the white side. Mark Chow says, "When I lived there, it was mostly white people. At least visually, I can remember only white people." Interview with Mark Chow, July 13, 2022. See also census maps at the University of Washington's Segregated Seattle website, depts.washington.edu/civilr/maps_race_seattle.htm.

86 "with a delightful Chinese twist": Joyce Chen, who opened her first restaurant in Boston a decade after Ruby Chow's Dinner Club opened, also famously called her dumplings "Peking ravioli," and they are now referred to also as "ravs" or "Boston potstickers."

87 "The tongs are not": Frank Chin, "The Three Kingdoms," pp. 361–62.

88 "You need to eat better": Eunice Lam, his brother Peter's girlfriend, then wife, wrote of him at the time, "Back then Bruce Lee had pimples all over his face, even his back, and he had sores." *Beijing Youth Daily*, June 13, 2018, trans. Monica Ying.

88 "You're in my household": Interview with Mark Chow, July 21, 2022.

88 "peeling shrimp": This section is deeply informed by interviews with Mark Chow. I'm indebted to his generosity.

88 they all soon returned to work: Jesse Glover, *Bruce Lee Between Wing Chun and Jeet Kune Do* (self-published, 1976), p. 17.

90 "I didn't forget you!!": From the original letter. This last P.S. portion is not included in the transcription of the letter in Bruce Lee, *Letters of the Dragon: Correspondence 1958–1973*, ed. John Little (Tuttle, 1998), p. 22.

90 "cry my heart out": Eunice Lam/Lam Yin-ni, "The Inside World of Bruce Lee," in Wong Shun Leung, *Bruce Lee: His Unknowns in Martial Arts Learning* (Hong Kong: Bruce Lee Jeet-kune-do Club, 1977), p. 63; Eunice Lam, "Bruce Lee Is Actually Very Gentle," July 21, 2008, yule.sohu.com/20080721/n258270375.shtml, trans. Sze K. Chan. This web page cites the *Southern Metropolis Daily* but appears to be one of many reprints across the Chinese-language web. The original is from her former column in *Nam Dou Dai Pai Dong* (南都大牌檔).

Chapter 10: The Student

91 an "exchange program": Nile Thompson and Carolyn J. Marr with Tom G. Heuser, "Seattle Public Schools, 1862–2000: Ballard High School," in *Building for Learning: Seattle Public School Histories, 1862–2000* (Seattle Public Schools, rev. ed., 2002), historylink.org/file/10458. In one sense, the exchange program worked. At Ballard, Sue Ann met the man who became her first husband. Interview with Sue Ann Kay, March 31, 2022.

474   NOTES

91 at the University of Minnesota: Thompson, Marr, and Heuser, *Seattle Public Schools, 1862–2000*.

91 only three Black students and one Japanese American were enrolled as full-time students: Quintard Taylor, *The Forging of a Black Community: Seattle's Central District from 1870 through the Civil Rights Era* (University of Washington Press, 1994), p. 211.

91 Martin Luther King Jr. test lines: Isolde Raftery, "Martin Luther King Workshopped His 'I Have a Dream' Speech in Seattle," KUOW.org, Jan. 20, 2019, kuow.org/stories/what-martin-luther-king-jr-told-seattle-the-one-time-he-visited.

91 Stokely Carmichael: Priscilla Long, "Stokely Carmichael Speaks to 4,000 at Seattle's Garfield High School on April 19, 1967," Historylink.org, Mar. 2, 2002, historylink.org/file/3715.

91 equal parts white, Black, Asian, and other: Alice Ito and Mayumi Tsutakawa, "Roger Shimomura Interview," Densho Digital Archive, Mar. 18 and 20, 2023, ddr.densho.org/media/ddr-densho-1000/ddr-densho-1000-142-transcript-6e3d832f04.htm.

91 with racial epithets: Anne Collins Goodyear, "Roger Shimomura: An American Artist," *American Art* 27, no. 1 (Spring 2013), p. 71.

92 "the sunset side of the mountain": Interview with Doug Palmer, June 28, 2022; Joan Singler, Jean Durning, Betty Lou Valentine, and Maid Adams, *Seattle in Black and White: The Congress of Racial Equality and the Fight for Equal Opportunity* (University of Washington Press, 2011), p. 8.

92 a western one: See the "Segregated Seattle" maps created by the University of Washington's Seattle Civil Rights & Labor History Project for 1950 and 1960, depts.washington.edu/civilr/maps_race_seattle.htm; David Wilma, "President Roosevelt Approves Loan for Yesler Terrace Public Housing Project in Seattle on December 2, 1939," Historylink.org, Jan. 1, 1999, historylink.org/File/2105.

92 "A bad husband cannot be a good man": From Bruce Lee's copy of Wilfred D. Best, *The Student's Companion* (Collins, 1958). Courtesy of the Wing Luke Museum.

92 "I know what is wrong": Bruce Lee Diary, entry from Jan. 21 and 22, 1960. Courtesy of the Bruce Lee Family Archive.

93 might do to them: Interview with Mark Chow, July 21, 2022.

94 "getting into childhood fights": Jesse Glover, *Bruce Lee Between Wing Chun and Jeet Kune Do* (self-published, 1976), p. 1.

94 "When Ron's mother came to the door": Glover, *Bruce Lee Between Wing Chun and Jeet Kune Do*, pp. 5–7.

96 broken his hand: "Years later Bruce Lee told me that James Lee had said that he wanted to impress us with the fact that he could hurt us, just in case we had something up our sleeves. Bruce also said that there was a good chance that James Lee might have been drinking." Glover, *Bruce Lee Between Wing Chun and Jeet Kune Do*, pp. 10–11.

96 the Chong Wah Association building: Doug Palmer notes that Jesse Glover, in his autobiography, *Bruce Lee Between Wing Chun and Jeet Kune Do*, recalls seeing Bruce first performing at Seafair. However, Bruce arrived in Seattle a month after the 1959 Seafair, which took place in the first week of August. Doug Palmer, *Bruce Lee: Sifu, Friend and Big Brother* (Chin Music Press, 2020), p. 21.

It's possible that the event in Chinatown was an affiliated event after the official proceedings or, perhaps more likely, related to the Mid-Autumn Moon Festival activities, which would have occurred two weeks after he arrived. Regardless, it had to have happened during the fall. According to Doug Palmer, citing Bruce Lee's own diaries, Bruce records his first meeting with Jesse in January 1960.

96 popping his knuckles for effect: Glover, *Bruce Lee Between Wing Chun and Jeet Kune Do*, p. 12.

96 the new kid who worked for Ruby Chow: An early article covered some of his Hong Kong movies, but was written for a youthful, non-Chinese audience. Frank Lynch, "Seattle Scene: A Budding Star of Chinese Movies," *Seattle Post-Intelligencer*, no date, likely 1960. From the Bruce Lee archives. Reprinted in part in *Words from the Dragon*, pp. 22–24.

97 and many more: Taken from Bruce Lee's diary. Courtesy of the Bruce Lee Family Archive. See also Doug Palmer, *Bruce Lee: Sifu, Friend and Big Brother*, p. 21.

97 "forty movements on the dummy": Hawkins Cheung, "Bruce Lee's Hong Kong Years: Cleaning Up the Mess the 'Little Dragon' Left Behind," *Inside Kung Fu*, Nov. 1991. Available at hawkinscheung.com/html/hcarticle1.htm.

97 spilling his whole story: Glover, *Bruce Lee Between Wing Chun and Jeet Kune Do*, p. 13.

Chapter 11: A Central District Story

99 "January 8, 1960": From his original diary. Courtesy Bruce Lee Family Archive. It's a small three-year cloth-cover diary made in Tokyo and meant to cover 1959, 1960, 1961. He signs the inside cover as December 31, 1959. The printed date for this entry is 1月 8 日. The year is marked as "19—." Bruce fills in the year as "1961" but

writes alongside it, "Fri." January 8, 1960, was a Friday. It's safe to infer that the entry is from January 8, 1960. See also Doug Palmer, *Bruce Lee: Sifu, Friend and Big Brother* (Chin Music Press, 2020), p. 21.

99 "some respect for Chinese": Jesse Glover in Fiaz Rafiq, *Bruce Lee Conversations: The Life and Legacy of a Legend* (HNL Publishing, 2009), p. 24.

99 "I threw jabs, hooks, and haymakers": Glover, *Bruce Lee Between Wing Chun and Jeet Kune Do* (self-published, 1976), p. 14.

99 *siu lum tao*: Paul Bax, *Number One: Reflections from Bruce Lee's First Student, Jesse Glover* (self-published, 2016), p. 194; Paul Bax, "The Jesse Glover Interview," in *Disciples of the Dragon: Reflections from the Students of Bruce Lee* (Outskirts Press, 2008), p. 15.

99 "January 10, 1960": Diary entry. "To night" is written with the odd gap. Courtesy Bruce Lee Family Archive.

100 five dollars from his family: Diary entry, Jan. 25, 1960.

100 "able to speak Chinese": Glover, *Bruce Lee Between Wing Chun and Jeet Kune Do*, p. 50.

100 "effective swings of Choy Li Fut": Glover, *Bruce Lee Between Wing Chun and Jeet Kune Do*, p. 40.

100 "before he could spit it out": Glover, *Bruce Lee Between Wing Chun and Jeet Kune Do*, p. 66.

100 practice his self-defense more: Diary entry, Feb. 5, 1960.

100 "little more than an advanced beginner": Glover, *Bruce Lee Between Wing Chun and Jeet Kune Do*, p. 18.

100 "made money by collecting money": Interview with Leroy Garcia, July 8, 2023.

100 "the scars to prove it": James DeMile in Paul Bax, *Number One*, p. 41

102 "You are about to witness": From Bruce's notes for his presentation. Courtesy Bruce Lee Family Archive.

102 what fighting is really like: James Halpin, "The Little Dragon: Bruce Lee," in Thomas A. Green and Joseph R. Svinth, eds., *Martial Arts in the Modern World* (Praeger, 2003), p. 114, reprinted in David Brewster and David M. Buerge, eds., *The Washingtonians: A Biographical Portrait of the State* (Sasquatch Press, 1989), p. 421; Rafiq, *Bruce Lee Conversations*, p. 28.

For Halpin's account, DeMile seems to have exaggerated the story a bit, suggesting that Bruce issued the challenge from the stage after dismantling "some sucker." In subsequent tellings, however, such as in his interview with Fiaz Rafiq and in the filmed interview with World of Martial Arts TV in the next note, he describes himself issuing a challenge to Lee. I've chosen the latter here.

102 "like a drunken monkey": "James DeMile Interview Pt. 1, Meeting Bruce Lee," World of Martial Arts Television, YouTube, Dec. 11, 2012, youtube.com/watch?v=itaRaDuuc54.

102 "In a blink": Rafiq, *Bruce Lee Conversations*, p. 28.

102 "devil children": Interview with Leroy Garcia, July 8, 2022.

103 "Like most other Japanese immigrants of the day": Taky Kimura, *Regards from the Dragon: Seattle*, rev. ed., compiled by David Tadman (Empire Books, 2009), p. xviii.

103 "so they will be good to us": Interview with Andy Kimura, Jan. 18, 2023.

103 "and the Declaration of Independence": Mark Jacobs, "Jeet Kune Do Community Bids Farewell to Taky Kimura," BlackBeltmag.com, June 27, 2021; "Tracking the Dragon 94 Ft. Taky Kimura," posted by George Brennan, YouTube, youtube.com/watch?v=tl2ttq6Fs4Y. Both of these sources are apparently no longer available on the web.

103 to "watch them": Interview with Andy Kimura, Jan. 18, 2023.

104 They traveled in fear and silence: For a moving documentary account, see Lawson Fusao Inada, ed., *Only What We Could Carry: The Japanese American Internment Experience* (Heyday Books, 2000).

104 "until they sent me to the camps": Halpin, "The Little Dragon: Bruce Lee," p. 122.

104 the 442nd Regimental Combat Team: David F. Bonner. "The 442nd as a Fighting Unit," *Military Review*, July-August 2022, pp. 129–38, armyupress.army.mil/Journals/Military-Review/English-Edition-Archives/July-August-2022/nisei/.

104 the so-called Indian Wars: Violet Cristoforo, "Poetic Reflections of the Tule Lake Internment Camp" and a haiku by Min Morimoto, in Inada, ed., *Only What We Could Carry*, pp. 328, 331.

104 the government labeled "disloyal": Susan Kamei has shown how the Loyalty Questionnaires grew out of the debates caused by the 442nd. Susan Kamei, *When Can We Go Back to America? Voices of Japanese American Incarceration During World War II* (Simon & Schuster, 2021), pp. 202–12. For a more visceral account, read John Okada's 1957 classic of Asian American literature, *No-No Boy*.

104 an ordeal: Violet de Cristoforo, "Poetic Reflections of the Tule Lake Internment Camp," in Inada, ed., *Only What We Could Carry*, p. 326.

476 NOTES

104 without anesthesia: Interview with Andy Kimura, Jan. 18, 2023.
104 They maintained their own roads and safety: Monica Sone, *Nisei Daughter* (University of Washington Press, 1953; rev. ed. 1979), p. 195; Roger Shimomura, *Shadows of Minidoka* (Lawrence Art Center, 2011) p. 96.
105 "and no possessions": Taky Kimura, *Regards from the Dragon: Seattle*, p. xix.
105 without his hair cut: "Tracking the Dragon 94 Ft. Taky Kimura," posted by George Brennan, YouTube, youtube.com/watch?v=tl2ttq6Fs4Y.
105 not to put her arm around him in public: Robert Clouse, *Bruce Lee: The Biography* (Unique Publications, 1988), p. 38.
105 "I was not worthy": Tommy Gong, *The Evolution of a Martial Artist* (Bruce Lee Enterprises, 2013), p. 20.
105 "half-ashamed even to be alive": Halpin, "The Little Dragon: Bruce Lee," p. 122.
106 "worse than anyone else": Taky Kimura, *Regards from the Dragon: Seattle*, p. xxviii.
106 "'You just refuse to recognize it": Interview with Andy Kimura, Jan. 18, 2023; Taky Kimura, *Regards from the Dragon: Seattle*, p. xxiii; Bruce Thomas, *Bruce Lee: Fighting Spirit* (Blue Snake Books, 1994), 36-7.
106 "Why do you put up with this shit?": Interview with Andy Kimura, January 26, 2023.
107 Around that time: Joe Cowles, in Paul Bax, *Disciples of the Dragon: Reflections from the Students of Bruce Lee* (Outskirts Press, 2008), p. 72.

Part IV: The Man Who Thinks He Can, 1961–1962

109 "The boxers will bring": Joyce Carol Oates, *On Boxing*. Updated and Expanded Edition (Harper Perennial, 2006), p. 9.

Chapter 12: Blood on the Floor

110 "I didn't spar with Bruce": Paul Bax, *Number One: Reflections from Bruce Lee's First Student, Jesse Glover* (self-published, 2016), p. 74.
110 "I tried to crush Bruce": Bax, *Number One*, p. 41.
110 "He had what they called": Interview with Leroy Garcia, July 8, 2022.
110 "We tried not to really hurt": Bax, *Number One*, pp. 43, 74.
111 "girls, philosophy, and Chinese history": Jesse Glover, *Bruce Lee Between Wing Chun and Jeet Kune Do* (self-published, 1976), p. 27.
111 One night, the guys: Interview with Andy Kimura, Jan. 18, 2023.
111 his English and history homework: Jesse Glover, "Remember Edward C. Hart: November 8, 1924–December 3, 1998," "Knowing Is Not Enough": *The Official Newsletter of Jun Fan Jeet Kune Do* 2, no. 4 (Winter 1999), p. 10.
111 nights on the town: James DeMile has said that Bruce was accosted one night by racist thugs who wanted to beat him up for dancing with a blond woman. Fiaz Rafiq, *Bruce Lee Conversations: The Life and Legacy of a Legend* (HNL Publishing, 2009), p. 31. Leroy Garcia confirms that Bruce and his then-wife Sherry were involved in an incident with a group of white men but that it was over a parking spot they had taken from Bruce.
111 took the gang: *The Orphan* lobby cards for Seattle and San Francisco, dated 1961, announcing September 15 and 16 screenings. The lobby cards had Ng Cho-fan hailing Bruce as "a new talent": "You will see!" They were written in traditional Chinese.
112 "bawled and cheered": Frank Lynch, "Seattle Scene: A Budding Star of Chinese Movies," *Seattle Post-Intelligencer*, no date, likely 1960. From the Bruce Lee archives. Reprinted in part in John Little, ed., *Bruce Lee: Words of the Dragon, Interviews, 1958–1973* (Tuttle, 1997), pp. 22–24.
112 "opportunities here were greater": Glover, *Bruce Lee Between Wing Chun and Jeet Kune Do*, p. 48.
112 "best Gung Fu man in the world": Glover, *Bruce Lee Between Wing Chun and Jeet Kune Do*, p. 38.
112 "dreams and reality": Glover, *Bruce Lee Between Wing Chun and Jeet Kune Do*, p. 40.
112 "That sounds good": Interview with Mark Chow, July 21, 2022.
112 Yuen Cho Choi: Yuen Cho Choi, *Book 5: Shaolin Diamond Fist* (self-published, 1953), trans. Sze K. Chan. *Sifu* Yuen Cho Choi was apparently a prolific writer, and Bruce had a few of his books. He wrote of this two-finger push-up in *Book 2: Secrets of Kung Fu: Plum Flower Wooden Stumps* that the technique came from Sideward Dragon Qigong. Translated by Sze K. Chan.
112 "looking a job for me": From Bruce Lee's diary, Jan. 4, 1960. Courtesy of the Bruce Lee Family Archive.
113 Bruce dispatched quickly": Paul Bax, *Disciples of the Dragon: Reflections from the Students of Bruce Lee* (Outskirts Press, 2008), p. 39.

113 "Bruce said that": Glover, *Bruce Lee Between Wing Chun and Jeet Kune Do*, p. 17.
113 "It was funny to watch": Glover, *Bruce Lee Between Wing Chun and Jeet Kune Do*, p. 49.
113 "Over here, they don't fight": Interview with Ben Der, Jan. 27, 2022.
114 "It's power, Bruce": Interview with Leroy Garcia, July 13, 2022.
114 "I don't think he liked": Paul Bax, *Disciples of the Dragon*, deluxe ed. (self-published, 2019), p. 39.
115 "The main focus": Rafiq, *Bruce Lee Conversations*, p. 29.
115 "how to beat me?": Bax, *Disciples of the Dragon*, 2008, p. 110.
115 Yoichi Nakachi was: Bax, *Disciples of the Dragon*, 2008, pp. 19–20; interview with Leroy Garcia, July 13, 2022; Taky Kimura, *Regards from the Dragon: Seattle*, rev. ed., compiled by David Tadman (Empire Books, 2009), p. 141.
115 "for us to fight": Interview with Leroy Garcia, July 13, 2022.
115 "We told him": Glover, *Bruce Lee Between Wing Chun and Jeet Kune Do*, p. 42.
115 "He challenged Bruce": Interview with Leroy Garcia, July 8, 2022.
116 "punch him, kick him": Glover, *Bruce Lee Between Wing Chun and Jeet Kune Do*, pp. 43–44; interview with Leroy Garcia, July 13, 2022.
116 "for them to stop": Glover, *Bruce Lee Between Wing Chun and Jeet Kune Do*, p. 45; interview with Leroy Garcia, July 13, 2022.
116 red with blood: Interview with Leroy Garcia, July 13, 2022.
116 eye socket was cracked: Jesse Glover in Bax, *Disciples of the Dragon*, p. 19.
116 "Twenty-two seconds": Interview with Leroy Garcia, July 13, 2022. The description of this fight and its lead-up is also drawn from Glover, *Bruce Lee Between Wing Chun and Jeet Kune Do*, pp. 42–45; Bruce Thomas, *Bruce Lee: Fighting Spirit* (Blue Snake Books, 1994), pp. 44–45; Paul Bax, "Ed Hart Interview," in *Disciples of the Dragon, Volume 1*, 2008, pp. 26–27.
116 "I've seen a lot of fights": Interview with Leroy Garcia, July 13, 2022.

Chapter 13: Dance Away

117 2.6 grade point average: His Edison transcript shows him graduating with three As, seven Bs, five Cs, three Ds, and one passed class, but a later University of Washington transcript shows he finished Edison with a 2.6 GPA. His college transcript was reprinted after his death in *Hawaii's Kung Fu and Other Martial Arts (Split Second)*, June 1974, p. 7. Courtesy of Perry Lee.
117 "go to the university without him": "Profiles: The Legacy of Ruby Chow," KIRO-TV, Seattle, 2006, youtube.com/watch?v=x4tuzSr7eTU.
117 "better than winning the lottery!": Robert Lee, *Bruce Lee, My Brother* (Masterpiece Films, 2010), p. 125, trans. Sze K. Chan. He was specifically referring to a horse-race track lottery game that boasted notoriously long odds.
117 "Drama," Bruce answered: A copy of his college transcript received sometime in 1973 or 1974 had "Drama" listed under "Major," with a slash through it, and "PRE MAJ" typed in, with a handwritten date "5-2-61," the equivalent of "Undeclared." He took two classes in drama in his time at UW, a class in theater speech in his first quarter, and a children's theater class in the spring of 1962. *Hawaii's Kung Fu and Other Martial Arts (Split Second)*.
118 "you're one of them": Interview with Lawrence Matsuda, Apr. 13, 2022.
118 "and showing off": Alice Ito and Mayumi Tsutakawa, "Roger Shimomura Interview," Densho Digital Archive, Mar. 18 and 20, 2023, ddr.densho.org/media/ddr-densho-1000/ddr-densho-1000-142-transcript-6e3d832f04.htm.
118 somehow getting over: Skip Ellsworth in Paul Bax, *Disciples of the Dragon: Reflections from the Students of Bruce Lee* (Outskirts Press, 2008), p. 38.
119 She was book smart: Interview with Amy Sanbo, Sept. 14, 2018.
119 "with force": Bao Nguyen interview with Amy Sanbo, Apr. 24, 2019.
119 "to anyone for anything": This section is constructed from interviews Amy Sanbo gave to me and Bao Nguyen on separate occasions. See also Charlotte LeFevre, "The Lady and the Dragon," *Northwest Asian Weekly*, Dec. 1, 2007; and Tom Bleecker, *Unsettled Matters: The Life and Death of Bruce Lee* (Gilderoy Publications, 1996), pp. 33–42. Bleecker has also posted audio from his 1992 interviews with Amy Sanbo and Lonny Kaneko in three parts on YouTube under "Amy Sanbo Video Series": youtube.com/watch?v=IP5vSL_wcGU, youtube.com/watch?v=5vqHwfK3dWo, and youtube.com/watch?v=wjF1GbcaVXk.
119 Roger. whom she had been dating: Interview with Amy Sanbo, Sept. 14, 2018. Amy and Roger had dated starting when she arrived at the University of Washington in 1958 through 1961, when Roger graduated from

UW and was deployed to Korea. Amy saw him off at the airport sometime late in the spring or early in the summer. Soon, Roger said, "I got letters from two or three guys saying that I should know she's seeing a lot of Bruce Lee... and you know, I'm eight thousand miles away, I mean, if I weren't, if I was living there, what was I gonna do?... And so I just thought, I don't really care." "Roger Shimomura interview," Densho Digital Archive.

120 thought to herself: Interview with Amy Sanbo, Sept. 14, 2018.

120 "No. 27. Are you willing": See Cherstin M. Lyon, "Questions 27 and 28," *Densho Encyclopedia*, encyclopedia.densho.org/Questions_27_and_28/.

121 "holding their children as hostages": Interview with George Takei, Mar. 4, 2024.

121 "Very competitive": Interview with Amy Sanbo, Sept. 14, 2018. See also Bleecker, *Unsettled Matters*, pp. 35–36, and Bleecker's "Amy Sanbo Video Series," video 1 of 3.

122 Some mornings he cooked up ginger beef: James Halpin, "The Little Dragon: Bruce Lee," in Thomas A. Green and Joseph R. Svinth, eds., *Martial Arts in the Modern World* (Praeger, 2003), p. 123. In my interview with Linda Lee Cadwell, she was surprised to learn this. He had never made ginger beef for her.

122 "forty percent me": Bleecker, *Unsettled Matters*, pp. 38–39.

122 "Bruce was one of these people": Bleecker, *Unsettled Matters*, p. 36; interview with Amy Sanbo, Sept. 14, 2018.

122 "80 percent today": Bleecker, *Unsettled Matters*, pp. 38–39.

123 "A girl must be like a blossom": Lyrics here are from "Song of the King" from *The King and I*. Lyrics by Oscar Hammerstein II. Music by Richard Rodgers. Copyright © 1951 by Richard Rodgers and Oscar Hammerstein II. Copyright Renewed. Williamson Music owner of publication and allied rights throughout the world. International Copyright Secured. All Rights Reserved. Reprinted by Permission of Hal Leonard LLC

123 "I was looking at your eyes": Bleecker, "Amy Sanbo Video Series," video 1 of 3; interview with Amy Sanbo, Sept. 14, 2018.

Chapter 14: The Ghosts and the Moon

125 "In the restaurant entrance": Billy Potts, "Young Bruce Lee, Part 1: Street Brawling and Cha-Cha Dancing in Seattle," *Zolima City Mag*, Nov. 19, 2020, zolimacitymag.com/young-bruce-lee-part-i-street-brawling-and-cha-cha-dancing-in-seattle-chinatown/.

125 For years the workers: Interview with Mark Chow, July 21, 2022.

125 "even in his sleep": Robert Clouse, *Bruce Lee: The Biography* (Unique Publications, 1988), p. 25.

126 "my mother was very strong-willed": Interview with Mark Chow, July 21, 2022.

126 "Don't talk to him": Interview with Mark Chow, July 21, 2022.

126 elders in the community: Interview with Jacquie Kay, Apr. 21, 2022.

126 "looked over the room": Potts, "Young Bruce Lee, Part 1."

126 "on his way to greatness": Taky Kimura, *Regards from the Dragon: Seattle*, rev. ed., compiled by David Tadman (Empire Books, 2009), p. 197.

127 demonstrate the diversity: Jesse Glover, *Bruce Lee Between Wing Chun and Jeet Kune Do* (self-published, 1976), p. 40.

127 KCTS Channel 9: John Little, ed., *Bruce Lee: Words of the Dragon, Interviews, 1958–1973* (Tuttle, 1997), p. 25.

127 In the third episode: Interview with Leroy Garcia, July 13, 2022.

127 "Zen is grounded precisely": Alan Watts, *Zen Buddhism* (James Ladd Delkin, 1948), republished in Alan Watts, *Zen: A Short Introduction* (New World Library, 2019), pp. 38–39.

127 "Those who speak do not know": Alan Watts, *The Way of Zen* (Pantheon, 1957), p. 12. This translation is taken from Arthur Waley, *The Way and Its Power: A Study of the Tao Te Ching and Its Place in Chinese Thought* (Grove Press, 1958), p. 210.

128 "SIMPLICITY DIRECTNESS FREEDOM": This was inscribed on p. 83 in his copy of Watts's *The Way of Zen*, on the first page of chapter 4, "The Rise and Development of Zen."

128 In a paper he had written: Interview with Jacquie Kay, May 10, 2022. See also "Margaret Walters: Former Teacher and Student Advisor to Bruce Lee," *Hawaii's Kung Fu and Other Martial Arts (Split Second)*, June 1974, pp. 5, 7. Courtesy of Perry Lee.

128 "the spontaneity of the universe": Bruce Lee, "The Tao of Gung Fu" paper.

128 "talking about at lunch": Interview with Amy Sanbo and Lisa Yamamoto, Sept. 14, 2018; Bleecker, "Amy Sanbo Video Series," video 1 of 3.

128 like Skip's frat brothers: Interview with Amy Sanbo and Lisa Yamamoto, Sept. 14, 2018; Amy Sanbo interview with Bao Nguyen, Apr. 24, 2019.

128 than any of them did: Interview with Amy Sanbo, Sept. 14, 2018; James Halpin, "The Little Dragon: Bruce Lee," in Thomas A. Green and Joseph R. Svinth, eds., *Martial Arts in the Modern World* (Praeger, 2003) p. 122.

128 "he had control": Interview with Amy Sanbo, Sept. 14, 2018.

128 "I heard you're looking for me": Interview with Doug Palmer, Oct. 12, 2018.

129 "dealing with people": Doug Palmer, *Bruce Lee: Sifu, Friend and Big Brother* (Chin Music Press, 2020), p. 57.

129 "all of the students except Roger": Palmer, *Bruce Lee: Sifu, Friend and Big Brother*, p. 32.

129 "a whole new audience": Interview with Leroy Garcia, July 13, 2022.

129 "always been Jesse to him": Glover, *Bruce Lee Between Wing Chun and Jeet Kune Do*, p. 62.

129 "a bloody nose": Glover, *Bruce Lee Between Wing Chun and Jeet Kune Do*, p. 71.

130 detained in a Canadian immigration jail: Paul Bax, *Disciples of the Dragon: Reflections from the Students of Bruce Lee* (Outskirts Press, 2008), pp. 54–55.

Chapter 15: American Fictions

132 "We'll live on the Peak, Amy": Interview with Amy Sanbo, Sept. 14, 2018; Tom Bleecker, *Unsettled Matters: The Life and Death of Bruce Lee* (Gilderoy Publications, 1996), p. 40.

132 "Bruce was still such a child yet": Interview with Amy Sanbo, Sept. 14, 2018. Previous biographies have Bruce still together with Amy until well into 1963, but her diploma is dated June 9, 1962, with a double major in Far Eastern and Slavic Studies. Interview with Lisa Yamamoto, Feb. 18, 2022.

132 "the emotions he felt": Jesse Glover, *Bruce Lee Between Wing Chun and Jeet Kune Do* (self-published, 1976), p. 26.

132 he was Chinese: Interview with Leroy Garcia, July 13, 2022; Bao Nguyen interview with Leroy Garcia, Apr. 22, 2019.

133 "U Introduced to Gung Fu": Weldon Johnson, "Mike Lee Hope for Rotsa Ruck—U Introduced to Gung Fu," *Seattle Times*, 1963 (clipping found in the Bruce Lee Family Archive, no date given) reproduced in John Little, ed., *Bruce Lee: Words of the Dragon, Interviews, 1958–1973* (Tuttle, 1997), pp. 24–26.

134 "away from the practice sessions": Glover, *Bruce Lee Between Wing Chun and Jeet Kune Do*, p. 62.

134 "Act One of the Bruce Lee movie": Interview with Leroy Garcia, July 13, 2022.

134 "I told them": Fiaz Rafiq, *Bruce Lee Conversations: The Life and Legacy of a Legend* (HNL Publishing, 2009), p. 37.

134 "make everybody call him *sifu*": Billy Potts, "Young Bruce Lee, Part 1: Street Brawling and Cha-Cha Dancing in Seattle," *Zolima City Mag*, Nov. 19, 2020, zolimacitymag.com/young-bruce-lee-part-i-street-brawling-and-cha-cha-dancing-in-seattle-chinatown/.

134 a bloody nose and a bruised sternum: Potts, "Young Bruce Lee, Part 1."

135 "he used them to be aggressive!": Bruce Thomas, *Bruce Lee: Fighting Spirit* (Blue Snake Books, 1994), p. 33.

135 By the end of 1962: Geoffrey C. Ward and Ken Burns, *The Vietnam War: An Intimate History* (Knopf, 2017), p. 56.

135 "If your GPA dropped below a 2.0": Interview with Lawrence Matsuda, Apr. 13, 2022.

135 dropped to 1.84: University of Washington transcript in *Hawaii's Kung Fu and Other Martial Arts* (Split Second); Tan Vinh, "A Rare, Personal Glimpse of Bruce Lee's Seattle Years," *Seattle Times*, Oct. 3, 2014.

136 "How could a kid": Taky Kimura, *Regards from the Dragon: Seattle*, rev. ed., compiled by David Tadman (Empire Books, 2009), p. 184.

136 shaking his head: Linda Lee, *Bruce Lee: The Man Only I Knew* (Warner Paperback Library, 1975), pp. 65–66.

136 "Americans ignore history": Frances FitzGerald, *Fire in the Lake: The Vietnamese and the Americans in Vietnam* (Little Brown/Back Bay, 1972), pp. 7–8.

136 "I think they all thought": Interview with Linda Lee Cadwell, May 2, 2023.

137 "This letter is hard to understand": Draft letter to Pearl Tso, from Bruce Lee Family Archive. This has been published in heavily edited form in Bruce Lee, *Letters of the Dragon: Correspondence 1958–1973*, ed. John Little (Tuttle, 1998). It may have been taken from this draft. In the archive, this draft goes on for several pages without a clear end. It is not clear from the archive if Bruce sent the version in *Letters*, or which, if any, version he may have sent. Here I use the text from the draft in the archive.

139 "the assistant sales manager": A. J. Liebling, *The Sweet Science* (Viking, 1956; repr. ed., North Point Press, 2004), p. 5.

480 NOTES

139 "very reliable and trustworthy": Eunice Lam, "Bruce Lee Is Actually Very Gentle," yule.sohu.com /20080721/n258270375.shtml, July 21, 2008, trans. Sze K. Chan.

139 "a passing boat": The Bruce Lee archives contain multiple undated versions of the poem, "Boating on Lake Washington," with slight differences in each. One has "1960" scribbled in pencil (the poem that is rendered in black ink), but to my eyes, the penciled date doesn't appear to be in his handwriting. The Lee family dates this version of the poem to 1963 and has reprinted a copy of it in Bruce Lee, *In My Own Process* (Genesis Publications, 2024), p. 59.

139 "I'll race you": Interview with Abe Santos, Feb. 24, 2017.

Part V: Simplicity Directness Freedom, 1962–1964

141 "To me, great musicians": Miles Davis with Quincy Troupe, *Miles: The Autobiography* (Simon and Schuster, 1989), pp. 182–83, 400.

Chapter 16: Mavericks

142 Wally Jay had learned boxing: Interview with Leon Jay, Jan. 14, 2023. See also Wally Jay, *Small-Circle Jujitsu* (Black Belt/Ohara Publications, 1989), and Wally Jay, *Small Circle Jujitsu: History and Practice* (self-published, 2020). Mahalo nui no ku'u 'ohana'o Jay!

142 white GIs: Charles Russo, *Striking Distance: Bruce Lee and the Dawn of Martial Arts in America* (University of Nebraska Press, 2016), p. 90. The Jay family has kept archives of photos of Okazaki's graduating classes in the 1940s, and they are striking both for their diversity and size.

143 were soundly whipped: Interview with Leon Jay, Jan. 14, 2023; interview with Brad Burgo, Jan. 22, 2023.

143 "I knew it!": Leon Jay said, "It was something if you see success coming from a Chinese man in a Japanese art." Interview with Leon Jay, Jan. 14, 2023; interview with Brad Burgo, Jan. 22, 2023; interview with James Mussels, Jan. 6, 2023.

143 their friend George Lee: "The 'Knowing Is Not Enough' Interview: Allen Joe," *"Knowing Is Not Enough": The Official Newsletter of Jun Fan Jeet Kune Do* 1, no. 4 (Winter 1998), p. 62.

143 "the real deal": "The 'Knowing Is Not Enough' Interview: Allen Joe," pp. 62, 67.

143 Allen called James "Killer": Tommy Gong, *The Evolution of a Martial Artist* (Bruce Lee Enterprises, 2013), p. 52.

144 "a model than a *gung fu* man": "The 'Knowing Is Not Enough' Interview: Allen Joe," p. 65.

144 like a rag doll: Allen Joe with Svetlana Kim and Dmitri Bobkov, *The Last of the Four Musketeers* (Balboa Press, 2015), p. 66. Gong, *The Evolution of a Martial Artist*, pp. 47–48. "The 'Knowing Is Not Enough' Interview: Allen Joe," pp. 7–11.

144 for his build: Interview with Greglon Lee, July 13, 2023.

144 "You guys sure did!": Interview with Greglon Lee, July 13, 2023.

145 "Yim Wing Chun": Interview with Greglon Lee, July 13, 2023.

145 with mink coats: Interview with Greglon Lee, July 13, 2023.

146 alliteration with *karate*: Russo, *Striking Distance*, p. 74.

146 no more than ten dollars: Interview with Leo Fong, March 21, 2018; Charles Russo, "James Yimm Lee and T. Y. Wong: A Rivalry that Shaped the Chinese Martial Arts in America," *Kung Fu Tea* blog, Sept. 1, 2016, chinesemartialstudies.com/2016/09/01/james-yimm-lee-and-t-y-wong-a-rivalry-that-shaped-the-chinese-martial-art-in-america/comment-page-1/; Russo, *Striking Distance*, p. 75.

146 "I wasted three and a half years": James Yimm Lee, *Wing Chun Kung Fu: Chinese Art of Self-Defense*, technical adviser, Bruce Lee (Black Belt Books, 1972), p. 5.

146 "See I can break 'em too!": Charles Russo, "James Yimm Lee and T. Y. Wong."

146 "in disgust": James Yimm Lee, *Wing Chun Kung Fu: Chinese Art of Self-Defense*, p. 5.

147 "everyone who knew him": Ralph Castro in Sid Campbell and Greglon Lee, *Remembering the Master: Bruce Lee, James Yimm Lee, and the Creation of Jeet Kune Do* (Blue Snake Books, 2006), p. 85.

147 rumbled with marines: Gene Ching, "Great American Great Grandmaster," KungFuMagazine.com, Jan./Feb. 2010, kungfumagazine.com/magazine/article.php?article=871. For more on the legendary Pearl City Tavern and its island-wide rep, see "Pearl City Tavern," *Images of Old Hawai'i* blog, Jan. 8, 2022, imagesofoldhawaii.com/pearl-city-tavern/.

147 police, bouncers, security guards: Interview with Greglon Lee, July 13, 2023; Russo, *Striking Distance*, p. 75.

147 "they were big brutes": Interview with Greglon Lee, July 13, 2023.

147 at the Lees' doorstep: My money is on the latter. Charles Russo's *Striking Distance* has Bruce showing up on the Lees' doorstep. The certainty of what was thought to be a definitive account in Sid Campbell and Greglon Lee's two-book series *The Dragon and the Tiger* has been cast into doubt by Greglon himself, who says that he

NOTES 481

had never scrutinized or secured an editor for Sid Campbell's text. For his part, Greglon says he believes the two first met in person after Bruce's dance class.

147 "he will become world famous": Interview with Greglon Lee, July 13, 2023.
147 "training methods to the cicumstances": Campbell and Lee, *Remembering the Master*, p. 9.
147 "that has ever happened": Ralph Castro in Campbell and Lee, *Remembering the Master*, p. 87.
148 a man half his age: "The 'Knowing Is Not Enough' Interview: Allen Joe," p. 48.
148 "they could mentor him": Interview with Greglon Lee, July 13, 2023; Russo, *Striking Distance*, p. 82.

Chapter 17: Homecoming

149 wielding a knife: Doug Palmer, *Bruce Lee: Sifu, Friend and Big Brother* (Chin Music Press, 2020), p. 72; interview with Lanston Chinn, July 7, 2022.
149 "what was happening in that town": Interview with Lanston Chinn, July 7, 2022.
149 "rain and wind and punishing frost": Translated from the original by Sze K. Chan.
149 what to say to each other: Phoebe Lee, Agnes Lee, Robert Lee, and Peter Lee, *Lee Siu Loong: Memories of the Dragon*, compiled by David Tadman (Bruce Lee Club, 2004), p. 7.
150 minor in commercial art: Draft letter to Pearl Tso, from Bruce Lee archives.
150 leave the country: Linda Lee, *Bruce Lee: The Man Only I Knew* (Warner Paperback Library, 1975), p. 66.
150 "how he got through Freshman English 101": "Margaret Walters: Former Teacher and Student Advisor to Bruce Lee," *Hawaii's Kung Fu and Other Martial Arts (Split Second)*, June 1974, p. 5.
150 "skip the country": Margaret Walters," *Hawaii's Kung Fu and Other Martial Arts (Split Second)*, June 1974, p. 6; Linda Lee, *Bruce Lee: The Man Only I Knew*, p. 66.
151 "struck it rich": Phoebe Lee, Agnes Lee, Robert Lee, and Peter Lee, *Lee Siu Loong*, pp. 9, 11.
151 "Aren't you proud of me?": Robert Lee as told to Tony Page, "My Brother, Bruce: Reminiscences by Robert Lee," *Fighting Stars*, Aug. 1983, p. 45.
151 "everyone around him": Phoebe Lee, Agnes Lee, Robert Lee, and Peter Lee, *Lee Siu Loong*, p. 6.
151 "businessmen in Western suits": Robert Clouse, *Bruce Lee: The Biography* (Unique Publications, 1988), pp. 45-46.
151 "a magical summer": Phoebe Lee, Agnes Lee, Robert Lee, and Peter Lee, *Lee Siu Loong*, p. 71.
152 he would acquire: Palmer, *Bruce Lee: Sifu, Friend and Big Brother*, pp. 100, 105; interview with Doug Palmer, Oct. 12, 2018.
152 "Remember to dress sharp": Palmer, *Bruce Lee: Sifu, Friend and Big Brother*, p. 91.
152 "Can you show me": "Amy Pak Interview," in Chaplin Chang and Roger Lo, *The Bruce Lee They Knew* (Infolink Publishing, 2003), p. 184, trans. Sze K. Chan; Bruce Thomas, *Bruce Lee: Fighting Spirit* (Blue Snake Books, 1994), p. 52.
153 "as he got off the ferry!": Interview with Doug Palmer, Oct. 12, 2018; Palmer, *Bruce Lee: Sifu, Friend and Big Brother*, p. 122.
153 a primary method of comparison: "Bruce Lee in the 1980s: William Cheung and Dan Inosanto," *Fighting Stars*, Aug. 1983, p. 44.
153 the Tao itself in action: Bruce Lee, "The 'Chi Sao' of Wing Chun," *The 1969 Black Belt Yearbook*, p. 25, reprinted in *The Best of Bruce Lee* (Rainbow Publications, 1974), p. 63.
153 "through which its flow can pass": Bruce Lee, "The 'Chi Sao' of Wing Chun," p. 26.
153 in sticking hands: Jesse Glover, *Bruce Lee Between Wing Chun and Jeet Kune Do* (self-published, 1976), p. 52.
153 "to say so directly": Palmer, *Bruce Lee: Sifu, Friend and Big Brother*, pp. 129-30.
153 "I didn't realize it at the time": Interview with Doug Palmer, Oct. 12, 2018.
154 "your money when you need it": M. Uyehara, "Bruce Lee: The Man, the Fighter, the Superstar," in Editors of *Black Belt* magazine, eds., *The Legendary Bruce Lee* (Ohara Publications, 1986), p. 14.
154 he saw his father alive: Uyehara, "Bruce Lee: The Man, the Fighter, the Superstar," p. 14.

Chapter 18: Things Disclose Themselves

155 "on our doorstep with a suitcase": Conrad Wesselhoeft, "What It Was Like to Have Bruce Lee As a Houseguest," *Seattle Weekly*, Nov. 24, 2015.
155 physically fit enough to serve: Linda Lee, *Bruce Lee: The Man Only I Knew* (Warner Paperback Library, 1975), p. 66.

482 NOTES

156 made a mean oyster beef: Linda Lee, *The Bruce Lee Story* (Ohara Publications, 1989), pp. 12, 14. The space is also described in Barbara Manning, "A History of 4750 University Way Northeast, Seattle, Washington," no date, likely 2019, pauldorpat.com/wp-content/uploads/2020/11/4750-University-Way-Manning-report.pdf.

156 share of the profits: Taky Kimura, *Regards from the Dragon: Seattle*, rev. ed., compiled by David Tadman (Empire Books, 2009), p. 128.

156 *break the rules*: Adapted from a letter he wrote to Fred Sato, in Bruce Lee, *Letters of the Dragon: Correspondence 1958–1973*, ed. John Little (Tuttle, 1998), p. 75.

156 "what man lives for": Bruce Lee, "Me and Jeet Kune Do," in John Little, ed., *Bruce Lee: Words of the Dragon, Interviews, 1958–1973* (Tuttle, 1997), p. 124.

156 "was Chinese martial arts": Bruce Lee, "Me and Jeet Kune Do."

157 "in this big *gweilo* world": Interview with Jacquie Kay, May 10, 2022.

158 "his incredible speed and snap": Bruce Lee, *Chinese Gung Fu: The Philosophical Art of Self-Defense* (Black Belt Books, 1963; repr. ed., 2008), p. 4.

158 "unnecessary wasted motions": Bruce Lee, *Chinese Gung Fu*, p. 88.

158 "Its philosophy is based": Bruce Lee, *Chinese Gung Fu*, p. 6.

159 "interdependent on each other": Bruce Lee, *Chinese Gung Fu*, p. 39.

160 "The great mistake in swordsmanship": This line would also become a favorite of LeBron James. In transcribing the note, Bruce universalized the quote by taking out the specific references to swordsmanship. Ichiun was the disciple of Sekiun, credited with bringing *wu hsin* into the art of Japanese swordsmanship as *mujushin-ken*. The original quote is from the second essay on Zen and swordsmanship in Daisetz T. Suzuki, *Zen and Japanese Culture* (Bollingen Foundation/Princeton University Press, 1959; repr. ed., 1970), p. 177.

160 "because it is empty": These lines are underlined in his copy of the book, which is now in the collection of the Wing Luke Museum. Eugen Herrigel, *Zen in the Art of Archery* (Pantheon, 1953), p. 59.

160 *Wu hsin*, Bruce wrote: Here is Suzuki's translation of seventeenth-century Buddhist prelate Takuan Sōhō's "Letter to Yagyū Tajima No Kami Munenori on the Mystery of Prajñā Immovable": "For instance, suppose ten men are opposing you, each in succession ready to strike you with a sword. As soon as one is disposed of, you will move on to another without permitting the mind to 'stop' with any. However rapidly one blow may follow another, you leave no time to intervene between the two. Every one of the ten will thus be successively and successfully dealt with. This is possible only when the mind moves from one object to another without being 'stopped' or arrested by anything. If the mind is unable to move on in this fashion, it is sure to lose the game somewhere between the two encounters." Daisetz T. Suzuki, *Zen and Japanese Culture*, p. 98. See also Takuan Sōhō, *The Unfettered Mind: Writings from a Zen Master to a Master Swordsman*, translated by William Scott Wilson (Kodansha International, 1986, 2002), pp. 31–32.

160 "As soon as he stops": Bruce Lee, "The Tao of Gung Fu" paper.

160 "the art of artlessness, the principle of no-principle": Bruce Lee, "The Tao of Gung Fu."

160 "the line of creation": *Tao, the Great Luminant: Essays from the Huai Nan Tzu*, trans. Evan Morgan (1933; repr. ed., Forgotten Books, 2008), pp. 50–51. Also accessible at: https://sacred-texts.com/tao/tgl/tgl1.htm.

160 "it is not divided": Bruce Lee, "The Tao of Gung Fu." Again, the first sentence here directly quotes from Morgan's translation of the section called "Greatness of Yieldingness Illustrated by Water," p. 51.

160 shaping its flow to the terrain: Chapter 6, Lines 27 and 28, in Sun Tzu, *The Art of War*, trans. Samuel Griffiths (Oxford University Press, 1963), p. 101.

161 "strike in a straight line": As one corrections officer put it, "Untrained people fight the force, not the emptiness." Sgt. Rory Miller, *Meditations on Violence: A Comparison of Martial Arts Training & Real World Violence* (YMAA Publication Center, 2008), p. 147.

161 "avoidance of injury to all things": Chapter 33 in *Chuang Tzŭ: Mystic, Moralist, and Social Reformer*, trans. Herbert Giles (Bernard Quaritch, 1889), www.gutenberg.org/files/59709/59709-h/59709-h.htm.

161 "Good weapons are instruments of fear": Laozi, chapter 31, *Tao Te Ching*, trans. Gia-Fu Feng and Jane English with Toinette Lippe (Vintage, 1972; repr. ed. 2011), unpaginated.

161 "himself and his opponent": Bruce Lee, "The Tao of Gung Fu."

161 "Martial arts are sportslike only": Barry Allen, *Striking Beauty: A Philosophical Look at the Asian Martial Arts* (Columbia University Press, 2015), p. 141, also see pp. 133–36.

162 "greed, anger, and folly": Here he was alluding to Suzuki, *Zen and Japanese Culture*, pp. 89–90.

162 "necessary for him": Suzuki, *Zen and Japanese Culture*, p. 62. The disquieting relationship between Suzuki's work and the Japanese military is explored in Brian Daizen Victoria's *Zen at War*, 2nd. ed. (Rowman & Littlefield, 2006). For another perspective, see Richard Jaffe's Introduction to *Selected Works of D. T. Suzuki*, vol 1, Richard Jaffe, ed. (University of California Press, 2015).

162 "observed like a funeral": Laozi, *Tao Te Ching*, chapter 31, trans. Gia-Fu Feng and Jane English with Toinette Lippe (Vintage, 1972; repr. ed., 2011), unpaginaged.

For a contrast in thinking about the ethics of sword fighting, Bruce would surely have been familiar with chapter 30 of the *Zhuangzi*, "Talking About Swords," in which the Taoist master humbles a fight-crazy emperor into reconsidering his sword fighting bloodlust.

162 the form of riddles: *The Book of Lieh-Tzu: A Classic of Tao*, trans. A. C. Graham (Columbia University Press, 1960; repr. ed., 1990), pp. 37–38.

162 "Respond like an echo": In his original paper, he had quoted the following translation, citing Zhuangzi, misattributing the lines to the "Huai Nan Tzu / Tao the Great Illuminant": "Establish nothing in regard to oneself. Let things be what they are, move like water, rest like a mirror, respond like an echo, pass quickly like the non-existent, and be quiet as purity. Those who agree are harmonious. Those who gain, lose. Do not precede others, always follow them." From Fung Yu-Lan, *A History of Chinese Philosophy*, vol. 1, trans. Derk Bodde (Princeton University Press, 1953), p. 173.

But later he found the A. C. Graham translation of the same passage, and this translation, reproduced here, would become the one he would regularly cite for the rest of his life.

A final note: scholars will notice that I've conflated Laozi, Liezi, and Zhuangzi with the books that bear their names. I recognize there is substantial debate and discourse around their individual historicity, as well as the authorship of these books. I have made a choice here in favor of the storytelling.

162 meekness and humility: "The Tao of Gung Fu."

163 "rise above them all": Raymond B. Blakney, translation, 1955 in "Tao of Gung Fu" paper.

163 "trying to have us live": D. T. Suzuki, *An Introduction to Zen Buddhism* (Evergreen/Black Cat, 1964), p. 64.

163 countercultural instruments for self-actualization: For discussion of American Taoism as cultural appropriation, see Cai Juemin, "A False Dao?: Popular Daoism in America," *Journal of Daoist Studies* 13 (2000), pp. 106–35; Steve Bradbury, "The American Conquest of Philosophical Taoism," in *Translation East and West: A Cross-Cultural Approach*, Cornelia N. Moore and Lucy Lower, eds. (College of Languages, Linguistics, and Literature and the East West Center, University of Hawai'i, 1992), pp. 29–41. See also James Brown, "The Zen of Anarchy: Japanese Exceptionalism and the Anarchist Roots of the San Francisco Poetry Renaissance," *Religion and American Culture: A Journal of Interpretation* 19, no. 2 (Summer 2009), p. 219. Watts, for his part, was loudly critical of the Beats and their lifestyle.

163 who practiced Buddhism: For discussion of the differences and tensions between Japanese American Buddhists and white convert Buddhists, see Michael Masatsugu, "'Beyond This World of Transiency and Impermanence': Japanese Americans, Dharma Bums, and the Making of American Buddhism during the Early Cold War Years," *Pacific Historical Review* 77, no. 3 (Aug. 2008), pp. 423–51.

Chapter 19: This Is It!

164 "My mother was a toughie": Interview with Linda Lee Cadwell, May 2, 2023.

165 "stir up trouble": Madeline Crowley, *We Lived Here: Stories of Seattle's Central Area* (Chin Music Press, 2020), pp. 57–58.

165 not *what is expected in our family*: Crowley, *We Lived Here*. p, 53.

165 "and find out?": Interview with Sue Ann Kay, March 31, 2022; Linda Lee, *The Bruce Lee Story* (Ohara Publications, 1989), p. 7.

165 "for the physicality of it": Interview with Linda Lee Cadwell, May 2, 2023.

165 What did I get myself: Linda Lee, *The Bruce Lee Story*, p. 7.

166 "call, I think, 'hazel'": John Little, ed., *Bruce Lee: Words of the Dragon, Interviews, 1958–1973* (Tuttle, 1997), p. 36.

166 "THIS IS IT": This text is taken from Bruce's informational flyer headed "THIS IS IT!" Courtesy Bruce Lee Family Archive.

167 "how to write perfectly": Interview with Linda Lee Cadwell, May 2, 2023.

167 "'No, only you and me'": Linda Lee, *The Bruce Lee Story*, pp. 11–12.

167 "To live content with small means": Bruce Lee, *Letters of the Dragon: Correspondence 1958–1973*, ed. John Little (Tuttle, 1998), p. 32.

168 "My Symphony": The poem was actually excerpted from an 1841 letter in which Channing describes to a friend the simple kind of life he wanted to live. In the twentieth century, it became widely known as an inspirational poem. The original passage is in Octavius Brooks Frothingham, *Memoir of William Henry Channing* (Houghton and Mifflin, 1866), p. 166.

168 "everything perfect": Linda Lee, *Bruce Lee: The Man Only I Knew* (Warner Paperback Library, 1975), p. 28.

484 NOTES

168 "germinates no more": These quotes were written in one of Bruce's notebooks. Because some of them have been reprinted on the internet without context, they have been attributed to him. But the original authors of these quotes are: "Fame is climbing..." Josh Billings; "The essential thing is..." Paul Valery; "Some of us..." William Feather; "It is always the secure..." Gilbert Keith Chesterton; "Knowing is not..." Johann Wolfgang von Goethe; "Nothing is so aggravating..." Oscar Wilde; "Analysis kills..." Henri Frederic Amiel.

169 "Meet me in fifteen minutes": Linda Lee, *Bruce Lee: The Man Only I Knew*, p. 10.

169 "'We gotta get there!'": Interview with Linda Lee Cadwell, May 2, 2023.

169 "fast-growing karate sect": "Sport: Violent Repose," *Time*, Mar. 3, 1961.

169 suited for the movie screen: Leilani Parker, *Memories of Ed Parker, Sr. Grandmaster of American Kenpo Karate* (Delsby Publications, 2013), p. 62.

169 "such a natural athlete": Parker, *Memories of Ed Parker*, p. 62.

170 it was Ed Parker: Chris Trevino, "Bruce Lee Put U.S. Martial Arts on the Grand Stage in Long Beach 50 Years Ago," *Long Beach Press-Telegram*, Sept. 1, 2017.

170 "'doing' something 'about' combat": Dan Inosanto and George Foon, *Jeet Kune Do: The Art and Philosophy of Bruce Lee* (Know Now Publishing, 1980), p. 48.

170 "everybody looks the same": Interview with Dan Inosanto, Sept. 26, 2023.

170 "patternized mechanical robot": Bruce Lee, *The Tao of Gung Fu*, ed. John Little (Tuttle, 1997), pp. 18–19.

170 "the judges and referees": Paul Bax, *Disciples of the Dragon: Reflections from the Students of Bruce Lee* (Outskirts Press, 2008), p. 177.

170 "meet this guy": Trevino, "Bruce Lee Put U.S. Martial Arts on the Grand Stage in Long Beach 50 Years Ago."

170 "what lies in the martial arts world": Parker, *Memories of Ed Parker*, p. 62.

171 "You shouldn't miss it": Alan Ward, "'Gung Fu' Would Have Helped Liston," *Oakland Tribune*, May 1, 1964.

171 six times as many in Los Angeles: There were 58,000 in SF in 1960; see Nami Sumida, "Six Maps Show How San Francisco's Asian Population Has Changed," *San Francisco Chronicle*, Apr. 11, 2022, https://www.sfchronicle.com/projects/2022/san-francisco-asian-population/. There were 11,676 in Oakland; see bayareacensus.ca.gov/cities/Oakland50.htm. There were 15,159 in Santa Clara County; see bayareacensus.ca.gov/counties/SantaClaraCounty50.htm. And in Los Angeles, there were more than 109,000 Asians; see laalmanac.com/population/po20.php. There were 17,000 in Seattle; see https://historylink.org/File/9341.

171 wasting his time in the Pacific Northwest: Jesse Glover, *Bruce Lee Between Wing Chun and Jeet Kune Do* (self-published, 1976), p. 91.

171 "a form of paralysis": Interview with Leo Fong, Mar. 21, 2018; Charles Russo, *Striking Distance: Bruce Lee and the Dawn of Martial Arts in America* (University of Nebraska Press, 2016), pp. 6–7.

171 "any wasted motions": Russo, *Striking Distance*, pp. 6–7.

172 for his poor eyesight: "Bruce Lee in the 1980s: William Cheung and Dan Inosanto," *Fighting Stars*, Aug. 1983, p. 44. William Cheung said, "Also, a lot of people do not realize that Bruce was very nearsighted. And he was always conscious of that. So if he was in a confrontation, he would always throw the first punch. He couldn't see four feet away." Dan Inosanto added, "He couldn't see without his glasses. That's probably why he closed the gap so fast." Bruce would later name this technique the "progressive indirect attack." As Dan Inosanto described it to me, "It appeared to you that he was really far away but he'd make a motion *like that* and then he's closer than you think. I think he got that from *The Art of War*: 'When my enemy advances, I retreat. When my enemy retreats, I advance.'" Interview with Dan Inosanto, Sept. 26, 2023.

172 "Bruce left the stage to mixed applause": Charles Russo, *Striking Distance*, p. 9.

172 "talking bad afterward": Interview with Leo Fong, Mar. 21, 2018.

172 "training all you want": Interview with Greglon Lee, July 13, 2023.

172 through the plate-glass window: Russo, *Striking Distance*, pp. 113–14.

173 "He would speak": Interview with Lanston Chinn, July 7, 2022.

173 "what's the right thing to do": Interview with Lanston Chinn, July 7, 2022.

173 "that was very clever": Interview with Linda Lee Cadwell, May 2, 2023.

173 ship his furniture and books: The Allied Van Lines moving contract for the pickup of his goods is signed by Taky Kimura and dated July 20, 1964. Courtesy of the Bruce Lee Family Archive.

173 "When I took Bruce to the airport": Linda Lee, *The Bruce Lee Story*, p. 16.

Part VI: A Bigger Stage, 1964–1965

175 "Do not press": Chapter 7, Verse 36. Sun Tzu. *The Art of War*. Translated by Lionel Giles. classics.mit.edu/Tzu/artwar.html.

Chapter 20: Openings

176 show Bruce around the city: Interview with Dan Inosanto, Sept. 26, 2023.
176 "always getting drunk!": Interview with Dan Inosanto, Sept. 26, 2023; Perry William Kelly, *Dan Inosanto: The Man, the Teacher, the Artist* (Paladin Press, 2000), p. 20.
176 an arcing front kick: Fiaz Rafiq, *Bruce Lee Conversations: The Life and Legacy of a Legend* (HNL Publishing, 2009), p. 92.
176 the virtues of simplicity and directness: Bao Nguyen interview with Barney Scollan, July 5, 2019; Rafiq, *Bruce Lee Conversations*, p. 92.
176 "the nucleus of an atom": Jhoon Rhee, *Bruce Lee and I* (MVM Books, 2000), p. ix.
177 "for whatever reason": Interview with Barney Scollan, Mar. 15, 2024.
177 "who can do anything": Paul Bax, *Disciples of the Dragon: Reflections from the Students of Bruce Lee* (Outskirts Press, 2008), pp. 86–87.
177 "You know we have that": Interview with Dan Inosanto, Sept. 26, 2023; Fran Colberg, "Kali . . . Teaching An Old Martial Art New Tricks," *Black Belt*, Sept. 1975, p. 52.
177 Long Beach Municipal Auditorium: Charles Russo, *Striking Distance: Bruce Lee and the Dawn of Martial Arts in America* (University of Nebraska Press, 2016), p. 117.
177 dozens of referees and judges: Leilani Parker, *Memories of Ed Parker, Sr. Grandmaster of American Kenpo Karate* (Delsby Publications, 2013), pp. 67, 69.
178 for *him* to continue: "Hawaiians Dominate the First International Karate Championships," *Black Belt*, Jan. 1965, p. 62.
178 Filipino martial arts to North American audiences: "Hawaiians Dominate the First International Karate Championships"; Joseph T. Arriola, "Meet the Man Who Inherited Flor Villabrille's 'Death Stick,'" *Black Belt*, July 1994, pp. 35–36.
178 the headliner slot: "Hawaiians Dominate the First International Karate Championships."
178 "our industry would prosper": Parker, *Memories of Ed Parker*, p. 62.
178 *than any style or system*: Russo, *Striking Distance*, p. 120; "The 'Knowing Is Not Enough' Interview: Richard Bustillo," *"Knowing Is Not Enough": The Official Newsletter of Jun Fan Jeet Kune Do* 4, no. 3 (Fall 1999), p. 4. The original quote from Jiddu Krishnamurti is, "The individual is of first importance, not the system; and as long as the individual does not understand the total process of himself, no system, whether of the left or of the right, can bring order and peace to the world." Krishnamurti, *Education and the Significance of Life* (1953), https://jkrishnamurti.org/content/chapter-1-education-and-significance-life.
178 *can get the job done*: Interview with Barney Scollan, Mar. 15, 2024; Bao Nguyen interview with Barney Scollan, July 5, 2019.
178 with the one-inch punch: Interview with Barney Scollan, Mar. 15, 2024.
178 roar of applause: Joe Hyams, *Zen in the Martial Arts* (Bantam, 1979) pp. 9–10.
178 "the masses that were gathered": Bao Nguyen interview with Barney Scollan, July 5, 2019.
179 "It was very frustrating": Dan Inosanto and George Foon, *The Filipino Martial Arts* (Know Now Publishing, 1980), p. 9.
179 "I felt there was no need": Linda Lee, *The Bruce Lee Story* (Ohara Publications, 1989), p. 18.
179 "strength, honesty, purity, and loyalty": Taky Kimura, *Regards from the Dragon: Seattle*, rev. ed., compiled by David Tadman (Empire Books, 2009), p. 189.
179 "any girl you'll find again": Robert Clouse, *Bruce Lee: The Biography* (Unique Publications, 1988), p. 51.
179 "There was no 'down on bended knee'": Interview with Linda Lee Cadwell, May 2, 2023.
179 "I *knew* I wanted to be": Linda Lee, *The Bruce Lee Story*, p. 18.
180 "a treasured and guarded custom": Jack Johnson, *My Life in the Ring and Out* (1927; repr. ed., Proteus, 1977), p. 26.
180 "for the races to mix": *Loving v. Virginia*, Supreme Court of the United States, 388 U.S. 1, Decided June 12, 1967, majority opinion by Chief Justice Earl Warren, law2.umkc.edu/faculty/projects/ftrials/conlaw/loving.html.
181 "the obliteration of racial pride": *Loving v. Virginia*, citing State of Virginia's 1965 decision in *Naim v. Naim*, 197 Va. 80, 87 S.E.2d 749. One of the more mind-bending arguments used by the State of Virginia before the Supreme Court was that because intermarriage bans punished white and Black alike, they did not violate the Equal Protection Clause of the Fourteenth Amendment. Similar thinking has been the bedrock for recent legal arguments against affirmative action and other racial equity policies.
181 overturning the state's anti-miscegenation laws: Washington State did not have an intermarriage ban

486 NOTES

in 1964, but it had its own terrible history. Black, Filipino, Chinese, and Japanese Americans joined together to stop the passage of anti-miscegenation laws as late as 1937. Courts still disenfranchised spouses of color when their white partners died. See Stefanie Johnson, "Blocking Racial Intermarriage Laws in 1935 and 1937," Seattle Civil Rights and Labor History Project, University of Washington, https://depts.washington.edu/civilr /antimiscegenation.htm.

181 marriage between a white person and a non-white person: The percentage of non-Hispanic Blacks who favored interracial marriage that year was 56 percent. As late as 1995, a majority of US whites disapproved of interracial marriage. See Frank Newport, "In U.S., 87% Approve of Black-White Marriage, vs. 4% in 1958," Gallup, July 25, 2013, news.gallup.com/poll/163697/approve-marriage-blacks-whites.aspx.

181 "A friend of mine": Linda Lee, *The Bruce Lee Story*, p. 18.

181 "His father, mother, and even the entire family": Robert Chan in Chaplin Chang and Roger Lo, *The Bruce Lee They Knew* (Infolink Publishing, 2003), pp. 42–43, trans. Sze K. Chan.

181 "welcome me to the family": Linda Lee, *The Bruce Lee Story*, p. 19. One article from *TV Picture Life* had the author Fredda Dudley Balling writing, "Bruce's mother only wrote one superb sentence: 'If she is your choice, she is ours. We welcome her to the family.'" However, much of this article—meant to paint a wholesome romantic view of interracial marriage—is invented, even hallucinated. Fredda Dudley Balling, "Bruce Lee: Love Knows No Geography," *TV Picture Life*, presumably Nov. 1966. Reprinted in John Little, ed., *Bruce Lee: Words of the Dragon, Interviews, 1958–1973* (Tuttle, 1997), pp. 39, 73–75. In an extensive note, the editor John Little fact checks this article.

181 "I do think that": Interview with Linda Lee Cadwell, May 2, 2023.

181 "What do you know": Madeline Crowley, *We Lived Here: Stories of Seattle's Central Area* (Chin Music Press, 2020), p. 54.

182 *to wait a year?*: Interview with Linda Lee Cadwell, May 2, 2023.

182 *support their daughter?*: Interview with Lanston Chin, July 7, 2022.

182 "They didn't know": Interview with Linda Lee Cadwell, May 2, 2023.

182 have a "yellow baby": Interview with Linda Lee Cadwell, May 2, 2023.

182 *look down on you?*: Crowley, *We Lived Here*, p. 55.

183 never intended for the races to mix: Interview with Linda Lee Cadwell, May 2, 2023. Also see Linda Lee, *The Bruce Lee Story*, p. 19; Clouse, *Bruce Lee: The Biography*, pp. 55–56; Tom Bleecker, *Unsettled Matters: The Life and Death of Bruce Lee* (Gilderoy Publications, 1996), p. 46.

183 "better do it in a church": Linda Lee, *The Bruce Lee Story*, p. 19; Clouse, *Bruce Lee: The Biography*, p. 56.

183 "nor was there a photographer present": Linda Lee, *Bruce Lee: The Man Only I Knew* (Warner Paperback Library, 1975), p. 31.

Chapter 21: Training Floor

184 Others threw bottles, rocks, and bricks: For more on the Birmingham campaign, see Paul Kix, *You Have to Be Prepared to Die Before You Begin to Live: Ten Weeks in Birmingham That Changed America* (Celadon, 2023).

184 "affects all indirectly": Martin Luther King Jr. "Letter from a Birmingham Jail," Apr. 16, 1963, www .africa.upenn.edu/Articles_Gen/Letter_Birmingham.html.

184 the Free Speech Movement: Interview with Barney Scollan, March 15, 2024; Bao Nguyen interview with Barney Scollan, July 5, 2019.

184 "a lot of other stuff going on": Interview with Linda Lee Cadwell, May 2, 2023.

185 "I fed those people": Robert Clouse, *Bruce Lee: The Biography* (Unique Publications, 1988), p. 62.

185 a degree in philosophy: Bruce Lee, *Letters of the Dragon: Correspondence 1958–1973*, ed. John Little (Tuttle, 1998), p. 41.

185 "Within the first year": Ernest Benavidez in Sid Campbell and Greglon Lee, *Remembering the Master: Bruce Lee, James Yimm Lee, and the Creation of Jeet Kune Do* (Blue Snake Books, 2006), p. 68.

185 "keep up with them": Bob Baker in Campbell and Lee, *Remembering the Master*, pp. 38–39.

185 physique-building progress: George Lee in Campbell and Lee, *Remembering the Master*, p. 34.

186 "at such a great pace": Bob Baker in Campbell and Lee, *Remembering the Master*. p. 40.

186 became longtime friends: Leo Fong in Campbell and Lee, *Remembering the Master*, p. 55.

188 "between art and combat": Interview with Leo Fong, Mar. 21, 2018.

188 "a sound and an echo": Interview with Leo Fong, Mar. 21, 2018; Leo Fong in Campbell and Lee, *Remembering the Master*, p. 56.

189 inspired by the real Cotton Club–type establishments: See Arthur Dong's delightful 1989 documentary,

Forbidden City USA, or the book of the same name. Arthur Dong, *Forbidden City U.S.A.: Chinatown Nightclubs, 1936–1970* (DeepFocus Productions, 2015).

189 Through the 1950s, youth gangs: Victor G. Nee and Bret de Bary Nee, *Longtime Californ': A Documentary Study of an American Chinatown* (1972; repr. ed., Stanford University Press, 1986), p. 338; Bill Lee, *Chinese Playground: A Memoir* (self-published, 2014), pp. 67–68.

189 active participants in public violence: See Lee, *Chinese Playground*, pp. 84–86; Nee and Nee, *Longtime Californ'*, pp. 343–44.

189 back alleys, and movie theaters: Lee, *Chinese Playground*, pp. 66–94.

189 "Now it's just the opposite": Nee and Nee, *Longtime Californ'*, p. 338.

189 increased sixfold: Nee and Nee, *Longtime Californ'*, p. 338.

189 "This was now their Chinatown": Lee, *Chinese Playground*, pp. 69–70. "It also came down to what was seen in the locker room. Essentially the ABCs were circumcised and the FOBs were not. Ridiculous as it seemed, one's foreskin, or lack of, could determine your fate," Bill Lee wrote. There is an odd irony of this in relationship to Bruce's Asian American story. In 1963, he had gotten circumcised in Hong Kong, a passage into becoming an ABC. Yet he would be regarded by the *gung fu* establishment in Chinatown—old and young—as an FOB.

190 "a dissident with bad manners": Charles Russo, *Striking Distance: Bruce Lee and the Dawn of Martial Arts in America* (University of Nebraska Press, 2016), pp. 6, 129.

190 "He didn't like the Chinese there": Interview with Linda Lee Cadwell, May 2, 2023.

190 "'when he hit me!'": Bruce Lee's undated notes of a conversation with James Yimm Lee. From the Bruce Lee Family Archive. A similar conversation is published as a discussion between Bruce, James, and Leo Fong as "A Discussion on Chinese Gung Fu," in Bruce Lee, *The Tao of Gung Fu*, ed. John Little (Tuttle, 1997), pp. 163–68.

Chapter 22: The Boxer from Toisan

191 "all the good martial arts": Interview with Dan Inosanto, Sept. 26, 2023.

191 "Why would you kick high": Charles Russo, *Striking Distance: Bruce Lee and the Dawn of Martial Arts in America* (University of Nebraska Press, 2016), p. 131. Much of this section is based on Russo's excellent account.

192 "Get up here right now": Interview with Dan Inosanto, Sept. 26, 2023.

192 "We began cheering": Russo, *Striking Distance*, pp. 132–33.

192 a torrent of cigarettes flew toward it: In a second version—told to Wong Jack Man, who had not been there, but later circulated by him and his students—Bruce invited up his friend George Long, a White Crane expert. He explained to the crowd he would be demonstrating his one-inch punch. He outfitted Long with a pad. But then either Long moved or Bruce missed. And the crowd roared. Bruce threw the punch again, this time knocking back his target. But now, George complained, "That's not fair. You said you'd only punch me once." At this the crowd began laughing, booing, and jeering Bruce. George departed the stage as a torrent of cigarettes flew toward it. That these different versions have been told only enhances the Rashomon qualities of everything about the subsequent fight and its aftermath. Versions of this story are included in Michael Dorgan, "Shaolin Master Wong Jack Man's Last Interview," 2017, Hunyuan Martial Arts Academy of San Jose, taichisanjose.com/wong-jack-man-interview; and Rick L. Wing, *Showdown in Oakland: The Story Behind the Wong Jack Man–Bruce Lee Fight* (Kindle ebook, self-published, 2013). However, Wong's account was secondhand. I've chosen here to go with the version that Charles Russo has described in his book, as he has directly sourced it from multiple attendees.

192 his new book for sale: Wing, *Showdown in Oakland*, location 753.

192 "my school in Oakland": Russo, *Striking Distance*, p. 134.

192 backing down from a fight: Russo, *Striking Distance*, p. 134.

192 the effectiveness of Wing Chun: Wing, *Showdown in Oakland*, location 896; Russo, *Striking Distance*, pp. 134–35.

192 when the time came: Interview with Leo Fong, Mar. 21, 2018. See also Paul Bax, *Disciples of the Dragon: Reflections from the Students of Bruce Lee* (Outskirts Press, 2008), p. 127.

192 "Chickenshit son of a bitch": Interview with Leo Fong, Mar. 21, 2018.

192 "not instigating it": Wing, *Showdown in Oakland*, location 923.

193 in brush calligraphy: Russo, *Striking Distance*, p. 134; Wing, *Showdown in Oakland*, location 1030.

194 "Wong had just recently": Linda Lee, *Bruce Lee: The Man Only I Knew* (Warner Paperback Library, 1975), pp. 67–68, 71–72. Note her choice of the word "presumably," a nuance that disappears in countless subsequent accounts.

194 "not supposed to teach non-Chinese": Interview with Linda Lee Cadwell, May 2, 2023.

488 NOTES

194 a master of multiple systems: Wing, *Showdown in Oakland*, location 454; interview with Michael Dorgan, Oct. 5, 2022.

195 "to America and the world": Michael Dorgan, "Shaolin Master Wong Jack Man's Last Interview."

195 *jing wu*: For more details on *jing wu*, see Benjamin Judkins and Jon Nielson, *The Creation of Wing Chun: A Social History of the Southern Chinese Martial Arts* (State University of New York Press, 2015), p. 137; and Brian Kennedy and Elizabeth Guo, *Jingwu: The School That Transformed Kung Fu* (Blue Snake Books, 2010).

195 Huo Yianjia: Bruce spoke to his Cantonese American friends in the United States with excitement about making a movie about the hero they knew as Fok Yuen Gap, 霍元甲. According to Kennedy and Guo's excellent *Jingwu: The School That Transformed Kung Fu*, the fight actually never happened, nor did a second challenge, by a British boxer (pp. 73–78). In both instances the Europeans seem to have forfeited or walked away. However, these stories have passed into modern mythos through *Fist of Fury* and subsequent movies, from Jackie Chan's *New Fist of Fury* and Jet Li's *Fist of Legend* to countless more-recent movies from the Chinese industry that advance nationalist themes.

196 more than fifty forms from multiple styles: Interview with Michael Dorgan, Sept. 28, 2022. Wing, *Showdown in Oakland*, location 531.

196 "doing these public shows": Dorgan, "Shaolin Master Wong Jack Man's Last Interview."

196 "he wasn't chatty": Interview with Michael Dorgan, Oct. 5, 2022.

196 the best way to do it: In an endnote, Matthew Polly notes, "Others have suggested it was David who put that idea in Wong Jack Man's head. Having learned of Wong's ambitions to open his own school, David specifically sought him out and talked him into fighting Bruce Lee." Matthew Polly, *Bruce Lee: A Life* (Simon & Schuster, 2018), pp. 152, 532.

Russo's reporting has Chin speaking of Wong's intention to open a school, but not that Chin had intended to fight himself. But questions have been raised if Chin had really planned to fight. "Why Wong Jack Man, of all the people in the Chinatown martial arts community, had stepped forward remains a matter of much debate," Russo wrote. "Among the more prevalent perspectives is the idea that Wong had been manipulated into the entire affair, the new kid in town naively lured into a fight without realizing the stakes." Russo, *Striking Distance*, pp. 134–35.

196 "to exchange skills with Bruce Lee": Dorgan, "Shaolin Master Wong Jack Man's Last Interview."

196 Wong Jack Man and David Chin: Wing, *Showdown in Oakland*, locations 940, 945.

197 "after the performance": Taky Kimura, *Regards from the Dragon: Seattle*, rev. ed., compiled by David Tadman (Empire Books, 2009), pp. 52–33.

197 apparently motivated to make something happen: Wing, *Showdown in Oakland*, location 938; Russo, *Striking Distance*, p. 135.

197 "Okay, set the date": Russo, *Striking Distance*, p. 135.

197 "when he comes downhill": Chapter 7, verse 33. There is also this: "Whoever is first in the field and awaits the coming of the enemy, will be fresh for the fight; whoever is second in the field and has to hasten to battle will arrive exhausted." Chapter 6, verse 1. Sun Tzu, *The Art of War*, trans. Lionel Giles, classics.mit.edu/Tzu/artwar.html.

197 Ben Der had moved back: Interview with Ben Der, Jan. 27, 2022.

197 just for hanging out: Russo writes, "His nickname, Ya Ya, was a reference to his constantly yammering mouth. One longtime Chinatown resident remembers Wu as 'the sort of guy that always had to insert himself into things.'" Russo, *Striking Distance*, p. 134.

197 "'beat up by Wong Jack Man!'": Interview with Ben Der, Jan. 27, 2022.

197 two other friends eager for a show: Russo writes, "They were all at least a decade older than both Wong Jack Man and David Chin and carried the feel of mischievous hanger-on types, people who wanted to feel close to the action." Russo, *Striking Distance*, p. 137.

198 descended into a yard area: Interview with Linda Lee Cadwell, May 2, 2023.

198 shortly after Wong and Chin: Wing, *Showdown in Oakland*, location 1229.

198 Wong Jack Man would only remember: Michael Dorgan, *No Fight No Blame: A Journalist's Life in Martial Arts* (self-published, 2023), p. 82.

198 did not recall him being there: Michael Dorgan, "Bruce Lee's Toughest Fight," *Official Karate*, July 1980. Accessible at Hunyuan Martial Arts Academy of San Jose, taichisanjose.com/articles-bruce-lee-toughest-fight.

Interview with Linda Lee Cadwell, May 2, 2023.

198 recalled fifteen people: Dorgan, *No Fight No Blame*, p. 82.

198 David Chin insisted Chen: Polly, *Bruce Lee: A Life*, p. 535.

198 "'We're challenging you'": Interview with Linda Lee Cadwell, May 2, 2023.

198 David Chin would deny: Polly, *Bruce Lee: A Life*, pp. 533–34.
198 "locked the door": Dorgan, "Shaolin Master Wong Jack Man's Last Interview."
198 "therefore had to punish [him]": *Chinese Pacific Weekly*, in Wing, *Showdown in Oakland*, location 1727.
198 "It's all out!": Dorgan, "Shaolin Master Wong Jack Man's Last Interview"; Linda Lee, *Bruce Lee: The Man Only I Knew*, p. 72; interview with Linda Lee Cadwell, May 2, 2023.

Chapter 23: The Fight

199 his Northern Shaolin kicks: Michael Dorgan, *No Fight No Blame: A Journalist's Life in Martial Arts* (self-published, 2023), p. 85.
199 under his long sleeves: Rick L. Wing, *Showdown in Oakland: The Story Behind the Wong Jack Man-Bruce Lee Fight* (Kindle ebook, self-published, 2013), location 928.
199 "The challenge was real": Wing, *Showdown in Oakland*, location 1420; Mathew Polly, *Bruce Lee: A Life* (Simon & Schuster, 2018), p. 156.
199 "He really wanted": Dorgan, *No Fight No Blame*, p. 84.
199 "attack unguarded spots": Chapter 11, verse 19 in Sun Tzu, *The Art of War*, trans. Lionel Giles, classics.mit.edu/Tzu/artwar.html.
199 "if I seriously hurt him": Michael Dorgan, "Shaolin Master Wong Jack Man's Last Interview," 2017, Hunyuan Martial Arts Academy of San Jose, taichisanjose.com/wong-jack-man-interview.
199 "I don't think so": Polly, *Bruce Lee: A Life*, p. 535.
200 "they were scaring everyone in the room": Dorgan, "Shaolin Master Wong Jack Man's Last Interview."
200 punching the back of Wong's head: Interview with Barney Scollan, Mar. 15, 2024.
200 buckled him: Polly, *Bruce Lee: A Life*, p. 156; Charles Russo, *Striking Distance: Bruce Lee and the Dawn of Martial Arts in America* (University of Nebraska Press, 2016), p. 140. Both these accounts are from David Chin's description of the fight. See also Wing, *Showdown in Oakland*, location 1422.
200 on a step or a floorboard: Wing, *Showdown in Oakland*, location 1465; Polly, *Bruce Lee: A Life*, pp. 156–57; Russo, *Striking Distance*, pp. 140–41.
200 Do you yield?: Interview with Linda Lee Cadwell, May 2, 2023.
200 Linda would say: Interview with Linda Lee Cadwell, May 2, 2023.
200 "not more than seven minutes": Russo, *Striking Distance*, p. 141.
200 "so winded that he could not go on": Dorgan, "Shaolin Master Wong Jack Man's Last Interview"; interview with Michael Dorgan, Oct. 5, 2022.
200 "'Get the fuck out of here!'": Interview with Leo Fong, Mar. 21, 2018.
200 a decisive blow: In 1965, he wrote to James, "The more I think of him to have fought me without getting blasted bad, the more I'm pissed off! If I just took my time, anger screwed me up—that bum is nothing!" Bruce Lee, *Letters of the Dragon: Correspondence 1958–1973*, ed. John Little (Tuttle, 1998), p. 124. He told Dan Inosanto, "I chased him and, like a fool, kept punching his head and back; my fists were already swelling from his hard head. Then I did something I'd never done before: I just put my arm round his neck and knocked him on his ass. I kept whacking him as he lay on the floor—until he gave up. I was so tired I could hardly punch him." Bruce Thomas, *Bruce Lee: Fighting Spirit* (Blue Snake Books, 1994), p. 63.
201 "That was the revelation": Interview with Linda Lee Cadwell, May 2, 2023.
201 "The mood was sullen": Russo, *Striking Distance*, p. 141.
201 "they set him up": Interview with Ben Der, Jan. 27, 2022.
201 "I would tell people it was a draw": Russo, *Striking Distance*, p. 143.
201 Wong agreed: In 2017, Wong told Dorgan, "Before we left, Bruce Lee asked me not to discuss the fight with anyone and I agreed. But later he bragged to people that he had won, which is why I then issued a public challenge on the front page of a local Chinese newspaper, inviting him to fight me in an open arena filled with witnesses. He did not respond." Dorgan, "Shaolin Master Wong Jack Man's Last Interview."
201 Jin Yong: Later he would champion Bruce's sister-in-law, Eunice Lam, whose columns in the paper sealed her reputation as a glamorous but world-weary celebrity.
201 "the shadow follows the form": Wing, *Showdown in Oakland*, location 1678.
201 "in the last encounter": Wing, *Showdown in Oakland*, location 1684. Wing credits Gordon Lew for the translations.
202 "were bursting green": Wing, *Showdown in Oakland*, location 1669. Translated by Gordon Lew. "National art" is the translation for *guoshu*, a common Mandarin Chinese term for the Chinese fighting arts, what Cantonese called *gung fu*, dating back at least to the Jing Wu era.

202 brothers in the art: Wing, *Showdown in Oakland*, location 1596.

202 not make enemies: Wing, *Showdown in Oakland*, location 1596.

202 shaking in his boots: Robert Clouse, *Bruce Lee: The Biography* (Unique Publications, 1988), p. 59.

202 "two sheets of paper as proof": It may be possible that these papers were David Chin's letters. Wing, *Showdown in Oakland*, location 1727. Translated by Gordon Lew.

203 "not even in the area": Wing, *Showdown in Oakland*, location 1738. Translated by Gordon Lew.

203 none other than David Chin: Wing. *Showdown in Oakland*, location 1800. Translated by Gordon Lew.

203 "any injuries or hurt feelings": Wing, *Showdown in Oakland*, location 1822.

203 and attacked: Wing, *Showdown in Oakland*, location 1897. Translated by Gordon Lew.

203 "as the beginning": Wing, *Showdown in Oakland*, location 1897.

203 "with their own eyes": Wing, *Showdown in Oakland*, location 1904.

203 there were Chinese: Russo, *Striking Distance*, pp. 146–48.

204 Linda cited the experience of Al Dacascos: Linda Lee, *Bruce Lee: The Man Only I Knew* (Warner Paperback Library, 1975), pp. 72, 74. Al Dacascos describes the encounter in his autobiography, *Legacy: Through the Eyes of the Warrior* (Kaizen Quest Publishing, 2016), pp. 47–48. No fight ever ensued, as the *gung fu* men left after learning of his deep Hawai'i connections to Ming Lum and Adriano Emperado.

204 If a scroll or a threat had been real: John Little has speculated that Bing Chan, a student of Lau Bun, had inserted an ultimatum into either or both of the letters to honor his master's wishes. The theory presumes a generalissimo's shot-calling power that the seventy-five-year-old Lau likely could not have possessed in 1964, three years before his death, amid the major cultural and demographic changes going on in Chinatown in the mid-sixties. See John Little, *Wrath of the Dragon: The Real Fights of Bruce Lee* (ECW, 2023), p. 100.

204 enforce such an edict or how: Interview with Linda Lee Cadwell, May 2, 2023. Since her 1975 memoir, she has been consistent on this point.

204 They maintained that nothing of the sort: Wing, *Showdown in Oakland*, locations 940, 945.

204 some of Bruce's closest friends agreed: Russo, *Striking Distance*, p. 146.

204 "gossipy small-town politics": Interview with Leo Fong, Mar. 21, 2018. Leo Fong added that when he was studying in Chinatown from 1960 to 1962, he met a number of non-Chinese who were studying under Lau Bun and T. Y. Wong—including Al Novak, Bob Baker, David Cox, and the Macias brothers.

204 Al Dacascos himself believed: Dacascos, *Legacy*, pp. 48, 79.

205 "wound down in unison": Russo, *Striking Distance*, p. 151. It would also be a mistake to attribute this widespread change to Bruce Lee's performance in a secret—if later sensationalized—fight. Even after the Long Beach event, Bruce was still a relative unknown in the States, and certainly during his lifetime never commanded such fealty—if anyone ever even could in the notoriously fractious *gung fu* world.

205 "if you did that against Wong Jack Man": Interview with Leo Fong, Mar. 21, 2018. See also his interview with Paul Bax, *Disciples of the Dragon: Reflections from the Students of Bruce Lee* (Outskirts Press, 2008), p. 126.

206 "like a linebacker cutting off a runner": Interview with Leo Fong, Mar. 21, 2018.

206 "Wait till I assemble everything": Taky Kimura, *Regards from the Dragon: Seattle*, rev. ed., compiled by David Tadman (Empire Books, 2009), pp. 82–85. Undated, but likely late 1965 or early 1966.

206 "scare hell out of them": Bruce Lee, *Letters of the Dragon*, p. 107.

206 "phony demonstration": Dorgan, "Shaolin Master Wong Jack Man's Last Interview." Bruce's full DayTimer entry for Saturday, Apr. 6, 1968, reads: "Flight 441 Leave: 4:55pm Arrive: 5:40pm 7:00pm—Civic Auditorium, San Francisco—phony demonstration (James, Ted, Mike)." Courtesy of the Bruce Lee Family Archive.

206 He quipped: Interview with Harvey Dong, Dec. 21, 2023.

206 "not only as a loser but a villain": Dorgan, "Bruce Lee's Toughest Fight," *Official Karate*, July 1980. Accessible at Hunyuan Martial Arts Academy of San Jose, taichisanjose.com/articles-bruce-lee-toughest-fight.

207 "If I had to do it over, I wouldn't": Dorgan, "Bruce Lee's Toughest Fight."

Book II: Mirror

209 "I'm Asian American": Ken Chen, "Corky Lee and the Work of Seeing." N+1. January 25, 2003: www.nplusonemag.com/online-only/online-only/corky-lee-and-the-work-of-seeing/

Part VII: Broken Mirrors, 1966–1967

211 "You are minor character": Jill Lepore, "Chan, The Man." *The New Yorker*. August 2, 2010. www.newyorker.com/magazine/2010/08/09/chan-the-man.

Chapter 24: The Screen Test

212 one in two hundred Americans: "The Rise of Asian Americans (2012)" AAPIData website. Posted April 25, 2024. aapidata.com/issue-focus/the-rise-of-asian-americans-2012/. Data for US Census found in U.S. Department of Commerce, Bureau of the Census. *Current Population Reports: Population Estimates*. Series P-25, No, 323. January 14, 1966. www2.census.gov/library/publications/1966/demographics/P25-323.pdf

212 "it was an accident": Mike Plane (Mito Uyehara), "Super Star Bruce Lee: An Acclaimed Phenomenon," in Editors of *Black Belt* magazine, eds., *The Legendary Bruce Lee* (Ohara Publications, 1986), p. 71.

212 "the 'role of a lifetime'": Stanley Fish, "Just Published: Minutiae Without Meaning," *New York Times*, Sept. 7, 1999.

213 "here I am, a Chinese": Alex Ben Block, "Bruce Lee's Last Interview." *Martial Arts Legends*, December 1995, p. 23.

213 On Friday, February 5, 1965: William Dozier letter to Bruce Lee, Jan. 25, 1965, courtesy William Dozier Archives at the University of Wyoming American Heritage Center.

213 "I just knew it was going to be a boy!": Interview with Helen Hendricks, partial article recovered from archive, undated, likely 1966.

213 "blond, gray-eyed Chinaman": Linda Lee, *The Bruce Lee Story* (Ohara Publications, 1989), p. 71; Flora Rand, "I Want My Son to Be a Mixed-Up Kid!," *TV Radio Mirror*, Nov. 1966. Reprinted in John Little, ed., *Bruce Lee: Words of the Dragon, Interviews, 1958–1973* (Tuttle, 1997), p. 48.

214 stepping into his crime-solving shoes: "Lorenzo Semple. Jr. Interview, Part 1 of 3—EmmyTVLegends .org," interview by Lee Goldberg, Television Academy Foundation, Feb. 4, 2011, interviews.televisionacademy .com/interviews/lorenzo-semple-jr?clip=1#interview-clips. See video at youtube.com/watch?v=-R8BST_TZ uU&t=16s. Bruce also discussed this in his appearance on *The Pierre Berton Show*, Canadian Broadcasting Corporation, 1971.

214 "a Chinese James Bond": Bruce Lee, *Letters of the Dragon: Correspondence 1958–1973*, ed. John Little (Tuttle, 1998), p. 54; *Pierre Berton Show*.

214 shoot the audition: Bruce Lee letter to William Dozier, Feb. 21, 1965, William Dozier Archives.

215 "We are not like that": Edward Sakamoto, "Anna May Wong and the Dragon-Lady Syndrome," *Los Angeles Times*, July 12, 1987.

215 "Keep California White": Brian Niiya, "James D. Phelan," *Densho Encyclopedia*, updated Aug. 28, 2013, encyclopedia.densho.org/James_D._Phelan/.

215 the Production Code: Motion Picture Production Code, productioncode.dhwritings.com/multipleframes _productioncode.php.

215 what is and is not *acceptable*: I am indebted to Rashad Robinson for this distinction and insight. See Rashad Robinson, "Changing Our Narrative About Narrative," Othering and Belonging Institute, Apr. 18. 2018, belonging.berkeley.edu/changing-about-narrative.

215 "dying a thousand deaths" on-screen: "Milestones," *Time*, Feb. 10, 1961, content.time.com/time/subscriber /printout/0,8816,872153,00.html.

216 preserve the fictions of whiteness: Arthur Dong's essential documentary and book, *Hollywood Chinese*, reproduces industry magazine articles featuring extensive makeup instructions to create yellowface. Arthur Dong, *Hollywood Chinese: The Chinese in American Feature Films* (Angel City Press, 2019), pp. 92–98.

216 did "not seem beautiful enough": Graham Russell Gao Hodges, *Anna May Wong: From Laundryman's Daughter to Hollywood Legend* (Palgrave Macmillan, 2004), pp. 153–54; Katie Gee Salisbury, *Not Your China Doll: The Wild and Shimmering Life of Anna May Wong* (Dutton, 2024), p. 250. She was not the only one who seemed too Oriental for Hollywood. Hodges writes, "In his reports on tests for Mary Wong, Keye Luke, and other Chinese actors, [associate producer and casting exec Albert] Lewin argued that, despite their ethnicity, they did not fit his conception of what Chinese people looked like."

216 as beneath her: Salisbury, *Not Your China Doll*, p. 256. See also Hodges, *Anna May Wong*, pp. 152–54. Hodges believes that Anna May Wong was a victim of the Hays Code (the Motion Picture Production Code), which banned sexual miscegenation, meaning that even if a white lead was playing a role in Blackface or Yellowface, a person of color could not play their lover or spouse.

216 an imperturbable cool: Hodges, *Anna May Wong*, p. 163. Besides Hodges's book, this section benefits from the flowering of many excellent book-length biographies and studies on Anna May Wong, including Yunte Huang, *Daughter of the Dragon: Anna May Wong's Rendezvous with American History* (Liveright, 2023); Anthony B. Chan, *Perpetually Cool: The Many Lives of Anna May Wong* (Scarecrow Press, 2007); Salisbury, *Not Your China Doll*; and Shirley Jennifer Lim, *Anna May Wong: Performing the Modern* (Temple University Press, 2019).

216 "the screen's foremost Oriental villainess": "Milestones," *Time*, Feb. 10, 1961.

217 "a trend for exotic people": Brian Jamieson, dir., *To Whom It May Concern: Ka-Shen's Journey*, documentary (Redwind Productions, 2009).

217 "Uh, Miss Kwan": Jamieson, *To Whom It May Concern*.

218 climb to proper assimilation: "Success Story of One Minority in the U.S," *U.S. News and World Report*, Dec. 26,1966, pp. 73–78; Robert G. Lee, *Orientals: Asian Americans in Popular Culture* (Temple University Press, 1999), p. 151.

218 could not stay in whites-only hotels: Interview with Nancy Kwan, Apr. 21, 2023.

218 "After [*Flower Drum Song*]": Arthur Dong, dir., *Hollywood Chinese*, documentary (Deep Focus Productions, 2007).

218 "worse than the actresses": Interview with Nancy Kwan, Apr. 21, 2023.

219 "the yellow peril incarnate in one man": Sax Rohmer, *The Mystery of Dr. Fu Manchu* (Methuen Publishing, 1913, reprint Jarrold & Sons, 1929) p. 13. First serialized in 1911, it would be published as a book in 1913. The author told an interviewer, "In ancient Saxon, 'sax' means 'blade,' 'rohmer' equals 'roamer.'" Cay Van Ash and Elizabeth Sax Rohmer, *Master of Villainy: A Biography of Sax Rohmer* (Bowling Green University Popular Press, 1972), p. 39.

219 an Asian invasion from all directions: John Kuo Wei Tchen and Dylan Yeats, "Introduction: Yellow Peril Incarnate," in John Kuo Wei Tchen and Dylan Yeats, eds., *Yellow Peril! An Archive of Anti-Asian Fear* (Verso, 2014), pp. 11–14.

219 no one would speak to him: Christopher Frayling, *The Yellow Peril: Dr. Fu Manchu & The Rise of Chinaphobia* (Thames & Hudson, 2014) pp. 66–67.

219 "But that is a different matter": Van Ash and Rohmer, *Master of Villainy*, pp. 72–73.

220 "outwit the Orientals": Norman Sklarewitz, "The New Bad Guys: Orientals Take Over as TV, Film Villains," *Wall Street Journal*, Oct. 12, 1966.

220 "I think about it all the time, okay?": Dong, *Hollywood Chinese*, p. 53.

221 "the light dainty steps of a woman": Earl Derr Biggers, *The House Without a Key* (Bobbs-Merrill, 1925), p. 76.

221 "knew very little about Hawai'i": Jill Lepore, *The Story of America: Essays on Origins* (Princeton University Press, 2012), p. 269.

221 "a correct portrayal of the race": Barbara Gregorich, "Earl Derr Biggers," *Harvard Magazine*, Mar. 1, 2000, harvardmagazine.com/2000/03/earl-derr-biggers-html.

221 "fortune-cookie English": Elaine Kim, "Preface," in *Charlie Chan Is Dead: An Anthology of Contemporary Asian American Fiction*, ed. Jessica Hagedorn (Penguin, 1993), p. xiii.

221 "Tongue often hang man": See Yunte Huang, "Appendix I: A List of Charlie Chanisms," *Charlie Chan: The Untold Story of the Honorable Detective and His Rendezvous with American History* (Norton, 2010); "Aphorisms: The Collected Sayings of Charlie Chan," Charlie Chan Family Home, charliechan.org/the-aphorisms/.

221 Charlie's second-generation ABC sons: Dong, *Hollywood Chinese*, p. 64.

222 "success stories": Robert G. Lee, *Orientals*, pp. 149–50, citing original articles from 1966; "Success Story of One Minority in the U.S," *U.S. News and World Report*; William Peterson, "Success Story: Japanese-American Style," *New York Times Magazine*, Jan. 9, 1966.

222 "There is racist hate and racist love": Frank Chin and Jeffery Paul Chan, "Racist Love," in Richard Kostelanetz, ed., *Seeing Through Shuck* (Ballantine Books, 1972), p. 65.

222 "A white man teaches us how to be Chinese": Victor G. Nee and Bret de Bary Nee, *Longtime Californ': A Documentary Study of an American Chinatown* (1972; repr. ed., Stanford University Press, 1986), p. 385.

223 "play exactly what he is": Frank Chin, "Keye Luke Interview on His Career in the Motion Picture Industry," part 1, Apr. 16, 1971, California Revealed, californiarevealed.org/do/7edbef37-6dbe-4923-9cf9-25966e03f0fb. But Luke also insisted that Warner Oland had been "a remarkable man, a complete artist. He studied Chinese philosophy, he took trips to China, collected things and brought them back, and he practiced calligraphy."

223 "a series of coincidences": Frank Chin, "Keye Luke Interview."

224 from stage left toward Bruce: The *I Am Bruce Lee* video also identifies the assistant director as George Trendle, the creator of *The Green Hornet*. Matthew Polly does not believe this is him, and it makes no sense that Trendle would have been the assistant director on an audition for *Number One Son*, which was not even his property. Polly, *Bruce Lee: A Life* (Simon & Schuster, 2018), p. 536.

Chapter 25: Number One

227 "Bruce had this idea": Interview with Linda Lee Cadwell, May 2, 2023.

227 "'How could you have done this?'": Robert Clouse, *Bruce Lee: The Biography* (Unique Publications, 1988), p. 62.

227 "To Chinese": Robert Lee as told to Tony Page, "My Brother, Bruce: Reminiscences by Robert Lee," *Fighting Stars*, Aug. 1983, pp. 45-46.

227 "There is no hurry about it": William Dozier letter to Bruce Lee, Feb. 17, 1965, courtesy William Dozier Archives at the University of Wyoming American Heritage Center.

228 "in his early twenties": William Dozier, "You Can't Tell the Players Without a Program: A Hollywood Glossary" (unpublished, undated, likely 1970s), p. iii, William Dozier Archives.

228 "pure escapism" and "unreality": William Dozier interview with Fletcher Markle, *Telescope*, CBC, 1966, available online as "Batman and William Dozier," youtube.com/watch?v=rkvR4PGqBhA.

228 "a slam-bang one-hour action-adventure series": "Number One Son: A New One Hour Television Series. Presentation by Lorenzo Semple, Jr." (undated, likely 1965), p. 3. Courtesy of the Bruce Lee Family Archive.

228 "bouncing around with a pigtail": Maxwell Pollard, "In Kato's Gung-Fu, Action Is Instant," *Black Belt*, Nov. 1967, p. 14. Reprinted in Editors of *Black Belt* magazine, eds., *The Legendary Bruce Lee* (Ohara Publications, 1986), p. 41.

229 "he moves cool": "Number One Son," pp. 5, 7, 9, 15.

229 "race problem in any episode": "Number One Son," pp. 4, 15.

229 "involving mind control and murder": Daryl Joji Maeda, *Like Water: A Cultural History of Bruce Lee* (New York University Press, 2022), p. 157.

229 "NUMBER ONE SON of the fabled Charlie Chan": "Number One Son," p. 16.

229 "believe that it could happen": William Dozier letter to Lorenzo Semple, Apr. 20, 1965, William Dozier Archives.

229 "Gung Fu fighting techniques": Bruce Lee Letter to William Dozer, Apr. 28, 1965, William Dozier Archives.

230 "He was kind of fried": Interview with Lanston Chinn, July 7, 2022.

230 "I've ever seen!": Linda Lee, *Bruce Lee: The Man Only I Knew* (Warner Paperback Library, 1975), pp. 31-32.

230 "She just liked Bruce": Interview with Linda Lee Cadwell, May 2, 2023.

230 "the number-one spoiled child": Clouse, *Bruce Lee: The Biography*, p. 65.

230 "Brandon was hell on wheels": Interview with Linda Lee Cadwell, May 2, 2023.

230 from Uncle Siu Hon-Sang: Wong Shun Leung, *Bruce Lee: His Unknowns in Martial Arts Learning* (Hong Kong: Bruce Lee Jeet-kune-do Club, 1977), pp. 36-37.

230 "no limit limitation": Bruce Lee, *Letters of the Dragon: Correspondence 1958–1973*, ed. John Little (Tuttle, 1998), p. 55.

231 "what they were saying": Interview with Linda Lee Cadwell, May 2, 2023.

231 "speak English clearly": William Dozier letter to Bruce Lee, July 2, 1965.

232 "Thank you!": Bruce Lee letter to William Dozier, August 10, 1965.

232 "Bill got a call": Lorenzo Semple, Jr., "Requiem for a Cheeky 'Batman,'" *Variety*, July 9, 2008, variety.com/2008/film/markets-festivals/requiem-for-a-cheeky-batman-1117988712/.

232 "the metaphor of life as theater": Susan Sontag, "Notes on 'Camp,'" *Partisan Review* 31, no. 4 (Fall 1964), monoskop.org/images/5/59/Sontag_Susan_1964_Notes_on_Camp.pdf.

232 "it would be funny": William Dozier interview with Fletcher Markle, *Telescope*.

233 *Superman* and *Dick Tracy* were already off the table: Joel Eisner, *The Official Batman Batbook* (Titan Books, 1987), pp. 4-5.

233 "launching pad for you": William Dozier letter to Bruce Lee, Nov. 23, 1965, William Dozier Archives.

233 an article in *Life* magazine: Taky Kimura, *Regards from the Dragon: Seattle*, rev. ed., compiled by David Tadman (Empire Books, 2009), pp. 82-83.

233 numbered twenty million, mostly kids: "This Day In History—January 30—'The Lone Ranger' Debuts on Detroit Radio," History.com, updated Jan. 27, 2021, history.com/this-day-in-history/the-lone-ranger-debuts-on-detroit-radio.

234 "unless they were stopped": Martin Grams and Terry Salomonson, *The Green Hornet: A History of Radio, Motion Pictures, Comics, and Television* (OTR Publishing, 2010), p. 10.

234 by confronting evildoers: The TV version of the Green Hornet softened Britt Reid's playboy status—Trendle wanted him to be more of a workingman. But it also added a twist. Crime bosses had framed his muckraking father for murder, and he had died broken spirited in prison. Just as Bruce Wayne is avenging the murder of his parents, Reid is avenging his father's death. From "William Dozier's Plea for Renewal," in Grams and Salomonson, *The Green Hornet*, p. 777.

234 "a custom in some parts of the Orient": Grams and Salomonson, *The Green Hornet*, p. 74.

494 NOTES

234 "usual Japanese immobility and austereness": Grams and Salomonson, *The Green Hornet*, p. 135.

234 changed Kato to a Filipino: Grams and Salomonson, *The Green Hornet*, pp. 78, 372.

235 "an Oriental": Grams and Salomonson, *The Green Hornet*, p. 318. See also Maeda, *Like Water*, p. 166.

235 a "good for nothing sucker": Kimura, *Regards from the Dragon*, pp. 64–67.

Chapter 26: The Sum of All Projections

236 "a multimillion-dollar business potential": "TV: Zap! Pow! It's Batman and Robin," *New York Times*, Jan. 13, 1966.

236 "a human-being Indian on television": Leroy F. Aarons, "Batman's Boy Has a Black Belt Rival," *Washington Post*, Aug. 30, 1966. Reprinted in John Little, ed., *Bruce Lee: Words of the Dragon, Interviews, 1958–1973* (Tuttle, 1997), p. 60.

237 with his chop: William Dozier letter to Bruce Lee, Feb. 14, 1966, courtesy William Dozier Archives at the University of Wyoming American Heritage Center.

237 But his pay stub would never reflect it: William Dozier, "TV Estimate. Series: The Green Hornet. Production No. #9800. Series Budget," compiled May 26, 1966, revised July 13, 1966, p. 1A. From the William Dozier Archives.

Also see Martin Grams and Terry Salomonson, *The Green Hornet: A History of Radio, Motion Pictures, Comics, and Television* (OTR Publishing, 2010), pp. 726–50.

237 "this job is most satisfying": Bruce Lee, *Letters of the Dragon: Correspondence 1958–1973*, ed. John Little (Tuttle, 1998), p. 53

237 "the largest privately built apartment development west of Chicago": "712-Unit Project Finished on Coast," *New York Times*, Sept. 23, 1962, p. 18R.

237 "electronic huge elevators": Bruce Lee, *Letters of the Dragon*, pp. 70–71.

237 The Lees settled into a twenty-third-floor apartment: Interview with Linda Lee Cadwell, May 2, 2023; "The higher, the more expensive": Bruce Lee, *Letters of the Dragon*, p. 71.

237 lived on the twelfth floor: Burt Ward with Stanley Ralph Ross, *Boy Wonder: My Life In Tights* (Logical Figments Books, 1995), p. 57.

237 "was his hair": Interview with Peter Chin, Dec. 15, 2023; Peter Chin, *The Last Disciple: My Memoirs with Bruce Lee* (Ignite Press, 2024), p. 82.

237 Paul Newman, James Garner, and Vic Damone: Bruce Lee, *Letters of the Dragon*, pp. 68–69.

238 to Steve McQueen: Marc Eliot, *Steve McQueen: A Biography* (Three Rivers Press, 2011), p. 148. Steve McQueen had just shot a film in Japan called *The Sand Pebbles*. Bruce had briefly been considered for a role that went to Mako, whose performance was honored with Oscar and Golden Globe nominations.

238 Bruce told Taky: Bruce Lee, *Letters of the Dragon*, p. 73; Taky Kimura, *Regards from the Dragon: Seattle*, rev. ed., compiled by David Tadman (Empire Books, 2009), pp. 60–61.

238 "how low we had been": Linda Lee, *Bruce Lee: The Man Only I Knew* (Warner Paperback Library, 1975), p. 95.

238 "Simplicity is the cherished quality": Jon Thurber, "Jeff Corey, 88, Blacklist Led Actor to Teaching," *Los Angeles Times*, Aug. 19, 2002.

238 "This cat is very Zen-ish": Kimura, *Regards from the Dragon*, pp. 60–61.

238 "as The Weapon": Bill Irvin, "Hornet's Sidekick a Blur on Film," *Chicago American*, Aug. 23, 1966, in Little, ed., *Bruce Lee: Words of the Dragon*, p. 67. Caps in original.

238 "Simplicity—to express": Letter from Bruce Lee to William Dozier, June 21, 1966. Excerpt reprinted in Bruce Lee, *Letters of the Dragon*, pp. 77–78.

239 "Carry on": Letter from William Dozier to Bruce Lee, June 23, 1966, William Dozier Archive.

239 understand his Hong Kong accent: Van Williams interview included in *Game of Death: Alternative Version*, extras (Arrow Video, 2023).

239 "he was hard to understand": Van Williams interview, *Game of Death*.

239 "not exactly striving for reality": Peter Bart, "More Chartreuse Than Campy," *New York Times*, May 8, 1966. Also published as Peter Bart, "Here Comes The Green Hornet," *Milwaukee Journal*, May 15, 1966.

240 "a nice guy": Van Williams interview, *Game of Death*.

240 "I can tell the producers": P. M. Clepper, "Dearly Simple Fighter," *Saint Paul Dispatch*, July 18, 1966. Reprinted in Little, ed., *Bruce Lee: Words of the Dragon*, pp. 64–66.

240 "who can say 'Britt Reid'": Clepper, "Dearly Simple Fighter." He would repeat this joke for years. See Little, ed., *Bruce Lee: Words from the Dragon*, p. 151.

240 "but Fu Manchu": Willard Clopton, Jr., "Kato Likes Puns, Preys on Words," *Washington Post*, May 1967 (day unknown). Reprinted in Little, ed., *Bruce Lee: Words of the Dragon*, p. 82. The Asian American film critic Irving Paik dated this joke back to the 1930s, when the Fu Manchu radio serials were in their heyday. Irving Paik, "That Oriental Feeling," in Amy Tachiki, Eddie Wong, Franklin Odo with Buck Wong, eds., *Roots: An Asian American Reader* (UCLA Asian American Studies Center, 1971), pp. 30–31.

240 "can't all be Wong": Clopton, "Kato Likes Puns, Preys on Words"; Yunte Huang, *Daughter of the Dragon: Anna May Wong's Rendezvous with American History* (Liveright, 2023), p. 307.

240 "understanding what was going on": Clepper, "Kato Likes Puns, Preys on Words." He told another journalist, "My father was a star of Chinese opera, but Chinese opera is about as tough on the American ear as anything ever heard. I'd rather listen to jazz." "Likes Jazz," *Reno Evening Gazette and Nevada State Journal*, Dec. 17, 1966, p. 8.

241 "the role of Kato": Sara, "Robin's New Love Rival," *TV/Radio Show*, Oct. 1966. Reprinted in Little, ed., *Bruce Lee: Words of the Dragon*, p. 32.

241 certified circulation was four hundred thousand: Estelle Tucker, "Statement of Ownership, Management and Circulation," *TV and Movie Screen*, 1966 (date unknown, likely November or December), p. 72. This statement's "date of filing" is Oct. 1, 1966.

241 "Marriage is a friendship": Fredda Dudley Balling, "Bruce Lee: 'Our Mixed Marriage Brought Us a Miracle of Love!," *TV and Movie Screen*, 1966 (date unknown, likely November or December). Reprinted in Little, ed., *Bruce Lee: Words of the Dragon*, p. 45.

241 "like some women": Flora Rand, "I Want My Son to Be a Mixed-Up Kid!," *TV/Radio Mirror*, Nov. 1966. Reprinted in Little, ed., *Bruce Lee: Words of the Dragon*, p. 48.

241 "instead of *potatoes*": Jane Allen, "What's It REALLY Like to Live a Mixed Marriage!," magazine unknown, undated (likely 1966). This article, along with many others from the period, are included in a scrapbook in the Bruce Lee Family Archive.

241 much bigger than themselves: Jane Allen wrote, "She might well have expected some surprise, if not outright opposition, from the homefront when she introduced Bruce to her folks. But Linda insists there was never any friction in the Emory [sic] household from the moment when Bruce first crossed the threshold to their official engagement some months later. 'My parents really liked him, especially my mother,' she said with a sincerity that is hard to contrive. 'I mean they liked him for *himself*. They didn't think of him as that *Chinese boy*, but that boy, *Bruce Lee*. That didn't take much trying because *anyone* who meets him is immediately sold on him.'" Jane Allen, "What's It REALLY Like to Live a Mixed Marriage!"

241 "the same everywhere": Flora Rand, "I Want My Son to Be a Mixed-Up Kid!"

241 *TV Picture Life*: "Love Knows No Geography," Ibid. Unfortunately the copy in the scrapbook in the Bruce Lee Family Archive does not include any information on the cover date. Based on the accompanying articles included in that physical clipping I surmise that the article may have appeared in a regional edition, perhaps a West Coast version, of *TV Picture Life*, November 1966. In most editions I've seen that are available now on sites such as eBay, it seems that a "bonus section" on *Lost in Space* ran in its place elsewhere. One could speculate that the article was only published in certain regional editions, and further conclude that interracial marriage was still taboo for national print. But I haven't been able to verify the provenance of the article.

241 a delirious kind of fan fiction: Balling, "Love Knows No Geography." See John Little's notes on this article in *Bruce Lee: Words of the Dragon*, pp. 73–75.

241 "explain it": Balling, "Love Knows No Geography."

242 "as I looked around": Ted Thomas, "The Ted Thomas Interview." *Martial Arts Legends*, December 1995, p. 86.

242 He gave *gung fu* seminars: "Gung Fu Topic of Discussions," *Nevada State Journal and Reno Evening Gazette*, Dec. 31, 1966, p. 7.

242 "it was all over": Matthew Polly, *Bruce Lee: A Life* (Simon & Schuster, 2018), p. 186.

243 "'No more of that stuff, Bruce!'": Van Williams interview, *Game of Death*.

243 "hit the man": Gene LeBell in Guy Scutter, dir., *Bruce Lee, Martial Arts Master*, documentary (Merlin Group/Canal, 1993).

243 "not good sportsmanship": John Corcoran interview with Stirling Silliphant, transcript, undated, part 2, pp. 7–8. Courtesy of the Stirling Silliphant Papers at UCLA. Portions of these interview transcripts were published in three parts in *Kick Magazine* from July through Sept. 1980.

243 "That's un-American": Interview with Andre Morgan, May 12, 2023.

243 the white guys guffawed: Polly, *Bruce Lee: A Life*, pp. 187, 242.

244 roared with laughter: LeBell in *Bruce Lee, Martial Arts Master*.

496   NOTES

244 "disrespect" for "American stuntmen": Joe Rogan, "Episode 1675—Quentin Tarantino," *The Joe Rogan Experience*, June 2021.
244 "I don't want to do it anymore": Van Williams interview, *Game of Death*.

Chapter 27: Mirrors and Smoke

245 "Like a blotter on legs": Jack Dempsey, *Championship Fighting: Explosive Punching and Aggressive Defense* (Simon & Schuster, 1950), pp. 15, 17.
245 "something other than to sell merchandise": William Dozier, "You Can't Tell the Players Without a Program: A Hollywood Glossary" (unpublished, undated, likely mid-1970s), p. 80, courtesy William Dozier Archive at the University of Wyoming American Heritage Center.
245 "rugs, and peanut butter!": ABC Merchandising, "The Impact of Merchandising," *Supplement to Modern Retailer*, Oct. 1966. See also "Hornet's Nest," *Newsweek*, July 18, 1966, p. 96.
246 "Tarzan beat us": Taky Kimura, *Regards from the Dragon: Seattle*, rev. ed., compiled by David Tadman (Empire Books, 2009), pp. 90–91.
246 Dozier blamed Trendle for backgrounding Kato: Martin Grams and Terry Salomonson, *The Green Hornet: A History of Radio, Motion Pictures, Comics, and Television* (OTR Publishing, 2010), p. 320.
246 "the one that did all the fighting": Bao Nguyen interview with Jeff Chinn, Sept. 13, 2019.
246 scheduled for the week before the Thanksgiving holiday: Grams and Salomonson, *The Green Hornet*, pp. 734–35.
247 "not be overdone": Grams and Salomonson, *The Green Hornet*, p. 338.
247 Dan Inosanto, who served as: Charles Lucas and Fran Colberg, "Duel to the Death With Bruce Lee!," *Black Belt Magazine's Best of Bruce Lee #2*, 1975, p. 61.
247 The fan mail was telling a clear story: Mito Uyehara, *Bruce Lee: The Incomparable Fighter* (Ohara Publications, 1988), p. 70; Grams and Salomonson, *The Green Hornet*, p. 320.
247 "He stood alone": Interview with Perry Lee, May 5, 2023.
247 "The Cobra from the East": The treatment is dated Oct. 28, 1966. Courtesy of the Bruce Lee Family Archive.
248 "in his off hours?": Grams and Salomonson, *The Green Hornet*, pp. 777–78.
248 "make use of this opportunity, buddy": Kimura, *Regards from the Dragon*, pp. 86–87.
249 "That makes me look like an idiot": Van Williams interview included in *Game of Death: Alternative Version*, extras (Arrow Video, 2023); John Little, ed., *Bruce Lee: Words of the Dragon, Interviews, 1958–1973* (Tuttle, 1997), pp. 72–73.
249 "We'll see how great": Little, ed., *Bruce Lee: Words of the Dragon*, p. 73.
249 "I couldn't keep a straight face anymore": Uyehara, *Bruce Lee: The Incomparable Fighter*, p. 72.
249 "nice to have you with Twentieth Century-Fox": William Self letter to Bruce Lee, Jan. 17, 1967, Bruce Lee Family Archive. The die had been cast. According to Grams and Salomonson, Dozier had sent a letter to Trendle on January 3 to tell him that ABC was likely canceling the show. Grams and Salomonson, *The Green Hornet*, p. 343.
250 "I couldn't protect myself": Maxwell Pollard, "In Kato's Gung-Fu, Action Is Instant," *Black Belt*, Nov. 1967, p. 14. Reprinted in Editors of *Black Belt* magazine, eds., *The Legendary Bruce Lee* (Ohara Publications, 1986), p. 41.
251 "Chan would be a ski instructor": Willard Clopton, Jr., "Kato Likes Puns, Preys on Words," *Washington Post*, May 1967 (date unknown). Reprinted in Little, ed., *Bruce Lee: Words of the Dragon*, pp. 81–82.

In a letter to Taky Kimura, undated but likely from early 1967, Bruce discussed traveling to Seattle to see him after his appearance in Washington, DC, and wrote, "Also, the good news is that Dozier will probably pick up the option—according to my agent—and Fitzsimon, the vice president is working on a 1 hr. series for me."

251 "to do whatever is necessary to protect himself": *Malcolm X Speaks* (Grove Press, 1965) pp. 49, 68.
251 "one Black soldier ain't coming back": Diane C. Fujino, *Samurai Among Panthers: Richard Aoki on Race, Resistance, and a Paradoxical Life* (University of Minnesota Press, 2012), p. 131.
251 through solidarity work: Harvey C. Dong, "The Origins and Trajectory of Asian American Political Activism in the San Francisco Bay Area, 1968–1978," PhD dissertation in Ethnic Studies, University of California at Berkeley, 2002, pp. 42–43.
251 on his bed beside each other: Interview with Harvey Dong, Dec. 21, 2023.
252 sold them a .357 Magnum: Bobby Seale, *Seize the Time* (Random House, 1970), pp. 72–73, 79–85.
252 "from racist police oppression and brutality": See "The Black Panther Party's Ten-Point Program," ucpress.edu/blog/25139/the-black-panther-partys-ten-point-program/.

252 "That was awesome": Fujino, *Samurai Among Panthers*, p. 135.

252 "before it is too late": Cynthia Deitle Leonardatos, "California's Attempts to Disarm the Black Panthers," *San Diego Law Review* 36, no. 4 (1999), p. 971, digital.sandiego.edu/sdlr/vol36/iss4/3.

253 "learn to defend ourselves": Stephen Shames and Bobby Seale, *Power to the People, The World of the Black Panthers* (Abrams, 2016), p. 51.

253 "we pursue!": Sun Tzu, *The Art of War*, trans. Samuel B. Griffith (Oxford University Press, 1963), p. 51.

253 "specifically our own": Interview with Dan Inosanto, Sept. 26, 2023; quoted in "Introduction," *The Art of War*, trans. Griffith, p. 55.

Grffith cites Mao Zedong, "On Protracted War" (May 1938). A similar quote is also in "Problems of Strategy in China's Revolutionary War" (Dec. 1936). The Little Red Book contains a modification of the same idea from another source: "Now, there are two different attitudes towards learning from others. One is the dogmatic attitude of transplanting everything, whether or not it is suited to our conditions. This is no good. The other attitude is to use our heads and learn those things which suit our conditions, that is, to absorb whatever experience is useful to us. That is the attitude we should adopt." Quoted from Mao Zedong, "On the Correct Handling of Contradictions Among the People" (Feb. 27, 1957). In Mao Zedong, *Quotations from Chairman Mao Tse-Tung* (People's Press, 1966, Reprint, 2019, Marxists Internet Archive), p. 140.

Part VIII: Warrior State of Mind, 1967–1969

255 "All art is martial art": Frank Chin, "Come All Ye Asian American Writers of the Real and the Fake," in *The Big Aiiieeeee! An Anthology of Chinese American and Japanese American Literature*. Edited by Jeffery Paul Chan, Frank Chin, Lawson Fusao Inada, and Shawn Wong. Meridian Books, 1991. p. 35.

Chapter 28: The Names, Part 1

256 "'the intercepting fist style'": Dan Inosanto and George Foon, *Jeet Kune Do: The Art and Philosophy of Bruce Lee* (Know Now Publishing, 1980), pp. 66–67.

256 "'the Way or the ultimate reality'": Maxwell Pollard, "In Kato's Gung-Fu, Action Is Instant," *Black Belt*, Nov. 1967, p. 14. Reprinted in Editors of *Black Belt* magazine, eds., *The Legendary Bruce Lee* (Ohara Publications, 1986), p. 41.

256 "when the enemy does not move": Interview with Peter Chin, Dec. 15, 2023. Peter explained that Bruce was fond of the *Romance of the Three Kingdoms* and the wisdom of the military strategist Zhuge Liang, who is often credited with this saying. My thanks to Sze K. Chan.

256 "strike second but land first": For more on the martial ideas herein, see Barry Allen, *Striking Beauty: A Philosophical Look at the Asian Martial Arts* (Columbia University Press, 2015), pp. 21–23. Also see Ryan Ohl, *Jun Fan Gung Fu: Origins & Evolution* (self-published, 2023), p. 74.

As an aside, the homonymic *Jit Kune*—"Immediate fist" (即拳)—was the name of a fundamental Northern Shaolin form, one of the first he had learned from Siu Hon-Sang before leaving Hong Kong. They may sound similar, but there is no direct relationship between the two.

256 both at the same time: Interview with Peter Chin, Dec. 15, 2023.

257 licensed Kung Fu Kato schools: Jhoon Rhee in *Bruce Lee 1940–1973* (Ohara Publications, 1974), p. 57; Inosanto and Foon, *Jeet Kune Do*, p. 50.

257 managing satellites across the country: George Dillman in Paul Bax, *Disciples of the Dragon: Reflections from the Students of Bruce Lee* (Outskirts Press, 2008), pp. 209–10.

257 he didn't want to prostitute himself: Interview with Peter Chin, Dec. 11, 2024.

257 "'Kato—Mothers, bring your little boys'": J. D. Bethea, "Don't Call It Karate—It's Martial Art," *Washington Star*, Aug. 16, 1970. Reprinted in John Little, ed., *Bruce Lee: Words of the Dragon, Interviews, 1958–1973* (Tuttle, 1997), p. 97.

257 "No Afilliation With": Tommy Gong, *The Evolution of a Martial Artist* (Bruce Lee Enterprises, 2013), pp. 97, 163.

257 earned advanced belts with Ed Parker: Bremer said they jokingly called themselves "the Turncoats." Jose M. Fraguas, *Jeet Kune Do Conversations* (Unique Publications, 2001), p. 22.

257 "There were only twelve of us": Richard Bustillo, compiled by John Little, "The Wisdom of Bruce Lee: Training in the Modern World"; *"Knowing Is Not Enough": The Official Newsletter of Jun Fan Jeet Kune Do*. Vol. 2, No. 3. Fall 1998. p. 3.

258 "quit after a few weeks": Dan Lee in "Bruce Lee as Seen Through the Eyes of Students of Jeet Kune Do," in *Bruce Lee 1940–1973*, pp. 48–9.

258 "wearing two chest protectors": Steve Golden in Bax, *Disciples of the Dragon*, p. 189.

258 "a kick is just a kick": Bruce Lee, *Tao of Jeet Kune Do*, ed. Gilbert Johnson (Ohara Publications, 1975), p. 70; Alan Watts, *The Way of Zen* (Pantheon, 1957), p. 144; D. T. Suzuki, *Essays in Zen Buddhism* (Rider &

Company/Buddhist Society of London, 1950), p. 24. Watts translates Ching-yüan's words this way: "Before I had studied Zen for thirty years, I saw mountains as mountains, and waters as waters. When I arrived at a more intimate knowledge, I came to the point where I saw that mountains are not mountains, and waters are not waters. But now that I have got its very substance I am at rest. For it's just that I see mountains once again as mountains, and waters once again as waters."

258 "three stages of cultivation": He seems to be influenced here again by D. T. Suzuki, who vividly relates this notion of the stages of cultivation to a beginner swordsman in his first chapter on "Zen and Swordsmanship" in *Zen and Japanese Culture* (Bollingen Foundation/Princeton University Press, 1959; repr. ed., 1970), pp. 99–100.

258 "it becomes 'It hits!'": Gong, *The Evolution of a Martial Artist*, pp. 157–58.

With his "it hits" note, Bruce is paraphrasing from Eugen Herrigel, *Zen in the Art of Archery* (Pantheon, 1953), pp. 51–53, and D. T. Suzuki, *Zen and Japanese Culture*, pp. 99–100. Of course, this idea then appears in *Enter The Dragon*.

259 "a ranking system of no ranking": Pollard, "In Kato's Gung-Fu, Action Is Instant."

259 "When they would spar": Interview with Diana Lee Inosanto, Nov. 18, 2021.

259 "starts hauling people": Interview with Dan Inosanto, Sept. 26, 2023.

260 "Those years it's between Wing Chun and Choy Li Fut": Interview with Peter Chin, Dec. 15, 2023.

261 "So I went there": Shannon Lee interview with Ted Wong, Sept. 4, 2002, courtesy of Shannon Lee and the Bruce Lee Family Archive.

261 "You need to work": "The 'Knowing Is Not Enough' Interview: Ted Wong," *"Knowing Is Not Enough": The Official Newsletter of Jun Fan Jeet Kune Do* 1, no. 3 (Fall 1997), pp. 4, 7.

262 He was in a neck brace for weeks: Interview with Mito Uyehara, Sept. 20, 2023.

262 hit from behind by a car: Gong, *The Evolution of a Martial Artist*, p. 105.

Chapter 29: The Names, Part 2

263 "the Oriental world is going Western": "McLuhan's War," *Time*, Dec. 11, 1972, content.time.com/time/subscriber/printout/0,8816,878088,00.html; P. Mansaram, "An Unpublished Interview with Marshall McLuhan," *McLuhan Galaxy* blog, interview from 1967, posted Jan. 7, 2013, mcluhangalaxy.wordpress.com/2013/01/07/an-unpublished-interview-with-marshall-mcluhan-1967-by-artist-p-mansaram/.

263 "not even the Orientals": Duke Ellington, spoken introduction, *The Afro-Eurasian Eclipse* (Fantasy Records, 1971).

263 They were younger: Japanese, who were then the largest Asian ethnic group in the US, tended to be a little older—at a median age of 32.3—while Chinese and Filipinos were well below the US median of 28.1, at 26.6 and 26.2 years of age, respectively. US Department of Commerce, Bureau of the Census, *Subject Reports: Japanese, Chinese, and Filipinos in the United States* (US Government Printing Office, 1973).

264 "what is the movies?": Maxine Hong Kingston, *The Woman Warrior: Memoirs of a Girlhood Among Ghosts* (Alfred A. Knopf, 1976; repr. ed., Vintage International, 1989), pp. 7–8.

264 form a party caucus: Interview with Victoria "Vicci" Wong, Jan. 3, 2024.

264 that supported conscientious objectors: Interview with Victoria "Vicci" Wong, Jan. 3, 2024; interview with Lillian Fabros Bando, Jan. 17, 2024.

265 "You have to find your own group": Interview with Victoria "Vicci" Wong, Jan. 3, 2024.

266 "came out an Asian American": Interview with Victoria "Vicci" Wong, Jan. 3, 2024.

266 "We Asian-Americans believe": "AAPA General Philosophy Statement, June 1968," in "Fact Sheet: Asian-American Political Alliance," flyer, Sept. 17, 1968, courtesy of the University of California at Berkeley Ethnic Studies Library collection.

266 "other people struggling against war": Interview with Jeffrey Thomas Leong, Jan. 10, 2024.

266 there were AAPA chapters at: W. K Quon and V. Wong, "An Understanding of AAPA," undated flyer, likely early 1969. University of California at Berkeley Ethnic Studies Library collection.

266 Similar Asian American organizations: William Wei, *The Asian American Movement* (Temple University Press, 1993), pp. 24, 123, 287.

267 their children could proudly join: Wei, *The Asian American Movement*, pp. 25–26; Karen Ishizuka, *Serve the People* (Verso Books, 2016), pp. 91–94.

267 Asian Council for Equality: Ishizuka, *Serve the People*, pp. 89–91. See also Bob Santos, *Humbows, not Hot Dogs! Memoirs of a Savvy Asian American Activist* (Chin Music Press, 2018).

267 "It seemed like all of us": Ishizuka, *Serve the People*, pp. 72, 75.

267 The idea of the Asian American: See Viet Thanh Nguyen, "Palestine Is in Asia: An Asian American Ar-

gument for Solidarity," *The Nation*, Jan. 29, 2024. Originally presented in his Harvard Norton Lecture, Dec. 5, 2023. Also see Viet Thanh Nguyen, *To Save and to Destroy: Writing as an Other* (Belknap Press, 2025).

267 "a New World Consciousness": Karen Umemoto, "'On Strike! San Francisco State College Strike, 1968–69: The Role of Asian American Students," *Amerasia Journal* 15, no. 1 (1989), p. 15.

268 "the primary stage of yellow consciousness": Amy Uyematsu, "The Emergence of Yellow Power in America," *Gidra*, Oct. 1969, pp. 8, 9, 10.

268 "without fear of death": Larry Kubota, "Yellow Power!: Necessary but Not Sufficient," *Gidra*, Apr. 1969, p. 3.

269 "you take his life": The quote is taken from D. T. Suzuki's germinal chapter on "Zen and the Samurai" in his classic *Zen and Japanese Culture*. Specifically, it is from a note on Yamamoto Tsunemoto's nineteenth-century *bushido* text, *The Hagakure*. Suzuki, *Zen and Japanese Culture*, p. 74.

269 "forget about pride and pain": The full quote is this: "Approach Jeet Kune Do with the idea of mastering the will. Forget about winning and losing; forget about pride and pain. Let your opponent graze your skin and you smash into his flesh; let him smash into your flesh and you fracture his bones; let him fracture your bones and you take his life! Do not be concerned with your escaping safely—lay your life before him!" Bruce Lee, *Tao of Jeet Kune Do*, p. 12; Suzuki, *Zen and Japanese Culture*, pp. 74, 177. Those interested in better understanding Bruce's inspirations should also see James Bishop, *Who Wrote the Tao? The Literary Sourcebook of the Tao of Jeet Kune Do* (Promethean Press, 2022), p. 12.

269 "*simple, direct*, and *non-classical*": Maxwell Pollard, "In Kato's Gung-Fu, Action Is Instant," *Black Belt*, Nov. 1967, p. 14. Reprinted in Editors of *Black Belt* magazine, eds., *The Legendary Bruce Lee* (Ohara Publications, 1986), p. 41.

270 "Bruce's concept was": John Scura, "Bruce Lee—the Instructor," *Fighting Stars*, Spring 1977, p. 29.

270 Bruce told the *Black Belt* editors: "Bruce Lee Talks Back," *Black Belt*, Jan. 1968, p. 25.

270 "It's going to be different in 1970": Interview with Dan Inosanto, Sept. 26, 2023; Pete McCormack, dir., *I Am Bruce Lee*, documentary (Network Entertainment, Bruce Lee Enterprises, and Leeway Media Group in association with Spike TV, 2012).

270 "don't fuss over it": Dan Inosanto and George Foon, *Jeet Kune Do: The Art and Philosophy of Bruce Lee* (Know Now Publishing, 1980), p. 67.

Chapter 30: Stand!

271 "All sophomore and junior years": Kareem Abdul-Jabbar, *Giant Steps: The Autobiography of Kareem Abdul-Jabbar* (Bantam, 1983), p. 165.

271 "There I was": Kareem Abdul-Jabbar and Raymond Obstfeld, *Becoming Kareem: Growing Up On and Off the Court* (Little Brown, 2017), p. 6.

271 "big jungle n——r": Abdul-Jabbar and Obstfeld, *Becoming Kareem*, p. 38.

271 "Right then and there I knew": Lew Alcindor with Jack Olson, "My Story," *Sports Illustrated*, Oct. 1969, p. 95.

272 because of death threats: John Matthew Smith, *The Sons of Westwood: John Wooden, UCLA, and the Dynasty That Changed College Basketball* (University of Illinois Press, 2013), p. 97.

272 "Why should they ask me": Dave Zirin, *A People's History of Sports in the United States* (New Press, 2008), p. 147.

272 for draft evasion: "License for Bout Is Called Illegal," *New York Times*, Feb. 26, 1966.

272 "make a stand against this kind of thing": Zirin, *A People's History of Sports in the United States*, p. 163; Harry Edwards, *The Revolt of the Black Athlete* (Free Press, 1969), p. 53.

272 "Black Hitlers": Edwards, *The Revolt of the Black Athlete*, p. 72; John Matthew Smith, "'It's Not Really My Country': Lew Alcindor and the Revolt of the Black Athlete," *Journal of Sport History* 36, no. 2 (Summer 2009), p. 224.

273 without fouling: Abdul-Jabbar and Obstfeld, *Becoming Kareem*, pp. 245–46.

273 "your entire inner self trained": Abdul-Jabbar, *Giant Steps*, p. 185.

273 "before he could do anything else": Interview with Mito Uyehara, Sept. 20, 2023; Mito Uyehara, *Bruce Lee: The Incomparable Fighter* (Ohara Publications, 1988), pp. 105–11.

273 "got down to business": Abdul-Jabbar and Obstfeld, *Becoming Kareem*, pp. 246–48.

274 "beat a tall guy!": Fiaz Rafiq, *Bruce Lee Conversations: The Life and Legacy of a Legend* (HNL Publishing, 2009), p. 69.

274 punches and kicks on the bag: Rafiq, *Bruce Lee Conversations*, p. 164.

274 "his shin and thigh with a kick": Harold Heffernan, "$500 an Hour Going Rate for Top Tutor on Violence," *Star Press* (Muncie, IN), June 17, 1969, p. 18.

500 NOTES

274 Big Lew could rattle the rim: Interview with Mito Uyehara, Sept. 20, 2023.
274 "staring at his belly button": Interview with Doug Palmer, June 28, 2022.
274 "deal with people and attack him": Abdul-Jabbar, *Giant Steps*, p. 188.
274 "Nothing was for art's sake": John Scura, "The Dragon and the Franchise," *Fighting Stars*, Apr. 1976, pp. 40, 41.
275 "one kick practiced 10,000 times": Abdul-Jabbar and Obstfeld, *Becoming Kareem*, p. 248.
275 "which I could relate to": Abdul-Jabbar, *Giant Steps*, p. 186.
275 "where are we going to move?" Shahan Mufti, *American Caliph: The True Story of a Muslim Mystic, a Hollywood Epic, and the 1977 Siege of Washington, DC* (Farrar, Straus and Giroux, 2022), pp. 71–72; Abdul-Jabbar, *Giant Steps*, pp. 170–71.
275 "I had better things to do": Abdul-Jabbar, *Giant Steps*, p. 171.
275 "but they didn't know me": Abdul-Jabbar, *Giant Steps*, pp. 170, 181. He revealed his name at a June 3, 1971, press conference.
275 "jealous of my privacy": Abdul-Jabbar, *Giant Steps*, p. 183.
276 they often ate in the kitchen: Interview with Peter Chin, Dec. 15, 2023; Rafiq, *Bruce Lee Conversations*, p. 145; interview with Mito Uyehara, Sept. 20, 2023. My thanks to Evan Jackson Leong for first recounting these stories to me.
276 "We both had experienced discrimination": Abdul-Jabbar and Obstfeld, *Becoming Kareem*, p. 249.
276 a "valet to the stars": Bao Nguyen interview with Kareem Abdul-Jabbar, Nov. 3, 2019; Abdul-Jabbar, *Giant Steps*, p. 189.
276 he told a shocked Bruce: Bruce Lee, *In My Own Process* (Genesis Publications, 2024), p. 186; Scura, "The Dragon and the Franchise," p. 40.
276 "he'd gone to school in Hong Kong": Bao Nguyen interview with Kareem Abdul-Jabbar, Nov. 3, 2019.
276 "He can be very difficult": Roger Kahn, "Kareem Arrives," *Beyond the Boys of Summer* (McGraw-Hill, 2005), p. 50.
276 "'good guys and bad guys in all races'": Uyehara, *Bruce Lee: The Incomparable Fighter*, p. 110.
276 Bruce couldn't stop laughing: Uyehara, *Bruce Lee: The Incomparable Fighter*, p. 110.
277 "He had to keep up a kind of mystique": Davis Miller, *The Tao of Bruce Lee* (Vintage, 2000), p. 168.
277 "Bruce needed friends": Abdul-Jabbar, *Giant Steps*, p. 189.
277 "he was still Bruce Lee": Abdul-Jabbar, *Giant Steps*, p. 190.
278 "We call it the war of the flea": Robert Smith, Richard Axen, and DeVere Pentony, *By Any Means Necessary: The Revolutionary Struggle at San Francisco State* (Jossey-Bass, 1970), pp. 144–45.
278 "On and on and on": William Barlow and Peter Shapiro, *An End to Silence: The San Francisco State Student Movement in the 60s* (Pegasus/Bobbs-Merrill, 1971), p. 223.
278 "between Black, brown and yellow people": Barlow and Shapiro, *An End to Silence*, p. 227.
279 its third in six months: Barlow and Shapiro, *An End to Silence*, p. xiii.
279 "but simply thoughtlessness": Daryl Maeda, *Chains of Babylon: The Rise of Asian America* (University of Minnesota Press, 2009), pp. 48–49.
279 "*Nisei* social groups should cease to exist": Maeda, *Chains of Babylon*, p. 49.
279 "the adventure of relocation": Gerald W. Haslam and Janice E. Haslam, *In Thought and Action: The Enigmatic Life of S. I. Hayakawa* (University of Nebraska Press, 2011), p. 317.
279 "The relocation forced them out": S. I. Hayakawa, "Testimony Before Subcommittee on Administrative Law and Government Relations, U.S. House of Representatives," Apr. 28, 1986.
279 help Negroes assimilate quicker: Maeda, *Chains of Babylon*, p. 57.
279 end the strike by December 2: Barlow and Shapiro, *An End to Silence*, p. 253; Smith, Axen, and Pentony, *By Any Means Necessary*, p. 207.
279 "we'll forgive him for Pearl Harbor": Maeda, *Chains of Babylon*, p. 58; Gerald Haslam, "Hayakawa Among the Conservatives," *Boom: A Journal of California* 1, no. 4 (Winter 2011), p. 11.
279 "bring Black and white together": "Hayakawa's Role—Man in the Middle," *San Francisco Chronicle*, Nov. 27, 1968, p. 7.
280 "I'm the college president!": Jerry Carroll, "Sound and Fury at SF State," *San Francisco Chronicle*, Dec. 3, 1968, p. 1.
280 a "bravura performance": Carroll, "Sound and Fury at SF State."

280 "and common thieves": Karen Umemoto, "On Strike: San Francisco State College Strike, 1968–1969," in Min Zhou and James V. Gatewood, eds., *Contemporary Asian America: A Multidisciplinary Reader* (New York University Press, 2000), p. 72.

280 "urging the Negro to imitate the Sansei": "S.I. Rips Gidra!," *Gidra* 1, no. 2 (May 1969), p. 1.

280 a "banana," and "really white": Laura Ho, "Pigs Pickets & a Banana," and Alan Nishio, "The Oriental as a 'Middleman Minority,'" *Gidra* 1, no. 2 (May 1969), p. 3; Hsieh Yu-Hsien, "Editorial from San Francisco State," *Asian American Political Alliance* newspaper 1, no. 2 (Jan. 1969).

280 "could never have gotten away with it": Maeda, *Chains of Babylon*, p. 65.

280 offer Asian American Studies courses that year: "Movement Chronology," *Gidra*, Jan. 1970, p. 14.

280 "broader and more varied in its character": Malcolm Collier and Dan Gonzales, "Origins," in Russell Jeung, Karen Umemoto, Harvey Dong, Eric Mar, Lisa Hirai Tsuchitani, and Arnold Pan, eds., *Mountain Movers: Student Activism & The Emergence of Asian American Studies* (UCLA Asian American Studies Press, 2019), p. 52.

Part IX: Above and Below Sunset, 1968–1970

283 "Marginalization is a sword": Charles Gaines, "The Theater of Refusal: Black Art and Mainstream Criticism," in *The Theater of Refusal: Black Art and Mainstream Criticism*, Catherine Lord, ed. (The Regents of the University of California, 1993), p. 17.

Chapter 31: Plateaus

284 "become a black belt": Taki Theodoracopulos, "Celebrity Kicks," *Esquire*, Sept. 1980, p. 85.

284 twenty-five dollars an hour: Bruce Lee, *Letters of the Dragon: Correspondence 1958–1973*, ed. John Little (Tuttle, 1998), p 68; J. D. Bethea in John Little, ed., *Bruce Lee: Words of the Dragon, Interviews, 1958–1973* (Tuttle, 1997), p. 97.

284 "They can afford it": *The Evolution of a Martial Artist* (Bruce Lee Enterprises, 2013), p. 110; Linda Lee, *Bruce Lee: The Man Only I Knew* (Warner Paperback Library, 1975), p. 98.

284 "middle-aged macho syndrome": John Little, "Enter the Dragon: The Making of a Classic Movie," essay included in *Enter the Dragon* DVD, 25th Anniversary Special Edition (Warner Home Video, 1998), p. 32.

285 "the highest-priced martial artist in the United States": Harold Heffernan, "$500 an Hour Going Rate for Top Tutor on Violence," *Star Press* (Muncie, IN), June 17, 1969, p. 18.

285 "taste my cup of tea?": Bruce Lee, "Liberate Yourself from Classical Karate," *Black Belt*, Sept. 1971, p. 25. Widely reprinted, including in Editors of *Black Belt* magazine, eds., *The Legendary Bruce Lee* (Ohara Publications, 1986).

285 "The usefulness of a cup is in its emptiness": He may have been inspired by the wording of Arthur Waley's translation of the *Tao Te Ching*, chapter 11, in *The Way and Its Power: A Study of the Tao Te Ching and Its Place in Chinese Thought* (Grove Press, 1958), 155. Waley's more oblique take was: "But it is on the space where there is nothing that the usefulness of the vessel depends."

286 "everything he wanted": Marshall Terrill, *Steve McQueen: Portrait of an American Rebel* (Donald I. Fine Books, 1993), p. 149.

286 "That guy": Mito Uyehara, *Bruce Lee: The Incomparable Fighter* (Ohara Publications, 1988), p. 121.

286 "Just to get to his front door": Uyehara, *Bruce Lee: The Incomparable Fighter*, p. 126.

286 "running after them": Terrill, *Steve McQueen*, pp. 251–52.

286 Steve phoned the house: Interview with Peter Chin, Dec. 15, 2023.

287 "I'm calm, Steve": Terrill, *Steve McQueen*, pp. 270–71.

287 "street-fighting technique for Steve": Terrill, *Steve McQueen*, p. 181.

287 "gives me advice on acting": Uyehara, *Bruce Lee: The Incomparable Fighter*, p. 126.

287 "Bruce," Steve said: This source is, at their request, confidential.

287 the rare millionaire writer: "Television: The Fingers of God," *Time*, Aug. 9, 1963.

287 another bodyguard's mouth: John Corcoran interview with Stirling Silliphant, transcript, undated, part 1, p. 10. Courtesy of the Stirling Silliphant Papers at UCLA. Through Jay Sebring, Bruce had actually met Vic Damone in Vegas, but their meeting nowhere near resembled this story. This excerpt is also included in the *Circle of Iron* DVD extras, which say that these interviews took place in early 1980.

288 "I can tell we have a lot of work with you": Corcoran interview with Silliphant, part 2, p. 3.

288 $275 an hour: Nat Segaloff, *Stirling Silliphant: The Fingers of God* (BearManor Media, 2013), p. 92.

288 "understand a kick": Alex Ben Block, *The Legend of Bruce Lee* (Dell, 1974), pp. 49–50.

502 NOTES

288 when fighting trained boxers or street fighters: James Tugend, transcript of interview with Stirling Silliphant, for *Fighting Stars*, unpublished, undated, likely late 1973. Stirling Silliphant Papers at UCLA. The article ran as James Tugend, "Stirling Silliphant's World of Oscars, Emmies, and Gung-Fu," *Fighting Stars*, Feb. 1974, pp. 22–27.

288 "If it kills you, it kills you": Robert Clouse, *Bruce Lee: The Biography* (Unique Publications, 1988), p. 72.

289 "I remember that afternoon so vividly": Segaloff, *Stirling Silliphant*, pp. 93–94.

289 reading Fritz Perls's books on Gestalt therapy: Interview with Leo Fong, Mar. 21, 2018. Bruce's library includes heavily underlined copies of Perls's *Gestalt Theory Verbatim* and *In and Out the Garbage Pail*, among other titles. Wing Luke Museum collection.

289 "Period": Jim Whitmore, "New Meanings of Aggression: An Interview with Stirling Silliphant," *Deadly Hands of Kung Fu*, no. 25 (June 1976) p. 39.

289 "I opened all my windows": Segaloff, *Stirling Silliphant*, pp. 93–94.

289 "mark them as women": Uyehara, *Bruce Lee: The Incomparable Fighter*, p. 73.

290 "some people who like to sleep": Interview with Nancy Kwan, Apr. 21, 2023.

291 "demolish Marlowe's office": Segaloff, *Stirling Silliphant*, p. 95.

291 "he tried too hard": Matthew Polly, *Bruce Lee: A Life* (Simon & Schuster, 2018), p. 250.

291 "harmless enough to flirt with": Sharon Farrell with Jessie Dee Young, *Sharon Farrell: "Hollywood Princess" from Sioux City, Iowa* (self-published, 2013), p. 130.

291 "do tricks in front of Steve to impress him": Terrill, *Steve Mcqueen*, p. 150.

292 "and work out a little": Uyehara, *Bruce Lee: The Incomparable Fighter*, pp. 122–23.

292 her eye on McQueen: In her autobiography, which reads like a romance novel in which she plays a free-spirited, sometimes tragic protagonist, Sharon Farrell spins a love triangle between Bruce, Steve, and herself. She also claims to have had an affair with Che Guevara in 1959, at the age of eighteen, while in Cuba to shoot her debut movie, *Kiss Her Goodbye*. See Farrell with Young, *Sharon Farrell*.

Chapter 32: The Seeker

293 "the great American secular religion": Richard Lingeman, "How to Lose Friends and Alienate People," *New York Times*, Aug. 13, 1995.

293 "Whatever the mind of man": Napoleon Hill, *Think and Grow Rich* (1937; repr. ed., Highroads Media, 2004), p. 41. There have been many reprints over the years. The version Bruce probably read was the 1956 edition.

293 "occupy your mind": Hill, *Think and Grow Rich*, p. 74. In this, Hill's words had much in common with the vulgar and still circulated 19th-century Western mistranslation of the *Dhammapada*: "All that we are is the result of what we have thought." In this way, the idea—rooted in cultural misunderstanding—has served as another strange hinge between Asian philosophy and American self-help literature. See *Sacred Books of the East, Vol. 10: The Dhammapada and Sutta Nipata*, by Max Müller and Max Fausböll [1881]. sacred-texts.com/bud/sbe10/sbe1003.htm.

294 "young, foolish, and with grand visions": Linda Lee, *The Bruce Lee Story* (Ohara Publications, 1989), p. 87.

294 He had a hanging bag: Linda Lee, *The Bruce Lee Story*, p. 88.

295 "I can't even buy a new pair of glasses": Interview with Nancy Kwan, Apr. 21, 2023.

295 "do everything faster and faster": Robert Clouse, *Bruce Lee: The Biography* (Unique Publications, 1988), p. 80.

295 "I was experiencing": Jhoon Rhee, Bruce Lee and I (MVM Books, 2000), p. 98.

296 carry a handgun everywhere: Marshall Terrill, *Steve McQueen: Portrait of an American Rebel* (Donald I. Fine Books, 1993), pp. 186–88.

296 "especially when you have a family": Mito Uyehara, *Bruce Lee: The Incomparable Fighter* (Ohara Publications, 1988), p. 124.

296 "warding off blows": Vincent Bugliosi with Curt Gentry, *Helter Skelter: The True Story of the Manson Murders* (W. W. Norton, 1974; repr. ed., 1994), p. 41.

296 "far from being a fighter": Uyehara, *Bruce Lee: The Incomparable Fighter*, p. 124.

296 "roaming around at random": Interview with Linda Lee Cadwell, May 2, 2023.

297 did Polanski breathe more easily: Roman Polanski, *Roman by Polanski* (Morrow, 1984), pp. 317–18.

297 $85.12: Bank records from the Bruce Lee Family Archive.

297 "a Chinese word meaning 'beautiful'": Letter from Bruce Lee to Jhoon Goo Rhee, March 4, 1969, in *Letters from the Dragon*, p. 113.

NOTES 503

298 On September 25, 1968: In his Day-Timer, Bruce scrawled, "12:00pm Stirling to meet Steve McQueen."
298 "We met with Steve": Corcoran Silliphant transcripts. Transcript 4, p. 13.
298 "Nah," Steve said: Clouse, *Bruce Lee: The Biography*, p. 84.
298 "I'm not going to carry you on my back": Clouse, *Bruce Lee: The Biography*, p. 84.
298 "he won't do this film with me?": John Corcoran interview with Stirling Silliphant, transcript, undated, part 4, pp. 13-14. Courtesy of the Stirling Silliphant Papers at UCLA.
298 "how gigantic Bruce's self-belief was?" Corcoran interview with Silliphant, part 4, pp. 13-14.
298 knocked down a few pegs: This narrative would be apotheosized in Albert Goldman's bilious, bigoted two-part series for *Penthouse* in 1983. He wrote, "So long as Lee was living in obscurity in Los Angeles, a married man with two children, a coach for movie stars who were studying the martial arts, an occasional performer on TV or in films, he was able to manage his life comfortably. He was cheerful, self-contained, considerate of others, and so dedicated to his training ideals that he would never smoke or drink, much less experiment with drugs ... The truth is that all the years Lee had lived in California, he had been a soul on ice. Like many aliens, especially those from the Orient, he had adopted a mask and suppressed or sublimated many of his most basic character traits ... In life, Lee was a loser." Albert Goldman, "The Life and Death of Bruce Lee," *Penthouse*. January 1983, pp. 64-66, 214, 222-230. February 1983, pp. 54-57, 184-189. In Quentin Tarantino's novelized *Once Upon a Time ... in Hollywood*, he writes of his version of Bruce Lee that "he had a game plan in mind. Like Charles Manson, this spiritual *sifu* stuff was just a side gig. The way Charles Manson wanted to be a rock star, Bruce Lee wanted to be a movie star." Quentin Tarantino, *Once Upon a Time ... in Hollywood* (Harper Perennial, 2021), p. 206.
299 "keeping our star in shape": Marshall Terrill, *Steve McQueen: The Life and Legend of a Hollywood Icon* (Triumph Books, 2010), p. 288.
299 in the University library reading books: Letter from Mark Silliphant to Stirling Silliphant, Oct. 27, 1968. Stirling Silliphant Papers at UCLA.
299 send Steve updates: Letter from Stirling Silliphant to Steve McQueen, Oct. 4, 1968. From the Stirling Silliphant Papers at UCLA Special Collections.
299 Coburn had risen to fame: Interview with Peter Chin, Dec. 15, 2023. See also Robyn L. Coburn, *Dervish Dust: The Life and Words of James Coburn* (Potomac Books, 2021); Sean MacCauley, "Get to Know James Coburn, the Ultimate Sixties Tough Guy," GQ, Sept. 3, 2015, gq-magazine.co.uk/article/james-coburn-the-ultimate-sixties-tough-guy.
299 "relates everything to martial arts or the martial arts to everything": Uyehara, *Bruce Lee: The Incomparable Fighter*, p. 114.
299 talked Eastern philosophy for hours: Clouse, *Bruce Lee: The Biography*, p. 83.
300 "the returning to his original sense of freedom": Notes found in the Bruce Lee Family Archive. Undated, likely 1969.
300 writer named Shelly Burton: Nat Segaloff, *Stirling Silliphant: The Fingers of God* (BearManor Media, 2013), p. 97.
301 "with another writer": Letter from Stirling Silliphant to Shelly Burton, Dec. 12, 1969. Courtesy Stirling Silliphant Papers at UCLA.
301 and technical adviser: Letter from Bruce Lee to Jhoon Goo Rhee, Mar. 4, 1969, in Bruce Lee, *Letters of the Dragon*, p. 113. It seems that Silliphant never got the project to the script stage.
301 "Seeing that he was": Clouse, *Bruce Lee: The Biography*, p. 84.
301 "Script is definitely": Bruce Lee letter to Stirling Silliphant, undated, written in advance of January 26, 1970, meeting. Courtesy Stirling Silliphant Papers.
301 "It was evident to me": Corcoran interview with Silliphant, part 3, p. 2.
301 Bruce "was beginning to accept": Corcoran Silliphant transcripts. Transcript 4, P. 5. Stirling's language here suggests he is projecting onto Bruce his own feelings about Bruce's ceiling.
301 "as high as Bruce could aspire": Corcoran interview with Silliphant, part 4, p. 5.

Chapter 33: What Is Freedom?

302 "possessed by nothing": Interview with Dan Inosanto, Sept. 26, 2023; Dan Inosanto, "Introduction," in Larry Hartsell, *Jeet Kune Do: Entering to Trapping to Grappling* (Unique Publications, 1984), p. vi.
302 "He was like the beacon": "Bruce Lee Touched the Lives of the Greats," *Black Belt Magazine's Best of Bruce Lee #2* (Rainbow Publications, 1975), p. 45.
302 "a lot of things to himself": Bruce Thomas, *Bruce Lee: Fighting Spirit* (Blue Snake Books, 1994), pp. 97-98.
302 "just flowing energy": Interview with Mito Uyehara, Sept. 20, 2023.
302 "pointed himself in another": Thomas, *Bruce Lee: Fighting Spirit*, pp. 97-98.

302 "You can't organize truth": *Words of the Dragon*, p. 95. Reprinted from an article by J.D. Bethea, "Don't call it karate—it's martial art." *Washington Star*, Aug. 16, 1970, p.S6.

302 as his interests shifted, every three months: Interview with Dan Inosanto, Sept. 26, 2023.

303 "They have to be involved": Taky Kimura, *Regards from the Dragon: Seattle*, rev. ed., compiled by David Tadman (Empire Books, 2009), p. 148.

303 "Keep it to yourself and close friends": Bruce Lee, *Letters of the Dragon: Correspondence 1958-1973*, ed. John Little (Tuttle, 1998), p. 112.

303 "True observation begins": Bruce Lee, "Liberate Yourself from Classical Karate," *Black Belt*, Sept. 1971, p. 25. Italics from the original.

303 "That was a moment of discovery": Interview with Jeffrey Thomas Leong, Jan. 10, 2024.

303 "Freedom is acquired by conquest": Paolo Freire, *Pedagogy of the Oppressed* (Herder and Herder, 1972), p. 31.

303 "We do not have to 'gain' freedom": Notes of Bruce Lee in the Bruce Lee Family Archive. This has also been edited and reproduced in Bruce Lee, *Artist of Life*, ed. John Little (Tuttle, 1999), p. 177.

304 "a truth that transcends styles or disciplines": Bruce Lee, "Liberate Yourself from Classical Karate."

305 Readers wrote in: Letter from Phil Davis, "By the Way," *Black Belt*, Aug. 1968, p. 3. Also see letters in *Dear Bruce Lee: A Compilation of Sentimental, Remorseful, Controversial Letters on the Superstar* (Ohara Publications, 1980), pp. 22-27, 61-63.

305 "a curriculum that will fit everybody": Interview with Dan Inosanto, Sept. 26, 2023.

305 "because it is very easy for a member": "The 'Knowing Is Not Enough' Interview—Bruce Lee: The Dan Lee Interview, Part 2," *Knowing Is Not Enough: The Official Newsletter of Jun Fan Jeet Kune Do* 2, no. 3 (Fall 1998), p. 10.

305 "Death is a renewal": These lines are also paraphrased in Bruce Lee, *Tao of Jeet Kune Do*, ed. Gilbert Johnson (Ohara Publications, 1975), p. 16. Krishnamurti, *Freedom from the Known*, pp. 17, 103-4. In his notes, he excerpts the last sentence. From the Bruce Lee Family Archive.

306 "you must die to everything of yesterday": This line is also included in the *Tao of Jeet Kune Do*, p. 16. Krishnamurti, *Freedom from the Known*, p. 17. The original quote is, "To be free of all authority, of your own and that of another, is to die of everything to yesterday, so that your mind is always fresh, always young, innocent, full of vigour and passion."

306 "to understand each other": Dan Inosanto in Brian White, dir., *Legacy of the Dragon*, documentary, 2001.

306 "I would be very disappointed if you did": Dan Inosanto in *Bruce Lee 1940-1973*, p. 44.

306 "We both bought long African evening gowns, kaftans": Steve Kerridge and Darren Chua, *Bruce Lee: Mandarin Superstar* (On the Fly Productions, 2018), unpaginated.

306 "I started showing Bruce how to ski": Kerridge and Chua, *Bruce Lee: Mandarin Superstar*, unpaginated.

306 "Though I had a few falls": Bruce Lee, *Letters of the Dragon*, p. 128.

306 "I hate skiing": Kerridge and Chua, *Bruce Lee: Mandarin Superstar*, unpaginated.

307 "All in all the group is not my type": Bruce Lee, *Letters of the Dragon*, p. 128.

307 offered five thousand dollars from one of the millionaire guests: J. D. Bethea, in John Little, ed., *Bruce Lee: Words of the Dragon, Interviews, 1958-1973* (Tuttle, 1997), p. 97.

307 "an hour about nothing important": Uyehara, *Bruce Lee: The Incomparable Fighter*, p. 75.

307 "especially the people in Hong Kong": Bao Nguyen interview with Robert Chua Wah-Peng, May 25, 2019.

Part X: Action Action, 1970-1972

309 "Hexagram 39": Alfred Huang, *The Complete I Ching. 10th Anniversary Edition.* (Inner Traditions, 1998/2010), pp. 320, 323.

Chapter 34: Water Above, Mountain Below

310 For four days in April: Gary Ka-wai Cheung, *Hong Kong's Watershed: The 1967 Riots* (Hong Kong University Press, 2009), pp. 9-11.

310 "Only one of eight ten- to fourteen-year-olds was in school": Cheung, *Hong Kong's Watershed*, p. 4.

310 "give them education too?": Frank Welsh, *A History of Hong Kong* (HarperCollins, 1993), p. 468.

310 disgust at government corruption: Cheung, *Hong Kong's Watershed*, pp. 13-14.

310 updated an emergency evacuation plan: Cheung, *Hong Kong's Watershed*, pp. 95-99.

310 fifty-one were dead: Cheung, *Hong Kong's Watershed*, pp. 223-24.

310 grown by 36 percent: I. C. Jarvie, *Window on Hong Kong: A Sociological Study of the Hong Kong Film Industry and Its Audience* (University of Hong Kong Centre of Asian Studies, 1977), p. 54.

310 as Hong Kongers: Steve Tsang, *A Modern History of Hong Kong* (I. B. Tauris, 2007), pp. 180–96.
311 a "new *wuxia* century": Stephen Teo, *Chinese Martial Arts Cinema: The Wuxia Tradition* (Edinburgh University Press, 2009), p. 91; Kinnia Yau Shuk-ting, "Interactions Between Japanese and Hong Kong Cinemas," in Meaghan Morris, Siu Leung Lik, and Stephen Chan Ching-kiu, eds., *Hong Kong Connections: Transnational Imagination in Action Cinema* (Duke University Press/Hong Kong University Press, 2005), pp. 34–48.
311 "sick men of Asia" tropes: Teo, *Chinese Martial Arts Cinema*, pp. 30–32.
311 the return of the repressed: Richard James Havis, "The Special Effects That Enlivened Early Martial Arts Movies in Hong Kong, from Flying Swords and Palm Rays to Men in Monster Suits," *South China Morning Post*, Sept. 5, 2021.
311 "tragic men who defy": Chang Cheh, "Creating the Martial Arts Film and the Hong Kong Cinema Style," in Stephen Teo, trans., *The Making of Martial Arts Film—As Told by Filmmakers and Stars* (Hong Kong Film Archive, 1999), p. 22.
311 violence was their last resort: Teo, *Chinese Martial Arts Cinema*, p. 100.
312 "That's too low": Interview with Peter Chin, Dec. 15, 2023; Chang Cheh, *A Retrospective of Hong Kong Films Over the Last Thirty Years*, 2nd ed. (Commercial Press, 2019), pp. 102–103, trans. Winnie Fu.
312 "or appearing on shows": Bruce Lee, *Letters of the Dragon: Correspondence 1958–1973*, ed. John Little (Tuttle, 1998), p. 132.
313 "jealous of my success": "Bruce Quitting Boxing for Acting," *Star* (Hong Kong), Apr. 4, 1970, p. 1. Reprinted in John Little, ed., *Bruce Lee: Words of the Dragon, Interviews, 1958–1973* (Tuttle, 1997), p. 94.
313 Uncle Walter Tso Tat-Wah organized: "Iron Fist Lee Siu Loong," from *Wah Kiu Yat Po*, Apr. 16, 1970, in Lee Siu Loong, *The Rise of the Mandarin Superstar: Old Hong Kong Newspaper Collection* (Volume 1: 1970–71), trans. Sai Loong (self-published, Kindle, 2006), loc. 182. See also Steve Kerridge and Darren Chua, *Bruce Lee: Mandarin Superstar* (On the Fly Productions, 2018). Thanks also to Winnie Fu.
313 "When I was over at the house": Peter Gast, "Shek Kin: Bruce Lee's Favorite Villain," *Inside Kung Fu*, Sept. 1985, p. 57.
313 the pop singer "Sum Sum": Bao Nguyen interview with Sylvia Lai, May 25, 2019.
314 looked up in astonishment: Mito Uyehara, *Bruce Lee: The Incomparable Fighter* (Ohara Publications, 1988), pp. 76–7.
314 "Every single person knew about him! Everyone!": Bao Nguyen interview with Sylvia Lai, May 25, 2019.
314 Bruce had been assassinated: "Unicorn Reveals Lee's Letter Which Claimed Safe and Sound," in *Wah Kiu Yat Po*, Mar. 1, 1971; "Lee Siu Loong Has Intention to Return to HK to Make Movie," in *Kung Sheung Evening News*, Mar. 11, 1971. Both in Lee Siu Loong, *The Rise of the Mandarin Superstar*. Thanks also to Winnie Fu.
314 "I only have twenty dollars each week": Interview with Linda Lee Cadwell, May 2, 2023.
315 After a full day of work on Friday, May 29: Bruce's Day-Timer for the 29th reads, "Script meeting all day (19)." In a letter dated August 25, 1970, Stirling apologizes to Bruce for not having delivered the script and asks for his patience. From the Stirling Silliphant Papers at UCLA Special Collections Library.
315 he felt his back pop: Shannon Lee, *Be Water, My Friend: The Teachings of Bruce Lee* (Flatiron Books, 2020), p. 135.
315 "never going to do *gung fu* again": Interview with Linda Lee Cadwell, May 2, 2023.
315 "When friends visited him": Mito Uyehara in Editors of *Black Belt* magazine, eds., *The Legendary Bruce Lee* (Ohara Publications, 1986), p. 10.
315 "Back set back": Bruce Lee's 1970 Day-Timer. The strange rendering of "set back" is in the original. Courtesy the Bruce Lee archive.
315 "how bad his back was": Interview with Linda Lee Cadwell, May 2, 2023.
315 his desk, his chair, his bed: Linda Lee, *The Bruce Lee Story* (Ohara Publications, 1989), p. 89.
315 he was really scared: Interview with Peter Chin, Dec. 15, 2023; Mito Uyehara in *Bruce Lee 1940–1973* (Ohara Publications, 1974), p. 37.
315 "not going to have a long life": Interview with Peter Chin, Dec. 15, 2023.
315 $2.73: Checkbook bank account records for May 8, 1970. Bruce Lee Family Archive.
316 "a disgrace for his wife to work": Linda Lee, *The Bruce Lee Story*, p. 95.
316 *Commentaries on the Martial Way*, a nod to the Chinese classics: After his death, many of these raw notes would be republished—often fragmented and without citations or context—in books like *Tao of Jeet Kune Do* and the volumes that would comprise *The Bruce Lee Library*. Bruce may not have intended them to be published in such a form. After he came to disdain systems and schools, Bruce had decided against publishing some of his writings, including the first draft of *Tao of Jeet Kune Do* and a book on Wing Chun with James Yimm Lee.

In the first few years following Bruce's death, Linda Lee tangled with the insurance companies over Bruce's life policy and with Raymond Chow and Golden Harvest over moneys that were due to the family. Still mourning his death and wishing to see his ideas receive a greater circulation to round out the image of Bruce Lee, she turned to publishing. It was in this context that she worked with a ghostwriter to publish her 1975 biography of Bruce under the title *Bruce Lee: The Man Only I Knew* in the United States and *The Life and Tragic Death of Bruce Lee* in the UK.

During this period, she also worked with a *Black Belt* editor, a former student of Bruce's, named Gilbert Johnson to compile what was published as *Tao of Jeet Kune Do* in 1975. Dan Inosanto also played a role in advising on the production of this book, which drew extensively from Bruce's *Commentaries on the Martial Way*. They were likely never meant for mass public consumption.

In the 1990s, Linda and Shannon Lee compiled and bound the extensive, if still incomplete, *Commentaries* to give to Bruce's closest friends as gifts. A fair portion of these notes—again, largely without citation—found their way into the John Little–edited collection of books for Tuttle called *The Bruce Lee Library*. In this way, many quotes that he had transcribed from portions of books that he had found intriguing were marketed as his own and would come to be attributed to him in subsequent years.

More recently, scholars such as Paul Bishop, Richard Torres, Ryan Ohl, and others have attempted to rectify these errors. This very welcome attention may help to place Bruce's work in its proper context while also shedding light on how eclectic, deep, and close a reader and how layered, synthetic, and creative a thinker Bruce Lee actually was.

316 "if anyone called or came over": Linda Lee, *The Bruce Lee Story*, p. 95.
316 for another night of comfortless sleep: These cards are kept in the Bruce Lee Family Archive. Interview with Shannon Lee, Feb. 26, 2024.

Chapter 35: A Journey from the West

317 "the definitive and classical martial arts film": John Corcoran interview with Stirling Silliphant, transcript, undated, part 4, p. 15. Courtesy of the Stirling Silliphant Papers at UCLA.
317 "It's about time we had an Oriental hero": John Little, ed., *Bruce Lee: Words of the Dragon, Interviews, 1958–1973* (Tuttle, 1997), p. 98.
317 "I can just about taste it": Editors of *Black Belt* magazine, eds., *The Legendary Bruce Lee* (Ohara Publications, 1986), p. 27.
317 "one can have peace of mind": Bruce's 1971 Day-Timer. Courtesy of the Bruce Lee Family Archive. Translated by Sze K. Chan.
317 "the carry on of the living": This paragraph from untitled treatment notes by Bruce Lee, undated. From Bruce Lee Family Archive.
318 "can a person know himself": Stirling Silliphant, "Pingree-Panpiper Productions Present a Film by James Coburn, Bruce Lee, Stirling Silliphant: The Silent Flute," Oct. 19, 1970, Stirling Silliphant Papers at UCLA.
320 "something to remember": Corcoran interview with Silliphant, part 4, pp. 15–16.
321 "shoot somewhere in the country": Corcoran interview with Silliphant, part 4, p. 16.
321 "We had to get him laid": Kerridge and Chua, *Bruce Lee: Mandarin Superstar*, unpaginated.
321 "it's pissing me off!": Steve Kerridge and Darren Chua, *Bruce Lee: Mandarin Superstar* (On the Fly Productions, 2018), unpaginated; Linda Lee, *Bruce Lee: The Man Only I Knew* (Warner Paperback Library, 1975), p. 24.
321 "at the back of Jimmy's head": Robert Clouse, *Bruce Lee: The Biography* (Unique Publications, 1988), p. 87.
322 "buses coming over": Kerridge and Chua, *Bruce Lee: Mandarin Superstar*, unpaginated.
322 "He had no idea": Clouse, *Bruce Lee: The Biography*, pp. 87, 90.
322 Three men ran out: Clouse, *Bruce Lee: The Biography*, 87, 90.
322 "I thought I saw poverty": Mito Uyehara, *Bruce Lee: The Incomparable Fighter* (Ohara Publications, 1988), p. 115.
322 Maybe it was just Steve and Bruce's weird competitive friendship: Interviews with Peter Chin, Dec. 15, 2023, and Dec. 11, 2024.
322 "You're a Chinese in a white man's world": Alex Ben Block, *The Legend of Bruce Lee* (Dell, 1974), p. 52. In other interviews Silliphant would often return to this point—that although he had been one of Bruce's biggest patrons, he had never seen his explosive success coming. When he heard Bruce ego-tripping like this, he told John Corcoran, "I thought, 'Bruce, don't break your heart. How can I tell you that the bottom line is that you are a Chinese in a Caucasian film industry?'" Corcoran interview with Silliphant, part 4, p. 1.
323 sent legal papers: Memorandum of Agreement between Pingree Productions and Panpiper, Apr. 5, 1971, Stirling Silliphant Papers at UCLA.

323 abruptly canceled his martial arts appointments with him: Bruce Lee's 1971 Day-Timer. Courtesy of the Bruce Lee Family Archive.

323 even outraged: Clouse, *Bruce Lee: The Biography*, p. 90

323 "my one chance of a lifetime": Uyehara, *Bruce Lee: The Incomparable Fighter*, p. 115.

323 "a security guard if I have to": Tony Page, "My Brother, Bruce: Reminiscences by Robert Lee," *Fighting Stars*, Aug. 1983, p. 47.

Chapter 36: The Teacher and the Warrior

324 "the spirit of your Jeet Kune Do truly is": John Corcoran interview with Stirling Silliphant, transcript, undated, part 3, p. 2. Courtesy of the Stirling Silliphant Papers at UCLA.

324 When he brought it to Paramount: Corcoran interview with Silliphant, part 3, p. 3.

324 locked the producer in a bear hug: Guy Scutter, dir., *Bruce Lee, Martial Arts Master*, documentary (Merlin Group/Canal, 1993). "Our introduction tended to favor him somewhat more than me," Rogosin said. "But I had control of the scripts after that which he became aware of."

324 "But I had felt blind": Corcoran interview with Silliphant, part 3, p. 3.

326 other books on acting and moviemaking: He copied quotes from Kazan interviews into an orange-covered notebook he entitled *Here Comes the Warrior*. From the Bruce Lee Family Archive. The Bruce Lee library collection at the Wing Luke Museum includes over two dozen titles on acting alone, and many dozens more on criticism and the craft from Stanley Kauffmann's *A World on Film* to Raymond Spottiswoode's *A Grammar of the Film*.

326 "Western, Modern, Others?": These are from pages of notes from the Bruce Lee Family Archive.

326 "The Chinese are quiet": In his notes he intended to source these photos from the Sutro Library, California State Library, and California Historical Society. Mark Twain, *Roughing It* (1872), online-literature.com /twain/roughing-it/55/.

327 Chinatown squad at bay: These details are taken from notebooks and scraps of notes Bruce took on this project, likely in the period between 1969 and early 1971. None of these are explicitly dated. I've taken my best guess about their sequencing. Courtesy of the Bruce Lee Family Archive.

327 Stirling Silliphant to help him edit it: The copy that I saw has Stirling Silliphant's name appearing above Bruce's, but it is crossed out. Perhaps Silliphant's secretary had retyped this draft. Courtesy of the Bruce Lee Family Archive.

327 a helper of the weak: In the *Number One Son* treatment, Semple follows the opening scene by introducing the series, saying "In A Nutshell . . . this is a slam-bang, one-hour action-adventure series . . . with a couple of unique differences, which we'll get to in a minute." Bruce leads off with, "In A Nutshell . . . this is a half-hour Western ACTION adventure series . . . with a couple of differences, which we'll go into in a minute." Ellipses here are from the originals. Both documents courtesy of the Bruce Lee Family Archive.

327 "walk blithely off": This line as well as previous ones—"a very cool customer" and "lithe and pantherlike"—of course, directly echo Semple's *Number One Son* presentation. Courtesy of the Bruce Lee Family Archive.

328 "These men have enormous power": Mito Uyehara, *Bruce Lee: The Incomparable Fighter* (Ohara Publications, 1988), p. 101.

329 he knew it could be conveyed through film: "Ed Spielman, 'The Kung Fu Characters,'" Autry National Center, June 11, 2013, vimeo.com/channels/autryoralhistory/87947946.

329 "*Those* Chinese guys were *us*": "Ed Spielman, 'The Kung Fu Characters.'"

329 "Bruce himself had been working": Linda Lee, *Bruce Lee: The Man Only I Knew* (Warner Paperback Library, 1975), p. 131.

330 submitted it on April 30, 1970: Matthew Polly, *Bruce Lee: A Life* (Simon & Schuster, 2018), p. 279.

330 "We talked about it a lot": Fred Weintraub, *Bruce Lee, Woodstock, and Me* (Brooktree Canyon Press, 2011), p. 5.

330 it was likely near presentation-ready shape: One line from the treatment shows up in a much-refined form in Stirling Silliphant's *Longstreet* script for "The Way of the Intercepting Fist": "To accept defeat, to learn to die is to be liberated from it." The first draft of the *Longstreet* script was written on May 12, 1971 (from the Bruce Lee Family Archive), and the script was finalized on shoot day, June 22, 1971; see Steve Kerridge and Darren Chua, *Bruce Lee: Mandarin Superstar* (On the Fly Productions, 2018). In the *Ah Sahm/Warrior* treatment, the line appears as, "If you are to learn something you must learn how to die!" That the Longstreet rendering feels like a refinement strongly suggests that the treatment preceded the *Longstreet* script.

331 with his fellow dinner guests Ted Ashley and Sy Weintraub: Bruce's letter to Ted Ashley in the wake of the *Kung Fu* snub suggests it may have been Ashley to whom he had pitched the series. "Again, thank you kindly for your kind participation on the initial stage of 'The Warrior,'" Bruce wrote on December 16, 1971. *Letters from the Dragon*, p. 163. Jerry Leider, who served as the head of the TV division, reported directly to Ashley, and to

508 NOTES

331 whom Tom Kuhn reported, may have also been involved in these meetings. The Day-Timer lists meetings with Ashley, Leider, and Kuhn in September.

331 "Greetings from Los Angeles": Jhoon Rhee, pp. 138–43, Also reprinted in *Letters of the Dragon*, pp. 144–45.

331 "Warner deal fell": It might have read "fell through," but a water stain has stolen the last word from us for all time. Courtesy of the Bruce Lee Family Archive.

Chapter 37: The Fighter's Instant

332 "Bruce taught me": John Corcoran interview with Stirling Silliphant, transcript, part 1, undated, p. 6. Courtesy of the Stirling Silliphant Papers at UCLA.

332 made up 70 percent: Yip Man-Fung, *Martial Arts Cinema and Hong Kong Modernity* (Hong Kong University Press, 2017), p. 7.

332 in Clearwater Bay: Felix Dennis and Don Atyeo, *Bruce Lee: King of Kung Fu* (Straight Arrow Books, 1974), p. 39.

332 "military boarding schools": Dennis and Atyeo, *Bruce Lee*, p. 39.

332 $250 a month: Dennis and Atyeo, *Bruce Lee*, p. 39.

Dylan Cheung, "Fields of Fury: The Rise of Golden Harvest," essay included with *Bruce Lee at Golden Harvest*, DVD boxed set (Arrow Films, 2023), p. 140.

332 "like the Hollywood of the 1930s": Jonathan Kandell, "Run Run Shaw, Chinese-Movie Giant of the Kung Fu Genre, Dies at 106," *New York Times*, Jan. 6, 2014; Dennis and Atyeo, *Bruce Lee*, p. 40.

333 With a handshake: Interview with Andre Morgan, May 12, 2023; Bao Nguyen interview with Andre Morgan, Apr. 22, 2019.

333 Run Run refused: Cheung, "Fields of Fury," p. 141.

334 his feeling of betrayal: Citing Andre Morgan, Matthew Polly has written that the triggering incident was when Jimmy Wang Yu, fresh off his success with *The Chinese Boxer*, decided to publicly leave Shaw Brothers, despite having years left on his contract. When Yu fled to Taiwan, Shaw filed for a court injunction to try to force Yu to stop working, and then, just to be petty, took out print ads warning producers that Yu was still under contract. Yu's actions certainly increased tensions between Shaw and Golden Harvest. However, much of this occurred after Chow left Shaw in late April and filed incorporation papers on May 5. *The Chinese Boxer* was released on November 27. Wong Ain-ling, ed., *The Shaw Screen: A Preliminary Study* (Hong Kong Film Archive, 2003), p. 377; Matthew Polly, *Bruce Lee: A Life* (Simon & Schuster, 2018), pp. 300–301.

334 deals, from Manila and Saigon to London and Rome: Interview with Andre Morgan, Mar. 7, 2023.

334 "His charisma stuck in my mind": Lu Tajiri, "Raymond Chow of Golden Harvest," *Fighting Stars*, Apr. 1974, p. 13.

334 in tracking Bruce down: Interview with Andre Morgan, Mar. 7, 2023.

334 "knows how to put things together": Bao Nguyen interview with Robert Chua Wah-Peng, May 25, 2019.

334 Gladys Liu Liang Hua: Andre Morgan also notes that she had kids attending school in Los Angeles at the time. Interview with Andre Morgan, Mar. 7, 2023.

334 "all of our other contract stars accordingly": Bey Logan, *Hong Kong Action Cinema* (Overlook Press, 1995), p. 27.

335 three years before: "Unicorn Exposing Some Unknown Deeds of Bruce Lee," in Bruce Thomas, *Bruce Lee: Fighting Spirit* (Bruce Lee Jeet-kune-do Club, 1978), p. 27.

335 "Bruce laughed it off": Linda Lee, *Bruce Lee: The Man Only I Knew* (Warner Paperback Library, 1975), p. 134.

335 "a bit of a hippy!": Bey Logan, *Hong Kong Action Cinema*, p. 27.

335 tried to pair Bruce with Chang Cheh: Bey Logan, *Hong Kong Action Cinema*, p. 26.

335 launching into a detailed critique: Steve Kerridge and Darren Chua, *Bruce Lee: Mandarin Superstar* (On the Fly Productions, 2018), unpaginated.

335 "together I am sure we can build something": Bao Nguyen, dir., *Be Water*, documentary, 2020. Polly, *Bruce Lee: A Life*, p. 302.

335 "any number of pictures you can get!": Interview with Andre Morgan, Mar. 7, 2023.

335 "must have done a good job!?": Bruce Lee, *Letters of the Dragon: Correspondence 1958–1973*, ed. John Little (Tuttle, 1998), p. 147.

336 surrounded by squatter settlements: Cheung, "Fields of Fury," p. 147.

336 as Bruce was telling: Dennis and Atyeo, *Bruce Lee*, p. 48.

336 "sophisticated as in the United States": Interview with Linda Lee Cadwell, May 2, 2023.

336 But Weintraub assured him: Fred Weintraub, *Bruce Lee, Woodstock, and Me* (Brooktree Canyon Press, 2011), p. 7.
336 "You're just starting to get hot": Corcoran interview with Silliphant, part 4, p. 5.
336 "Set your sights on Hong Kong instead": Linda Lee, *Bruce Lee: The Man Only I Knew*, p. 131.
336 "pay your hotel bill": Corcoran interview with Silliphant, part 4, pp. 6–7.
337 "They won't do that to me": Corcoran interview with Silliphant, part 4, p. 7
337 "Send for us when you can": Interview with Linda Lee Cadwell, May 2, 2023.
337 "things are going my way": Bruce Lee, *Letters of the Dragon*, p. 148.

Book III: Echo

338 "Heaven produces the teeming multitude": *A Source Book in Chinese Philosophy*. Translated by Wing Tsit-Chan (Princeton University Press, 1963), p. 5.

Part XI: The New Hero, 1971–1972

339 "truth often sounds paradoxical": "(Chapter) Seventy-Eight" in Lao Tsu, *Tao Te Ching*, trans. Gia-Fu Feng and Jane English with Toinette Lippe (Vintage Books, 1972; repr. ed., 2000), unpaginated.

Chapter 38: Us Against the World

342 "Uncle Tongs": Ling-chi Wang, "Chinatown in Transition," *Amerasia Journal* 33 no. 1 (2007), pp. 39, 41.
342 F.U.C.K.U.: Asian American Community Center Archive Group, *Stand Up: An Archive Collection of the Bay Area Asian American Movement 1968–1974* (Eastwind Books, 2009), p. 82.
342 "ripe for rebellion": Harvey Dong, "The Origins and Trajectory of Asian American Political Activism in the San Francisco Bay Area, 1968–1978," PhD Dissertation in Ethnic Studies, University of California at Berkeley, 2002, p. 50.
343 Harvey Dong, a born fighter: Interview with Harvey Dong, Dec. 21, 2023.
343 where the men shot pool and pinball: Fred Ho, "Alex Hing," in Fred Ho with Carolyn Antonio, Diane Fujino, and Steve Yip, eds., *Legacy to Liberation: Politics and Culture of Revolutionary Asian Pacific America* (AK Press/Big Red Media, 2000), pp. 284–85.
343 the I-Hotel was: Estella Habal, *San Francisco's I-Hotel: Mobilizing the Filipino American Community in the Anti-Eviction Movement* (Temple University Press, 2007), p. 34.
343 "the Manifest Destiny of the Financial District": Calvin Trillin, "Some Thoughts on the International Hotel," *New Yorker*, Dec. 1977, p. 116.
343 The I-Hotel and the adjacent Victory Building occupied: Habal, *San Francisco's I-Hotel*, pp. 3–4, 11.
343 "too valuable to permit poor people to park": Chester Hartman, *City for Sale: The Transformation of San Francisco*, revised and updated ed. (University of California Press, 2002), p. 71.
343 Joining Tino's Barber Shop: Habal, *San Francisco's I-Hotel*, pp. 34–5; interviews with Harvey Dong, Dec. 21, 2023, and Aug. 1, 2024.
344 With six hundred dollars they opened Everybody's Bookstore: Interviews with Harvey Dong, Dec. 21, 2023, and Aug. 1, 2024.
344 Carlos Bulosan's *America Is in the Heart*: Asian American Community Center Archive Group, *Stand Up*, pp. 96–103; interviews with Harvey Dong, Dec. 21, 2023, and Aug. 1, 2024.
344 "China was called": Asian American Community Center Archive Group, *Stand Up*, p. 117.
344 "Now, the people have": Emil De Guzman, "International Hotel," *Gidra*, Nov. 1970, p. 5.
344 "Some of the old men": Interview with Harvey Dong, Aug. 1, 2024.
345 "all over the place": Bruce Lee, *Letters of the Dragon: Correspondence 1958–1973*, ed. John Little (Tuttle, 1998), p. 148.
345 a family friend Tony Lau Wing: Bao Nguyen interview with Tony Lau Wing, May 27, 2019; "Interview with Tony Lau Wing," *The Big Boss* DVD extras, in *Bruce Lee at Golden Harvest* DVD boxed set (Arrow Video, 2023). Undated, likely 2000s.
345 Kowloon's China Drama Academy and other schools: See Jackie Chan with Jeff Yang, *I Am Jackie Chan* (Ballantine, 1999); Jackie Chan with Zhu Mo, *Never Grow Up* (Gallery Books, 2018); Yung Sai-shing, "Moving Body: The Interactions Between Chinese Opera and Action Cinema," in Meaghan Morris, Si Keung Li, and Stephen Chan Ching-kiu, eds., *Hong Kong Connections: Transnational Imagination in Action Cinema* (Duke University Press/Hong Kong University Press, 2005), pp. 24–26.
345 "those above him with indifference": "Interview with Tony Lau Wing."

510 NOTES

346 pioneered the use: Yung Sai-shing, "Moving Body," pp. 25-26; Yu Mo-Wan, "Martial Arts Directors in Hong Kong Cinema—Hang Yingjie," p. 85; and "Chan Siu-Pang" in "Martial Arts Techniques and Special Effects," p. 69, in Stephen Teo, trans., *The Making of Martial Arts Film—As Told by Filmmakers and Stars* (Hong Kong Film Archive, 1999) p. 85.

347 "Three Leg Lee": Matthew Polly, *Bruce Lee: A Life* (Simon & Schuster, 2018), p. 309.

347 "like it was his own project": "Interview with Tony Lau Wing."

347 "no feeling for it at all": Lu Tajiri, "Raymond Chow of Golden Harvest," *Fighting Stars*, Apr. 1974, p. 13.

347 "an anti-capitalist/anti-colonialist screed": Walter Chaw, "The Big Boss," essay included with *Bruce Lee at Golden Harvest* DVD boxed set, p. 12.

348 "Right now if I say": Chaplin Chang and Roger Lo, *The Bruce Lee They Knew* (Infolink Publishing, 2003), p. 20, trans. Sze K. Chan.

348 "I told him": Chang and Lo, *The Bruce Lee They Knew*, p. 20, trans. Sze K. Chan.

348 "'Wait a minute'": Chang and Lo, *The Bruce Lee They Knew*, p. 22, trans. Sze K. Chan.

348 "He seemed obsessed": Chang and Lo, *The Bruce Lee They Knew*, p. 25, trans. Sze K. Chan.

350 "All of a sudden": Interview with Linda Lee Cadwell, May 2, 2023.

350 surpassing the Julie Andrews movie: "Big Boss Still Rules the Roost," *China Mail*, Nov. 6, 1971. The big winner that weekend was Lo Wei, who had directed both *The Big Boss* and *Vengeance of a Snow Girl*.

350 grossed HKD $3.2 million: John Little, ed., *Bruce Lee: Words of the Dragon, Interviews, 1958–1973* (Tuttle, 1997), p. 115.

350 "Good? You will know": Bao Nguyen interview with Tony Lau Wing, May 27, 2019.

351 "how could he make it in America?": "Interview with Tony Lau Wing."

Chapter 39: The Mid-Pacific Man

352 "I was once asked where I spent most of my time": "Well Traveled," *Nevada State Journal and Reno Evening Gazette*, Nov. 19, 1966.

352 "Mid-Pacific Man": John Little, ed., *Bruce Lee: Words of the Dragon, Interviews, 1958–1973* (Tuttle, 1997), pp. 110-14, 149-54

352 Alexander Hume Ford: Alexander Hume Ford is best remembered now by surfers. He was the founder of the Outrigger Canoe Club, a storied waterman's institution. When he opened it in 1908, he made it a segregated whites-only club. Duke Kahanamoku helped desegregate it later.

352 the native fruits of paradise: Alexander Hume Ford, "Editorial Comment: Americanizing Hawaii," *The Mid-Pacific Magazine* 1, no. 2 (Feb. 1911), p. 193; Alexander Hume Ford, "Introduction to 'An Appeal to Hawaii,'" *The Mid-Pacific Magazine* 16, no. 1 (July 1918), p. 17.

352 "might be expected to do": Jack Moore, "Bruce Lee—The $3 Million Box-Office Draw," *Sunday Post-Herald*, Nov. 21, 1971. Reprinted in Little, ed., *Bruce Lee: Words of the Dragon*, pp. 113–14.

353 "the exotic Oriental support player": Jack Moore, "Superstar Bruce Lee?," *Off Duty*, Pacific ed., Nov. 1972. Reprinted in Little, ed., *Words of the Dragon*, p. 149. Moore's editors may have seen Bruce as akin to a "tragic mulatto," judging by their pull quotes: "Charlie Chan's No. 1 Son. That's What Hollywood Actors Do for a Living"; "Lee Si-lung Has Made It Big While Bruce Lee Is Still Struggling," pp. 8, 9 in original.

353 a thousand fans greeted: "Lee Siu Loong Found His Fame in Foreign Land; Enjoy Making Mandarin Movies," *Kung Sheung Daily News*, Sept. 7, 1971. Reprinted in *Lee Siu Loong, Rise of the Mandarin Superstar: Old Hong Kong Newspaper Collection (Volume 1: 1970–71)*, trans. Sai Loong (self-published, Kindle, 2006).

353 "learn the art of dying": John J. O'Connor, "In the Name of the Law Is the Name of the Game," *New York Times*, Sept. 19, 1971, p. D19.

353 "I wasn't about to give up": Fred Weintraub, *Bruce Lee, Woodstock, and Me* (Brooktree Canyon Press, 2011), p. 3. Citing Howard Friedlander, Lee biographer Matthew Polly writes that the film was sunk by the arrival at Warner Bros. of Dick Zanuck—another person who had trained in *karate* with Stirling Silliphant—and his number two, David Brown, in March 1970. However, Dick Zanuck and David Brown were actually not sacked from 20th Century-Fox until December 31, 1970, and did not step in to Warner Bros. until later in 1971. In *Bruce Lee: The Intercepting Fist*, Steve Kerridge and Darren Chua reprint the cover of Spielman and Friedlander's updated screenplay, dated Sept. 8, 1970. It is more likely that the film was torpedoed by Ted Ashley in advance of the shake-up or as late as the early months of 1971. Polly notes that Weintraub submitted drafts for *Kelsey* to Warner Bros. higher-ups in March and April of 1971. Matthew Polly, *Bruce Lee: A Life* (Simon & Schuster, 2018), pp. 280, 281; Steve Kerridge and Darren Chua, *Bruce Lee: The Intercepting Fist* (On the Fly Productions, 2020), unpaginated.

354 "What's a kung fu?": Bao Nguyen interview with Tom Kuhn, May 18, 2019.

354 "The room was exploding": Bao Nguyen interview with Tom Kuhn, May 18, 2019.

NOTES

354 "Supporting? Maybe": Bao Nguyen interview with Tom Kuhn, May 18, 2019.
355 on October 12: Steve Kerridge and Darren Chua, *Bruce Lee: The Intercepting Fist*. By this time, Spielman and Friedlander were no longer on contract. They were not involved in the final drafts written in the fall of 1971. Those were overseen by an in-house ABC-TV writer named Herman Miller.
355 "So we made a bet": Bao Nguyen interview with Nancy Kwan, May 11, 2019.
355 "our lives were changing": Linda Lee, *The Bruce Lee Story* (Ohara Publications, 1989), p. 107.
356 "What I am trying to do": John Hardie, "The Man With a Stomach Like a Brick Wall," *The Star* (Hong Kong), Nov. 1971, exact date not given, in Little, ed., *Bruce Lee: Words of the Dragon*, p. 108.
356 "Far out": Bruce Lee, *Letters of the Dragon: Correspondence 1958–1973*, ed. John Little (Tuttle, 1998), p. 113. This article was dated November 21,1971.
356 we can only speculate as to why: Matthew Polly believes *The Warrior* may have still been on the table for discussion with Warner Bros. Yet Bruce had met with executives for the *Kung Fu* role in September 1971. However, there is no evidence in the Bruce Lee Family Archive that any further refinement had gone into *The Warrior* treatment to align it with the completed *Kung Fu* screenplay, and no further documents beyond the rough treatment. It's very unlikely that at that point Bruce's treatment could have been viewed as a viable alternative to the *Kung Fu* screenplay, which had been through and was still undergoing revisions by the time Bruce met Tom Kuhn. Polly, *Bruce Lee: A Life*, p. 334.
357 "like the Deep South": Bruce Lee, *Letters of the Dragon*, p. 113.
357 "a lot of adjusting": Bruce Lee, *Letters of the Dragon*, p. 114.
357 *The Concrete Children*: The *Concrete Children* proposal is included in the Bruce Lee Family Archive. Steve Kerridge and Darren Chua also describe it in *Bruce Lee: The Intercepting Fist*, unpaginated.
357 while offering Bruce 49 percent: Contracts viewed in the Bruce Lee Family Archive; interview with Peter Chin, Dec. 15, 2023.
357 "He needs me more than I need him!" Interview with Peter Chin, Dec. 15, 2023.
357 As one headline: "Will Bruce Lee Stay in Hong Kong or Return to the U.S.? Audiences Have Taken a Deep Interest in the Development of the Matter," *Wah Kiu Yat Po*, Dec. 2, 1972. Article from the Hong Kong Film Archive sourced by Winnie Fu, translated by Sze K. Chan.
358 speculated on how much he might be paid: "Will Li hit Hollywood—or HK?" *The China Mail*, November 25, 1971.
358 "I am leaving all things to them": "Will Li hit Hollywood—or HK?" *The China Mail*, ibid.
358 "caught in a dilemma": "Will Bruce Lee Stay in Hong Kong or Return to the U.S.?"
358 "With the compensation he is getting right now": Starry, "Raymond Chow and Bruce Lee Show Support for Wei Ping-ao at Cilaxy Night Club," *Kung Sheung Daily News*, Dec. 4, 1972. Article from the Hong Kong Film Archive sourced by Winnie Fu, translated by Sze K. Chan.
358 "no longer need to go back to the U.S.": Qi Xia, "Bruce Lee May Stay in Hong Kong for an Extended Period of Time," *Kung Sheung Daily News*, Dec. 2, 1971. Article from the Hong Kong Film Archive sourced by Winnie Fu, translated by Sze K. Chan.
358 "Lee is now in Hong Kong": "'Big Boss' Hong Kong's New Boxoffice Champ," *Variety*, Dec. 8, 1971, p. 24.
359 "WHEN YOU RETURN TO THE STATES": Kerridge and Chua, *Bruce Lee: The Intercepting Fist*, unpaginated.

Chapter 40: Yellow-Faced Chinese

360 "He might be too authentic": Fred Weintraub, *Bruce Lee, Woodstock, and Me* (Brooktree Canyon Press, 2011), p. 6.
360 "find something else for him": Bao Nguyen interview with Tom Kuhn, May 18, 2019.
360 "Tom was right": Weintraub, *Bruce Lee, Woodstock, and Me*, p. 6.
360 Shooting began in December 1971: "WB-TV's Pix for ABC," *Variety*, Dec. 22, 1971, p. 48.
360 David Carradine: Tom Kuhn told Bao Nguyen, "First of all, the Carradine name was known in Hollywood because of his father, John Carradine, who had been a, not a major star but a second-level star, nevertheless," Kuhn told Bao Nguyen. "David was certainly not a star, but a well-enough-known name that his name on a television series would at least kick off some kind of a reminder. So yeah, I think it was a benefit for the show to have his name attached to it." Bao Nguyen interview with Tom Kuhn, May 18, 2019.
360 "They put a little tiny corner": "Remembering David Carradine," National Public Radio, June 4, 2009. Original interview by Terry Gross in 1991. www.npr.org/2009/06/04/104959308/remembering-david-carradine.
361 "give the Asian look some kind of authenticity": Bao Nguyen interview with Tom Kuhn, May 18, 2019.
361 "George Takei, as I recall, led the charge": Bao Nguyen interview with Tom Kuhn, May 18, 2019.

512 NOTES

361 "He made some martial arts movement at superspeed": Interview with George Takei, Mar. 4, 2024.

361 "obvious person to play it was Bruce": Interview with George Takei, Mar. 4, 2024.

362 *My Husband, the Enemy:* Ellen Endo, "There's Hope for TV," *Rafu Shimpo,* Oct. 21, 1971.

362 "the cream of Hollywood's Oriental actor colony": "Television Reviews: Kung Fu," *Variety,* Mar. 1, 1972, p. 44.

362 "what the initial fuss was about": Matthew Polly has written that Takei was leading an organization called the Association of Asian/Pacific American Artists and that the organization decided out of pragmatism to support *Kung Fu*. However, this organization did not come into existence until 1990. The term "Asian/Pacific American" did not come into popular usage until the late 1980s. Polly may have conflated this protest with the actions of an organization that James Hong led two decades later against the yellowface casting of Jonathan Pryce in *Miss Saigon* on Broadway. Matthew Polly, *Bruce Lee: A Life* (Simon & Schuster, 2018), p. 325. See Helen Zia, *Asian American Dreams: The Emergence of An American People* (Farrar, Straus and Giroux, 2000), p. 126. Interview with George Takei, Mar. 4, 2024.

362 "a failure of the movement to get representation": Interview with George Takei, Mar. 4, 2024.

362 "ABC got a lot of flak for it": Bao Nguyen interview with Tom Kuhn, May 18, 2019.

362 "a hero in a white man's world": Linda Lee, *Bruce Lee: The Man Only I Knew* (Warner Paperback Library, 1975), pp. 131, 134.

362 "He just couldn't understand it": Bao Nguyen, dir., *Be Water*, documentary (ESPN Films, 2020).

363 "captured on video": *The Pierre Berton Show,* Dec. 9, 1971. It has also been reproduced as "Bruce Lee—The Lost Interview" on various DVDs.

365 "Dear Ted": An edited version of this letter appears in Bruce Lee, *Letters of the Dragon: Correspondence 1958–1973,* ed. John Little (Tuttle, 1998), pp. 162–63. Original letter from the Bruce Lee Family Archive.

366 "The truth is, I am an American-born Chinese": Bruce Lee, "Me and Jeet Kune Do," in John Little, ed., *Bruce Lee: Words of the Dragon, Interviews, 1958–1973* (Tuttle, 1997), p. 124.

367 the joyous old toast: The saying is an adapted excerpt of a phrase from the *Book of Rites* in the Chapter entitled "Li Yun," paragraph 18. ctext.org/liji/li-yun?searchu=故聖人耐以天下為一家，以中國為一人者，非意之也，必知其情，辟於其義，明於其利，達於其患，然後能為之%E3%80%82&searchmode=showall#result.

Chapter 41: Fists and Mayhem

368 *The Intercepting Fist:* Bruce was still calling the movie *The Intercepting Fist* in mid-November, after shooting had begun and the Lee-Baker trailer was being screened in theaters. See Steve Kerridge and Darren Chua, *Bruce Lee: The Intercepting Fist* (On the Fly Productions, 2020), unpaginated, and Little, ed., *Words of the Dragon,* p. 115. An article from Malaysia on Nov. 13, 1971, also notes "The Intercepting Fists, Bruce's second Mandarin film, has started shooting this week at Golden Harvest's new studios at Hammer Hill Road, Kowloon." Sze Ping, "Film News from Hong Kong," *Sarawak Tribune,* Nov. 13, 1971. This suggests perhaps a parallel with the *Kung Fu/Warrior* episode of Bruce misidentifying his own work, whether intentionally or not.

368 publicize Bruce's still unnamed next film: Kerridge and Chua, *Bruce Lee: The Intercepting Fist,* unpaginated.

368 barely written a word: Kerridge and Chua, *Bruce Lee: The Intercepting Fist,* unpaginated; Matthew Polly, *Bruce Lee: A Life* (Simon & Schuster, 2018), p. 337.

369 fell thirteen floors to the street: Robert Clouse, *Bruce Lee: The Biography* (Unique Publications, 1988), p. 105.

369 and her uncomfortable: Linda Lee, *The Bruce Lee Story* (Ohara Publications, 1989), p. 112; Polly, *Bruce Lee: A Life,* p. 354.

369 "I'm not going to fight with anybody": John Little, ed., *Bruce Lee: Words of the Dragon, Interviews, 1958–1973* (Tuttle, 1997), p. 115.

369 "control my anger": Daniel Lee, "The 'Knowing Is Not Enough' Interview: Bruce Lee—Part 1." "'Knowing Is Not Enough': The Official Newsletter of Jun Fan Jeet Kune Do.* Vol. 2, No. 2. Summer 1998.

369 if they were confronted in the streets: Interview with Tony Lau Wing, *The Big Boss* DVD; Polly, *Bruce Lee: A Life,* p. 346.

369 "Hong Kong's a small place": Interview with Nancy Kwan, Apr. 21, 2023.

370 stepped in to rewrite the script: Interview with Andre Morgan, March 7, 2023.

370 "just kept quiet": Bey Logan, *Hong Kong Action Cinema* (Overlook Press, 1995), p. 29.

370 "fresh and new for the audience": Interview with Tony Lau Wing, *The Big Boss* DVD extras, in *Bruce Lee at Golden Harvest* DVD boxed set (Arrow Video, 2023).

370 "learning everything about films": Nora Miao interview from extras for *Fist of Fury*, in *Bruce Lee at Golden Harvest* DVD boxed set (Arrow Video, 2023). Filmed in 1993. See also Steve Kerridge and Darren Chua, *Bruce Lee: The Intercepting Fist,* unpaginated.

370 greyhound reports on the radio: Kerridge and Chua, *Bruce Lee: The Intercepting Fist*, unpaginated; Linda Lee, *The Bruce Lee Story*, p. 113.

370 "he made his point": Logan, *Hong Kong Action Cinema*, p. 29.

370 "feelings accumulated over time": Nora Miao interview from extras for *Fist of Fury*.

371 actually punked out: Brian Kennedy and Elizabeth Guo, *Jingwu: The School That Transformed Kung Fu* (Blue Snake Books, 2010), pp. 76–78. See also Kerridge and Chua, *Bruce Lee: The Intercepting Fist*.

371 explicitly banned Chinese: Robert A. Bickers and Jeffrey N. Wasserstrom, "Shanghai's 'Dogs and Chinese Not Admitted' Sign: Legend, History, and Contemporary Symbol," *China Quarterly* 142 (June 1995), pp. 444–66; Paul Theroux, "Shanghai: The Talk of People's Park," *New York Times Magazine*, Apr. 3, 1988, nytimes.com/1988/04/03/magazine/shanghai-the-talk-of-people-s-park.html. Most seem to agree that until 1928, Europeans did ban from Hongkou Park dogs that did not belong to them and Chinese who were not servants. A picture of a sign dated 1917 that doesn't explicitly name a ban on Chinese is reproduced in Kerridge and Chua's *Bruce Lee: The Intercepting Fist*.

371 "Chen Zhen is": Kerridge and Chua, *Bruce Lee: The Intercepting Fist*, unpaginated.

372 "I had a hard time": "Bruce Lee friend and co-star Bob Baker," from *Tracking the Dragon* VHS videotape. Film is from a 1990 conference in the UK of the same name. YouTube, posted by Greg Probert, youtube.com/watch?v=GrPCxlFD2sU&t=93s.

372 "I just about pulled": "Bruce Lee friend and co-star Bob Baker."

372 than William Goldman's: "The 'Knowing Is Not Enough' Interview—Bruce Lee: The Dan Lee Interview, Part 2," *Knowing Is Not Enough: The Official Newsletter of Jun Fan Jeet Kune Do* 2, no. 3 (Fall 1998), p. 9.

372 "his attitude upset me": Kerridge and Chua, *Bruce Lee: The Intercepting Fist*, unpaginated.

372 Raymond Chow stepped in again: Kerridge and Chua, *Bruce Lee: The Intercepting Fist*, unpaginated.

372 "worthwhile death": The 'Knowing Is Not Enough' Interview—Bruce Lee: The Dan Lee Interview, Part 2," p. 10.

372 "Boy am I happy for you!": Linda Lee, *The Bruce Lee Story*, p. 113.

372 top-grossing movies of the year: Kinnia Yau Shuk-ting, "Interactions Between Japanese and Hong Kong Cinemas," in Meaghan Morris, Siu Leung Lik, and Stephen Chan Ching-kiu, eds., *Hong Kong Connections: Transnational Imagination in Action Cinema* (Duke University Press/Hong Kong University Press, 2005), pp. 44–45.

372 "I could hardly believe my eyes": Phil Ochs, "Requiem for a Dragon Departed," in *I'm Gonna Say It Now: The Writings of Phil Ochs*, ed. David Cohen (Backbeat Books, 2020), pp. 225–26. Originally published in *Los Angeles Weekly News*, Sept. 21–28, 1973.

373 "their domestic film producers": Editors of *Black Belt* magazine, eds., *The Legendary Bruce Lee* (Ohara Publications, 1986), p. 77.

373 "these riots going on now!": Interview with Nancy Kwan, Apr. 21, 2023.

Part XII: Watch Me Now, 1972–1973

375 "Such disfiguring of senses": Cathy Park Hong, *Minor Feelings: An Asian American Reckoning* (One World, 2020), p. 55.

Chapter 42: The World Stage

376 weekly box office take: Cobbett Steinberg, *Reel Facts: The Movie Book of Records* (Vintage Books, 1982), p. 48.

376 desegregate their hiring practices: Ed Guerrero, *Framing Blackness: The African American Image in Film* (Temple University Press, 1993), pp. 84–85.

376 on a $2.2 million budget: Guerrero, *Framing Blackness*, p. 81.

377 saved MGM Studios from bankruptcy: Amy Abugo Ongiri, "*Shaft*: Power Moves," Criterion.com, June 21, 2022, criterion.com/current/posts/7834-shaft-power-moves. Also included in *Shaft* Blu-Ray/DVD (Criterion Collection, 2022); Elvis Mitchell, "A Black Gumshoe Who Built a Genre Is Back on the Job," *New York Times*, Apr. 30, 2000.

377 from collapse: David Desser, "The Kung Fu Craze: Hong Kong Cinema's First American Reception," in Poshek Fu and David Desser, eds., *Hong Kong Cinema: History, Arts, Identity* (Cambridge University Press, 2000), p. 24.

377 "elegant and sexy": Ben Okri, "Grace Wales Bonner," *The Happy Reader* 14 (Winter 2019), p. 21.

378 "I think you better keep": Interview with Andre Morgan, May 12, 2023.

379 "Who are you?": "One on One—Andre Morgan," Al-Jazeera English, Aug. 22 2009, youtube.com/watch?v=k99kkou6ioA.

514 NOTES

380 "the Chinese words which I have in mind": Pang Cheng Lian, "Inside Bruce Lee," *The New Nation* (Singapore), Aug. 14, 1972. Reprinted in John Little, ed., *Bruce Lee: Words of the Dragon, Interviews, 1958–1973* (Tuttle, 1997), p. 133.

381 paying fixers and off-duty police: Steve Kerridge, *Bruce Lee: Legends of the Dragon* (Hate Media, 2013), pp. 56, 63, 80.

381 "defeat all the whites in the film": "An Interview with Bruce Lee's Mother," in Bruce Thomas, *Bruce Lee: Fighting Spirit* (Blue Snake Books, 1994), p. 61.

382 "all but onanistic": Tony Rayns, "Bruce Lee and Other Stories," in *A Study of Hong Kong Cinema in the Seventies*, a publication of the 8th Hong Kong International Film Festival, Apr. 12–27, 1984 (Hong Kong Urban Council, 1984), p. 29. He originally explored these ideas, suggesting they were linked to a kind of Freudian death drive, in Tony Rayns, "Bruce Lee: Narcissism and Nationalism," in *A Study of the Hong Kong Martial Arts Film* (Hong Kong International Film Festival, Apr. 3, 1980), p. 112.

382 "Lee shows himself": Stephen Teo, *Hong Kong Cinema: The Extra Dimensions* (British Film Institute, 1997), p. 114.

382 "To the West": Teo, *Hong Kong Cinema*, pp. 113–14, 120.

384 "A foreigner being beaten": Darren Chua, "Premiere of the Dragon," *Bruce Lee Forever* 02 (Jan./Feb. 2023), pp. 6, 9.

385 leaders quickly moved to censor: See Chia Poteik, "Martial Arts and the Triad Gangs," *The Straits Times* (Singapore), Mar. 29, 1974, p. 16, eresources.nlb.gov.sg/newspapers/Digitised/Article/straitstimes 19740329-1.2.74.

385 politicians established a national body: Poteik, "Martial Arts and the Triad Gangs." The Martial Arts Instruction Bill was passed in March 1974. Politicians argued that as many as one-third of martial arts schools were fronts for triads.

385 "can't just pretend it does not exist": Pang Cheng Lian in Little, ed., *Words of the Dragon*, pp. 138–39.

385 "An action film borders": Piera Kwan, "The Violence Cult," *Hong Kong Standard*, Feb. 10, 1973. Reprinted in Little, ed., *Words of the Dragon*, pp. 155–57.

Chapter 43: The Cost

386 how to vanish: I'm deeply indebted to Susan Rogers, who closely watched Prince rise from stardom to superstardom with *Purple Rain*, for these insights, and to Pooja Nansi for introducing us.

386 "I have to take responsibility": Notes from the Bruce Lee Family Archive. His manifesto took many drafts, suggesting that he was perhaps continuing to work on this in the last year of his life. Also published as "Another Actor Speaks His Mind" in John Little, ed., *Bruce Lee: Artist of Life* (Tuttle Publishing, 1999), p. 222.

386 "the dirtiest business": Interview with Peter Chin, Dec. 11, 2024.

387 "form of relaxation to me nowadays": Bruce Lee, *Letters of the Dragon: Correspondence 1958–1973*, ed. John Little (Tuttle, 1998), pp. 168–69.

387 "I'm glad you showed up": Interview with Dan Inosanto, Sept. 26, 2023.

387 "Strangers would stop at my door": Mito Uyehara, *Bruce Lee: The Incomparable Fighter* (Ohara Publications, 1988), p. 138.

387 "everybody knows where to find you": Interview with Linda Lee Cadwell, May 2, 2023.

388 "there were a lot of sharks": Interview with Doug Palmer, Oct. 12, 2018.

388 "When Noriko had to use the toilet": Doug Palmer, *Bruce Lee: Sifu, Friend, and Big Brother* (Chin Music Press, 2020), pp. 188–89.

388 "the possibility of them being kidnapped": Interview with Doug Palmer, Oct. 12, 2018.

388 "in a small place like Hong Kong": H. S. Chow, "Action Man Bruce Likes the Quiet Life," *China Mail*, July 25, 1972. Reprinted in John Little, ed., *Bruce Lee: Words of the Dragon, Interviews, 1958–1973* (Tuttle, 1997), p. 122.

388 "Yeah, it's very costly": Bao Nguyen interview with Nancy Kwan, May 11, 2019.

388 "To stop Bruce getting too focused": Interview with Andre Morgan, March 7, 2023.

388 retired martial artist: John Little, *Bruce Lee: A Warrior's Journey* (Contemporary Books, 2001), pp. 85–90.

389 didn't feel comfortable in the role: Taky said he also had pressing export-import business at his grocery in October. See Little, *Bruce Lee: A Warrior's Journey*, pp. 80–81.

389 procure three more: "*Enter the Dragon* Producer Andre Morgan," *The Bruce Willow Podcast*, June 28, 2020, youtube.com/watch?v=yXgnfo-Uauc; interview with Andre Morgan, Mar. 7, 2023.

391 "stay in Southeast Asia all the time": Piera Kwan, "The Violence Cult," *Hong Kong Standard*, Feb. 10, 1973. Reprinted in Little, ed., *Words of the Dragon*, pp. 155–57.

391 "I had to prove not only": Interview with Andre Morgan, Mar. 7, 2023.
392 "how Bruce was in the fights": Fred Weintraub, *Bruce Lee, Woodstock, and Me* (Brooktree Canyon Press, 2011), p. 8.
392 "enjoy it that much more": Letter from Bruce Lee Family Archive dated July 3, 1972. The draft is written in Linda's handwriting, and reprinted undated in Bruce Lee, *Letters of the Dragon*, p. 165–66.
392 "So I went to Hong Kong": Fred Weintraub interview, *Game of Death: Alternative Versions*, in *Bruce Lee at Golden Harvest* Blu-Ray DVD boxed set (Arrow Films, 2023).

Chapter 44: Representations

393 "here you are": Henry Kissinger to President Richard Nixon, "My Talks with Chou En-lai," top-secret memo, July 14, 1971, National Security Archive at George Washington University, nsarchive2.gwu.edu/NSAEBB/NSAEBB66/ch-40.pdf.
393 "an exuberant novelty act": "Fist of Fury," *Variety*, Nov. 1, 1972.
393 "half the audiences were non-Chinese": "U.S. Publisher Arrives in Hong Kong for Consultations with Hong Kong Film Producers Bruce Lee and Run Run Shaw," Pagoda Films Press Release, undated, likely Jan. 1973, Bruce Lee Family Archive.
393 entertainment for the riotous diversity: For a detailed and lively history of this indie movie milieu and the rise of kung fu film in the United States, see Gracy Hendrix and Chris Poggiali, *These Fists Break Bricks* (Mondo Books, 2021). For a parallel history from the UK, see the brilliant Steve Kerridge's *Everybody Was Kung Fu Fighting* (On the Fly Productions, 2021).
394 "We're not going to show it": Interview with Lillian Fabros Bando, Jan. 17, 2024.
394 "everybody's jumping up and down": Interview with Vicci Wong, Jan. 3, 2024.
394 "the explosion of Chinese made films": "U.S. Publisher Arrives In Hong Kong for Consultations with Hong Kong Film Producers Bruce Lee and Run Run Shaw." Pagoda Films Press Release, January 11, 1973. From the Bruce Lee Archive.
394 hoping to put behind him: Robert Clouse, *The Making of Enter the Dragon* (Unique Publications, 1987), p. 25.
395 "his very lithe and agile cash cow": Fred Weintraub, *Bruce Lee, Woodstock, and Me* (Brooktree Canyon Press, 2011), pp. 10–11.
395 "'Sign the contract, Raymond'": Weintraub, *Bruce Lee, Woodstock, and Me*, p. 12.
395 "how the economics would really work": Bao Nguyen interview with Andre Morgan, Apr. 22, 2019.
395 Concord ponied up: Contract between Warner Brothers, Sequoia Pictures, and Concord Productions, Nov. 3, 1972, Bruce Lee Family Archive.
395 "I didn't know anything about Hong Kong": Michael Allin commentary on *Enter the Dragon* DVD, from *Bruce Lee at Golden Harvest* boxed set (Arrow Films, 2023).
396 "high chroma reds, golds, and blues": See Fred Weintraub and Tom Kuhn, dirs., *Bruce Lee: The Curse of the Dragon*, documentary, 1993; also Shannon Lee, dir., *No Way As Way*, documentary, 2013. Both on the *Enter the Dragon* DVD from *Bruce Lee at Golden Harvest* boxed set. *Bruce Lee: The Curse of the Dragon* is widely available. *No Way As Way* is also on the fortieth-anniversary DVD of *Enter the Dragon*.
396 The treatment: Michael Allin, *Blood and Steel*, treatment "from an idea by Fred Weintraub and Paul Heller," Aug. 26. 1972. Courtesy of the Bruce Lee Family Archive.
396 scoffed at the tiny budget: John Kelly, "Robert Clouse: Bruce Lee's Trusted Ally," *Inside Kung Fu*, Aug. 1987, p. 42.
397 "very dedicated": Kelly, "Robert Clouse: Bruce Lee's Trusted Ally," p. 41.
397 would receive one hundred thousand dollars: According to Andre Morgan, Bruce received one hundred thousand dollars, Chow was to receive twenty-five thousand, and Sequoia was to receive twenty-five thousand. Interview with Andre Morgan, May 12, 2023. That sum of $100,000 would be worth $740,000 in 2024 US dollars.

Chapter 45: The Proud Dragon

398 "who was trying to take advantage of me": Editors of *Black Belt* magazine, eds., *The Legendary Bruce Lee* (Ohara Publications, 1986), p. 77.
398 promote it as a new Bruce Lee film: Bey Logan, *Hong Kong Action Cinema* (Overlook Press, 1995), p. 31
398 "He was wearing": John Corcoran interview with Stirling Silliphant, transcript, undated, part 4, pp. 6, 9. Courtesy of the Stirling Silliphant Papers at UCLA.
398 "What was I supposed to do?": Alex Ben Block, *The Legend of Bruce Lee* (Dell, 1974), pp. 86–87.
398 "He had many faults": Tony Crawley, "Game Interview: Stirling Silliphant," *Game Magazine* (UK), Fall 1976. Courtesy of the Stirling Silliphant Papers at UCLA.

516 NOTES

398 "He meant a great deal to me": Tony Crawley, "Game Interview: Stirling Silliphant."
399 "implicated by your fame": "Bruce Lee and Nora Miao—Close Friends. Their Families Have a Close Relation," *Bruce Lee: His Privacy and Anecdotes* (Bruce Lee Jeet-kune-do Club, 1976), p. 52.
399 "not to let fame get to him!": Matthew Polly, *Bruce Lee: A Life* (Simon & Schuster, 2018), pp. 399–400.
399 "I felt real bad and disappointed": Mito Uyehara, *Bruce Lee: The Incomparable Fighter* (Ohara Publications, 1988), p. 79.
399 to Yip's family home to apologize: Polly, *Bruce Lee: A Life*, p. 400.
399 "If you do not take yourself as a superman": Wong Shun Leung, *Reminiscence of Bruce Lee* (Bruce Lee Jeet-kune-do Club, 1978), pp. 55–56.
400 "Another reason to stay home more": Interview with Linda Lee Cadwell, May 2, 2023.
400 "get at Bruce for their own reasons": Michael Kaye, "Exit the Dragon," *Penthouse*, international ed., vol. 10, no. 3 (1975), p. 28.
400 "Friends like you, comes once in a blue moon": "Letter to Jon Y. Lee—January 9, 1973," in Bruce Lee, *Letters of the Dragon: Correspondence 1958–1973*, ed. John Little (Tuttle, 1998), p. 176. Jon was James Lee's brother.
401 keeping the title of *Blood and Steel*: A small review in *Box Office* magazine for *Fist of Fury* in November mentioned Warner Bros. was making Lee's next movie, *Blood and Steel*. "Foreign Language Film Reviews: Fist of Fury," *Box Office*, Nov. 13, 1972, p. B6; Polly, *Bruce Lee: A Life*, p. 408.
401 "Asia's first superstar": "Enter the Dragon," *Newsweek*, Jan. 29, 1973, p. 46.
401 made Bruce's preferred title its headline: "Enter the Dragon," *Newsweek*.
402 "Extremes, though contrary, have the like effects": The 1962 letter to Pearl published in *Letters of the Dragon* excludes this section. From the Bruce Lee Family Archive.
402 "go too far to an extreme": Document from the Bruce Lee Family Archive, undated, likely 1959 or 1960, trans. Sze K. Chan.
402 "his continued physical fitness": Linda Lee, *Bruce Lee: The Man Only I Knew* (Warner Paperback Library, 1975), p. 14.
402 "how long I can keep this up": Linda Lee, *Bruce Lee: The Man Only I Knew*, p. 11.

Chapter 46: The Weight

403 unsuitable for Asian audiences: Chaplin Chang and Roger Lo, *The Bruce Lee They Knew* (Infolink Publishing, 2003), pp. 149–150, trans. Sze K. Chan.
403 "juvenile": John Kelly, "Robert Clouse: Bruce Lee's Trusted Ally," *Inside Kung Fu*, Aug. 1987, p. 103.
403 "It was his dream": Linda Lee interview in *Enter the Dragon* DVD extras, in *Bruce Lee at Golden Harvest* DVD boxed set, 2023. This is also included in earlier US DVD versions of *Enter the Dragon*.
403 "All my life": From the original document in the Bruce Lee Family Archive. Excerpts were published in edited form in Linda Lee, *Bruce Lee: The Man Only I Knew* (Warner Paperback Library, 1975), pp. 48–49, and John Little, ed., *Bruce Lee: Artist of Life* (Tuttle Publishing, 1999), p. 237. In his language of "self-actualization" and "self-image actualization" he was borrowing from Fritz Perls. The language of "blindly following propaganda, organized truths, etc." comes from Krishnamurti. The last "All my life" is scrawled almost incomprehensibly.
404 lured him with a forty-thousand-dollar contract: Matthew Polly, *Bruce Lee: A Life* (Simon & Schuster, 2018), p. 409. The first mention of *Enter the Dragon* in *Variety* on Jan. 10, 1973—five days before shooting was to commence—actually lists John Saxon's name before Bruce's. "'Dragon' and 'Harris' onto Warner's Slate," *Variety*, Jan. 10, 1973, p. 6.
404 not the one playing Roper: Robert Clouse, *The Making of Enter the Dragon* (Unique Publications, 1987), p. 30.
404 the low fee was "exploiting" him: John Little, "*Enter the Dragon*: The Making of a Classic Movie," essay included in *Enter the Dragon* DVD, 25th Anniversary Special Edition (Warner Home Video, 1998), p. 14.
405 "I don't want any part of it": Interview with Linda Lee Cadwell, May 2, 2023.
406 Weintraub promised to do it: Polly, *Bruce Lee: A Life*, pp. 407–408.
406 "if you were still awake by that time": Steve Jacques, "Enter the Dragon," *Fighting Stars*, Oct. 1974, p. 8.
406 "The main thing": From Bruce's annotated script for *Enter the Dragon*, dated Dec. 26, 1972. The title page reads, "BLOOD AND STEEL"—and then on the next line below it, "ENTER, THE DRAGON." Courtesy of the Bruce Lee Family Archive.
407 "They could have up and left": Interview with Linda Lee Cadwell, May 2, 2023.
407 "Linda was the peacemaker": Interview with Andre Morgan, May 12, 2023.

407 "at this late hour": Robert Clouse, *Bruce Lee: The Biography* (Unique Publications, 1988), p. 149.
407 "This is a coproduction": Interview with Linda Lee Cadwell, May 2, 2023.
408 "Let's play it straight here": Kelly, "Robert Clouse: Bruce Lee's Trusted Ally," p. 103.
409 each with two birds inside: Clouse, *The Making of* Enter the Dragon, pp. 181–82.
409 a torrent of curses at him and the crew: Fred Weintraub, *Bruce Lee, Woodstock, and Me* (Brooktree Canyon Press, 2011), pp. 21–22.
409 the couch would be red: Weintraub, *Bruce Lee, Woodstock, and Me*, pp. 18–20.
409 "The Chinese say yes to everything": Weintraub, *Bruce Lee, Woodstock, and Me*, p. 141.
409 "thought they were imbeciles": Clouse, *The Making of* Enter the Dragon, p. 104.
409 steered her into Communist Chinese waters: Clouse, *The Making of* Enter the Dragon, p. 175.
410 push the director off the roof: Polly, *Bruce Lee: A Life*, p. 416; Clouse, *The Making of* Enter the Dragon, p. 177.
410 "whatever the problem was disappeared": Paul Heller interview in *Game of Death: Alternative Versions* in *Bruce Lee at Golden Harvest* DVD boxed set (Arrow Films, 2023).
410 receive twelve stitches: Clouse, *The Making of* Enter the Dragon, pp. 160, 165, 167.
410 Bob took twelve takes' worth: Bey Logan, *Hong Kong Action Cinema* (Overlook Press, 1995), p. 39.
410 "followed by loss of strength": "(Chapter) Thirty" in Laozi, *Tao Te Ching*, trans. Gia-Fu Feng and Jane English with Toinette Lippe (Vintage Books, 1972; repr. ed., 2000), unpaginated.
410 recognize the carpenters and plasterers: Clouse, *The Making of* Enter the Dragon, pp. 120, 122.
410 called them "brother": Peter Bennett letter to P. Alston and Mito Uyehara at Rainbow Publications, Mar. 19, 1974, Bruce Lee Family Archive.
410 "squat down on the ground and talk": Clouse, *The Making of* Enter the Dragon, pp. 120, 122.
410 double their pay: Chaplin Chang and Roger Lo, *The Bruce Lee They Knew* (Infolink Publishing, 2003), p. 40, trans. Sze K. Chan.
411 "It's a Chinese thing": Bao Nguyen interview with Angela Mao, Feb. 4, 2019.
411 target of challenges from extras: For more, see John Little, *Wrath of the Dragon: The Real Fights of Bruce Lee* (ECW, 2023).
411 rolling film of the encounter: Clouse, *The Making of* Enter the Dragon, p. 158.
411 "Your *gung fu* isn't real": Bennett letter to Alston and Uyehara; Wong Shun Leung, *Reminiscence of Bruce Lee* (Bruce Lee Jeet-kune-do Club, 1978), p. 56.
411 "If I don't have real *gung fu*": Wong, *Reminiscence of Bruce Lee*, p. 56.
411 "This after Bruce help him, right?": Clouse, *The Making of* Enter the Dragon, p. 180.
411 another kick into his solar plexus: Bennett letter to Alston and Uyehara.
411 "He did not make any sound": Wong, *Reminiscence of Bruce Lee*, p. 56.
411 said his *sifu* had been wrong: Bennett letter to Alston and Uyehara.
411 "Seeing his appearance": Wong, *Reminiscence of Bruce Lee*, pp. 56–57.
412 take him to the hospital right away: Clouse, *The Making of* Enter the Dragon, pp. 158–59. See also Henry Wong interview in Chang and Lo, *The Bruce Lee They Knew*.
412 so that he could destroy it": Wong, who had been filming pickup shots and behind-the-scenes shots for a possible documentary, told Bruce there was other footage on the roll that he needed to preserve. Bruce let it go. But American technicians at Warner Bros. later destroyed it. Fans everywhere still mourn the loss. Clouse, *The Making of* Enter the Dragon, pp. 158–59.
412 "He was like a wounded beast": Wong, *Reminiscence of Bruce Lee*, p. 57.
412 "shatter her image as she walked by them": Little, "*Enter the Dragon*: The Making of a Classic Movie," p. 26. See also Clouse, *The Making of* Enter the Dragon, pp. 119, 121.
412 "somebody else's rice bowl": Paul Heller in Guy Scutter, dir., *Bruce Lee, Martial Arts Master*, documentary (Merlin Group/Canal, 1993).
412 "That's you and me": Clouse, *The Making of* Enter the Dragon, p. 193.

Chapter 47: The Names, Part 3

414 "It was a ludicrous, awful film": Aljean Harmetz, "Karate Films Deliver a Low Blow to Subtlety," *Los Angeles Times*, Jan. 6, 1974.
414 changed the movie's title five more times: Charles Lucas, "Profile of a Great American Fad," *Black Belt*, Oct. 1974, pp. 54, 56.

518 NOTES

414 "battering savagery": "5 Fingers of Death," *Variety*, Mar. 21, 1973, p. 18.

414 taken in ten million dollars worldwide: "Hong Kong Chop-Socky Pix & Cannes," *Variety*, May 30, 1973, p. 20.

414 "like a babysitter": Alex Ben Block, *The Legend of Bruce Lee* (Dell, 1974), p. 116.

415 "Who Will Get Superstar Li?": "Who Will Get Superstar Li?," *China Mail*, Mar. 2, 1973, p. 1.

415 "Bruce Will Make": "Bruce Will Make Film for Shaws," *The Star* (Hong Kong), Mar. 3, 1973, p. 1.

415 Bruce had demanded the record amount: Stephen Teo, *Chinese Martial Arts Cinema: The Wuxia Tradition* (Edinburgh University Press, 2009), p. 78.

415 *Variety* declared that Bruce: Jack Pitman, "Kung-Fu Chopping Big B.O.," *Variety*, May 2, 1973, pp. 5, 22. This is probably also the first printed use of the term "chop-socky," which appears in the headline on page 22.

415 The United States Catholic Conference: "Catholics Find MPAA Over-Permissive on Violence; Condemn Hong Kong Pix," *Variety*, June 13, 1973, p. 7.

415 the "Hong Kong-made 'chop-socky'": Robert J. Landry, "Global Slant at Cannes Fest: From Kung-Fu to Italo-U.S. Deals," *Variety*, May 9, 1973, p. 1.

415 "advertising as soon as possible?": Memo is dated Apr. 9, 1973. Reprinted in Dave Friedman, *Enter the Dragon: A Photographer's Journey* (self-published, 2013), p. 237.

416 like a kids' flick: Fred Weintraub, *Bruce Lee, Woodstock, and Me* (Brooktree Canyon Press, 2011), p. 17.

416 thinking it sounded like a monster movie: Friedman, *Enter the Dragon*, p. 8.

416 "alternative titles": Reproduced in Friedman, *Enter the Dragon*, p. 234.

416 sit through a Fu Manchu flick: Advertisement for Oakland and UA Hayward Drive-Ins, *The Daily Review* (Hayward, CA), June 9, 1973, p. 7.

416 the name BRUCE LEE: Michele Lomax, "A Big Day for Kung Fu Fans," *San Francisco Examiner*, Aug. 23, 1973, p. 30.

416 "an ovation": Michele Lomax, "Up to Our Fists in Kung Fu," *San Francisco Examiner*, June 1, 1973. Her note about the audiences being "predominantly black" comes in the last paragraph, so I've added it in parentheses here. In a contemporanous piece, Gene Siskel noted that 75 percent of the audiences in Chicago for kung fu movies were Black. Siskel, "Chicks to Chops Shift in Movie," *Oakland Tribune*, May 29, 1973, p. 35.

416 "Black adolescents wandered the aisles": Harmetz, "Karate Films Deliver a Low Blow to Subtlety."

417 "That black youth was not mimicking Bruce Lee": Jeff Furumura, "Kung-Fu Films: Big Bucks & Low Flying Kicks," *Gidra*, Feb. 1974, p. 9. Italics in original.

417 "I'm 'brother.' Boom!": Interview with Leon Jay, Jan. 14, 2023. See also Michele Lomax, "Bruce Lee's Last Film—Also His Best," *San Francisco Examiner*, Aug. 22, 1973, p. 31.

417 "to a point where it's ridiculous": Michael Kaye, "Exit the Dragon," *Penthouse* international ed., vol. 10, no. 3 (1975), p. 27.

417 Bruce, Betty, and Linda had met: Matthew Polly, *Bruce Lee: A Life* (Simon & Schuster, 2018), pp. 355–56.

417 suicide attempt at the end of 1972: Mito Uyehara, *Bruce Lee: The Incomparable Fighter* (Ohara Publications, 1988), p. 138. Matthew Polly covers these allegations as well. Polly, *Bruce Lee: A Life*, pp. 410–11.

418 "the fuckingest action motion picture that has ever been made": Bruce Lee, *Letters of the Dragon: Correspondence 1958–1973*, ed. John Little (Tuttle, 1998), p. 178.

418 as if he had dropped his glasses: Linda Lee, *Bruce Lee: The Man Only I Knew* (Warner Paperback Library, 1975), p. 94.

418 "making a loud noise and was shaking": Block, *The Legend of Bruce Lee*, p. 111.

418 "He's very sick": Linda Lee, *Bruce Lee: The Man Only I Knew*, p. 195.

419 "He had very irregular respiration": Toby Russell, dir., George Tan, prod., *Death by Misadventure: The Mysterious Life of Bruce Lee* (VideoAsia, 2003).

419 "he would die": Linda Lee, *Bruce Lee: The Man Only I Knew*, p. 195.

419 "You never write": Bruce Thomas, *Bruce Lee: Fighting Spirit* (Blue Snake Books, 1994), p. 195.

419 "everything was fine": Linda Lee, *Bruce Lee: The Man Only I Knew*, p. 14.

419 Dilantin: Linda Lee, *The Bruce Lee Story* (Ohara Publications, 1989), p. 153.

420 Bruce invited: Interview with Peter Chin, Dec. 15, 2023. Interview with Mitoshi Uyehara, Sept. 20, 2023.

420 laughing the same way every time: Interview with Mitoshi Uyehara, Sept. 20, 2023.

420 "Hold this cushion": Interview with Mitoshi Uyehara, Sept. 20, 2023.

420 "I hope we can return": Uyehara, *Bruce Lee: The Incomparable Fighter*, p. 142. When she and Bruce had been in Los Angeles two months before, she had told Uyehara, "Hong Kong is too hard for the kids. It's crowded

and I don't like to have them being exposed to the publicity." Mike Plane (Mito Uyehara), "Super Star Bruce Lee: An Acclaimed Phenomenon," *Fighting Stars*, Oct. 1973, p. 21.
420 "You almost lost your *sifu*": John Scura, "Bruce Lee—the Instructor," *Fighting Stars*, Spring 1977, p. 32.
420 the subject turned to getting old: Interview with Dan Inosanto, Sept. 26, 2023.
420 "You only get wiser": Maxwell Pollard, "In Kato's Gung Fu, Action Is Instant," *Black Belt*, Nov. 1967, p. 20.
420 "I don't think I would like that at all": Bao Nguyen, dir., *Be Water*, documentary (ESPN Films, 2020).
420 "He really dreaded that": Steve Rubenstein, "In the Shadow of a Legend," *Black Belt*, Aug. 1974, p. 20.
420 Peter worried: Interview with Peter Chin, December 11, 2024. 走火入魔 literally means "walking fire into a demon," and is a recognized condition in Asian psychiatry. Translation by Sze K. Chan.
420 "I'm never going to be like that": Interview with Peter Chin, Dec. 15, 2023.
421 a $1.35 million policy with Lloyds of London: Tom Bleecker, *Unsettled Matters: The Life and Death of Bruce Lee* (Gilderoy Publications, 1996), pp. 145–46. According to Bleecker, the sum of the policies came to nearly USD $1.6 million, which in 2024 dollars is about $11.2 million.
421 "It's unlucky": "An Interview with Bruce's Mother," in Thomas, *Bruce Lee: Fighting Spirit*, pp. 57–58.
421 "We've got it": Robert Clouse, *The Making of* Enter the Dragon (Unique Publications, 1987), p. 197.
421 "They went bananas": Robert Clouse, *Bruce Lee: The Biography* (Unique Publications, 1988), p. 167.
421 make five movies for Warner Bros.: "Bruce Li Scoops a Superstar Salary," *China Mail*, June 28, 1973.
421 "After spending a full two hours": Ted Ashley cable to Bruce Lee, June 7, 1973, Bruce Lee Family Archive.
421 "Following up on Ted": Dick Lederer cable to Bruce Lee, June 7, 1973, Friedman, Enter the Dragon.
422 "Dear Ted, Just": Letter from Bruce Lee to Ted Ashley, June 8, 1973, Bruce Lee Family Archive.
422 "AS REQUESTED": Ted Ashley cable to Bruce Lee, received June 13, 1973, Bruce Lee Family Archive.
422 "I am so relieved": Bruce Lee cable to Ted Ashley, June 16, 1973, Bruce Lee Family Archive.

Chapter 48: The Light of Stars

423 it hit number one: Desser, "The Kung Fu Craze: Hong Kong Cinema's First American Reception," in Poshek Fu and David Desser, eds., *Hong Kong Cinema: History, Arts, Identity* (Cambridge University Press, 2000), pp. 22–23.
423 "I won't carry Jim": Alex Ben Block, *The Legend of Bruce Lee* (Dell, 1974), p. 87.
423 "hear him out": July 20, 1973, letter to Adrian Marshall, Bruce Lee Family Archive. Reprinted in Bruce Lee, *Letters of the Dragon: Correspondence 1958–1973*, ed. John Little (Tuttle, 1998), p. 183.
423 "I must be very, very careful": Bruce Thomas, *Bruce Lee: Fighting Spirit* (Blue Snake Books, 1994), p. 199.
424 largest showcase yet for Asian martial arts: David Carradine was considered as a co-headliner, but he was later replaced by Keye Luke. It did become one of the largest expos to date, with a reported crowd of ten thousand at the Los Angeles Sports Arena on August 17. Linda Lee accepted an honor for Bruce. "Budo Under the Big Top," *Black Belt*, Jan. 1974, p. 36. Interview with Mito Uyehara, Sept. 20, 2023.
424 He told Mito: Interview with Mito Uyehara, Sept. 20, 2023.
424 He snapped back: Thomas, *Bruce Lee: Fighting Spirit*, p. 198.
424 "He was kind of down": Interview with Peter Chin, Dec. 11, 2024.
424 "nervous, suspicious, and hard to get along with": Jesse Glover, *Bruce Lee Between Wing Chun and Jeet Kune Do* (self-published, 1976), p. 90.
424 "What are *you* doing, Bruce?": Interview with Nancy Kwan, Apr. 21, 2023.
425 "that he had done it before": Maria Yi, "A Collection of Bruce's Funny Deeds," in *Bruce Lee: His Privacy and Anecdotes* (Bruce Lee Jeet-kune-do Club, 1976), p. 60.
425 As Linda was leaving for lunch: Linda Lee, *Bruce Lee: The Man Only I Knew* (Warner Paperback Library, 1975), p. 10.
425 Raymond came by: Matthew Polly, *Bruce Lee: A Life* (Simon & Schuster, 2018), p. 440.
426 "But I was there, I saw him": Bao Nguyen, dir., *Be Water*, documentary (ESPN Films, 2020).
426 "The friend asked her to turn on the four o'clock news": Nguyen, dir., *Be Water*.
426 When Taky Kimura arrived: Thomas, *Bruce Lee: Fighting Spirit*, p. 201.
426 "Let him have his moment to cry": Nguyen, dir., *Be Water*.
426 On July 25th . . . : This section is based on Linda Lee's account in *The Bruce Lee Story* (Ohara Publications, 1989), pp. 160 and 162; Felix Dennis and Don Atyeo's account in *Bruce Lee: King of Kung Fu* (Straight Arrow Books, 1974), pp. 76–78; and Wu Shih, dir., *Bruce Lee: The Man and the Legend* (Golden Harvest, 1973).

520 NOTES

428 "Long after the coffin was gone": Dennis and Atyeo, *Bruce Lee: King of Kung Fu*, p. 77.
428 had purchased to transport Bruce: Interview with Andre Morgan, Mar. 7, 2023.
428 "Do you want him buried with his kind?": Polly, *Bruce Lee: A Life*, p. 5.
428 "I am not standing here": Linda Lee's eulogy for Bruce Lee, courtesy of the Bruce Lee Family Archive.
429 "I broke down": Glover, *Bruce Lee Between Wing Chun and Jeet Kune Do*, p. 90.

Part XIII: Afterlives, 1973–Now

431 "Death is a return": *The Book of Lieh-Tzu: A Classic of Tao*. Translated by A.C. Graham (Columbia University Press, 1960, 1990), p. 25.

Chapter 49: The World Is a Ghetto

432 In 1973, kung fu movies took in: "Variety Chart Summary 1973," *Variety*, May 8, 1974, p. 68; "$11,106,237 to Chop Socky Pic in U.S. Playoff," *Variety*, May 8, 1974, p. 68. *Enter the Dragon* had taken in $3.8 million and ranked eighteenth, *The Chinese Connection* $2.3 million and *Fists of Fury* $1.5 million. Together this take would be $7.6 million, or $75.5 million in 2024 dollars. At eighth, *The Getaway* grossed $5.2 million.
432 "conveys the West's antipathy": Stephen Teo, *Hong Kong Cinema: The Extra Dimensions* (British Film Institute, 1997), p. 117.
433 "I'm looking at this fucking line": Interview with Andre Morgan, Mar. 7, 2023.
433 "Lee had an ego": Lou Gaul, "Beating a Path Toward Superstardom," *Fighting Stars*, Dec. 1975, p. 44. He would say in another interview: "I think it was harder for Bruce to break into show business than for me because when Bruce was doing his thing, he was the one who had to pave the way. He's Chinese." Jim Kelly would also say, "Bruce didn't have anyone to open up the doors for him as far as his nationality is concerned, but I did." *Black Belt Magazine's Best of Bruce Lee #2*, 1975, p. 48.
434 "It is not the vulgarity of James Arness pistol-whipping": Phil Ochs, *I'm Gonna Say It Now: The Writings of Phil Ochs*, ed. David Cohen (Backbeat Books, 2020), p. 225.
434 "the finger pointing to the moon": Alan Watts, *Zen Buddhism* (James Ladd Delkin, 1948), republished in Alan Watts, *Zen: A Short Introduction* (New World Library, 2019), p. 38.
435 "When the opponent expands": These lines may have been influenced by Miyamoto Musashi's "Scroll of Water" in *The Book of Five Rings*. He had written, "Here is what I call the flowing-water strike: you are fighting an equal battle with your opponent and each of you is searching for an opening. In this situation, when your opponent tries in haste to back off or disengage his sword or push yours back, you expand your body and your mind." Miyamoto Musashi, *The Complete Book of Five Rings*, ed. and trans. Kenji Tokitsu (Shambhala Press, 2000), p. 54.
435 1962 letter to Pearl Tso: The 1962 letter to Pearl published in *Letters of the Dragon* excludes this section. It reads, "Inside my mind, opposition have become mutually cooperative instead of mutually exclusive. In practice, when my opponent expands, I contract; when he contracts, I expand—to fit my movements harmoniously and continuously into that of my opponent without striving or resisting." Bruce Lee Family Archive.
435 "With regards to the philosophy": Bey Logan, *Hong Kong Action Cinema* (Overlook Press, 1995), p. 40.
435 "I think we were all": Paul Heller commentary in *Enter the Dragon* DVD, *Bruce Lee at Golden Harvest* boxed set (Arrow Video, 2023). This commentary track is widely available on US *Enter the Dragon* DVDs.
435 "After fan protests": Matthew Polly, *Bruce Lee: A Life* (Simon & Schuster, 2018), p. 586.

Chapter 50: Melancholia and Memory

436 "Although we do not have the final autopsy report": Felix Dennis and Don Atyeo, *Bruce Lee: King of Kung Fu* (Straight Arrow Books, 1974), p. 80.
436 "I appeal to you": Linda Lee, *Bruce Lee: The Man Only I Knew* (Warner Paperback Library, 1975), p. 204.
437 offering conflicting theories of death: The literature here is too vast to cite. Three of the most recent theories can be found in Matthew Polly, *Bruce Lee: A Life* (Simon & Schuster, 2018), pp. 455–73; "The Death of Bruce Lee," *History's Greatest Mysteries*, episode 3 (History Channel, 2021); and Priscila Villalvazo with Raul Fernandez-Prado, Maria Dolores Sánchez Niño, Sol Carriazo, Beatriz Fernández-Fernández, Alberto Ortiz, and Maria Vanessa Perez-Gomez, "Who Killed Bruce Lee? The Hyponatraemia Hypothesis," *Clinical Kidney Journal* 15, no. 12 (2022): pp. 2169–76.
437 "Personalities and narratives projected": Gloria Steinem, *Marilyn: Norma Jean* (1986; ebook ed., Open Road Media, 2013), p. 10.
437 "We felt it wouldn't last": Charles Lucas, "The Cult of Bruce Lee," *Fighting Stars*, Aug. 1975, p. 6.
437 she found herself: Charles Lucas, "They All Had Faces Like Bruce," *Fighting Stars*, Aug. 1975, pp. 22–29.
438 And even Lee Bruce: For an entertaining, sometimes poignant treatment of this period, its movies, and their "stars," see David Gregory, dir., *Enter the Clones of Bruce* (Severin Films, 2023).

NOTES 521

438 Flicks like: See Chris Poggiali, "Exit the Dragon, Enter the Clones," in *Legacy of Dragon, Volume 1*, Book included in the *Game of Clones: Bruceploitation Volume 1* boxed set (Severin Films, 2024).

438 a "biopic": Kenneth Turan, "The Apotheosis of Bruce Lee," *American Film*, Oct. 1975, p. 67.

438 The Shaw Brothers released: Poggiali, "Exit the Dragon, Enter the Clones," p. 39.

438 "Not only did he walk and talk like him": Douglas Jeffrey, "Friends and Family Mourn Tragic Death of Brandon Lee," *Black Belt*, July 1993, p. 96.

438 "I moved around a lot": John Little, "Brandon Lee's Final Martial Arts Interview," *Black Belt*, Aug. 1993, p. 28.

439 Brandon had organized his classmates: Interview with Linda Lee Cadwell, May 2, 2023.

439 "My father was a martial artist first": Jim Coleman, "Bruce Lee's Son Speaks Out!," *Black Belt*, Apr. 1986, p. 104.

440 "I feel almost possessed by the spirit of Bruce": For years David Carradine pursued the lead for *The Silent Flute*, which he eventually accomplished in a version retitled *Circle of Iron* (1978). He played, as Bruce had been slated to, the blind man (thankfully no longer named Ah Sahm), the Monkey Man, and the Panther Man. In 1974, he told *Fighting Stars* magazine, "I never met him, but I feel really possessed by him. It's weird." See Rick Shively, "Caine, the Magnificent Grasshopper," *Fighting Stars*, June 1974, p. 27. Martial arts film scholar Chris Poggiali notes Carradine was saying this as early as January 1974. Richard James Havis, "Why the kung fu in Circle of Iron, from an idea by Bruce Lee, would have left him unhappy," *South China Morning Post*, November 3, 2024. When Brandon was asked about his co-star's quote, he gently parried the question.

440 But with some of his most intimate friends: Michael Hainey, "Quentin Tarantino, Brad Pitt, and Leonardo DiCaprio Take You Inside *Once Upon a Time . . . in Hollywood*," *Esquire*, May 21, 2019, https://www.esquire.com/entertainment/movies/a27458589/once-upon-a-time-in-hollywood-leonardo-dicaprio-brad-pitt-quentin-tarantino-interview/; Shannon Colleary, "Remembering Former Love Brandon Lee 20 Years After His Death on the set of 'The Crow,'" *Medium*, Mar. 3, 2014, medium.com/@shannoncolleary/does-anyone-remember-brandon-lee-82d6f8c88697.

440 Marvel Comics head Stan Lee reportedly: Eric Francisco, "Stan Lee Tried to Make a Shang Chi Movie Starring Bruce Lee's Son," *Inverse*, Nov. 23, 2018, inverse.com/article/51139-stan-lee-shang-chi-movie-or-tv-show-bruce-lee-son.

440 "the action hero of the 90s": Chris Hicks, "Brandon Lee Follows In His Dad's Shoes, But He Hopes To Win Respect As An Actor In His Own Right." *Deseret News*, July 24, 1992. www.deseret.com/1992/7/24/18996080/brandon-lee-follows-in-his-dad-s-shoes-but-he-hopes-to-win-respect-as-an-actor-in-his-own-right/.

441 "Suddenly I felt this bolt": Shannon Lee, *Be Water, My Friend: The Teachings of Bruce Lee* (Flatiron Books, 2020), p. 151.

441 "What I remember of that": Shannon Lee, *Be Water, My Friend*, p. 152.

441 "I was in constant pain": Shannon Lee, *Be Water, My Friend*, p. 153.

442 She smiles: I am thankful to Bao Nguyen for capturing this image in *Be Water*. I am also grateful to Linda Lee Cadwell for, without an ounce of pretense and with an abundance of grace and generosity, revealing this side of herself.

Chapter 51: How We Use Our Hands

443 the Asian American awakening: I am indebted to the work of Karen Ishizuka and Karen Tei Yamashita for this idea.

444 "And so I am": Beau Sia, "Chasing Bruce Lee," *Dope and Wack* album (self-released, 2001).

444 Dozens of elderly tenants who had remained in the hotel: Estella Habal, *San Francisco's I-Hotel: Mobilizing the Filipino American Community in the Anti-Eviction Movement* (Temple University Press, 2007), pp. 146–47.

445 "Feeling power, wielding power": Karen Tei Yamashita, *I-Hotel* (Coffee House Press, 2010), p. 599.

445 veteran of both World Wars: Habal, *San Francisco's I-Hotel*, pp. 96–97.

445 "By saving the Hotel": Habal, *San Francisco's I-Hotel*, p. 106.

445 After midnight the police attacked: Habal, *San Francisco's I-Hotel*, pp. 147–55.

445 One of the last to be removed: James Sobredo, "I-Hotel Eviction Summary: Historical Essay," FoundSF, Fall 1997, foundsf.org/index.php?title=I-Hotel_Eviction_Summary.

445 "I am crippled": Habal, *San Francisco's I-Hotel*, p. 206.

446 lobby for a consolidated census category: See Yen Le Espiritu, *Asian American Panethnicity: Bridging Institutions and Identities* (Temple University Press, 1992).

446 find the "Chinaman": This section is based on the following accounts: Michael Moore, "The Man Who Killed Vincent Chin," *Detroit Free Press Sunday*, Aug. 30, 1987, available at rumble.media/the-man-who-killed-vincent-chin-by-michael-moore/; Helen Zia, *The Vincent Chin Legacy Guide*, 2nd. ed. (Vincent Chin Institute

and Smithsonian Asian Pacific American Center, 2022–23), pp. 12–13; Renee Tajima-Pena and Christina Choy, dirs., *Who Killed Vincent Chin?* (Film News Now and WTVS, 1987).

446 The jade pendant: Helen Zia, *The Vincent Chin Legacy Guide*, 2nd. ed., pp. 12–13. The breaking of a jade pendant is commonly thought to be a sign of ill fortune. It is simply heartbreaking to think of Vincent Chin's fate in relation to Bruce's moment of emergence as Cheng Chao-An in *The Big Boss*.

446 "Instead of attending Vincent's wedding": Helen Zia, *The Vincent Chin Legacy Guide*, 2nd. ed., pp. 12–13.

447 A family friend told: Helen Zia, *The Vincent Chin Legacy Guide*, 2nd. ed., p. 14.

447 the Asian American population grew by 81 percent: Anny Budiman and Neil G. Ruiz, "Key facts About Asian Americans, a Diverse and Growing Population," Pew Research Center, Apr. 29, 2021, pewresearch.org/short-reads/2021/04/29/key-facts-about-asian-americans/.

447 45 percent of us do not have one: "Examining Educational, Workforce, and Earning Divides in the Asian American and Pacific Islander Community," New American Economy Research Fund, May 13, 2021, https://research.newamericaneconomy.org/report/aapi-examine-educational-workforce-earning-divides/.

447 Those with college degrees: "Examining Educational, Workforce, and Earning Divides."

447 this head-spinning diversity: As one example, see Nami Sumida. "Charts Show Detailed Look into California's Growing Asian American Population," *San Francisco Chronicle*, Oct. 20, 2023, https://www.sfchronicle.com/projects/2023/california-asian-population-growth/.

448 During the pandemic: Josh Margolin, "FBI Warns of Potential Surge in Hate Crimes Against Asian Americans amid Coronavirus," ABC News, Mar. 27, 2020, https://abcnews.go.com/US/fbi-warns-potential-surge-hate-crimes-asian-americans/story?id=69831920. See also "Community Reports to Stop AAPI Hate: 2020–2022 Key Findings," Stop AAPI Hate, Nov. 2023, https://stopaapihate.org/wp-content/uploads/2023/10/23-SAH-TaxonomyReport-KeyFindings-F.pdf.

449 Viet Thanh Nguyen argued: Viet Thanh Nguyen, "Palestine Is in Asia: An Asian American Argument for Solidarity," *The Nation*, Jan. 29, 2024, thenation.com/article/world/palestine-asia-orientalism-expansive-solidarity/. See also Viet Thanh Nguyen, *To Save and To Destroy: Writing As An Other (The Charles Norton Lectures)* (Belknap Press, 2025).

449 "a metaphor for the struggle": James Baldwin, *The Cross of Redemption: Uncollected Writings* (Vintage, 2010), p. 41.

449 "and what is crucial here": Baldwin, *The Cross of Redemption*, p. 43.

450 The difference between the hero and the mere celebrity: Joseph Campbell with Bill Moyers. *The Power of Myth* (Anchor, 1988), p. xiv.

450 "Bruce began to practice *gung fu*": "An Interview with Bruce's Mother" in Bruce Thomas, *Bruce Lee: Fighting Spirit* (Blue Snake Books, 1994), p. 59.

451 "Bruce was giving dignity": Interview with Andre Morgan, Mar. 7, 2023.

Index

A

ABCs (American-born Chinese), 189
Abdul-Jabbar, Kareem (Lew Alcindor), 271–277, 294, 298, 314, 335, 388, 389, 426
Adams, Eddie, 300
Adventures of Fong Sai Yuk, The, 311
Afro-Eurasian Eclipse, The (Ellington), 263
Ah Sahm, 17, 330–331
Ahn, Philip, 362
Alcindor, Lew. *See* Abdul-Jabbar, Kareem (Lew Alcindor)
Ali, Bisha, 448
Ali, Muhammad, 186, 272, 434
alien land laws, 215
All Hong Kong Cha-Cha Championships, 60–61
All-American Girl, 448
Allen, Barry, 161
Allen, Jane, 495n241
Allin, Michael, 395–396, 397, 404, 405–406
American Born Chinese, 448
American Broadcasting Company (ABC)
    Batman and, 232–233, 236
    The Green Hornet and, 233, 240, 241, 245, 249
    Japanese American Citizens League and, 361–362
    Kung Fu and, 354, 360, 361, 362
    Longstreet and, 324
    rank of, 228
    risk taking by, 376n
American Citizens for Justice, 447
Amiel, Henri Frederic, 484n168
Amorous Lotus Pan, The, 191
"anchor babies" (term), 12
Andrews, Julie, 314, 350
Angel Island, 17–18, 76
anti-immigrant sentiment, 15–17, 19, 21, 76
anti-miscegenation laws, 180–181
antitrust legislation, 376
anti-war protests, 264–265, 268fig
Antonioni, 423
Aoki, Richard, 251–252, 265
Araki, Greg, 448
Arca, Flora, 259
Art of War (Sun Tzu), 253, 278
Ashley, Linda, 328
Ashley, Ted, 284, 328–329, 331, 335, 353, 355–357, 360, 365–366, 392, 394, 401, 408, 415–418, 421–422, 428

Asian American Movement, 267
Asian American Political Alliance (AAPA), 266–267, 277, 343, 344
Asian Americans
    activism of, 263–269, 277–281, 303, 342–344, 444–445, 450fig
    increase in population of, 447
    solidarity and, 449
    use of term, 3–4, 265–266
    violence against, 446–447, 448
    See also individual people
Asian Americans for Action, 267
Asian Community Center, 343
Asian Council for Equality, 267
Asian Legal Services, 343
Asian/Pacific American Artists, Association of, 512n362
Asiatic Barred Zone, 3–4, 17, 76, 447
Assassin, The, 311
Astaire, Fred, 123
Atyeo, Don, 332, 428
Au Wing Nien, 313
Aubrey, Jim, 287, 336
Autobiography of Malcolm X, The, 272
Auyeung Tin, 65
Ayson, Felix, 445

B

Bad Day at Black Rock, 80
Baker, Bob, 172, 185, 186, 350, 355, 368, 370, 371–372
Baldwin, James, 449–450
Ballard High School, 91
Bankhead, Tallulah, 236
Basquiat, Jean-Michel, 125
Batchelor, Denzil, 180n
Batman, 233, 235, 236, 237, 239, 245, 248–249
Battle of Hong Kong, The, 27
Be Water, My Friend (Lee), 441
Beatles, 284
Beatty, Warren, 169, 213–214
beimo (comparison fights), 49, 57, 80
Belasco, William, 230, 231, 232, 233, 235
Benavidez, Ernest, 185
Benn, Jon, 384
Bergman, Ingrid, 295
Berkeley, student protests in, 280
Berton, Pierre, 363–365, 366, 367, 405

Bevacqua, Art, 301
Big Boss, The, 2, 336, 345–351, 348–349fig, 353, 355–357, 365, 368, 371–372, 382, 384–385, 387–388, 391–392, 394, 395, 414–415, 432
Big Brother of Tangshan, The (*The Big Boss*), 345–351
Biggers, Earl Derr, 220–221
Billings, Josh, 484n168
Billy Jack, 378, 394
Birth of Mankind, The, 10–11fig, 41
Birth of the Dragon, The, 207
birthright citizenship, 20–21
Black audiences, 376, 393–394, 416–417
Black Belt, 145, 178, 249, 250, 262, 269, 270, 273, 303–305, 353, 386, 420, 424, 506n316
Black Belt Yearbook, 391
Black Champion (Farr), 180n
Black Lives Matter, 449, 451
Black Panther Party for Self-Defense, 5, 251–252, 264, 265, 342
Black Power, 91, 222, 251
Blackwell, Chris, 433
Blaxploitation, 376–377
Block, Alex Ben, 437
Blondie, 290
"Bloody Saturday" (Wong), 24–25, 25fig
Blowup, 423
"Boating on Lake Washington" (Lee), 139
Bob Marley and the Wailers, 433
Boggs, Grace Lee, 251
Bonanza, 236, 290, 324
Bonner, Grace Wales, 376
Bonnie and Clyde, 396
Book of the Five Rings (Musashi), 159, 276
Bosman, Charles Henri Maurice, 13
Boxer from Shantung, The, 393
Boxer Rebellion/Uprising, 52, 193, 195
Boxing (Haislet), 316
boxing tournament, 61–62
Breakfast at Tiffany's, 284
Bremer, Bob, 257
Bronson, Charles, 336
Brooke, Walter, 237
Brown, David, 510n353
Brown, Jim, 272
Bruce Lee in G.O.D., 389
Bruce Lee Library, The, 505n316
Bruce Lee Story, The (Lee), 437n
Bruce Lee: The Man Only I Knew (Lee), 24, 193, 437, 506n316
Bruce Lee: The Man, the Legend, 437
Bruceploitation, 6, 391, 437, 438, 444
bubonic plague, 28–29
Buck, Pearl, 216
Buddhism, 157
Bugliosi, Vincent, 296

Bullitt, 285, 287, 421
Burning of the Red Lotus Temple, The, 311
Burton, Shelly, 300–301
Bustillo, Richard, 257, 438
Butterfly Lovers tragedy, 311

C

Cabales, Angel, 179
Cadwell, Bruce, 442
Cadwell, Linda Lee. *See* Lee, Linda (later Cadwell)
camp, 232, 236
Campbell, Cindy, 433
Campbell, Joseph, 450
Campbell, Sid, 480–481n147
Caniff, Milt, 395
Capri, Ahna, 404
Carmichael, Stokely, 91, 222, 251
Carradine, David, 360–361, 362, 391, 439
Carradine, John, 360
Carson, Johnny, 423
Catch a Fire (Bob Marley and the Wailers), 433
Cathay Organization (MP&GI), 67, 312, 333, 368n
Cathay Studios, 217
centerline theory, 156
Central Pacific Railroad, 15
Cha, Louis (Jin Yong), 44, 201
cha-cha, 58–59, 60–61, 65, 69, 74, 75, 76, 79, 80, 96, 129
Chamberlain, Wilt, 276
Championship Fighting (Dempsey), 180, 245
Chan, Amy (Pak Yan), 58
Chan, Bing, 191, 192–193, 196, 203, 205
Chan, Charlie, 214, 218, 220–221
Chan, Jackie, 5, 345, 438n, 488n195
Chan, Jeffery Paul, 222
Chan, Robert, 181, 427
Chan, Unicorn, 34, 40, 312, 314, 334–335, 398
Chan, Wayne, 256
Chan King-Sam, 368
Chan Po-Chu, Connie, 334n
Chan Siu-Pang, 346
Chan Tat Fu, 313
Chan Wah Shun, 50
Chandler, Raymond, 290
Chang, Chaplin, 403, 410, 412
Chang, Grace, 59
Chang, Ying-Jen, 80–81
Chang Apana, 221
Chang Cheh, 67, 191, 311, 318, 333, 335
Chang Chung-Wen, Diana, 191, 201, 202, 203
Chang Tseng-Chai, 312
Channing, William Henry, 168
Charlie Chan and the Curse of the Dragon Queen, 221n

Charlie Chan in Shanghai, 222*fig*
Chaw, Walter, 347
Cheat, The, 214
Chen, Joyce, 87
Chen, William, 198
Chen Zhen, 385
Cheng Ching, Michael, 314
Cheng Pei-Pei, 334, 335
Chesterton, Gilbert Keith, 484n168
Cheung, Hawkins, 53, 57, 59, 61, 71, 89–90, 97
Cheung Cheuk-hing, William
    cha-cha and, 61
    comparison to, 42, 69
    correspondence with, 185, 303
    departure of, 63
    fighting and, 49
    friendship with Lee, 47–48, 61
    on Junction Road Eight Tigers, 46
    Lee on, 100
    Lee's childhood and, 40–41
    on Lee's ego, 61
    on Lee's eyesight, 484n172
    Triads and, 43–44
    Wing Chun and, 53–54
    with Wong Shun Leung, 57–58
    Yip Man and, 50
Cheung King-sin, 254–255*fig*
Cheung Wing-sit, 468n51
chi sao, 53, 54
Chiang, Cecilia, 87
Chiang, David, 312, 346, 350
Chicago Defender, 279
Chicano movement, 264
Chieh Yuan, 389
Chik Yiu-Cheong, Ricky, 380
Children's Crusade, 184
Chin, David, 192, 193, 196, 197, 199–200, 201, 203, 204
Chin, Frank, 19, 86, 87, 222–223
Chin, Peter, 237, 257, 260, 261, 294, 311–312, 315, 357, 386, 389, 420, 423, 428
Chin, Tsai, 220
Chin, Vincent, 446–447
Chin Chien, 41
China Doll, 217n
China Drama Academy, 345
China Mail, 357–358, 415
Chinatown, 284
Chinatown, San Francisco, 18, 28–29, 78, 188–190
Chinese American Citizens Alliance, 80
Chinese Association of Dancers, 79
Chinese Boxer, The, 333, 335, 346, 350, 397, 508n334
Chinese Connection, The, 414–415, 416, 423, 432
Chinese Exclusion Act (1882), 16, 19, 20, 21, 76, 326

Chinese Gung Fu (Lee), 158
Chinese Karate Kung-Fu (Lee and Wong), 146
Chinese Pacific Weekly, 202–203, 204, 206
Chinese Progressive Association, 343
Chinese Student Club, 265, 277
Chinese Youth Club, 93, 96
Ching, Alice, 145
Ch'ing-yüan Wei-hsin, 258
Chinn, Lanston, 149, 151, 156, 173, 182, 230, 246
Chin-Woo-Yuen Family Association, 197
Cho, Margaret, 448
Chong Wah Association, 87
Chop Chop, 364
Chor Yuen, 334n, 415
Chow, Mark, 87, 125, 126
Chow, Ping, 73*fig*, 82–83, 85–86, 87–88, 89*fig*, 93, 129
Chow, Raymond
    in Beverly Hills, 396
    The Big Boss and, 345–347
    Brandon and, 369
    compensation and, 410
    Concord Productions and, 357
    contract negotiations with, 335–336, 365
    Enter the Dragon (Blood and Steel) and, 403, 406, 414
    Fist of Fury and, 372
    The Game of Death and, 425
    Huo Yuanjia film and, 368
    international ambitions of, 377, 380
    Lee's illness and death and, 418, 420, 425–426, 436, 437, 438, 506n316
    Morgan and, 377–379
    Shaw and, 333–334
    Silliphant and, 398
    Ting Pei and, 417
    The Way of the Dragon and, 380–381
    Weintraub and, 394–395
Chow, Ruby, 82–89, 89*fig*, 93, 96, 112–113, 117, 125–126, 134–135, 155, 205, 342, 428
Chow, William, 142, 145
Chow Gar Praying Mantis clan, 57
Choy Li Fut, 50–51, 81, 188
Chu, Jon, 448
Chu Shong-Tin, 53
Chua, Robert, 334
Chua Wah-Peng, Robert, 307
Chung, Betty, 408
Chung Chang-Wha, 414
circumcision, 487n189
Citizen's Return Certificate, 22
Civil Exclusion Orders, 103, 104
Civil Rights Act (1964), 91
civil rights movement, 184, 251–253

Cleaver, Eldridge, 266
Clepper, P. M., 240
Closing the Gap, 172, 176, 192
Clouse, Anna, 412
Clouse, Robert, 396–397, 403, 404, 406, 408–410, 412, 419, 421, 432–433, 437
Coburn, James, 287, 299–300, 302, 308–309*fig*, 312–313, 317, 321–323, 336, 362, 423, 428
Cohen, Rob, 440
Collier, Malcolm, 280
Come Drink with Me, 311, 333, 334, 346
Commentaries on the Martial Way (Lee), 316
Concord Productions, 357, 365, 379, 380, 394, 395, 414, 423, 437
Concrete Children, The, 357
Confucius, 317
Congress of Racial Equality, 251
Conrad, Robert, 177
Coolidge, Calvin, 17
Corcoran, John, 506n322
Corey, Jeff, 238, 239, 290
Cotton Comes to Harlem, 376
Courtship of Eddie's Father, The, 324
Cox, David, 185
Crazy Rich Asians, 448
crime syndicates, organized, 43–44
Crimson Kimono, The, 80
Crosnier, Roger, 316
Crow, The, 440–441
Cuidera, Chuck, 364n
Cultural Revolution, 310

D

Dacascos, Al, 204
Damone, Vic, 237, 284, 501n287
Dangcil, Linda, 290
Darker than Amber, 396, 404
Darling Girl, 60, 60*fig*
Daughter of the Dragon, 219–220, 220*fig*, 440
Davis, Bette, 236
Davis, Ossie, 376
De Guzman, Emil, 344
Dean, James, 67
Deep Thrust: The Hand of Death, 415
"Definite Chief Aim" (Lee), 293
Delgado, Louis, 294
DeMile, James
    book project and, 158
    children of, 227
    closing of schools and, 306
    curricula and, 302
    end of training and, 134
    in Hong Kong, 389
    with Lee, 110–111
    Lee's dissatisfaction and, 153
    on Lee's teaching, 129
    on Lee's training, 114–115
    performing, 129
    photograph of, 108–109*fig*
    in school, 101–102
    The Silent Flute and, 314–315
    as single father, 230
    Wong Jack Man fight and, 202, 206, 212
DeMille, Cecil B., 23, 214
Dempsey, Jack, 180, 186, 245, 253
Dennis, Felix, 428
Der, Ben, 53, 58, 71, 79, 80, 113, 197, 201
desegregation, 184, 194
DeWitt, John, 103
Dhammapada, 502n293
Dick Tracy, 233
Diêm, President, 155
Diller, Barry, 354
Dillman, George, 257
Dillon, Richard, 326
dim mak, 93
Dirty Harry, 421
DJ Kool Herc, 433
Djeng, Frank, 382n
Dobbins, Benny, 243, 244, 247
Dong, Arthur, 220, 491n216
Dong, Harvey, 343, 344, 416
Donovan, Bea, 87
Doohan, Jimmy, 361
Dorgan, Michael, 193, 196, 199, 206
Douglass, Frederick, 20, 303
Downs, Hugh, 81
Dozier, William
    background of, 228
    Batman and, 236
    correspondence with, 365
    The Green Hornet and, 234–235, 236–237, 238–239, 245–246, 247–249
    "A Hollywood Glossary" by, 245
    Lee's acting and, 227, 238
    Number One Son and, 229, 231–232, 233
    recruitment of Lee by, 213, 214
    screen test and, 223n
    Silliphant and, 288
Dr. Zhivago, 423
Dragon (biopic), 204
Dragon and the Tiger, The (Campbell and Lee), 480–481n147
Dragon Dies Hard, The, 438
Dragon Inn, 311
Dragon: The Bruce Lee Story, 440
Dreams of Glass, 396
Drums of Fu Manchu, 220*fig*
Dudley Balling, Fredda, 241–242, 486n181

Dumke, Glenn, 278–279
Durkins, James, 88n

E

East West Players theater company, 361
East Wind Modern Kung Fu Club, 147
Eastwind, 343
Eastwood, Clint, 285, 336
Easy Rider, 318
Ebens, Ronald, 446–447
Edison Tech, 92, 96–97, 117
Edwards, Blake, 169, 177, 284, 314, 353
Edwards, Harry, 272, 276
Eisner, Will, 364n
Ellington, Duke, 263
Ellsworth, Skip, 101, 113, 118, 130, 429
Elms, Gary, 62
Emery, Joan, 164, 165, 172–173
Emery, Linda (later Lee). *See* Lee, Linda (later Cadwell)
Emery, Vivian, 164, 181–182, 183, 227, 230
Emperado, Adriano, 142
Eng, Esther, 22, 23
Enjoy Yourself Tonight, 313–314, 334
Enter the Dragon (Blood and Steel), 6, 374–375*fig*, 379–380, 395–398, 401, 404–413, 407*fig*, 414–417, 421–424, 432–435, 437, 498n258
Everybody's Bookstore, 344, 416
Everything Everywhere All at Once, 448
Exorcist, The, 404, 405

F

Fabros, Lillian, 264–265, 394
Fairbanks, Douglas, 215
Farr, Finis, 180n
Farrell, Sharon, 291, 292
Feather, William, 484n168
Fellini, 423
Fencing with the Foil (Crosnier), 316
Fencing with the Sabre (Crosnier), 316
feng shui, 125
Fighting Stars magazine, 437
Filipino Agricultural Laborers Association, 259
Final Game of Death, The, 389
Finishing the Game, 4
Fish, Stanley, 212
Fist of Fury, 29, 69, 186, 195, 227, 340–341*fig*, 370–373, 379, 382n, 384–385, 388, 391–395, 414–415, 451, 488n195
Fist of Legend, 488n195
Fist of Unicorn, 398
Fists of Fury, 415, 417, 432
FitzGerald, Frances, 136

FitzSimmons, Charles, 284
Five Fingers of Death, 414, 415
Flower Drum Song, 188–189, 217, 218, 290
Floyd, George, 451
Fong, Benson, 335, 362
Fong, Bryant, 342
Fong, Leo, 172, 185–189, 192, 198–200, 204–206, 274, 289, 335, 337, 343
Fong, Mona, 334–335
Fong Yue Ting v. United States, 463n17
Ford, Alexander Hume, 352
"Four Olds," 310
Fox, 376n
Francis, Arlene, 81
Franciscus, James, 324
Frand, Harvey, 355
Free Speech Movement, 184
Free University for Chinatown Kids, Unincorporated (F.U.C.K.U.), 342
Freire, Paulo, 303
French Connection, The, 414
Fresh Off the Boat, 448
Friedkin, William, 404, 414
Friedlander, Howard, 329–330, 510n353
Friedman, Milton, 33
From the Highway, 312
Fu Manchu, 218–219, 220, 221
Fukui, David, 119
Fuller, Samuel, 80
Fundamentals of Boxing (Ross), 187
Fung, Leung, 333
Fung Fung, 35
Fung Yu-Lan, 162
Furumura, Jeff, 417
Furutani, Warren, 267

G

Galileo High School, 189
Gallery of Madame Liu-Tsong, The, 214
Game of Death Redux, The, 389
Game of Death, The, 388–389, 390–391*fig*, 391, 423, 424, 425, 437, 438n
gangs, in Chinatown, 189
Garagiola, Joe, 275
Garcia, Leroy, 92, 101, 110–116, 127, 129, 132, 134, 426
Garfield High School, 91
Garner, James, 237, 290, 363
Gaumont, 377
Gee, Emma, 264, 267
Gee Yau Seah Academy, 192, 196, 265
Geisha Boy, The, 217n
Gentry, Curt, 296
Gestalt therapy, 289
Getaway, The, 432

Gidra, 267–268, 417
Ginsberg, Allen, 127
Giron, Lee, 179
Glover, Jesse, 94–102, 101*fig*, 105, 108–109*fig*, 110–116, 126–127, 129–130, 132, 134, 153, 158, 426, 429
Glover, Mary, 19
Go for Broke! 216
Godfather, The, 414, 433
Goethe, Johann Wolfgang von, 484n168
Golden, Steve, 257–258
Golden Gate Girl, 23
Golden Harvest Pictures, 333–337, 342, 344–351, 359, 368–369, 372, 377–379, 381, 384, 387–388, 391, 405, 410, 413–414, 506n316
Golden Hour show, 334
Goldman, Albert, 298
Gomez, Juan, 142
Gong Lum v. Rice, 187n
Gonzales, Dan, 280
Good Earth, The (Buck), 216, 362
"Gossip: And Satan Came Also" (Wotherspoon), 125
Gough, Lloyd, 237
Graham, A. C., 483n162
Grandview Theatre, 23
Grant, Ulysses S., 16
Grantham, Alexander, 43
Green Hornet, The, 5, 212, 233–234, 236–241, 244–251, 256–257, 260–261, 284, 306–307, 361, 366, 376n
Greenway Productions, 213, 233, 284
Griffith, Samuel, 253
Guan Yin, 161
Guess Who's Coming to Dinner, 241
Guevara, Che, 502n292
Guiding Light, The, 55
gun control legislation, 252–253
Gunn, Moses, 416
Gunn, Rocky, 391
Gunsmoke, 228

H

Hagakure, 269
Hagedorn, Jessica, 343
Haislet, Edwin, 316
Hall, Howard, 100, 101fig, 113, 115–116, 133
Hall, Juanita, 218n
ham (hexagram), 8
Han Ying-Chieh, 346, 348, 370, 371n
Hanna-Barbera, 423
Harmetz, Aljean, 416
Harris, Kamala Devi, 5
Harrison, George, 284

Hart, Ed, 96, 100, 105, 110–111, 113, 114, 115–116, 133, 429
Hart-Celler Act (1965), 189, 205, 212, 352, 447
Hartsell, Larry, 257
Hatchet Men, The (Dillon), 326
Have Gun Will Travel, 228
Hawai'i, 80, 81, 145, 177, 266, 352
Hawaii Five-O, 290, 324
Hayakawa, Samuel Ichiye, 279–280
Hayakawa, Sessue, 23, 214–215, 219, 440
Hayashi, Tokutaro (Raymond Toyo), 234
Hays Code. *See* Production Code
Heartaches, 23
Hearts and Minds, 319
Heller, Paul, 394–397, 405, 408–410, 412, 419, 421, 433–435
Hendrix, Jimi, 336
Hennessy, Dick, 437
Here Comes the Bride, 290
Here Comes the Warrior, 326
Herman, Justin, 343
Herrigel, Eugen, 160, 498n258
Hesse, Herman, 316
Hill, Napoleon, 112, 137, 293–294, 299, 356, 365
Hing Chung Wah Opera Troupe, 13
History of Chinese Philosophy, A (Fung), 162
Hitchcock, Alfred, 228
Ho, Leonard, 333, 368, 370
Ho Chi Minh, 253
Ho Kom Tong, 13–14
Ho Oi-Yu, Grace (later Li). *See* Li Oi-Yu, Grace (née Ho)
Hoffer, Eric, 316
Hokubei Mainichi, 280
Holden, William, 218
Holly, Lauren, 440
Hollywood Chinese (Dong), 491n216
"Hollywood Glossary, A" (Dozier), 245
Hom, Nancy, 343
Home (television show), 81
Hong, James, 218, 361, 362
Hong Fook Tong, 19
Hong Kong
 after war, 33
 changes in, 310–311, 313
 creation story of, 33–34
 film industry in, 32, 34, 37, 52, 55, 310–313, 332–333, 350
 fires in, 43
 media landscape of, 313
 political unrest in, 65
 population growth in, 43
 Sino-Japanese War and, 26–27
 unrest in, 310
Hong Kong Film Censorship Authority, 384
Hong Kong Standard, 385

Hooks, Pat, 100, 101, 101*fig*
Hop Sing Tong, 84, 87
Hopper, Dennis, 318
Hotung, Clara, 14
Hotung, Robert, 13
Howe, James Wong, 216
Huai Nan Tzu (The Huainanzi), 160, 300, 471n70
Huang, Alfred, 8
Huang, Eddie, 448
Huang Feng, 334
Hubbs, Gil, 412
Huen, Floyd, 265
Huerta, Dolores, 264
Hui, Michael, 313
Hui, Rebu, 400, 426, 428
Hui, Sam, 313, 400
Hum, Tony, 256
Hung, Sammo, 345
Hung Sing school, 81, 82
Huo Yuanjia, 69, 195, 368, 371, 379
Hutton, Bobby, 252, 253
Hutton, Eliza, 441
Hwang In-Shik, 381, 389
Hyams, Joe, 284, 324

I

I Am Bruce Lee, 223n
I Ching: The Book of Changes, 8, 100, 137
I Hotel (Yamashita), 445
I Wor Kuen, 343
Ichioka, Victor, 265
Ichioka, Yuji, 264, 267
Ichiun, Odagiri, 160
Iijima, Kazu, 266–267
immigration, limitations on, 15–17
Immigration Act (1917), 17
Immigration Act (1924), 17, 472n76
Immigration and Nationality Act (Hart-Celler; 1965), 189, 205, 212, 352, 447
In Living Color, 376n
"In My Own Process" (Lee), 403–404
In the Face of Demolition, 55
Infancy, 10–11fig, 41, 111, 334
Inosanto, Dan
    Ashley and, 328
    background of, 179, 259–260
    closing of schools and, 306
    curricula and, 302, 305
    The Green Hornet and, 247
    in Hong Kong, 389
    "intercepting fist style" and, 256
    Jeet Kune Do and, 270, 302
    Jun Fan Gung Fu Institute and, 257, 258, 259
    on Lee, 61n, 302
    Lee's children and, 438
    Lee's daughter and, 295
    Lee's fame and, 387
    Lee's illness and death and, 420, 426, 428
    Lees' move and, 294
    on Lee's style, 484n172
    Mao and, 253
    one-inch punch and, 176
    photographs of, 254–255*fig*
    Sun Sing Theatre event and, 191–192
    Tao of Jeet Kune Do and, 506n316
    training with Lee and, 191
Inosanto, Diana, 259, 426
Inosanto, Lilia, 260
Inosanto, Sebastian and Mary Arca, 259–260
Inside Karate, 193
Intercepting Fist, The, 350, 359, 368
Intercollegiate Chinese for Social Action (ICSA), 277
International Hotel (I-Hotel), 342, 343, 344, 416, 444, 450*fig*
International Karate Championship, 169–170, 176, 177–179, 286
interracial marriage, opposition to, 180–181, 182–183
Invincible Boxer, The, 414
Ironside, 290
Island Judo Jujitsu Club, 142
Iwamatsu, Makoto "Mako," 246, 361

J

Jack Johnson and His Times (Batchelor), 180n
Jackson, Herb, 261, 294
Jackson, John, 100
Jacobs, Pete, 257
James, LeBron, 482n160
Japanese American Citizens League, 361–362
Japanese American Film Company, 215n
Japanese Americans, in wartime concentration camps, 94, 103–104, 279
Japanese War Bride, 217n, 241
Jay, Bernice, 142
Jay, Leon, 417
Jay, Wally, 142–143, 158, 170–171, 186
Jeet Kune Do, 262, 269–270, 274, 288, 302, 304, 314, 324, 345, 353, 389
Jeffries, James, 180
Ji Han-Jae, 389
Jin Wah Sing Dramatic and Musical Association, 129
Jin Yong (Louis Cha), 44, 197, 201
Jing Mo Athletic Association, 206
Jing Mo Tai Yuk Woey, 195
Jing Wu Anniversary Book, 69

Jing Wu Association, 195, 368
Jing Wu Athletic Association, 69
Jing Wu Men, 195
Joe, Allen, 143–144, 148, 185
Joe Boys, 189
John Adams High School, 79
Johnson, Dwayne, 448
Johnson, Gilbert, 437, 506n316
Johnson, Jack, 180
Johnson, Lyndon, 184, 236
Johnson, Pat, 286, 437
Journey to the East, 423
Jowett, George F., 68
Joy Luck Club, The, 448
Joy Ride, 448
Judkins, Ben, 49
Jun Fan Gung Fu Institute, 5, 156, 171–173, 195, 197–198, 212, 248, 257–258, 261, 270, 302–303, 305–306
Junction Road Eight Tigers, 46–47

K

Kaelemakule, Paul, 142
Kahanamoku, Duke, 510n352
Kam Fong Chun, 290
Kam Yuen, 206
Kamaka, Clifford, 81
Kamiyama, Sôjin, 221
Kaneko, Lonny, 120, 122
Karloff, Boris, 223
Kato, Shuzo, 95, 117
Katsu, Shintaro, 369, 380
Kawachi, Ken, 142
Kay, Jacquie, 117, 157–158
Kay, Moses, 93
Kay, Roger, 93, 127
Kay, Sue Ann, 91, 93, 164, 165
Kazan, Elia, 325
Kearney, Denis, 15
Kearney Street Workshop, 343
Kelly, Jim, 404, 432–433
Kelsey, 353
Kendrick, Baynard, 324
Kennedy, John F., 135, 155, 184, 189
Kennedy, Robert, 277, 296
Kerouac, Jack, 127
Keung, Chan "Baldhead," 197
Khan, Nahnatchka, 448
Khor, Denise, 215n
Kid, The, 35–37, 41
Kim, Elaine, 221
Kimura, Haruyo, 102–105
Kimura, Masafusa, 116
Kimura, Suejiro, 102–105

Kimura, Takauki "Taky"
  Abdul-Jabbar and, 274
  background of, 102–105, 121
  book project and, 158
  closing of schools and, 306
  correspondence with, 230, 235, 238, 246, 247, 248
  curricula and, 302
  friendship with Lee, 101, 105–106, 111, 139
  The Game of Death and, 423
  in Hong Kong, 389
  as instructor, 156
  International Karate Championship and, 176, 178
  Jun Fan Gung Fu Institute and, 173
  Lee's illness and death and, 419, 426, 428
  Lee's marriage and, 183
  Lee's new system and, 206
  Lee's school and, 166
  Linda and, 179
  performing, 129, 191
  photographs of, 108–109*fig*, 140–141*fig*, 174–175*fig*
  rental space and, 133
  ROTC and, 135–136
  Seattle students and, 212
  training with Lee and, 126
  in West Los Angeles, 237
  Wong Jack Man fight and, 197
Kin Mon (Sturdy Citizen's Club) school, 81, 95–96, 145, 186, 192, 253
King, Martin Luther, Jr., 91, 184, 277, 296, 366
King, Rodney, 443
King and I, The, 123
King Boxer, 394, 414
King George V School, 46, 62
King Hu, 311, 333, 346
King of the Chinese Boxers, The, 336, 368
Kingston, Maxine Hong, 264
Kiss Her Goodbye, 502n292
Kissinger, Henry, 393, 433
Knackfuss, Hermann, 219
Kochiyama, Yuri, 251, 267
Kong, Buck Sam, 204–205
Koo, Joseph, 451
Korean War, 248n, 263
Kosuke Kawada, 27
Krishnamurti, Jiddu, 178, 305–306, 316, 389
Ku Klux Klan, 184, 186
Kubota, Larry, 268–269
Kubota, Takayuki, 177–178
Kuhn, Tom, 354–355, 356, 360, 361, 362
Kum Hon restaurant, 79
Kung Fu, 111, 206, 328–330, 353–355, 356–357, 359, 360, 362, 365, 376n, 391
Kung Fu: The Movie, 439–440

Kurosawa, 299, 329
Kuwa, George, 221
Kwan, Piera, 385
Kwan Ka-shen, Nancy, 217–218, 223, 290, 295, 355, 362, 369, 373, 388, 423, 424
Kwan Tak-Hing, 44

L

La Salle College, 41, 44–45, 56–57, 369
La Strada, 423
Lacoste, Johnny, 179
Lady from Shanghai, The, 412
Lady Whirlwind, 415
Lai, Michael, 41–42, 46
Lai, Sylvia, 313, 314
Laird, Donald and Eleanor, 137
Lake View Cemetery, 428
LaLanne, Jack, 143
Lam, Eunice, 90, 129, 139, 152, 312
Lam, Victor, 311, 335
Lam Ching-ying, 345, 370, 399
Langford, Charles, 418–419
Laozi, 7, 161, 162, 410
Largusa, Ben, 177, 178
Lau Bun (Wong On), 81–82, 188, 191, 204, 205
Lau Wing, Tony, 345, 347, 350–351, 369, 370, 399
Lau Yee Nam, 19
Laughlin, Tom, 378
Law Chi, 334
Law Kar, 311
Lawther, John Dobson, 316
Lazenby, George, 423, 425
Le Mans, 286
Lean, 423
LeBell, "Judo" Gene, 243–244, 290
Lederer, Dick, 416, 421–422
Lee (Li), Agnes Chow Fung, 14, 31, 31*fig*, 427
Lee (Li), Peter Chung Sum, 14, 24, 31*fig*, 40, 41, 45, 74–75, 89*fig*, 125, 139, 427
Lee (Li), Phoebe Chow Yuen, 8, 14, 26, 27, 32, 33, 46, 427
Lee, Bill, 189
Lee, Bob and Harriet, 80, 143, 144
Lee, Brandon Bruce Gwok Ho
  ABC promotion and, 241
  Abdul-Jabbar and, 275
  acting career of, 439–441, 443
  after Lee's death, 438
  birth of, 213
  death of, 441
  in Hong Kong, 230, 312, 314, 355, 369, 387
  journalism and, 420
  Lee's back injury and, 315
  Lee's father and, 227
  Lee's illness and death and, 427–428
  photographs of, 439*fig*
Lee, Bruce Jun Fan
  Abdul-Jabbar and, 273–277
  Allen and, 143–144
  arrival of in U.S., 76, 77*fig*, 78
  Ashley and, 417–418
  back injury and, 315–316, 317
  Berton interview and, 363–365, 367
  birth of, 12, 19–20
  birth of daughter and, 295
  book project and, 158
  boxing tournament and, 61–62
  on Bruce as teenager, 57
  cha-cha and, 65, 69, 74, 75, 76, 79, 80, 96, 129
  challenges issued by, 64
  Chang and, 311–312
  as child actor, 10–11*fig*, 35, 36, 38–39*fig*, 47*fig*
  childhood of, 24, 30–33, 40–42, 46–48
  Chinatown and, 189–190
  with Chows, 89*fig*
  confrontation between extra and, 411–412
  in *Darling Girl*, 60*fig*
  death of, 2, 425–429, 436–437
  death of father and, 227
  departure of for the U.S., 71
  departure of from U.S. after birth, 22–23
  draft board and, 79, 150, 155, 156
  drawings made by, 59–60
  dubbed movies of, 378
  English and, 92
  Enter the Dragon (*Blood and Steel*) and, 396–397, 401, 403, 405–413, 414, 421–422
  fame of, 386–388, 398–399, 417
  father's addiction and, 55
  fear of failure and, 70
  financial stresses on, 294–295, 297, 301, 323, 324
  Fist of Fury and, 370–373, 393
  Fist of Unicorn and, 398
  Fong and, 188
  on freedom, 303–304
  with friends, 110–111, 113
  funeral of, 427*fig*
  The Game of Death and, 388–389, 391
  Glover and, 96–97, 98–100, 101*fig*
  Golden Harvest Pictures and, 335–337, 342, 344–347, 348–351
  The Green Hornet and, 234–235, 236–237, 238–241, 242–243, 244, 246–251
  on *gung fu*, 137–138
  guns and, 114
  on Hollywood career, 212
  homeownership and, 294
  in Hong Kong, 150–153, 312, 313–314, 355–359, 368

Lee, Bruce Jun Fan (*cont.*)
   illness of, 418–421
   "intercepting fist style" and, 256
   International Karate Championship and, 178–179
   interviews with, 132–133
   in Japan, 74–75
   Jay and, 142–143
   Jeet Kune Do and, 269–270, 302, 304
   Kay family and, 93–94
   Kung Fu and, 329–330, 362
   learning Wing Chun, 53–54
   Lee (James) and, 147–148
   Linda and, 167–169, 171
   loneliness of, 149
   Longstreet and, 324, 353
   in Los Angeles, 237–238
   Manson murders and, 296
   marriage plans and, 179–180, 181–183
   married life of, 184–185
   McQueen and, 286–287, 291–292, 294
   Morgan and, 378–379
   motivational ideas and, 293, 299
   move to Seattle and, 82–83
   Nakachi fight and, 115–116
   Number One Son and, 228–230, 231–232, 233
   Palmer and, 128–129
   Parker and, 169, 170
   philosophy and, 159–163
   photographs of, 1*fig*, 31*fig*, 73*fig*, 140–141*fig*, 154*fig*, 159*fig*, 174–175*fig*, 208–209*fig*, 210–211*fig*, 254–255*fig*, 282–283*fig*, 308–309*fig*, 338–339*fig*, 340–341*fig*, 348–349*fig*, 374–375*fig*, 381–382*fig*, 390–391*fig*, 407*fig*, 430–431*fig*, 439*fig*
   Polanski and, 297
   popularity of, 240–241, 307
   Project Leng and, 297–299
   rooftop fight and, 62–63
   ROTC and, 135–136, 150
   Sanbo and, 119–120, 121–124, 131–132
   at school, 42, 44–45, 56–57, 79, 117, 477n117
   screen test and, 213–214, 223–226
   in Seattle, 84, 87–93
   The Silent Flute and, 299–301, 317–318, 321–323
   Silliphant and, 288
   on status of Asians in U.S., 366
   stresses on, 401–402
   stuntmen and, 243–244
   Sun Sing Theatre event and, 191–192
   as symbol of unity, 3
   Taky and, 105–106
   as teacher, 108–109*fig*, 112, 129, 133–134, 155–156, 166–167, 185–186, 257–259, 284–285, 302–303
   as teen actor, 55–56
   travel to U.S. and, 74–76
   trip to Hong Kong and, 310
   Tso and, 136–138
   TV series proposed by, 326–328, 330–331
   20th Century-Fox contract and, 231
   unified theory of martial arts and, 157
   at University of Washington, 117–118, 122, 127–128, 135, 149–150, 157–158, 171
   wages for, 237
   The Way of the Dragon and, 379–382, 384–385
   Weintraub negotiations and, 394–395
   Wing Chun Kung Fu and, 401
   Wong Jack Man fight and, 193–194, 196–207, 261
   with Wong Shun Leung, 57–58
   writings of, 68–69, 70–71
   with Yip Man, 54*fig*, 57
   See also individual movies
Lee, Christopher, 220, 416
Lee, Dan, 257–258, 294, 305, 369, 372
Lee, Erika, 17, 21
Lee, George, 80, 172, 185, 186, 198, 206, 258, 304
Lee, Greglon, 147, 148, 400, 401, 480–481n147
Lee, James Yimm, 80, 95–96, 99, 140–141*fig*, 143–148, 158, 169, 172, 185–186, 190–191, 198, 200, 248, 343, 366, 400–401
Lee, Jason Scott, 440
Lee, Katherine, 147, 185
Lee, Linda (later Cadwell)
   ABC promotion and, 241
   Abdul-Jabbar and, 273–274
   after Lee's death, 436, 437, 438
   Ashley and, 392
   background of, 164–166
   Balling interview with, 241–242
   The Big Boss and, 350
   birth of daughter and, 295
   Brandon and, 227, 230
   correspondence with, 306–307, 312, 345
   dating Lee, 167–169
   Enter the Dragon (Blood and Steel) and, 380, 403, 405, 406–407
   eviction and, 249
   financial stresses on, 301, 314, 323, 324
   Golden Harvest offer and, 336, 337
   The Green Hornet and, 237
   homeownership and, 294
   in Hong Kong, 230–231, 355, 369, 387, 400, 401
   Kung Fu and, 329–330, 362
   later life of, 442
   Lee and, 171
   on Lee and Chinatown, 190
   on Lee learning Wing Chun, 54
   Lee's back injury and, 315–316
   on Lee's childhood, 24, 45

Lee's diary and, 68
Lee's illness and death and, 418–420, 425–426, 427–429, 506n316
Lee's stresses and, 401–402, 417
in Los Angeles, 238
Manson murders and, 296
marriage plans and, 179–180, 181–183
married life of, 184–185
photographs of, 140–141*fig*, 166*fig*, 407*fig*, 439*fig*
pregnancy and, 172–173
prejudice and, 204
screen test and, 212–213, 214
Shaw Brothers and, 335
on Tso, 136
at University of Washington, 167
Wong Jack Man fight and, 193–194, 198, 200, 201, 202, 204, 205, 206
Lee, Mike (brother of Jesse Glover), 100, 108–109*fig*, 429
Lee, Perry, 247
Lee, Robert Jun Fai
boxing tournament and, 62
cha-cha championship and, 60–61
childhood of, 27
death of father and, 227
on father, 45, 46
father's addiction and, 55
on Lee as child, 34, 48
Lee's departure and, 68, 71
Lee's illness and death and, 420, 426, 427, 428
Lee's teenage years and, 59
Lee's visit home and, 151
move to U.S. and, 295
on parents' arrival in U.S., 19
Lee, Shannon E., 295, 315, 355, 369, 387, 427–428, 438, 439*fig*, 441–442, 448–449, 506n316
Lee, Stan, 440
Lee Gam-Kwan, Larry, 312
Lee Jun Fai, Robert (brother), 14, 24
Lee Ka Tai, Steve, 45
Lee Sun-Fung, 65
Legend of Bruce Lee, The (Block), 437
Legend of Jimmy Blue Eyes, The, 396
Legend of the Condor Heroes (Jin Yong), 197
Lei Day, 170–172
Leider, Jerry, 354, 355, 356, 359, 360, 362
Lennon, John, 284
Leong, Jeffrey Thomas, 266, 303
Leong, Russell, 343
Lepore, Jill, 221
Leung, Gou, 314
Leung, Margaret "Man Lan," 58, 60, 60*fig*
Leung, Richard, 114
Leung Bik, 50
Leung Jan, 50

Leung Sheung, 51, 153
Leung Sing Por, 313
Lewis, Jerry, 60, 111
Lewis, Joe, 177, 269, 294
Li, Jane, 142, 143
Li, Jet, 488n195
Li Hoi Chuen
after war, 30, 31–32
background of, 12–13
Ching Ming for, 312
death of, 226
departure of for Hong Kong, 22–23
departure of for the U.S., 14–15
in film, 32–33, 35, 45–46, 47*fig*
Lee's childhood and, 24, 26, 27, 32, 42
Lee's departure and, 71
Lee's education and, 117
Lee's film career and, 65
Lee's move to Seattle and, 82, 87–88
Lee's travel to U.S. and, 75
Lee's visit home and, 151, 154
opium addiction and, 55, 56
photographs of, 31*fig*, 154*fig*
Quan Ging Ho and, 78
retirement of, 68
in U.S., 17–20
Li Jun Biu, 13
Li Jung Teung, 14, 24
Li Ka-Shing, 310
Li Oi-Yu, Grace (née Ho)
after war, 30
background of, 12, 13–14
departure of for Hong Kong, 22
departure of for the U.S., 14–15
Hoi Chuen's addiction and, 55, 56
Japanese and, 26
on Lee, 450
Lee's childhood and, 24, 32, 33, 41, 42, 45, 46, 48
Lee's departure and, 68, 71
Lee's fighting and, 64
Lee's illness and death and, 420–421, 426, 428
Lee's move to Seattle and, 82, 87–88
Lee's teenage years and, 59
move to U.S. and, 295
photograph of, 31*fig*
Quan Ging Ho and, 78
in U.S., 17–18, 19–20
The Way of the Dragon and, 381
Liang, Lucas, 393
Liang Tzu-peng, 32
Liberace, 236
Liebling, A. J., 139
Liezi, The, 162
Lim, Adele, 448
Lim, Louisa, 34, 36

534 INDEX

Lin, Justin, 448–449
Lingeman, Richard, 293
Little, John, 490n204
Little Orphan Annie, 233
Little Red Book, 251–252, 253
Little Sister, The, 290
Liu Liang Hua, Gladys, 334, 335–336, 347, 424
Lo Dai-Wai, David, 314, 334
Lo Ting, 33–34
Lo Wei, 334, 346, 347, 348–349, 368, 369, 370, 372, 379, 424
Lok Gong Mui, 13
Lomax, Michele, 416
Lombardo, Goffredo, 377
Lone Ranger Show, The, 233–234
Long, George, 487n192
Longstreet, 324–325, 331, 335, 353, 363, 405
Loren, Sophia, 423
Los Angeles Times, 416
Louie, Joe, 189
Louie, Sam, 82
Love, Part 2, 55
Love Eterne, The, 311
Love Is a Many-Splendored Thing, 329
Loving, Richard and Mildred Jeter, 180–181
Loving v. Virginia, 180–181, 241
Lu Xun, 34
luʻau, 170–172
Lucas, Charles, 437
Luen Yang, Gene, 448
Luke, Keye, 111, 221, 222–223, 222fig, 234, 238, 360, 362, 404
Luke, Wing, 84
Lung Chi Chuen Choy Li Fut school, 62
Lup Mo studio, 191
Lynch, Frank, 111–112

M

Ma, Dick, 392, 394, 405, 414
Ma Kin Fung, 195
Machado, Lena, 171
Magnificent Seven, The, 299
Majority of One, A, 217
Mambo Girl, 59, 60
"Man Who Thinks He Can, The" (Wintle), 106
Mandarin Theatre, 14, 18, 19, 22
Manilatown, 343
Manson, Charles, 296–297
Mao Ying, Angela, 334, 405, 408, 410–411, 415
Mao Zedong, 253, 278, 310, 360, 393
Mar, Trisha, 125, 126
Mar Jim Sing, 84, 85
Mar Seung Gum. *See* Chow, Ruby
March on Washington, 184
Markle, Fletcher, 223n

Marley, Bob, 433, 434
Marlowe, 290–291
Marshall, Adrian, 314–315, 425
Martin, 376n
Martin, Dean, 290
Mason, Richard, 217
Matsuda, Larry, 117–118, 120, 135, 267
Matsuda, Minn, 267
Mattson, George, 170
McCulloch, Dave, 164
McLuhan, Marshall, 263
McQueen, Steve, 213, 238, 284–287, 291–292, 294, 296–299, 314, 322, 335, 363, 428, 432
MGM Studios, 216, 336, 353, 376–377, 423
Miao, Nora, 370, 371, 381, 398–399, 405
Miao Ker Hsiu, Nora, 334
Mid-Pacific, The, 352
Mid-Pacific Man (term), 352
military draft, 135
Miller, Herman, 511n355
Milwaukee Bucks, 276
Ming Pao Daily, 201–202
Mirakian, Anthony, 177
Mirikitani, Janice, 343
Miss Saigon, 512n362
Mission Impossible, 421
Mitchell, Jimmy, 142
Mitose, James, 142
mixed martial arts, origins of, 142
Miyabe, Takamitsu "Tak," 100–101
Modern Commando Science of Guerilla Self-Defense for the Home Front, The (Jowett), 68
Modern Karate Kung Fu (Lee), 95
Modern King-Fu Karate (Lee), 146
Monroe, Marilyn, 398, 437
Moore, Jack, 352, 356, 357
Morehouse, Laurence, 316
Morgan, Andre, 333, 377–379, 384, 388, 391, 395, 406–407, 409–410, 412, 425, 428, 433, 439, 451, 508n334
Morgan, Evan S., 160, 471n70
Mori, Tomi, 79
Ms. Marvel, 448
Mulford, Don, 252
Murray, George, 278
Musashi, Kareen Miyamoto, 159–160, 276, 329, 435
My Husband, the Enemy, 362
My Life in the Ring and Out (Johnson), 180n
My Son Ah Cheung, 35–37
"My Symphony" (Channing), 168
Mystery of Dr. Fu-Manchu, The, 219

N

Nagy, Ivan, 423
Naim v. Naim, 485n181

Nakachi, Yoichi, 115–116, 189, 204, 206
Nakamura, Bob, 361
Napier, Sam, 265
National General Pictures, 395, 414–415, 423
National Karate Championships, 250
National Rifle Association, 252–253
Nelson, Clara, 182
New Culture movement, 195
New Fist of Fury, 488n195
New Nation, 385
New York Herald-Tribune, 216
New York Times, 236, 237
Newman, Paul, 213, 237
Newsweek, 401, 415
Newton, Huey, 251–252
Ng Cho-Fan, 38–39fig, 55–56, 65, 66, 67
Ng Mui, 51–52
Ngai, Mae, 17, 472n76
Ngan Jai, 30, 34
Ngan Ma, 30
Nguyen, Bao, 360
Ni Kuang, 368
Nichols, Nichelle, 361
Nielson, Jon, 49
Nishio, Alan, 362
Nishioka, Hayward, 424
Nitz, Michael, 446–447
Nixon, Richard, 205, 360, 367, 377, 393
Nom Wah Tea Parlor, 85
Norris, Chuck, 177, 269, 286, 290, 294, 381, 384, 404, 437
"Notes on 'Camp'" (Sontag), 232
Notorious, 228
Novak, Al, 81, 147, 172, 185
Number One Son, 214, 228–230, 231–232, 233, 327, 360, 381, 391, 396n
Nuyen, France, 217

O

Oakland Tribune, 170
Oath of the Sword, The, 79, 215n
O'Brien, Noel, 81
Ochs, Phil, 372–373, 434
O'Connor, John J., 353
O'Hara, Maureen, 284
Ohara Publications, 437
Ohshima, Tsutomu, 177, 178
Okazaki, Henry, 142, 145
Okazaki, Stephen, 448
Oko, Yoko, 284
Oland, Warner, 221, 222fig, 223
Olympics, boycott of, 272, 275
Once Upon a Time . . . in Hollywood, 244, 503n298
One-Armed Swordsman, The, 67, 311
one-inch punch, 134, 172, 176, 178, 305

opium addiction, 55, 56
opium trade, 28
Opium Wars, 25–26, 28, 43
Organization of Afro-American Unity, 251
Oriental Art of Self-Defense, The, 127, 132
Oriental Book Sales, 145
"Oriental Problem," 221
Orphan, The, 38–39fig, 65–67, 96, 111–112, 122, 152, 167, 311
Orphan Generation, 310–311
Orphan's Tragedy, An, 55, 111–112
Our Man Flint, 299
Outrigger Canoe Club, 510n352

P

Pacific Citizen, 280
Page Act (1875), 16
Pagoda Theater, 393–394
Pai, Daniel K., 257
Paik, Irving, 495n240
Pak Hok Pai White Crane clan, 57
Pak Yan, 152, 154
Pak Yin, 66
Palmer, Doug, 108–109fig, 128–129, 151–153, 155, 169, 203–204, 274, 387–388
Palmer, Doug, Sr., 155, 173
Palmer, Ida, 155
Pan, Zebra, 370
pandemic, 4, 448
Pang, Brother Henry, 45
Pang Cheng Lian, 385
Paramount Studios, 260, 324, 353, 357, 361, 363
Park, Edward L., 221
Park, Randall, 448
Park, Robert Ezra, 221
Park Hong, Cathy, 442
Parker, Ed
  book project and, 158
  Edwards and, 284n
  fighting style and, 142
  Inosanto and, 179, 260
  International Karate Championship and, 169–170, 176, 177–178
  Lee and, 147, 169, 170
  Lee's discovery and, 213, 214
  Lee's reputation and, 189
  McQueen and, 286
  school opened by, 145
  students of, 257
  Time article and, 169
  in *The Wrecking Crew*, 290
Parks, Gordon, Jr., 376
Parks, Gordon, Sr., 376–377
Past Lives, 448
Peace and Freedom Party, 264–265

Peale, Norman Vincent, 293, 316
Pearl Harbor, 26, 103, 145
Pedagogy of the Oppressed (Freire), 303
Penn, Arthur, 396
Penthouse, 503n298
People's Liberation Army, 253
Perls, Fritz, 289
Perry, Matthew C., 205
Phantom of Chinatown, 223
Phelan, James Duval, 28–29, 215
philosophy, 156–157, 159–163
Philippine American Collegiate Endeavor (PACE), 267, 277
Pink Panther series, 284
Playhouse 90, 228
Poitier, Sidney, 241
Polanski, Roman, 284, 290, 296–297, 306–307, 313, 314
police violence, 94–95
Pollard, Maxwell, 250
Polly, Matthew, 22n, 27, 193, 196, 199, 244, 508n334, 510n353, 512n362
Ponti, Carl, 423
Porter, Leroy, 95
Poteet, Jerry, 257
Potts, Billy, 126
prajña, 157
President Coolidge, SS, 12, 17
President Pierce, 25
President Wilson, SS, 71
Presley, Elvis, 145, 169, 179, 257n, 423
Production Code, 215, 243, 491n216
Project Leng, 297–299
Proyas, Alex, 440
Pryce, Jonathan, 512n362
Psychology of Coaching (Lawther), 316

Q

Quan Ging Ho, 78–79, 82
qigong, 70
Quinn, Anthony, 295
Quo, Beulah, 361
Quotations from Chairman Mao Tse-Tung (Little Red Book), 251–252, 253

R

Rafu Shimpo, 250
Raiders, 189
Rainer, Luise, 216
Raisin in the Sun, 217
Randall, David, 29
Rank, 377
Rapid Fire, 440, 441, 443
Rasch, Philip, 316

Rayns, Tony, 382
Reagan, Ronald, 253, 278–279, 280
Rebel Without a Cause, 65
Rediffusion TV (RTV), 313, 314, 334
redlining maps, 78
Reisbord, David, 419
Reivers, The, 291, 298
Relyea, Robert, 299
Return of the Dragon, The, 380n
Rhee, Jhoon, 176, 177, 178, 250, 295, 297, 306, 317, 331, 380, 412, 424
Riley, Walter L., 150
Robbing the Dead, 23
Robbins, Tony, 293
Robinson, Sugar Ray, 186
Robles, Al, 343
Roethke, Theodore, 122
Rogosin, Joel, 324
Rohmer, Sax (Arthur Henry Ward), 219
Romance of the Three Kingdoms, 497n256
Roosevelt, Franklin Delano, 103, 135
Rosemary's Baby, 284
Rosner, Rick, 353
Ross, Barney, 187
Roundtree, Richard, 376
Ruby Chow's Chinese Dinner Club, 84, 86
Russell, Bill, 272
Russo, Charles, 81, 82, 172, 191, 193, 199, 201, 205, 480n147

S

"Saigon Execution" (Adams), 300
Saint Paul Dispatch, 240
samurai chanbara genre, 311
San Francisco State University, strike at, 278–280
San Jose Asian American Political Alliance, 267
Sanbo, Emiko (Amy), 119–120, 121–124, 128, 131, 137
Sand Pebbles, The, 260, 285
Sarafian, Richard, 318
Sarmiento, Max, 179
Sato, Fred, 95, 112, 114, 127, 237
Savage, Milo, 243
Saxon, John, 404
Sayonara, 241
Schifrin, Lalo, 420, 421
Scollan, Barney, 176–177, 178–179, 184
Screen Gems, 353
Seale, Bobby, 251–252, 253
Seattle Daily Times, 132
Seattle Dojo, 93, 95, 105
Seattle Post-Intelligencer, 111, 113
Seattle World's Fair, 132, 137, 143
Sebring, Jay, 177, 179, 213–214, 237–238, 284, 290, 296

INDEX 537

Seeker, 297, 300
segregation, 4, 91–92, 218, 280
Self, William, 249
Semple, Lorenzo, Jr., 228, 229, 232–233, 327, 396n
Sen Yung, Victor, 236, 324, 360, 362
Sequoia Pictures, 394, 395, 397
Seven Samurai, 299, 329
Shaft, 376–377, 416
Shaolin boxing forms, 69
Shaw, Frank, 79
Shaw, Run Run, 313, 332–335, 342, 388, 394, 414, 415, 423
Shaw Brothers, 191, 311, 312, 325, 329, 332–334, 346, 349–350, 393
Shek Kin, 313, 374–375*fig*, 404, 412
Shih, Vincent, 157
Shimomura, Roger, 118, 122, 123
Shortcomings, 448
Showdown in Oakland, 193
Sia, Beau, 444
Sick Man of Asia trope, 27–29
Silent Flute, The, 299–301, 313–315, 317–323, 324, 331, 336, 365, 396–398, 423
Silliphant, Mark, 299–300
Silliphant, Stirling
    advice from, 336–337
    background of, 287–288
    on fights in film, 243
    film roles for Lee from, 290–291
    Fist of Fury and, 398
    importance of to Lee, 285
    Lee's back injury and, 317
    Longstreet and, 324, 325, 335, 353, 405
    presentation for TV series and, 327
    Project Leng and, 295, 297–299
    The Silent Flute and, 300–301, 313, 314–315, 317–318, 320–323
    timing and, 332
    training with Lee, 288–289
    TV projects and, 357
Sima Qian, 69
Simpsons, The, 376n
Sims, Bennett, 329
Sinatra, Frank, 169, 213, 287
Sing Lee Theater, 191
Sino-Japanese War, Second, 26–27
Siu Hon-Sang, 69, 195, 202, 230
Siu Sang Yik, 13
Siu Son-Hang, 312
Sixteenth Street Baptist Church bombing, 184
Slomanski, Hank, 179
Sly and the Family Stone, 277
smallpox, 27–28
Sniffen, Darrell, 143
Snyder, Gary, 127
So Siu Siu, 152

Soft Arts Academy, 192
Solitary Swan in a Sea of Humanity, A (Auyeung), 65
Song, Celine, 448
Sontag, Susan, 232
Sound of Music, The, 350, 358
Source Book in Chinese Philosophy, A, 159*fig*, 316
Sources of Chinese Tradition, 316
South Pacific, 216–217, 241, 329
Spielman, Ed, 329–330
Sports Medicine for Trainers (Morehouse and Rasch), 316
St. Francis Xavier, 57, 61–62, 64
St. George school, 62
St. Stephen's College, 50
"Stand!" 277
Stanford, Leland, 15
Stanislavski method, 238, 285
Star, 415
Star Ferry riots, 310, 311
Star Trek, 260, 361
Steen, Allen, 177
Steinem, Gloria, 437
Steinmetz, Charles, 137
Steppenwolf (Hesse), 316
Stewart, Benny, 278
Stewart, Jackie, 307
Stone, Mike, 177, 269, 290, 294
Stone, W. Clement, 137
Stop the Draft Week, 264, 265
Story of Daisy, The, 399
Streisand, Barbra, 437
Striker, Fran, 233
Striking Distance (Russo), 193, 480n147
Student Nonviolent Coordinating Committee, 251, 264
stuntmen, 243–244, 345, 347, 399, 410
Sturges, John, 80, 299
Success System That Never Fails, The (Stone), 137
Sun Sing Theatre, 191–192, 198
Sun Tzu, 160, 161, 197, 199, 253
Sun Yee On Triad, 47, 61
Sun Yuk Fung, 202
Sunn Jue, Joseph, 23
Super Fly, 376, 394, 397
Superman, 233
Suzuki, Daisetz T., 160, 162, 163, 258, 269, 300, 498n258
Sweet Sweetback's Baadasssss Song, 376
Syquia, Luis and Serafin, 343
Sze Tai, Lady, 13

T

tai chi, 7
tai chi chuan, 7
Tajima-Peña, Renee, 448

Tak Sun, 40
Takei, George, 121, 361, 362
Tam Sau-Chen, 129
Tannenbaum, Tom, 284, 335, 353, 354, 357
Tao, 7
Tao, The Great Luminant, 471n70
"Tao of Gung Fu" paper (Lee), 70, 128, 144, 150, 157, 160, 163, 478n128, 482n160
Tao of Jeet Kune Do (Lee), 270, 315, 437, 504n306, 506n316
Tao Te Ching (Laozi), 7, 127, 163, 278, 501n285
Taoism, 127–128, 157, 159, 160
Tarantino, Quentin, 244, 298, 503n298
Tarkington, Rockne, 404
Tarzan, 246, 284
Tate, Sharon, 290, 296
Taylor, George, 127
Technique of Handling People, The (Laird and Laird), 137
Ten-Point Program, 252
Teo, Stephen, 32, 382, 432
Terry and the Pirates, 395
"Theory of Fighting, A," 68–69
They Call Me Bruce, 4
They Call Us Bruce (podcast), 444
Thief of Bagdad, The, 215
Think and Grow Rich (Hill), 137, 293
Third World Liberation Front (TWLF), 278, 303, 343
Third World Strike, 278–280, 278fig
This Is It! (Watts), 157
Thomas, Bruce, 134
Thomas Crown Affair, The, 285, 286
three stages of cultivation, 258
Thunderstorm, 151
Ti Lung, 312, 346, 350
Tien, James, 346, 347, 348
Tien Chuen, James, 334, 389
Tiger Force, 353, 357
Time, 169, 216
Ting Pei, Betty, 417, 423, 424, 425, 436, 438
Titanus, 377, 423
Today show, 275
Toll of the Sea, The, 215
Tonight Show, 423
Torrenueva, Joe, 179, 213, 257
Touch of Zen, A, 311, 346
Toyo, Raymond (Tokutaro Hayashi), 234
Tracy, Al, 176–177
Tracy, Will, 177
transcontinental railroad, 15
Trendle, George Washington, 233–234, 245–246, 247, 492n224

Triads, 43–44, 47
Trias, Robert, 145n, 177, 257n
Trillin, Calvin, 343
Tropper, Jonathan, 448–449
True Story of Wong Fei-Hung, The, 44
Truman, Harry, 228, 248n
Trump, Donald J., 4, 293
Tso, Eva, 59, 151, 152
Tso, Howard, 260
Tso, Pearl, 59, 136–138, 401–402, 435
Tso Tat-Wah, Walter, 59, 313
Tsu, Irene, 423
Tsui Sheung-tin, 469n53
Tsunemoto, Yamamoto, 499n269
Tule Lake concentration camp, 104, 119, 121
Tunney, Gene, 245
TV and Movie Screen, 241
TV Picture Life, 241, 486n181
TVB, 313, 333, 334
TV/Radio Mirror, 241
TV/Radio Show, 240–241
Twain, Mark, 326
20th Century-Fox
    Belasco and, 230
    Chan and, 221
    Dozier and, 213, 228
    The Green Hornet and, 233, 249
    Lee's meeting at, 284
    Lee's option agreement with, 231
    The Silent Flute and, 398
Two Opium Addicts Sweep a Long Dike, 56

U

Umeki, Miyoshi, 324
Union Film Enterprises, 56
United Artists, 376
United Farm Workers, 259, 264
Urquidez, Benny, 441
Uyehara, Mitoshi "Mito"
    Abdul-Jabbar (Alcindor) and, 273, 274, 276
    background of, 250
    Black Belt and, 145, 249
    correspondence with, 289, 314, 317, 322, 323, 328, 387, 398, 399
    Expo and, 423–424
    Fist of Fury and, 373
    Lee's back injury and, 315
    Lee's illness and death and, 420
    Manson murders and, 296
    McQueen, Steve, 291
    McQueen and, 286, 287
    Tao of Jeet Kune Do and, 315

Ting Pei and, 417
training with Lee and, 261, 294, 302
Wing Chun Kung Fu and, 400–401
Uyematsu, Amy, 267–268

V

Vajna, Andy, 387, 423
Valery, Paul, 484n168
Van Peebles, Melvin, 376
Vanishing Point, 318
Variety, 358–359, 362, 393, 414, 415, 418
Vengeance! 312, 346
Vengeance of a Snow Girl, 349–350
Victoria, Brian Daizen, 482n162
Viet Thanh Nguyen, 267, 319, 449
Vietnam War, 135–136, 155, 184, 236, 251, 253n, 263, 319, 384
Villabrille, Floro, 178
Visual Communications, 361

W

Wagner, Wende, 237
Wah Ching, 189
Wah Keung (Strong Chinese) Kung Fu Club, 81
Waley, Arthur, 501n285
Walk in the Spring Rain, A, 295
Wall, Bob, 381, 404, 410
Wall Street Journal, 220
Walters, Margaret, 70n, 128, 150, 156, 160
Wan Dai Hu, 50–51
Wan Kam Leung, 399
Wang, Robert, 41, 56
Wang, Wayne, 448
Wang Yu, Jimmy, 333, 346, 350, 358, 368, 372, 380, 508n334
War, 433
War Relocation Authority, 120–121
Ward, Arthur Henry (Sax Rohmer), 219
Ward, Burt, 237, 248–249
Warner Bros.
contract negotiations with, 394, 395, 401
Enter the Dragon (*Blood and Steel*) and, 397, 405, 406–408, 415, 421
The Exorcist and, 404
Five Fingers of Death and, 414
Kung Fu and, 330–331
Shaft and, 377
The Silent Flute and, 321, 323, 324
Warner Bros. Television, 354, 355, 356, 357, 359, 363
Warren, Earl, 485n180
Warrior, The, 17, 330, 356, 358, 359, 363, 364, 380, 384, 397, 449

Warrior's Journey, The, 389
water
importance of to Lee, 7–8, 160–161
Lee on, 70
screen test and, 224
Watts, Alan, 127, 137, 157, 160, 258, 433
Way of the Dragon, The, 374–375fig, 380–382, 381–382fig, 384–385, 388, 398, 405, 414, 438n
Way of the Tiger, the Sign of the Dragon, The, 328, 330
Way of Zen, The (Watts), 127, 157
Wealth Is Like a Dream, 33, 34, 47fig
Wei Min Bao, 344
Wei Min She, 343
Weintraub, Fred, 328–329, 335–336, 353–354, 360, 391–395, 397, 404–409, 415–416, 419–420, 433–435
Weintraub, Sy, 284, 314, 317, 328, 331, 395, 423
Wei-Ping Ao, Paul, 382n
Welles, Orson, 412
Wells, Frank, 421
West, Adam, 239
West Side Story, 217
Westmoreland, William, 319
"What Is an Actor?" (Lee), 386
When Tae Kwon Do Strikes, 412
Whisky a Go Go, 237–238
White & White, 22
Whitfield Barracks, 30
Wild Wild West, The, 246
Wilde, Oscar, 484n168
Wilhelm II, Kaiser, 219
Williams, Elmo, 423
Williams, Howard, 153
Williams, Van, 237, 239–240, 242–243, 244, 247, 249
Wing, Rick, 192, 193
Wing Chun, 42, 48, 50, 52–54, 68, 80
Wing Chun Kung Fu, 401
Wing Luke Museum, 90n
Wintle, Walter, 106
Wong, Anna May, 2, 214–215, 216, 218n, 219, 223, 240, 336, 362, 440
Wong, Ark, 179, 204
Wong, Doc Fai, 205
Wong, H. S. "Newsreel," 24–25, 25fig, 27, 216
Wong, Henry, 411–412
Wong, Kenneth, 192
Wong, Lawrence, 334
Wong, Leland, 343
Wong, T. Y., 81, 95–96, 145, 146, 158, 186, 189–190, 192, 204
Wong, Ted, 140–141fig, 260–262, 294, 438, 441
Wong, Victoria, 264–265, 266, 394

Wong Fei-Hung, 59, 311, 404
Wong Jack Man, 190, 192–196, 197–207, 212, 261
Wong Jim, James, 42, 45, 451
Wong Kim Ark, 21–22
Wong Man-Lei, Mary, 151
Wong Shee, 84
Wong Shun Leung (Gong Sau), 49–50, 57–58, 62–64, 69, 71, 80, 100, 153, 399–400, 411–412, 423
Woo, Charlie, 96, 100, 108–109*fig*, 133, 158
Woo, Peter, 418
Wood, Natalie, 169
Wooden, John, 271, 274
Woodstock, 329
Workingmen's Party, 15
World Is a Ghetto, The (War), 433
World of Suzie Wong, The, 217–218, 290, 408
World War II, 103
Wotherspoon, George, 125
Wrecking Crew, The, 290
Wu, Madame, 87
Wu, Ronald "Ya Ya," 193, 196, 197
Wu Chia Hsiang, 345, 346–347
wu hsin, 160
Wu Ngan, 30, 40, 307, 369, 400
Wu Pang, 44
wu wei, 160
wuxia novels/films, 67, 90, 197, 311, 333, 334, 346

X

X, Malcolm, 251, 272

Y

Yamamoto, John, 131–132
Yamashita, Karen Tei, 444–445
Yang, Jeff, 444
Ye Jianying, 393
Yellow Peril, 15, 16*fig*, 219, 220, 222, 432
yellowface, 216, 219, 221, 223, 360–361, 362, 391, 440, 512n362

Yellow-Faced Tiger, The, 379
Yeoh, Michelle, 448
Yeung, Bolo, 410
Yeung, Fook, 82–83, 88, 89*fig*, 93, 114, 127, 429
Yeung Sze, 404
Yi, Maria, 334, 347, 424–425
Yim Sheung Mo, 195
Yim Wing Chun, 51–52
Yim Yee, 51–52
Yimm Look On, 145
yin and *yang*, 7, 158, 159, 401–402
Yip Man, 42, 47–48, 50–54, 54*fig*, 57, 69, 70, 153, 230, 399
Young, Mark, 26
Young Rock, 448
Yu, Kelvin, 448
Yu, Phil, 444
Yu Leung, 32, 34
Yuen, Corey, 345
Yuen Fai, 81
Yuen Po-Wan, 35
Yung Hwa Studios, 368n

Z

Zanuck, Dick, 510n353
Zanuck, Richard, 287
Zatoichi, 111, 272, 275, 318
Zatoichi versus the One-Armed Swordsman, 380
Zen, 127
Zen and Japanese Culture (Suzuki), 498n258
Zen at War (Victoria), 482n162
Zen Buddhism, 127
Zen Buddhism and Its Influence on Japanese Culture (Suzuki), 162
Zen Flesh, Zen Bones, 285
Zen in the Art of Archery (Herrigel), 160, 498n258
Zhang Shichuan, 311
Zhuangzi, 161, 300, 483n162
Zhuge Liang, 497n256
Zia, Helen, 446–447

About MARINER BOOKS

MARINER BOOKS traces its beginnings to 1832, when William Ticknor cofounded the Old Corner Bookstore in Boston, from which he would run the legendary firm Ticknor and Fields, publisher of Ralph Waldo Emerson, Harriet Beecher Stowe, Nathaniel Hawthorne, and Henry David Thoreau. Following Ticknor's death, Henry Oscar Houghton acquired Ticknor and Fields and, in 1880, formed Houghton Mifflin, which later merged with venerable Harcourt Publishing to form Houghton Mifflin Harcourt. HarperCollins purchased HMH's trade publishing business in 2021 and reestablished their storied lists and editorial team under the name Mariner Books.

Uniting the legacies of Houghton Mifflin, Harcourt Brace, and Ticknor and Fields, Mariner Books continues one of the great traditions in American bookselling. Our imprints have introduced an incomparable roster of enduring classics, including Hawthorne's *The Scarlet Letter*, Thoreau's *Walden*, Willa Cather's *O Pioneers!*, Virginia Woolf's *To the Lighthouse*, W.E.B. Du Bois's *Black Reconstruction*, J.R.R. Tolkien's *The Lord of the Rings*, Carson McCullers's *The Heart Is a Lonely Hunter*, Ann Petry's *The Narrows*, George Orwell's *Animal Farm* and *Nineteen Eighty-Four*, Rachel Carson's *Silent Spring*, Margaret Walker's *Jubilee*, Italo Calvino's *Invisible Cities*, Alice Walker's *The Color Purple*, Margaret Atwood's *The Handmaid's Tale*, Tim O'Brien's *The Things They Carried*, Philip Roth's *The Plot Against America*, Jhumpa Lahiri's *Interpreter of Maladies*, and many others. Today Mariner Books remains proudly committed to the craft of fine publishing established nearly two centuries ago at the Old Corner Bookstore.